1 MONTH OF
FREE
READING

at

www.ForgottenBooks.com

By purchasing this book you are eligible for one month membership to ForgottenBooks.com, giving you unlimited access to our entire collection of over 1,000,000 titles via our web site and mobile apps.

To claim your free month visit:
www.forgottenbooks.com/free984246

ISBN 978-0-260-90212-2
PIBN 10984246

JOURNAL

OF THE

HONORABLE SENATE

JANUARY SESSION, 1903.

JOURNAL

OF THE

HONORABLE SENATE

JANUARY SESSION, 1903.

WEDNESDAY, January 7, 1903.

At 11 o'clock in the forenoon, on the first Wednesday of January, in the year of our Lord one thousand nine hundred and three, being the day prescribed by the constitution for the Legislature of New Hampshire to assemble, the following named persons, elected Senators, assembled in the capitol, in the city of Concord in said state, and His Excellency the Governor, attended by the Honorable Council, having come into the senate chamber, took and subscribed the oaths of office, and were duly qualified as Senators, agreeably to the provisions of the constitution, namely:

District No. 1—William F. Allen.
2—Henry W. Keyes.
3—George E. Whitney.
4—Joseph Lewando.
5—Alvah E. Burnell.
6—
7—John B. Cooper.
8—Fred J. Marvin.
9—Marcellus H. Felt.
10—Ferdinand A. Stillings.
11—James G. Fellows.
12—John H. Neal.

13—Levi A. Fuller.
14—Franklin Ripley.
15—Aaron M. Wilkins.
16—James Lightbody.
17—John C. Bickford.
18—Thomas J. Foley.
19--Charles W. Hoitt.
20—Jason E. Tolles.
21—Arthur E. Hoyt.
22—Lucien Thompson.
23—Allen D. Richmond.
24—

His Excellency the Governor and the Honorable Council then withdrawing, the Senate was called to order by Thomas F. Clifford, clerk of the last session.

The clerk stated that the first business was the selection of a temporary presiding officer.

On motion of Senator Wilkins, Senator Bickford was chosen temporary presiding officer.

The clerk requested Senators Felt and Burnell to conduct the temporary presiding officer to the chair.

On motion of Senator Tolles, it was unanimously voted that Senator Marvin cast one ballot for Charles W. Hoitt as President.

Senator Marvin cast one ballot and Charles W. Hoitt having a majority of all votes cast, was declared elected President.

The chair requested Senators Foley and Lewando to conduct the President to the chair.

The President, having assumed the chair, addressed the Senate as follows:

Senators:

I tender you my thanks for the unanimous election to the highest office in your body, and assure you of my deep appreciation therefor. In the discharge and performance of the duties of the position I call on you and each of you to assist me, that we may have clean, fair, and just legislation, a clear examination and discrimination as to matters brought up for consideration by this honorable body, believing as I do, that as good, yes, even better judgment is demanded in deciding what should not be passed to become law, as in the favorable consideration of those bills which are passed and do become the law of the state.

I ask the full and prompt attendance of the senators that each and all of the districts sending us here may know that they are represented, that their interests are cared for, that their confidence was not misplaced in selecting us for their senators. I ask that the business presented may be well considered, and not delayed but pushed along to final action and disposition, that the session, so far as this body is concerned may be brought to a close in a reasonably short time. Senators, thanking you again, I await your pleasure.

On motion of Senator Stillings, the following resolution was adopted:

Resolved, That Thomas F. Clifford, as clerk, be elected by acclamation; that Louis A. Thorp, as assistant clerk, be elected by acclamation; that William H. Weston, as sergeant-at-arms, be elected by acclamation; that Herbert A. McElwain, as messenger, be elected by acclamation; and that Hiram E. Currier, as doorkeeper, be elected by acclamation; and that Thomas F. Clifford, Louis A. Thorp, William H. Weston, Herbert A. McElwain, Hiram E. Currier, are hereby elected for the several positions named, respectively.

Thereupon Thomas F. Clifford, Louis A. Thorp, William H. Weston, Herbert A. McElwain, and Hiram E. Currier, appeared, signified to their acceptance and were duly sworn to the faithful discharge of their duties.

A true copy. Attest:

THOMAS F. CLIFFORD,
Clerk for 1901–1902.

On motion of Senator Hoyt of District No. 21, the following resolution was adopted:

Resolved, That the clerk of the Senate be authorized to furnish, at the expense of the state, during the session of 1903, two such daily newspapers, printed within the state, to the members and officers of the Senate, as such members and officers may select, and to the Governor and Council.

On motion of Senator Ripley, the following resolution was adopted :

Resolved, That the secretary of state be requested to furnish the Senate the official returns of votes from the various senatorial districts for the state.

On motion of Senator Whitney, the following resolution was adopted :

Resolved, That the returns of votes in the several senatorial districts be referred to a select committee of three, with instructions to examine and count the same, and report to the Senate whether any vacancies exist, and, if so, in what senatorial district.

The President appointed as members of such committee Senators Whitney, Cooper, and Marvin.

On motion of Senator Allen, the following resolution was adopted :

Resolved, That the rules of the Senate for the last session be the rules of the Senate for the present session, until otherwise ordered.

On motion of Senator Neal, the following resolution was adopted :

Resolved, That, until otherwise ordered, the Senate will meet at 11 o'clock in the forenoon and at 2 o'clock in the afternoon.

On motion of Senator Lightbody, the following resolution was adopted :

Resolved, That the House of Representatives be informed that the Senate, having assembled, has organized by the choice of Charles W. Hoitt as president, Thomas F. Clifford as clerk, Louis A. Thorp as assistant clerk, William H. Weston as sergeant-at-arms, Herbert A. McElwain as messenger, Hiram E. Currier as doorkeeper, and is now ready to proceed with the business of the session.

On motion of Senator Tolles, the Senate voted to take a recess subject to the call of the President.

(Recess.)

The Senate having reassembled, the Hon. Edward N. Pearson, secretary of state, appeared and presented the returns of votes for senators for the various senatorial districts, as returned to the secretary's office, which were referred to the select committee on returns.

The following message was received from the House of Representatives by its clerk:

HOUSE MESSAGE.

Mr. President:

The House of Representatives has adopted the following resolution:

Resolved, That the Honorable Senate be informed that the House of Representatives has organized by the election of Harry M. Cheney as speaker, James M. Cooper as clerk, Harrie M. Young as assistant clerk, and John K. Law as sergeant-at-arms, and is now ready to proceed with the business of the session.

The following report from the select committee appointed to examine the votes cast in the various senatorial districts of the state was read, accepted, and adopted:

The select committee to whom were referred the returns of votes for senators in the several senatorial districts, have attended to their duties, and having examined the returns made to the secretary of state, as well as the records in the office of said secretary, beg leave to report that they find the state of the vote returned in the several districts as follows:

DISTRICT NO. 1.

William F. Allen had	2,545
Manasah Perkins had	2,273

and William F. Allen, having a majority of all the votes cast, is elected.

DISTRICT NO. 2.

Henry W. Keyes had	2,291
Samuel B. Page had	1,554
All others had	2

and Henry W. Keyes, having a majority of all the votes cast, is elected.

DISTRICT No. 3.

George E. Whitney had	2,305
Albion T. Clark had	1,104

and George E. Whitney, having a majority of all the votes cast, is elected.

DISTRICT No. 4.

Joseph Lewando had	2,366
Henry F. Dorr had	1,335
Moses C. Spokesfield had	160

and Joseph Lewando, having a majority of all the votes cast, is elected.

DISTRICT No. 5.

Alvah W. Burnell had	2,290
Frank R. Marston had	1,813

and Alvah W. Burnell, having a majority of all the votes cast, is elected.

DISTRICT No. 6.

Elmer S. Tilton had	1,957
Harry W. Daniell had	1,915
Daniel E. Knowles had	212

and no person appearing to have a majority of all the votes cast, there is apparently no choice. The two constitutional candidates are Elmer S. Tilton and Harry W. Daniell.

DISTRICT No. 7.

John B. Cooper had	2,024
Ora D. Blanchard had	1,267
All others had	2

and John B. Cooper, having a majority of all the votes cast, is elected.

DISTRICT NO. 8.

Henry A. Hurlin had 1,526
Fred J. Marvin had 1,717

and Fred J. Marvin, having a majority of all the votes cast, is elected.

DISTRICT NO. 9.

Marcellus H. Felt had 2,364
John Gage had 1,389
All others had 1

and Marcellus H. Felt, having a majority of all the votes cast, is elected.

DISTRICT NO. 10.

Ferdinand A. Stillings had . . . 1,525
William A. J. Giles had 998
All others had 1

and Ferdinand A. Stillings, having a majority of all the votes cast, is elected.

DISTRICT NO. 11.

James G. Fellows had 2,156
George W. Lane had 1,876
All others had 2

and James G. Fellows, having a majority of all the votes cast, is elected.

DISTRICT NO. 12.

John Herbert Neal had 2,005
Eugene C. Foss had 1,403

and John Herbert Neal, having a majority of all the votes cast, is elected.

DISTRICT NO. 13.

Levi A. Fuller had 1,096
Daniel W. Bill had . . . . . 625.

and Levi A. Fuller, having a majority of all the votes cast, is
elected.

DISTRICT NO. 14.

Franklin Ripley had	1,310
George E. Whitcomb had	745

and Franklin Ripley, having a majority of all the votes cast, is
elected.

DISTRICT NO. 15.

Aaron M. Wilkins had	1,317
George G. Tolford had	1,004
All others had	1

and Aaron M. Wilkins, having a majority of all the votes cast,
is elected.

DISTRICT NO. 16.

James Lightbody had	1,062
Edward H. Murphy had	539

and James Lightbody, having a majority of all the votes cast, is
elected.

DISTRICT NO. 17.

John C. Bickford had	1,606
John E. Coffin had	751
All others had	1

and John C. Bickford, having a majority of all the votes cast, is
elected.

DISTRICT NO. 18.

William Marcotte had	2,057
Thomas J. Foley had	2,991

and Thomas J. Foley, having a majority of all the votes cast, is
elected.

DISTRICT NO. 19.

Charles W. Hoitt had	1,415
Henry H. Davis had	1,038

Frank A. Burbank had 79
All others had 3

and Charles W. Hoitt, having a majority of all the votes cast, is elected.

DISTRICT NO. 20.

Josiah N. Woodward had 1,460
Jason E. Tolles had 1,733
Joseph E. Bassett had 96
All others had 3

and Jason E. Tolles, having a majority of all the votes cast, is elected.

DISTRICT NO. 21.

Arthur E. Hoyt had 2,148
Emery N. Eaton had 1,299
All others had 1

and Arthur E. Hoyt, having a majority of all the votes cast, is elected.

DISTRICT NO. 22.

Lucien Thompson had 1,354
Charles S. Clifford had 718

and Lucien Thompson, having a majority of all the votes cast, is elected.

DISTRICT NO. 23.

Allen D. Richmond had 1,461
Valentine M. Coleman had . . . 1,246

and Allen D. Richmond, having a majority of all the votes cast, is elected.

DISTRICT NO. 24.

Joseph H. Gardiner had 791
Calvin Page had 849
Ira C. Seymour had 444
All others had 1

and no person appearing to have a majority of all the votes cast, there is apparently no choice. Joseph H. Gardiner having deceased, the two constitutional candidates are Calvin Page and Ira C. Seymour.

> Respectfully submitted,
> GEORGE E. WHITNEY,
> JOHN B. COOPER,
> FRED J. MARVIN,
> *Committee.*

On motion of Senator Keyes, the following resolution was adopted :

Resolved, That a message be sent to the House of Representatives that from an examination of the returns of votes there appear to be vacancies in Senatorial Districts Nos. 6 and 24; that Elmer S. Tilton and Harry W. Daniell are the two constitutional candidates in District No. 6; that Calvin Page and Ira C. Seymour are the two constitutional candidates in District No. 24; and that the Senate is ready to meet the House in convention at such time as the House may suggest, for the purpose of filling the vacancies in the Senate, agreeable to the provisions of the constitution.

On motion of Senator Thompson, the Senate adjourned

AFTERNOON.

The following message was received from the House of Representatives by its clerk :

HOUSE MESSAGE.

Mr. President :

The House of Representatives has adopted the following resolution, in the adoption of which it asks the concurrence of the Honorable Senate :

Resolved, That a committee of five, consisting of the Speaker and four members, be appointed by the chair to report on the subject of proper rules of procedure in this House, and that they, with such members as the Senate may join, be a committee on Joint Rules of the Senate and House of Representatives.

On motion of Senator Fuller, the foregoing resolution was concurred in.

On motion of Senator Thompson, the Senate adopted the following resolution :

Resolved, That a committee of two, consisting of the President and one Senator, be appointed by the chair as a committee on Joint Rules of the Senate and House of Representatives to act with a similar committee on the part of the House.

The President appointed as member of such committee on the part of the Senate, Senator Bickford.

On motion of Senator Cooper, the following resolution was adopted :

Resolved, by the Senate, the House of Representatives concurring, That the joint rules of the last Legislature be the joint rules of this Legislature until otherwise ordered.

The following message was received from the House of Representatives by its clerk :

HOUSE MESSAGE.

Mr. President :

The House of Representatives concurs with the Honorable Senate in the adoption of the following resolution :

Resolved, by the Senate, the House of Representatives concurring, That the joint rules of the last Legislature be the joint rules of this Legislature until otherwise ordered.

The House of Representatives has adopted the following resolution :

Resolved, That the Honorable Senate be notified that the House of Representatives will be ready to meet the Senate in joint convention for the purpose of canvassing the votes for Governor and Councilors, for the election of a commissary-general agreeably to the provisions of the constitution, and for the purpose of filling vacancies in Senatorial Districts Nos. 6 and 24, at 3 o'clock this afternoon.

On motion of Senator Burnell, the Senate met the House of Representatives in joint convention for the purpose of canvassing the votes for Governor and Councilors, for the election of a commissary-general, and for the purpose of filling vacancies in Senatorial Districts Nos. 6 and 24, agreeably to the provisions of the constitution.

(See House proceedings.)

Upon returning to the Senate chamber, the Honorable Edward N. Pearson, secretary of state, appeared and introduced Elmer S. Tilton, senator from District No. 6, and Calvin Page, senator from District No. 24; each of whom had taken and subscribed the oath of office before His Excellency the Governor, and were duly qualified as senators agreeably to the provisions of the constitution.

On motion of Senator Stillings, the Senate adjourned.

THURSDAY, JANUARY 8, 1903.

The Senate met according to adjournment.

The reading of the journal having been commenced, on motion of Senator Tolles, the rules were so far suspended that its further reading was dispensed with.

On motion of Senator Allen, the Senate voted to take a recess until 11 : 45 o'clock.

(Recess.)

The Senate having reassembled, the following message was received from the House of Representatives by its clerk :

HOUSE MESSAGE.

Mr. President:

The House of Representatives has adopted the following resolution :

Resolved, That the House of Representatives is ready to meet the Honorable Senate in joint convention for the purpose of receiving His Excellency the Governor, and any communication he may be pleased to make, and for the transaction of such other business as may properly come before such convention.

On motion of Senator Hoyt of District No. 21, the Senate met the House of Representatives in joint convention :

(See House proceedings.)

Upon returning to the Senate chamber, on motion of Senator Keyes, the following resolution was adopted :

Resolved, That when the Senate adjourns, it adjourn to meet to-morrow morning at 9 o'clock, and when it adjourns to-morrow morning it adjourn to meet next Monday evening at 7:30 o'clock.

On motion of Senator Bickford, the Senate adjourned.

FRIDAY, JANUARY 9, 1903.

The Senate met according to adjournment.

Senator Stillings, having assumed the chair, read the followlowing communication :

NASHUA, N. H., January 9, 1903.

Senator Stillings :

Please preside for me at the morning session to-day, of the New Hampshire Senate, and oblige,

Yours truly,

CHARLES W. HOITT,

President.

The journal was read and approved.

On motion of Senator Allen, the Senate adjourned.

MONDAY, JANUARY 12, 1903.

The Senate met according to adjournment.

Senator Stillings, having assumed the chair, read the following communication :

NASHUA, N. H., January 12, 1903.

Senator Stillings :

Please preside for me at the evening session to-night, of the New Hampshire Senate, and oblige,

Yours truly,

CHARLES W. HOITT,

President.

The journal was read and approved.

On motion of Senator Fellows, the Senate adjourned.

TUESDAY, JANUARY 13, 1903.

The Senate met according to adjournment.

The journal was read and approved.

The President announced the following standing and joint standing committees :

STANDING COMMITTEES.

On the Judiciary.—Senators Bickford, Page, Ripley, Allen, and Tolles.

On Revision of the Laws.—Senators Wilkins, Fuller, Hoyt, Lewando, and Page.

On Banks.—Senators Lightbody, Stillings, Keyes, Tolles, and Cooper.

On Finance.—Senators Lewando, Richmond, Wilkins, Bickford, and Ripley.

On Agriculture.—Senators Thompson, Fuller, Marvin, Burnell, and Wilkins.

On Railroads.—Senators Keyes, Cooper, Neal, Fellows, and Tolles.

On Education.—Senators Ripley, Thompson, Felt, Tilton, and Lightbody.

On Incorporations.—Senators Richmond, Whitney, Foley, Allen, and Keyes.

On Public Health.—Senators Stillings, Whitney, Felt, Neal, and Bickford.

On Elections.—Senators Fellows, Whitney, Bickford, Marvin, and Hoyt.

On Claims.—Senators Allen, Fuller, Stillings, Marvin, and Tilton.

On Towns and Parishes.—Senators Fuller, Bickford, Burnell, Allen, and Marvin.

On Roads, Bridges, and Canals.—Senators Hoyt, Keyes, Stillings, Wilkins, and Marvin.

On Asylum for Insane.—Senators Felt, Fellows, Ripley, Richmond, and Foley.

On State Prison and Industrial School.—Senators Cooper, Hoyt, Thompson, Page, and Fellows.

On Manufactures.—Senators Whitney, Lightbody, Allen, Tilton and Cooper.

On Soldiers' Home.—Senators Neal, Fuller, Felt, Foley, and Lewando.

On Fisheries and Game.—Senators Tilton, Cooper, Burnell, Lewando, and Richmond.

On Labor.—Senators Page, Neal, Whitney, Thompson, and Foley.

On Military Affairs.—Senators Tolles, Whitney, Lightbody, Keyes, and Lewando.

On Rules.—President Hoitt, Senators Page, and Neal.

JOINT STANDING COMMITTEES.

On Engrossed Bills.—Senators Burnell and Wilkins.

On State Library.—Senator Stillings.

On State House and State House Yard.—Senator Fellows.

LEAVE OF ABSENCE.

Senator Page was granted leave of absence for the day on account of business engagements.

Senator Tolles, of District No. 20, gave notice that on to-morrow, or some subsequent day, he would ask leave to introduce a bill entitled "An act in amendment of the charter of the Salem Water-Works Company."

Senator Thompson, of District No. 22, gave notice that on to-morrow, or some subsequent day, he would ask leave to introduce a bill entitled "An act to amend section 1 of an act of June 1814, incorporating the Congregational Society in Durham."

On motion of Senator Stillings, the following resolution was adopted :

Resolved, That the clerk be authorized to procure the services of a stenographer, whose duty it shall be to attend the sessions of the Judiciary Committee, and when not so engaged to assist the clerk of the Senate.

On motion of Senator Thompson, the following resolution was adopted :

Resolved, That the clerk of the Senate be instructed to procure twenty-six copies of Hon. William M. Chase's revised edition of the Public Statutes; and furnish one copy to each member and to the clerk and assistant clerk of the Senate.

On motion of Senator Bickford, the following resolution was adopted:

Resolved, That when the Senate adjourns it adjourn to meet Wednesday, January 14, at 11 o'clock a. m.

On motion of Senator Felt, the Senate adjourned.

WEDNESDAY, JANUARY 14, 1903.

The Senate met according to adjournment.

The journal was read and approved.

Agreeably to previous notice, Senator Thompson introduced the following entitled bill which was read a first and second time and referred to the Committee on Revision of the Laws:

An act to amend section 1 of an act of June, 1814, incorporating the Congregational Society in Durham.

Agreeably to previous notice, Senator Tolles introduced the following entitled bill which was read a first and second time and referred to the Committee on Incorporations:

An act in amendment of the charter of the Salem Water-Works Company and legalizing and confirming the acts of said corporation in relation thereto.

On motion of Senator Tolles, the following resolution was adopted:

Resolved, That the clerk be authorized to procure the services of a stenographer, whose duties it shall be to attend the sessions of the Committee on Revision of the Laws and other committees of the Senate, and when not so engaged, to assist the clerk and members of the Senate as they may require.

The following message was received from the House of Representatives by its clerk:

HOUSE MESSAGE.

Mr. President:

The House of Representatives has adopted the following resolution:

WHEREAS, William H. Getchell has been elected chaplain of the House of Representatives for the present session,

Resolved, That prayers be offered in the House five minutes before the hour fixed for the first session each day, and that His Excellency the Governor, the Council, and the Honorable Senate be informed thereof, and be invited to attend.

The House of Representatives has adopted the following resolution, in the passage of which it asks the concurrence of the Honorable Senate :

Resolved, by the House of Representatives, the Senate concurring, That a committee of three on the part of the House be appointed to confer with a like committee on the part of the Senate, to make assignment of rooms to the various committees and employees of both branches of the legislature, and the Speaker has appointed as members of such committee on the part of the House, Mr. Morgan of Manchester, Mr. Darling of Whitefield, and Mr. Drake of Freedom.

On motion of Senator Lightbody, the foregoing resolution was concurred in.

The President appointed as members of such committee on the part of the Senate, Senators Burnell, Marvin, and Richmond.

On motion of Senator Bickford, the following resolution was adopted :

Resolved, That the Senate accept the invitation to attend prayers, extended by the House of Representatives.

On motion of Senator Keyes, the following resolution was adopted :

Resolved, That a committee of three be appointed, to whom is referred the message of His Excellency the Governor, and that they be instructed to report what reference should be made of the several recommendations made therein.

The President appointed as members of such committee, Senators Keyes, Bickford, and Cooper.

LEAVE OF ABSENCE.

On motion of Senator Tolles, leave of absence was granted to Senator Ripley for the remainder of the week.

Senator Lightbody, of District No. 16, gave notice that on to-morrow, or some subsequent day, he would ask leave to introduce a bill entitled "An act to exempt the Young Men's Christian Association of Manchester, N. H., from taxation."

Senator Bickford, of District No. 17, gave notice that on to-morrow, or some subsequent day, he would ask leave to introduce bills with the following titles :

An act to change the name of The Woman's Auxiliary to the City Missionary Society of Manchester.

An act in amendment of section 3 of chapter 252 of the Public Statutes, relating to examinations, appeals, bail, and recognizances.

An act relative to bail in criminal cases.

An act in amendment of section 14 of chapter 264 of the Public Statutes, relating to offenses against the police of towns.

The following message was received from the House of Representatives by its clerk :

HOUSE MESSAGE.

Mr. President :

The House of Representatives has passed the following joint resolution, in the passage of which it asks the concurrence of the Honorable Senate :

Joint resolution favoring the establishment of a national forest reserve in the White Mountain region.

The following joint resolution sent up from the House of Representatives was read a first time :

Joint resolution favoring the establishment of a national forest reserve in the White Mountain region.

On motion of Senator Page, the rules were so far suspended that the second reading of the joint resolution was dispensed with.

On motion of the same Senator, the rules were so far suspended that the joint resolution was read a third time and passed.

On motion of Senator Hoyt of District No. 21, the Senate adjourned.

AFTERNOON.

On motion of Senator Stillings, the Senate adjourned.

THURSDAY, JANUARY 15, 1903.

The Senate met according to adjournment.

The journal was read and approved.

The following report from the Special Committee on Assignment of Rooms was accepted and adopted:

The Special Committee on the Assignment of Rooms to the several committees of the Senate report the following assignments:

STANDING COMMITTEES.

On Agriculture, room No. 11.

On Incorporations, adjutant-general's office.

On the Judiciary, room No. 11.

On Revision of the Laws, senate reception room.

On Railroads, adjutant-general's office.

On Banks, adjutant-general's office.

On Finance, room No. 6.

On Manufactures, room No. 11.

On Roads, Bridges, and Canals, senate reception room.

On Education, office of superintendent of public instruction.

On Military Affairs, adjutant-general's office.

On Claims, room No. 11.

On Towns and Parishes, room No. 11.

On State Prison and Industrial School, adjutant-general's office.

On Elections, room No. 11.

On Asylum for the Insane, room No. 6.

On Labor, labor commissioner's office.

On Soldier's Home, adjutant-general's office.

On Fisheries and Game, state library room.

On Public Health, office of board of health.

On Rules, senate reception room.

JOINT STANDING COMMITTEES.

On Engrossed Bills, secretary of state's office.

On State Library, state library.

On State House and State House Yard, state library room.

Employees, senate chamber and reception room.

A. W. BURNELL,
For the Committee.

On motion of Senator Lewando, the following resolution was adopted:

Resolved, That when the Senate adjourns this morning it adjourn to meet to-morrow morning at 9.30 o'clock, and when it adjourns to-morrow morning it adjourn to meet next Monday evening at 7.30 o'clock.

Senator Lewando, for the Committee on Revision of the Laws, to whom was referred "An act to amend section 1 of an act of June, 1814, incorporating the Congregational Society in Durham," reported the same without amendment and recommended its passage.

The report was accepted and the bill ordered to a third reading on Tuesday morning next, at 11 o'clock.

Senator Page, of District No. 24, gave notice that on to-morrow, or some subsequent day, he would ask leave to introduce a bill entitled "An act to amend chapter 192 of the Public Statutes, relating to insolvent estates."

Senator Tolles, of District No. 20, gave notice that on to-morrow, or some subsequent day, he would ask leave to introduce a bill entitled "An act amending the charter of the Nashua Light, Heat, and Power Company of Nashua."

Senator Foley, of District No. 18, gave notice that on to-morrow, or some subsequent day, he would ask leave to introduce a bill entitled "An act amending section 14, chapter 180 of the Public Statutes, relating to hours of labor of women and minors under the age of eighteen years in manufacturing or mechanical establishments."

On motion of Senator Foley, the following resolution was adopted:

Resolved, That two new committees be established to be known as the "Committee on Forestry," and the "Committee on Public Improvements."

The President announced the following additional standing committees:

On Forestry.—Senators Keyes, Allen, Cooper, Hoyt of District No. 21, and Lewando.

On Public Improvements.—Senators Stillings, Lightbody, Tolles, Whitney, and Thompson.

LEAVE OF ABSENCE.

Senators Wilkins and Page were granted leave of absence for Tuesday, January 20, on account of important business.

Senator Wilkins, at his request, was excused from further service on the Committee on Engrossed Bills, and the President appointed Senator Keyes to fill the vacancy.

On motion of Senator Tilton, the Senate adjourned.

FRIDAY, JANUARY 16, 1903.

The Senate met according to adjournment.

Senator Stillings, having assumed the chair, read the following communication:

NASHUA, N. H., Jan. 16, 1903.

Senator Stillings :

Please preside for me at to-day's session of the New Hampshire Senate, and oblige

CHARLES W. HOITT,
President.

The reading of the journal having been commenced, on motion of Senator Fellows the rules were so far suspended that further reading was dispensed with.

On motion of Senator Allen, the Senate adjourned.

MONDAY, JANUARY 19, 1903.

The Senate met according to adjournment.

Senator Allen, having assumed the chair, read the following communication :

NASHUA, N. H., Jan. 19, 1903.

Senator Allen :

Please preside for me at to-night's session of the New Hampshire Senate, and oblige

CHARLES W. HOITT,
President.

The journal was read and approved.

On motion of Senator Keyes, the Senate adjourned.

TUESDAY, JANUARY 20, 1903.

The Senate met according to adjournment.

The journal was read and approved.

On motion of Senator Burnell, the following resolution was adopted :

Resolved, That the Senate proceed to the choice of a United States Senator at 12 o'clock noon, to-day, for the term of six years from the fourth day of March, A. D. 1903, in accordance with the provisions of the laws of the United States.

The following message was received from the House of Representatives by its clerk :

HOUSE MESSAGE.

Mr. President :

The Speaker has named as members of the joint standing committees of the House and Senate, on the part of the House :

On Engrossed Bills.—Messrs. Willis of Concord and Converse of Lyme.

On State Library.—Messrs. Wheeler of Haverhill, Hayes of Dover, and Libby of Gorham.

On State House and State House Yard.—Messrs. Lintott of Nashua, Fellows of Brentwood, and Hill, E. J., of Concord.

The House of Representatives has passed bills with the following titles, in the passage of which it asks the concurrence of the Honorable Senate:

An act in amendment of the charter of the city of Dover, creating a board of police commissioners for said city and fixing the salaries of the officers in the police department.

An act authorizing the Manchester Mills to increase its capital stock.

The following entitled bill sent up from the House of Representatives, was read a first and second time, and referred to the Committee on Incorporations.

An act authorizing the Manchester Mills to increase its capital stock.

The following entitled bill sent up from the House of Representatives, was read a first and second time:

An act in amendment of the charter of the city of Dover, creating a board of police commissioners for said city, and fixing the salaries of the officers in the police department.

On motion of Senator Richmond, the rules were so far suspended that the bill was read a third time by its title and passed.

The following entitled Senate bill was taken up, read a third time, passed, and sent to the House of Representatives for concurrence:

An act to amend section 1 of an act of June, 1814, incorporating the Congregational Society in Durham.

Agreeably to previous notice, Senator Bickford introduced the following entitled bills, which were severally read a first and second time, and referred to the Committee on Judiciary:

An act to exempt certain property of the Manchester Young Men's Christian Association from taxation.

An act to change the name of the Woman's Auxiliary to the City Missionary Society of Manchester.

An act in amendment of section 14 of chapter 264 of the Public Statutes, relating to offenses against the police of towns.

The Committee on Rules made the following report:

That Senate Rule No. 25 be amended by striking out the words " a committee on Asylum for the Insane," and substituting in the place thereof the words " a committee on State Hospital;" and further amend Rule 25 by adding after the words " a committee on Public Health," the words "a committee on Forestry; and a committee on Public Improvements."

CHARLES W. HOITT,
CALVIN PAGE,
JOHN H. NEAL,
Committee on Rules.

The report was accepted and laid on the table under Senate Rule No. 34.

The following report from the Committee on Engrossed Bills was read and accepted:

The Committee on Engrossed Bills have carefully examined and found correctly engossed the following joint resolution:

Joint resolution favoring the establishment of a national forest reserve in the White Mountain region.

A. W. BURNELL,
For the Committee.

On motion of Senator Hoyt of District No. 21, the Senate voted to take a recess until 11.55 o'clock.

(Recess.)

The Senate, having reassembled, proceeded by a *viva voce* vote to name one person for Senator in Congress from the state of New Hampshire.

The following Senators named Jacob H. Gallinger:

Senators Allen, Keyes, Lewando, Burnell, Tilton, Felt, Stillings, Fellows, Neal, Fuller, Lightbody, Bickford, Hoitt of District No. 19, Hoyt of District No. 21, Thompson, and Richmond.

The following Senators named John M. Mitchell:

Senators Foley and Tolles.

Sixteen Senators named Jacob H. Gallinger.

Two Senators named John M. Mitchell.

And, Jacob H. Gallinger being named as the choice of a majority of the votes cast, it is ordered that the name of Jacob H. Gallinger be entered upon the Journal of the Senate as the choice of a majority of the Senators for Senator of the United States from the State of New Hampshire for the term of six years from the 4th day of March, A. D., 1903.

On motion of Senator Keyes, the Senate adjourned.

AFTERNOON.

Senator Tolles, of District No. 20, gave notice that on to-morrow, or some subsequent day, he would ask leave to introduce a bill entitled "An act in amendment of section 128, chapter 59 of the Laws of 1895, entitled 'An act to revise and amend Title 13 of the Public Statutes, relating to militia.'"

On motion of Senator Thompson, the Senate adjourned.

WEDNESDAY, JANUARY 21, 1903.

The Senate met according to adjournment.

The journal was read and approved.

The following message was received from the House of Representatives by its clerk :

HOUSE MESSAGE.

Mr. President:

The House of Representatives has passed a bill with the following title, in the passage of which it asks the concurrence of the Honorable Senate:

An act to allow the city of Nashua to appropriate money for the celebration of its semi-centennial.

The House of Representatives has passed the following resolution :

Resolved, That the Honorable Senate be notified that the House of Representatives will be ready to meet the Senate in

joint convention at 12 o'clock noon, to-day, January 21, for
the purpose of proceeding to the election of a United States
Senator for the full term of six years from March 4, 1903,
according to the law, and for the election of a secretary of
state and state treasurer.

The following entitled bill sent up from the House of Representatives was read a first and second time, and referred
to the Committee on Military Affairs:

An act to allow the city of Nashua to appropriate money for
the celebration of its semi-centennial.

(Senator Page in the chair.)

On motion of Senator Thompson, the Senate voted to recall
the bill from the Committee on Military Affairs.

Senator Tolles offered the following amendment:

Amend section one of said bill by striking out the words "a
sum not exceeding one thousand dollars" in the second line
of said section, and insert in lieu thereof the words, "such
sum as the city council may determine."

The question being stated,

Shall the amendment be adopted?

(Discussion ensued.)

Senator Felt moved to amend the amendment by inserting
the words "not to exceed twenty-five thousand dollars."

The question being stated,

Shall the amendment to the amendment be adopted?

(Discussion ensued.)

Senator Felt withdrew his motion to amend the amendment.

The question recurring,

Shall the amendment be adopted?

The affirmative prevailed on a *viva voce* vote.

On motion of Senator Foley, the rules were so far suspended that the bill as amended was read a third time, passed,
and sent to the House of Representatives for concurrence in
Senate amendment.

(President in the chair.)

Senator Keyes for the Committee on Incorporations, to whom was referred "An act authorizing the Manchester Mills to increase its capital stock," reported the same without amendment and recommended its passage.

The report was accepted, and, on motion of Senator Keyes, the rules were so far suspended that the bill was read a third time and passed.

On motion of Senator Foley, the following resolution was adopted:

Resolved, That the clerk of the Senate be and hereby is instructed immediately to request from the secretary of the convention of 1902 to revise the constitution, that he transmit to the Senate certified copies of the resolutions of said convention relating to the subjects of passes and trusts, and to report the same to the Senate as soon as they are received by him.

On motion of Senator Bickford, the following resolution was adopted: .

Resolved, That the Senate meet the House of Representatives in joint convention at 12 o'clock noon, for the purpose of proceeding to the election of a United States Senator for the term of six years from March 4, 1903, and for the election of secretary of state and state treasurer.

Senator Thompson of District No. 22 gave notice that on to-morrow, or some subsequent day, he would ask leave to introduce a bill entitled "An act to authorize the State Board of Agriculture to appoint a state nursery inspector and to provide for the protection of trees and shrubs from injurious insects and diseases."

On motion of Senator Lewando, the Senate met the House of Representatives in joint convention.

(See House proceedings.)

The Senate reassembled.

Agreeably to previous notice, Senator Tolles introduced the following entitled bill, which was read a first and second time and referred to the Committee on Incorporations:

An act amending the charter of the Nashua Light, Heat, and Power Company of Nashua.

Agreeably to previous notice, the same senator introduced the following entitled bill, which was read a first and second time, and referred to the Committee on Military Affairs:

An act in amendment of section 128 chapter 59 of the Laws of 1895, entitled "An act to revise and amend Title 13 of the Public Statutes, relating to the militia."

On motion of Senator Felt, the Senate adjourned.

AFTERNOON.

The following message was received from His Excellency the Governor, by the Honorable Edward N. Pearson, secretary of state:

THE STATE OF NEW HAMPSHIRE.

JANUARY 21, 1903.

COUNCIL CHAMBER,

To the Honorable Senate:

I hereby transmit the following reports:

Of the Secretary of State,
Of the State Treasurer,
Of the Adjutant-General,
Of the Insurance Commissioner,
Of the Bank Commissioners,
Of the Commissioner of Labor,
Of the Registrar of Vital Statistics,
Of the Attorney-General,
Of the Superintendent of Public Instruction,
Of the State Normal School,
Of the State Board of Health,
Of the Commission to Consider the Question of a State Sanatorium for Consumptives,
Of the Trustees of the School for the Feeble-Minded,
Of the Forestry Commission,
Of the State Library,

Of the Commissioners of Lunacy,

Of the Board of Equalization,

Of the Commission to ascertain and exactly determine the position of each New Hampshire regiment in the siege of Vicksburg,

Of the Fish and Game Commission,

Of the Industrial School,

Of the Board of Charities and Corrections,

Of the State Hospital,

Of the Cattle Commission.

NAHUM J. BACHELDER,

Governor.

The President announced that the several reports would be referred as follows :

Of the Secretary of State,

To the Committee on Revision of the Laws.

Of the State Treasurer,

To the Committee on Finance.

Of the Adjutant-General,

To the Committee on Military Affairs.

Of the Insurance Commissioner,

To the Committee on Incorporations.

Of the Bank Commissioners,

To the Committee on Banks.

Of the Commissioner of Labor,

To the Committee on Labor.

Of the Registrar of Vital Statistics,

To the Committee on Public Health.

Of the Attorney-General,

To the Committee on the Judiciary.

Of the Superintendent of Public Instruction,

To the Committee on Education.

Of the State Normal School,

To the Committee on Education.

Of the State Board of Health,

To the Committee on Public Health.

Of the Commission to Consider the Question of a State Sanatorium for Consumptives,

To the Committee on Public Health.

Of the Trustees of the School for the Feeble-Minded,

To the Committee on Judiciary.

Of the Forestry Commission,

To the Committee on Forestry.

Of the State Library,

To the Committee on State Library.

Of the Commissioners of Lunacy,

To the Committee on State Hospital.

Of the Board of Equalization,

To the Committee on Finance.

Of the Committee to ascertain and exactly determine the position of each New Hampshire regiment in the siege of
Vicksburg,

To the Committee on Military Affairs.

Of the Fish and Game Commission,

To the Committee on Fisheries and Game.

Of the Industrial School,

To the Committee on State Prison and Industrial School.

Of the Board of Charities and Corrections,

To the Committee on the Judiciary.

Of the State Hospital,

To the Committee on State Hospital.

Of the Cattle Commission,

To the Committee on Agriculture.

The report of the Committee on Rules was taken from the
table and adopted.

LEAVE OF ABSENCE.

The Committee on Roads, Bridges and Canals was granted
leave of absence for the remainder of the week.

Agreeably to previous notice, Senator Foley introduced the
following entitled bill, which was read a first and second time,
and referred to the Committee on Labor:

An act in amendment of section 14 of chapter 180 of the

Public Statutes, relating to hours of labor of women and minors under the age of eighteen years in manufacturing establishments.

The following message was received from the House of Representatives by its clerk :

Mr. President:

The House of Representatives has passed the following entitled bills, in the passage of which it asks the concurrence of the Honorable Senate :

An act to repeal chapter 200 of the Laws of 1899, entitled " An act to amend chapter 207 of the Laws of 1895, relating to the police court of Haverhill."

An act to establish a police court in the town of Haverhill.

An act relating to persons employed under and by virtue of an act of Congress relating to the surveys of the geological survey of the United States.

An act to change the name of Dodge's Falls Dam and Manufacturing Company to " Ryegate Paper Company."

An act providing a seal for the State Board of Agriculture.

An act to amend the charter of the New Hampshire Odd Fellows' Widows' and Orphans' Home, approved August 15, 1883.

An act to amend chapter 69 of the Laws of 1901, entitled " An act to protect the Ammonoosuc river in Carroll, Bethlehem, Littleton, Lisbon, and Bath, and its tributaries from pollution by sawdust and other waste."

An act amending section 11 of chapter 63 of the Session Laws of 1897, entitled " Practice of Medicine."

The following entitled bills, sent up from the House of Representatives, were severally read a first and second time and referred,—

TO THE COMMITTEE ON THE JUDICIARY :

An act to change the name of Dodge's Falls Dam and Manufacturing Company to " Ryegate Paper Company."

An act relating to persons employed under and by virtue of an act of Congress relating to the surveys of the geological survey of the United States.

An act to establish a police court in the town of Haverhill.

An act to amend chapter 69 of the Laws of 1901, entitled "An act to protect the Ammonoosuc river in Carroll, Bethlehem, Littleton, Lisbon, and Bath, and its tributaries from pollution by sawdust and other waste."

An act to repeal chapter 200 of the Laws of 1899, entitled "An act to amend chapter 207 of the Laws of 1895, relating to the police court of Haverhill."

An act amending section 11 of chapter 63 of the Session Laws of 1897, entitled "Practice of Medicine."

TO THE COMMITTEE ON INCORPORATIONS:

An act to amend the charter of the New Hampshire Odd Fellows' Widows' and Orphans' Home, approved August 15, 1883.

TO THE COMMITTEE ON AGRICULTURE:

An act providing a seal for the State Board of Agriculture.

Agreeably to previous notice, Senator Bickford introduced the following entitled bill, which was read a first and second time, and referred to the Committee on the Judiciary:

An act in relation to bail in criminal cases.

(Senator Bickford in the chair.)

LEAVE OF ABSENCE.

Senators Ripley and Allen were granted leave of absence for the remainder of the week.

On motion of Senator Lightbody, the Senate adjourned.

THURSDAY, JANUARY 22, 1903.

The Senate met according to adjournment.

The journal was read and approved.

The following telegram was read by the President:

"Phœnix, Ariz., January 21, 1903.
To the President of Senate, Concord, N. H.:

The twenty-second legislative assembly of the territory of Arizona send greeting to the Legislature of the State of New Hampshire and respectfully prays that your honorable body request its representative in the Senate of the United States to favor the passage of the omnibus statehood bill.

J. C. EVANS,
Chief Clerk.

Agreeably to previous notice, Senator Page introduced the following entitled bill, which was read a first and second time, and referred to the Committee on the Judiciary:

An act in amendment of chapter 192 of the Public Statutes, relating to insolvent estates.

Agreeably to previous notice, Senator Thompson introduced the following entitled bill, which was read a first and second time, and referred to the Committee on Agriculture:

An act to authorize the State Board of Agriculture to appoint a state nursery inspector, and to provide for the protection of trees and shrubs from injurious insects and diseases.

Senator Lewando for the Committee on Military Affairs, to whom was referred "An act in amendment of section 128 chapter 59 of the Laws of 1895, entitled 'An act to revise and amend Title 13 of the Public Statutes relating to militia,'" reported the same with the following amendment and recommended its passage:

After section 1 add, "Sect. 2. This act shall take effect upon its passage."

The report was accepted, amendment adopted, and the bill laid on the table to be printed.

Senator Tolles for the Committee on the Judiciary, to whom was referred "An act to change the name of the Woman's Auxiliary to the City Missionary Society of Manchester," reported the same without amendment and recommended its passage.

The report was accepted, and on motion of Senator Bickford, the rules were so far suspended that the bill was read a third time by its title, passed, and sent to the House of Representatives for concurrence.

Senator Tolles for the Committee on the Judiciary, to whom was referred "An act in amendment of section 14 of chapter 264 of the Public Statutes, relating to offenses against the police of towns, reported the same in a new draft and recommended its passage.

The report was accepted and the bill, in its new draft, was read a first and second time and laid on the table to be printed.

Senator Tolles for the Committee on the Judiciary, to whom was referred "An act to repeal chapter 200 of the Laws of 1899, entitled 'An act to amend chapter 207 of the Laws of 1895, relating to the police court of Haverhill,'" reported the same without amendment and recommended its passage.

The report was accepted and the bill ordered to a third reading this afternoon at 2 o'clock.

Senator Tolles for the Committee on the Judiciary, to whom was referred "An act amending section 11 of chapter 63 of the Session Laws of 1897, entitled 'Practice of Medicine,'" reported the same without amendment and recommended its passage.

The report was accepted, and on motion of Senator Felt, the rules were suspended and the bill was read a third time by its title and passed.

Senator Thompson, of District No. 22, gave notice that on to-morrow, or some subsequent day, he would ask leave to introduce a bill entitled "An act in amendment of the charter of the Plymouth Guaranty Savings Bank."

Senator Neal, of District No. 12, gave notice that on to-morrow, or some subsequent day, he would ask leave to introduce a bill entitled "An act in amendment of chapter 174 of the Public Statutes, relating to marriages."

The following report from the Committee on Engrossed Bills was read and accepted:

The Committee on Engrossed Bills have carefully examined and found correctly engrossed the following entitled bills:

An act in amendment of the charter of the city of Dover, creating a board of police commissioners for said city, and fixing the salaries of the officers of the police department.

An act authorizing the Manchester Mills to increase its capital stock.

A. W. BURNELL,
For the Committee.

On motion of Senator Foley, the following resolution was adopted:

Resolved, That when the Senate adjourns this afternoon, it adjourn to meet at 9.30 o'clock to-morrow morning, and when it adjourns to-morrow morning it be to meet at 7.30 o'clock Monday evening.

The following message was received from the House of Representatives by its clerk:

HOUSE MESSAGE.

Mr. President:

The House of Representatives has voted to concur with the Honorable Senate in its amendment to the following entitled bill:

An act to allow the city of Nashua to appropriate money for the celebration of its semi-centennial.

The House of Representatives has passed the following entitled bills, in the passage of which it asks the concurrence of the Honorable Senate:

An act to promote cleanliness and to protect the public from the disease commonly known as consumption.

An act in amendment of an act approved March 26, 1895, entitled "An act in amendment of an act incorporating the Newmarket Manufacturing Company, approved June 12, 1823, and 'An act in amendment thereof approved July 7, 1881.'"

An act in amendment of section 1 chapter 185 Laws of 1901, entitled "An act authorizing the Hillsborough County Convention to raise money for the building and repairing of court house."

The following entitled bills sent up from the House of Representatives were severally read a first and second time and referred,—

To the Committee on Public Health:

An act to promote cleanliness and to protect the public from the disease commonly known as consumption.

To the Committee on Revision of the Laws:

An act in amendment of section 1 chapter 185 Laws of 1901, entitled "An act authorizing the Hillsborough County Convention to raise money for the building and repairing of court house."

To the Committee on Incorporations:

An act in amendment of an act approved March 26, 1895, entitled "An act in amendment of an act incorporating the Newmarket Manufacturing Company, approved June 12, 1823, and 'An act in amendment thereof approved July 7, 1881.'"

On motion of Senator Stillings, the Senate adjourned.

AFTERNOON.

Senator Bickford, of District No. 17, gave notice that on to-morrow, or some subsequent day, he would ask leave to introduce a bill entitled "An act to revive, renew, and amend the charter of the Knights of Pythias Building Association of Manchester, passed at the session of 1895, and approved March 29, 1895."

Senator Page, of District No. 24, gave notice that on to-morrow, or some subsequent day, he would ask leave to introduce a bill entitled "An act to repeal chapter 112 of the Public Statutes, relating to the sale of spirituous or intoxicating liquor and the amendments thereof and thereto."

The following entitled House bill was read a third time and passed:

An act to repeal chapter 200 of the Laws of 1899, entitled "An act to amend chapter 207 of the Laws of 1895, relating to the police court of Haverhill."

On motion of Senator Burnell, the Senate adjourned.

FRIDAY, JANUARY 23, 1903.

The Senate met according to adjournment.

The journal was read and approved.

On motion of Senator Stillings, the Senate adjourned.

MONDAY, JANUARY 26, 1903.

The Senate met according to adjournment.

The journal was read and approved.

Senator Bickford having assumed the chair, read the following communication:

Nashua, N. H., January 26, 1903.

Senator Bickford:

Please preside for me at the evening session to-night, of the New Hampshire Senate, and oblige,

CHARLES W. HOITT,

President.

Senator Tilton, of District No. 6, gave notice that on to-morrow, or some subsequent day, he would ask leave to introduce a Joint resolution in relation to a fish-hatching house at Laconia.

Senator Bickford, of District No. 17, gave notice that on to-morrow, or some subsequent day, he would ask leave to introduce a bill entitled "An act to regulate, restrict, and control the sale of spirituous and intoxicating liquors."

Senator Fuller, of District No. 13, gave notice that on to-morrow, or some subsequent day, he would ask leave to introduce a bill entitled "An act to incorporate the National Trust Company."

Senator Cooper, of District No. 7, gave notice that on to-morrow, or some subsequent day, he would ask leave to introduce a bill entitled "An act relating to highways, highway agents, and street commissioners."

On motion of Senator Fuller, the Senate adjourned.

TUESDAY, JANUARY 27, 1903.

The Senate met according to adjournment.

The journal was read and approved.

The following entitled Senate bills, having been printed, were taken from the table and ordered to a third reading this afternoon at 2 o'clock:

An act in amendment of section 128, chapter 59 of the Laws of 1895, entitled "An act to revise and amend Title 13 of the Public Statutes relating to the militia."

An act in amendment of section 14 of chapter 264 of the Public Statutes, relating to offenses against the police of towns.

Senator Tolles for the Committee on the Judiciary, to whom was referred an act entitled "An act in relation to bail in criminal cases," reported the same without amendment and recommended its passage.

The same Senator for the Committee on the Judiciary, to whom was referred a bill entitled "An act to amend chapter 69 of the Laws of 1901, entitled 'An act to protect the Ammonoosuc river in Carroll, Bethlehem, Littleton, Lisbon, and Bath, and its tributaries from pollution by sawdust and other waste,'" reported the same without amendment and recommended its passage.

The reports were accepted and bills were severally laid on the table to be printed.

Senator Tolles for the Committee on the Judiciary, to whom was referred a bill entitled "An act to change the name of Dodge's Fall Dam and Manufacturing Company to 'Ryegate Paper Company,'" reported the same without amendment and recommended its passage.

The same Senator for the Committee on the Judiciary, to whom was referred a bill entitled "An act to establish a police court in the town of Haverhill," reported the same without amendment and recommended its passage.

The reports were accepted and the bills were severally ordered to a third reading this afternoon at 2 o'clock.

The following report from the Committee on Engrossed Bills was read and adopted:

The Committee on Engrossed Bills have examined bills with the following titles and find them correctly engrossed:

An act amending section 11 of chapter 63 of the Session Laws of 1897, entitled "Practice of Medicine."

An act to repeal chapter 200 of the Laws of 1899, entitled "An act to amend chapter 207 of the Laws of 1895, relating to the police court of Haverhill."

An act to allow the city of Nashua to appropriate money for the celebration of its semi-centennial.

HENRY W. KEYES,
For the Committee.

Agreeably to previous notice, Senator Thompson introduced the following entitled bill, which was read a first and second time and referred to the Committee on Education :

An act to amend chapter 93 section 15 of the Public Statutes, as amended by chapter 61 of the Session Laws of 1901, relating to scholars.

Agreeably to previous notice, Senator Lewando introduced the following entitled bill, which was read a first and second time and referred to the Committee on Banks :

An act in amendment of the charter of the Plymouth Guaranty Savings Bank.

Agreeably to previous notice, Senator Fuller introduced the following entitled bill, which was read a first and second time and referred to the Committee on Banks :

An act to incorporate the National Trust Company.

Agreeably to previous notice, Senator Cooper introduced the following entitled bill, which was read a first and second time and referred to the Committee on Roads, Bridges, and Canals :

An act relating to highways, highway agents, and street commissioners.

Agreeably to previous notice, Senator Neal introduced the following entitled bill, which was read a first and second time and referred to the Committee on Labor :

An act relating to the time required for filing notice of intention of marriage and the consent of parents to the marriage of minors.

Agreeably to previous notice, Senator Page introduced the following entitled bill, which was read a first and second time and referred to the Committee on the Judiciary :

An act to repeal chapter 112 of the Public Statutes, relating to the sale of spirituous or intoxicating liquor and all amendments thereof and thereto.

Agreeably to previous notice, Senator Tilton introduced a Joint resolution in relation to a fish-hatching house at Laconia, which was read a first and second time and referred to the Committee on Fisheries and Game.

The following message was received from the House of Representatives by its clerk :

Mr. President:

The House of Representatives has passed bills with the following titles, in the passage of which it asks the concurrence of the Honorable Senate :

An act authorizing the Concord & Montreal Railroad, lessor, to acquire the Concord Street Railway and other property, to issue bonds to pay therefor, and authorizing a physical connection of the Manchester Street Railway with the electric branches of the Concord & Montreal Railroad.

An act to extend the charter for the building of the Claremont Street Railway.

The following entitled bills sent up from the House of Representatives were severally read a first and second time and referred,—

To the Committee on Railroads :

An act to extend the charter for the building of the Claremont Street Railway.

An act authorizing the Concord & Montreal Railroad, lessor, to acquire the Concord Street Railway and other property, to issue bonds to pay therefor, and authorizing a physical connection of the Manchester Street Railway with the electric branches of the Concord & Montreal Railroad.

PETITIONS PRESENTED AND REFERRED.

To the Committee on Public Health :

By Senator Keyes, petition of the Lakeport Union of the Woman's Christian Temperance Union and 43 other like petitions, asking the Senate to pass a bill with penalty attached, to prohibit expectoration in public buildings and public conveyances and upon sidewalks.

On motion of Senator Burnell, the Senate adjourned.

AFTERNOON.

The following entitled House bills were severally read a third time and passed :

An act to establish a police court in the town of Haverhill.

An act to change the name of Dodge's Falls Dam and Manufacturing Company to "Ryegate Paper Company."

The following entitled Senate bills were severally read a third time, passed, and sent to the House of Representatives for concurrence.

An act in amendment of section 128 chapter 59 of the Laws of 1895, entitled "An act to revise and amend Title 13 of the Public Statutes, relating to militia."

An act in amendment of section 14 of chapter 264 of the Public Statutes, relating to offenses against the police of towns.

On motion of Senator Ripley, the Senate voted to take a recess until 2.45 o'clock.

(Recess.)

The Senate reassembled.

Agreeably to previous notice, Senator Bickford introduced the following entitled bill, which was read a first and second time and referred to the Committee on Incorporations :

An act to revive, renew and amend the charter of the Knights of Pythias Building Association of Manchester.

Senator Stillings for the Committee on Public Health, to whom was referred a bill entitled "An act to promote cleanliness and to protect the public from the disease commonly known as consumption," reported the same without amendment and recommended its passage.

The report was accepted and the bill ordered to a third reading to-morrow morning at 11 o'clock.

(Senator Hoyt of District No. 21 in the chair.)

Senator Richmond for the Committee on Incorporations, to whom was referred a bill entitled "An act in amendment of the charter of the Salem Water-Works Company, and legalizing and confirming the acts of said corporation in relation thereto," reported the same without amendment and recommended its passage.

The report was accepted and the bill laid upon the table to be printed.

President Hoitt was granted leave of absence for Wednesday, January 28.

On motion of Senator Bickford, the Senate adjourned.

WEDNESDAY, JANUARY 28, 1903.

The Senate met according to adjournment.

(Senator Stillings in the chair.)

The reading of the journal having been commenced, on motion of Senator Fuller, the rules were so far suspended that its further reading was dispensed with.

The following entitled Senate bill was read a third time, passed, and sent to the House of Representatives for concurrence :

An act in amendment of the charter of the Salem Water-Works Company, and legalizing and confirming the acts of said corporation in relation thereto.

The following entitled House bill, having been printed, was taken up and ordered to a third reading this afternoon at 2 o'clock :

An act to promote cleanliness and to protect the public from the disease commonly known as consumption.

Senator Richmond offered the following resolution :

Resolved, That, until otherwise ordered, the Senate will meet at 11 o'clock in the forenoon, and at 3 o'clock in the afternoon.

The resolution was declared lost on a viva voce vote.

Senator Cooper for the Committee on Railroads, to whom was referred a bill entitled " An act to extend the charter for the building of the Claremont Street Railway," reported the same without amendment and recommended its passage.

The report was accepted and the bill ordered to a third reading this afternoon at 2 o'clock.

Senator Keyes for the Committee on Railroads, to whom was referred a bill entitled "An act authorizing the Concord & Montreal Railroad, lessor, to acquire the Concord Street Railway and other property, to issue stock and bonds to pay therefor, and authorizing a physical connection of the Manchester Street Railway with the electric branches of the Concord & Montreal Railroad," reported the same without amendment and recommended its passage.

The report was accepted.

The question being stated,

Shall the bill be read a third time?

Senator Bickford moved to lay the bill, together with the report, on the table.

The question being stated,

Shall the bill, together with the report, be laid on the table?

The motion prevailed on a viva voce vote.

Senator Page demanded the yeas and nays.

The clerk proceeded to call the roll.

The following Senators voted in the affirmative:

Senators Allen, Marvin, Felt, Fuller, Ripley, Wilkins, Lightbody, Bickford, and Foley.

The following Senators voted in the negative:

Senators Keyes, Lewando, Burnell, Tilton, Cooper, Fellows, Neal, Tolles, Hoyt of District No. 21, Thompson, Richmond, and Page.

Nine Senators having voted in the affirmative and twelve Senators having voted in the negative, the negative prevailed.

The question recurring,

Shall the bill be read a third time?

The affirmative prevailed on a viva voce vote, and the bill was ordered to a third reading this afternoon at 2 o'clock.

The following message was received from the House of Representatives by its clerk:

HOUSE MESSAGE.

Mr. President:

The House of Representatives has passed bills with the following titles, in the passage of which it asks the concurrence of the Honorable Senate:

An act to unite the school districts of the town of Rollinsford.

An act in amendment of chapter 78 of the Laws of 1897, relating to biennial elections.

An act authorizing the city of Dover to exempt from taxation the property of the Hayes Hospital.

An act to abolish the Board of Library Commissioners.

An act to amend chapter 92 of the Public Statutes, relating to duties of school boards.

An act reviving and continuing the charter of the Warner and Kearsarge Road Company and amendments to said charter.

An act to amend chapter 93, in relation to scholars.

An act to amend chapter 95 of the Public Statutes, relating to the trustees of the State Normal School.

An act to provide for obtaining the testimony of non-resident directors, officers, and agents of New Hampshire corporations, and the production of corporate books, records, and papers.

An act in relation to the salary of the state reporter.

The following entitled bills sent up from the House of Representatives were severally read a first and second time and referred:

To the Committee on the Judiciary:

An act in relation to the salary of the state reporter.

An act in amendment of chapter 78 of the Laws of 1897, relating to biennial elections.

An act authorizing the city of Dover to exempt from taxation the property of the Hayes Hospital.

An act to provide for obtaining the testimony of non-resident directors, officers, and agents of New Hampshire corporations, and the production of corporate books, records, and papers.

To the Committee on State Library:

An act to abolish the Board of Library Commissioners.

To the Committee on Railroads:

An act reviving and continuing the charter of the Warner and Kearsarge Road Company and amendments to said charter.

To the Committee on Education :

An act to unite the school districts of the town of Rollinsford.

An act to amend chapter 92 of the Public Statutes, relating to duties of school boards.

An act to amend chapter 93, in relation to scholars.

An act to amend chapter 95 of the Public Statutes, relating to the trustees of the State Normal School.

LEAVE OF ABSENCE.

Senator Tolles was granted leave of absence for the afternoon session.

On motion of Senator Lightbody, the Senate adjourned.

AFTERNOON.

(Senator Keyes in the chair.)

The following entitled House bill was read a third time :

An act authorizing the Concord & Montreal Railroad, lessor, to acquire the Concord Street Railway and other property, to issue stock and bonds to pay therefor, and authorizing a physical connection of the Manchester Street Railway with the electric branches of the Concord & Montreal Railroad.

The question being stated,

Shall the bill pass ?

(Discussion ensued.)

The affirmative prevailed on a *viva voce* vote and the bill passed.

The following entitled House bills were severally read a third time and passed :

An act to promote cleanliness and to protect the public from the disease commonly known as consumption.

An act to extend the charter for the building of the Claremont Street Railway.

Senator Lightbody for the Committee on Education, to whom was referred a bill entitled "An act to amend chapter 92 of the Public Statutes, relating to the duties of school boards," reported the same without amendment and recommended its passage.

Senator Thompson for the Committee on Education, to whom was referred a bill entitled "An act to amend chapter 95 of the Public Statutes, relating to the trustees of the State Normal School," reported the same without amendment and recommended its passage.

The reports were accepted and the bills were severally ordered to a third reading to-morrow morning at 11 o'clock.

Senator Lewando for the Committee on Fisheries and Game, to whom was referred a "Joint resolution in relation to a fish-hatching house at Laconia," reported the same without amendment and recommended its passage.

The report was accepted and the joint resolution laid on the table to be printed.

The following report from the Committee on Engrossed Bills was read and accepted:

The Committee on Engrossed Bills have carefully examined and found correctly engrossed the following entitled bill:

An act to establish a police court in the town of Haverhill.

HENRY W. KEYES,

For the Committee.

The following message was received from the House of Representatives by its clerk:

HOUSE MESSAGE.

Mr. President:

The House of Representatives has passed a bill with the following title, in the passage of which it asks the concurrence of the Honorable Senate:

An act to extend the time of the charter of the Keene, Marlow & Newport Electric Railway Co.

The following entitled bill sent up from the House of Representatives was read a first and second time and referred:

To the Committee on Railroads:

An act to extend the time of the charter of the Keene, Marlow & Newport Electric Railway Company.

On motion of Senator Marvin, the Senate adjourned.

THURSDAY, JANUARY 29, 1903.

The Senate met according to adjournment.

The reading of the journal having been commenced, on motion of Senator Keyes, the rules were so far suspended that its further reading was dispensed with.

The following entitled House bills were severally read a third time and passed :

An act to amend chapter 95 of the Public Statutes, relating to the trustees of the State Normal School.

An act to amend chapter 92 of the Public Statutes, relating to duties of school boards.

Joint resolution in relation to a fish hatching house Laconia, having been printed, was taken from the table and ordered to a third reading this afternoon at 2 o'clock.

Senator Fuller, for the Committee on Agriculture, to whom was referred a bill entitled "An act providing a seal for the State Board of Agriculture," reported the same without amendment and recommended its passage.

Senator Burnell, for the Committee on Agriculture, to whom was referred a bill entitled "An act to authorize the State Board of Agriculture to appoint a state nursery inspector, and to provide for the protection of trees and shrubs from injurions insects and disease," reported the same without amendment and recommended its passage.

The reports were accepted and the bills severally laid on the table to be printed.

Senator Stillings, for the Committee on State Library, to whom was referred a bill entitled "An act to abolish the Board of Library Commissioners," reported the same without amendment and recommended its passage.

The report was accepted, and on motion of Senator Stillings, the rules were so far suspended that the bill was read a third time and passed.

The following report from the Committee on Engrossed Bills was read and accepted :

The Committee on Engrossed Bills have examined bills with the following titles and find them correctly engrossed :

An act authorizing the Concord & Montreal Railroad, lessor, to acquire the Concord Street Railway and other property, to issue stock and bonds to pay therefor, and authorizing a physical connection of the Manchester Street Railway with the electric branches of the Concord & Montreal Railroad.

An act to extend the charter for the building of the Claremont Street Railway.

An act to promote cleanliness and to protect the public from the disease commonly known as consumption.

An act to change the name of Dodge's Falls Dam and Manufacturing Company to "Ryegate Paper Company."

A. W. BURNELL,
For the Committee.

On motion of Senator Tilton, the following resolution was adopted:

Resolved, That when the Senate adjourn this afternoon, it be to meet Friday morning at 9.30 o'clock, and when it then adjourns it be to meet Monday evening at 7.30 o'clock.

On motion of Senator Keyes, the Senate adjourned.

AFTERNOON.

Joint resolution in relation to a fish hatching house at Laconia, was read a third time, passed, and sent to the House of Representatives for concurrence.

The following entitled Senate bill having been printed was taken from the table, and on motion of Senator Bickford, the rules were so far suspended that the bill was read a third time, passed, and sent to the House of Representatives for concurrence:

An act in relation to bail in criminal cases.

The following message was received from the House of Representatives by its clerk:

HOUSE MESSAGE.

Mr. President:

The House of Representatives has passed bills with the following titles, in the passage of which it asks the concurrence of the Honorable Senate:

An act in amendment of chapter 78 of the Laws of 1901, entitled "An act providing for a judiciary system consisting of two courts."

An act to amend chapter 241 of the Session Laws of 1893, entitled "An act to establish the city of Laconia" and repealing chapter 200 of the Laws of 1901, entitled "An act to amend chapter 241 of the Session Laws of 1893, entitled 'An act to establish the city of Laconia.'"

The following entitled bill sent up from the House of Representatives was read a first and second time:

An act in amendment of chapter 78 of the Laws of 1901, entitled "An act providing for a judiciary system consisting of two courts."

On motion of Senator Lewando, the rules were so far suspended that the bill was read a third time by its title and passed.

The following entitled bill sent up from the House of Representatives was read a first and second time:

An act to amend chapter 241 of the Session Laws of 1893, entitled "An act to establish the city of Laconia," and repealing chapter 200 of the Laws of 1901, entitled "An act to amend chapter 241 of the Session Laws of 1893, entitled 'An act to establish the city of Laconia.'"

Senator Tilton moved that the rules be so far suspended that the bill be read a third time by its title at the present time.

The question being stated,

Shall the rules be suspended?

(Discussion ensued.)

Senator Page demanded the yeas and nays.

The clerk proceeded to call the roll.

The following Senators voted in the affirmative:

Senators Keyes, Whitney, Lewando, Burnell, Tilton, Cooper, Felt, Stillings, Fellows, Neal, Fuller, Ripley, Wilkins, Lightbody, Hoyt of District No. 21, and Thompson.

The following Senators voted in the negative :

Senators Marvin, Foley, Tolles, and Page.

Seventeen Senators having voted in the affirmative and four Senators having voted in the negative, the affirmative prevailed, the rules were suspended, and the bill was read a third time by its title.

The question being stated,

Shall the bill pass?

The affirmative prevailed on a *viva voce* vote.

Senator Page demanded the yeas and nays.

The clerk proceeded to call the roll.

The following Senators voted in the affirmative :

Senators Keyes, Whitney, Lewando, Burnell, Tilton, Cooper, Felt, Stillings, Fellows, Neal, Fuller, Ripley, Wilkins, Lightbody, Bickford, Hoyt of District No. 21, and Thompson.

The following Senators voted in the negative :

Senators Marvin, Foley, Tolles, and Page.

Seventeen Senators having voted in the affirmative and four Senators having voted in the negative, the affirmative prevailed, and the bill passed.

On motion of Senator Lightbody, the following resolution was adopted :

Resolved, That the clerk procure for the use of the Senate, sixty copies of the Gilmore manual of the New Hampshire Senate.

On motion of Senator Fuller, the Senate adjourned.

* * *

FRIDAY, JANUARY 30, 1903.

The Senate met according to adjournment.

The reading of the journal having been commenced, on motion of Senator Keyes, the rules were so far suspended that its further reading was dispensed with.

The following report from the Committee on Engrossed Bills was read and accepted :

The Committee on Engrossed Bills have examined and found correctly engrossed the following entitled bill :

An act to amend chapter 241 of the Session Laws of 1893, entitled "An act to establish the City of Laconia," and repealing chapter 200 of the Laws of 1901, entitled "An act to amend chapter 241 of the Session Laws of 1893, entitled 'An act to establish the City of Laconia.'"

HENRY W. KEYES,
For the Committee.

On motion of Senator Allen, the Senate adjourned.

MONDAY, FEBRUARY 2, 1903.

The Senate met according to adjournment.

The journal was read and approved.

On motion of Senator Burnell, the Senate adjourned.

TUESDAY, FEBRUARY 3, 1903.

The Senate met according to adjournment.

The journal was read and approved.

On motion of Senator Keyes, the following resolution was adopted:

Resolved, That, until otherwise ordered, the Senate will meet at 11 o'clock in the forenoon and at 3 o'clock in the afternoon.

The following entitled Senate and House bills, having been printed, were taken from the table, and severally ordered to a third reading this afternoon at 3 o'clock:

An act to authorize the State Board of Agriculture to appoint a state nursery inspector and to provide for the protection of trees and shrubs from injurious insects and diseases.

An act to amend chapter 69 of the Laws of 1901, entitled "An act to protect the Ammonoosuc river in Carroll, Bethlehem, Littleton, Lisbon, and Bath, and its tributaries, from pollution by sawdust and other waste."

The following message was received from the House of Representatives by its clerk:

Mr. President:

The House of Representatives has passed the following entitled bills, and joint resolutions, in the passage of which it
asks the concurrence of the Honorable Senate :

An act to amend chapter 79 of the Laws of 1899, entitled
"An act to amend chapter 184 of the Public Statutes, relating
to the times and places of holding courts of probate within and
for the county of Grafton."

An act to amend chapter 183 of Session Laws of 1897, entitled "An act to authorize the village fire precinct of Wolfeborough to construct and maintain an electric plant."

An act relating to salary of justice of police court of Nashua,
in case of vacancy in office of justice.

An act to extend the time for the location, construction, and
completion of the railroad of the Moosilauke Railroad Company.

An act to authorize the city of Concord to appropriate money
for the celebration of its semi-centennial.

An act in amendment of the charter of the city of Concord,
providing for the election of overseers of the poor.

An act in amendment of the charter of the city of Concord,
authorizing the establishment of precincts within said city for
the collection of garbage.

An act to establish the salary of the justice of the police
court of Concord.

An act in amendment of section 15, chapter 93 of the Public
Statutes as amended in 1901, relating to scholars.

An act in amendment of section 11, chapter 79 of the Session Laws of 1901, relating to the fish and game commissioners.

Joint resolution appropriating money to be expended for a
monument at Vicksburg, Miss.

The following entitled bills and joint resolution sent up from
the House of Representatives were severally read a first and
second time and referred,—

To the Committee on the Judiciary :

An act in amendment of section 15, chapter 93 of the Public
Statutes as amended in 1901, relating to scholars.

An act in amendment of the charter of the city of Concord, providing for the election of overseers of the poor.

To the Committee on Revision of the Laws :

An act to amend chapter 79 of the Laws of 1899, entitled "An act to amend chapter 184 of the Public Statutes, relating to the times and places of holding courts of probate within and for the county of Grafton."

An act relating to salary of associate justice of the police court of Nashua, in case of vacancy in office of justice.

An act to establish the salary of the justice of the police court of Concord.

An act to amend chapter 183 of Session Laws of 1897, entitled "An act to authorize the village fire precinct of Wolfeborough to construct and maintain an electric plant."

To the Committee on Military Affairs :

Joint resolution appropriating money to be expended for a monument at Vicksburg, Miss.

To the Committee on Fisheries and Game :

An act in amendment of section 11, chapter 79 of the Session Laws of 1901, relating to the fish and game commissioners.

To the Committee on Railroads :

An act to extend the time for the location, construction, and completion of the railroad of the Moosilauke Railroad Company.

To the Committee on Finance :

An act to authorize the city of Concord to appropriate money for the celebration of its semi-centennial.

To the Committee on Public Improvements :

An act in amendment of the charter of the city of Concord, authorizing the establishment of precincts within said city for the collection of garbage.

Senator Tolles, for the Committee on the Judiciary, to whom was referred a bill entitled "An act in amendment of chapter 192 of the Public Statutes, relating to insolvent estates," reported the same in new draft and recommended its passage.

The report was accepted and the bill, in its new draft, was read a first and second time and laid on the table to be printed.

Senator Neal, for the Committee on Public Health, reported

a bill entitled "An act in amendment of chapter 171 of the Public Statutes, relating to life insurance," and recommended its passage.

The report was accepted and the bill reported from the committee was read a first and second time and laid on the table to be printed.

The following report from the Committee on Engrossed Bills was read and accepted:

The Committee on Engrossed Bills have examined bills with the following titles and find them correctly engrossed:

An act to abolish the Board of Library Commissioners.

An act to amend chapter 92 of the Public Statutes, relating to duties of school boards.

An act to amend chapter 95 of the Public Statutes, relating to the trustees of the State Normal School.

An act in amendment of chapter 78 of the Laws of 1901, entitled "An act providing for a judiciary system consisting of two courts."

A. W. BURNELL,
For the Committee.

PETITIONS PRESENTED AND REFERRED.

To the Committee on the Judiciary:

By President Hoitt, petition of Boscawen Lodge, No. 127, I. O. G. T., and Mrs. John T. Fowler and others of Newfields, asking the Senate to retain the present prohibitory law and prevent the passage of a high license local option bill.

LEAVE OF ABSENCE.

The Committee on Education was granted leave of absence from to-day's session.

The following communication and certified copies of resolutions adopted by the Constitutional Convention of 1902, were received by the clerk and laid before the Senate:

CONCORD, N. H., Feb. 3, 1903.

THOMAS F. CLIFFORD, ESQ.,

Clerk of the Senate,

Concord, N. H.

Sir: Enclosed herewith please find a certified copy of the amendment to the Constitution, as passed by the recent Convention to revise the Constitution, pertaining to the regulation and control of trusts.

Also a certified copy of the resolution introduced by Mr. Leach of Franklin, on the subject of free passes, and a transcript of my journal relating thereto.

Very respectfully yours,

T. H. MADIGAN, JR.,

Secretary of the Convention to Revise the Constitution.

On motion of Mr. Chandler of Concord the various resolutions on the subject of free passes, together with the substitute resolution of Mr. Leach of Franklin, were recalled from the Committee of the Whole.

The question was upon the adoption of the resolution offered by Mr. Leach of Franklin:

Resolved, That the Committee report to the Convention in favor of the indefinite postponement of all proposed amendments relating to free passes, with the recommendation that the Legislature consider the subject and enact such legislation, if any, as in their opinion the public good may require.

The yeas and nays were ordered taken upon the question, and 221 gentlemen having voted in the affirmative and 101 in the negative the motion prevailed.

I hereby certify that the above is a true copy of the record.

T. H. MADIGAN, JR.,

Secretary of the Convention of 1902 to Revise the Constitution.

TRUSTS.

Article 82 of the Constitution is amended by adding the following: Free and fair competition in the trades and industries is an inherent and essential right of the people, and should be protected against all monopolies and conspiracies which tend to hinder or destroy it. The size and functions of all corporations should be so limited and regulated as to prohibit fictitious capitalization, and provision should be made for the supervision and government thereof.

Therefore, all just power possessed by the state is hereby granted to the General Court to enact laws to prevent the operations within the state of all persons and associations, and all trusts and corporations, foreign or domestic, and the officers thereof, who endeavor to raise the price of any article of commerce or to destroy free and fair competition in the trades and industries through combination, conspiracy, monopoly, or any other unfair means; to control and regulate the acts of all persons, associations, corporations, trusts, and officials doing business within the state; to prevent fictitious capitalization; and to authorize civil and criminal proceedings in respect to all the wrongs herein declared against.

I hereby certify that the above is a true copy of the record.

T. H. MADIGAN, JR.,
Secretary of the Convention of 1902 to Revise the Constitution.

On motion of Senator Page, it was voted that action on the foregoing resolutions be indefinitely postponed.

(Senator Richmond in the chair.)

On motion of Senator Tolles, the Senate adjourned.

AFTERNOON.

The following entitled Senate bill was read a third time, passed, and sent to the House of Representatives for concurrence:

An act to authorize the State Board of Agriculture to appoint a state nursery inspector, and to provide for the protection of trees and shrubs from injurious insects and diseases.

The following entitled House bill was read a third time and passed:

An act to amend chapter 69 of the Laws of 1901, entitled "An act to protect the Ammonoosuc river in Carroll, Bethlehem, Littleton, Lisbon, and Bath, and its tributaries, from pollution by sawdust and other waste."

The following message was received from the House of Representatives by its clerk:

HOUSE MESSAGE.

Mr. President:

The House of Representatives has passed bills with the following titles, in the passage of which it asks the concurrence of the Honorable Senate:

An act in amendment of chapter 44 of the Laws of 1893, relating to the powers and duties of the Forestry Commission with respect to public parks.

An act in amendment of section 9, chapter 105 of the laws passed January session, 1901, relating to political caucuses and conventions.

An act to authorize the city of Portsmouth to raise money and issue bonds for a new high schoolhouse.

An act to amend section 4 of chapter 96 of the Laws of 1901, and section 6 of chapter 92 of the Public Statutes, relating to courses of study.

An act confirming and legalizing the organization and acts of the Berlin Street Railway.

An act in amendment of the charter of the Wells River Bridge, and authorizing the Concord & Montreal Railroad to hold stock therein.

An act to establish the Lisbon village district.

The following entitled bills sent up from the House of Representatives were severally read a first and second time and referred:

To the Committee on Railroads:

An act confirming and legalizing the organization and acts of the Berlin Street Railway.

An act in amendment of the charter of the Wells River Bridge, and authorizing the Concord & Montreal Railroad to hold stock therein.

To the Committee on the Judiciary:

An act in amendment of section 9, chapter 105 of the laws passed January session, 1901, relating to political caucuses and conventions.

To the Committee on Education:

An act to amend section 4 of chapter 96 of the Laws of

1901, and section 6 of chapter 92 of the Public Statutes, relating to courses of study.

To the Committee on Finance:

An act to authorize the city of Portsmouth to raise money and issue bonds for a new high schoolhouse.

To the Committee on Forestry:

An act in amendment of chapter 44 of the Laws of 1893, relating to the powers and duties of the Forestry Commission with respect to public parks.

To the Committee on Towns and Parishes:

An act to establish the Lisbon village district.

Senator Stillings, for the Committee on Public Improve_ ments, reported a bill, entitled "An act to provide for the improvement of public roads," and recommended its passage.

The report was accepted, and the bill reported from the Committee was read a first and second time, and laid on the table to be printed.

Senator Lewando, for the Committee on Revision of Laws, to whom was referred a bill, entitled " An act in amendment of section 1, chapter 185, Laws of 1901, entitled ' An act authorizing the Hillsborough county convention to raise money for the building and repairing of court houses,' " reported the same with the following amendment, and recommended its passage: Said act is hereby amended by striking out the words " together with such committee as the said county convention may appoint," in the sixteenth and seveneenth lines; also strike out the word " such " after the word " in " in the twentieth line, and insert in the same line after the word " denominations " the words " of one hundred, five hundred, and ten hundred dollars," so that said section as amended shall read as follows:

" Section 1.   The county convention for Hillsborough county, for the years 1901 and 1902, is authorized to vote a sum of money not exceeding one hundred and thirty thousand dollars for the purchase of land, and the erection, completion, and furnishing of a court house and county offices in the city of Nashua, and for the purchase of land and buildings and the making additions to and alterations and repairs of such buildings so purchased in Manchester, or for the erection and completion of a building in the city of Manchester, and the furnishing thereof for court house and county office purposes, and to empower the county commissioners of said county to borrow a sufficient sum of money for such purpose, and to issue the bonds of the county therefor in denominations of one hundred, five hundred, and ten hundred, and at such rate of interest not exceeding three per cent. per annum, payable at such time and place as they may determine, and all bonds thus issued and sold to individuals living in said county of Hillsborough shall be exempt from taxation."

The report was accepted.

The question being stated,

Shall the amendment be adopted?

On motion of Senator Lewando, the bill was recommitted for further consideration.

On motion of Senator Foley, the Senate adjourned.

WEDNESDAY, FEBRUARY 4, 1903.

The Senate met according to adjournment.

The reading of the journal having commenced, on motion of Senator Keyes, the rules were so far suspended that its further reading was dispensed with.

The following entitled House bill, having been printed, was taken from the table and ordered to a third reading this afternoon at 3 o'clock: ·

An act providing a seal for the State Board of Agriculture.

The following entitled Senate bill, having been printed, was taken from the table and ordered to a third reading this afternoon at 3 o'clock:

An act to provide for the improvement of public roads.

Senator Tolles moved to reconsider the vote whereby the bill was ordered to a third reading.

The motion prevailed on a *viva voce* vote.

On motion of the same Senator, the bill was referred to the Committee on Public Improvements.

The following message was received from the House of Representatives by its clerk:

HOUSE MESSAGE.

Mr. President:

The House of Representatives has passed the following entitled bills and joint resolution, in the passage of which it asks the concurrence of the Honorable Senate:

An act to amend an act to establish a corporation by the name of the trustees of the N. H. Conference Seminary and the N. H. Female College, approved December 29, 1852, and other acts amending the same.

An act in amendment of sections 1, 3, and 4 of chapter 72 of the Public Statutes, relating to the discontinuance of highways.

An act in amendment of the charter of the Walpole Electric Light & Power Company.

An act to repeal the charter of the Massabesic Horse Railroad Company.

An act to amend chapter 92, Public Statutes, relating to school boards.

An act in amendment of the charter of the Colby Academy, providing for filling vacancies and election of members.

An act to incorporate the First Free Baptist church of Franconia.

An act to amend chapter 179 of the Public Statutes, relating to guardians of insane persons and spendthrifts.

An act to permit executors and administrators to resign.

An act to amend sections 54 and 58, chapter 78 of the fish and game laws.

An act to amend the charter of the North Shore Water Company.

An act in amendment of the charter of the Exeter Gas Light Company.

An act to incorporate the Walpole Water & Sewer Company.

An act to encourage the planting and perpetuation of forests.

An act to authorize the town of Lancaster to exempt certain property from taxation, and to ratify its doings in the same.

Joint resolution to provide for a forest examination of the White Mountain region.

The following entitled bills and joint resolution, sent up from the House of Representatives, were severally read a first and second time, and referred:

To the Committee on the Judiciary:

An act to amend an act to establish a corporation by the name of the trustees of the N. H. Conference Seminary and the N. H. Female College, approved December 29, 1852, and other acts amending the same.

An act to amend chapter 179 of the Public Statutes, relating to guardians of insane persons and spendthrifts.

An act in amendment of the charter of the Colby Academy, providing for filling vacancies and election of members.

An act to amend the charter af the North Shore Water Company.

To the Committee on the Revision of the Laws :

An act to permit executors and administrators to resign.

An act in amendment of sections 1, 3, and 4 of chapter 72 of the Public Statutes, relating to the discontinuance of highways.

To the Committee on Incorporations:

An act to incorporate the First Free Baptist church of Franconia.

An act to incorporate the Walpole Water & Sewer Company.

An act in amendment of the charter of the Walpole Electric Light & Power Company.

An act in amendment of the charter of the Exeter Gas Light Company.

To the Committee on Forestry:

An act to encourage the planting and perpetuation of forests.

Joint resolution to provide for a forest examination of the White Mountain region.

To the Committee on Railroads :

An act to repeal the charter of the Massabesic Horse Railroad Company.

To the Committee on Education :

An act to amend chapter 92, Public Statutes, relating to school boards.

To the Committee on Fisheries and Game:

An act to amend sections 54 and 58, chapter 78 of the fish and game laws.

To the Committee on Towns and Parishes:

An act to authorize the town of Lancaster to exempt certain property from taxation, and to ratify its doings in the same.

Senator Tolles, for the Committee on the Judiciary, to whom was referred a bill entitled " An act in relation to the salary of the state reporter," reported the same without amendment, and recommended its passage.

The report was accepted and the bill ordered to a third reading this afternoon at 3 o'clock.

On motion of Senator Ripley, the following entitled House bill was recalled from the Committee on the Judiciary:

An act in amendment of section 15 of chapter 93 of the Public Statutes, as amended in 1901, relating to scholars.

Senator Page moved that the bill be returned to the House of Representatives.

Senator Thompson moved to lay the motion offered by the Honorable Senator from District No. 24, together with the bill, on the table.

Senator Bickford rose to a point of order, stating that said bill was not physically before the Senate.

The Chair ruled that the point of order was not well taken.

The question being stated,

Shall the motion to lay the bill, and motion of the Honorable Senator from District 24, on the table, prevail?

The affirmative prevailed on a *viva voce* vote.

(Senator Neal in the chair.)

Senator Lightbody, for the Committee on Education, to whom was referred a bill entitled " An act to amend chapter 93, in relation to scholars," reported the same without amendment and recommended its passage.

The report was accepted and the bill laid on the table to be printed.

The same Senator, for the same committee, to whom was referred a bill entitled " An act to amend chapter 93, section 15 of the Public Statutes, as amended by chapter 61 of the Session Laws of 1901, relating to scholars," reported the same with the following amendment and recommended its passage : Amend by striking out section 2 and insert in place thereof the following :

SECT. 2. Nothing in this act shall be construed as relating to the routine duties of his office in Concord.

Further amend by adding the following section :

SECT. 3. This act shall take effect upon its passage.

The report was accepted.

The question being stated,

Shall the amendments be adopted ?

The affirmative prevailed on a *viva voce* vote, and the bill was laid on the table to be printed.

On motion of Senator Bickford, the rules were so far suspended that all bills in order for a third reading this afternoon at 3 o'clock were made in order for a third reading at the present time.

The following entitled House bills were severally read a third time and passed :

An act in relation to the salary of the state reporter.

An act providing a seal for the State Board of Agriculture.

The following entitled Senate bills, having been printed, were taken from the table and severally ordered to a third reading this afternoon at 3 o'clock.

An act in amendment of chapter 192 of the Public Statutes, relating to insolvent estates.

An act in amendment of chapter 171 of the Public Statutes, relating to life insurance.

On motion of Senator Thompson, the Senate adjourned.

AFTERNOON.

The following message was received from the House of Representatives by its clerk :

HOUSE MESSAGE.

Mr. President:

The House of Representatives has passed bills with the

following titles, in the passage of which it asks the concurrence of the Honorable Senate:

An act to legalize the town meetings in Dorchester for years 1896, 1897, 1898, 1899, and 1900.

An act to repeal an act of the legislature of 1842, entitled "An act to annex Richard Pickering of Newington to school district No. 1 in Portsmouth," approved June 22, 1842.

An act to legalize the biennial election of the town of Effingham, held November 4th, 1902.

An act to legalize and confirm the warrant for, and the votes and proceedings at, the biennial election and meeting in Stratham, held the fourth day of November, 1902.

An act to legalize the biennial election of the town of Conway, held November 4, 1902.

An act to legalize and confirm the selectmen's warrant for and the votes and proceedings thereunder, at the biennial election and meeting in the town of Columbia, held in said town on the fourth day of November, A. D. 1902.

The House of Representatives has adopted the following resolution:

Resolved, That the Honorable Senate be requested to return to the House of Representatives the following entitled bill: "An act in amendment of section 15, chapter 93 of the Public Statutes, as amended in 1901, relating to scholars."

On motion of Senator Thompson, the following entitled bill was taken from the table:

An act in amendment of section 15 of chapter 93 of the Public Statutes, as amended in 1901, relating to scholars.

On motion of the same Senator, the request of the House of Representatives asking to have the bill returned was granted.

On motion of Senator Foley, the Senate voted to take a recess for 30 minutes.

(Recess.)

The Senate reassembled.

The following entitled bills sent up from the House of Representatives were severally read a first and second time and referred:

To the Committee on Elections:

An act to legalize the biennial election of the town of Conway, held November 4, 1902.

An act to legalize the biennial election of the town of Effingham, held November 4th, 1902.

An act to legalize the town meetings in Dorchester for years 1896, 1897, 1898, 1899, and 1900.

An act to legalize and confirm the selectmen's warrant for and the votes and proceedings thereunder, at the biennial election and meeting in the town of Columbia, held in said town on the fourth day of November, A. D. 1902.

An act to legalize and confirm the warrant for, and the votes and proceedings at, the biennial election and meeting in Stratham, held the fourth day of November, 1902.

To the Committee on Education:

An act to repeal an act of the Legislature of 1842, entitled "An act to annex Richard Pickering of Newington to school district No. 1, in Portsmouth," approved June 22, 1842.

The following entitled Senate bills were severally read a third time, passed, and sent to the House of Representatives for concurrence:

An act in amendment of chapter 171 of the Public Statutes, relating to life insurance.

An act in amendment of chapter 192 of the Public Statutes, relating to insolvent estates.

Senator Stillings, for the Committee on Public Improvements, to whom was referred a bill entitled "An act in amendment of the charter of the city of Concord authorizing the establishment of precincts within said city for the collection of garbage," reported the same without amendment and recommended its passage.

Senator Burnell, for the Committee on Fisheries and Game, to whom was referred a bill entitled "An act in amendment of section 11, chapter 79 of the Session Laws of 1901, relating to the fish and game commissioners," reported the same without amendment and recommended its passage.

Senator Lightbody, for the Committee on Military Affairs, to whom was referred Joint resolution appropriating money to be expended for a monument at Vicksburg, Miss., reported the same without amendment and recommended its passage.

Senator Ripley, for the Committee on Finance, to whom was referred the following entitled bills:

An act to authorize the city of Concord to appropriate money for the celebration of its semi-centennial.

An act to authorize the city of Portsmouth to raise money and, issue bonds for a new high schoolhouse, reported the same without amendment and recommended their passage.

Senator Richmond, for the Committee on Incorporations, to whom was referred the following entitled bills:

An act in amendment of the charter of the Walpole Electric Light and Power Company.

An act to revive, renew, and amend the charter of the Knights of Pythias Building Association of Manchester, reported the same without amendment and recommended their passage.

The reports were accepted and the bills and joint resolution were severally ordered to a third reading to-morrow morning at 11 o'clock.

The following report from the Committee on Engrossed Bills was read and accepted:

The Committee on Engrossed Bills have examined bills with the following titles and find them correctly engrossed:

An act to amend chapter 69 of the Laws of 1901, entitled "An act to protect the Ammonoosuc river in Carroll, Bethlehem, Littleton, Lisbon, and Bath, and its tributaries, from pollution by sawdust and other waste."

An act in relation to the salary of the state reporter.

A. W. BURNELL,
For the Committee.

On motion of Senator Keyes, the Senate adjourned.

THURSDAY, FEBRUARY 5, 1903.

The Senate met according to adjournment.

The reading of the journal having been commenced, on

motion of Senator Fuller, the rules were so far suspended that its further reading was dispensed with.

The following entitled House bills and House joint resolution were severally read a third time and passed:

An act in amendment of section 11, chapter 79 of the Session Laws of 1901, relating to the fish and game commissioners.

An act in amendment of the charter of the city of Concord, authorizing the establishment of precincts within said city for the collection of garbage.

An act to authorize the city of Portsmouth to raise money and issue bonds for a new high school house.

An act to authorize the city of Concord to appropriate money for the celebration of its semi-centennial.

Joint resolution appropriating money to be expended for a monument at Vicksburg, Miss.

The following entitled House bills in order for third reading at the present time were severally taken up, and

On motion of Senator Keyes, the bills were laid on the table.

An act to incorporate the Walpole Water and Sewer Company.

An act in amendment of the charter of the Walpole Electric Light and Power Company.

The following entitled Senate bill was read a third time, passed, and sent to the House of Representatives for concurrence:

An act to revise, renew, and amend the charter of the Knights of Pythias Building Association of Manchester.

The following entitled House bill, having been printed, was taken from the table and ordered to a third reading this afternoon at 3 o'clock:

An act to amend chapter 93, in relation to scholars.

Senator Fuller, for the Committee on Revision of the Laws, to whom was referred a bill entitled "An act to amend chapter 183 of Session Laws of 1897, entitled 'An act to authorize the village fire precinct of Wolfeborough to construct and maintain an electric plant,' " reported the same without amendment and recommended its passage.

Senator Keyes, for the Committee on Railroads, to whom was referred a bill entitled "An act reviving and continuing the charter of the Warner and Kearsarge Road Company, and amendments to said charter," reported the same without amendment and recommended its passage.

Senator Hoyt of District No. 21, for the Committee on Revision of the Laws, to whom was referred a bill entitled "An act to amend chapter 79 of the Laws of 1899, entitled 'An act to amend chapter 184 of the Public Statutes, relating to the times and places of holding courts of probate within and for the county of Grafton," reported the same without amendment and recommended its passage.

Senator Page, for the Committee on Revision of the Laws, to whom was referred a bill entitled "An act relating to salary of associate justice of police court of Nashua, in case of vacancy in office of justice," reported the same without amendment and recommended its passage.

The reports were accepted and the bills severally ordered to a third reading this afternoon at 3 o'clock.

Senator Tolles, for the Committee on the Judiciary, to whom was referred a bill entitled "An act to provide for obtaining the testimony of non-resident directors, officers, and agents of New Hampshire corporations and the production of corporate books, records, and papers," reported the same with the following resolution :

Resolved, That it is inexpedient to legislate.

The report was accepted.

The question being stated,

Shall the resolution be adopted?

Senator Keyes moved to lay the bill and resolution on the table.

The question being stated,

Shall the bill and resolution be laid on the table?

The affirmative prevailed on a *viva voce* vote.

Senator Page rose to a question of privilege, and then demanded the yeas and nays.

The clerk proceeded to call the roll.

The following named Senators voted in the affirmative:

Senators Keyes, Whitney, Lewando, Burnell, Cooper, Felt, Fellows, Neal, Lightbody, and Hoyt of District No. 21.

The following Senators voted in the negative:

Senators Ripley, Wilkins, Bickford, Foley, Tolles, Richmond, and Page.

Ten senators having voted in the affirmative and seven senators having voted in the negative, the affirmative prevailed and the bill was laid on the table.

The following report from the Committee on Engrossed Bills was read and accepted:

The Committee on Engrossed Bills have examined a bill with the following title and find it correctly engrossed:

An act providing a seal for the State Board of Agriculture.

HENRY W. KEYES,
For the Committee.

The following message was received from the House of Representatives by its clerk:

HOUSE MESSAGE.

Mr. President:

The House of Representatives has passed bills with the following titles, in the passage of which it asks the concurrence of the Honorable Senate:

An act to incorporate the New Hampshire Genealogical Society.

An act to authorize the town of Lancaster to acquire property for the protection of its water supply.

The following entitled bills sent up from the House of Representatives were severally read a first and second time and referred:

To the Committee on Education:

An act to incorporate the New Hampshire Genealogical Society.

To the Committee on Incorporations:

An act to authorize the town of Lancaster to acquire property for the protection of its water supply.

On motion of Senator Hoyt of District No. 21, the Senate adjourned.

AFTERNOON.

The following entitled House bills were severally read a third time and passed:

An act reviving and continuing the charter of the Warner and Kearsarge Road Company, and amendments to said charter.

An act to amend chapter 79 of the Laws of 1899, entitled "An act to amend chapter 184 of the Public Statutes, relating to the times and places of holding courts of probate within and for the county of Grafton."

An act relating to salary of associate justice of police court of Nashua, in case of vacancy in office of justice.

An act to amend chapter 93, in relation to scholars.

An act to amend chapter 183 of Session Laws of 1897, entitled "An act to authorize the village fire precinct of Wolfeborough to construct and maintain an electric plant."

Senator Tolles, for the Committee on the Judiciary, to whom was referred a bill entitled "An act to amend an act to establish a corporation by the name of the trustees of the N. H. Conference Seminary and the N. H. Female College, approved December 29, 1852, and other acts amending the same," reported the same without amendment and recommended its passage.

The report was accepted and on motion of Senator Hoyt of District No. 21, the rules were so far suspended that the bill was read a third time and passed.

Senator Tolles, for the Committee on the Judiciary, to whom was referred the following entitled House bills, reported the same without amendment and recommended their passage:

An act authorizing the city of Dover to exempt from taxation the property of the Hayes Hospital.

An act in amendment of the charter of the city of Concord, providing for the election of overseers of the poor.

An act to amend the charter of the North Shore Water Company.

An act in amendment of the charter of the Colby Academy, providing for filling vacancies and election of members.

An act to amend chapter 179 of the Public Statutes, relating to guardians of insane persons and spendthrifts.

Senator Lewando, for the Committee on Revision of the Laws, to whom was referred a bill entitled "An act in amendment of sections 1, 3, and 4, of chapter 72 of the Public Statutes, relating to the discontinuance of highways," reported the same without amendment and recommended its passage.

The reports were accepted and the bills severally ordered to a third reading Tuesday morning next at 11 o'clock.

On motion of Senator Hoyt of District No. 21, the following resolution was adopted:

Resolved, That when the Senate adjourns, it adjourn to meet at 9.30 o'clock to-morrow morning, and when it adjourns to-morrow morning, it be to meet Monday evening at 7.30 o'clock.

On motion of Senator Bickford, the Senate adjourned.

FRIDAY, FEBRUARY 6, 1903.

The Senate met according to adjournment.

The reading of the journal having been commenced, on motion of Senator Keyes, the rules were so far suspended that its further reading was dispensed with.

On motion of the same Senator, the Senate adjourned.

MONDAY, FEBRUARY 9, 1903.

The Senate met according to adjournment.

The journal was read and approved.

On motion of Senator Fuller, the Senate adjourned.

TUESDAY, FEBRUARY 10, 1903.

The Senate met according to adjournment.

The journal was read and approved.

The following entitled House bills were severally read a third time and passed :

An act to amend the charter of the North Shore Water Company.

An act in amendment of the charter of the city of Concord, providing for the election of overseers of the poor.

An act in amendment of the charter of the Colby Academy, providing for filling vacancies and election of members.

An act in amendment of sections 1, 3, and 4 of chapter 72 of the Public Statutes, relating to the discontinuances of highways.

An act to amend chapter 179 of the Public Statutes, relating to guardians of insane persons and spendthrifts.

An act authorizing the city of Dover to exempt from taxation the property of the Hayes Hospital.

The following message was received from the House of Representatives by its clerk :

HOUSE MESSAGE.

Mr. President:

The House of Representatives has passed bills with the following titles, in the passage of which it asks the concurrence of the Honorable Senate:

An act to incorporate the Portsmouth & Newcastle Street Railway Company.

An act to establish water-works in Enfield village fire district in the town of Enfield.

An act in amendment of an act to incorporate the North Conway & Mount Kearsarge Railroad, passed June session 1883, and all subsequent acts relating to the same.

An act authorizing the town of Hudson to construct water-works and establish an electric light plant.

An act in amendment of the charter of the city of Dover, creating a board of street and park commissioners for said city.

An act in relation to the town of Newmarket and the Newmarket Water-Works.

An act to incorporate the Littleton, Franconia & Bethlehem Electric Railway Company.

The following entitled bills sent up from the House of Representatives were severally read a first and second time and referred :

To the Committee on Railroads :

An act to incorporate the Portsmouth & Newcastle Street Railway Company.

An act to incorporate the Littleton, Franconia & Bethlehem Electric Railway Company.

An act in amendment of an act to incorporate the North Conway & Mount Kearsarge Railroad, passed June session 1883, and all subsequent acts relating to the same.

The following entitled bill sent up from the House of Representatives was read a first and second time, and on motion of Senator Page, the rules were so far suspended that the bill was read a third time and passed :

An act in relation to the town of Newmarket and the Newmarket Water-Works.

On motion of Senator Page, the rules were so far suspended that the following entitled bills sent up from the House of Representatives were severally read a first and second time by their titles and referred :

To the Committee on the Judiciary :

An act authorizing the town of Hudson to construct water-works and establish an electric light plant.

To the Committee on Incorporations :

An act to establish water-works in Enfield village fire district, in the town of Enfield.

The following entitled bill sent up from the House of Representatives was read a first and second time :

An act in amendment of the charter of the city of Dover, creating a board of street and park commissioners for said city.

Senator Thompson moved that the rules be so far suspended that the bill be in order for a third reading at the present time.

The question being stated,

Shall the rules be suspended?

(Discussion ensued.)

The negative prevailed on a *viva voce* vote.

Senator Thompson called for a division.

One Senator voted in the affirmative and fourteen Senators voted in the negative. The negative prevailed, and the bill was referred to the Committee on the Judiciary.

On motion of Senator Keyes, the following entitled House bill was taken from the table :

An act to incorporate the Walpole Water and Sewer Company.

On motion of the same Senator, the rules were so far suspended that the bill was placed back on its second reading for purpose of amendment.

On motion of the same Senator, the following amendment was adopted :

Amend section 3 by inserting in the seventh line after the word "Walpole" the following, viz. : —"excepting that part of said town which lies northerly of a line drawn from the southwest corner of the town of Langdon near Table Rock, so called, on Fall Mountain, to the east end of the present stone arch bridge of the Boston & Maine Railroad Company across the Connecticut river at Bellows Falls, Vermont."

On motion of Senator Thompson, the rules were so far suspended that the bill as amended was read a third time by its title, passed, and sent to the House of Representatives for concurrence in Senate amendment.

On motion of Senator Keyes, the following entitled bill was taken from the table, read a third time, and passed.

An act in amendment of the charter of the Walpole Electric Light and Power Company.

Senator Whitney offered the following resolution :

Resolved, That the House of Representatives be requested to return to the Senate the following entitled Senate bill, which was passed by the Senate February 4 :

An act in amendment of chapter 171 of the Public Statutes, relating to life insurance.

The question being stated,

Shall the resolution be adopted ?

(Discussion ensued.)

The negative prevailed on a *viva voce* vote, and the resolution was not adopted.

On motion of Senator Keyes, the following resolution was adopted:

Resolved, That His Excellency the Governor be requested to return to the Senate the following entitled House bill for purpose of amending the title:

An act to amend chapter 93, in relation to scholars.

The foregoing entitled bill having been returned to the Senate, on motion of Senator Keyes, the following amendment was adopted:

Amend the title to the bill by inserting after the figures "93" the following: "of the Public Statutes"; so that the title as amended shall read: "An act to amend chapter 93 of the Public Statutes, in relation to scholars."

The bill with amended title was sent to the House of Representatives for concurrence in Senate amendment.

The following report from the Committee on Engrossed Bills was read and accepted:

The Committee on Engrossed Bills have examined and found correctly engrossed the following entitled bills and joint resolution:

An act to authorize the city of Concord to appropriate money for the celebration of its semi-centennial.

An act to authorize the city of Portsmouth to raise money and issue bonds for a new high school house.

An act in amendment of the charter of the city of Concord, authorizing the establishment of precincts within said city for the collection of garbage.

An act in amendment of section 11, chapter 79 of the Session Laws of 1901, relating to the fish and game commissioners.

An act to amend "An act to establish a corporation by the name of Trustees of the N. H. Conference Seminary and the N. H. Female College, approved Dec. 29, 1852, and other acts amending the same."

An act to amend chapter 183 of Session Laws of 1897 entitled "An act to authorize the village fire precinct of Wolfeborough to construct and maintain an electric plant."

An act relating to salary of associate justice of police court of Nashua, in case of vacancy in office of justice.

An act to amend chapter 79 of the Laws of 1899, entitled "An act to amend chapter 184 of the Public Statutes, relating to the times and places of holding courts of probate within and for the county of Grafton."

An act reviving and continuing the charter of the Warner & Kearsarge Road Company, and amendments to said charter.

Joint resolution appropriating money to be expended for a monument at Vicksburg, Miss.

HENRY W. KEYES,
For the Committee.

The following entitled Senate bill, having been printed, was taken from the table and ordered to a third reading this afternoon at 3 o'clock:

An act to amend chapter 93, section 15 of the Public Statutes, as amended by chapter 61 of the Session Laws of 1901, relating to scholars.

On motion of Senator Neal, the Senate adjourned.

AFTERNOON.

The following entitled Senate bill was read a third time, passed, and sent to the House of Representatives for concurrence:

An act to amend chapter 93, section 15 of the Public Statutes, as amended by chapter 61 of the Session Laws of 1901, relating to scholars.

On motion of Senator Bickford, the Senate adjourned.

WEDNESDAY, FEBRUARY 11, 1903.

The Senate met according to adjournment.

The reading of the journal having been commenced, on motion of Senator Wilkins, the rules were so far suspended that its further reading was dispensed with.

LEAVE OF ABSENCE.

On motion of Senator Stillings, leave of absence was granted Senator Burnell for the remainder of the week on account of sickness.

The following message was received from the House of Representatives by its clerk:

HOUSE MESSAGE.

Mr. President:

The House of Representatives has passed bills with the following titles, in the passage of which it asks the concurrence of the Honorable Senate:

An act to incorporate the Derry Savings Bank of Derry.

An act to enable the town of Greenville to acquire, own, and operate an electric power and lighting plant.

An act in amendment of section 3, chapter 209 of the Public Statutes, relating to exemptions from serving as jurors.

An act in amendment of section 27, chapter 154 of the Public Statutes, relating to the calling of proprietors' meetings.

An act in amendment of section 4 of chapter 206 of the Laws of 1897, being "An act to incorporate the Bethlehem Electric Light Company."

An act amending chapter 92 of the Public Statutes, in relation to school boards.

An act to establish a new apportionment for the assessment of public taxes.

An act in amendment of chapter 82 of the Laws of 1897, concerning the preservation and inspection of ballots.

The following entitled bills sent up from the House of Representatives were severally read a first and second time and referred:

To the Committee on Revision of the Laws:

An act in amendment of chapter 82 of the Laws of 1897, concerning the preservation and inspection of ballots.

An act in amendment of section 4 of chapter 206 of the Laws of 1897, being "An act to incorporate the Bethlehem Electric Light Company."

To the Committee on the Judiciary :

An act in amendment of section 27, chapter 154 of the Public Statutes, relating to the calling of proprietors' meetings.

An act in amendment of section 3, chapter 209 of the Public Statutes, relating to exemptions from serving as jurors.

To the Committee on Education :

An act amending chapter 92 of the Public Statutes, in relation to school boards.

To the Committee on Banks :

An act to incorporate the Derry Savings Bank in Derry.

To the Committee on Incorporations :

An act to enable the town of Greenville to acquire, own, and operate an electric power and lighting plant.

On motion of Senator Lewando, the rules were so far suspended that the following entitled bill sent up from the House of Representatives was read a first and second time by its title and referred to the Committee on Finance :

An act to establish a new apportionment for the assessment of public taxes.

Senator Bickford, under a suspension of the rules, sixteen Senators having actually voted in favor thereof, introduced a bill entitled :

" An act to incorporate the Ossipee Water and Electric Company," which was read a first and second time and referred to the Committee on Incorporations.

Senator Lightbody, for the Committee on Banks, to whom was referred a bill entitled " An act in amendment of the charter of the Plymouth Guaranty Savings Bank," reported the same with the following amendment and recommended its passage: Amend said bill by striking out section 2 and substituting in place thereof the following : Section 2. Said bank shall within thirty days after the passage of this act notify the general depositors of the foregoing amendment to the charter in such manner as the bank commissioners shall approve. Further amend said bill by adding the following section : Section 3. This act shall take effect on its passage.

The report was accepted, amendments adopted, and the bill laid upon the table to be printed.

On motion of Senator Keyes, the following resolution was adopted:

Resolved, That when the Senate adjourns this morning it adjourn to meet to-morrow morning at 11 o'clock.

On motion of Senator Thompson, the Senate adjourned.

THURSDAY, FEBRUARY 12, 1903.

The Senate met according to adjournment.

The journal was read and approved.

LEAVE OF ABSENCE.

The Committee on State Hospital was granted leave of absence for Tuesday afternoon, February 17.

On motion of Senator Page, the following resolution was adopted:

Resolved, That when the Senate adjourns this morning it adjourn to meet this afternoon at 2 o'clock.

Senator Lewando, for the Committee on Revision of the Laws, to whom was referred a bill entitled "An act to establish the salary of the justice of the police court of Concord," reported the same without amendment and recommended its passage.

The report was accepted and the bill ordered to a third reading this afternoon at 2 o'clock.

On motion of Senator Keyes, the following entited House bill was taken from the table:

An act to provide for obtaining the testimony of non-resident directors, officers, and agents of New Hampshire corporations, and the production of corporate books, records, and papers.

The question being stated,

Shall the resolution of the committee that it is inexpedient to legislate be adopted?

The negative prevailed on a *viva voce* vote.

Senator Keyes offered the following amendment

6

Amend section 5 by striking out the present section of the bill and inserting in place thereof the following : "Section 5. If any such director, officer, or agent shall wilfully neglect or refuse to appear and produce books, records, or papers, or to testify or to give his deposition as required in such order or summons, the superior court in its discretion may thereupon appoint a receiver to manage and control such corporation until the reasonable and just orders of the court shall be complied with, and when such orders shall have been complied with such receiver shall be discharged."

The question being stated,

Shall the amendment be adopted?

(Discussion ensued.)

Senator Tolles moved to recommit the bill to the Committee on the Judiciary.

The question being stated,

Shall the bill be recommitted?

(Discussion ensued.)

Senator Foley demanded the yeas and nays.

The clerk proceeded to call the roll.

The following named Senators voted in the affirmative :

Senators Marvin, Ripley, Wilkins, Bickford, Foley, Tolles, Richmond, and Page.

The following named Senators voted in the negative :

Senators Allen, Keyes, Whitney, Lewando, Tilton, Cooper, Felt, Stillings, Fellows, Neal, Fuller, Lightbody, Hoyt of District No. 21, and Thompson.

Eight Senators having voted in the affirmative and fourteen Senators having voted in the negative, the negative prevailed and the motion to recommit was lost.

The question recurring,

Shall the amendment offered by the Honorable Senator from District No. 2 be adopted?

(Discussion ensued.)

Senator Bickford offered to substitute, as an amendment to the amendment offered by the Honorable Senator from District No. 2, the following :

" If any such director, officer, or agent shall neglect or refuse to appear, produce books, records, or papers, or to testify
or give his deposition as required by such order or summons,
he shall be individually liable for the debts or damage that
may be assessed by the court in the case pending and the
court may order execution against such director, officer, or
agent and the corporation or against either as the plaintiff
shall elect or the court may deem just.   If such proceeding
wherein the order or summons is issued is pending before a
court of law or equity and the corporation of which such person is a director, officer, or agent is a party defendant in such
proceedings, the neglect or refusal of such person to appear,
produce books, records, or papers, or to testify, or give his deposition as aforesaid, shall be deemed *prima facie* evidence in
such proceedings against said corporation that he would testify
to the truth of all matters alleged against said corporation in
the plaintiff's declaration, bill, information, or complaint ; if
such corporation is summoned as witness and shall neglect to
appear and answer after due notice from the court, served upon
the clerk or a resident director of such corporation, or upon a
non-resident director, service in the manner provided in section 2 of this act for summoning a proper officer or agent, said
corporation shall be adjudged chargeable for the amount of
the judgment which may be recovered by the plaintiff against
the defendant."

The question being stated,

Shall the proposed amendment be adopted ?

(Discussion ensued.)

The negative prevailed on a *viva voce* vote.

The question recurring,

Shall the amendment offered by the Honorable Senator from
District No. 2 be adopted ?

The affirmative prevailed on a *viva voce* vote.

Senator Bickford offered the following amendment :

Amend section 2 of said act by inserting after the word
" court " and before the word " may " in the second line of said
section as shown in the printed bill, the following words : " upon

notice to the defendant." Further amend said section by striking out the word "may" in the eighth line of said section as printed and insert instead thereof the word "shall." Further amend said section by striking out all after the word "to" in the ninth line of said section as printed, and the words "of abode of" in the tenth line of said section as printed, so that said section as amended shall read as follows:

"Upon petition of any party to such proceedings any justice of the Superior Court upon notice to the defendant may issue such order as shall seem to the court to be reasonable and just, requiring such director, officer, or agent to appear and testify in such proceeding, and upon such order the clerk of the Superior Court for any county may issue a summons requiring such director, officer, or agent to appear and comply with the terms of said order. Such summons shall be served by delivering in hand to the person summoned, either within or without the state, an attested copy thereof, and such summons may require the person so summoned to produce books, records, and papers as aforesaid in connection with his testimony."

The question being stated,

Shall the amendment be adopted?

(Discussion ensued.)

The affirmative prevailed on a *viva voce* vote.

Senator Bickford offered the following amendment:

Amend section 3 of said bill by inserting after the word "proceeding" in the first and second lines of said section as printed and before the word "any" the following words: "after neglect or refusal to appear and testify as required in section 2 of this act," so that said section as amended shall read:

"Upon the petition of any party to such proceeding, after neglect or refusal to appear and testify as may be required in section 2, any justice of the Superior Court may issue a commission to any special commissioner for that purpose appointed by the court, authorizing such commissioner to summon or cause to be summoned such director, officer, or agent to appear before him and give his deposition for use in such proceeding, and such summons may require the person so summoned to produce books, records, and papers as aforesaid in connection with his deposition."

The question being stated,

Shall the amendment be adopted?

(Discussion ensued.)

Senator Stillings moved to reconsider the vote whereby the Senate adopted the amendment offered by the Honorable Senator from District No. 17 to section 2 of said bill.

The question being stated,

Shall the vote be reconsidered?

Senator Page demanded the yeas and nays.

The clerk proceeded to call the roll.

The following named Senators voted in the affirmative:

Senators Allen, Keyes, Whitney, Lewando, Tilton, Cooper, Marvin, Felt, Stillings, Fellows, Neal, Fuller, Hoyt of District 21, and Thompson.

The following named Senators voted in the negative:

Senators Ripley, Wilkins, Lightbody, Bickford, Foley, Tolles, Richmond, and Page.

Fifteen Senators having voted in the affirmative, and eight Senators having voted in the negative, the affirmative prevailed.

Senator Page rose to a question of personal privilege, and asked a ruling from the chair on the question whether a member who was absent from the Senate chamber at the time the vote on the foregoing amendment was taken, now had a right to vote on the question of reconsideration. The chair ruled that if the question had been raised in due season it would have been well taken but was now out of order.

The question being stated,

Shall the amendment offered by the Honorable Senator from District No. 17 to section 2 of said bill be adopted?

(Discussion ensued.)

Senator Page moved that the Senate adjourn.

The negative prevailed on a *viva voce* vote,

The question recurring,

Shall the amendment offered by the Honorable Senator from
District No. 17 to section 2 of said bill be adopted?

The negative prevailed on a *viva voce* vote, and the amendment was not adopted.

The question recurring,

Shall the amendment offered by the Honorable Senator from
District No. 17 to section 3 of said bill be adopted?

The negative prevailed on a *viva voce* vote, and the amendment was not adopted.

Senator Bickford offered the following amendment: Amend
section 4 of said bill by adding at the end the words "Providing said witness shall be summoned to come from another state
into this state, he shall be paid double fees for his travel and
attendance."

The question being stated,

Shall the amendment be adopted?

(Discussion ensued.)

The affirmative prevailed on a *viva voce* vote, and the amendment was adopted.

Senator Page offered the following amendment: Amend
said bill by striking out all of section 6.

The question being stated,

Shall the amendment be adopted?

On motion of Senator Tolles, the Senate adjourned.

AFTERNOON.

Senator Keyes called for the unfinished business of the morning, being the consideration of the following entitled House
bill: "An act to provide for obtaining the testimony of non-
resident directors, officers, and agents of New Hampshire corporations, and the production of corporate books, records, and
papers."

The question being stated,

Shall the amendment offered by the Honorable Senator from
District No. 24 to strike out all of section 6 be adopted?

(Discussion ensued.)

The negative prevailed on a *viva voce* vote, and the amendment was not adopted.

Senator Page offered the following amendment: Amend said bill by adding at the end of section 7 the following words: "but its provisions shall not apply to any suit or legal proceeding now pending in any court in this state," so that said section 7 as amended shall read as follows: "Section 7. This act shall take effect upon its passage, but its provisions shall not apply to any suit or legal proceeding now pending in any court in this state."

The question being stated,

Shall the amendment be adopted?

(Discussion ensued.)

The negative prevailed on a *viva voce* vote.

Senator Page demanded the yeas and nays.

The clerk proceeded to call the roll.

The following named Senators voted in the affirmative:

Senators Bickford, Richmond, and Page.

The following named Senators voted in the negative:

Senators Allen, Keyes, Whitney, Lewando, Tilton, Cooper, Marvin, Felt, Stillings, Foley, Neal, Fuller, Ripley, Wilkins, Lightbody, Tolles, Hoyt of District No. 21, and Thompson.

Three Senators having voted in the affirmative, and eighteen Senators having voted in the negative, the negative prevailed, and the amendment was not adopted.

Senator Keyes offered the following amendment: Amend the amendment to section 5 of said bill as adopted this morning by inserting after the word "discretion" in the fourth line of said amended section the words "upon notice and hearing," so that the amendment to said section shall read as follows: "Section 5. If any such director, officer, or agent shall wilfully neglect or refuse to appear, produce books, records, or papers, or to testify or give his deposition as required by such order or summons, the Superior Court in its discretion, upon notice and hearing, may thereupon appoint a receiver to manage and control such corporation until the reasonable and just orders of the court shall be complied with, and when such orders shall have been complied with, such receiver shall be discharged."

The question being stated,

Shall the amendment to the section as amended be adopted?

(Discussion ensued.)

The affirmative prevailed on a *viva voce* vote, and the amendment was adopted.

Senator Page moved to lay the bill as amended on the table to be printed.

The question being stated,

Shall the bill as amended be laid on the table to be printed?

The negative prevailed on a *viva voce* vote.

The question being stated,

Shall the bill be ordered to a third reading?

Senator Keyes moved that the rules be so far suspended that the bill be in order for a third reading at the present time.

The question being stated,

Shall the rules be suspended?

(Discussion ensued.)

The negative prevailed on a *viva voce* vote.

Senator Keyes called for a division.

At the request of Senator Wilkins, Senator Keyes withdrew his call for a division, and the bill was ordered to a third reading Tuesday forenoon, February 17, at 11 o'clock.

The following entitled House bill was read a third time and passed:

An act to establish the salary of the justice of the police court of Concord.

The following message was received from the House of Representatives by its clerk:

HOUSE MESSAGE.

Mr. President:

The House of Representatives has passed bills with the following titles, and joint resolutions, in the passage of which it asks the concurrence of the Honorable Senate:

An act to punish embezzlement by executors, administrators, guardians, and trustees.

An act in addition to chapter 58 of the Public Statutes, relating to the appraisal of taxable real estate.

An act in amendment of chapter 23 of the Laws of 1901, entitled "An act to establish a laboratory of hygiene."

An act to change the name of Station lake in the town of Springfield.

An act relating to domestic insurance companies.

An act to enable the city of Manchester to appropriate money toward the armory rent of Camp Derwin No. 184, Spanish War Veterans.

An act to change the name of the body of water formerly called Munsonville pond, lying in the towns of Nelson and Stoddard.

An act in amendment of the charter of the city of Berlin.

An act to exempt from taxation real estate reservations of the Appalachian Mountain Club.

An act in relation to milk tickets.

Joint resolution in favor of the Granite State Deaf Mute Mission.

The House of Representatives has voted to concur with the Honorable Senate in its amendment to the following entitled bill:

An act to incorporate the Walpole Water and Sewer Co.

The House of Representatives has voted to concur with the Honorable Senate in its amendment to the title of the following entitled bill:

An act to amend chapter 93, in relation to scholars.

The following entitled bills and joint resolution sent up from the House of Representatives were severally read a first and second time and referred,—

To the Committee on the Judiciary:

An act in amendment of the charter of the city of Berlin.

An act relating to domestic insurance companies,

An act in addition to chapter 58 of the Public Statutes, relating to the appraisal of taxable real estate.

An act to punish embezzlement by executors, administrators, guardians, and trustees.

To the Committee on Finance:

Joint resolution in favor of the Granite State Deaf Mute Mission.

An act in amendment of chapter 23 of the Laws of 1901, entitled "An act to establish a laboratory of hygiene."

To the Committee on Towns and Parishes:

An act to change the name of the body of water formerly called Munsonville pond, lying in the towns of Nelson and Stoddard.

An act to change the name of Station lake in the town of· Springfield.

To the Committee on Military Affairs:

An act to enable the city of Manchester to appropriate money toward the armory rent of Camp Derwin No. 184, Spanish War Veterans.

To the Committee on Agriculture:

An act in relation to milk tickets.

To the Committee on Public Improvements:

An act to exempt from taxation real estate reservations of the Appalachian Mountain club.

On motion of Senator Page, the following resolution was adopted:

Resolved, That when the Senate adjourns it adjourn to meet to-morrow morning at 9.30 o'clock, and when it adjourns to-morrow it adjourn to meet next Monday evening at 7.30 o'clock.

The following entitled Senate bill, having been printed, was taken from the table and ordered to a third reading Tuesday morning next at 11 o'clock:

An act in amendment of the charter of the Plymouth Guaranty Savings Bank.

On motion of Senator Foley, the Senate adjourned.

FRIDAY, FEBRUARY 13, 1903.

The Senate met according to adjournment.

The reading of the journal having been commenced, on motion of Senator Stillings, the rules were so far suspended that its further reading was dispensed with.

On motion of the same Senator, the Senate adjourned.

MONDAY, FEBRUARY, 16, 1903.

The Senate met according to adjournment.

The journal was read and approved.

On motion of Senator Felt, the Senate adjourned.

TUESDAY, FEBRUARY 17, 1903.

The Senate met according to adjournment.

The journal was read and approved.

The following message was received from His Excellency the Governor, by the Honorable Edward N. Pearson, secretary of state:

THE STATE OF NEW HAMPSHIRE.

COUNCIL CHAMBER, February 13, 1903.

To the Honorable Senate:

I hereby transmit the following reports:

Of the Railroad Commissioners,

Of the Soldiers' Home,

Of the State Prison,

Of the Boulevard Commissioners.

NAHUM J. BACHELDER,
Governor.

The President announced that the several reports would be referred as follows:

Of the Railroad Commissioners,

To the Committee on Railroads.

Of the Soldiers' Home,

To the Committee on Soldiers' Home.

Of the State Prison,

To the Committee on State Prison and Industrial School.

Of the Boulevard Commissioners,

To the Committee on Public Improvements.

The following report from the Committee on Engrossed Bills was read and accepted:

The Committee on Engrossed Bills have examined bills with the following titles, and find them correctly engrossed:

An act to amend the charter of the North Shore Water Company.

An act to amend chapter 93 of the Public Statutes, in relation to scholars.

An act in amendment of the charter of the Salem Water-Works Company, and legalizing and confirming the acts of said corporation in relation thereto.

An act in relation to the town of Newmarket, and the Newmarket water-works.

An act in amendment of sections 1, 3, and 4 of chapter 72 of the Public Statutes, relating to the discontinuance of highways.

An act authorizing the city of Dover to exempt from taxation the property of the Hayes Hospital.

An act in amendment of the charter of the city of Concord, providing for the election of overseers of the poor.

An act in amendment of the charter of the Colby Academy, providing for filling vacancies and election of members.

An act to amend chapter 179 of the Public Statutes, relating to guardians of insane persons and spendthrifts.

An act in amendment of the charter of the Walpole Electric Light & Power Company.

An act to incorporate the Walpole Water & Sewer Company.

HENRY W. KEYES,

For the Committee.

The following entitled Senate bill was read a third time, passed and sent to the House of Representatives for concurrence:

An act in amendment of the charter of the Plymouth Guaranty Savings Bank.

The following entitled House bill was read a third time:

"An act to provide for obtaining the testimony of non-resident directors, officers, and agents of New Hampshire corporations, and the production of corporate books, records, and papers."

The question being stated,

Shall the bill pass?

(Discussion ensued.)

Senator Page offered the following resolution :

WHEREAS, The Constitution of this State requires the supreme court to advise the Senate upon any important question of law, when requested, and House bill No. 103, now before the Senate, involves legal questions of great importance regarding which there is doubt, therefore, be it

Resolved, That the supreme court be requested to advise the Senate as to the validity, constitutionality, and possibility of making operative the legislation contained in, and proposed by, said House bill No. 103, and, especially, as to the proper answer to the following questions involved in said bill, viz.:

1. Has any court in this state, or can it have, the power to compel the attendance as a witness, of non-residents of another state, before any court in this state, or any magistrate in this or any other state, by summons served in another state and without any service of such summons in this state?

2. If the answer to the above question is *no*, can any court in this state be given the power to punish any person, or corporation, for not complying with an order which the court has no power to make, or responding to a summons which the court has no power to issue?

3. If a court in this state has, or can be given, the power to order, or summon, a non-resident witness to appear and testify, as above, has any court in this state, or can it be given, the power to punish, or put in the hands of a receiver, any domestic corporation of which such witness may be a director, because such witness does not comply with such order or summons?

Resolved, That an attested copy of said House bill No. 103, with any amendments thereto proposed by the Senate, and an attested copy of this resolution be immediately delivered by the clerk of the Senate to the chief justice of the supreme court.

The same Senator moved that the whole matter lie upon the table until an answer from the supreme court to the foregoing questions be received.

The question being stated,

Shall the whole matter lie upon the table?

(Discussion ensued.)

The negative prevailed on a *viva voce* vote.

Senator Page demanded the yeas and nays.

The clerk proceeded to call the roll.

The following Senators voted in the affirmative:

Senators Fuller, Ripley, Wilkins, Bickford, Foley, Richmond, and Page.

The following Senators voted in the negative:

Senators Allen, Keyes, Lewando, Burnell, Tilton, Cooper, Fel't, Stillings, Fellows, Neal, Lightbody, and Thompson.

Seven Senators having voted in the affirmative, and twelve Senators having voted in the negative, the negative prevailed.

The question being stated,

Shall the bill pass?

(Discussion ensued.)

Senator Page moved that the further consideration of the bill be postponed until Tuesday next.

The question being stated,

Shall the bill be postponed?

The negative prevailed on a *viva voce* vote.

The question recurring,

Shall the bill pass?

(Discussion ensued.)

The affirmative prevailed on a *viva voce* vote, the bill passed, and was sent to the House of Representatives for concurrence in Senate amendments.

The following message was received from the House of Representatives by its clerk:

HOUSE MESSAGE.

Mr. President:

The House of Representatives has passed bills with the following titles, in the passage of which it asks the concurrence of the Honorable Senate:

An act to provide for taking depositions outside this state, and depositions within this state for use in other states.

An act severing the homestead farm of Hiram S. Stevens from the school district of the town of Middleton and annexing the same to the town of Wakefield for school purposes.

An act relative to the issue of bonds, coupon notes, and other evidences of indebtedness of street railway or other railroad companies.

An act to allow the town of Hampton to readopt chapter 29, in the Laws of 1893, in relation to the repair of highways.

The following entitled bills sent up from the House of Representatives were severally read a first and second time and referred :

To the Committee on the Judiciary :

An act relative to the issue of bonds, coupon notes, and other evidences of indebtedness of street railway or other railroad companies.

An act to provide for taking depositions outside this state and depositions within this state for use in other states.

To the Committee on Revision of the Laws :

An act to allow the town of Hampton to readopt chapter 29, in the Laws of 1893, in relation to the repair of highways.

An act severing the homestead farm of Hiram S. Stevens from the school district of the town of Middleton and annexing the same to the town of Wakefield for school purposes.

On motion of Senator Felt, the Senate adjourned.

AFTERNOON.

Senator Keyes, for the Committee on Incorporations, to whom was referred a bill entitled "An act to authorize the town of Lancaster to acquire property for the protection of its water supply," reported the same without amendment and recommended its passage.

Senator Keyes, for the Committee on Railroads, to whom was referred the following entitled bills : "An act to extend the time for the location, construction, and completion of the railroad of the Moosilauke Railroad Company,"

"An act in amendment of the charter of the Wells River Bridge, and authorizing the Concord and Montreal Railroad to hold stock therein,"

"An act confirming and legalizing the organization and acts of the Berlin Street Railway," reported the same without amendment and recommended their passage.

The reports were accepted and the bills were severally ordered to a third reading to-morrow morning at 11 o'clock.

. Senator Keyes, for the Committee on Railroads, to whom was referred a bill entitled "An act to incorporate the Littleton, Franconia & Bethlehem Electric Railway Company," reported the same without amendment and recommended its passage.

The report was accepted, and on motion of Senator Keyes, the rules were so far suspended that the bill was read a third time by its title and passed.

Senator Keyes, for the Committee on Incorporations, to whom was referred a bill entitled "An act amending the charter of the Nashua Light, Heat and Power Co. of Nashua," reported the same with the following amendment and recommended its passage : Amend by striking out section 3 and substituting therefor the following :

SECT. 3. This act shall be submitted for acceptance to the voters of said town at the next town election, that the same may be legally submitted, and if accepted by a majority of those voting thereon at such election it shall thereupon take full effect.

The report was accepted and amendment adopted.

On motion of Senator Keyes, the rules were so far suspended that the bill was read a third time, passed, and sent to the House of Representatives for concurrence in Senate amendment.

Senator Keyes, for the Committee on Incorporations, to whom was referred a bill entitled "An act in amendment of an act approved March 26, 1895, entitled an act in amendment of an act incorporating the Newmarket Manufacturing Co., approved June 12, 1823, and an act in amendment thereof, approved July 7, 1881," reported the same in a new draft and recommended its passage.

The report was accepted, and the bill, in its new draft, was read a first and second time and ordered to a third reading to-morrow morning at 11 o'clock

LEAVE OF ABSENCE.

Senator Hoyt of District No. 21 was granted leave of absence from Wednesday's session on account of death in his family.

On motion of Senator Thompson, the Senate adjourned.

WEDNESDAY, FEBRUARY 18, 1903.

The Senate met according to adjournment.

The reading of the journal having been commenced, on motion of Senator Fuller, the rules were so far suspended that its further reading was dispensed with.

The following entitled House bills were severally read a third time and passed :

An act confirming and legalizing the organization and acts of the Berlin Street Railway.

An act in amendment of the charter of the Wells River Bridge and authorizing the Concord & Montreal Railroad to hold stock therein.

An act to extend the time for the location, construction, and completion of the railroad of the Moosilauke Railroad Company.

An act to authorize the town of Lancaster to acquire property for the protection of its water supply.

The following entitled House bill, in Senate new draft, was read a third time, passed, and sent to the House of Representatives for concurrence:

An act in amendment of an act approved March 26, 1895, entitled "An act in amendment of an act incorporating the Newmarket Manufacturing Company, approved June 12, 1823, and an act in amendment thereof, approved July 7, 1881."

Senator Lewando, for the Committee on Forestry, to whom was referred the following entitled bill and joint resolution :

"An act in amendment of chapter 44 of the Laws of 1893, relating to the powers and duties of the Forestry Commission with respect to public parks,"

Joint resolution to provide for a forest examination of the White Mountain region, reported the same without amendment and recommended their passage.

Senator Ripley, for the Committee on Finance, to whom was referred the following entitled bill and joint resolution :

"An act in amendment of chapter 23 of the Laws of 1901, entitled 'An act to establish a laboratory of hygiene,'"

Joint resolution in favor of the Granite State Deaf Mute

Mission, reported the same without amendment and recommended their passage.

Senator Tolles, for the Committee on the Judiciary, to whom was referred a bill entitled " An act in amendment of the charter of the city of Dover, creating a board of street and park commissioners for said city," reported the same without amendment and recommended its passage.

Senator Keyes for the Committee on Railroads, to whom was referred a bill entitled "An act in amendment of an act to incorporate the North Conway and Mount Kearsarge Railroad, passed June session 1883, and all subsequent acts relating to the same," reported the same without amendment and recommended its passage.

Senator Richmond, for the Committee on Incorporations, to whom was referred the following entitled bills :

"An act to amend the charter of the New Hampshire Odd Fellows', Widows', and Orphans' Home, approved August 15, 1883,"

"An act to establish water-works in Enfield village fire district, in the town of Enfield,"

"An act to incorporate the Ossipee Water and Electric Co.," reported the same without amendment and recommended their passage.

Senator Fuller, for the Committee on Towns and Parishes, to whom was referred the following entitled bills :

"An act to change the name of Station Lake, in the town of Springfield,"

"An act to change the name of the body of water formerly called Munsonville pond, lying in the towns of Nelson and Stoddard,"

"An act to authorize the town of Lancaster to exempt certain property from taxation and to ratify its doings in the same,"

"An act to establish the Lisbon village district," reported the same without amendment and recommended their passage.

Senator Marvin, for the Committee on Elections, to whom was referred the following entitled bills :

"An act to legalize the town-meeting in Dorchester for the years 1896, 1897, 1898, 1899, and 1900,"

"An act to repeal an act of the legislature of 1842, entitled an act to annex Richard Pickering of Newington to School District No. 1 in Portsmouth, approved June 22, 1842,"

"An act to legalize the biennial election of the town of Conway, held November 4th, 1902,"

"An act to legalize and confirm the warrant for, and the votes and proceedings at, the biennial election and meeting in Stratham, held the fourth day of November, 1902."

"An act to legalize the biennial election of the town of Effingham, held November 4th, 1902,"

"An act to legalize and confirm the selectmen's warrant for and the votes and proceedings thereunder at the biennial election and meeting in the town of Columbia, held in said town the fourth day of November, A. D. 1902," reported the same without amendment and recommended their passage.

The reports were accepted, and the bills and joint resolutions were severally ordered to a third reading this afternoon at 3 o'clock.

Senator Burnell, for the Committee on Fisheries and Game, to whom was referred a bill entitled "An act to amend sections 54 and 58, chapter 78 of the fish and game laws," reported the same with the following amendment and recommended its passage :

Amend section 1 of the bill by striking out the number "78" and inserting in place the number "79."

The report was accepted, amendment adopted, and the bill ordered to a third reading this afternoon at 3 o'clock.

The following message from the Committee on Engrossed Bills was read and accepted :

The Committee on Engrossed Bills have examined bills with the following titles and find them correctly engrossed :

An act to establish the salary of the justice of the police court of Concord.

An act in amendment of chapter 192 of the Public Statutes, relating to insolvent estates.

A. W. BURNELL,
For the Committee.

Senator Burnell, under suspension of the rules, sixteen Senators having actually voted in favor thereof, introduced a bill entitled :

"An act to incorporate the Jackson Water-Works Company," which was read a first and second time and referred to the Committee on Incorporations.

On motion of Senator Stillings, the Senate voted to take a recess for five minutes.

(Recess.)

The Senate reassembled.

The following message was received from the House of Representatives by its clerk :

HOUSE MESSAGE.

Mr. President:

The House of Representatives has passed bills with the following titles, in the passage of which it asks the concurrence of the Honorable Senate :

An act to authorize the Connecticut River Railroad Company to acquire stock of the Vermont Valley Railroad.

An act amending section 4, chapter 40 of the Public Statutes, relating to towns.

An act in amendment of section 2, chapter 2555, Laws of 1861, entitled "An act to incorporate the Alpha Delta Phi Society."

An act in relation to reports and increase of stock and bonds of corporations owning stock in railways.

An act to enable the state board of health to prevent contaminated water being furnished for domestic consumption.

An act in relation to smallpox.

An act to amend chapter 94 of the Public Statutes, in relation to the superintendent of public instruction.

An act in amendment of the act relating to the terms of the superior court in Grafton county.

An act authorizing the town of Peterborough to exempt from taxation the improvements or new buildings to be erected on the Tarbell block lot.

An act to annex a certain island in Lake Winnipesaukee,

now owned and occupied by George W. Sherwell, being one of the group of islands known as the Aunt Dolly islands, to the town of Meredith.

An act to change the name of the New Hampshire Health and Accident Insurance Company and to further define its powers and privileges.

The House of Representatives has concurred with the Honorable Senate in the passage of the following entitled bill:

An act in amendment of chapter 192 of the Public Statutes, relating to insolvent estates.

(Senator Fuller in the chair.)

The following entitled bills, sent up from the House of Representatives, were severally read a first and second time and referred.

To the Committee on Revision of the Laws:

An act authorizing the town of Peterborough to exempt from taxation the improvements or new buildings to be erected on the Tarbell block lot.

An act in amendment of section 2, chapter 2555, Laws of 1861, entitled: "An act to incorporate the Alpha Delta Phi Society."

An act amending section 4, chapter 40 of the Public Statutes relating to towns.

To the Committee on the Judiciary:

An act to change the name of the New Hampshire Health and Accident Insurance Company and to further define its powers and privileges.

An act in amendment of the act relating to the terms of the superior court in Grafton county.

To the Committee on Public Health:

An act in relation to smallpox.

An act to enable the State Board of Health to prevent contaminated water being furnished for domestic consumption.

To the Committee on Railroads:

An act to authorize the Connecticut River Railroad Company to acquire stock of the Vermont Valley Railroad.

An act in relation to reports and increase of stock and bonds of corporations owning stock in railways.

To the Committee on Education:

An act to amend chapter 94 of the Public Statutes, in relation to the superintendent of public instruction.

To the Committee on Towns and Parishes:

An act to annex a certain island in Lake Winnipesaukee, now owned and occupied by George W. Sherwell, being one of the group of islands known as the Aunt Dolly Islands, to the town of Meredith.

On motion of Senator Fellows, the Senate adjourned.

AFTERNOON.

On motion of Senator Burnell, the Senate voted to take a recess until 4 o'clock.

(Recess.)

The Senate reassembled.

(Senator Thompson in the chair.)

The following entitled House bills and House joint resolutions were severally read a third time and passed.

An act in amendment of chapter 23 of the Laws of 1901, entitled: "An act to establish a laboratory of hygiene."

An act to legalize the biennial election of the town of Conway, held November 4, 1902.

An act to amend the charter of the New Hampshire Odd Fellows', Widows', and Orphans' Home, approved August 15, 1883.

An act to establish water-works in Enfield village fire district in the town of Enfield.

An act to establish the Lisbon village district.

An act to legalize and confirm the selectmen's warrant for and the votes and proceedings thereunder at the biennial election and meeting in the town of Columbia held in said town on the fourth day of November, A. D. 1902.

An act in amendment of chapter 44 of the Laws of 1893, relating to the powers and duties of the Forestry Commission with respect to public parks.

An act to legalize and confirm the warrant for, and the votes and proceedings at, the biennial election and meeting in Stratham, held the fourth day of November, 1902.

An act to legalize the town meetings in Dorchester for years 1896, 1897, 1898, 1899, and 1900.

An act to repeal an act of the legislature of 1842, entitled "An act to annex Richard Pickering of Newington to school district No. 1 in Portsmouth," approved June 22, 1842.

An act in amendment of an act to incorporate the North Conway & Mount Kearsarge Railroad, passed June session 1883, and all subsequent acts relating to the same.

An act to change the name of the body of water formerly called Munsonville pond, lying in the towns of Nelson and Stoddard.

An act to authorize the town of Lancaster to exempt certain property from taxation and to ratify its doings in the same.

An act in amendment of the charter of the city of Dover, creating a board of street and park commissioners for said city.

An act to legalize the biennial election of the town of Effingham, held November 4th, 1902.

An act to change the name of Station lake in the town of Springfield.

Joint resolution to provide for a forest examination of the White Mountain region.

Joint resolution in favor of the Granite State Deaf Mute Mission.

The following entitled House bill was read a third time and passed :

An act to amend sections 54 and 58, chapter 78 of the fish and game laws.

On motion of Senator Tilton, the title of the bill was amended by striking out its present title and substituting in place thereof the following :

An act to amend sections 54 and 58 of chapter 79 of the Laws of 1901, relating to the fish and game laws of the state.

The bill as amended was sent to the House of Representatives for concurrence in Senate amendments.

On motion of Senator Bickford, the rules were so far suspended that the following entitled Senate bill was read a third time by its title, passed, and sent to the House of Representatives for concurrence :

An act to incorporate the Ossipee Water and Electric Company.

The following message was received from the House of Representatives by its clerk :

Mr. President:

The House of Representatives has passed bills with the following titles and joint resolution, in the passage of which it asks the concurrence of the Honorable Senate :

An act to amend an act passed at the January session 1903, entitled :

"An act to amend chapter 241 of the Session Laws of 1893, entitled 'An act to establish the city of Laconia,' " and repealing chapter 200 of the Laws of 1901, entitled "An act to amend chapter 241 of the Session Laws of 1893, entitled 'An act to establish the city of Laconia.' "

An act in amendment of chapter 202 of the Laws of 1889, entitled : "An act to establish water-works in the town of Wolfeborough as amended by chapter 191 of the Laws of 1891."

An act to amend section 1, chapter 184 of the Public Statutes, relative to the times and places for holding courts of probate ; repealing chapter 29 of the Session Laws of 1901.

An act to equalize school privileges in the town of Littleton.

Joint resolution making appropriation for repairs on buildings erected by the state for the New Hampshire Veterans' Association at the Weirs.

On motion of Senator Bickford, the rules were so far suspended that the following entitled bill sent up from the House of Representatives was read a first and second time by its title :

An act to amend an act passed at the January session, 1903, entitled An act to amend chapter 241 of the Session Laws of 1893, entitled "An act to establish the city of Laconia," and repealing chapter 200 of the Laws of 1901, entitled "An act to amend chapter 241 of the Session Laws of 1893, entitled 'An act to establish the city of Laconia.' "

Senator Fuller moved that the rules be so far suspended that the bill be read a third time by its title at the present time.

(Discussion ensued.)

The negative prevailed on a *viva voce* vote, and the bill was referred to the Committee on the Judiciary.

The following entitled bills and joint resolution sent up from the House of Representatives were severally read a first and second time and referred.

To the Committee on Military Affairs:

Joint resolution making appropriation for repairs on buildings erected by the state for the New Hampshire Veterans' Association at the Weirs.

To the Committee on Education:

An act to equalize school privileges in the town of Littleton.

To the Committee on Revision of the Laws:

An act to amend section 1, chapter 184 of the Public Statutes, relative to the times and places for holding courts of probate; repealing chapter 29 of the Session Laws of 1901.

To the Committee on Incorporations:

An act in amendment of chapter 202 of the Laws of 1889, entitled "An act to establish water-works in the town of Wolfeborough as amended by chapter 191 of the Laws of 1891."

(President in the chair.)

Senator Lewando, under a suspension of the rules, sixteen Senators having actually voted in favor thereof, introduced a bill entitled:

"An act to incorporate the First Congregational Church of Wolfeborough, New Hampshire."

On motion of Senator Bickford, the rules were so far suspended that the bill was read a first and second time by its title and referred to the Committee on Incorporations.

On motion of Senator Wilkins, the Senate adjourned.

THURSDAY, FEBRUARY 19, 1903.

The Senate met according to adjournment.

The reading of the journal having been commenced, on motion of Senator Keyes, the rules were so far suspended that its further reading was dispensed with.

Senator Lightbody, for the Committee on Education, to whom was referred a bill entitled "An act to incorporate the New Hampshire Genealogical Society," reported the same without amendment and recommended its passage.

Senator Lewando, for the Committee on Revision of the Laws, to whom was referred the following entitled bills:

"An act in amendment of chapter 82 of the Laws of 1897, concerning the preservation and inspection of ballots."

"An act in amendment of section 4 of chapter 206 of the Laws of 1897, being an act to incorporate the Bethlehem Electric Light Company," reported the same without amendment and recommended their passage.

Senator Tolles, for the Committee on the Judiciary, to whom was referred the following entitled bills:

"An act to punish embezzlement by executors, administrators, guardians, and trustees,"

"An act authorizing the town of Hudson to construct waterworks and establish an electric light plant,"

"An act to provide for taking depositions outside this state and depositions within this state for use in other states,"

"An act relative to the issue of bonds, coupon notes, and other evidences of indebtedness of street railway or other railroad companies,"

"An act in amendment of section 3, chapter 209 of the Public Statutes, relating to exemptions from serving as jurors,"

"An act in addition to chapter 58 of the Public Statutes, relating to the appraisal of taxable real estate,"

"An act in amendment of section 27, chapter 154 of the Public Statutes, relating to the calling of proprietors' meetings,"

"An act in amendment of the charter of the city of Berlin," reported the same without amendment and recommended their passage.

The reports were accepted, and the bills severally ordered to a third reading this afternoon at 3 o'clock.

Senator Tolles, for the Committee on the Judiciary, to whom was referred a bill entitled "An act to exempt certain property of the Manchester Young Men's Christian Association from taxation," reported the same in a new draft and recommended its passage.

The report was accepted, and the bill, in its new draft, was read a first and second time and ordered to a third reading this afternoon at 3 o'clock.

The following message was received from the House of Representatives by its clerk:

HOUSE MESSAGE.

Mr. President:

The House of Representatives has passed the following entitled bill and joint resolutions, in the passage of which it asks the concurrence of the Honorable Senate:

An act to authorize the Governor with the consent of the council to cause the original maps and surveys by the town proprietors of New Hampshire to be mounted and preserved.

Joint resolution to provide for completing the painting and decorating of the walls of the state library building.

Joint resolution in favor of the New Hampshire State Hospital.

Joint resolution appropriating money to aid Dartmouth College in the education of New Hampshire students.

Joint resolution appropriating money to complete the payment of expenses of the recent constitutional convention.

The following entitled bill and joint resolutions sent up from the House of Representatives were severally read a first and second time and referred:

To the Committee on State Hospital:

Joint resolution in favor of the New Hampshire State Hospital.

To the Committee on Finance:

Joint resolution appropriating money to aid Dartmouth College in the education of New Hampshire students.

To the Committee on Education:

An act to authorize the Governor with the consent of the council to cause the original maps and surveys by the town proprietors of New Hampshire to be mounted and preserved.

To the Committee on Claims:

Joint resolution appropriating money to complete the payment of expenses of the recent constitutional convention.

Joint resolution to provide for completing the painting and decorating of the walls of the state library building.

On motion of Senator Marvin, the Senate voted to take a recess for fifteen minutes.

(Recess.)

The Senate reassembled.

Senator Bickford, for the Committee on the Judiciary, reported the following entitled bill:

"An act in relation to state officials, commissioners, trustees, or other persons having control of public funds."

The bill reported from the committee was read a first and second time and ordered to a third reading this afternoon at 3 o'clock.

On motion of Senator Tilton, the following resolution was adopted:

Resolved, That when the Senate adjourns this morning it adjourn to meet at 2 o'clock this afternoon.

On motion of Senator Bickford, the rules were so far suspended that bills in order for a third reading this afternoon at 3 o'clock were made in order for a third reading at the present time.

The following entitled House bills were severally read a third time and passed:

An act in amendment of section 4 of chapter 206 of the Laws of 1897, being an act to incorporate the Bethlehem Electric Light Company.

An act to punish embezzlement by executors, administrators, guardians, and trustees.

An act to incorporate the New Hampshire Genealogical Society.

An act in amendment of section 3, chapter 209 of the Public Statutes, relating to exemption from serving as jurors.

An act relating to domestic insurance companies.

(Senator Bickford in the chair.)

An act in addition to chapter 58 of the Public Statutes, relating to the appraisal of taxable real estate.

An act providing for taking depositions outside this state, and depositions within this state for use in other states.

An act relative to the issue of bonds, coupon notes, and other evidences of indebtedness of street railway or other railroad companies.

An act in amendment of section 27, chapter 154 of the Public Statutes, relating to the calling of proprietors' meetings.

On motion of Senator Hoitt of District No. 19, the rules were so far suspended that the following entitled House bills were severally read a third time by their titles and passed:

An act authorizing the town of Hudson to construct waterworks and establish an electric light plant.

An act in amendment of the charter of the city of Berlin.

The following entitled Senate bill, in new draft, was read a third time, passed, and sent to the House of Representatives for concurrence.

An act to exempt certain property of the Manchester Young Men's Christian Association from taxation.

The following entitled Senate bill was read a third time, passed, and sent to the House of Representatives for concurrence:

An act in relation to state officials, commissioners, trustees, or other persons having control of public funds.

Senator Tolles, for the Committee on the Judiciary, to whom was referred a bill entitled An act to amend an act passed at the January session, 1903, entitled "An act to amend chapter 241 of the Session Laws of 1893," entitled "An act to establish the city of Laconia," and repealing chapter 200 of the Laws of 1901, entitled "An act to amend chapter 241 of the Session Laws of 1893, entitled 'An act to establish the city of Laconia,'" reported the same without amendment and recommended its passage.

The report was accepted.

Senator Tilton moved that the rules be so far suspended that the bill be read a third time by its title.

The question being stated,

Shall the rules be suspended?

The affirmative prevailed on a *viva voce* vote.

Senator Page demanded the yeas and nays.

The clerk proceeded to call the roll.

The following named Senators voted in the affirmative:

Senators Allen, Keyes, Lewando, Tilton, Marvin, Felt, Fellows, Neal, Fuller, Ripley, Wilkins, Bickford, Hoitt of District No. 19, and Hoyt of District No. 21.

The following named Senators voted in the negative:

Senators Foley, Richmond, and Page.

Fourteen Senators having voted in the affirmative and three Senators having voted in the negative, the affirmative prevailed and the rules were suspended.

The bill was read a third time by its title.

The question being stated,

Shall the bill pass?

(Discussion ensued.)

The affirmative prevailed on a *viva voce* vote.

On motion of Senator Wilkins, the rules were so far suspended that the following entitled bill was put back on its second reading for purpose of amendment.

An act in amendment of chapter 82 of the Laws of 1897, concerning the preservation and inspection of ballots.

On motion of the same Senator, the following amendment was adopted:

Amend section 1 by striking out the figures "17" in the first line of said section, and insert in place thereof the figure "1."

The bill was then ordered to a third reading this afternoon at 2 o'clock.

LEAVE OF ABSENCE.

Senator Cooper was granted leave of absence for the remainder of the week on account of sickness.

On motion of Senator Tilton, the Senate adjourned.

AFTERNOON.

The following entitled House bill was read a third time, passed, and sent to the House of Representatives for concurrence in Senate amendment :

An act in amendment of chapter 82 of the Laws of 1897, concerning the preservation and inspection of ballots.

On motion of Senator Keyes, the following resolution was adopted :

Resolved, That when the Senate adjourns this afternoon it adjourn to meet to-morrow morning at 9.30 o'clock, and when it adjourns to-morrow morning it adjourn to meet Monday afternoon at 2 o'clock.

Senator Tolles, for the Committee on the Judiciary, to whom was referred the following entitled bills :

"An act in amendment of the act relating to the terms of the superior court in Grafton county,"

"An act to change the name of the New Hampshire Health and Accident Insurance Company and to further define its powers and privileges," reported the same without amendment and recommended their passage.

Senator Keyes, for the Committee on Railroads, to whom was referred a bill entitled "An act to repeal the charter of the Massabesic Horse Railroad Company," reported the same without amendment and recommended its passage.

The reports were accepted and the bills severally ordered to a third reading Tuesday forenoon next at 11 o'clock.

On motion of Senator Lightbody, the Senate adjourned.

FRIDAY, February 20, 1903.

The Senate met according to adjournment.

The reading of the journal having been commenced, on motion of Senator Stillings, the rules were so far suspended that its further reading was dispensed with.

On motion of Senator Stillings, the Senate adjourned.

MONDAY, FEBRUARY 23, 1903.

The Senate met according to adjournment.

Senator Stillings having assumed the chair, read the following communication:

NASHUA, N. H., Feb. 23, 1903.

Senator Stillings:

Please preside for me at the session to-day of the New Hampshire Senate, and oblige

CHARLES W. HOITT,
President.

The journal was read and approved.

On motion of Senator Lightbody, the Senate adjourned.

TUESDAY, FEBRUARY 24, 1903.

The Senate met according to adjournment.

The journal was read and approved.

The following entitled House bills were severally read a third time and passed:

An act to change the name of the New Hampshire Health and Accident Insurance Company, and to further define its powers and privileges.

An act in amendment of the act relating to the terms of the superior court in Grafton county.

An act to repeal the charter of the Massabesic Horse Railroad Company.

(Senator Fuller in the chair.)

The following report from the Committee on Engrossed Bills was read and accepted:

The Committee on Engrossed Bills have examined and found correctly engrossed the following entitled bills and joint resolutions:

An act to amend an act passed at the January session 1895, entitled "An act to amend chapter 241 of the Session Laws of 1893," entitled "An act to establish the city of Laconia," and repealing chapter 200 of the Laws of 1901, entitled "An act to amend chapter 241 of the Session Laws of 1893, entitled 'An act to establish the city of Laconia.'"

Senator Lewando, for the Committee on Revision of the Laws, to whom was referred the following entitled bills:

"An act to amend section 1, chapter 184 of the Public Statutes, relative to the times and places for holding courts of probate, repealing chapter 29 of the Session Laws of 1901,"

"An act in amendment of section 2, chapter 2555, Laws of 1861, entitled 'An act to incorporate the Alpha Delta Phi Society,'"

"An act to permit executors and administrators to resign," reported the same without amendment and recommended their passage.

Senator Felt, for the Committee on Education, to whom was referred a bill entitled "An act to unite the school districts of the town of Rollinsford," reported the same without amendment and recommended its passage.

Senator Tilton, for the Committee on Education, to whom was referred a bill entitled "An act amending chapter 92 of the Public Statutes, in relation to school boards," reported the same without amendment and recommended its passage.

Senator Lightbody, for the Committee on Education, to whom was referred a bill entitled "An act to amend chapter 94 of the Public Statutes, in relation to the superintendent of public instruction," reported the same without amendment and recommended its passage.

Senator Thompson, for the Committee on Education, to whom was referred a bill entitled "An act to equalize school privileges in the town of Littleton," reported the same without amendment and recommended its passage.

Senator Ripley, for the Committee on Education, to whom was referred a bill entitled "An act to amend section 4 of chapter 96 of the Laws of 1901, and section 6 of chapter 92 of the Public Statutes, relating to courses of study," reported the same without amendment and recommended its passage.

Senator Lewando, for the Committee on Military Affairs, to whom was referred a bill entitled "An act to enable the city of

8

Manchester to appropriate money toward the armory rent of Camp Derwin, No. 184, Spanish-American War Veterans," reported the same without amendment and recommended its passage.

The reports were accepted and the bills severally ordered to a third reading this afternoon at 3 o'clock.

The following message was received from the House of Representatives by its clerk:

HOUSE MESSAGE.

Mr. President:

The House of Representatives has voted to concur with the Honorable Senate in its amendments to the following entitled bill:

An act to amend sections 54 and 58 of chapter 79 of the Laws of 1901, relating to the fish and game laws of the state.

The House of Representatives has passed bills and a joint resolution with the following titles, in the passage of which it asks the concurrence of the Honorable Senate:

Joint resolution in favor of Charles H. Roberts.

An act in amendment of chapter 86 of the Public Statutes, in relation to state aid to indigent deaf and dumb, blind, and feeble-minded persons.

An act explanatory of the powers of the courts in reference to the fees of commissioners in certain cases.

An act to amend the charter of the New England and Louisiana Land Company.

An act to amend the charter of Brown's Lumber Company of Whitefield, approved July 1, 1874.

An act in relation to the settlement of paupers.

The following entitled bills and joint resolution were severally read a first and second time and referred:

To the Committee on the Judiciary:

An act to amend the charter of the New England and Louisiana Land Company.

An act to amend the charter of Brown's Lumber Company of Whitefield, approved July 1, 1874.

An act explanatory of the powers of the courts in reference to the fees of commissioners in certain cases.

To the Committee on Finance :

An act in amendment of chapter 86 of the Public Statutes, in relation to state aid to indigent deaf and dumb, blind, and feeble-minded persons.

To the Committee on Revision of the. Laws :

An act in relation to the settlement of paupers.

To the Committee on Claims :

Joint resolution in favor of Charles H. Roberts.

(President in the chair.)

Senator Bickford, for the Committee on the Judiciary, reported the following entitled bills, which were severally read a first and second time and laid on the table to be printed :

An act in amendment of section 4 of chapter 37 of the Session Laws of 1895, entitled "An act providing for the appointment of bail commissioners for towns and cities."

An act in amendment of section 29, chapter 266 of the Public Statutes, relating to trespasses and malicious injuries.

Senator Thompson, under a suspension of the rules, sixteen Senators having actually voted in favor thereof, introduced a Joint resolution authorizing the trustees of the N. H. College of Agriculture and the Mechanic Arts to permit certain real estate in Durham to be used as the site of a public library, which was read a first and second time and referred to the Committee on the Judiciary.

LEAVE OF ABSENCE.

Senator Ripley was granted leave of absence on account of business engagements.

On motion of Senator Fuller, the Senate adjourned.

AFTERNOON.

The following entitled House bills were severally read a third time and passed :

An act to equalize school privileges in the town of Littleton.

An act to permit executors and administrators to resign.

An act amending chapter 92 of the Public Statutes, in relation to school boards.

An act to enable the city of Manchester to appropriate money toward the armory rent of Camp Derwin, No. 184, Spanish-American War Veterans.

An act to unite the school districts of the town of Rollinsford.

An act to amend section 1, chapter 184 of the Public Statutes, relative to the times and places for holding courts of probate, repealing chapter 29 of the Session Laws of 1901.

An act to amend section 4 of chapter 96 of the Laws of 1901, and section 6 of chapter 92 of the Public Statutes, relating to courses of study.

An act in amendment of section 2, chapter 2555 of Laws of 1861, entitled "An act to incorporate the Alpha Delta Phi Society."

An act to amend chapter 94 of the Public Statutes, in relation to the superintendent of public instruction.

The following report from the Committee on Engrossed Bills was read and accepted:

The Committee on Engrossed Bills have examined, and found correctly engrossed, the following entitled bills and joint resolutions:

An act to punish embezzlement by executors, administrators, guardians, and trustees.

An act in amendment of the charter of the city of Dover, creating a board of street and park commissioners for said city.

An act to incorporate the New Hampshire Genealogical Society.

An act to establish the Lisbon village district.

An act in amendment of an act to incorporate the North Conway & Mount Kearsarge Railroad, passed June session 1883, and all subsequent acts relating to the same.

An act to establish water-works in Enfield village fire district in the town of Enfield.

An act relating to domestic insurance companies.

An act confirming and legalizing the organization and acts of the Berlin Street Railway.

An act to authorize the town of Lancaster to exempt certain property from taxation, and to ratify its doings in the same.

An act to incorporate the Littleton, Franconia & Bethlehem Electric Railway Company.

An act in amendment of chapter 44 of the Laws of 1893, relating to the powers and duties of the forestry commission with respect to public parks.

An act in amendment of section 3, chapter 209 of the Public Statutes, relating to exemptions from serving as jurors.

An act authorizing the town of Hudson to construct waterworks and establish an electric light plant.

An act to legalize and confirm the selectmen's warrant for, and the votes and proceedings thereunder, at the biennial election and meeting in the town of Columbia, held in said town on the fourth day of November, A. D. 1902.

Joint resolution in favor of the Granite State Deaf Mute Mission.

Joint resolution to provide for a forest examination of the White Mountain region.

An act to legalize town-meetings in Dorchester for the years 1896, 1897, 1898, 1899, and 1900.

An act to legalize and confirm the warrant for, and the votes and proceedings at, the biennial election and meeting in Stratham, held the fourth day of November, 1902.

An act in amendment of the charter of the Wells River Bridge, and authorizing the Concord & Montreal Railroad to hold stock therein.

An act to legalize the biennial election of the town of Effingham, held November 4th, 1902.

An act to change the name of the body of water formerly called Munsonville pond.

An act to repeal an act of the legislature of 1842, entitled "An act to annex Richard Pickering of Newington to school district No. 1 in Portsmouth," approved June 22, 1842.

An act to change the name of Station Lake in the town of Springfield.

An act to legalize the biennial election of the town of Conway, held November 4, 1902.

An act to extend the time for the location, construction, and completion of the railroad of the Moosilauke Railroad Company.

An act to amend the charter of the New Hampshire Odd Fellows', Widows', and Orphans' Home, approved August 15, 1883.

An act in addition to chapter 58 of the Public Statutes, relating to the appraisal of taxable real estate.

An act in amendment of chapter 23 of the Laws of 1901, entitled "An act to establish a laboratory of hygiene."

An act relative to the issue of bonds, coupon notes, and other evidences of indebtedness of street railway or other railroad companies.

An act in amendment of the charter of the city of Berlin.

An act to amend sections 54 and 58 of chapter 79 of the Laws of 1901, relating to the fish and game laws of the state.

An act in amendment of section 4 of chapter 206 of the Laws of 1897, being an act to incorporate the Bethlehem Electric Light Company.

An act in amendment of section 27, chapter 154 of the Public Statutes, relating to the calling of proprietors' meetings.

An act to authorize the town of Lancaster to acquire property for the protection of its water supply.

An act to provide for taking depositions outside this state, and depositions within this state for use in other states.

A. W. BURNELL,
For the Committee.

Senator Allen, for the Committee on Claims, to whom was referred Joint resolution appropriating money to complete the payment of expenses of the recent constitutional convention, reported the same without amendment and recommended its passage.

Senator Tilton, for the Committee on Claims, to whom was referred Joint resolution to provide for completing the painting and decorating of the walls of the state library building, reported the same without amendment and recommended its passage.

Senator Richmond, for the Committee on Incorporations, to whom was referred a bill entitled "An act in amendment of chapter 202 of the Laws of 1889, entitled 'An act to establish water-works in the town of Wolfeborough as amended by chapter 191 of the Laws of 1891,'" reported the same without amendment and recommended its passage.

Senator Lewando, for the Committee on Military Affairs, to whom was referred Joint resolution making appropriation for repairs on buildings erected by the state for the New Hampshire Veterans' Association at the Weirs, reported the same without amendment and recommended its passage.

Senator Thompson, for the Committee on Public Improvements, to whom was referred a bill entitled "An act to exempt from taxation real estate reservations of the Appalachian Mountain Club," reported the same without amendment and recommended its passage.

Senator Tilton, for the Committee on Claims, to whom was referred Joint resolution in favor of Charles H. Roberts, reported the same without amendment and recommended its passage.

The reports were accepted, and the bills and joint resolutions were severally ordered to a third reading to-morrow morning at 11 o'clock.

Senator Richmond, for the Committee on Incorporations, to whom was referred a bill entitled "An act to incorporate the Jackson Water-Works Company," reported the same without amendment and recommended its passage.

The report was accepted and on motion of Senator Burnell, the rules were so far suspended that the bill was read a third time by its title, passed and sent to the House of Representatives for concurrence.

Senator Stillings, for the Committee on Public Health, to whom was referred a bill entitled "An act to enable the State Board of Health to prevent contaminated water being furnished for domestic consumption," reported the same with the following amendment and recommended its passage:

Amend section (one) 1 by striking out in line seven the words "and the directors of corporations," and inserting in their place the words "or corporation official or agent;" and in line eight inserting between the words "fine" and "not" the words "of not less than one hundred dollars and."

The report was accepted, amendments adopted, and the bill ordered to a third reading to-morrow morning at 11 o'clock.

Senator Stillings, for the Committee on Public Improvements, to whom was referred a bill entitled "An act to provide for the improvement of public roads," reported the same in a new draft and recommended its passage.

The report was accepted and on motion of Senator Page, the rules were so far suspended that the bill, in its new draft, was read a first and second time by its title and laid on the table to be printed.

Senator Allen, for the Committee on Claims, reported a Joint resolution in favor of Arthur E. Clarke, which was read a first and second time and ordered to a third reading to-morrow morning at 11 o'clock.

Senator Page moved to reconsider the vote whereby the following entitled House bill passed:

An act to change the name of the New Hampshire Health and Accident Insurance Company and to further define its powers and privileges.

The question being stated,

Shall the vote be reconsidered?

The affirmative prevailed on a *viva voce* vote.

On motion of the same Senator, the rules were so far suspended that the bill was placed back on its second reading for the purpose of amendment.

The same Senator offered the following amendment:

Amend by striking out the words "New Hampshire" in the second line of section (one) 1 and inserting instead the words "State Security," so that said section as amended shall read: "Section 1. The name of the New Hampshire Health and Accident Insurance Company is hereby changed to 'State Security Life and Accident Company' hereinafter called the Company."

The amendment was adopted and on motion of the same
Senator, the rules were so far suspended that the bill was read
a third time, passed and sent to the House of Representatives
for concurrence in Senate amendment.

The following message was received from the House of Representatives by its clerk:

HOUSE MESSAGE.

Mr. President:

The House of Representatives has passed bills and a joint
resolution with the following titles, in the passage of which
it asks the concurrence of the Honorable Senate:

Joint resolution in favor of John K. Law and others.

An act to enable the Hedding Campmeeting Association to
fund its indebtedness.

An act to incorporate the Nashua and Hollis Electric Railroad Company.

An act to encourage the use of wide tires on certain vehicles
constructed before January 1, 1900, and now in use in New
Hampshire.

The House of Representatives has passed the following
resolution:

Resolved, That the Honorable Senate be requested to return
to the House of Representatives the following entitled House
bill: "An act in relation to the settlement of paupers."

The following entitled bills and joint resolution sent up from
the House of Representatives were severally read a first and
second time and referred:

To the Committee on Claims:

Joint resolution in favor of John K. Law and others.

To the Committee on Railroads: •

An act to incorporate the Nashua & Hollis Electric Railroad Company.

To the Committee on the Judiciary:

An act to enable the Hedding Campmeeting Association
to fund its indebtedness.

To the Committee on Agriculture:

An act to encourage the use of wide tires on certain

vehicles constructed before January 1, 1900, and now in use in New Hampshire.

On motion of Senator Lightbody, the following entitled bill was recalled from the Committee on Labor and referred to the Committee on Public Health :

An act relating to the time required for filing notice of intention of marriage and the consent of parents to the marriage of minors.

On motion of Senator Burnell, the Senate adjourned.

WEDNESDAY, FEBRUARY 25, 1903.

The Senate met according to adjournment.

The reading of the journal having been commenced, on motion of Senator Fuller, the rules were so far suspended that its further reading was dispensed with.

The following entitled House bills and House joint resolutions were severally read a third time and passed :

An act in amendment of chapter 202 of the Laws of 1899, entitled "An act to establish water-works in the town of Wolfeborough, as amended by chapter 191 of the Laws of 1891."

An act to exempt from taxation real estate reservations of the Appalachian Mountain Club.

Joint resolution in favor of Charles H. Roberts.

Joint resolution appropriating money to complete the payment of expenses of the recent constitutional convention.

Joint resolution making appropriations for repairs on buildings erected by the state for the New Hampshire Veterans' Association at The Weirs.

Joint resolution to provide for completing the painting and decorating of the walls of the state library building.

The following entitled House bill was read a third time, passed, and sent to the House of Representatives for concurrence in Senate amendment :

An act to enable the State Board of Health to prevent contaminated water being furnished for domestic consumption.

Senate joint resolution in favor of Arthur E. Clarke was read a third time, passed, and sent to the House of Representatives for concurrence.

(Senator Allen in the chair.)

The following message was received from the House of Representatives by its clerk:

HOUSE MESSAGE.

Mr. President:

The House of Representatives has voted to concur with the Honorable Senate in its amendments to the following entitled bill:

An act in amendment of chapter 82 of the Laws of 1897, concerning the preservation and inspection of ballots.

The House of Representatives concurs with the Honorable Senate in the passage of the following entitled bills:

An act to amend section 1 of an act of June, 1814, incorporating the Congregational Society of Durham.

An act in relation to bail in criminal cases.

An act to revive, renew, and amend the charter of the Knights of Pythias Building Association of Manchester.

An act in amendment of section 14 of chapter 264 of the Public Statutes, relating to offenses against the police of towns.

An act to change the name of the Woman's Auxiliary to the City Missionary Society of Manchester.

The House of Representatives has passed bills with the following titles, in the passage of which it asks the concurrence of the Honorable Senate:

An act in amendment of chapter 215, Laws of 1895, entitled "An act to confirm the organization of the Androscoggin Hospital Association."

An act in amendment of chapter 51 of the Public Statutes, relating to cemeteries.

An act relating to agreed lines between adjoining owners.

An act to incorporate the Omicron Deuteron Charge of the Theta Delta Chi.

An act to incorporate the Manchester Fire Insurance Company of New Hampshire.

An act to amend section 2, chapter 179 of the Public Statutes, relating to the appointment of guardians of insane persons.

An act in amendment of section 34 of chapter 43 of the Public Statutes, in regard to the incompatibility of certain town offices.

An act in addition to chapter 153, Public Statutes, creating section 20 of said chapter.

An act incorporating the Maynesboro Fire Insurance Company.

An act to amend section 1 of chapter 46, Session Laws of 1895, relating to annual enumeration of school children.

An act providing for the appointment of guardians for minors in certain cases.

An act to reimburse the town or county for aid furnished paupers.

An act in amendment of chapter 91, section 8, Laws of 1897, relating to the duties of the State Board of Charities and Correction.

An act amending the charter of the Newmarket Electric Light, Power, and Heat Company.

An act authorizing the Mt. Pleasant Hotel Company to increase its capital stock.

An act providing for the purchase of a bond for the deputy state treasurer.

The following entitled bills, sent up from the House of Representatives, were severally read a first and second time and referred,—

To the Committee on the Judiciary:

An act providing for the appointment of guardians for minors in certain cases.

An act relating to agreed lines between adjoining owners.

An act in amendment of chapter 51 of the Public Statutes, relating to cemeteries.

An act in amendment of chapter 91, section 8, Laws of 1897, relating to the duties of the State Board of Charities and Correction.

An act in addition to chapter 153, Public Statutes, creating section 20 of said chapter.

To the Committee on Incorporations:

An act to incorporate the Omicron Deuteron Charge of the Theta Delta Chi.

An act authorizing the Mt. Pleasant Hotel Company to increase its capital stock.

An act amending the charter of the Newmarket Electric Light, Power, and Heat Company.

An act to incorporate the Maynesboro Fire Insurance Company.

An act to incorporate the Manchester Fire Insurance Company of New Hampshire.

An act to amend section 2, chapter 179 of the Public Statutes, relating to the appointment of guardians of insane persons.

To the Committee on Revision of the Laws:

An act in amendment of chapter 215, Laws of 1895, entitled "An act to confirm the organization of the Androscoggin Hospital Association.

An act in amendment of section 34 of chapter 43 of the Public Statutes, in regard to the incompatibility of certain town offices.

An act providing for the purchase of a bond for the deputy state treasurer.

To the Committee on Education:

An act to amend section 1 of chapter 46, Session Laws of 1895, relating to annual enumeration of school children.

To the Committee on Towns and Parishes:

An act to reimburse the town or county for aid furnished paupers.

Senator Felt, for the Committee on State Hospital, to whom was referred Joint resolution in favor of the New Hampshire State Hospital, reported the same without amendment and recommended its passage.

The report was accepted and the joint resolution ordered to a third reading this afternoon at 3 o'clock.

On motion of Senator Tolles, the Senate voted to take a recess of fifteen minutes.

(Recess.)

The Senate reassembled.

On motion of Senator Tolles, the Senate adjourned.

AFTERNOON.

Joint resolution in favor of the New Hampshire State Hospital, was read a third time and passed.

Senator Ripley, for the Committee on Finance, to whom was referred Joint resolution appropriating money to aid Dartmouth College in the education of New Hampshire students, reported the same without amendment and recommended its passage.

Senator Keyes, for the Committee on Railroads, to whom was referred the following entitled bills :

An act to extend the time of the charter of the Keene, Marlow and Newport Electric Railway Company,

An act to authorize the Connecticut River Railroad Company to acquire stock of the Vermont Valley Railroad,

An act to incorporate the Nashua and Hollis Electric Railroad Company, reported the same without amendment and recommended their passage.

Senator Tolles, for the Committee on the Judiciary, to whom was referred the following entitled bills :

An act in amendment of section nine (9), chapter one hundred and five (105) of the laws passed January session, 1901, relating to political caucuses and conventions,

An act to enable the Hedding Campmeeting Association to fund its indebtedness,

An act to amend the charter of Brown's Lumber Company of Whitefield, approved July 1, 1874,

An act explanatory of the powers of the courts in reference to the fees of commissioners in certain cases, reported the same without amendment and recommended their passage.

The reports were accepted and the bills and joint resolution were severally ordered to a third reading to-morrow morning at 11 o'clock.

Senator Lewando, for the Committee on Revision of the Laws, to whom was referred a bill entitled "An act in amendment of section 1, chapter 185, Laws 1901, entitled 'An act authorizing the Hillsborough county convention to raise money for building and repairing of court houses,' " reported the same in a new draft and recommended its passage.

The report was accepted, and the bill, in its new draft, was read a first and second time, and ordered to a third reading to-morrow morning at 11 o'clock.

Senator Tolles, for the Committee on the Judiciary, to whom was referred Senate joint resolution authorizing the trustees of the " N. H. College of Agriculture and the Mechanic Arts " to permit certain real estate in Durham to be used as the site of a public library, reported the same without amendment and recommended its passage.

The report was accepted and the joint resolution laid on the table to be printed.

Senator Lightbody, for the Committee on Education, to whom was referred a bill entitled "An act to amend chapter 92, Public Statutes, relating to school boards," reported the same with the following amendment and recommended its passage :

Strike out section 2 and substitute therefor

Section 2. Not more than ten dollars shall be expended for the flag, flagstaff and appliances for any one schoolhouse, and the school board shall have the same control over its preservation and display that it has over the other district property.

Also add

Section 3. This act shall take effect upon its passage.

The report was accepted, amendments adopted, and the bill ordered to a third reading to-morrow morning at 11 o'clock.

On motion of Senator Wilkins, it was voted to grant the request of the House of Representatives, asking to have the following entitled bill returned :

An act in relation to the settlement of paupers.

The following message was received from the House of Representatives by its clerk :

HOUSE MESSAGE.

Mr. President:

The House has voted to concur with the Honorable Senate in its amendments to the following entitled bill :

An act to provide for obtaining the testimony of non-resident directors, officers, and agents of New Hampshire corporations and the production of corporate books, records, and papers.

The House of Representatives concurs with the Honorable Senate in the passage of the following entitled bill in Senate new draft sent down from the Honorable Senate:

An act in amendment of an act approved March 26, 1895, entitled "An act in amendment of an act incorporating the Newmarket Manufacturing Company, approved June 12, 1823," and an act in amendment thereof approved July 7, 1881.

The House of Representatives refuses to concur with the Honorable Senate in the passage of the following entitled bill sent down from the Honorable Senate:

An act to amend chapter 93, section 15 of the Public Statutes, as amended by chapter 61 of the Session Laws of 1901, relating to scholars.

The House of Representatives has passed bills with the following titles, in the passage of which it asks the concurrence of the Honorable Senate:

An act to incorporate the Pittsfield Light and Power Company.

An act to change the name of the South Congregational Society of Newmarket, N. H., now located in Newfields, N. H.

The following entitled bill sent up from the House of Representatives was read a first and second time and referred to the Committee on Revision of the Laws:

An act to change the name of the South Congregational Society of Newmarket, N. H., now located in Newfields, N. H.

On motion of Senator Felt, the rules were so far suspended that the following entitled bill sent up from the House of Representatives was read a first and second time by its title and referred to the Committee on Incorporations:

An act to incorporate the Pittsfield Light and Power Company.

The following report from the Committee on Engrossed Bills was read and accepted:

The Committee on Engrossed Bills have examined and found correctly engrossed the following entitled bills and joint resolutions:

An act amending chapter 92 of the Public Statutes, in relation to school boards.

An act to amend section 4 of chapter 96 of the Laws of 1901, and section 6 of chapter 92 of the Public Statutes, relating to courses of study.

An act to repeal the charter of the Massabesic Horse Railroad Company.

An act to permit executors and administrators to resign.

An act to amend chapter 94 of the Public Statutes, in relation to the superintendent of public instruction.

An act in amendment of chapter 82 of the Laws of 1897, concerning the preservation and inspection of ballots.

An act in amendment of the act relating to the terms of the superior court in Grafton county.

An act to equalize school privileges in the town of Littleton.

An act to enable the city of Manchester to appropriate money toward the armory rent of Camp Derwin, No. 184, Spanish American War veterans.

An act to unite the school districts of the town of Rollinsford.

An act in amendment of section 2, chapter 2555, Laws of 1861, entitled "An act to incorporate the Alpha Delta Phi Society."

An act to amend section 1, chapter 184 of the Public Statutes, relative to the times and places for holding courts of probate, repealing chapter 29 of the Session Laws of 1901.

An act to amend section 1 of an act of June, 1814, incorporating the Congregational Society in Durham.

An act to change the name of "The Woman's Auxiliary to the City Missionary Society of Manchester."

An act in amendment of section 14 of chapter 264 of the Public Statutes, relating to offenses against the police of towns.

An act in relation to bail in criminal cases.

An act to revive, renew, and amend the charter of the Knights of Pythias Building Association of Manchester.

Joint resolution in favor of Charles H. Roberts.

An act to provide for obtaining the testimony of non-resident

9

directors, officers, and agents of New Hampshire corporations and the production of corporate books, records, and papers.

A. W. BURNELL,
For the Committee.

On motion of Senator Felt, the Senate adjourned.

THURSDAY, FEBRUARY 26, 1903.

The Senate met according to adjournment.

The reading of the journal having been commenced, on motion of Senator Ripley, the rules were so far suspended that its further reading was dispensed with.

The following entitled House bill was read a third time, passed, and sent to the House of Representatives for concurrence in Senate amendments:

An act to amend chapter 92, Public Statutes, relating to school boards.

The following entitled House bill, in Senate new draft, was read a third time, passed, and sent to the House of Representatives for concurrence:

An act in amendment of section 1, chapter 185, Laws of 1901, entitled "An act authorizing the Hillsborough county convention to raise money for the building and repairing of court houses."

The following entitled House bills and joint resolution were severally read a third time and passed:

An act to authorize the Connecticut River Railroad Company to acquire stock of the Vermont Valley Railroad.

An act to amend the charter of Brown's Lumber Company of Whitefield, approved July 1, 1874.

An act explanatory of the powers of the courts in reference to the fees of commissioners in certain cases.

An act to incorporate the Nashua and Hollis Electric Railroad Company.

An act to enable the Hedding Campmeeting Association to fund its indebtedness.

An act in amendment of section nine (9), chapter one hundred and five (105) of the laws passed January session, 1901, relating to political caucuses and conventions.

An act to extend the time of the charter of the Keene, Marlow, and Newport Electric Railway Company.

Joint resolution appropriationg money to aid Dartmouth College in the education of New Hampshire students.

The following entitled Senate bill having been printed was taken from the table :

An act to provide for the improvement of public roads.

Senator Keyes moved to make the bill a special order for Wednesday next at 11 o'clock.

The question being stated,

Shall the motion prevail?

(Discussion ensued.)

Senator Keyes withdrew his motion, and the bill was ordered to a third reading this afternoon at 3 o'clock.

On motion of Senator Keyes, the following resolution was adopted :

Resolved, That when the Senate adjourns this morning it adjourn to meet to-morrow morning at 9.30 o'clock, and when it adjourns to-morrow it adjourn to meet Monday afternoon at 2 o'clock.

The following entitled Senate bills having been printed, were taken from the table, and ordered a third reading Tuesday morning next at 11 o'clock :

An act in amendment of section 29, chapter 266 of the Public Statutes, relating to trespasses and malicious injuries.

An act in amendment of section 4 of chapter 37 of the Session Laws of 1895, entitled " An act providing for the appointment of bail commissioners in cities and towns."

Senator Wilkins moved that all bills in order for a third reading this afternoon be made in order for a third reading at the present time.

On motion of Senator Thompson, the motion of Senator Wilkins was laid on the table.

Senator Lightbody, for the Committee on Education, to whom was referred a bill entitled "An act to authorize the

Governor with the consent of the Council to cause the original maps and surveys by the town proprietors of New Hampshire to be mounted and preserved," reported the same without amendment, and recommended its passage.

Senator Lewando, for the Committee on Revision of the Laws, to whom was referred a bill entitled "An act authorizing the town of Peterborough to exempt from taxation the improvements on new buildings to be erected on the Tarbell block lot," reported the same without amendment, and recommended its passage.

Senator Marvin, for the Committee on Towns and Parishes, to whom was referred a bill entitled "An act to annex a certain island in Lake Winnipesaukee now owned and occupied by George W. Sherwell, being one of the group of islands known as the Aunt Dolly islands, to the town of Meredith," reported the same without amendment, and recommended its passage.

Senator Fuller, for the Committee on Towns and Parishes, to whom was referred a bill entitled "An act to reimburse the town or county for aid furnished paupers," reported the same without amendment, and recommended its passage.

The reports were accepted, and the bills severally ordered to a third reading Tuesday morning next at 11 o'clock.

Senator Lewando, for the Committee on Revision of the Laws, to whom was referred a bill entitled "An act to allow the town of Hampton to re-adopt chapter 29 in the Laws of 1893, in relation to repair of highways," reported the same with the following resolution:

Resolved, That it is inexpedient to legislate.

The report was accepted and the resolution adopted.

On motion of Senator Thompson, it was voted to take from the table the motion, offered by the Honorable Senator from District No. 15, that all bills in order for a third reading this afternoon be made in order for a third reading at the present time.

The question being stated,

Shall the motion offered by the Honorable Senator from District No. 15 prevail?

The negative prevailed on a *viva voce* vote.

The following message was received from the House of Representatives by its clerk :

HOUSE MESSAGE.

Mr. President:

The House of Representatives has voted to concur with the Honorable Senate in its amendments to the following entitled bills :

An act to enable the State Board of Health to prevent contaminated water being furnished for domestic consumption.

An act to change the name of the New Hampshire Health and Accident Insurance Company, and to further define its powers and privileges.

The House of Representatives has passed the following resolution :

Resolved, That the Honorable Senate be requested to return to the House of Representatives the following entitled bill :

An act to establish a new apportionment for the assessment of public taxes.

The House of Representatives has passed bills with the following titles, in the passage of which it asks the concurrence of the Honorable Senate :

An act to amend chapter 95 of the Public Statutes, relating to Normal School.

An act relative to the salary of the register of probate for Coös county.

An act relating to the salary of the register of probate for the county of Cheshire.

An act in relation to the salary of the judge of probate for Merrimack county.

An act in relation to the salary of the register of probate for Strafford county.

An act in relation to the salary of the judge of probate for Strafford county.

An act relating to the salary of the judge of probate for the county of Rockingham.

An act fixing office hours in state offices.

An act to provide for a more economical and practical expenditure of money appropriated by the state for the construction and repair of highways.

On motion of Senator Lewando, the request of the House of Representatives was granted, asking that the Senate return the following entitled bill :

An act to establish a new apportionment for the assessment of public taxes.

The following entitled bills sent up from the House of Representatives were severally read a first and second time and referred,—

To the Committee on the Judiciary :

An act in relation to the salary of the judge of probate for Strafford county.

An act relating to the salary of the judge of probate for the county of Rockingham.

An act in relation to the salary of the judge of probate for Merrimack county.

An act relative to the salary of the register of probate for Coös county.

An act relating to the salary of the register of probate for the county of Cheshire.

An act in relation to the salary of the register of probate for Strafford county.

An act fixing office hours in state offices.

To the Committee on Finance :

An act to amend chapter 95 of the Public Statutes, relating to Normal School.

On motion of Senator Thompson, the rules were so far suspended that the following entitled bill sent up from the House of Representatives was read a first and second time by its title and referred to the Committee on Roads, Bridges, and Canals :

An act to provide for a more economical and practical expenditure of money appropriated by the state for the construction and repair of highways.

On motion of Senator Foley, the Senate adjourned.

FRIDAY, FEBRUARY 27, 1903.

The Senate met according to adjournment.

Senator Thompson having assumed the chair, read the following communication :

NASHUA, N. H., February 27, 1903.

Senator Thompson :

Please preside for me at the morning session, Friday, February 27, 1903, of the New Hampshire Senate, and oblige

CHARLES W. HOITT,

President.

The reading of the journal having been commenced, on motion of Senator Keyes, the rules were so far suspended that its further reading was dispensed with.

On motion of the same Senator, the Senate adjourned.

MONDAY, MARCH 2, 1903.

The Senate met according to adjournment.

The journal was read and approved.

On motion of Senator Cooper, the Senate adjourned.

TUESDAY, MARCH 3, 1903.

The Senate met according to adjournment.

The journal was read and approved.

The following entitled House bills were severally read a third time and passed :

An act to reimburse the town or county for aid furnished paupers.

An act to annex a certain island in Lake Winnipesaukee now owned and occupied by George W. Sherwell, being one of the group of islands known as the Aunt Dolly islands, to the town of Meredith.

An act to authorize the Governor, with the consent of the council, to cause the original maps and surveys by the town proprietors of New Hampshire to be mounted and preserved.

An act authorizing the town of Peterborough to exempt from taxation the improvements or new buildings to be erected on the Tarbell block lot.

The following entitled Senate bills were severally read a third time, passed, and sent to the House of Representatives for concurrence:

An act in amendment of section 4 of chapter 37 of the Session Laws of 1895, entitled "An act providing for the appointment of bail commissioners for cities and towns."

An act in amendment of section 29, chapter 266 of the Public Statutes, relating to trespasses and malicious injuries.

The following entitled Senate bill in order for a third reading was taken up, and on motion of Senator Stillings, the rules were so far suspended that the bill was placed back on its second reading for the purpose of amendment:

"An act to provide for the improvement of public roads."

On motion of the same Senator, the following amendments were adopted:

Amend said bill by striking out section seventeen (17) and substituting therefor the following, viz.:

SECT. 17.   This act shall not repeal, derogate from, nor in any way affect the provisions of a bill entitled "An act to provide for a more practical and economical expenditure of money appropriated by the state for the construction and repairs of highways," provided said entitled bill shall become a law.

Further amend said bill by striking out section eighteen (18) and substituting therefor the following, viz.:

SECT. 18.   All other acts and parts of acts, except as provided in this bill, and especially mentioned in section seventeen, being inconsistent with this act, are hereby repealed.

Further amend said bill by adding the following section:

SECT. 19.   This act shall take effect upon its passage.

On motion of Senator Tolles, the rules were so far suspended that the bill was read a third time by its title and passed.

On motion of Senator Stillings, the following amendment to the title of the bill was adopted :

Amend by striking out the present title and substituting therefor the following, viz.:

"An act to provide for the coöperation of the state with towns and cities in the construction and repairs of highways, and for the establishment of the office of state highway engineer."

The bill was then sent to the House of Representatives for concurrence.

The following message was received from the House of Representatives by its clerk :

HOUSE MESSAGE.

Mr. President:

The House of Representatives has passed joint resolutions and bills with the following titles, in the passage of which it asks the concurrence of the Honorable Senate :

Joint resolution in favor of raising Squam bridge in Holderness and Little Squam bridge in Ashland, and of improving navigation in Squam lake and connecting waters.

An act relative to the enlargement of the state library building.

Joint resolution to provide a nursery for the growth and distribution of forest seedling trees within the state at cost.

Joint resolution to appropriate a sum of money to pay Arthur W. Dudley a balance due him for money expended and labor performed in making surveys for the state.

Joint resolution in favor of screening the outlet of Forest lake.

An act to incorporate the Hampstead & Haverhill Street Railway Company.

An act to incorporate the Chester, Fremont & Brentwood Street Railway Company.

An act to incorporate the Epping, Brentwood & Kingston Street Railway.

An act to incorporate the Goffs Falls, Litchfield & Hudson Street Railway Company.

An act to provide for a bounty on hedgehogs.

An act authorizing the town of Littleton to establish or acquire a water and electric light plant.

The House of Representatives has voted to concur with the Honorable Senate in its amendments to the following entitled bill:

An act to amend chapter 92, Public Statutes, relating to school boards.

The House of Representatives refuses to concur with the Honorable Senate in the passage of the following entitled bill sent down from the Honorable Senate:

An act in amendment of the charter of the Plymouth Guaranty Savings Bank.

The House of Representatives concurs with the Honorable Senate in the passage of the following entitled bill, with amendments, in the passage of which amendments the House asks the concurrence of the Honorable Senate:

An act to authorize the State Board of Agriculture to appoint a state nursery inspector, and to provide for the protection of trees and shrubs from injurious insects and diseases.

Amend section 6 by adding at the close of said section the words "The cost of said inspection shall not exceed $300 annually."

Amend by adding the following:

"SECT. 8.   This act shall take effect upon its passage."

The Senate concurred with the House of Representatives in its amendments to the foregoing entitled Senate bill.

The following entitled bills and joint resolutions sent up from the House of Representatives were read a first and second time and referred,—

To the Committee on Public Improvements:

An act relative to the enlargement of the state library building.

To the Committee on Claims:

Joint resolution to appropriate a sum of money to pay Arthur W. Dudley a balance due him for money expended and labor performed in making surveys for the state.

To the Committee on Forestry:

Joint resolution to provide a nursery for the growth and distribution of forest seedling trees within the state at cost.

To the Committee on Roads, Bridges, and Canals:

Joint resolution in favor of raising Squam bridge in Holderness and Little Squam bridge in Ashland, and of improving navigation in Squam lake and connecting waters.

To the Committee on Fisheries and Game:

An act to provide for a bounty on hedgehogs.

Joint resolution in favor of screening the outlet of Forest lake.

On motion of Senator Bickford, the rules were so far suspended that the following entitled bills sent up from the House of Representatives were severally read a first and second time by their titles and referred,—

To the Committee on Incorporations:

An act authorizing the town of Littleton to establish or acquire a water and electric light plant.

To the Committee on Railroads:

An act to incorporate the Goffs Falls, Litchfield & Hudson Street Railway Company.

An act to incorporate the Epping, Brentwood & Kingston Street Railway.

An act to incorporate the Hampstead & Haverhill Street Railway Company.

An act to incorporate the Chester, Fremont & Brentwood Street Railway Company.

The following report from the Committee on Engrossed Bills was read and accepted: ·

The Committee on Engrossed Bills have examined, and found correctly engrossed, the following entitled bills and joint resolutions:

An act to enable the State Board of Health to prevent contaminated water being furnished for domestic consumption.

Joint resolution in favor of the New Hampshire State Hospital.

An act in amendment of chapter 202 of the Laws of 1889, entitled "An act to establish water-works in the town of Wolfeborough," as amended by chapter 191 of the Laws of 1891.

An act in amendment of an act approved March 26, 1895, entitled "An act in amendment of an act incorporating the

Newmarket Manufacturing Company, approved June 12, 1823, and an act in amendment thereof, approved July 7, 1881."

Joint resolution making appropriation for repairs on buildings erected by the state for the New Hampshire Veterans' Association at the Weirs.

Joint resolution appropriating money to complete the payment of expenses of the recent constitutional convention.

An act to exempt from taxation real estate reservations of the Appalachian Mountain Club.

Joint resolution to provide for completing the painting and decorating of the walls of the state library building.

An act to change the name of the New Hampshire Health and Accident Insurance Company, and to further define its powers and privileges.

An act to incorporate the Nashua & Hollis Electric Railroad Company.

An act to enable the Hedding Campmeeting Association to fund its indebtedness.

An act explanatory of the powers of the courts in reference to the fees of commissioners in certain cases.

An act to extend the time of the charter of the Keene, Marlow & Newport Electric Railway Company.

An act to authorize the Connecticut River Railroad Company to acquire stock of the Vermont Valley Railroad.

Joint resolution appropriating money to aid Dartmouth College in the education of New Hampshire students.

An act to amend the charter of Brown's Lumber Company of Whitefield, approved July 1, 1874.

An act in amendment of section nine (9), chapter one hundred and five (105), of the laws passed January session, 1901, relating to political caucuses and conventions.

An act to amend chapter 92, Public Statutes, relating to school boards.

> A. W. BURNELL,
> *For the Committee.*

Senator Neal, for the Committee on Public Health, to whom was referred a bill entitled "An act in relation to smallpox," reported the same without amendment and recommended its passage.

The report was accepted and the bill ordered to a third reading this afternoon at 3 o'clock.

Senator Keyes, for the Committee on Roads, Bridges, and Canals, to whom was referred a bill entitled "An act to provide for a more economical and practical expenditure of money appropriated by the state for the construction and repair of highways," reported the same without amendment and recommended its passage.

The report was accepted, and on motion of Senator Keyes, the rules were so far suspended that the bill was read a third time by its title and passed.

On motion of Senator Fellows, the Senate adjourned.

AFTERNOON.

The following entitled House bill was read a third time and passed :

An act in relation to smallpox.

Senator Neal, for the Committee on Public Health, to whom was referred a bill entitled "An act relating to the time required for filing notice of intention of marriage and the consent of parents to the marriage of minors," reported the same without amendment and recommended its passage.

The report was accepted and the bill laid on the table to be printed.

Senator Lightbody, for the Committee on Banks, reported the following entitled bill and recommended its passage :

An act to incorporate the Whitefield Loan and Trust Company.

The bill reported from the committee was read a first and second time and laid on the table to be printed.

Senator Fuller, for the Committee on Agriculture, to whom was referred a bill entitled "An act to encourage the use of wide tires on certain vehicles constructed before Jan. 1st, 1900, and now in use in New Hampshire," reported the same with the following amendments, and recommended its passage :

Strike out the word "councils" in the first line of section 1, and insert in its place the word "assessors." Also strike out the word "highway" before the word "tax" in the third line of section 1.

The report was accepted, amendments adopted, and the bill ordered to a third reading to-morrow morning at 11 o'clock.

Senator Richmond, for the Committee on Incorporations, to whom was referred a bill entitled "An act authorizing the town of Littleton to establish or acquire a water and electric light plant," reported the same with the following amendment and recommended its passage:

Amend by adding at the end of section 3 the following:

Provided, however, that entry upon and taking of property, rights and estate, laid out and taken for the purpose of this act, shall not be postponed by reason of any failure of the parties to agree upon the compensation to be paid or by reason of proceedings being instituted by either party for the assessment of damages as provided in this act, by the said town or district, as the case may be, but said municipal corporation may enter upon, take and occupy such property, rights and estate by filing a bond to the satisfaction of the Superior Court or the clerk thereof, conditioned on the payment of all damages that may be afterwards agreed upon or allowed in any case.

The report was accepted, amendment adopted, and the bill ordered to a third reading to-morrow morning at 11 o'clock.

Senator Fuller, for the Committee on Agriculture, to whom was referred a bill entitled "An act in relation to milk tickets," reported the same without amendment and recommended its passage.

Senator Lightbody, for the Committee on Banks, to whom was referred a bill entitled "An act to incorporate the Derry Savings Bank of Derry," reported the same without amendment and recommended its passage.

Senator Richmond, for the Committee on Incorporations, to whom was referred a bill entitled "An act in amendment of the charter of the Exeter Gas Light Company," reported the same without amendment and recommended its passage.

Senator Tolles, for the Committee on the Judiciary, to whom was referred the following entitled bills :

"An act in amendment of chapter 51 of the Public Statutes, relating to cemeteries,"

"An act in relation to the salary of the register of probate for Strafford county,"

"An act relating to the salary of the register of probate for the county of Cheshire,"

"An act relative to the salary of the register of probate for Coös county,"

"An act in relation to the salary of the judge of probate for Merrimack county,"

"An act relating to the salary of the judge of probate for the county of Rockingham,"

"An act in relation to the salary of the judge of probate for Strafford county,"

"An act relating to agreed lines between adjoining owners," reported the same without amendment and recommended their passage.

The reports were accepted and the bills were severally ordered to a third reading to-morrow morning at 11 o'clock.

The following message was received from the House of Representatives by its clerk :

HOUSE MESSAGE.

Mr. President :

The House of Representatives has passed bills with the following titles, in the passage of which it asks the concurrence of the Honorable Senate :

An act to incorporate the Uncanoonuc Incline Railway & Development Company.

An act to establish a State Sanatorium for Consumptives.

On motion of Senator Lewando, the rules were so far suspended that the following entitled bill sent up from the House of Representatives was read a first and second time by its title and referred to the Committee on Public Health :

An act to establish a State Sanatorium for Consumptives.

On motion of Senator Tilton, the rules were so far suspended that the following entitled bill sent up from the House of Representatives was read a first and second time by its title and referred to the Committee on Railroads:

An act to incorporate the Uncanoonuc Incline Railway & Development Company.

On motion of Senator Wilkins, the Senate voted to take a recess for fifteen minutes.

(Recess.)

The Senate reassembled.

Senator Keyes, for the Committee on Incorporations, to whom was referred a bill entitled "An act to incorporate the Omicron Deuteron Charge of the Theta Delta Chi," reported the same without amendment and recommended its passage.

Senator Richmond, for the Committee on Incorporations, to whom was referred a bill entitled "An act to incorporate the Manchester Fire Insurance Company of New Hampshire," reported the same without amendment and recommended its passage.

The reports were accepted and the bills severally ordered to a third reading to-morrow morning at 11 o'clock.

Senator Tilton, for the Committee on Claims, to whom was referred Joint resolution in favor of John K. Law and others, reported the same with the following amendment and recommended its passage:

"That John Demerritt be allowed the sum of thirty-three dollars and twenty cents.

"That George W. Johnson be allowed the sum of seventeen dollars and fifty cents."

The report was accepted, amendment adopted, and the Joint resolution was ordered to a third reading to-morrow morning at 11 o'clock.

Senator Bickford, for the Committee on the Judiciary, reported the following entitled bill and recommended its passage:

"An act in amendment of sections 6 and 7 of chapter 270 of the Public Statutes, relating to lotteries, gambling and wagers."

The bill reported from the committee was read a first and second time and laid on the table to be printed.

Senator Wilkins, for the Committee on Revision of the Laws, reported the following entitled bill and recommended its passage :

"An act enabling the city of Concord to appropriate money for observing Memorial Day."

The bill reported from the committee was read a first and second time and ordered to a third reading to-morrow morning at 11 o'clock.

On motion of Senator Hoyt of District No. 21, the Senate adjourned.

———————

WEDNESDAY, MARCH 4, 1903.

The Senate met according to adjournment.

The reading of the journal having been commenced, on motion of Senator Keyes, the rules were so far suspended that its further reading was dispensed with.

The following entitled House bill and Joint resolution were severally read a third time, passed and sent to the House of Representatives for concurrence in Senate amendments :

An act to encourage the use of wide tires on certain vehicles constructed before January 1, 1900, and now in use in New Hampshire.

Joint resolution in favor of John K. Law and others.

On motion of Senator Keyes, the rules were so far suspended that the following entitled House bill was read a third time by its title, passed, and sent to the House of Representatives for concurrence in Senate amendments :

An act authorizing the town of Littleton to establish or acquire a water and electric light plant.

The following entitled House bills were severally read a third time and passed :

An act relative to the salary of the register of probate for Coös county.

An act relating to the salary of the register of probate for the county of Cheshire.

10

An act in relation to the salary of the judge of probate for Merrimack county.

An act in relation to the salary of the register of probate for Strafford county.

An act relating to the salary of the judge of probate for the county of Rockingham.

An act in relation to the salary of the judge of probate for Strafford county.

An act to incorporate the Manchester Fire Insurance Company of New Hampshire.

An act relating to agreed lines between adjoining owners.

An act in amendment of the charter of the Exeter Gas Light Company.

An act in amendment of chapter 51 of the Public Statutes, relating to cemeteries.

An act to incorporate the Derry Savings Bank of Derry.

The following entitled Senate bill was read a third time, passed, and sent to the House of Representatives for concurrence:

An act enabling the city of Concord to appropriate money for observing Memorial Day.

The following entitled House bill was read a third time and passed:

"An act to incorporate the Omicron Deuteron Charge of the Theta Delta Chi."

On motion of Senator Keyes, the title to the bill was amended by adding the word "Fraternity."

The bill was sent to the House of Representatives for concurrence in Senate amendment.

The following entitled House bill in order for a third reading was taken up:

An act in relation to milk tickets.

Senator Page moved that the rules be so far suspended that the bill be placed back on its second reading for purpose of amendment.

The question being stated,

Shall the rules be suspended?

(Discussion ensued.)

The affirmative prevailed on a *viva voce* vote.

On motion of Senator Bickford, the bill was laid on the table.

Senator Neal, for the Committee on Public Health, to whom was referred a bill entitled "An act to establish a state sanatorium for consumptives," reported the same without amendment and recommended its passage.

Senator Marvin, for the Committee on Roads, Bridges, and Canals, to whom was referred Joint resolution in favor of raising Squam bridge in Holderness, and Little Squam bridge in Ashland, and of improving navigation in Squam lake and connecting waters, reported the same without amendment and recommended its passage.

Senator Lewando, for the Committee on Revision of the Laws, to whom was referred the following bills:

"An act providing for the purchase of a bond for the deputy state treasurer,"

"An act to change the name of the South Congregational Society in Newmarket, N. H., now located in Newfields, N. H.," reported the same without amendment and recommended their passage.

The reports were accepted, and the bills were severally ordered to a third reading this afternoon at 3 o'clock.

Senator Lewando, for the Committee on Revision of the Laws, to whom was referred the following entitled bills:

" An act amending section 4, chapter 40 of the Public Statutes, relating to towns,"

" An act in amendment of section 34 of chapter 43 of the Public Statutes, in regard to the incompatibility of certain town offices," reported the same with the following resolution:

Resolved, That it is inexpedient to legislate.

The reports were accepted and the resolution adopted.

On motion of Senator Bickford, the following entitled bill was taken from the table:

An act in relation to milk tickets.

On motion of the same Senator, the following amendment was adopted : Amend section 1 by inserting the word "bread" after the word "for" in the first line.

On motion of the same Senator, the rules were so far suspended that the bill was read a third time by its title and passed.

On motion of the same Senator, the title was amended by inserting the words "and bread" after the word "milk."

The bill as amended was sent to the House of Representatives for concurrence in Senate amendments.

The following message was received from the House of Representatives by its clerk :

HOUSE MESSAGE.

Mr. President: ·

The House of Representatives has passed bills and joint resolutions with the following titles, in the passage of which it asks the concurrence of the Honorable Senate :

An act in amendment of chapter 262 of the Public Statutes, relating to coroners and coroners' inquests.

An act to provide for the assessment and collection of an annual state tax for the term of two years.

An act to ratify the doings of the town of Northumberland in purchasing the stock of the Northumberland Water Company.

An act to provide for the care and support of the dependent insane by the state.

Joint resolution in favor of the Board of Registration in Dentistry.

An act in amendment of chapter 107 of the Session Laws of 1901, relating to the inspection of milk.

An act in amendment of section 1 of chapter 196 of the Public Statutes, relating to the descent of intestate estates.

An act to change the name of the Gorham Five Cent Savings Bank.

An act to permit the town of Gorham to exempt certain property from taxation.

An act in amendment of sections 4, 5, and 9 of chapter 85 of the Public Statutes, entitled "Support of county paupers."

An act to exempt soldiers and sailors of the Spanish-American War from paying a poll tax.

The following entitled bills and joint resolution sent up from the House of Representatives were severally read a first and second time and referred,—

To the Committee on Banks:

An act to change the name of the Gorham Five Cent Savings Bank.

To the Committee on State Hospital:

An act to provide for the care and support of the dependent insane by the state.

To the Committee on Towns and Parishes:

An act to ratify the doings of the town of Northumberland in purchasing the stock of the Northumberland Water Company.

To the Committee on Finance:

An act to provide for the assessment and collection of an annual state tax for the term of two years.

(Senator Wilkins in the chair.)

Joint resolution in favor of the Board of Registration in Dentistry.

To the Committee on Revision of the Laws:

An act in amendment of sections 4, 5, and 9 of chapter 85 of the Public Statutes, entitled "Support of county paupers."

An act to permit the town of Gorham to exempt certain property from taxation.

To the Committee on the Judiciary:

An act in amendment of chapter 262 of the Public Statutes, relating to coroners and coroners' inquests.

An act in amendment of section 1 of chapter 196 of the Public Statutes, relating to the descent of intestate estates.

An act to exempt soldiers and sailors of the Spanish-American War from paying a poll tax.

An act in amendment of chapter 107 of the Session Laws of 1901, relating to the inspection of milk.

On motion of Senator Keyes, the Senate voted to recall the following entitled House bill from the Committee on Incorporations, and said bill was referred to the Committee on the Judiciary:

An act to amend section 2, chapter 179 of the Public Statutes, relating to the appointment of guardians of insane persons.

Senator Tilton, under a suspension of the rules, sixteen senators having actually voted in favor thereof, introduced the following entitled bill, which was read a first and second time and referred to the Committee on Fisheries and Game:

An act in amendment of section 56, chapter 79 of the Laws of '1901' relating to fish and game.

On motion of Senator Felt, the Senate adjourned.

AFTERNOON.

The following entitled House bills and joint resolution were severally read a third time and passed:

An act providing for the purchase of a bond for the deputy state treasurer.

An act to change the name of the South Congregational Society of Newmarket, N. H., now located in Newfields, N. H.

Joint resolution in favor of raising Squam bridge in Holderness and Little Squam bridge in Ashland, and of improving navigation in Squam lake and connecting waters.

On motion of Senator Page, the rules were so far suspended that the following entitled bill was read a third time by its title and passed:

An act to establish a state sanatorium for consumptives.

The following entitled Senate bills and Senate joint resolution having been printed were taken from the table and severally ordered to a third reading to-morrow morning at 11 o'clock:

An act relating to the time required for filing notice of intention of marriage and the consent of parents to the marriage of minors.

An act to incorporate the Nutfield Loan and Trust Company.

An act in amendment of sections 6 and 7, chapter 70 of the Public Statutes, relating to lotteries, gambling, and wagers.

Joint resolution authorizing the trustees of the N. H. College of Agriculture and the Mechanic Arts to permit certain real estate in Durham to be used as the site of a public library.

Senator Keyes, for the Committee on Incorporations, to whom was referred a bill entitled "An act to enable the town of Greenville to acquire, own, and operate an electric power and lighting plant," reported the same without amendment and recommended its passage.

Senator Ripley, for the Committee on Finance, to whom was referred the following entitled bills :

"An act in amendment of chapter 86 of the Public Statutes, in relation to state aid to indigent deaf and dumb, blind, and feeble-minded persons,"

"An act to amend chapter 95 of the Public Statutes, relating to Normal School," reported the same without amendment and recommended their passage.

The reports were accepted and the bills were severally ordered to a third reading to-morrow morning at 11 o'clock.

Senator Burnell, for the Committee on Fisheries and Game, to whom was referred a bill entitled "An act in amendment of section 56, chapter 79 of the Laws of 1901, relating to fish and game," reported the same without amendment and recommended its passage.

The report was accepted and the bill laid on the table to be printed.

Senator Thompson, for the Committee on Public Improvements, to whom was referred a bill entitled "An act relative to the enlargement of the state library building," reported the same without amendment and recommended its passage.

The report was accepted.

Senator Bickford offered the following amendment :

Amend by striking out "state library" and inserting instead thereof "state house."

The amendment was not adopted on a *viva voce* vote.

The bill was then ordered to a third reading to-morrow morning at 11 o'clock.

Senator Bickford, for the Committee on the Judiciary, reported the following entitled bill, which was read a first and second time and laid on the table to be printed :

An act in amendment of sections 1, 2, and 5, chapter 105 of the Session Laws of 1901, approved March 22, 1901, and as amended at the session of 1903.

Senator Cooper, for the Committee on Railroads, reported the following entitled bill, which was read a first and second time and laid on the table to be printed:

An act to amend the charter of the Newport and George's Mills Electric Railway Company.

The following report from the Committee on Engrossed Bills was read and accepted :

The Committee on Engrossed Bills have examined, and found correctly engrossed, the following entitled bills:

An act to annex a certain island in Lake Winnipesaukee, now owned and occupied by George W. Sherwell, being one of the group of islands known as the Aunt Dolly islands, to the town of Meredith.

An act to authorize the governor with the consent of the council to cause the original maps and surveys by the town proprietors of New Hampshire to be mounted and preserved.

An act to reimburse the town or county for aid furnished paupers.

An act authorizing the town of Peterborough to exempt from taxation the improvements on new buildings to be erected on the Tarbell block lot.

An act in relation to smallpox.

An act to authorize the state board of agriculture to appoint a state nursery inspector, and to provide for the protection of trees and shrubs from injurious insects and diseases.

An act to provide for a more economical and practical expenditure of money appropriated by the state for the construction and repair of highways.

A. W. BURNELL,
For the Committee.

On motion of Senator Ripley, the Senate adjourned.

THURSDAY, March 5, 1903.

The Senate met according to adjournment.

The reading of the journal having been commenced, on motion of Senator Fuller, the rules were so far suspended that its further reading was dispensed with.

The following entitled House bills were severally read a third time and passed:

An act in amendment of chapter 86 of the Public Statutes, in relation to state aid to indigent deaf and dumb, blind, and feeble-minded persons.

An act to amend chapter 95 of the Public Statutes, relating to Normal School.

An act relative to the enlargement of the state library building.

On motion of Senator Page, the rules were so far suspended that the following entitled House bill was read a third time by its title and passed:

An act to enable the town of Greenville to acquire, own, and operate an electric power and lighting plant.

The following entitled Senate bills and Senate joint resolution were severally read a third time, passed, and sent to the House of Representatives for concurrence:

An act relating to the time required for filing notice of intention of marriage and the consent of parents to the marriage of minors.

An act in amendment of sections 5 and 7 of chapter 270 of the Public Statutes, relating to lotteries, gambling, and wagers.

Joint resolution authorizing the trustees of the N. H. College of Agriculture and the Mechanic Arts to permit certain real estate in Durham to be used as the site of a public library.

On motion of Senator Page, the rules were so far suspended that the following entitled Senate bill was read a third time by its title, passed, and sent to the House of Representatives for concurrence:

An act to incorporate the Nutfield Loan and Trust Company.

Senator Lightbody, for the Committee on Banks, to whom

was referred a bill entitled "An act to change the name of the Gorham Five Cent Savings Bank," reported the same without amendment and recommended its passage.

Senator Keyes, for the Committee on Incorporations, to whom was referred a bill entitled "An act to incorporate the First Free Baptist Church of Franconia," reported the same without amendment and recommended its passage.

Senator Felt, for the Committee on State Hospital, to whom was referred a bill entitled "An act to provide for care and support of the dependent insane by the state," reported the same without amendment and recommended its passage.

Senator Ripley, for the Committee on Finance, to whom was referred a bill entitled "An act to provide for the assessment and collection of an annual state tax for the term of two years," reported the same without amendment and recommended its passage.

Senator Ripley, for the Committee on Finance, to whom was referred Joint resolution in favor of the Board of Registration in dentistry, reported the same without amendment and recommended its passage.

Senator Burnell, for the Committee on Fisheries and Game, to whom was referred Joint resolution in favor of screening the outlet of Forest lake, reported the same without amendment and recommended its passage.

Senator Burnell, for the Committee on Fisheries and Game, to whom was referred a bill entitled "An act to provide for bounty on hedgehogs," reported the same without amendment and recommended its passage.

Senator Keyes, for the Committee on Railroads, to whom was referred the following entitled bills :

"An act in relation to reports and evidences of stock and bonds of corporations owning stock in railways,"

"An act to incorporate the Goffs Falls, Litchfield and Hudson Street Railway Company," reported the same without amendment and recommended their passage.

Senator Lewando, for the Committee on Revision of the Laws, to whom was referred the following entitled bills :

"An act in amendment of chapter 215, Laws 1895, entitled

'An act to confirm the organization of the Androscoggin Hospital Association,'"

"An act in amendment of sections 4, 5, and 9 of chapter 85 of the Public Statutes, entitled 'Support of county paupers,'"

"An act to permit the town of Gorham to exempt certain property from taxation," reported the same without amendment and recommended their passage.

Senator Marvin, for the Committee on Towns and Parishes, to whom was referred the following entitled bills:

"An act severing the homestead farm of Hiram S. Stevens from the school district of the town of Middleton, and annexing the same to the town of Wakefield for school purposes,"

"An act to ratify the doings of the town of Northumberland in purchasing the stock of the Northumberland Water Company," reported the same without amendment and recommended their passage.

The reports were accepted and the bills and joint resolutions were severally ordered to a third reading this afternoon at 3 o'clock.

Senator Marvin, for the Committee on Roads, Bridges, and Canals, to whom was referred a bill entitled "An act relating to highways and highway agents and street commissioners," reported the same with the following amendment and recommended its passage: Amend section 1 by striking out the words "once in every month from the first day of April to the first day of November in each year," and inserting therefor the following: "once in every sixty days from the first of May to the first of October in each year," so that said section as amended shall read as follows:

SECT. 1. Every highway agent and street commissioner in this state shall cause all loose stones, lying within the travelled part of every highway in his town or city, to be removed at least once in every sixty days from the first of May to the first of October in each year, and stones so removed shall not be left in the gutter nor upon the side of the travelled part of the highway so as to be liable to work back or be brought back into the travelled part thereof for the use of road machines or other machines used in repairing highways.

The report was accepted, amendment adopted, and the bill ordered to a third reading this afternoon at 3 o'clock.

Senator Keyes, for the Committee on Railroads, to whom was referred a bill entitled "An act to incorporate the Hampstead and Haverhill Street Railway Company," reported the same with the following amendment and recommended its passage : Amend section 1 by adding in the thirteenth line after the word "Atkinson" the words "to Atkinson Depot, thence."

The report was accepted, amendment adopted, and on motion of Senator Hoyt of District 21, the rules were so far suspended that the bill was read a third time by its title, passed, and sent to the House of Representatives for concurrence in Senate amendment.

The following message from the Committee on Engrossed Bills was read and accepted :

The Committee on Engrossed Bills have examined and found correctly engrossed the following entitled bills and joint resolutions :

An act relating to the salary of the judge of probate for the county of Rockingham.

An act in relation to the salary of the judge of probate for Strafford county.

An act in relation to the salary of the judge of probate for Merrimack county.

An act in relation to the salary of the register of probate for Strafford county.

An act relating to the salary of the register of probate for the county of Cheshire.

An act relative to the salary of the register of probate for Coös county.

An act to incorporate the Derry Savings Bank of Derry.

An act in amendment of the charter of the Exeter Gas Light Company.

An act to incorporate the Manchester Fire Insurance Company of New Hampshire.

An act relating to agreed lines between adjoining owners.

An act in amendment of chapter 51 of the Public Statutes, relating to cemeteries.

An act to establish a state sanatorium for consumptives.

HENRY W. KEYES,

For the Committee.

On motion of Senator Keyes, the following resolution was adopted:

Resolved, That when the Senate adjourns this afternoon, it adjourn to meet at 9.30 o'clock to-morrow morning, and that when it adjourns to-morrow morning, it adjourn to meet at 2 o'clock Monday afternoon, and that when it adjourns Monday afternoon, it adjourn to meet at 11 o'clock Wednesday morning.

On motion of Senator Page, the following resolution was adopted:

Resolved, That when the Senate adjourns this forenoon, it adjourn to meet at 2 o'clock this afternoon, and that all bills in order for a third reading at 3 o'clock this afternoon be in order at 2 o'clock.

The following message was received from the House of Representatives by its clerk:

HOUSE MESSAGE.

Mr. President:

The House of Representatives concurs with the Honorable Senate in the passage of the following joint resolution:

Joint resolution in relation to a fish hatching house at Laconia.

The House of Representatives has voted to concur with the Honorable Senate in its amendments to the following entitled bills and joint resolutions:

An act to encourage the use of wide tires on certain vehicles constructed before January 1, 1900, and now in use in New Hampshire.

An act authorizing the town of Littleton to establish or acquire a water and electric light plant.

Joint resolution in favor of John K. Law and others.

An act in relation to milk and bread tickets.

The House of Representatives has passed bills and joint

resolutions with the following titles, in the passage of which it asks the concurrence of the Honorable Senate:

An act to provide for the daily publication of the journals of the Senate and House of Representatives.

An act for the promotion of horticulture.

An act relating to books of deposit issued by savings banks when lost, destroyed, or assigned.

·An act to authorize the managers of the New Hampshire Soldiers' Home to procure an adequate supply of water for the use of said home.

An act to provide, in common with the state of Vermont, for the acquisition, building, and maintenance of free bridges across the Connecticut river.

An act in amendment of section 4 of chapter 162 of the Public Statutes, fixing the salaries of the members of the board of bank commissioners.

An act in amendment of section 1 of chapter 3 of the Laws of 1893, fixing the salary of the clerk of the board of bank commissioners.

An act in amendment of section 17 of chapter 285 of the Public Statutes, relating to the state prison.

An act in amendment of chapter 119 of the Public Statutes, relating to the inspection and licensing of boats, their engineers and pilots.

Joint resolution in favor of screening the outlet to Penacook lake in the city of Concord.

Joint resolution for an appropriation for the construction of a screen across the outlet of Lake Winnisquam at East Tilton, in the county of Belknap.

Joint resolution for lighting the lighthouse on Loon island in Sunapee lake, repairing the cable connected therewith, improving the light service, placing and maintaining buoys on said lake, and removing obstructions to navigation in said lake.

Joint resolution in favor of maintaining buoys and placing lights in Squam lake.

Joint resolution in favor of appropriating money for screening the outlet of Tewksbury's pond in the town of Grafton.

Joint resolution appropriating money for screening the outlet of Highland lake in the town of Andover.

Joint resolution appropriating money for screening the outlet of Pleasant pond in New London.

Joint resolution for screening the outlet of Merry Meeting lake in the town of New Durham.

Joint resolution for an appropriation for screening Crystal lake in Gilmanton.

Joint resolution in favor of the New Hampshire School for Feeble-Minded Children.

Joint resolution to appropriate money for the screening of Armington pond, so called, in the town of Piermont.

Joint resolution to encourage the breeding and exhibiting of thoroughbred animals.

Joint resolution for screening the outlet to Center pond in the town of Stoddard.

Joint resolution in favor of Ella F. Densmore of Charlestown, Mary F. Lombard of Acworth, Frank G. Smith of Waltham, Massachusetts, Eugene P. Smith of Newport, and George E. Shattuck of Hinsdale.

(Senator Felt in the chair.)

The following entitled bills and joint resolutions sent up from the House of Representatives were severally read a first and second time and referred:

To the Committee on Roads, Bridges, and Canals:

An act to provide, in common with the state of Vermont, for the acquisition, building, and maintenance of free bridges across the Connecticut river.

To the Committee on State Prison and Industrial School:

An act in amendment of section 17 of chapter 285 of the Public Statutes, relating to the state prison.

To the Committee on Claims:

Joint resolution in favor of Ella F. Densmore of Charlestown, Mary F. Lombard of Acworth, Frank G. Smith of Waltham, Massachusetts, Eugene P. Smith of Newport, and George E. Shattuck of Hinsdale.

To the Committee on Soldiers' Home:

An act to authorize the managers of the New Hampshire Soldiers' Home to procure an adequate supply of water for the use of said home.

To the Committee on Agriculture:

An act for the promotion of horticulture.

To the Committee on the Judiciary:

An act to provide for the daily publication of the journals of the Senate and House of Representatives.

An act relating to books of deposit issued by savings banks, when lost, destroyed, or assigned.

An act in amendment of chapter 119 of the Public Statutes, relating to the inspection and licensing of boats, their engineers and pilots.

To the Committee on Finance:

An act in amendment of section 1 of chapter 3 of the Laws of 1893, fixing the salary of the clerk of the board of bank commissioners.

An act in amendment of section 4 of chapter 162 of the Public Statutes, fixing the salaries of the members of the board of bank commissioners.

Joint resolution for lighting the lighthouse on Loon island in Sunapee lake, repairing the cable connected therewith, improving the light service, placing and maintaining buoys on said lake, and removing obstructions to navigation in said lake.

Joint resolution in favor of maintaining buoys and placing lights in Squam lake.

Joint resolution in favor of the New Hampshire School for Feeble-Minded Children.

To the Committee on Fisheries and Game:

Joint resolution for an appropriation for the construction of a screen across the outlet of Lake Winnisquam at East Tilton, in the county of Belknap.

Joint resolution for screening the outlet to Center pond in the town of Stoddard.

Joint resolution to appropriate money for the screening of Armington pond, so called, in the town of Piermont.

Joint resolution for an appropriation for screening Crystal lake in Gilmanton.

Joint resolution for screening the outlet of Merry Meeting lake in the town of New Durham.

Joint resolution appropriating money for screening the outlet of Pleasant pond in New London.

Joint resolution appropriating money for screening the outlet of Highland lake in the town of Andover.

Joint resolution in favor of appropriating money for screening the outlet of Tewksbury's pond in the town of Grafton.

Joint resolution in favor of screening the outlet of Penacook lake in the city of Concord.

The following joint resolution sent up from the House of Representatives was read a first and second time:

Joint resolution to encourage the breeding and exhibiting of thoroughbred animals.

Senator Page moved that the joint resolution be referred to the Committee on Public Health.

The question being stated,

Shall the bill be referred to the Committee on Public Health?

(Discussion ensued.)

The negative prevailed on a *viva voce* vote.

On motion of Senator Thompson, the joint resolution was referred to the Committee on Agriculture.

(President in the chair.)

On motion of Senator Cooper, the Senate adjourned.

AFTERNOON.

The following entitled House bills and joint resolution were severally read a third time and passed:

An act in amendment of chapter 215, Laws of 1895, entitled " An act to confirm the organization of the Androscoggin Hospital Association."

An act to sever the homestead farm of Hiram S. Stevens from the school district of the town of Wakefield for school purposes.

An act to permit the town of Gorham to exempt certain property from taxation.

11

An act to ratify the doings of the town of Northumberland in purchasing the stock of the Northumberland Water Company.

An act in amendment of sections 4, 5, and 9 of chapter 85 of the Public Statutes, entitled " Support of county paupers."

An act to provide for the care and support of the dependent insane by the state.

An act to provide for the assessment and collection of an annual state tax for the term of two years.

An act in relation to the reports and increase of stock and bonds of corporations owning stock in railroads.

Joint resolution in favor of the Board of Registration in Dentistry.

The following entitled House bill was read a third time :

An act to provide for a bounty on hedgehogs.

Senator Page moved that the bill be made a special order for Thursday next at 11 o'clock.

The question being stated,

Shall the bill be made a special order for Thursday next at 11 o'clock?

(Discussion ensued.)

The negative prevailed on a *viva voce* vote.

The bill passed.

On motion of Senator Bickford, the rules were so far suspended that the following entitled House bills in order for a third reading were read a third time by their titles and passed:

An act to incorporate the First Free Baptist Church of Franconia.

An act to incorporate the Goffs Falls, Litchfield and Hudson Street Railway Company.

Joint resolution in favor of screening the outlet of Forest lake was read a third time.

Senator Page moved that the bill be indefinitely postponed.

The question being stated,

Shall the bill be indefinitely postponed?

(Discussion ensued.)

The negative prevailed on a *viva voce* vote.

The joint resolution passed.

The following entitled Senate bill was read a third time, passed, and sent to the House of Representatives for concurrence:

An act relating to highways and highway agents and street commissioners.

The following entitled Senate bills having been printed were taken from the table and ordered to a third reading to-morrow morning at 9.30 o'clock:

An act in amendment of section 56, chapter 79, of the Laws of 1901, relating to fish and game.

An act in amendment of sections 1, 2, and 5, chapter 105, of the Session Laws of 1901, approved March 2, 1901, and as amended at the session of 1903.

An act to amend the charter of the Newport and George's Mills Electric Railway Company.

Senator Marvin, for the Committee on Claims, to whom was referred "Joint resolution in favor of Ella F. Densmore of Charlestown, Mary F. Lombard of Acworth, Frank G. Smith of Waltham, Massachusetts, Eugene P. Smith of Newport, and George E. Shattuck of Hinsdale," reported the same without amendment and recommended its passage.

The same Senator, for the same committee, to whom was referred "Joint resolution to appropriate a sum of money to pay Arthur W. Dudley a balance due him for money expended and labor performed in making surveys for the state," reported the same without amendment and recommended its passage.

Senator Tolles, for the Committee on the Judiciary, to whom was referred the following entitled bills:

"An act to exempt soldiers and sailors of the Spanish-American War from paying a poll tax,"

"An act in addition to chapter 153, Public Statutes, creating section 20 of said chapter," reported the same without amendment and recommended their passage.

Senator Burnell, for the Committee on Fisheries and Game, to whom was referred the following joint resolutions:

"Joint resolution for screening the outlet of Center pond in the town of Stoddard,"

"Joint resolution in favor of appropriating money for

screening the outlet of Tewksbury's pond in the town of Grafton,"

"Joint resolution for an appropriation for screening Crystal lake in Gilmanton,"

"Joint resolution for screening the outlet of Merry Meeting lake in the town of New Durham,"

"Joint resolution to appropriate money for the screening of Armington pond, so called, in the town of Piermont,"

"Joint resolution in favor of screening the outlet of Penacook lake in the city of Concord,"

"Joint resolution for an appropriation for the construction of a screen across the outlet of Lake Winnisquam at East Tilton, in the county of Belknap,"

"Joint resolution appropriating money for screening the outlet of Pleasant pond in New London,"

"Joint resolution appropriating money for screening the outlet of Highland lake in the town of Andover," reported the same without amendments and recommended their passage.

Senator Wilkins moved that all joint resolutions reported from the Committee on Fisheries and Game pertaining to screening be recommitted for the purpose of submitting the same in one report.

The question being stated,

Shall the joint resolutions reported from the Committee on Fisheries and Game be recommitted?

Senator Tilton demanded the yeas and nays.

Senator Wilkins withdrew his motion, and the bills and joint resolutions were severally ordered to a third reading to-morrow morning at 9.30 o'clock.

Senator Tolles, for the Committee on the Judiciary, to whom was referred the following entitled bills:

"An act in amendment of chapter 91, section 8, Laws 1897, relating to the duties of the State Board of Charities and Correction,"

"An act to amend section 2, chapter 179, of the Public Statutes, relating to the appointment of guardians of insane persons," reported the same with the resolution :—

That it is inexpedient to legislate.

The reports were accepted and the resolutions adopted.

On motion of Senator Page, the rules were so far suspended that the Joint resolution in favor of Ella F. Dinsmore of Charlestown, Mary F. Lombard of Acworth, Frank G. Smith of Waltham, Massachusetts, Eugene P. Smith of Newport, and George R. Shattuck of Hinsdale, was recommitted to the Committee on Claims.

On motion of Senator Tilton, the rules were so far suspended that all bills and joint resolutions in order for a third reading to-morrow morning at 9.30 o'clock were made in order for a third reading at the present time.

The following joint resolutions were severally read a third time and passed:

Joint resolution for screening the outlet of Merry Meeting lake in the town of New Durham.

Joint resolution in favor of screening the outlet of Penacook lake in the city of Concord.

Joint resolution for an appropriation for screening Crystal lake in Gilmanton.

Joint resolution in favor of appropriating money for screening the outlet of Tewksbury's pond in the town of Grafton.

Joint resolution appropriating money for screening the outlet of Pleasant pond in New London.

Joint resolution appropriating money for screening the outlet of Highland lake in the town of Andover.

Joint resolution to appropriate money for the screening of Armington pond, so called, in the town of Piermont.

Joint resolution for an appropriation for the construction of a screen across the outlet of Lake Winnisquam at East Tilton, in the county of Belknap.

Joint resolution for screening the outlet of Center pond in the town of Stoddard.

Joint resolution to appropriate a sum of money to pay Arthur W. Dudley a balance due him for money expended and labor performed in making surveys for the state.

On motion of Senator Tolles, the rules were so far suspended that all bills in order for a third reading were read a third time by their titles.

And following entitled House bills were severally read a third time and passed :

"An act to exempt soldiers and sailors of the Spanish-American War from paying a poll tax."

"An act in addition to chapter 154, Public Statutes, creating section 20 of said chapter."

And the following entitled Senate bills were severally read a third time, passed, and sent to the House of Representatives for concurrence :

"An act in amendment of section 56, chapter 79, of the Laws of 1901, relating to fish and game."

"An act in amendment of sections 1, 2, and 5, chapter 105 of the Session Laws of 1901, approved March 22, 1901, and as amended at the session of 1903."

"An act to amend the charter of the Newport and George's Mills Electric Railway Company."

The following message was received from the House of Representatives by its clerk:

HOUSE MESSAGE.

Mr. President:

The House of Representatives has passed the following entitled bills and joint resolution, in the passage of which it asks the concurrence of the Honorable Senate :

"An act in amendment of sections 2 and 3, chapter 42 of the Public Statutes, relating to government of town meetings."

"An act to legalize the annual school meeting in the town school district in the town of Franconia, in the year 1902, and to legalize the acts of said district at that meeting and the subsequent acts and proceedings of the district officers elected at said meeting."

"An act to legalize the warrant for a town meeting to be held in the town of Franconia on the second Tuesday of March, 1903."

"An act authorizing the city of Nashua to issue bonds and exempt the same from taxation."

" Joint resolution in favor of Horace L. Worcester."

"An act to authorize the Hudson, Pelham and Salem Electric

Railway Company to take leases of the railway and property of the Haverhill and Southern New Hampshire Street Railway Company, the Lawrence and Methuen Street Railway Company, and the Lowell and Pelham Street Railway Company."

"An act to incorporate the Milton Mills and Union Electric Railway Company."

"An act to amend chapter 243 of the Laws of 1901, creating the Grafton Improvement Company."

On motion of Senator Keyes, the rules were so far suspended that the following entitled bills sent up from the House of Representatives were severally read a first and second time by their titles and referred:

To the Committee on Railroads:

"An act to incorporate the Milton Mills and Union Electric Railway Company."

"An act to authorize the Hudson, Pelham and Salem Electric Railway Company to take leases of the railway and property of the Haverhill and Southern New Hampshire Street Railway Company, the Lawrence and Methuen Street Railway Company, and the Lowell and Pelham Street Railway Company."

To the Committee on the Judiciary:

"An act to legalize the annual school meeting of the town school district in the town of Franconia in the year 1902, and to legalize the acts of said district at that meeting and the subsequent acts and proceedings of the district officers elected at said meeting."

"An act authorizing the city of Nashua to issue bonds and exempt the same from taxation."

"An act to amend chapter 243 of the Laws of 1901, creating the Grafton Improvement Manufacturing and Power Company."

The following entitled bill sent up from the House of Representatives was read a first and second time by its title, and on motion of Senator Bickford, the rules were so far suspended that the bill was read a third time by its title and passed:

"An act to legalize the warrant for the town meeting to be held in the town of Franconia on the second Tuesday of March, 1903."

Joint resolution in favor of Horace L. Worcester, sent up from the House of Representatives, was read a first and second time, and on motion of Senator Allen, the rules were so far suspended that the joint resolution was read a third time and passed.

The following entitled bill sent up from the House of Representatives was read a first and second time by its title, and on motion of Senator Keyes, the rules were so far suspended that the bill was read a third time by its title and passed:

"An act in amendment of sections 2 and 3, chapter 427 of the Public Statutes, relating to government of town meetings."

On motion of Senator Keyes, the Senate adjourned.

FRIDAY, MARCH 6, 1903.

The Senate met according to adjournment.

The reading of the journal having been commenced, on motion of Senator Keyes, the rules were so far suspended that its further reading was dispensed with.

The following report from the Committee on Engrossed Bills was read and accepted:

The Committee on Engrossed Bills have examined, and found correctly engrossed, the following entitled bills and joint resolutions:

An act to enable the town of Greenville to acquire, own, and operate an electric power and lighting plant.

An act to incorporate the Ossipee Water and Electric Company.

An act to legalize the warrant for the town meeting to be held in the town of Franconia on the second Tuesday of March, 1903.

An act authorizing the town of Littleton to establish and acquire a water and electric light plant.

An act in relation to reports and increase of stock and bonds of corporations owning stock in railways.

An act in amendment of sections 4, 5, and 9 of chapter 85 of the Public Statutes, entitled "Support of county paupers."

An act to provide for the assessment and collection of an annual state tax for the term of two years.

An act in amendment of chapter 86 of the Public Statutes, in relation to state aid to indigent deaf and dumb, blind, and feeble-minded persons.

An act to amend chapter 95 of the Public Statutes, relating to Normal School.

An act in amendment of chapter 215, Laws 1895, entitled "An act to confirm the organization of the Androscoggin Hospital Association."

An act in amendment to chapter 153, Public Statutes, creating section 20 of said chapter.

An act to provide for a bounty on hedgehogs.

An act to ratify the doings of the town of Northumberland in purchasing the stock of the Northumberland Water Company.

An act relative to the enlargement of the state library building.

An act to exempt the soldiers and sailors of the Spanish-American War from paying a poll tax.

An act to incorporate the First Free Baptist church of Franconia.

An act to change the name of the Gorham Five Cents Savings Bank.

An act severing the homestead of Hiram S. Stevens from the school district of the town of Middleton, and annexing the same to the town of Wakefield for school purposes.

An act providing for the purchase of a bond for the deputy state treasurer.

An act in relation to milk and bread tickets.

An act to change the name of the South Congregational Society in Newmarket, New Hampshire, now located in Newfields, New Hampshire.

An act to encourage the use of wide tires on certain vehicles constructed before January 1, 1900, and now in use in New Hampshire.

An act to incorporate the Goffs Falls, Litchfield and Hudson Street Railway Company.

Joint resolution in relation to a fish hatching house at Laconia.

Joint resolution in favor of Horace L. Worcester.

Joint resolution in favor of appropriating money for screening the outlet of Pleasant pond in the town of New London.

Joint resolution for an appropriation for the construction of a screen across the outlet of Lake Winnisquam at East Tilton, in the county of Belknap.

Joint resolution for screening the outlet of Center pond in the town of Stoddard.

Joint resolution to appropriate money for the screening of Armington pond, so called, in the town of Piermont.

Joint resolution appropriating money for screening the outlet of Highland lake in the town of Andover.

Joint resolution for screening the outlet of Merry Meeting lake in the town of New Durham.

Joint resolution in favor of screening the outlet of Forest lake.

Joint resolution in favor of the Board of Registration in Dentistry.

Joint resolution in favor of screening the outlet of Penacook lake in the city of Concord.

Joint resolution in favor of appropriating money for screening the outlet of Tewksbury's pond in the town of Grafton.

Joint resolution for an appropriation for screening Crystal lake in Gilmanton.

Joint resolution in favor of raising Squam bridge in Holderness and Little Squam bridge in Ashland, and of improving navigation in Squam lake and connecting waters.

Joint resolution in favor of John K. Law and others.

An act to permit the town of Gorham to exempt certain property from taxation.

An act to incorporate the Hampstead and Haverhill Street Railway Company.

An act in amendment of sections 2 and 3, chapter 42 of the Public Statutes, relating to government of town meetings.

An act to provide for the care and support of the dependent insane by the state.

An act amending the charter of the Nashua Light, Heat and Power Company.

Joint resolution to appropriate a sum of money to pay Arthur W. Dudley a sum due him for money expended and labor performed in making surveys for the state.

HENRY W. KEYES,
For the Committee.

On motion of Senator Keyes, the Senate adjourned.

MONDAY, MARCH 9, 1903.

The Senate met according to adjournment.

Senator Stillings having assumed the chair, read the following communication:

NASHUA, N. H., March 9, 1903.

Senator Stillings:

Please preside for me at the session to-day of the New Hampshire Senate, and oblige

CHARLES W. HOITT,
President.

The journal was read and approved.

On motion of Senator Bickford, the Senate adjourned.

WEDNESDAY, MARCH 11, 1903.

The Senate met according to adjournment.

The journal was read and approved.

On motion of Senator Bickford, the Senate adjourned.

AFTERNOON.

The Committee on Rules submitted the following resolution:

Resolved, That printed copies of all bills ordered printed by the House of Representatives and sent up to the Senate for its consideration, shall, on reference to any committee, be immediately distributed by the sergeant-at-arms, and no report thereon shall be accepted from any committee until such distribution has been made.

CHARLES W. HOITT,
For the Committee.

On motion of Senator Bickford, the resolution was adopted.

The following message was received from the House of Representatives by its clerk:

HOUSE MESSAGE.

Mr. President:

The House of Representatives refuses to concur with the Honorable Senate in the passage of the following entitled bill sent down from the Honorable Senate:

An act in amendment of chapter 171 of the Public Statutes, relating to life insurance.

The House of Representatives concurs with the Honorable Senate in the passage of the following entitled bill:

An act amending the charter of the Nashua Light, Heat and Power Company of Nashua.

The House of Representatives has voted to concur with the Honorable Senate in its amendments to the following entitled bill:

An act to incorporate the Hampstead and Haverhill Street Railway Company.

The House of Representatives has passed bills and joint resolutions with the following titles, in the passage of which it asks the concurrence of the Honorable Senate:

Joint resolution in favor of William J. Patch.

An act to amend section 10, chapter 79 of the Session Laws of 1901, relating to the duties of the fish and game commissioners.

An act in amendment of section 1, chapter 67, Laws of 1889, relating to expenses of judges of the supreme court.

An act to provide for the holding of library institutes.

Joint resolution in favor of the Granite State Dairymen's Association.

The following entitled bills and joint resolutions sent up

from the House of Representatives were severally read a first and second time and referred:

To the Committee on the Judiciary:

An act in amendment of section 1, chapter 67, Laws of 1899, relating to expenses of judges of the supreme court.

To the Committee on Claims:

Joint resolution in favor of William J. Patch.

To the Committee on Finance:

Joint resolution in favor of the Granite State Dairymen's Association.

To the Committee on Fisheries and Game:

An act to amend section 10, chapter 79 of the Session Laws of 1901, relating to the duties of the Fish and Game Commissioners.

To the Committee on Education:

An act to provide for the holding of library institutes.

Senator Bickford, for the Committee on the Judiciary, to whom was referred the following entitled bills:

" An act authorizing the city of Nashua to issue bonds and exempt the same from taxation,"

"An act to provide for the daily publication of the journals of the Senate and House of Representatives,"

"An act in amendment of chapter 119 of the Public Statutes, relating to the inspection and licensing of boats, their engineers and pilots,"

"An act to legalize the annual school meeting of the town school district in the town of Franconia in the year 1902, and to legalize the act of said district at that meeting and the subsequent acts and proceedings of the district officers elected at said meeting," reported the same without amendment and recommended their passage.

The reports were accepted, and the bills severally ordered to a third reading to-morrow morning at 11 o'clock.

On motion of Senator Neal, the Senate adjourned.

THURSDAY, MARCH 12, 1903.

The Senate met according to adjournment.

The reading of the journal having been commenced, on motion of Senator Stillings, the rules were so far suspended that its further reading was dispensed with.

The following entitled House bills were severally read a third time and passed:

An act authorizing the city of Nashua to issue bonds and exempt the same from taxation.

An act to provide for the daily publication of the journals of the Senate and House of Representatives.

An act in amendment of chapter 119 of the Public Statutes, relating to the inspection and licensing of boats, their engineers and pilots.

An act to legalize the annual school meeting of the town school district in the town of Franconia in the year 1902, and to legalize the acts of said district at that meeting and the subsequent acts and proceedings of the district officers elected at said meeting.

Senator Fuller, for the Committee on Soldiers' Home, to whom was referred a bill entitled "An act to authorize the managers of the New Hampshire Soldiers' Home to procure an adequate supply of water for the use of said Home," reported the same without amendment and recommended its passage.

Senator Keyes, for the Committee on Railroads, to whom was referred a bill entitled "An act to authorize the Hudson, Pelham and Salem Electric Railway Company to take leases of the railway and property of the Haverhill and Southern New Hampshire Street Railway Company, the Lawrence & Methuen Street Railway Company, and the Lowell & Pelham Street Railway Company," reported the same without amendment and recommended its passage.

Senator Richmond, for the Committee on Incorporations, to whom was referred the following entitled bills:

"An act amending the charter of the Newmarket Electric Light, Heat and Power Company,"

"An act authorizing the Mt. Pleasant Hotel Company to increase its capital stock," reported the same without amendment and recommended their passage.

The reports were accepted and the bills severally ordered to a third reading this afternoon at 3 o'clock.

On motion of Senator Keyes, the Senate voted to take a recess until 11.45 o'clock.

(Recess.)

The Senate reassembled.

The following message was received from the House of Representatives by its clerk:

HOUSE MESSAGE.

Mr. President:

The House of Representatives has voted to concur with the Honorable Senate in its amendments to the following entitled bill:

An act to incorporate the Omicron Deuteron Charge of the Theta Delta Chi Fraternity.

The House of Representatives concurs with the Honorable Senate in the passage of the following entitled bills:

An act in amendment of the charter of the Salem Water-Works Company, and legalizing and confirming the acts of said corporation in relation thereto.

An act in amendment of section 128, chapter 59 of the Laws of 1895, entitled "An act to revise and amend Title 13 of the Public Statutes, relating to militia."

An act to incorporate the Ossipee Water and Electric Company.

The House of Representatives has passed the following entitled bills and joint resolution, in the passage of which it asks the concurrence of the Honorable Senate:

Joint resolution appropriating nine thousand dollars for additions and repairs to the Industrial School.

An act ratifying votes of the town of Littleton passed at its town meeting held on the 10th day of March, 1903.

An act to legalize and ratify the votes and proceedings at

the annual meeting in Newton, holden on the tenth day of March, 1903.

The following entitled bill and joint resolution sent up from the House of Representatives were severally read a first and second time and referred :

To the Committee on the Judiciary :

An act to legalize and ratify the votes and proceedings at the annual meeting in Newton, holden on the tenth day of March, 1903.

To the Committee on State Prison and Industrial School :

Joint resolution appropriating nine thousand dollars for additions and repairs to the Industrial School.

The following entitled bill sent up from the House of Representatives was read a first and second time, and on motion of Senator Keyes, the rules were so far suspended that the bill was read a third time and passed :

An act ratifying votes of the town of Littleton passed at its town meeting held on the 10th day of March, 1903.

The following report from the Committee on Engrossed Bills was read and accepted :

The Committee on Engrossed Bills have examined and found correctly engrossed the following entitled bills :

An act to incorporate the Omicron Deuteron Charge of the Theta Delta Chi Fraternity.

An act in amendment of section 128, chapter 59 of the Laws of 1895, entitled "An act to revise and amend Title 13 of the Public Statutes, relating to militia."

HENRY W. KEYES,
For the Committee.

On motion of Senator Fuller, the Senate adjourned.

AFTERNOON.

The following entitled House bills were severally read a third time and passed :

An act to authorize the Hudson, Pelham & Salem Electric Railway Company to take leases of the railway and property of the Haverhill & Southern New Hampshire Street Railway

Company, the Lawrence & Methuen Street Railway Company, and the Lowell & Pelham Street Railway Company.

An act to authorize the manager of the New Hampshire Soldiers' Home to provide an adequate supply of water for the use of said home.

An act authorizing the Mt. Pleasant Hotel Company to increase its capital stock.

On motion of Senator Richmond, the rules were so far suspended that the following entitled House bill was read a third time by its title and passed:

An act amending the charter of the Newmarket Electric Light, Heat, and Power Company.

Senator Bickford, for the Committee on the Judiciary, to whom was referred the following entitled bills:

"An act relating to books of deposit issued by savings banks when lost, destroyed, or assigned,"

"An act in amendment of section 1 of chapter 196 of the Public Statutes, relating to the descent of intestate estates," reported the same without amendment and recommended their passage.

Senator Richmond, for the Committee on Incorporations, to whom was referred a bill entitled "An act to incorporate the Pittsfield Light and Power Company," reported the same without amendment and recommended its passage.

The reports were accepted and the bills severally ordered to a third reading to-morrow morning at 11 o'clock.

Senator Bickford, for the Committee on the Judiciary, reported the following entitled bill which was read a first and second time and laid on the table to be printed:

An act in amendment of section 3 of chapter 7 of the Public Statutes, relating to the state house and yard.

The following message was received from the House of Representatives by its clerk:

HOUSE MESSAGE.

Mr. President:

The House of Representatives has passed bills with the following titles, in the passage of which it asks the concurrence of the Honorable Senate:

12

An act annexing certain islands in Lake Winnipesaukee to the town of Tuftonborough.

An act to authorize the Dover and Eliot Street Railway and the Eliot Bridge Company to transfer their properties and franchises to the Berwick, Eliot & York Street Railway.

An act to incorporate the Kearsarge Mountain Electric Railway Company.

An act to incorporate the New Ipswich, Greenville and Wilton Electric Railway Company.

An act to incorporate the History Commission of Concord.

The following entitled bills sent up from the House of Representatives were severally read a first and second time and referred :

To the Committee on Education :

An act to incorporate the History Commission of Concord.

To the Committee on Towns and Parishes :

An act annexing certain islands in Lake Winnipesaukee to the town of Tuftonborough.

On motion of Senator Bickford, the rules were so far suspended, that the following entitled bills sent up from the House of Representatives were severally read a first and second time by their titles and referred :

To the Committee on Railroads :

An act to incorporate the Kearsarge Mountain Electric Railway Company.

An act to incorporate the New Ipswich, Greenville and Wilton Electric Railway Company.

An act to authorize the Dover and Eliot Street Railway and the Eliot Bridge Company to transfer their properties and franchises to the Berwick, Eliot & York Street Railway.

On motion of Senator Foley, the Senate adjourned.

FRIDAY, MARCH 13, 1903.

The Senate met according to adjournment.

The reading of the journal having been commenced, on motion of Senator Fuller, the rules were so far suspended that its further reading was dispensed with.

The following entitled House bill was read a third time and passed:

An act in amendment of section 1 of chapter 196 of the Public Statutes, relating to the descent of intestate estates.

On motion of Senator Stillings, the rules were so far suspended that the following entitled House bill was read a third time by its title and passed:

An act to incorporate the Pittsfield Light and Power Company.

(Senator Thompson in the chair.)

The following entitled House bill was read a third time:

An act relating to books of deposit issued by savings banks when lost, destroyed, or assigned.

The question being stated,

Shall the bill pass?

(Discussion ensued.)

On motion of Senator Hoitt of District No. 19, the bill was indefinitely postponed.

(The President in the chair.)

The following report from the Committee on Engrossed Bills was read and accepted:

The Committee on Engrossed Bills have examined, and found correctly engrossed, the following entitled bills and joint resolutions:

An act to legalize the annual school meeting of the town school district in the town of Franconia in the year 1902, and to legalize the acts of said district at that meeting and the subsequent acts and proceedings of the district officers elected at said meeting.

An act to provide for the daily publication of the journals of the Senate and House of Representatives.

An act in amendment of chapter 119 of the Public Statutes relating to the inspection and licensing of boats, their engineers and pilots.

An act authorizing the city of Nashua to issue bonds and exempt the same from taxation.

An act ratifying votes of the town of Littleton passed at its town meeting held on the 10th day of March, 1903.

An act to incorporate the Jackson Water-Works Company.

An act in relation to state officials, commissioners, trustees, or other persons having control of public funds.

HENRY W. KEYES,

For the Committee.

Senator Bickford, for the Committee on the Judiciary, to whom was referred a bill entitled "An act to legalize and ratify the votes and proceedings at the annual meeting in Newton, on the the tenth day of March, 1903," reported the same without amendment and recommended its passage.

Senator Keyes, for the Committee on Forestry, to whom was referred "Joint resolution to provide a nursery for the growth and distribution of forest seedling trees within the state at cost," reported the same without amendment and recommended its passage.

The reports were accepted and the bill and joint resolution were severally ordered to a third reading Tuesday morning next at 11 o'clock.

The following message was received from the House of Representatives by its clerk:

HOUSE MESSAGE.

Mr. President:

The House of Representatives concurs with the Honorable Senate in the passage of the following entitled bills:

An act to incorporate the Jackson Water-Works Company.

An act in relation to state officials, commissioners, trustees, or other persons having control of public funds.

The House of Representatives has passed bills and a joint resolution with the following titles, in the passage of which it asks the concurrence of the Honorable Senate:

An act to incorporate the Swift River Railroad Company.

An act to incorporate the Prudential Fire Insurance Company.

An act in amendment of so much of chapter 264 of the Laws of the State of New Hampshire, passed at the January session,

1893, as relates to the establishing of a board of street and park commissioners for the city of Manchester.

An act to incorporate the Sons of Veterans' Memorial Hall Association.

An act to incorporate the Meredith and Ossipee Valley Railroad Company.

An act to amend section 16 of chapter 79 of the Session Laws of 1901, relating to the taking of deer.

An act authorizing the state treasurer to transfer certain sums of money to the literary fund for schools.

An act to amend the charter of the Bennington Water-Works Company.

An act to incorporate the Warren Water and Light Company.

An act to incorporate the Bellman Club of Manchester, N. H.

An act to incorporate the Dover Loan and Trust Company.

Joint resolution in favor of New Hampshire Soldiers' Home.

On motion of Senator Thompson, the rules were so far suspended that the following entitled bills sent up from the House of Representatives were severally read a first and second time by their titles and referred :

To the Committee on Incorporations :

An act to incorporate the Bellman Club of Manchester, N. H.

An act to incorporate the Prudential Fire Insurance Company.

An act to incorporate the Warren Water and Light Company.

An act to amend the charter of the Bennington Water-Works Company.

An act to incorporate the Dover Loan and Trust Company.

To the Committee on the Judiciary :

An act to incorporate the Sons of Veterans' Memorial Hall Association.

An act in amendment of so much of chapter 264 of the Laws of the State of New Hampshire, passed at the January session, 1893, as relates to the establishing of a board of street and park commissioners for the city of Manchester.

To the Committee on Railroads :

An act to incorporate the Swift River Railroad Company.

An act to incorporate the Meredith and Ossipee Valley Railroad Company.

To the Committee on Finance :

An act authorizing the state treasurer to transfer certain sums of money to the literary fund for schools.

To the Committee on Fisheries and Game :

, An act to amend section 16 of chapter 79 of the Session Laws of 1901, relating to the taking of deer.

Joint resolution in favor of New Hampshire Soldiers' Home, sent up from the House of Representatives, was read a first and second time and referred :

To the Committee on Soldiers' Home.

On motion of Senator Thompson, the following resolution was adopted :

Resolved, That when the Senate adjourns that it adjourn to meet next Monday afternoon at 2 o'clock.

On motion of Senator Allen, the Senate adjourned.

MONDAY, MARCH 16, 1903.

The Senate met according to adjournment.

The reading of the journal having been commenced, on motion of Senator Stillings, the rules were so far suspended that its further reading was dispensed with.

On motion of the same Senator, the Senate adjourned.

TUESDAY, MARCH 17, 1903.

The Senate met according to adjournment.

The journal was read and approved.

The following message was received from the House of Representatives by its clerk :

HOUSE MESSAGE.

Mr. President :

The House of Representatives concurs with the Honorable Senate in the passage of the following entitled bill :

An act to amend the charter of the Newport and George's Mills Electric Railway Company.

The House of Representatives deems it inexpedient to legislate on a bill with the following title, sent down from the Honorable Senate:

An act to amend chapter 93, section 15 of the Public Statutes, as amended by chapter 61 of the Session Laws of 1901, relating to scholars.

The House of Representatives has passed bills and a joint resolution with the following titles, in the passage of which it asks the concurrence of the Honorable Senate:

An act in amendment of the charter of the city of Manchester, establishing a board of assessors in place of the assessors provided under the chapter and laws of the state.

An act relating to the setting off by the legislature of territory of one town or city on to that of another town or city.

An act in amendment of section 79 of chapter 79 of the Laws of 1901, in regard to lobster traps.

An act relating to the salary of the judge of probate for the county of Carroll.

An act in amendment of Public Statutes, chapter 81, section 2, relating to telegraph, telephone, and electric light companies.

Joint resolution in favor of Horace S. Cummings.

An act to require non-residents to secure a license before hunting deer within the state of New Hampshire, and providing penalties for violation of its provisions.

The following entitled bills and joint resolution sent up from the House of Representatives were severally read a first and second time and referred:

To the Committee on the Judiciary:

An act relating to the salary of the judge of probate for the county of Carroll.

An act in amendment of the charter of the city of Manchester, establishing a board of assessors in place of the assessors provided under the chapter and laws of the state.

An act in amendment of Public Statutes, chapter 81, section 2, relating to telegraph, telephone, and electric light companies

To the Committee on Fisheries and Game :

An act in amendment of section 79 of chapter 79 of the Laws of 1901, in regard to lobster traps.

An act to require non-residents to secure a license before hunting deer within the state of New Hampshire, and providing penalties for violation of its provisions.

To the Committee on Towns and Parishes :

An act relating to the setting off by the legislature of territory of one town or city on to that of another town or city.

To the Committee on Finance :

Joint resolution in favor of Horace S. Cummings.

The following entitled Senate bill having been printed, was taken from the table and ordered to a third reading this afternoon at 3 o'clock.

An act in amendment of section 3 of chapter 7 of the Public Statutes, relating to the state house and yard.

The following entitled House bill was read a third time and passed :

An act to legalize and ratify the votes and proceedings at the annual meeting in Newton, holden on the tenth day of March, 1903.

Joint resolution to provide a nursery for the growth and distribution of forest seedling trees within the state at cost, was read a third time.

The question being stated,

Shall the bill pass ?

Senator Bickford moved that the joint resolution be indefinitely postponed.

The question being stated,

Shall the joint resolution be indefinitely postponed ?

(Senator Allen in the chair.)

(Discussion ensued.)

The affirmative prevailed on a *viva voce* vote, and the joint resolution was indefinitely postponed.

The following report from the Committee on Engrossed Bills was read and accepted :

The Committee on Engrossed Bills have examined and

found correctly engrossed the following entitled bills and joint resolutions:

An act to incorporate the Pittsfield Light and Power Company.

An act in amendment of section 1 of chapter 196 of the Public Statutes, relating to the descent of intestate estates.

An act to amend the charter of the Newport and George's Mills Electric Railway Company.

An act to authorize the Hudson, Pelham and Salem Electric Railway Company to take leases of the railway and property of the Haverhill & Southern New Hampshire Street Railway Company, the Lawrence & Methuen Street Railway Company, and the Lowell & Pelham Street Railway Company.

An act authorizing the Mt. Pleasant Hotel Company to increase its capital stock.

An act to authorize the managers of the N. H. Soldiers' Home to procure an adequate supply of water for the use of said home.

An act amending the charter of the Newmarket Electric Light, Power, and Heat Company.

HENRY W. KEYES,
For the Committee.

On motion of Senator Hoyt, of District No. 21, the Senate adjourned.

AFTERNOON.

Senator Fuller, for the Committee on Agriculture, to whom was referred a bill entitled "An act for the promotion of horticulture," reported the same without amendment and recommended its passage.

Senator Burnell, for the Committee on Fisheries and Game, to whom was referred the following entitled bills:

"An act to amend section 16 of chapter 79 of the Laws of 1901, relative to the taking of deer,"

"An act to amend section 10, chapter 79 of the Laws of 1901, relative to the duties of the fish and game commissioners," reported the same without amendment and recommended their passage.

Senator Ripley, for the Committee on Finance, to whom was referred the following entitled bills and joint resolution :

"An act authorizing the state treasurer to transfer certain sums of money to the literary fund for schools,"

"An act in amendment of section 1 of chapter 3 of the Laws of 1893, fixing the salary of the clerk of the board of bank commissioners,"

"An act in amendment of section 4 of chapter 162 of the Public Statutes, fixing the salaries of the members of the board of bank commissioners,"

"Joint resolution in favor of maintaining buoys and placing lights on Squam lake,"

"Joint resolution in favor of the Granite State Dairyman's Association,"

"Joint resolution for lighting the lighthouse on Loon island in Sunapee lake, repairing the cable connected therewith, improving the light service, placing and maintaining buoys on said lake and removing obstructions to navigation in said lake," reported the same without amendment and recommended their passage.

The reports were accepted and the bills and joint resolutions were severally ordered to a third reading to-morrow morning at 11 o'clock.

Senator Ripley, for the Committee on Finance, to whom was referred "Joint resolution in favor of Horace S. Cummings," reported the same without amendment and recommended its passage.

The report was accepted and on motion of Senator Bickford, the joint resolution and accompanying report were laid on the table.

The following entitled Senate bill was read a third time, passed, and sent to the House of Representatives for concurrence :

An act in amendment of section 3 of chapter 7 of the Public Statutes, relating to the state house and yard.

On motion of Senator Burnell, the Senate adjourned.

WEDNESDAY, MARCH 18, 1903.

The Senate met according to adjournment.

The reading of the journal having been commenced, on motion of Senator Keyes, the rules were so far suspended that its further reading was dispensed with.

The following entitled House bills and joint resolutions were severally read a third time and passed:

An act for the promotion of horticulture.

An act to amend section 16 of chapter 79 of the Session Laws of 1901, relating to the taking of deer.

An act authorizing the state treasurer to transfer certain sums of money to the literary fund for schools.

An act to amend section 10, chapter 79 of the Session Laws of 1901, relating to the duties of the fish and game commissioners.

An act in amendment of section 4 of chapter 162 of the Public Statutes, fixing the salaries of the members of the board of bank commissioners.

An act in amendment of section 1 of chapter 3 of the Laws of 1893, fixing the salary of the clerk of the board of bank commissioners.

Joint resolution in favor of the Granite State Dairyman's Association.

Joint resolution in favor of maintaining buoys and placing lights in Squam lake.

Joint resolution for lighting the lighthouse on Loon island in Sunapee lake, repairing the cable connected therewith, improving the light service, placing and maintaining buoys on said lake, and removing obstructions to navigation in said lake.

Senator Fuller, for the Committee on Soldiers' Home, to whom was referred "Joint resolution in favor of New Hampshire Soldiers' Home," reported the same without amendment and recommended its passage.

The report was accepted and the joint resolution ordered to a third reading this afternoon at 3 o'clock.

Senator Tilton, for the Committee on Fisheries and Game, reported the following entitled bill, which was read a first and second time:

"An act in amendment of section 14, chapter 79, Session Laws of 1901, relating to the powers of the fish and game commissioners."

On motion of Senator Tilton, the rules were so far suspended that the bill was read a third time, passed, and sent to the House of Representatives for concurrence.

The following report from the Committee on Engrossed Bills was read and accepted:

The Committee on Engrossed Bills have examined and found correctly engrossed the following entitled bills:

An act to legalize and ratify the votes and proceedings at the annual meeting in Newton, holden on the tenth day of March, 1903.

An act relating to highways and highway agents and street commissioners.

A. W. BURNELL.

For the Committee.

The following message was received from the House of Representatives by its clerk:

HOUSE MESSAGE.

Mr. President:

The House of Representatives concurs with the Honorable Senate in the passage of the following entitled bills:

An act relating to highways, highway agents, and street commissioners.

An act to amend section 52 of chapter 79 of the Laws of 1901, entitled "An act to revise the fish and game laws of the state."

An act in amendment of "An act to incorporate the Society of Social Friends," approved June 29, 1826, "An act to incorporate the United Fraternity," approved July 6, 1827, and "An act to incorporate the Philotechnic Society of the Chandler Scientific department of Dartmouth College," approved July 13, 1854, and to authorize the calling of meetings of said corporations respectively.

An act in amendment of section 13, chapter 59, Laws of 1895, relating to the bond of the adjutant-general.

An act in amendment of section 59, chapter 79 of the Session Laws of 1901, relating to the taking of black bass.

An act to change the name of the Manchester Heating and Lighting Company of Manchester, N. H.

An act to authorize the town of Gilmanton to exempt certain property from taxation.

An act to define the duties of the state treasurer with reference to public funds.

An act to incorporate the Derry and Salem Street Railway Company.

An act in amendment of sections 7 and 10, chapter 27, Laws of 1895, relating to street railways.

An act in amendment of section 13, chapter 27 of the Pamphlet Laws of 1895, relating to street railways.

Joint resolution providing for the repairs and construction of certain state highways, certain highways in unincorporated places, and certain roads in places where such roads cannot be maintained by any local municipality.

Joint resolution in favor of Green's basin in Lake Winnipesaukee.

Joint resolution in favor of the widow of Benjamin F. March of Mason.

Joint resolution in favor of placing and maintaining buoys and lights in Lake Winnipesaukee and adjacent waters.

The following entitled bills and joint resolutions sent up from the House of Representatives were severally read a first and second time and referred:

(Senator Tolles in the chair.)

To the Committee on Claims:

Joint resolution in favor of the widow of Benjamin F. March of Mason.

To the Committee on Finance:

An act to define the duties of the state treasurer with reference to public funds.

To the Committee on Military Affairs:

An act in amendment of section 13, chapter 59, Laws of 1895, relating to the bond of the adjutant-general.

To the Committee on Public Improvements:

Joint resolution in favor of Green's basin in Lake Winnipesaukee.

To the Committee on Towns and Parishes:

An act to authorize the town of Gilmanton to exempt certain property from taxation.

To the Committee on Roads, Bridges, and Canals:

. Joint resolution in favor of placing and maintaining buoys and lights in Lake Winnipesaukee and adjacent waters.

Joint resolution providing for the repairs and construction of certain state highways, certain highways in unincorporated places, and certain roads in places where such roads cannot be maintained by any local municipality.

To the Committee on Fisheries and Game:

An act in amendment of section 59, chapter 79 of the Session Laws of 1901, relating to the taking of black bass.

An act to amend section 52 of chapter 79 of the Laws of 1901, entitled "An act to revise the fish and game laws of the state."

To the Committee on Incorporations:

An act to change the name of the Manchester Heating and Lighting Company of Manchester, N. H.

An act in amendment of "An act to incorporate the Society of Social Friends," approved June 29, 1826, "An act to incorporate the United Fraternity," approved July 6, 1827, and "An act to incorporate the Philotechnic Society of the Chandler Scientific department of Dartmouth College," approved July 13, 1854, and to authorize the calling of meetings of said corporations respectively.

To the Committee on Railroads:

An act in amendment of section 13, chapter 27 of the Pamphlet Laws of 1895, relating to street railways.

An act in amendment of sections 7 and 10, chapter 27, Laws of 1895, relating to street railways.

An act to incorporate the Derry and Salem Street Railway Company.

(The President in the chair.)

On motion of Senator Felt, the Senate adjourned.

AFTERNOON.

Joint resolution in favor of New Hampshire Soldiers' Home was read a third time and passed.

Senator Marvin, for the Committee on Towns and Parishes, to whom was referred "An act annexing certain islands in Lake Winnipesaukee to the town of Tuftonborough," reported the same without amendment and recommended its passage.

Senator Lightbody, for the Committee on Education, to whom was referred the following entitled bills:

"An act to incorporate the History Commission of Concord,"

"An act to amend section 1 of chapter 46, Session Laws of 1895, relating to annual enumeration of school children," reported the same without amendment and recommended their passage.

The reports were accepted and the bills severally ordered to a third reading to-morrow morning at 11 o'clock.

Senator Tolles, for the Committee on Agriculture, to whom was referred a bill entitled "An act in amendment of chapter 107 of the Session Laws of 1901, relating to the inspection of milk," reported the same with the following amendment and recommended its passage:

Amend section 1 of said bill by striking out all after the word "follows" in the second line of said section, and insert instead thereof the following: " By adding at the end of said section the words 'provided, however, that any person selling only the product of his own cows shall be exempt from paying any fee for such license,' so that said section as amended shall read : "

SECTION 1. That section 4 of chapter 107 of the Laws of 1901 be amended as follows : By adding at the end of said section the words " provided, however, that any person selling only the product of his own cows shall be exempt from paying any fee for such license," so that said section as amended shall read :

" SECT. 4. Whoever goes about in carriages or makes a business of selling milk, skim-milk or cream, in any such city or town, or offering for sale, or having in his possession with intent to sell, milk, skim-milk or cream, unless a license has first been

obtained as provided in the preceding sections, shall be fined
not more than ten dollars for the first offense ; and for any subsequent offense he shall be fined fifty dollars, or be imprisoned not more than sixty days, or both; provided, however,
that any person selling only the product of his own cows shall
be exempt from paying any fee for such license."

Further amend said bill by adding the following section :

SECT. 2. All acts and parts of acts inconsistent with this
act are hereby repealed, and this act shall take effect upon its
passage.

The report was accepted, amendments adopted, and bill
ordered to a third reading to-morrow morning at 11 o'clock.

Senator Tolles, for the Committee on the Judiciary, to whom
was referred a bill entitled "An act in amendment of Public
Statutes, chapter 81, section 2, relating to telegraph, telephone,
and electric light companies," reported the same with the following amendment and recommended its passage :

Amend section 2 by adding the following :   " Provided, that
the provisions of this act shall not apply to any city in which
special laws relating to the subject matter of this bill are now
in force," so that said section as amended shall read :

SECT. 2. All acts and parts of acts inconsistent with this
act are hereby repealed, and this act shall take effect upon its
passage, provided, that the provisions of this act shall not apply
to any city in which special laws relating to the subject matter
of this bill are now in force.

The report was accepted, amendment adopted, and on motion of Senator Bickford, the rules were so far suspended that
the bill was read a third time, passed and sent to the House
of Representatives for concurrence in Senate amendment.

Senator Tolles, for the Committee on the Judiciary, to whom
was referred a bill entitled "An act relating to persons employed under and by virtue of an act of congress, relating to
the surveys of the geological survey of the United States,"
reported the same with the following resolution :

Resolved, That it is inexpedient to legislate.

The report was accepted and resolution adopted.

On motion of Senator Whitney, the Senate adjourned.

THURSDAY, March 19, 1903.

The Senate met according to adjournment.

The reading of the journal having been commenced, on motion of Senator Bickford, the rules were so far suspended that its further reading was dispensed with.

The following entitled House bills were read a third time and passed:

An act to incorporate the History Commission of Concord.

An act to amend section 1 of chapter 46, Session Laws of 1895, relating to annual enumeration of school children.

An act annexing certain islands in Lake Winnipesaukee to the town of Tuftonborough.

The following entitled House bill was read a third time, passed, and sent to the House of Representatives for concurrence in Senate amendments:

An act in amendment of chapter 107 of the Session Laws of 1901, relating to the inspection of milk.

On motion of Senator Bickford, "Joint resolution in favor of Horace S. Cummings," was taken from the table.

The question being stated,

Shall the joint resolution be read a third time?

The affirmative prevailed on a *viva voce* vote and the joint resolution was ordered to a third reading this afternoon at 3 o'clock.

Senator Ripley, for the Committee on Finance, to whom was referred "Joint resolution in favor of the New Hampshire School for Feeble-Minded Children," reported the same without amendment and recommended its passage.

Senator Lewando, for the Committee on Military Affairs, to whom was referred a bill entitled "An act in amendment of section 13, chapter 59, Laws of 1895, relating to the bond of the adjutant-general," reported the same without amendment and recommended its passage.

Senator Marvin, for the Committee on Roads, Bridges, and Canals, to whom was referred "Joint resolution in favor of placing and maintaining buoys and lights in Lake Winnipesaukee and adjacent waters," reported the same without amendment and recommended its passage.

13

Senator Thompson, for the Committee on Public Improvements, to whom was referred " Joint resolution in favor of Green's basin in Lake Winnipesaukee," reported the same without amendment and recommended its passage.

Senator Tilton, for the Committee on Claims, to whom was referred " Joint resolution in favor of the widow of Benjamin F. March of Mason," reported the same without amendment and recommended its passage.

The same Senator, for the same Committee, to whom was referred "Joint resolution in favor of William J. Patch," reported the same without amendment and recommended its passage.

Senator Burnell, for the Committee on Fisheries and Game, to whom was referred the following entitled bills :

" An act in amendment of section 59, chapter 79 of the Session Laws of 1901, relating to the taking of black bass,"

" An act to require non-residents to secure a license before hunting deer within the state of New Hampshire, and providing penalties for the violation of its provisions," reported the same without amendment and recommended their passage.

Senator Hoyt, for the Committee on State Prison and Industrial School, to whom was referred "Joint resolution appropriating nine thousand dollars for additions and repairs to the Industrial School," reported the same without amendment and recommended its passage.

The same Senator, for the same Committee, to whom was referred a bill entitled "An act in amendment of section 17 of chapter 285 of the Public Statutes, relating to the state prison," reported the same without amendment and recommended its passgge.

Senator Tolles, for the Committee on the Judiciary, to whom was referred the following entitled bills :

" An act to incorporate the Sons of Veterans' Memorial Hall Association,"

" An act relating to the salary of the judge of probate for the county of Carroll,"

" An act fixing office hours in state offices," reported the same without amendment and recommended their passage.

Senator Richmond, for the Committee on Incorporations, to whom was referred the following entitled bills :

"An act to incorporate the Maynesboro Fire Insurance Co.,"

" An act to incorporate the Dover Loan and Trust Co.,"

" An act to incorporate the Bellman Club of Manchester, N. H.,"

" An act to incorporate the Warren Water and Light Co.,"

"An act to amend the charter of the Bennington Water Works Co.,"

" An act to incorporate the Prudential Fire Insurance Co.," reported the same without amendment and recommended their passage.

Senator Keyes, for the Committee on Railroads, to whom was referred the following entitled bills :

" An act to incorporate the Uncanoonuc Incline Railway and Development Co.,"

"An act to incorporate the Swift River Railroad Co.,"

" An act to incorporate the Epping, Brentwood & Kingston Street Railway Co.,"

"An act in amendment of sections 7 and 10 chapter 27, Laws of 1895, relating to street railways,"

"An act to incorporate the Meredith and Ossipee Valley Railroad Co.,"

"An act in amendment of section 13, chapter 27 of the Pamphlet Laws of 1895, relating to street railways,"

" An act to incorporate the Derry and Salem Street Railway Co.,"

" An act to incorporate the New Ipswich, Greenville and Wilton Electric Railway Co.,"

"An act to incorporate the Milton Mills and Union Electric Railway Co.,"

" An act to authorize the Dover and Eliot Street Railway, and the Eliot Bridge Co. to transfer their properties and franchises to the Berwick, Eliot & York Street Railway," reported the same without amendment and recommended their passage.

The reports were accepted and the bills and joint resolutions were severally ordered to a third reading this afternoon at 3 o'clock.

Senator Marvin, for the Committee on Roads, Bridges, and Canals, to whom was referred " An act to provide in common with the state of Vermont for the acquisition, building, and maintenance of free bridges across the Connecticut river," reported the same with the following amendment and recommended its passage :

Insert after the word "devolve" in section 7, line 6, the word "equally," so that said section shall read as follows :

SECT. 7. Towns in this state into which bridges extend shall build all necessary roads to connect with said bridges, and maintain the same free of cost to the state. After the freeing of any bridge or the purchase by the state of a bridge from a town, the maintenance of the same shall devolve equally upon the several towns in this state and in the state of Vermont in which such bridges are located, subject to the supervision of the respective engineers or commissioners of New Hampshire and Vermont.

The report was accepted, amendment adopted, and the bill ordered to a third reading this afternoon at 3 o'clock.

Senator Marvin, for the Committee on Roads, Bridges, and Canals, to whom was referred " Joint resolution providing for the repairs and construction of certain state highways, certain highways in unincorporated places, and certain roads in places where such roads cannot be maintained by any local municipality," reported the same with the following amendment and recommended its passage :

That the sum of one hundred dollars ($100) be appropriated for repairing the Crotchet Mountain road, so called, in the town of Francestown, one half to be expended in 1903, and one half in 1904.

The report was accepted, amendment adopted, and the joint resolution ordered to a third reading this afternoon at 3 o'clock.

Senator Tolles, for the Committee on the Judiciary, to whom was referred a bill entitled " An act to amend chapter 243 of the Laws of 1901, creating the Grafton Improvement Manufacturing and Power Co.," reported the same with the following amendment and recommended its passage :

Amend section 5 by inserting after the word "river" and before the word "in" in the last line of said section, the words "in as free and convenient a manner as is afforded by the river."

The report was accepted, amendment adopted, and the bill ordered to a third reading this afternoon at 3 o'clock.

Senator Tolles, for the Committee on the Judiciary, to whom was referred a bill entitled " An act to amend the charter of the New England and Louisiana Land Co.," reported the same with the following resolution :

Resolved, That it is inexpedient to legislate.

The report was accepted and resolution adopted.

Senator Tolles, for the Committee on the Judiciary, reported the following entitled bills, which were severally read a first and second time and laid on the table to be printed :

"An act for the relief of the town of New Castle."

"An act in amendment of section 2 of chapter 5 of the Public Statutes, relating to the publication and distribution of statutes, journals, and reports."

"An act in amendment of section 2 of chapter 32 of the Laws of 1895, entitled 'An act in relation to printing the reports of certain state officers.' "

On motion of Senator Cooper, the rules were so far suspended that all bills and joint resolutions in order for a third reading this afternoon at 3 o'clock were made in order for a third reading at the present time.

On motion of Senator Tolles, the rules were further suspended and the following entitled House bills were severally read a third time by their titles and passed :

An act to incorporate the Prudential Fire Insurance Company.

An act to incorporate the Bellman Club of Manchester, N. H.

An act to incorporate the Maynesboro Fire Insurance Company.

An act fixing office hours in state offices.

An act to incorporate the Epping, Brentwood and Kingston Street Railway.

An act to incorporate the Derry and Salem Street Railway Company.

An act to incorporate the Sons of Veterans' Memorial Hall Association.

An act to incorporate the Uncanoonuc Incline Railway and Development Company.

An act to incorporate the Dover Loan and Trust Company.

An act to incorporate the Warren Water and Light Company.

An act to incorporate the Chester, Fremont & Brentwood Street Railway Company.

An act to incorporate the Milton Mills and Union Electric Railway Company.

An act to amend the charter of the Bennington Water-Works. Company.

An act to incorporate the New Ipswich, Greenville and Wilton Electric Railway Company.

An act in amendment of section 17 of chapter 285 of the Public Statutes, relating to the state prison.

An act in amendment of section 13, chapter 27 of the Pamphlet Laws of 1895, relating to street railways.

An act to incorporate the Meredith and Ossipee Valley Railroad Company.

An act in amendment of sections 7 and 10, chapter 27, Laws of 1895, relating to street railways.

An act in amendment of section 59, chapter 79 of the Session Laws of 1901, relating to the taking of black bass.

An act to authorize the Dover & Eliot Street Railway and the Eliot Bridge Company to transfer their properties and franchises to the Berwick, Eliot & York Street Railway.

An act to incorporate the Swift River Railroad Company.

An act relating to the salary of the judge of probate for the county of Carroll.

An act in amendment of section 13, chapter 59, Laws of 1895, relating to the bond of the adjutant-general.

The following entitled House bill was read a third time by its title:

"An act to require non-residents to secure a license before hunting deer within the state of New Hampshire and providing penalties for violation of its provisions."

The question being stated,

Shall the bill pass?

(Discussion ensued.)

The affirmative prevailed on a *viva voce* vote.

The following entitled House bills were severally read a third time by their title, passed, and sent to the House of Representatives for concurrence in Senate amendments:

An act to provide, in common with the state of Vermont, for the acquisition, building, and maintenance of free bridges across the Connecticut river.

An act to amend chapter 243 of the Laws of 1901, creating the Grafton Improvement Manufacturing and Power Company.

The following joint resolution was read a third time:

Joint resolution in favor of Horace S. Cummings.

The question being stated,

Shall the joint resolution pass?

(Discussion ensued.)

The affirmative prevailed on a *viva voce* vote.

Senator Page demanded the yeas and nays.

The clerk proceeded to call the roll.

The following named Senators voted in the affirmative:

Senators Allen, Whitney, Lewando, Burnell, Tilton, Cooper, Marvin, Felt, Stillings, Fellows, Neal, Lightbody, Bickford, Foley, Tolles, Hoyt of District No. 21, Thompson, Richmond.

The following named Senator voted in the negative:

Senator Page.

Nineteen Senators having voted in the affirmative, and one Senator having voted in the negative, the affirmative prevailed and the joint resolution passed.

The following joint resolutions were severally read a third time and passed:

Joint resolution in favor of Green's basin in Lake Winnipesaukee.

Joint resolution in favor of the New Hampshire School for Feeble-Minded Children.

Joint resolution in favor of the widow of Benjamin F. March of Mason.

Joint resolution appropriating nine thousand dollars for additions and repairs to the Industrial School.

Joint resolution in favor of placing and maintaining buoys and lights in Lake Winnipesaukee and adjacent waters.

Joint resolution in favor of William J. Patch.

On motion of Senator Tolles, the Senate adjourned.

AFTERNOON.

The Senate met according to adjournment.

Joint resolution providing for the repairs and construction of certain state highways, certain highways in unincorporated places, and certain roads in places where such roads cannot be maintained by any local municipality, was read a third time, passed and sent to the House of Representatives for concurrence in Senate amendments.

Senator Richmond, for the Committee on Incorporations, to whom was referred the following entitled bills:

"An act to change the name of the Manchester Heating and Lighting company of Manchester, N. H.,"

"An act in amendment of 'An act to incorporate the Society of Social Friends,' approved June 29, 1826, and 'An act to incorporate the United Fraternity,' approved July 6, 1827, and 'An act to incorporate the Philotechnic Society of the Chandler Scientific Department of Dartmouth College,' approved July 13, 1854, and to authorize the calling of meetings of said corporations respectively," reported the same without amendment and recommended their passage.

The reports were accepted and the bills severally ordered to a third reading to-morrow morning at 11 o'clock.

The following report from the Committee on Engrossed Bills was read and accepted:

The Committee on Engrossed Bills have examined, and found correctly engrossed, the following entitled bills and joint resolutions:

Joint resolution in favor of the Granite State Dairyman's Association.

Joint resolution in favor of maintaining buoys and placing lights on Squam lake.

An act authorizing the state treasurer to transfer certain sums of money to the literary fund for schools.

An act to amend section 10, chapter 79 of the Session Laws of 1901, relative to duties of the fish and game commissioners.

An act for the promotion of horticulture.

An act in amendment of section 1 of chapter 3 of the Laws of 1893, fixing the salary of the clerk of the board of bank commissioners.

An act in amendment of section 4 of chapter 162 of the Public Statutes, fixing the salaries of the members of the board of bank commissioners.

Joint resolution in favor of New Hampshire Soldiers' Home.

Joint resolution for lighting the lighthouse on Loon island in Sunapee lake, repairing the cable connected therewith, improving the light service, placing and maintaining buoys on said lake, and removing obstructions to navigation in said lake.

A. W. BURNELL,
For the Committee.

The following message was received from the House of Representatives by its clerk:

HOUSE MESSAGE.

Mr. President:

The House of Representatives concurs with the Honorable Senate in the passage of the following entitled bills:

An act enabling the city of Concord to appropriate money for observing Memorial Day.

The House of Representatives has voted to concur with the Honorable Senate in its amendments to the following entitled bill:

An act in amendment of Public Statutes, chapter 81, section 2, relating to telegraph, telephone and electric light companies.

The House of Representatives has passed bills with the following titles, in the passage of which it asks the concurrence of the Honorable Senate:

An act to incorporate the Caledonia Power Company.

An act to legalize and confirm the warrant for, and the votes and proceedings at, the annual election and meeting in Ward three in the city of Berlin, held the tenth day of March, 1903.

An act in amendment of chapter 98 of the Laws of 1901, relating to the duties of tree wardens.

An act in amendment of section 22, chapter 27, Laws of 1895, entitled "An act in relation to the incorporation, organization, and regulation of street railway companies and authorizing the use of electricity as motive power by existing steam railroads."

An act to incorporate the Peabody River Improvement Company.

The following entitled bills sent up from the House of Representatives were severally read a first and second time and referred:

To the Committee on Forestry:

An act in amendment of chapter 98 of the Laws of 1901, relating to the duties of tree wardens.

To the Committee on the Judiciary:

An act to legalize and confirm the warrant for, and the votes and proceedings at, the annual election and meeting in Ward three in the city of Berlin, held the tenth day of March, 1903.

To the Committee on Railroads:

An act in amendment of section 22, chapter 27, Laws of 1895, entitled "An act in relation to the incorporation, organization and regulation of street railway companies and authorizing the use of electricity as motive power by existing steam railroads."

To the Committee on Incorporations:

An act to incorporate the Caledonia Power Company.

An act to incorporate the Peabody River Improvement Company.

Senator Bickford, for the Committee on the Judiciary, reported the following entitled bill, which was read a first and second time:

An act to incorporate the Evangelical Congregational Church of Plaistow, N. H., and the North Parish of Haverhill, Mass.

On motion of Senator Tolles, the rules were so far suspended that the bill was read a third time by its title, passed, and sent to the House of Representatives for concurrence.

On motion of Senator Tolles, the Senate voted to take a recess until 4 o'clock.

(Recess.)

The Senate reassembled.

On motion of Senator Felt, the following resolution was adopted:

Resolved, That when the Senate adjourns, it be to meet to-morrow morning at 9.30 o'clock.

Senator Tilton moved to reconsider the vote whereby the following entitled House bill passed:

An act to amend section 16 of chapter 19 of the Session Laws of 1901, relating to the taking of deer.

The question being stated,

Shall the vote be reconsidered?

The affirmative prevailed on a *viva voce* vote.

On motion of the same Senator, the bill was recommitted to the Committee on Fisheries and Game.

On motion of Senator Bickford, the Senate adjourned.

FRIDAY, MARCH 20, 1903

The Senate met according to adjournment.

The reading of the journal having been commenced, on motion of Senator Bickford, the rules were so far suspended that its further reading was dispensed with.

The following entitled House bills were severally read a third time and passed:

An act to change the name of the Manchester Heating and Lighting Company of Manchester, N. H.

An act in amendment of "An act to incorporate the Society of Social Friends," approved June 29, 1826, "An act to incorporate the United Fraternity," approved July 6, 1827, and "An act to incorporate the Philotechnic Society of the Chandler

Scientific Department of Dartmouth College," approved July 13, 1854, and to authorize the calling of meetings of said corporations respectively.

The following entitled Senate bill having been printed was taken from the table:

An act for the relief of the town of New Castle.

On motion of Senator Page, the rules were so far suspended that the bill was read a third time by its title, passed, and sent to the House of Representatives for concurrence.

The following entitled Senate bills having been printed were taken from the table and ordered to a third reading Tuesday morning next at 11 o'clock:

An act in amendment of section 2 of chapter 32 of the Laws of 1895, entitled "An act in relation to printing the reports of certain state offices."

An act in amendment of section 2 of chapter 5 of the Public Statutes, relating to the publication and distribution of statutes, journals, and reports.

On motion of Senator Keyes, the rules were so far suspended that all bills in order for a third reading Tuesday morning next at 11 o'clock were made in order at the present time, and the following entitled Senate bills were severally read a third time, passed, and sent to the House of Representatives for concurrence:

An act in amendment of section 2 of chapter 32 of the Laws of 1895, entitled "An act in relation to the printing of the reports of certain state offices."

An act in amendment of section 2 of chapter 5 of the Public Statutes, relating to the publication and distribution of statutes, journals, and reports.

The following report from the Committee on Engrossed Bills was read and accepted:

The Committee on Engrossed Bills have examined, and found correctly engrossed, the following entitled bills and joint resolution:

Joint resolution in favor of Horace S. Cummings.

An act enabling the city of Concord to appropriate money for observing Memorial Day.

An act in amendment of Public Statutes, chapter 81, section 2, relating to telegraph, telephone, and electric light companies.

A. W. BURNELL,
For the Committee.

On motion of Senator Keyes, the Senate voted to take a recess until 11 o'clock.

(Recess.)

The Senate reassembled.

On motion of Senator Bickford, the following resolution was adopted:

Resolved, That when the Senate adjourns it be to meet Monday evening next at eight o'clock.

On motion of Senator Keyes, the Senate adjourned.

MONDAY, MARCH 23, 1903.

The Senate met according to adjournment.

Senator Keyes, having assumed the chair, read the following communication:

NASHUA, N. H., March 23, 1903.

Senator Keyes:

Please preside for me at the morning session to-day of the New Hampshire Senate, and oblige,

CHARLES W. HOITT,
President.

The journal was read and approved.

On motion of Senator Fuller, the Senate adjourned.

TUESDAY, MARCH 24, 1903.

The Senate met according to adjournment.

The journal was read and approved.

Senator Burnell, for the Committee on Fisheries and Game,

to whom was referred a bill entitled " An act in amendment of section 79 of chapter 79 of the Laws of 1901, in relation to lobster traps," reported the same with the following amendment and recommended its passage :

Amend section 1 of the bill by striking out in lines 26, 27, 28, and 29 of said section the words " but no indictment shall be maintained unless the name of the owner of the trap or traps shall be carved, painted, or printed in legible letters not less than three fourths of an inch in length on all buoys maintained with such traps."

The report was accepted, amendment adopted, and the bill ordered to a third reading this afternoon at 3 o'clock.

Senator Tilton, for the Committee on Fisheries and Game, to whom was referred a bill entitled " An act to amend section 16 of chapter 79 of the Session Laws of 1901, relating to the taking of deer," reported the same in new draft and recommended its passage.

The report was accepted and the bill in its new draft was read a first and second time.

On motion of Senator Tilton, the rules were so far suspended that the printing was dispensed with, and on motion of the same Senator, the rules were so far suspended that the bill was read a third time by its title, passed, and sent to the House of Representatives for concurrence in Senate new draft.

Senator Burnell, for the Committee on Fisheries and Game, to whom was referred a bill entitled An act to amend section 52 of chapter 79 of the Laws of 1901, entitled " An act to revise the fish and game laws of the state," reported the same without amendment and recommended its passage.

The report was accepted and the bill ordered to a third reading this afternoon at 3 o'clock.

Senator Tolles, for the Committee on the Judiciary, to whom was referred a bill entitled " An act to legalize and confirm the warrant for and the votes and proceedings at the annual election and meeting in Ward three in the city of Berlin, held the tenth day of March, 1903," reported the same without amendment and recommended its passage.

On motion of Senator Bickford, the rules were so far suspended that the bill was read a third time by its title and passed.

The following message was received from the House of Representatives by its clerk:

HOUSE MESSAGE.

Mr. President:

The House of Representatives concurs with the Honorable Senate in the passage of the following entitled bill :

An act in amendment of section 56, chapter 79 of the Laws of 1901, relating to fish and game.

The House of Representatives has voted to concur with the Honorable Senate in its amendments to the following entitled bills and joint resolution :

An act to amend chapter 243 of the Laws of 1901, creating the Grafton Improvement Manufacturing and Power Co.

An act in amendment of chapter 107 of the Session Laws of 1901, relating to the inspection of milk.

Joint resolution providing for the repairs and construction of certain state highways, certain highways in unincorporated places, and certain roads in places where such roads cannot be maintained by any local municipality.

The House of Representatives has passed the following entitled bills and joint resolutions, in the passage of which it asks the concurrence of the Honorable Senate :

Joint resolution to appropriate the sum of three hundred dollars for the purpose of turning Silver stream into Success pond in the township of Success, and to screen the outlet to said pond.

Joint resolution in favor of John M. Stanyan for soldier's pay and bounty.

Joint resolution to provide for the treatment of indigent consumptives.

An act in relation to the salary of the judge of probate for the county of Grafton.

An act to amend section 14 and section 15, chapter 286 of the Public Statutes, relating to the salaries of the judge and register of probate for Belknap county.

An act relating to the salary of the judge of probate of the county of Sullivan.

An act relating to the protection and preservation of ornamental and shade trees in the highways.

An act in amendment of section 1, chapter 31 of the Laws of 1897, entitled "An act in amendment of section 6 of chapter 83 of the Public Statutes, in relation to the settlement of paupers."

An act in amendment of section 1, chapter 83 of the Public Statutes, entitled "Settlement of paupers."

An act authorizing the Concord & Montreal Railroad, lessor, to vote on all stock owned by it in other corporations.

An act to incorporate the Mt. Belknap Electric Railway Company.

An act to incorporate the Candia and Deerfield Street Railway Company.

An act to incorporate the Connecticut River Power Company of New Hampshire.

An act in amendment of section 7, chapter 3, of the Laws of 1897, entitled "An act to regulate the licensing and registration of physicians and surgeons."

An act in amendment of the charter of the Exeter Gas, Electric Light and Power Company.

An act to incorporate the Manchester and Haverhill Street Railway Company.

An act to incorporate the Concord, Dover & Rochester Street Railway.

An act to incorporate the Dunbarton and Goffstown Street Railway Company.

An act to regulate the traffic in intoxicating liquor.

The following entitled bills and joint resolutions sent up from the House of Representatives were severally read a first and second time and referred:

To the Committee on the Judiciary:

An act in relation to the salary of the judge of probate for the county of Grafton.

An act to amend section 14 and section 15, chapter 286 of

the Public Statutes, relating to the salaries of the judge and register of probate for Belknap county.

An act relating to the salary of the judge of probate for the county of Sullivan.

To the Committee on Revision of the Laws:

An act in amendment of section 1, chapter 83 of the Public Statutes, entitled "Settlement of paupers."

An act in amendment of section 1, chapter 31 of the Laws of 1897, entitled "An act in amendment of section 6 of chapter 83 of the Public Statutes, in relation to the settlement of paupers."

To the Committee on Public Health:

An act in amendment of section 7, chapter 63 of the Laws of 1897, entitled "An act to regulate the licensing and registration of physicians and surgeons."

Joint resolution to provide for the treatment of indigent consumptives.

To the Committee on Public Improvements:

An act relating to the protection and preservation of ornamental and shade trees in the highways.

To the Committee on Incorporations:

An act in amendment of the charter of the Exeter Gas, Electric Light and Power Company.

To the Committee on Claims:

Joint resolution in favor of John M. Stanyan for soldier's pay and bounty.

To the Committee on Finance:

Joint resolution to appropriate the sum of three hundred dollars for the purpose of turning Silver stream into Success pond in the township of Success, and to screen the outlet of said pond.

On motion of Senator Keyes, the rules were so far suspended that the following entitled bills sent up from the House of Representatives were severally read a first and second time by their titles and referred:

To the Committee on Railroads:

An act authorizing the Concord & Montreal Railroad, lessor, to vote on all stocks owned by it in other corporations.

14

An act to incorporate the Manchester and Haverhill Street Railway Company.

An act to incorporate the Dunbarton and Goffstown Street Railway Company.

An act to incorporate the Candia and Deerfield Street Railway Company.

An act to incorporate the Concord, Dover and Rochester Street Railway.

An act to incorporate the Mt. Belknap Electric Railway Company.

To the Committee on Incorporations :

An act to incorporate the Connecticut River Power Company of New Hampshire.

On motion of Senator Thompson, the following entitled bill sent up from the House of Representatives was read a first and second time by its title and referred :

To the Committee of the Whole :

An act to regulate the traffic in intoxicating liquor.

On motion of Senator Bickford, the foregoing entitled bill was made a special order for immediate consideration upon the assembling of the Senate this afternoon as in the committee of the whole.

On motion of Senator Keyes, the rules were so far suspended that all bills in order for a third reading this afternoon at 3 o'clock were made in order for a third reading at the present time.

The following entitled House bill was read a third time and passed :

An act to amend section 52 of chapter 79 of the Laws of 1901, entitled " An act to revise the fish and game laws of the state."

The following entitled House bill was read a third time, passed, and sent to the House of Representatives for concurrence in Senate amendment :

An act in amendment of section 79 of chapter 79 of the Laws of 1901, in regard to lobster traps.

The following report from the Committee on Engrossed Bills was read and accepted :

The Committee on Engrossed Bills have examined and found correctly engrossed the following entitled bills and joint resolutions :

An act to amend section 1 of chapter 46, Session Laws of 1895, relating to annual enumeration of school children.

An act in amendment of section 59, chapter 79 of the Session Laws of 1901, relating to the taking of black bass.

An act in amendment of section 56, chapter 79 of the Laws of 1901, relating to fish and game.

An act to incorporate the History Commission of Concord.

Joint resolution in favor of William J. Patch.

An act to incorporate the Prudential Fire Insurance Company.

An act to change the name of the Manchester Heating and Lighting Company of Manchester, N. H.

An act to incorporate the Sons of Veterans' Memorial Hall Association.

Joint resolution in favor of placing and maintaining buoys and lights in Lake Winnipesaukee and adjacent waters.

An act to incorporate The Maynesborough Fire Insurance Company.

An act to amend the charter of the Bennington Water-Works Company.

An act in amendment of chapter 107 of the Session Laws of 1901, relating to the inspection of milk.

An act to authorize the Dover and Elliot Street Railway and the Eliot Bridge Company to transfer their property and franchises to the Berwick, Eliot and York Street Railway.

An act to incorporate the Chester, Fremont and Brentwood Street Railway Company.

An act to require non-residents to secure a license before hunting deer within the state of New Hampshire, and providing penalties for violation of its provisions.

A. W. BURNELL,
For the Committee.

On motion of Senator Tolles, the following resolution was adopted :

Resolved, That when the Senate adjourns, it be to meet **at** 2.30 o'clock this afternoon.

On motion of Senator Whitney, the Senate adjourned.

. AFTERNOON.

On motion of Senator Bickford, the following entitled bill was recalled from the Committee of the Whole and laid on the table to be printed:

An act to regulate the traffic in intoxicating liquor.

The following message was received from the House of Representatives by its clerk:

HOUSE MESSAGE.

Mr. President:

The House of Representatives has voted to concur with the Honorable Senate in its amendments to the following entitled bill:

An act to provide, in common with the state of Vermont, for the acquisition, building, and maintenance of free bridges across the Connecticut river.

The House of Representatives concurs with the Honorable Senate in the passage of the following entitled bill:

An act to exempt certain property of the Manchester Young Men's Christian Association from taxation.

The House of Representatives has passed bills with the following titles, in the passage of which it asks the concurrence of the Honorable Senate:

An act enabling the city of Manchester to build and operate an electric lighting plant for the purpose of lighting its streets and public buildings.

An act authorizing the city of Nashua to exempt the Highland Spring Sanatorium Company from taxation.

An act to revive the charter of the Colebrook Water Company, approved February 23, 1897.

An act to amend chapter 40, Laws of 1893, relating to inspectors of buildings.

An act to sever certain residences from the school district of the town of Wilmot and to annex the same to the school district of the town of New London.

The House of Representatives concurs with the Honorable Senate in the passage of the following entitled bill, with amendments, in the passage of which amendments the House asks the concurrence of the Honorable Senate:

An act relating to the time required for filing notice of intention of marriage, and the consent of parents to the marriage of minors.

Amend section 1 by inserting after the word "shall" in the second line of said section the words "in case either of the parties is a non-resident of this state."

Further amend said section by striking out all after the word "sections" in the fourth line of said section, so that said section shall read as follows:

SECTION 1. The notice of intention of marriage required by sections 5 and 6 of chapter 174 of the Public Statutes, shall, in case either of the parties is a non-resident of this state, be filed five days before the clerk shall issue a certificate setting forth the facts as required by said sections.

Amend the title by striking out the words "and the consent of parents to the marriage of minors," so that the title will read, "An act relating to the time required for filing notice of intention of marriage."

The Senate concurred with the House of Representatives in the foregoing amendments.

The following entitled bills sent up from the House of Representatives were severally read a first and second time and referred:

To the Committee on the Judiciary:

An act to revive the charter of the Colebrook Water Company, approved February 23, 1897.

An act to amend chapter 40, Laws of 1893, relating to inspection of buildings.

To the Committee on Public Improvements:

An act enabling the city of Manchester to build and operate an electric lighting plant for the purpose of lighting its streets and public buildings.

To the Committee on Towns and Parishes:

An act to sever certain residences from the school district of the town of Wilmot and to annex the same to the school district of the town of New London.

To the Committee on Incorporations:

An act authorizing the city of Nashua to exempt the Highland Spring Sanatorium Company from taxation.

Senator Tilton, for the Committee on Claims, to whom was referred Joint resolution in favor of Ella F. Densmore of Charlestown, Mary F. Lombard of Acworth, Frank G. Smith of Waltham, Massachusetts, Eugene P. Smith of Newport, and George E. Shattuck of Hinsdale, reported the same without amendments and recommended its passage.

The report was accepted and on motion of Senator Bickford, the joint resolution was laid on the table.

On motion of Senator Tolles, the following resolution was adopted:

Resolved, That when the Senate adjourns this afternoon it be to meet to-morrow morning at 10 o'clock.

Senator Tolles, for the Committee on the Judiciary, to whom was referred a bill entitled "An act in amendment of so much of chapter 264 of the Laws of the State of New Hampshire, passed at the January session, 1893, as relates to the establishing of a board of street and park commissioners for the city of Manchester," reported the same with the following resolution:

Resolved, That it is inexpedient to legislate.

The report was accepted and the resolution adopted.

Senator Tolles, for the Committee on the Judiciary, to whom was referred the following entitled bills:

"An act to amend section 14 and section 15, chapter 286 of the Public Statutes, relating to the salary of the judge and register of probate for Belknap county,"

"An act in relation to the salary of the judge of probate for the county of Grafton,"

"An act relating to the salary of the judge of probate of the county of Sullivan,"

"An act in amendment of section 1, chapter 67, Laws of 1899, relating to expenses of judges of the supreme court,"

"An act in amendment of the charter of the city of Manchester, establishing a board of assessors in place of the assessors provided under the chapter and laws of the state," reported the same without amendment and recommended their passage.

The reports were accepted and the bills severally ordered to a third reading to-morrow morning at 10 o'clock.

Senator Fuller, for the Committee on Towns and Parishes, to whom was referred a bill entitled "An act to authorize the town of Gilmanton to exempt certain property from taxation," reported the same with the following amendment and recommended its passage:

Amend by inserting after the word "from" in section 1, second line, the word "local."

The report was accepted.

The question being stated,

Shall the amendment be adopted?

(Discussion ensued.)

The affirmative prevailed on *viva voce* vote.

The bill was ordered to a third reading to-morrow morning at 10 o'clock.

Senator Tolles, for the Committee on the Judiciary, reported the following entitled bill:

"An act establishing the office of medical referee and amending chapter 262 of the Public Statutes, relating to coroner's inquests," and recommended its passage.

The bill reported by the committee was read a first and second time and laid on the table to be printed.

Senator Tolles, for the Committee on the Judiciary, reported the following entitled bill:

An act in amendment of An act entitled "An act for the enlargement and extension of water-works of the city of Portsmouth," approved March 10th, 1899, and recommended its passage.

On motion of Senator Page, the rules were so far suspended that the bill reported from the committee was read a first and second time by its title.

On motion of the same Senator, the rules were further suspended and the bill was read a third time by its title, passed, and sent to the House of Representatives for concurrence.

The following report from the Committee on Engrossed Bills was read and accepted:

The Committee on Engrossed Bills have examined and found correctly engrossed the following entitled bills and joint resolutions:

An act in amendment of section 17 of chapter 285 of the Public Statutes, relating to the state prison.

An act in amendment of section 13, chapter 27 of the Pamphlet Laws of 1895, relating to street railways.

An act to incorporate the Warren Water and Light Company.

An act to incorporate the Epping, Brentwood and Kingston Street Railway Company.

An act to incorporate the Derry and Salem Street Railway Company.

An act to incorporate the Milton Mills and Union Electric Railway Company.

An act to amend chapter 243 of the Laws of 1901, creating the Grafton Improvement Manufacturing and Power Company.

An act annexing certain islands in Lake Winnipesaukee to the town of Tuftonborough.

An act relating to the salary of the judge of probate of the county of Carroll.

Joint resolution in favor of Green's basin in Lake Winnipesaukee.

Joint resolution in favor of the widow of Benjamin F. March of Mason.

Joint resolution in favor of the New Hampshire School for Feeble-Minded Children.

An act to incorporate the Dover Loan and Trust Company.

An act to incorporate the Meredith and Ossipee Valley Railroad Company.

An act to incorporate the New Ipswich, Greenville and Wilton Electric Railway Company.

An act to incorporate the Uncanoonuc Incline Railway and Development Company.

An act to incorporate the Swift River Railroad Company.

An act to incorporate the Bellman Club of Manchester, N. H.

An act in amendment of section 13, chapter 59, Laws of 1895, relating to the bond of the adjutant-general.

Joint resolution appropriating nine thousand dollars for additions and repairs to the industrial school.

An act in amendment of sections 7 and 10, chapter 27, Laws of 1895, relating to street railways.

Joint resolution providing for the repairs and construction of certain state highways, certain highways in unincorporated places, and certain roads in places where such roads cannot be maintained by any local municipality.

An act in amendment of " An act to incorporate the Society of Social Friends," approved June 29, 1826, "An act to incorporate the United Fraternity," approved July 6, 1827, and " An act to incorporate the Philotechnic Society of the Chandler Scientific Department of Dartmouth College," approved July 13, 1854, and to authorize the calling of meetings of said corporations respectively.

An act fixing office hours in state offices.

An act to exempt certain property of the Manchester Young Men's Christian Association from taxation.

A. W. BURNELL,
For the Committee.

On motion of Senator Neal, the Senate adjourned.

WEDNESDAY, MARCH 25, 1903.

The Senate met according to adjournment.

The reading of the journal having been commenced, on motion of Senator Fuller, the rules were so far suspended that its further reading was dispensed with.

The following entitled House bills were severally read a third time and passed :

An act relating to the salary of the judge of probate of the county of Sullivan.

An act to amend section 14 and section 15, chapter 286 of the Public Statutes, relating to the salaries of the judge and register of probate for Belknap county.

An act in amendment of section 1, chapter 57, Laws of 1899, relating to expenses of judges of the supreme court.

An act in relation to the salary of the judge of probate for the county of Grafton.

An act in amendment of the charter of the city of Manchester, establishing a board of assessors in place of the assessors provided under the chapter and laws of the state.

On motion of Senator Bickford, the title to the foregoing bill was amended by striking out the word "chapter" after the word "the" and inserting in place thereof the word "charter."

The bill was then sent to the House of Representatives for concurrence in Senate amendment.

The following entitled House bill was read a third time, passed, and sent to the House of Representatives for concurrence in Senate amendment :

An act to authorize the town of Gilmanton to exempt certain property from taxation.

The following message was received from the House of Representatives by its clerk :

HOUSE MESSAGE.

Mr. President :

The House of Representatives has passed the following entitled bills and joint resolution, in the passage of which it asks the concurrence of the Honorable Senate:

Joint resolution for an appropriation for the benefit of the New Hampshire College of Agriculture and the Mechanic Arts.

An act to establish a new apportionment for the assessment of public taxes.

An act to amend chapter 60, section 3, of the Statute Laws of 1891, relating to dog licenses.

An act to enlarge the powers of towns and cities.

An act in amendment of section 20 of chapter 27 of the Public Statutes, entitled "County Commissioners."

An act to incorporate the New Hampshire Beneficiary Union.

An act to establish water-works in the town of Greenville.

An act to amend chapter 96 of the Session Laws of 1901, relating to high schools.

An act in relation to the settlement of paupers.

An act providing for a state system of highway construction and improvement and for the appointment of highway engineers.

An act to amend chapters 2 and 112 of the Public Statutes, and to provide for the better enforcement of the liquor laws.

An act in amendment of section 23 of chapter 79 of the Laws of 1901, in relation to fines.

An act in amendment of section 7 of chapter 59 of the Public Statutes, relating to the assessment and collection of taxes.

The following entitled bills and joint resolution sent up from the House of Representatives were severally read a first and second time and referred:

To the Committee on the Judiciary:

An act in amendment of section 20 of chapter 27 of the Public Statutes, entitled "County Commissioners."

An act to incorporate the New Hampshire Beneficiary Union.

An act in amendment of section 7 of chapter 59 of the Public Statutes and section 13 of chapter 60 of the Public Statutes, relating to the assessment and collection of taxes.

To the Committee on Agriculture:

Joint resolution for an appropriation for the benefit of the New Hampshire College of Agriculture and the Mechanic Arts.

An act to amend chapter 96 of the Session Laws of 1901, relating to high schools.

To the Committee on Towns and Parishes:

An act to enlarge the powers of towns and cities.

On motion of Senator Thompson, the rules were so far suspended that the following entitled bills sent up from the House of Representatives were severally read a first and second time by their titles and referred:

To the Committee on Incorporations:

An act to establish water-works in the town of Greenville.

To the Committee on Roads, Bridges, and Canals:

An act providing for a state system of highway construction and improvement and for the appointment of highway engineers.

On motion of Senator Tolles, the rules were so far suspended that the following entitled bill sent up from the House of Representatives was read a first and second time by its title and referred :

To the Committee on the Judiciary :

An act to amend chapters 2 and 112 of the Public Statutes, and to provide for the better enforcement of the liquor laws.

The following entitled bill sent up from the House of Representatives was read a first time :

An act in amendment of section 23 of chapter 79 of the Laws of 1901, in relation to fines.

The question being stated,

Shall the bill be read a second time?

On motion of Senator Page, the bill was laid on the table.

The following entitled bill sent up from the House of Representatives was read a first time :

An act in relation to the settlement of paupers.

The question being stated,

Shall the bill be read a second time?

The negative prevailed on a *viva voce* vote.

The following entitled bill sent up from the House of Representatives was read a first time :

An act to amend chapter 60, section 3 of the Statute Laws of 1891, relating to dog licenses.

The question being stated,

Shall the bill be read a second time?

On motion of Senator Page, the bill was indefinitely postponed.

On motion of Senator Lewando, the rules were so far suspended that the following entitled bill sent up from the House of Representatives was read a first and second time by its title :

An act to establish a new apportionment for the assessment of public taxes.

On motion of Senator Thompson, the rules were further suspended, and the bill was read a third time by its title and passed.

Senator Richmond, for the Committee on Incorporations, to whom was referred a bill entitled "An act to incorporate the First Congregational Church of Wolfeboro, New Hampshire," reported the same without amendment and recommended its passage.

The report was accepted, and on motion of Senator Bickford, the rules were so far suspended that the bill was read a third time by its title, passed, and sent to the House of Representatives for concurrence.

Senator Ripley, for the Committee on Finance, to whom was referred a bill entitled "An act to define the duties of the state treasurer with reference to public funds," reported the same with the following resolution:

Resolved, That it is inexpedient to legislate.

The report was accepted and resolution adopted.

Senator Richmond, for the Committee on Incorporations, to whom was referred a bill entitled "An act to incorporate the Connecticut River Power Company of New Hampshire," reported the same without amendment and recommended its passage.

Senator Marvin, for the Committee on Towns and Parishes, to whom was referred the following entitled bills:

"An act to sever certain residences from the school district of the town of Wilmot and to annex the same to the school district of the town of New London,"

"An act relating to the setting off by the legislature of territory of one town or city on to that of another town or city," reported the same without amendment and recommended their passage.

The reports were accepted and the bills severally ordered to a third reading this afternoon at 3 o'clock.

Senator Page offered the following resolution:

Resolved, By the Senate of the State of New Hampshire that application is hereby made to the Congress under the provision of Article Five of the constitution of the United States for the calling of a convention to propose an amendment to the constitution of the United States, making United States Senators elective in the several states by direct vote of the people; and, *resolved further*, that the clerk of the Senate is hereby directed to transmit copies of this application to the Senate of the United States, and copies to the members of the said Senate from this state, also to transmit copies hereof to the presiding officers of each of the legislatures now in session in the several states, requesting their coöperation.

The question being stated,

Shall the resolution be adopted?

(Discussion ensued.)

On motion of Senator Bickford, the resolution was laid on the table.

On motion of Senator Keyes, the following entitled House bill was taken from the table and referred to the Committee of the Whole:

An act to regulate the traffic in intoxicating liquor.

On motion of the same Senator, the Senate resolved itself into a Committee of the Whole for the purpose of considering the foregoing entitled House bill, and the President appointed Senator Felt as chairman of the committee.

IN COMMITTEE OF THE WHOLE.

(Senator Felt in the chair.)

SENATE.

(The President in the chair.)

Senator Felt, chairman of the Committee of the Whole, reported for the committee that it had made progress on the matter under consideration, and asked leave to sit again.

The report was accepted and leave to sit again was granted.

On motion of Senator Keyes, the following resolution was adopted:

Resolved, That when the Senate adjourns it be to meet this afternoon at 2.30 o'clock.

On motion of Senator Bickford, the Senate adjourned.

AFTERNOON.

On motion of Senator Thompson, the Senate resolved itself into a Committee of the Whole for the further consideration of the following entitled House bill:

"An act to regulate the traffic in intoxicating liquor," and the President appointed Senator Felt as chairman of this committee.

IN COMMITTEE OF THE WHOLE.

(Senator Felt in the chair.)

SENATE.

(The President in the chair.)

Senator Felt, chairman of the Committee of the Whole, reported that it had completed the work it had in hand, and asked leave to submit his report in writing later.

The verbal report was accepted and leave granted to submit a written report.

On motion of Senator Keyes, the Senate voted to take a recess until 7.30 o'clock.

(Recess.)

The Senate reassembled.

The following entitled House bills were severally read a third time and passed:

An act to sever certain residences from the school district of the town of Wilmot and to annex the same to the school district of the town of New London.

An act relating to the setting off by the legislature of territory of one town or city on to that of another town or city.

On motion of Senator Tolles, the rules were so far suspended that the following entitled House bill was read a third time by its title and passed:

An act to incorporate the Connecticut River Power Company of New Hampshire.

Senator Foley, for the Committee on Agriculture, to whom was referred Joint resolution for an appropriation for the benefit of the New Hampshire College of Agriculture and the Mechanic Arts, reported the same without amendment and recommended its passage.

Senator Richmond, for the Committee on Incorporations, to whom was referred the following entitled bills:

"An act in amendment of the charter of the Exeter Gas Light and Power Company,"

"An act authorizing the city of Nashua to exempt the Highland Springs Sanatorium Company from taxation," reported the same without amendments and recommended their passage.

Senator Keyes, for the Committee on Railroads, to whom was referred the following entitled bills:

"An act to incorporate the Mt. Belknap Electric Railway Company,"

"An act to incorporate the Candia and Deerfield Street Railway Company,"

"An act to incorporate the Concord, Dover and Rochester Street Railway Company,"

"An act authorizing the Concord & Montreal Railroad, lessor, to vote on all stock owned by it in other corporations,"

"An act to incorporate the Dunbarton and Goffstown Street Railway Company,"

"An act to incorporate the Manchester and Haverhill Street Railway Company,"

"An act in amendment of section 22, chapter 27, Laws of 1895, entitled 'An act in relation to the incorporation, organization, and regulation of street railway companies, and authorizing the use of electricity as motive power by existing steam railroads,'"

"An act to incorporate the Kearsarge Mountain Electric Railway Company," reported the same without amendments and recommended their passage.

The reports were accepted and the bills severally ordered to a third reading to-morrow morning at 11 o'clock.

The following message was received from the House of Representatives by its clerk:

HOUSE MESSAGE.

Mr. President:

The House of Representatives concurs with the Honorable Senate in the passage of the following entitled bills:

An act in amendment of section 14, chapter 79, Session Laws of 1901, relating to the powers of the fish and game commissioners.

An act in amendment of section 2 of chapter 5 of the Public

Statutes, relating to the publication and distribution of statutes, journals, and reports.

The House of Representatives has passed the following entitled bills and joint resolutions, in the passage of which it asks the concurrence of the Honorable Senate :

An act to amend chapter 184 of the Laws of 1897, entitled "An act to incorporate the Dalton Power Company," as amended by section 1, chapter 221 of the Laws of 1899.

An act to exempt certain property of the Keene Young Men's Christian Association from taxation.

An act to legalize a vote taken at the annual town meeting in Boscawen on the second Tuesday of March, A. D. 1903.

An act in amendment of section 19, chapter 57 of the Public Statutes, relating to the annual invoice of polls and taxable property.

An act in amendment of chapter 134 of the Public Statutes, relating to the practice of dentistry.

An act in relation to the administration of the state prison and to provide for necessary improvements and repairs.

An act for the better preservation of highways and accommodating public travel.

Joint resolution in favor of the widow of John W. Jewett of Claremont.

Joint resolution appropriating five hundred dollars for a monument to be erected at Hackensack, New Jersey, in memory of Gen. Enoch Poor.

Joint resolution appropriating money to be expended for the preservation of the muster rolls.

The following entitled bills and joint resolutions sent up from the House of Representatives were severally read a first and second time and referred :

To the Committee on Education :

An act to legalize a vote taken at the annual town meeting in Boscawen on the second Tuesday of March, A. D. 1903.

To the Committee on Finance :

Joint resolution appropriating money to be expended for the preservation of the muster rolls.

To the Committee on State Prison and Industrial School :

15

An act in relation to the administration of the state prison and to provide for necessary improvements and repairs.

To the Committee on the Judiciary :

An act in amendment of section 19, chapter 57 of the Public Statutes, relating to the annual invoice of polls and taxable property.

An act to exempt certain property of the Keene Young Men's Christian Association from taxation.

On motion of Senator Foley, the rules were so far suspended that the following entitled bill sent up from the House of Representatives was read a first and second time by its title and referred :

To the Committee on Incorporations :

An act to amend chapter 184 of the Laws of 1897, entitled "An act to incorporate the Dalton Power Company," as amended by section 1, chapter 221 of the Laws of 1899.

On motion of Senator Thompson, the rules were so far suspended that the following entitled bill sent up from the House of Representatives was read a first and second time by its title and referred :

To the Committee on Public Health :

An act in amendment of chapter 134 of the Public Statutes, relating to the practice of dentistry.

The following bill sent up from the House of Representatives was read a first time :

An act for the better preservation of highways and accommodating public travel.

The question being stated,

Shall the bill be read a second time?

The negative prevailed on a *viva voce* vote.

Joint resolution in favor of the widow of John W. Jewett of Claremont, sent up from the House of Representatives, was read a first and second time, and on motion of Senator Cooper, the rules were so far suspended that the joint resolution was read a third time and passed.

(Senator Bickford in the chair.)

Joint resolution appropriating five hundred dollars for a

monument to be erected at Hackensack, New Jersey, in memory of Gen. Enoch Poor, was read a first and second time.

Senator Hoitt of District No. 19 moved that the rules be so far suspended that the joint resolution be read a third time.

The question being stated,

Shall the rules be suspended?

(Discussion ensued.)

Senator Hoitt of District No. 19, withdrew his motion, and the joint resolution was referred to the Committee on Finance.

The following report from the Committee on Engrossed Bills was read and accepted:

The Committee on Engrossed Bills have examined and found correctly engrossed the following entitled bills:

An act to amend section 52 of chapter 79 of the Laws of 1901, entitled "An act to revise the fish and game laws of the state."

An act to legalize and confirm the warrant for, and the votes and proceedings at, the annual election and meeting in Ward three of the city of Berlin, held the tenth day of March, 1903.

An act relating to the time required for filing notice of intention of marriage.

An act to provide in common with the state of Vermont for the acquisition, building, and maintenance of free bridges across the Connecticut river.

A. W. BURNELL,
For the Committee.

On motion of Senator Tolles, the Senate voted to take a recess for ten minutes.

(Recess.)

The Senate reassembled.

LEAVE OF ABSENCE.

Senator Hoitt of District No. 19 was granted leave of absence for Thursday, March 26th, on account of death in the family.

Senator Felt, chairman of the Committee of the Whole, to whom was referred the following entitled bill, "An act to regulate the traffic in intoxicating liquor," having considered the

same, report the same with the following amendments and
recommend its passage :

Amend section 1 by inserting the word "firms" after the word
"include" in the third line of said section.

Amend section 5 by inserting the words "commissioner or"
after the word "any" in the eighth line of said section.

Amend section 6, fifth class, by inserting after the word
"only" in the third line of said fifth class the words "and for
dealers in hardware, paints, and decorating materials to sell
alcohol for mechanical and chemical uses only," so that said
fifth class as amended shall read :

Fifth Class. For retail druggists and apothecaries to sell
liquor of any kind for medicinal, mechanical, chemical, and
sacramental uses only, and for dealers in hardware, paints, and
decorating materials to sell alcohol for mechanical and chemical uses only.

Also amend section 6, seventh class, by striking out the
period after the figure 8, and insert in place thereof a comma
and add the words "in the discretion of the board of license
commissioners."

Further amend section 6, eighth class, by striking out the
word "and" after the word "distillers" in the first line of said
class, and insert in place thereof a comma; also amend said
eighth class by inserting after the word "brewer" in said line
the words "and bottlers."

Further amend said section 6 by adding at the end of said
section the words "all licenses granted prior to May 1st, 1904,
shall expire on that date, all licenses after May 1st, 1904, shall
expire May 1st of the following year, and all licensees shall pay
for the time from date of issue to the first day of the May following."

Amend section 7, first class, by striking out all after the word
"lodging" in said first class.

Further amend section 7, third class, by striking out the word
"twenty" and inserting in place thereof the word "eighteen."

Further amend section 7, third class, by striking out the word
"twenty" in the third line of said third class, and insert in
place thereof the word "eighteen."

Further amend said third class by striking out the word
·"twenty" in the fifth line of said third class, and insert in place
thereof the word "eighteen."

Further amend section 7, fourth class, by striking out the
word "twenty" in the third line of said fourth class, and insert
in place thereof the word "eighteen."

Further amend section 7, fourth class, by striking out the
word "twenty" in the fifth line and insert in place thereof the
word "eighteen."

Amend section 8, subdivision 3, by inserting after the word
"city" in the second line in said subdivision, the words "or
the adjoining town or city," so that said subdivision will read
as follows :

Three.   Who is not a citizen of the United States, and a resident of the state of New Hampshire, and of the town or city
or the adjoining town or city within which he desires to carry
on the liquor business for one year last prior to the filing of his
application ;

Further amend section 8, subdivision 7, by striking out after
the word "therefore" in the second line of said subdivision, the
words "shall receive a license."

Further amend section 8, subdivision 9, by inserting after the
word "him" in the tenth line of said subdivision the words
"provided, however, that no bond shall be accepted for a less
amount than five hundred dollars."

Amend section 9 by inserting after the word "on" in the
seventh line the words "or in any location where the traffic
shall be deemed by said board of license commissioners detrimental to the public welfare."

Amend section 10 by inserting after the word "duties" in
the fourteenth line of said section the words "also the sum of
one thousand dollars, or as much thereof as may be needed to
pay the necessary expenses of the state laboratory of hygiene
incurred under the provisions of this act, and all expenditures
shall be audited by the governor and council."

Amend section 13 by striking out after the word "die" in
the second line of said section the words "or cease to traffic in
liquor during the term for which said license was issued, such

person, or his duly authorized attorney, or his representative," and insert in place of the words so stricken out the words "his heirs, executors, or administrators."

Amend section 15 by striking out after the word "minor" in the third line of said section the words "unless accompanied by his parent or guardian."

Amend section 16, subdivision second, by striking out the word "ten" in the second line of said subdivision and inserting in place thereof the word "eleven."

Amend section 21 by inserting after the word "any" in the first line the word "commissioner"; also amend said section by inserting the word "selectman" after the word "agent" in the first line.

Amend section 24 by inserting after the word "the" and before the word "special" in the third line the words "commissioners and"

Amend section 31 by striking out in the first line of said section the words "first day" and inserting in place thereof the words "third Tuesday."

Further amend section 31 by striking out the word "and" in the next to the last line of said section, and inserting after the word "6th" and before the word "classes" in said line the words "and 8th."

The report was accepted and amendments adopted.

On motion of Senator Bickford, the rules were so far suspended that the bill was read a third time by its title.

Tha question being stated,

Shall the bill pass?

Senator Page demanded the yeas and nays.

The clerk proceeded to call the roll.

The following named Senators voted in the affirmative:

Senators Keyes, Lewando, Tilton, Cooper, Marvin, Neal, Lightbody, Bickford, Foley, Hoitt of District No. 19, Tolles, Hoyt of District No. 21, Thompson, Richmond, and Page.

The following named Senators voted in the negative:

Senators Burnell, Felt, Fellows, Fuller, and Wilkins.

Senators Stillings and Ripley paired.

Fifteen Senators having voted in the affirmative and five

Senators having voted in the negative, the affirmative prevailed, the bill passed, and was sent to the House of Representatives for concurrence in Senate amendments.

On motion of Senator Richmond, the Senate adjourned.

THURSDAY, MARCH 26, 1903.

The Senate met according to adjournment.

(Senator Keyes in the chair.)

The reading of the journal having been commenced, on motion of Senator Wilkins, the rules were so far suspended that its further reading was dispensed with.

Senator Lewando moved to reconsider the vote whereby the Senate adopted the resolution that it was inexpedient to legislate on the following entitled House bill :

An act to define the duties of the state treasurer with reference to public funds.

The question being stated,

Shall the vote be reconsidered?

The affirmative prevailed on a *viva voce* vote.

On motion of Senator Thompson, the bill was recommitted to the Committee on Finance.

Senator Hoyt of District No. 21 moved to reconsider the vote whereby the Senate voted to indefinitely postpone the following entitled House bill :

An act to amend chapter 60, section 3 of the Statute Laws of 1891, relating to dog licenses.

The question being stated,

Shall the vote be reconsidered?

The affirmative prevailed on a *viva voce* vote.

The bill was read a second time by its title and referred to the Committee on Public Improvements.

The following entitled House bills and joint resolution were severally read a third time and passed :

An act authorizing the city of Nashua to exempt the High-land Springs Sanatorium Company from taxation.

An act authorizing the Concord & Montreal Railroad, lessor, to vote on all stock owned by it in other corporations.

Joint resolution for an appropriation for the benefit of the New Hampshire College of Agriculture and the Mechanic Arts.

An act in amendment of section 22, chapter 27, Laws of 1895, entitled "An act in relation to the incorporation, organization and regulation of street railway companies and authorizing the use of electricity as motive power by existing steam railroads.

An act in amendment of the charter of the Exeter Gas, Electric Light and Power Company.

On motion of Senator Tilton, the rules were so far suspended that the following entitled House bills were severally read a third time by their titles and passed:

An act to incorporate the Mt. Belknap Electric Railway Company.

An act to incorporate the Kearsarge Mountain Electric Railway Company.

An act to incorporate the Candia and Deerfield Street Railway Company.

An act to incorporate the Manchester and Haverhill Street Railway Company.

An act to incorporate the Concord, Dover and Rochester Street Railway.

An act to incorporate the Dunbarton and Goffstown Street Railway Company.

The following message was received from the House of Representatives by its clerk:

HOUSE MESSAGE.

Mr. President:

The House of Representatives has voted to concur with the Honorable Senate in its amendments to the following entitled bills:

An act in amendment of the charter of the city of Manchester, establishing a board of assessors in place of the assessors provided under the charter and laws of the state.

An act authorizing the town of Gilmanton to exempt certain property from taxation.

The House of Representatives has passed a bill with the following title, in the passage of which it asks the concurrence of the Honorable Senate:

An act to provide suitable armory quartets for the National Guard at Manchester.

The foregoing entitled bill sent up from the House of Representatives was read a first and second time and referred:

To the Committee on Military Affairs.

The following entitled Senate bill having been printed was taken from the table and ordered to a third reading this afternoon at 3 o'clock:

An act establishing the office of medical referee and amending chapter 262 of the Public Statutes, relating to coroners' inquests.

Senator Lewando, for the Committee on Revision of the Laws, to whom was referred a bill entitled "An act in amendment of section 1, chapter 31 of the Laws of 1897, entitled 'An act in amendment of section 6 of chapter 83 of the Public Statutes,' in relation to the settlement of paupers," reported the same without amendment and recommended its passage.

Senator Marvin, for the Committee on Roads, Bridges, and Canals, to whom was referred a bill entitled "An act providing for a state system of highway construction and improvement, and for the appointment of highway engineers," reported the same without amendment and recommended its passage.

Senator Richmond, for the Committee on Incorporations, to whom was referred the following entitled bills:

"An act to incorporate the Peabody River Improvement Company,"

"An act to incorporate the Caledonia Power Company," reported the same without amendment and recommended their passage.

The reports were accepted and the bills severally ordered to a third reading this afternoon at 3 o'clock.

On motion of Senator Tolles, the following entitled House bill was recalled from the Committee on Public Improvements:

An act to amend chapter 60, section 3 of the Statute Laws of 1891, relating to dog licenses.

On motion of the same Senator, the rules were so far suspended that the bill was read a third time by its title and passed.

On motion of Senator Hoyt of District No. 21, the Senate voted to take a recess for 15 minutes.

(Recess.)

The Senate reassembled.

On motion of Senator Wilkins, the following resolution was adopted:

Resolved, That when the Senate adjourns this morning, it adjourn to meet this afternoon at 2 o'clock.

On motion of Senator Lewando, the Senate adjourned.

AFTERNOON.

On motion of Senator Tolles, the rules were so far suspended that the following entitled House bills were severally read a third time by their titles and passed:

An act in amendment of section 1, chapter 31 of the Laws of 1897, entitled " An act in amendment of section 6 of chapter 83 of the Public Statutes, in relation to the settlement of paupers."

An act to incorporate the Peabody River Improvement Company.

An act to incorporate the Caledonia Power Company.

An act providing for a state system of highway construction and improvement, and for the appointment of highway engineers.

The following entitled Senate bill was read a third time and passed:

An act establishing the office of medical referee and amending chapter 262 of the Public Statutes, relating to coroners' inquests.

On motion of Senator Thompson, the Senate voted to reconsider the vote whereby the bill passed.

On motion of Senator Bickford, the rules were so far suspended that the bill was placed back upon its second reading for the purpose of amendment.

On motion of Senator Felt, the following amendment was adopted:

Amend section 2 by striking out in the 4th line the word "Hillsborough," and insert the words "and Hillsborough" after the word "Grafton" in the 5th line; and further amend by inserting the word "each" after the word "three" in the 5th line.

The amendment was adopted and on motion of Senator Thompson, the rules were so far suspended that the bill was read a third time by its title, passed, and sent to the House of Representatives for concurrence.

Senator Hoyt of District No. 21, for the Committee on State Prison and Industrial School, to whom was referred a bill entitled "An act in relation to the state prison and to provide for necessary improvements and repairs," reported the same without amendment and recommended its passage.

Senator Tilton, for the Committee on Claims, to whom was referred Joint resolution in favor of John M. Stanyan for soldier's pay and bounty, reported the same without amendment and recommended its passage.

Senator Lewando, for the Committee on Military Affairs, to whom was referred a bill entitled "An act to provide suitable armory quarters for the National Guard at Manchester," reported the same without amendment and recommended its passage.

Senator Tolles, for the Committee on the Judiciary, to whom was referred the following entitled bills:

"An act to exempt certain property of the Keene Young Men's Christian Association from taxation,"

"An act to revive the charter of the Colebrook Water Company, approved February 23, 1897," reported the same without amendment and recommended their passage.

The reports were accepted and the bills severally ordered to a third reading to-morrow morning at 11 o'clock.

Senator Marvin, for the Committee on Elections, to whom was referred a bill entitled "An act to legalize a vote taken at the annual town meeting in Boscawen on the second Tuesday of March, 1903," reported the same with the following amendment and recommended its passage.

Insert after the word "taken" in the first line the following: "at the annual town meeting in Boscawen on the second Tuesday of March, 1903."

The report was accepted, amendment adopted, and the bill ordered to a third reading to-morrow morning at 11 o'clock.

Senator Foley, for the Committee on Agriculture, to whom was referred Joint resolution to encourage the breeding and exhibition of thoroughbred farm animals, reported the same with the following resolution:

Resolved, That it is inexpedient to legislate.

The report was accepted and resolution adopted.

Senator Tolles, for the Committee on the Judiciary, reported the following entitled bill and recommended its passage:

An act in relation to the powers and duties of the police commissioners of Manchester.

The report was accepted, and the bill reported from the committee, was read a first and second time, and on motion of Senator Page, the rules were so far suspended that the bill was read a third time by its title, passed, and sent to the House of Representatives for concurrence.

On motion of Senator Fuller, the rules were so far suspended that all bills and joint resolutions in order for a third reading to-morrow morning at 11 o'clock were made in order for a third reading at the present time.

Joint resolution in favor of John M. Stanyan for soldier's pay and bounty, was read a third time and passed.

On motion of Senator Fuller, the rules were so far suspended that the following entitled House bills in order for a third reading were severally read a third time by their titles and passed:

An act in relation to the administration of the state prison and to provide for necessary improvements and repairs.

An act to exempt certain property of the Keene Young Men's Christian Association from taxation.

An act to provide for suitable armory quarters for the National Guard at Manchester.

An act to revive the charter of the Colebrook Water Company, approved February 3, 1897.

The following entitled House bill was read a third time by its title, passed, and sent to the House of Representatives for concurrence in Senate amendments:

An act to legalize a vote taken at the annual meeting in Boscawen on the second Tuesday of March, A. D. 1903.

On motion of Senator Lewando, the Senate voted to take a recess subject to the call of the President.

(Recess.)

The Senate reassembled.

The following message was received from the House of Representatives by its clerk:

HOUSE MESSAGE.

Mr. President:

The House of Representatives has refused to concur with the Honorable Senate in the following amendments to a bill entitled "An act to regulate the traffic in intoxicating liquors."

Amend section 7, first class, by striking out all after the word "lodging" in said first class.

Amend section 16, subdivision second, by striking out the word "ten" in the second line of said subdivision and inserting in place thereof the word "eleven."

Amend section 31 by striking out the word "and" in the next to the last line of said section and inserting after the word "6th" and before the word "classes" in said line the words "and 8th," and has adopted the following resolution:

Resolved, That a committee of three members of the House be appointed by the Speaker to confer with a like committee on the part of the Senate in relation to the bill and amendments.

The Speaker has appointed as such committee on the part of the House, Messrs. Batchelder of Keene, Phillips of Franklin, and Small of Rochester.

On motion of Senator Thompson, the following resolution was adopted:

Resolved, That a committee of three be appointed by the President to confer with the House Committee of Conference in regard to the Senate amendments to House bill No. 473, entitled " An act to regulate the traffic in intoxicating liquor."

The President appointed as members of such committee Senators Bickford, Hoyt of District No. 21, and Page.

On motion of Senator Thompson, the Senate voted to take a recess of fifteen minutes.

(Recess.)

The Senate reassembled.

On motion of Senator Thompson, the following resolution was adopted :

Resolved, That when the Senate adjourns it adjourn to meet to-morrow morning at 9.30 o'clock, and that when it adjourns to-morrow morning it adjourn to meet next Monday afternoon at 2 o'clock.

The committee of conference upon the non-concurrence of the House of Representatives in the passage of certain amendments of the Senate to the following entitled House bill, "An act to regulate the traffic in intoxicating liquor," reported the same with a recommendation that the Senate recede from its position as to the following amendments :

Amend section 7, first class, by striking out all after the word " lodging " in said first class.

Amend section 16, subdivision second, by striking out the word " ten " in the second line of said subdivision, and insert in the place thereof the word " eleven."

Amend section 31 by striking out the word " and " in the next to the last line of said section, and inserting after the word " 6th " and before the word " classes " in said line the words " and 8th."

The committee further recommended that the following amendments be adopted :

Amend section 7, first class, by striking out the following words : " If the guest resorts to a house for food only, then he must partake of and pay for a meal costing not less than twenty-five cents."

Amend section 16, subdivision second, by adding at the end of said subdivision the words "unless the town or board of mayor and aldermen of the city where such licensee carries on business shall extend the hours not later than 11 o'clock at night, which said town or board of mayor and aldermen is hereby authorized to do."

> JOHN C. BICKFORD,
> ARTHUR E. HOYT,
> CALVIN PAGE,
> *Senate Conferees.*
>
> FREDERICK E. SMALL,
> LEWIS W. PHILLIPS,
> *House Conferees.*

The report was accepted, and on motion of Senator Bickford, the Senate voted to recede from the preceding amendments.

On motion of the same Senator, the Senate voted to adopt the amendments reported by the committee of conference.

On motion of Senator Fuller, the Senate adjourned.

FRIDAY, MARCH 27, 1903.

The Senate met according to adjournment.

The reading of the journal having been commenced, on motion of Senator Keyes, the rules were so far suspended that its further reading was dispensed with.

The following message was received from the House of Representatives by its clerk:

HOUSE MESSAGE.

Mr. President:

The House of Representatives has passed the following entitled bills and joint resolution, in the passage of which it asks the concurrence of the Honorable Senate:

An act in amendment of and in addition to section 3, chapter 105 of the Laws of 1901, in relation to political caucuses and conventions.

An act to provide for the representation of the state of New Hampshire and the exhibition of its products and attractions at the Louisiana Purchase Exposition at St. Louis in 1904.

An act to provide for a revision of the general and public laws.

An act in amendment of chapter 64, Laws of 1899, relating to Firemen's Relief Fund.

An act to incorporate the Sandwich Electric Railway Company.

An act to revive, amend, and extend the charter of the Alton and Gilmanton Electric Railway Company.

An act to revive, amend, and extend the charter of the Gilmanton and Barnstead Electric Railway Company.

An act to exempt from local taxation the hotel property that may be erected in the village of North Stratford in the town of Stratford.

An act in amendment of chapter 208 of the Session Laws of 1899, entitled "An act to incorporate the Walpole Electric Light and Power Company," and of an act passed at the present session.

Joint resolution relating to repairs upon the state house.

The House of Representatives has adopted the following concurrent resolution, in the passage of which it asks the concurrence of the Honorable Senate:

WHEREAS, It appears that all necessary legislative work may easily be accomplished by Friday, the 3d day of April; there fore be it

Resolved, By the House of Representatives, the Senate concurring, that the present session of the legislature be brought to a final adjournment on Friday, the 3d day of April, at 12 o'clock noon ; and be it further

Resolved, That all reports, bills and joint resolutions at that time pending in either branch of the legislature be indefinitely postponed.

On motion of Senator Keyes, the following amendment to the foregoing concurrent resolution was adopted:

Amend by striking out the words "Friday, the 3d day " and inserting in place thereof "Thursday, the 2d day."

The concurrent resolution as amended was sent to the House of Representatives for its concurrence.

The following entitled bills sent up from the House of Representatives were severally read a first and second time and referred :

To the Committee on the Judiciary :

An act in amendment of and in addition to section 3, chapter 105 of the Laws of 1901, in relation to political caucuses and conventions.

An act to provide for the revision of the general and public laws.

An act in amendment of chapter 64, Laws of 1899, relating to Firemen's Relief Fund.

To the Committee on Finance :

An act to exempt from local taxation the hotel property that may be erected in the village of North Stratford in the town of Stratford.

To the Committee on Public Improvements :

Joint resolution relating to repairs upon the state house.

On motion of Senator Keyes, the rules were so far suspended that the following entitled bills sent up from the House of Representatives were read a first and second time by their titles and referred :

To the Committee on Railroads :

An act to incorporate the Sandwich Electric Railway Company.

An act to revive, amend, and extend the charter of the Alton and Gilmanton Electric Railway Company.

An act to revive, amend and extend the charter of the Gilmanton and Barnstead Electric Railway Company.

To the Committee on Incorporation :

An act in amendment of chapter 208 of the Session Laws of 1899, entitled "An act to incorporate the Walpole Electric Light and Power Company," and of an act amending said act passed at the present session.

To the Committee on Finance :

An act to provide for the representation of the state of New

16

Hampshire and the exhibition of its products and attractions at the Louisiana Purchase Exposition at St. Louis in 1904.

The following report from the Committee on Engrossed Bills was read and accepted :

The Committee on Engrossed Bills have examined and found correctly engrossed the following entitled bill :

An act to regulate the traffic in intoxicating liquor.

HENRY W. KEYES,
For the Committee.

On motion of Senator Burnell, the Senate adjourned.

MONDAY, MARCH 30, 1903.

The Senate met according to adjournment.

The reading of the journal having been commenced, on motion of Senator Stillings, the rules were so far suspended that its further reading was dispensed with.

On motion of Senator Keyes, the Senate adjourned.

TUESDAY, MARCH 31, 1903.

The Senate met according to adjournment.

The journal was read and approved.

On motion of Senator Burnell, the following resolution was adopted :

Resolved, That the Governor be requested to return to the Senate the following entitled bill :

An act to amend section 14 and section 15, chapter 286 of the Public Statutes, relating to the salary of the judge and register of probate for Belknap county.

The foregoing entitled bill having been returned by His Excellency the Governor, it was moved by Senator Burnell that the Senate reconsider the vote whereby the bill passed.

The question being stated,

Shall the vote be reconsidered ?

The affirmative prevailed on a *viva voce* vote.

On motion of the same Senator, the rules were so far suspended that the bill was placed back on its second reading for the purposes of amendment.

On motion of the same Senator, the following amendment was adopted:

Amend section 2 by inserting after the word " six " in the fifth line of said section the word "hundred."

On motion of the same Senator, the rules were so far suspended that the bill was read a third time by its title, passed, and sent to the House of Representatives for concurrence in Senate amendment.

On motion of Senator Bickford, "Joint resolution in favor of Ella F. Densmore of Charlestown, Mary F. Lombard of Acworth, Frank G. Smith of Waltham, Massachusetts, Eugene P. Smith of Newport, and George E. Shattuck of Hinsdale," was taken from the table.

On motion of the same Senator, the following amendment was adopted:

Amend by striking out all after the word " only " in the 15th line and all of the 16th line.

Further amend by striking out all after the word " kin " in the 19th line, and insert instead thereof the following: " in the following shares : To George E. Shattuck of Hinsdale, the sum of eleven hundred dollars ($1,100); to Ella F. Densmore of Charlestown, four hundred forty dollars and fifty-two cents ($440.52); to Mary F. Lombard of Acworth, four hundred forty dollars and fifty-two cents ($440.52); to Frank G. Smith of Waltham, Massachusetts, four hundred forty dollars and fifty-two cents ($440.52); and to Eugene P. Smith of Newport, four hundred forty dollars and fifty-four cents ($440.54)."

On motion of Senator Allen, the rules were so far suspended that the joint resolution was read a third time, passed, and sent to the House of Representatives for concurrence in Senate amendments.

The following message was received from the House of Representatives by its clerk:

Mr. President:

The House of Representatives has voted to concur with the Honorable Senate in its amendments to the following entitled bill :

An act to legalize a vote taken at the annual town meeting in Boscawen on the second Tuesday of March, A. D. 1903.

The House of Representatives has passed bills with the following titles, in the passage of which it asks the concurrence of the Honorable Senate :

An act amending sections 37, 38, and 40 of chapter 59 of the Session Laws of 1895, as amended by chapter 25 of the Laws of 1901, in relation to the militia.

An act in relation to the Lisbon village district.

The following entitled bill sent up from the House of Representatives was read a first and second time and referred. :

To the Committee on Elections :

An act in relation to the Lisbon village district.

On motion of Senator Tolles, the rules were so far suspended that the following entitled bill sent up from the House of Representatives was read a first and second time by its title and referred :

To the Committee on Military Affairs :

An act amending sections 37, 38, and 40 of chapter 59 of the Session Laws of 1895, as amended by chapter 25 of the Laws of 1901, in relation to the militia.

Senator Burnell, for the Committee on Fisheries and Game, reported a Joint resolution appropriating money for screening the outlet of Sunapee lake.

The joint resolution reported from the committee was read a first and second time, and on motion of Senator Cooper, the rules were so far suspended that the joint resolution was read a third time, passed, and sent to the House of Representatives for concurrence.

Senator Wilkins, for the Committee on Finance, to whom was referred " Joint resolution to appropriate the sum of three hundred dollars for the purpose of turning Silver stream into Success pond in the township of Success, and to screen the outlet of said pond," reported the same without amendment and recommended its passage.

The report was accepted.

The question being stated,

Shall the bill be read a third time?

The negative prevailed on a *viva voce* vote.

Senator Lightbody, for the Committee on Banks, to whom was referred a bill entitled "An act to incorporate the National Trust Company," reported the same with the following resolution:

Resolved, That it is inexpedient to legislate.

The report was accepted and resolution adopted.

Senator Richmond, for the Committee on Incorporations, to whom was referred a bill entitled "An act to establish water-works in the town of Greenville," reported the same without amendment and recommended its passage.

Senator Wilkins, for the Committee on Finance, to whom was referred a " Joint resolution appropriating money to be expended for the preservation of the muster rolls," reported the same without amendment and recommended its passage.

The same Senator, for the same committee, to whom was referred a " Joint resolution appropriating five hundred dollars for a monument to be erected at Hackensack, N. J., in memory of Gen. Enoch Poor," reported the same without amendment and recommended its passage.

The reports were accepted, and the bill and joint resolutions severally ordered to a third reading this afternoon at 3 o'clock.

The following report from the Committee on Engrossed Bills was read and accepted:

The Committee on Engrossed Bills have examined and found correctly engrossed the following entitled bills and joint resolutions:

An act in amendment of section 1, chapter 31 of the Laws of 1897, entitled "An act in amendment of section 6 of chapter 83 of the Public Statutes, in relation to the settlement of paupers."

An act to incorporate the Caledonia Power Company.

Joint resolution in favor of John M. Stanyan for soldier's pay and bounty.

An act in relation to the administration of the state prison and to provide for necessary improvements and repairs.

An act to incorporate the Concord, Dover & Rochester Street Railway.

An act in amendment of the charter of the city of Manchester, establishing a board of assessors in place of the assessors provided under the charter and laws of the state. .

An act to revive the charter of the Colebrook Water Company, approved February 23, 1897.

An act to provide suitable armory quarters for the National Guard at Manchester.

An act in amendment of the charter of the Exeter Gas, Electric Light, and Power Company.

An act to exempt certain property of the Keene Young Men's Christian Association from taxation.

An act in amendment of section 22, chapter 27, Laws of 1895, entitled "An act in relation to the incorporation, organization, and regulation of street railway companies, and authorizing the use of electricity as motive power by existing steam railroads."

Joint resolution in favor of the widow of John W. Jewett of Claremont.

Joint resolution for an appropriation for the benefit of the New Hampshire College of Agriculture and the Mechanic Arts.

An act authorizing the Concord & Montreal Railroad, lessor, to vote on all stock owned by it in other corporations.

An act to incorporate the Manchester and Haverhill Street Railway Company.

An act authorizing the city of Nashua to exempt The Highland Spring Sanatorium Company from taxation.

An act relating to the setting off by the legislature of territory of one town or city on to that of another town or city.

An act to sever certain residences from the school district of the town of Wilmot, and to annex the same to the school district of the town of New London.

An act to incorporate the Mt. Belknap Electric Railway Company.

An act to incorporate the Kearsarge Mountain Electric Railway Company.

An act to incorporate the Peabody River Improvement Company.

An act providing for a state system of highway construction and improvement, and for the appointment of highway engineers.

An act to incorporate the Connecticut River Power Company of New Hampshire.

An act to incorporate the Dunbarton and Goffstown Street Railway Company.

A. W. BURNELL,
For the Committee.

On motion of Senator Felt, the Senate adjourned.

AFTERNOON.

The following entitled House bill and joint resolutions were severally read a third time and passed:

An act to establish water-works in the town of Greenville.

Joint resolution appropriating five hundred dollars for a monument to be erected at Hackensack, N. J., in memory of Gen. Enoch Poor.

Joint resolution appropriating money to be expended for the preservation of the muster rolls.

The following message was received from the House of Representatives:

HOUSE MESSAGE.

Mr. President:

The House of Representatives has passed the following entitled bills in the passage of which it asks the concurrence of the Honorable Senate:

An act in amendment of section 14, chapter 180, Public Statutes, relating to the hours of labor for women and minors in manufacturing or mercantile establishments.

An act to regulate the penalty for murder.

The following entitled bills sent up from the House of Representatives were severally read a first and second time and referred:

To the Committee on Labor:

An act in amendment of section 14, chapter 180, Public Statutes, relating to the hours of labor for women and minors in manufacturing or mercantile establishments.

To the Committee on the Judiciary:

An act to regulate the penalty for murder.

On motion of Senator Hoyt of District No. 21, the following resolution was adopted:

Resolved: That when the Senate adjourns this afternoon it be to meet to-morrow morning at 10 o'clock.

Senator Richmond, for the Committee on Incorporations, to whom was referred a bill entitled "An act to amend chapter 184 of the Laws of 1897, entitled 'An act to incorporate the Dalton Power Company,' as amended by section 1, chapter 221 of the Laws of 1899," reported the same without amendment and recommended its passage.

Senator Keyes, for the Committee on Forestry, to whom was referred a bill entitled "An act in amendment of chapter 98 of the Laws of 1901, relating to the duties of tree wardens," reported the same without amendment and recommended its passage.

Senator Keyes, for the Committee on Railroads, to whom was referred the following entitled bills:

"An act to revive, amend, and extend the charter of the Alton and Gilmanton Electric Railway Company,"

"An act to incorporate the Sandwich Electric Railway Company,"

"An act to revive, amend, and extend the charter of the Gilmanton and Barnstead Electric Railway Company," reported the same without amendment and recommended their passage.

The reports were accepted and the bills severally ordered to a third reading to-morrow morning at 10 o'clock.

Senator Keyes, for the Committee on Railroads, to whom was referred a bill entitled "An act to incorporate the Portsmouth & Newcastle Street Railway Company," reported the same with the following resolution:

Resolved, That it is inexpedient to legislate.

The report was accepted and the resolution adopted.

Senator Richmond, for the Committee on Incorporations, to whom was referred a bill entitled "An act in amendment of chapter 208 of the Session Laws of 1899, entitled 'An act to incorporate the Walpole Electric Light and Power Company,' and of an act amending said act, passed at the present session," reported the same without amendment and recommended its passage.

The report was accepted, and on motion of Senator Richmond, the rules were so far suspended that the bill was read a third time by its title and passed.

Senator Marvin, for the Committee on Towns and Parishes, to whom was referred a bill entitled "An act to enlarge the powers and duties of towns," reported the same with the following amendment and recommended its passage:

Strike out in section 1, third line, the words "amusement rooms."

The report was accepted and amendment adopted.

The question being stated,

Shall the bill be read a third time?

The negative prevailed on a *viva voce* vote.

Senator Fuller called for a division.

A division being taken, two Senators voted in the affirmative and twelve Senators voted in the negative, and the bill was refused a third reading.

Senator Keyes, for the Committee on Forestry, to whom was referred a bill entitled "An act to encourage the planting and preservation of forests," reported the same with the following amendment and recommended its passage:

Amend by striking out section 3 and inserting in place thereof the following:

SECT. 3. In order to facilitate the planting of trees as hereinbefore provided, the forestry commission is hereby authorized and directed to contract, without expense to the state, upon terms to be approved by the governor and council, with reputable nurserymen to provide, at a price to be determined upon, seeds and seedlings of timber or forest trees, to landowners for planting within this state, in accordance with the terms of section 1 of this act.

The report was accepted, amendment adopted, and the bill ordered to a third reading to-morrow morning at 10 o'clock.

Senator Lightbody, for the Committee on Education, to whom was referred a bill entitled "An act to amend chapter 96 of the Session Laws of 1901, relating to high schools," reported the same without amendment and recommended its passage.

The report was accepted.

The question being stated,

Shall the bill be read a third time?

The negative prevailed on a *viva voce* vote.

Senator Thompson called for a division.

(Discussion ensued.)

A division being taken, eleven Senators voted in the affirmative.

Senator Thompson demanded the yeas and nays.

The clerk proceeded to call the roll.

The following named Senators voted in the affirmative:

Senators Keyes, Lewando, Burnell, Cooper, Felt, Fuller, Wilkins, Lightbody, Hoitt of District No. 19, Hoyt of District No. 21, and Thompson.

The following named Senators voted in the negative:

Senators Foley and Richmond.

Eleven Senators having voted in the affirmative and two Senators having voted in the negative, the affirmative prevailed, and the bill was ordered to a third reading to-morrow morning at 11 o'clock.

On motion of Senator Page, the Senate voted to take a recess for ten minutes.

(Recess.)

The Senate reassembled.

Senator Lewando, for the Committee on Military Affairs, to whom was referred a bill entitled "An act amending sections 37, 38, and 40 of chapter 59 of the Session Laws of 1895, as amended by chapter 25 of the Laws of 1901, in relation to the militia," reported the same with the following amendment and recommended its passage :

Amend by striking out section 2 and inserting in place thereof the following :

SECT. 2. That section 98 of chapter 95 of the Laws of 1895, as amended by chapter 25 of the Laws of 1901, be amended by striking out the words "two dollars" after the words "band musicians" in the sixteenth line and inserting in place thereof the words "three dollars."

Further amend by adding the following section :

SECT. 3. All acts or parts of acts inconsistent with this act are hereby repealed, and this act shall take effect upon its passage.

The report was accepted and amendments adopted.

On motion of Senator Lightbody, the rules were so far suspended that the bill was read a third time by its title, passed, and sent to the House of Representatives for concurrence in Senate amendments.

Senators Ripley, Thompson, and Felt, for the Committee on Education, to whom was referred a bill entitled "An act to provide for the holding of library institutes," reported the same without amendment and recommended its passage.

Senators Lightbody and Tilton, a minority of the Committee on Education, to whom was referred a bill entitled "An act to provide for the holding of library institutes," reported the same with the following resolution :

Resolved, That it is inexpedient to legislate.

The reports were accepted.

Senator Lightbody moved that the report of the minority be substituted for that of the majority.

The question being stated,

Shall the minority report be substituted for that of the majority ?

(Discussion ensued.)

Senator Thompson rose to a point of order which was not sustained by the chair.

The question recurring,

Senate Ripley demanded the yeas and nays.

The clerk proceeded to call the roll.

The following named Senators voted in the affirmative:

Senators Lewando, Burnell, Cooper, Neal, Fuller, Lightbody, Bickford, Foley, Tolles, Hoyt of District No. 21, Richmond and Page.

The following named Senators voted in the negative: ·

Senators Allen, Keyes, Marvin, Felt, Ripley, Wilkins, Thompson.

Twelve Senators having voted in the affirmative and seven Senators having voted in the negative, the affirmative prevailed and the minority report was substituted for that of the majority.

The question being stated,

Shall the resolution reported by the minority of the committee that it is inexpedient to legislate be adopted?

The affirmative prevailed on a *viva voce* vote.

Senator Page moved that the resolution pertaining to the election of United States Senators by the people and the calling of a constitutional convention to amend the constitution of the United States be taken from the table.

The question being stated,

Shall the resolution be taken from the table?

The negative prevailed on a *viva voce* vote.

On motion of Senator Bickford, the Senate adjourned.

WEDNESDAY, APRIL 1, 1903.

The Senate met according to adjournment.

The reading of the journal having been commenced, on motion of Senator Bickford, the rules were so far suspended that its further reading was dispensed with.

On motion of Senator Tolles, the rules were so far suspended that the following entitled House bills were severally read a third time by their titles and passed:

An act to amend chapter 96 of the Session Laws of 1901, relating to high schools.

An act in amendment of chapter 98 of the Laws of 1901, relating to the duties of tree wardens.

An act to incorporate the Sandwich Electric Railway Company.

An act to amend chapter 184 of the Laws of 1897, entitled "An act to incorporate the Dalton Power Company," as amended by section 1, chapter 221 of the Laws of 1899.

An act to revive, amend, and extend the charter of the Gilmanton and Barnstead Electric Railway Company.

An act to revive, amend, and extend the charter of the Alton and Gilmanton Electric Railway Company.

The following entitled House bill was read a third time by its title, passed, and sent to the House of Representatives for concurrence in Senate amendments:

An act to encourage the planting and perpetuation of forests.

Senator Bickford, for the Committee on the Judiciary, reported the following entitled bill and recommended its passage:

An act relating to the use of trade marks and names.

The report was accepted and on motion of Senator Bickford, the rules were so far suspended that the bill reported from the committee was read a first and second time by its title.

On motion of the same Senator, the rules were so far suspended as to dispense with the printing, and the bill was read a third time by its title, passed, and sent to the House of Representatives for concurrence.

Senator Lewando, for the Committee on Revision of the Laws, to whom was referred a bill entitled "An act in amendment of section 1, chapter 83 of the Public Statutes, entitled 'Settlement of Paupers,'" reported the same without amendment and recommended its passage.

Senator Marvin, for the Committee on Elections, to whom was referred a bill entitled "An act in relation to the Lisbon village district," reported the same without amendment and recommended its passage.

Senator Neal, for the Committee on Public Health, to whom was referred the following entitled bills:

"An act in amendment of chapter 134 of the Public Statutes relating to the practice of dentistry,"

"An act in amendment of section 7, chapter 63 of the Laws of 1897, entitled 'An act to regulate the licensing and registration of physicians and surgeons,'" reported the same without amendment and recommended their passage.

Senator Tolles, for the Committee on the Judiciary, to whom was referred the following entitled bills :

"An act in amendment of section 7 of chapter 59 of the Public Statutes, and section 13 of chapter 60 of the Public Statutes, relating to the assessment and collection of taxes,"

"An act in amendment of chapter 64, Laws of 1899, relating to firemen's relief fund," reported the same without amendment and recommended their passage.

The reports were accepted and the bills severally ordered to a third reading this afternoon at 3 o'clock.

Senator Ripley, for the Committee on Finance, to whom was referred a bill entitled "An act to define the duties of the state treasurer with reference to public funds," reported the same without amendment and recommended its passage.

The report was accepted.

Senator Page offered the following amendment :

Amend by adding at the end of section 1 the following : " excepting the interest upon such funds as are paid to the treasurer for distribution to the towns and cities of the state, and the interest shall be distributed to such towns and cities proportionately in the same manner as said funds are distributed."

The amendment was adopted on a *viva voce* vote, and the bill ordered to a third reading this afternoon at 3 o'clock.

Senator Ripley, for the Committee on Finance, to whom was referred a bill entitled "An act to exempt from local taxation the hotel property that may be erected in the village of North Stratford in the town of Stratford," reported the same with the following amendment and recommended its passage.

Amend by adding at the end of section 1 the following words : "provided that the town shall so vote at any legal meeting of the voters thereof."

The report was accepted, amendment adopted, and the bill ordered to a third reading this afternoon at 3 o'clock.

Senator Tolles, for the Committee on the Judiciary, to whom was referred a bill entitled "An act to regulate the penalty for murder," reported the same with the following amendment and recommended its passage:

Amend section 1 by striking out the first eleven lines of said section and insert in place thereof the following:

SECTION 1. That section 5 of chapter 278 of the Public Statutes, as amended by section 1, chapter 24, Laws of 1899, is hereby repealed, and the following is substituted in place thereof.

The report was accepted, amendment adopted, and the bill ordered to a third reading this afternoon at 3 o'clock.

The following message was received from the House of Representatives by its clerk:

HOUSE MESSAGE.

Mr. President:

The House of Representatives has voted to concur with the Honorable Senate in its amendment to the concurrent resolu tion relative to final adjournment April 2.

The House of Representatives has voted to concur with the Honorable Senate in its amendments to the following entitled bill and joint resolutions:

An act to amend section 14 and section 15, chapter 286 of the Public Statutes, relating to the salaries of the judge and register of probate for Belknap county.

Joint resolution in favor of Ella F. Densmore of Charlestown, Mary F. Lombard of Acworth, Frank G. Smith of Waltham, Massachusetts, Eugene P. Smith of Newport, and George E. Shattuck of Hinsdale.

The House of Representatives has passed bills with the following titles, in the passage of which it asks the concurrence of the Honorable Senate:

An act in addition to and in amendment of section 10 of chapter 198 of the Public Statutes, relating to trustees of estates.

An act providing for the taxation of building and loan associations.

The following entitled bills sent up from the House of Representatives were severally read a first and second time and referred:

To the Committee on the Judiciary:

An act in addition to and in amendment of section 10 of chapter 198 of the Public Statutes, relating to trustees of estates.

To the Committee on Banks:

An act to provide for the taxation of building and loan associations.

On motion of Senator Wilkins, the rules were so far suspended that all bills in order for a third reading this afternoon at 3 o'clock were made in order for a third reading at the present time.

On motion of Senator Tolles, the rules were further suspended so that the following entitled bills were severally read a third time by their titles and passed:

An act in amendment of section 7, chapter 63 of the Laws of 1897, entitled "An act to regulate the licensing and registration of physicians and surgeons."

An act in amendment of chapter 134 of the Public Statutes, relating to the practice of dentistry.

An act in relation to the Lisbon village district.

(Senator Foley in the chair.)

An act in amendment of chapter 64, Laws of 1899, relating to firemen's relief fund.

An act in amendment of section 7 of chapter 59 of the Public Statutes, and section 13 of chapter 60 of the Public Statutes, relating to assessment and collection of taxes.

An act in amendment of section 1, chapter 83 of the Public Statutes, entitled "Settlement of Paupers."

(President in the chair.)

The following entitled House bills with amendments were severally read a third time by their titles, passed, and sent to the House of Representatives for concurrence in Senate amendments :

An act to define the duties of the state treasurer with reference to public funds.

An act to exempt from local taxation the hotel property that may be erected in the village of North Stratford in the town of Stratford.

The following entitled House bill was read a third time by its title and passed :

An act to regulate the penalty for murder.

On motion of Senator Page, the title was amended by striking out its present title and substituting in place thereof the following:

"An act in amendment of section 5, chapter 278 of the Public Statutes, as amended by section 1, chapter 24, Laws of 1899, relating to homicide and offenses against the person."

The bill was then sent to the House of Representatives for concurrence in Senate amendments.

The following report from the Committee on Engrossed Bills was read and accepted :

The Committee on Engrossed Bills have examined and found correctly engrossed the following entitled bills :

An act to incorporate the Candia and Deerfield Street Railway Company.

An act to amend chapter 60, section 3 of the Statute Laws of 1891, relating to dog licenses.

An act to legalize a vote taken at the annual meeting in Boscawen on the second Tuesday of March, 1903.

An act in amendment of chapter 208 of the Session Laws of 1899, entitled "An act to incorporate the Walpole Electric Light and Power Company," and of an act amending said act passed at the present session.

A. W. BURNELL,
For the Committee.

The following message was received from His Excellency the Governor by the Honorable Edward N. Pearson, Secretary of State :

To the Honorable Senate:

I herewith return House bill No. 298, entitled " An act to provide in common with the state of Vermont for the acquisition, building, and maintenance of the bridges across the Connecticut river, without my signature.

My reasons for the disapproval of this act are:

The bill is very loosely drawn. Its limitations are very few and by no means definite. But apparently it provides for the appointment of a civil engineer having a practical knowledge of bridge work who, in connection with a commission authorized by the state of Vermont, shall proceed after certain investigations to purchase and free all existing toll bridges over the Connecticut river between New Hampshire and Vermont; to construct new free bridges at such points or places as may seem to them best to promote the public welfare, and to reimburse such towns as have already expended any money in the freeing of bridges, upon condition that the state of Vermont shall assume half the expense incurred, and appropriates $20,000 for this work annually until the work is completed.

The boundary line between New Hampshire and Vermont is at high water mark on the Vermont side of the Connecticut. The bridges across the Connecticut are therefore all in New Hampshire except perhaps the western abutments. I see no good reason why we should ask Vermont to assume any part of the expense of the highways in New Hampshire, or why she should consent to any such proposition.

The logical result of the passage of this bill would be an agreement between the representatives of the two states that in justice we should pay three fourths or seven eighths of the cost of the acquirement of the toll bridges, the construction of such new ones as in the opinion of the commissioners and engineer may be desirable, and the reimbursement of the towns that have already freed the bridges in their territory, and having started with this scheme, the probabilities are that we should feel in duty bound to accept what was recommended by our engineer. It comes therefore to this, that the bill authorizes the freeing of all toll bridges over the Connecticut in New Hampshire, the construction of all needed new ones, and the reimbursement of all towns for all they have expended on such bridges at the expense of our state treasury. There is absolutely no limit in the bill as to the time during which we shall pay $20,000 annually, and that, when once begun, the project will not call for several times that sum each year, we have no guarantee. From the best information I can obtain, I judge that at least a quarter of a million dollars will be required to carry this plan to completion.

I see no reason why the state of New Hampshire should purchase, construct, or maintain bridges across the Connecticut river than across the Merrimack, the Contoocook, the Androscoggin, the Cocheco, or the Saco, and the passage of this act, it appears to me, would be unjust discrimination against the taxpayers of every section of the state, except the tier of towns along the Connecticut which are generally as well able to support their own highways as any, and which, so far as I am informed, do not ask for state aid of this kind.

I think we should avoid as far as practicable the adoption of projects which will entail upon those who come after us, for an indefinite period, financial burdens that they may not be able to bear without great sacrifices. We have now in the treasury a large sum received from the United States government which will be dissipated this year. The next legislature will not have it to draw upon, and if we are prudent we shall consider this fact and restrain ourselves from contracting necessary obligations which they will have to discharge. If this be so, the appropriation of $20,000 annually, practically a perpetuity, for such an object, cannot be defended.

According to the terms of this act, the work contemplated is not to be proceeded with unless the legislature of Vermont shall assume half the expense before the first of January, 1905. At that time another New Hampshire legislature will have been elected and be ready to assemble, and I think we may wisely leave to our immediate successors the question whether the condition of our treasury and the public need warrants the outlay proposed ascertaining meanwhile, if that is desirable, whether Vermont will join us and if so upon what terms,.

which can easily be done without giving to an engineer such vast, unlimited, and perpetual powers as this bill proposes.

N. J. BACHELDER,

Governor.

The question being stated,

Will the Senate upon reconsideration pass the bill, notwithstanding the objections of the Governor thereto?

Senator Bickford moved that the message, together with the bill, be laid on the table.

The question being stated,

Shall the message, together with the bill, be laid on the table?

The affirmative prevailed on a *viva voce* vote.

The following message was received from the House of Representatives by its clerk:

HOUSE MESSAGE.

Mr. President:

The House of Representatives concurs with the Honorable Senate in the passage of the following entitled bill:

An act relative to the use of trade marks and names.

The House of Representatives has voted to concur with the Honorable Senate in its amendments to the following entitled bills:

An act in amendment of section 5, chapter 278 of the Public Statutes, as amended by section 1, chapter 24, Laws of 1899, relating to homicide and offenses against the person.

An act to exempt from local taxation the hotel property that may be erected in the village of North Stratford in the town of Stratford.

An act to define the duties of the state treasurer with reference to public funds.

An act amending sections 37, 38, and 40, of chapter 59 of the Session Laws of 1895, as amended by chapter 25 of the Laws of 1901, in relation to the militia.

An act to encourage the planting and perpetuating of forests.

The House of Representatives has passed the following entitled bills and joint resolutions in the passage of which it asks the concurrence of the Honorable Senate:

Joint resolution in favor of John K. Law and others.

Joint resolution in favor of Albert T. Severance and others.

An act to legalize and confirm the school board's warrant and the votes and proceedings thereunder at the annual school meeting in the town of Newfields, held in said town on the 14th day of March, 1903.

An act for the relief of the town of New Castle.

The following joint resolution sent up from the House of Representatives was read a first time:

Joint resolution in favor of John K. Law and others.

The second reading of the joint resolution having been commenced, on motion of Senator Page, its further reading was dispensed with.

On motion of the same Senator, the rules were so far suspended that the joint resolution was made in order for a third reading at the present time.

The third reading of the joint resolution having been commenced, on motion of the same Senator its further reading was dispensed with.

The question being stated,

Shall the joint resolution pass?

The affirmative prevailed on a *viva voce* vote.

The following entitled bills and joint resolution sent up from the House of Representatives were severally read a first and second time and referred:

To the Committee on Claims:

Joint resolution in favor of Albert T. Severance and others.

To the Committee on Elections:

An act for the relief of the town of New Castle.

An act to legalize and confirm the school board's warrant and the votes and proceedings thereunder at the annual school meeting in the town of Newfields, held in said town on the 14th day of March, 1903.

On motion of Senator Page, the following entitled House bills were recalled from the committees to whom they had been referred:

An act to legalize and confirm the school board's warrant and votes and proceedings thereunder at the annual school meeting in the town of Newfields, held in said town on the 14th day of March, 1903.

An act for the relief of the town of New Castle.

On motion of the same Senator, the rules were so far suspended that the foregoing entitled bills were made in order for a third reading at the present time, and on motion of the same Senator, the rules were further suspended and the bills severally read a third time by their titles and passed.

Senator Lightbody, for the Committee on Public Improvements, to whom was referred a bill entitled "An act relating to the protection and preservation of ornamental and shade trees in the highways," reported the same with the following resolution :

Resolved, That it is inexpedient to legislate.

The report was accepted and resolution adopted.

Senator Tilton, for the Committee on Claims, to whom was referred " Joint resolution in favor of Albert T. Severance and others," reported the same without amendment and recommended its passage.

The report was accepted and the joint resolution ordered to a third reading this afternoon at 3 o'clock.

The following message was received from the House of Representatives by its clerk :

HOUSE MESSAGE.

Mr. President :

The House of Representatives has passed the following entitled bills in the passage of which it asks the concurrence of the Honorable Senate :

An act authorizing the license commissioners to license *bona fide* hotels in unorganized towns and places to sell intoxicating liquors.

An act relating to the printing of ballots provided for in an act entitled "An act to regulate the traffic in intoxicating liquor," approved March 27, 1903.

An act to renew an act to incorporate the Glen Junction Transfer Company, passed January session, 1897, and to amend the same.

The following entitled bills sent up from the House of Representatives were severally read a first and second time and referred:

To the Committee on Incorporations:

An act to renew an act to incorporate the Glen Junction Transfer Company, passed January session, 1897, and to amend the same.

To the Committee on the Judiciary:

An act authorizing the license commissioners to license *bona fide* hotels in unorganized towns and places to sell intoxicating liquors.

An act relating to the printing of ballots provided for in an act entitled "An act to regulate the traffic in intoxicating liquor," passed March 27, 1903.

On motion of Senator Keyes, the Senate adjourned.

AFTERNOON.

Joint resolution in favor of Albert T. Severance and others was read a third time.

On motion of Senator Bickford, the rules were so far suspended that the bill was placed back on its second reading for the purpose of amendment.

On motion of the same Senator, the bill was laid on the table.

Senator Richmond, for the Committee on Incorporations, to whom was referred a bill entitled "An act to renew an act to incorporate the Glen Junction Transfer Company," passed January session, 1897, and to amend the same, reported the same without amendment and recommended its passage.

Senator Neal, for the Committee on Public Health, to whom was referred "Joint resolution to provide for the treatment of indigent consumptives," reported the same without amendment and recommended its passage.

Senator Tolles, for the Committee on the Judiciary, to whom was referred the following entitled bills:

"An act in amendment of chapter 262 of the Public Statutes, relating to coroners and coroners' inquests,"

"An act in amendment of section 20 of chapter 27 of the Public Statutes, entitled ' County Commissioners,' "

"An act in addition to and in amendment to section 10 of chapter 198 of the Public Statutes, relating to trustees of estates,"

"An act authorizing the license commissioners to license *bona fide* hotels in unorganized towns and places to sell intoxicating liquor,"

"An act relating to the printing of ballots provided for in an act entitled 'An act to regulate the traffic in intoxicating liquor,' approved March 27, 1903," reported the same without amendments and recommended their passage.

The reports were accepted and the bills severally ordered to a third reading to-morrow morning at 11 o'clock.

Senator Tolles, for the Committee on the Judiciary, to whom was referred a bill entitled "An act to amend chapter 40, Laws of 1893, relating to inspectors of buildings," reported the same with the following amendment and recommended its passage:

Amend section 2 by striking out all after the word "inspector," in the 14th line of said section, and inserting in place thereof the following: "so far as the same relates to the building rules of such city or town or the safety of such building after erected for the purpose for which it is designed. If any such inspector shall refuse to approve of any plan submitted to him as aforesaid, any person aggrieved thereby may appeal from the decision of such inspector to the superior court for the county in which such city or town is situated, either in term time or vacation, and said court shall make such orders therein as justice may require."

The report was accepted, amendment adopted, and the bill ordered to a third reading to-morrow morning at 11 o'clock.

Senator Tolles, for the Committee on the Judiciary, to whom was referred a bill entitled "An act to amend chapters 2 and 112 of the Public Statutes, and to provide for a better enforcement of the liquor laws," reported the same with the following amendment and recommended its passage:

Amend by striking out sections 9 and 10 of said act. Renumber the succeeding sections. Further amend by striking out section 16 of said bill and inserting instead thereof the following : "Nothing in this act shall be construed to in any way conflict with, limit, or restrain any part or parts of an act passed at the January session, 1903, entitled 'An act to regulate the traffic in intoxicating liquor,' and this act shall be in force after the third Tuesday of May, 1903."

The report was accepted, amendment adopted, and the bill ordered to a third reading to-morrow morning at 11 o'clock.

Senator Tolles, for the Committee on the Judiciary, to whom was referred the following entitled bills, "An act in amendment of, and in addition to, section 3, chapter 105, Laws of 1901, in relation to political caucuses and conventions,"

"An act in amendment of chapter 78 of the Laws of 1897 relating to biennial elections,"

"An act to repeal chapter 112 of the Public Statutes, relating to the sale of spirituous or intoxicating liquor and all amendments thereto," reported the same with the following resolution :

Resolved, That it is inexpedient to legislate.

The reports were accepted and the resolution adopted.

Senator Ripley, for the Committee on Finance, to whom was referred a bill entitled "An act for the representation of the state of New Hampshire and the exhibition of its products and attractions at the Louisiana Purchase Exposition in St. Louis in 1904," reported the same with the following resolution :

Resolved, That it is inexpedient to legislate.

The report was accepted and resolution adopted.

Senators Foley, Neal, Whitney, and Thompson, for the Committee on Labor, to whom was referred a bill entitled "An act in amendment of section 14, chapter 180, Public Statutes, regulating the hours of labor for women and minors in manufacturing and mercantile establishments," reported the same with the following amendment and recommended its passage :

Strike out the word "short" in the 9th line thereof and insert in place thereof the word "shorter." Insert after the 12th line thereof the following :

"III. When it is necessary to make repairs to prevent interruption of the ordinary running of the machinery."

Senator Page, a minority of the Committee on Labor, to

whom was referred a bill entitled "An act in amendment of section 14, chapter 180, Public Statutes, regulating the hours of labor for women and minors in manufacturing and mercantile establishments," reported the same with the following resolution:

Resolved, That it is inexpedient to legislate.

The reports were accepted.

Senator Page moved to substitute the minority report for that of the majority.

The question being stated,

Shall the minority report be substituted for that of the majority?

(Discussion ensued.)

The affirmative prevailed on a *viva voce* vote.

Senator Foley demanded the yeas and nays.

The clerk proceeded to call the roll.

The following named Senators voted in the affirmative:

Senators Allen, Tilton, Cooper, Felt, Fellows, Fuller, Ripley, Wilkins, Lightbody, Hoyt of District No. 21, and Page.

The following named Senators voted in the negative:

Senators Marvin, Neal, Bickford, Foley, Tolles, Thompson, and Richmond.

Fifteen Senators having voted in the affirmative and seven Senators having voted in the negative, the affirmative prevailed, and the report of the minority was substituted for that of the majority.

The question being stated,

Shall the resolution reported by the minority be adopted?

The affirmative prevailed on a *viva voce* vote.

On motion of Senator Keyes, the rules were so far suspended that all bills in order for a third reading to-morrow morning at 11 o'clock were made in order for a third reading at the present time, and on motion of the same Senator, the rules were further suspended and the following entitled bills were severally read a third time by their title and passed:

An act in addition to and in amendment to section 10 of chapter 198 of the Public Statutes, relating to trustees of estates.

An act authorizing the license commissioners to license *bona fide* hotels in unorganized towns and places to sell intoxicating liquors.

An act in amendment of section 20 of chapter 27 of the Public Statutes, entitled "County Commissioners."

An act relating to the printing of ballots provided for in an act entitled "An act to regulate the traffic in intoxicating liquor," approved March 27, 1903.

An act in amendment of chapter 262 of the Public Statutes, relating to coroners and coroners' inquests.

An act to renew an act to incorporate the Glen Junction Transfer Company, passed January session, 1897, and to amend the same.

The following entitled House bills were severally read a third time by their titles, passed, and sent to the House of Representatives for concurrence in Senate amendments:

An act to amend chapters 2 and 112 of the Public Statutes, and to provide for a better enforcement of the liquor laws.

An act to amend chapter 40, Laws of 1893, relating to inspectors of buildings.

The following joint resolution was read a third time and passed:

Joint resolution to provide for the treatment of indigent consumptives.

On motion of Senator Bickford, Joint resolution in favor of Albert T. Severance and others, was taken from the table.

The same Senator offered the following amendment:

Amend by adding after the word "house," in the 12th line of said joint resolution, the following:

"That the sum of fourteen thousand dollars ($14,000) be and hereby is appropriated for each of the years 1903 and 1904, for the maintenance and to provide water. That forty-five hundred dollars be provided for equipment, laundry, painting buildings and general repairs, and that the sum of ten thousand dollars be appropriated for a school building, the same to include two school-rooms, sewing room, manual training room, and a hall to be used for religious and other purposes, for the New Hampshire School for the Feeble-Minded Children.

" That Warren F. Langley be allowed the sum of one hundred dollars in full payment of salary for attendance as member of the House of Representatives from the opening of the session until February 18, 1903."

The question being stated,

Shall the amendment be adopted?

(Discussion ensued.)

The affirmative prevailed on a *viva voce* vote.

On motion of the same Senator, the rules were so far suspended that the joint resolution was made in order for a third reading at the present time.

The reading of the joint resolution having been commenced, on motion of the same Sentor, its further reading was dispensed with.

The joint resolution passed and was sent to the House of Representatives for concurrence in Senate amendments.

Senator Bickford moved that the message of His Excellency the Governor upon a bill entitled "An act to provide, in common with the state of Vermont, for the acquisition, building, and maintenance of the bridges across the Connecticut river," together with the bill, be taken from the table and considered.

The question being stated,

Shall the message and bill be taken from the table?

The affirmative prevailed on a *viva voce* vote.

The question being stated,

Will the Senate upon reconsideration pass the bill, notwithstanding the objections of the Governor thereto?

(Discussion ensued.)

The President ordered the yeas and nays.

The clerk proceeded to call the roll.

The following named Senators voted in the affirmative:

Senators Allen, Cooper, Marvin, Neal, and Page.

The following named Senators voted in the negative:

Senator Keyes, Whitney, Lewando, Burnell, Tilton, Felt, Fellows, Fuller, Ripley, Wilkins, Lightbody, Bickford, Foley, Tolles, Hoyt of District No. 21, Thompson, and Richmond.

Five senators having voted in the affirmative, and seventeen Senators having voted in the negative, the negative prevailed, and the Senate refused to pass the bill, notwithstanding the objections of the Governor thereto.

Senator Thompson, under a suspension of the rules, sixteen Senators having actually voted in favor thereof, introduced a Joint resolution in favor of the owners of farm animals killed by order of the United States Department of Agriculture to stamp out the foot and mouth disease.

The joint resolution was read a first and second time, and on motion of the same Senator, the rules were so far suspended that the joint resolution was read a third time, passed, and sent to the House of Representatives for concurrence.

Senator Lightbody, for the Committee on Banks, to whom was referred a bill entitled "An act providing for the taxation of building and loan associations," reported the same without amendment and recommended its passage.

The report was accepted and on motion of the same Senator, the rules were so far suspended that the bill was made in order for a third reading at the present time, and on motion of the same Senator, the rules were further suspended and the bill was read a third time by its title.

The question being stated,

Shall the bill pass?

(Discussion ensued.)

The affirmative prevailed on a *viva voce* vote.

The following message was received from the House of Representatives by its clerk:

HOUSE MESSAGE.

Mr. President:

The House of Representatives concurs with the Honorable Senate in the passage of the following entitled bills sent down from the Honorable Senate:

An act in amendment of section 3 of chapter 7 of the Public Statutes, relating to the state house and yard.

An act in amendment of section 2 of chapter 32 of the Laws

of 1895, entitled "An act in relation to printing the reports of certain state officers."

Joint resolution appropriating money for screening the outlet of Lake Sunapee, so called.

An act to amend section 16 of chapter 79 of the Session Laws of 1901, relating to the taking of deer.

The House of Representatives refuses to concur with the Honorable Senate in the passage of the following entitled bill sent down from the Honorable Senate:

An act in amendment of an act entitled "An act for the enlargement and extension of water-works for the city of Portsmouth," approved March 10, 1899.

On motion of Senator Whitney, the Senate adjourned.

THURSDAY, APRIL 2, 1903.

The Senate met according to adjournment.

The reading of the journal having been commenced, on motion of Senator Fuller, the rules were so far suspended that its further reading was dispensed with.

Senator Tolles, for the Committee on the Judiciary, to whom was referred the following entitled bills:

"An act to incorporate The New Hampshire Beneficiary Union,"

."An act to provide for a revision of the general and public laws," reported the same with the following resolution:

Resolved, That it is inexpedient to legislate.

The reports were accepted and resolution adopted.

Senators Page, Tolles, and Allen, for the Committee on the Judiciary, to whom was referred a bill entitled "An act in amendment of section 19, chapter 57 of the Public Statutes, relating to the annual invoice of polls and taxable property," reported the same without amendment and recommended its passage.

Senators Bickford and Ripley, a minority of the Committee on the Judiciary, to whom was referred a bill entitled "An act in amendment of section 19, chapter 57 of the Public Statutes, relating to the annual invoice of polls and taxable property," reported the same with the following resolution :

Resolved, That it is inexpedient to legislate.

The reports were accepted.

Senator Bickford moved that the minority report be substituted for that of the majority.

The question being stated,

Shall the minority report be substituted for that of the majority?

(Discussion ensued.)

The affirmative prevailed on a *viva voce* vote.

The question being stated,

Shall the resolution reported by the minority be adopted ?

The affirmative prevailed on a *viva voce* vote.

Senator Thompson, for the Committee on Public Improvements, to whom was referred " Joint resolution relating to the repairs upon the state house," reported the same without amendment and recommended its passage.

The report was accepted.

On motion of the same Senator, the rules were so far suspended that the joint resolution was read a third time and passed.

Senators Bickford, Tolles, and Ripley, for the Committee on the Judiciary, to whom was referred a bill entitled "An act providing for the appointment of guardians for minors in certain cases," reported the same with the following amendment and recommended its passage.

Amend section 1 by striking out all after the word " commissioners " in the seventh line down to the word "such " in the eighth line.

Further amend by striking out section 2 and renumbering the following sections.

Amend section 2 as renumbered by striking out all after the word " repute " in the eighth line of said section.

Amend section 3 as renumbered by adding after the word " reasonable" in the eighth line of said section the words " subject to appeal, and no bond shall be required in any appeal under the provisions of this act."

Senators Page and Allen, a minority of the Committee on the Judiciary, to whom was referred a bill entitled "An act to provide for the appointment of guardians for minors in certain cases," reported the same without amendment and recommended its passage.

The reports were accepted.

Senator Page moved that the minority report be substituted for that of the majority.

(Discussion ensued.)

The affirmative prevailed on a *viva voce* vote.

Senator Tolles moved that the bill be indefinitely postponed.

The question being stated,

Shall the bill be indefinitely postponed?

The negative prevailed on a *viva voce* vote.

The question being stated,

Shall the bill be read a third time?

On motion of Senator Thompson, the rules were so far suspended that the bill was read a third time by its title and passed.

Senator Page offered the following resolution which was unanimously adopted by a rising vote:

WHEREAS, Our associate, the Honorable Senator from District No. 10, the Honorable Ferdinand A. Stillings, has by reason of serious illness been prevented from occupying his seat in this chamber for several weeks, and to-day, contrary to our expectations and greatly to our regret, we learn that he will be unable to join with us in the closing hours of the session, therefore

Resolved, That we tender to our associate our heartfelt sympathy in this his unfortunate affliction and his enforced detention from his business and our midst, and we earnestly hope that he will speedily be restored to health and to his friends.

Resolved, That these resolutions be entered upon the journal of the Senate and an attested copy thereof be sent to the Honorable Senator by the clerk.

The following message was received from the House of Representatives by its clerk:

HOUSE MESSAGE.

Mr. President:

The House of Representatives concurs with the Honorable Senate in the passage of the following entitled bills and joint resolution :

Joint resolution in favor of the owners of farm animals killed by order of the United States Department of Agriculture to stamp out the foot and mouth disease.

"An act establishing the office of medical referee, and amending chapter 262 of the Public Statutes, relating to coroners' inquests."

"An act in relation to the powers and duties of police commissioners of the city of Manchester."

The House of Representatives has voted to concur with the Honorable Senate in its amendments to the following entitled bills and joint resolution :

An act to amend chapters 2 and 112 of the Public Statutes, and to provide for a better enforcement of the liquor laws.

An act to amend chapter 40, Laws of 1893, relating to the inspectors of buildings.

"An act in amendment of section 1, chapter 85, Laws of 1901, entitled "An act authorizing the Hillsborough county convention to raise money for the building and repairing of court houses."

Joint resolution in favor of Albert T. Severance and others.

Senator Whitney, for a majority of the Committee on Public Improvements, to whom was referred a bill entitled "An act enabling the city of Manchester to build and operate an electric lighting plant for the purpose of lighting its streets and public buildings," reported the same with the following resolution :

Resolved, That it is inexpedient to legislate.

Senator Thompson, for a minority of the Committee on Public Improvements, to whom was referred a bill entitled "An act enabling the city of Manchester to build and operate an electric lighting plant for the purpose of lighting its streets and public buildings," reported the same without amendment and recommended its passage.

18

The reports were accepted.

Senator Thompson moved that the minority report be substituted for that of the majority.

The question being stated,

Shall the minority report be substituted for that of the majority?

The negative prevailed on a *viva voce* vote.

Senator Thompson demanded the yeas and nays.

The clerk proceeded to call the roll.

The following named Senators voted in the affirmative:

Senators Foley and Thompson.

The following named Senators voted in the negative:

Senators Allen, Keyes, Whitney, Lewando, Tilton, Cooper, Marvin, Felt, Fellows, Neal, Fuller, Ripley, Wilkins, Lightbody, Bickford, Tolles, Hoyt of District No. 21, Richmond, and Page.

Two Senators having voted in the affirmative and nineteen Senators having voted in the negative, the negative prevailed, and the minority report was not substituted for that of the majority.

The question being stated,

Shall the resolution reported by the majority, that it is inexpedient to legislate, be adopted?

The affirmative prevailed on a *viva voce* vote.

(Senator Tolles in the chair.)

The following message was received from the House of Representatives by its clerk:

HOUSE MESSAGE.

Mr. President:

The House of Representatives has adopted the following concurrent resolution, in the passage of which it asks the concurrence of the Honorable Senate:

Resolved, By the House of Representatives, the Senate concurring, that a committee, consisting of one from each county, be appointed by the House, with such as the Senate may join, to wait upon His Excellency the Governor, and inform him that the legislature has completed the business of the session and is ready to receive any communication he may be pleased to make. The Speaker has appointed as members of such committee on the part of the House Messrs. Small, White, Hoitt, Dow, Emerson, Jones, Dickerson, Matthews, Merrill, and Hicks.

On motion of Senator Page, the Senate concurred in the foregoing concurrent resolution sent up from the House of Representatives.

The President appointed as members of such committee on the part of the Senate, Senators Page, Tilton, and Marvin.

The following report from the Committee on Engrossed Bills was read and accepted:

The Committee on Engrossed Bills have examined, and found correctly engrossed, the following entitled bills and joint resolutions:

Joint resolution in favor of the owners of farm animals killed by order of the United States Department of Agriculture to stamp out the foot and mouth disease.

An act in relation to the powers and duties of police commissioners of the city of Manchester.

Joint resolution relating to repairs upon the state house.

An act providing for the appointment of guardians for minors in certain cases.

An act in amendment of section 1, chapter 185, Laws of 1901, entitled "An act authorizing the Hillsborough county convention to raise money for the building and repairing of court houses."

An act establishing the office of medical referee, and amending chapter 262 of the Public Statutes, relating to coroners' inquests.

Joint resolution in favor of Albert T. Severance and others.

An act to amend chapter 40, Laws of 1893, relating to inspectors of buildings.

An act to amend chapters 2 and 112 of the Public Statutes, and to provide for the better enforcement of the liquor laws.

Joint resolution appropriating five hundred dollars for a monument to be erected at Hackensack, New Jersey, in memory of Gen. Enoch Poor.

Joint resolution in favor of Ella F. Densmore of Charlestown, Mary F. Lombard of Acworth, Frank G. Smith of Waltham, Massachusetts, Eugene P. Smith of Newport, and George E. Shattuck of Hinsdale.

Joint resolution appropriating money to be expended for the preservation of the muster rolls.

An act to amend section 14 and section 15, chapter 286 of the Public Statutes, relating to the salaries of the judge and register of probate for Belknap county.

An act providing for a state system of highway construction and improvement, and for the appointment of highway engineers.

Joint resolution in favor of John K. Law and others.

An act in addition to and in amendment to section 10 of chapter 198 of the Public Statutes, relating to trustees of estates.

An act providing for the taxation of building and loan associations.

An act in amendment of chapter 262 of the Public Statutes, relating to coroners and coroners' inquests.

An act in amendment of section 20 of chapter 27 of the Public Statutes, entitled "County Commissioners."

Joint resolution to provide for the treatment of indigent consumptives.

An act relating to the printing of ballots provided for in an act entitled "An act to regulate the traffic in intoxicating liquor," approved March 27, 1903.

An act to renew an "Act to incorporate the Glen Junction Transfer Company," passed January session, 1897, and to amend the same.

An act authorizing the license commissioners to license *bona fide* hotels in unorganized towns and places to sell intoxicating liquor.

An act to revive, amend, and extend the charter of the Alton and Gilmanton Electric Railway Company.

An act to revive, amend, and extend the charter of the Gilmanton and Barnstead Electric Railway Company.

An act to amend chapter 96 of the Session Laws of 1901, relating to high schools.

An act in amendment of chapter 98 of the Laws of 1901, relating to the duties of tree wardens.

An act to amend chapter 184 of the Laws of 1897, entitled "An act to incorporate the Dalton Power Company," as amended by section 1, chapter 221 of the Laws of 1899.

An act amending sections 37, 38, and 40 of chapter 59 of the Session Laws of 1895, as amended by chapter 25 of the Laws of 1901, in relation to the militia.

An act in amendment of section 1 of chapter 67 of the Laws of 1899, relating to expenses of judges of the supreme court.

An act in amendment of section 14, chapter 79, Session Laws of 1901, relating to the powers of the fish and game commissioners.

An act to authorize the town of Gilmanton to exempt certain property from taxation.

An act in relation to the salary of the judge of probate for the county of Grafton.

An act relating to the salary of the judge of probate of the county of Sullivan.

An act in amendment of section 2 of chapter 5 of the Public Statutes, relating to the publication and distribution of statutes, journals, and reports.

An act in amendment of section 79 of chapter 79 of the Laws of 1901, in regard to lobster traps.

An act to establish a new apportionment for the assessment of public taxes.

An act in amendment of chapter 64, Laws of 1899, relating to firemen's relief fund.

An act to legalize and confirm the school board's warrant for and the votes and proceedings thereunder at the annual school district meeting in the town of Newfields, held in said town on the fourteenth day of March, 1903.

An act for the relief of the town of Newcastle.

An act in amendment of section 2 of chapter 32 of the Laws of 1895, entitled "An act in relation to printing the reports of certain state officers.

An act in amendment of section 3 of chapter 7 of the Public Statutes, relating to "the state house and yard."

An act in amendment of chapter 134 of the Public Statutes, relating to the practice of dentistry.

An act in amendment of section 5, chapter 278 of the Public Statutes, as amended by section 1, chapter 24, Laws of 1899, relating to homicide and offenses against the person.

An act to exempt from local taxation the hotel property that may be erected in the village of North Stratford in the town of Stratford.

An act to define the duties of the state treasurer with reference to public funds.

An act in amendment of section 1 of chapter 83 of the Public Statutes, entitled "Settlement of Paupers."

An act in amendment of section 7 of chapter 59 of the Public Statutes, and section 13 of chapter 60 of the Public Statutes, relating to the assessment and collection of taxes.

An act in amendment of section 7, chapter 63 of the Laws of 1897, entitled "An act to regulate the licensing and registration of physicians and surgeons."

An act to amend section 16 of chapter 79 of the Session Laws of 1901, relating to the taking of deer.

An act to incorporate the Sandwich Electric Railway Company.

An act to encourage the planting and perpetuation of forests.

An act relating to the use of trade marks and names.

An act in relation to the Lisbon village district.

Joint resolution appropriating money for screening the outlet of Sunapee lake, so called.

HENRY W. KEYES,
A. W. BURNELL,
Committee.

On motion of Senator Page, the Senate voted to take recess subject to the call of the President.

(Recess.)

The Senate reassembled.

(The President in the chair.)

By concurrent resolution previously adopted by the Senate

and the House of Representatives that all reports, bills, and joint resolutions pending in either branch of the legislature on Thursday, the 2d day of April, at 12 o'clock noon, be indefinitely postponed, the following entitled bills were indefinitely postponed:

SENATE BILL.

An act in amendment of section 14 of chapter 180 of the Public Statutes, relating to hours of labor of women and minors under the age of 18 years in manufacturing or mercantile establishments.

HOUSE BILL.

An act in amendment of section 23 of chapter 79 of the Laws of 1901, in relation to fines.

The following message was received from the House of Representatives:

HOUSE MESSAGE.

Mr. President:

By concurrent resolution previously adopted by the Senate and House of Representatives that all reports, bills, and joint resolutions pending in either branch of the legislature on Thursday, the 2d of April, at 12 o'clock noon, be indefinitely postponed, the following entitled bills sent down from the Honorable Senate were indefinitely postponed:

An act to provide for a more economical and practical expenditure of the money appropriated by the state for the construction and repairs of highways.

An act in amendment of section 29, chapter 266 of the Public Statutes, relating to trespasses and malicious injuries.

An act in amendment of sections 6 and 7 of chapter 270 of the Public Statutes, relating to lotteries, gambling, and wagers.

An act in amendment of section 4, chapter 37 of the Session Laws of 1895, entitled " An act providing for the appointment of bail commissioners for cities and towns."

An act to incorporate the First Congregational Church of Wolfeborough, N. H.

An act for the relief of the town of New Castle.

An act to incorporate the Evangelical Church of Plaistow, N. H., and the North Parish of Haverhill, Mass.

Senator Page, for the joint select committee appointed to wait upon His Excellency the Governor and inform him that the legislature had completed the business of the session, and was ready to receive any communication that he might be pleased to make, reported that they had attended to their duty and had been informed by His Excellency that he would in person make a communication to the legislature forthwith.

His Excellency Honorable Nahum J. Bachelder, attended by the Honorable Council, then appeared and made the following communication to the Senate:

THE STATE OF NEW HAMPSHIRE.
EXECUTIVE DEPARTMENT.

CONCORD, April 2, 1903.

To the Honorable Senate and House of Representatives:

I have signed or returned to the body in which they originated all the bills and joint resolutions submitted for my approval.

Having been informed by a joint committee of the Senate and House of Representatives that you have completed the business of the session and are ready to adjourn, I do, by the authority vested in the executive, hereby adjourn the legislature to the last Wednesday of December, in the year of our Lord one thousand nine hundred and four.

NAHUM J. BACHELDER,
Governor.

And thereupon, the President, in accordance with the proclamation of His Excellency the Governor, and by virtue of the authority vested in him, declared the Senate adjourned to the last Wednesday in December, in the year of our Lord one thousand nine hundred and four.

THOMAS F. CLIFFORD,
Clerk.

A true copy—Attest:

THOMAS F. CLIFFORD,
Clerk.

JOURNAL

OF THE

HOUSE OF REPRESENTATIVES

JANUARY SESSION, 1903.

JOURNAL

OF THE

HOUSE OF REPRESENTATIVES

JANUARY SESSION. 1903.

WEDNESDAY, JANUARY 7, 1903.

On the first Wednesday in January, in the year of our Lord one thousand nine hundred and three, being the day designated by the constitution for the assembling of that body, the one hundred and eighth General Court of the state of New Hampshire convened at the capitol in the city of Concord, and the Representatives-elect, having assembled in the hall of the House of Representatives, were called to order by Henry E. Brock, clerk of the House for the preceding session.

The clerk proceeded to call the roll and, three hundred and eighty-six members answering to their names, a quorum was declared present.

On motion of Mr. French of Moultonborough,—

Resolved, That a committee of two be appointed by the clerk to wait upon His Excellency the Governor, and inform him that a quorum of the House is assembled and requests his attendance.

The clerk appointed Messrs. French of Moultonborough and Small of Rochester as such committee.

His Excellency the Governor, having been informed that a quorum of the House was assembled, appeared, attended by the Honorable Council, and the following-named gentlemen, having presented their credentials, were duly qualified by His Excellency as members of the House of Representatives, by taking and subscribing to the oaths of office, agreeably to the provisions of the constitution :

ROCKINGHAM COUNTY.

Atkinson . . .	George A. Sawyer.
Auburn . . .	Albert E. Preston.
Brentwood . . .	D. Frank Fellows.
Candia	Edward E. Hubbard.
Chester	Augustus P. Morse.
Danville . . .	Mahlon B. Darbe.
Deerfield . . .	Woodbury R. White.
Derry	John P. Hardy.
	Greenleaf K. Bartlett.
	Albert E. Shute.
Epping	Joseph A. Edgerly.
Exeter	Edward E. Nowell.
	John Scammon.
	Albert T. Severance.
	Leonard F. Smith.
Fremont . . .	Andrew J. Brown.
Greenland . . .	Lorenzo D. Duntley.
Hampstead . . .	William A. Emerson.
Hampton . . .	William E. Lane.
Hampton Falls . .	James H. Brown.
Kingston . . .	George F. Quimby.
Londonderry . . .	William H. Crowell.
Newcastle . . .	James W. Pridham.
Newfields . . .	George L. Chase.
Newington . . .	Daniel W. Badger.
Newmarket . . .	Harry W. Haines.
	John E. Kent.
Newton . . .	Ezra N. George.
North Hampton . .	John W. Warner.
Northwood . . .	James A. Bickford.
Nottingham . . .	Edward F. Gerrish.
Plaistow . . .	John W. Sleeper.

Portsmouth—
 Ward 1 .   .   .   Henry P. Payne.
      .   Eben H. Blaisdell.
 Ward 2 .   .   .   Morris C. Foye.
          Howard O. Nelson.
      .   Harry B. Yeaton.
 Ward 3 .   .   .   William Cogan.
          Albert H. Adams.
 Ward 4 .   .   :   Sherman T. Newton.
 Ward 5 .   .   .   Jeremiah J. Couhig.
Raymond   .   .   .   Plummer B. Corson.
Rye   .   .   . ·   .   George H. Brown.
Salem   .   .   .   .   Daniel A. Abbott.
          Howard L. Gordon.
Sandown   .   .   .   Charles H. Young.
Seabrook   .   .   .   George C. Dow.
South Hampton   .   .   Frank B. Swain.
Stratham   .   :   .   Emmons B. Chase.
Windham   .   .   .   John E. Cochran.

STRAFFORD COUNTY.

Barrington   .   .   .   Frank L. Howe.
Dover—
 Ward 1 .   .   .   George Fred Mathes.
          Alvah T. Ramsdell.
 Ward 2 .   .   .   Frank M. Libby.
          John W. Jewell.
          William F. Nason.
 Ward 3 .   .   .   Arthur G. Whittemore.*
          Charles C. Bunce.
 Ward 4 .   .   .   Edward D. Smith.
          George D. Barrett.
          Frank L. Hayes.
 Ward 5 .   .   .   John H. Wesley.
Durham   .   .   .   Charles S. Langley.
Farmington   .   .   .   Charles F. York.
          John Tuttle.
Lee   .   ı   .   .   Ben F. Davis.
Madbury   .   .   .   Martin V. B. Felker.

Middleton	. . .	William B. Place.*
Milton .	. . .	John E. Townsend.
New Durham	. .	George H. Jones.
Rochester—		
Ward 1	. .	Joel W. McCrillis.
Ward 2	. .	Fred W. Crocker.
Ward 3	. .	Joseph Warren.
Ward 4	. .	Frederic E. Small.
		Simeon Bergeron.
Ward 5 .	. .	Horace L. Worcester.
Ward 6 .	. .	Albert Wallace.
Rollinsford	. . .	Michael B. Harrity.
Somersworth—		
Ward 1 .	. .	Burton Etter.
Ward 2 .	. .	Fred Wentworth.
Ward 3 .	. .	Pierre P. Demers.
Ward 4 .	. .	Dennis J. Murnane.
		Napoleon Boutin.
Ward 5 .	. .	Elisha C. Andrews.
Strafford	. . .	Victor L. Caverly.

BELKNAP COUNTY.

Alton	. . .	Charles L. Pinkham.
Barnstead	. .	Thomas L. Hoitt.
Belmont	. .	John M. Sargent.
Centre Harbor	. .	Edgar W. Smith.
Gilford .	. . .	Fred J. Potter.
Gilmanton	. .	Elbridge G. Clough.
Laconia—		
Ward 1 .	. .	Albert H. Davis.
		George E. Hull.
Ward 2 .	. .	Cleophas L. Fecteau.
		Wilber L. Prescott.
Ward 3 .	. .	Harry S. Chase.
Ward 4 .	. .	Frank A. Edwards.
		Charles L. Kimball.
Meredith	. .	Edmund Quimby.
New Hampton	. .	Frank P. Morrill.
Sanbornton .	. .	Otis S. Sanborn

Tilton . . . . George B. Rogers.
Frank L. Mason.

CARROLL COUNTY.

Albany . . . Horatio Littlefield.
Bartlett . . . Edgar A. Stevens.
Chatham . . . Dana A. Weeks.
Conway . . . Holmes B. Fifield.
Hiram H. Dow.
Walter R. Burnell.
Effingham . . . Seth J. Philbrick.
Freedom . . . Orren E. Drake.
Jackson . . . George P. Trickey.
Madison . . . Roscoe G. Greene.
Moultonborough . . James E. French.
Ossipee . . . Almon F. Abbott.
Sandwich . . . Charles B. Hoyt.
Tamworth . . . Albert S. Pollard.
Tuftonborough . . John A. Edgerly.
Wakefield . . . Simon Blake.
Wolfeborough . . John H. Beacham.
William J. Britton.

MERRIMACK COUNTY.

Allenstown . . . Henri T. Fontaine.*
Andover . . . Wilton P. Graves.
Boscawen . . . Almon G. Harris.
Bow . . . . David W. White.
Bradford . . . Harlan P. Morse.
Canterbury . . . John A. Beck.
Chichester . . . Charles A. Langmaid.
Concord—
Ward 1 . . . Eddie C. Durgin.
Joseph E. Symonds.
Ward 2 . . . Ross W. Cate.
Ward 3 . . . Joseph E. Shepard.
Ward 4 . . . James K. Kennedy.
Eben M. Willis.
Samuel J. Matson.

Concord—
 Ward 5 .   .   .   Almon W. Hill.
          Harley B. Roby.
 Ward 6 .   .   .   Frederic T. Woodman.
          Howard A. Kimball.
          Warren E. Emerson.
 Ward 7 .   .   .   Albert P. Davis.
          William W. Critchett.
          Horace O. Mathews.
 Ward 8 .   .   .   Edson J. Hill.
 Ward 9 .   .   .   William J. Ahern.
          James J. Donagan.
Danbury   .   .   .   Roy Litchfield.
Dunbarton   .   .   .   John Bunten.
Epsom   .   .   .   Walter H. Tripp.
Franklin—
 Ward 1 .   .   .   Lewis W. Phillips.
 Ward 2 .   .   .   Hector Morin.
          Seth W. Jones.
 Ward 3 .   .   .   Charles W. Adams.
          Curtis A. Davis.
Henniker   .   .   .   Arthur G. Preston.
Hill   .   .   .   George W. Twombly.
Hooksett   .   .   .   Spurzhie E. Worthley.
Hopkinton   .   .   .   Daniel F. Fisk.
Loudon   .   .   .   John B. Sanborn.
New London   .   .   Edwin F. Messer.
Northfield   .   .   .   Oscar P. Sanborn.
Pembroke   .   .   .   John G. Tallant.
          Levi L. Aldrich.
          Warren D. Foss.
Pittsfield   .   .   .   Frank D. Hutchins.
          John A. Walker, Jr.
Salisbury   .   .   .   Thomas R. Little.
Sutton   .   .   .   Herbert L. Pillsbury.
Warner   .   .   .   Mason T. Ela.
Webster   .   .   .   Irvin A. Burbank.
Wilmot   .   .   .   Warren F. Langley.*

HILLSBOROUGH COUNTY.

Amherst . . .	George E. Farley.
Antrim . . .	John N. P. Woodbury.
Bedford . . .	Ira Barr.
Bennington . . .	Frank B. Gould.
Brookline . . .	Linville M. Shattuck.
Deering . . .	James S. Craine.
Francestown . . .	Daniel B. Tobie.
Goffstown . . .	George Pattee.
	George L. Eaton.
Greenfield . . .	George H. Putnam.
Greenville . . .	Robert Brown, Jr.
Hancock . . .	Clarence H. Ware.
Hillsborough . .	Henry P. Whitaker.
	Walter J. A. Ward.
Hollis	Elbridge J. Farley.
Hudson . . .	Philip J. Connell.
Litchfield . . .	Isaac N. Center.
Lyndeborough . .	Andy Holt.
Manchester—	
Ward 1 . . .	John B. Cavanaugh.
	Olof P. Nyberg.
	Joseph W. Abbott.
Ward 2 . .	Robert R. Chase.
	John J. Donahue.
	Kirk C. Bartlett.
	James G. Taggart.
	John A. Sheehan.
Ward 3 . . .	Arthur S. Bunton.
	Frank E. Farrell.
	Victor C. Johnson.
	Joseph W. D. McDonald.
	Walter H. Wright.
	Amos G. Straw.*
Ward 4 . . .	Albert T. Barr.
	William H. Morgan.
	Amede Dubuc.
	Fred C. Darrah.

Manchester—

Ward 4 . . .	Orrin D. Carpenter.
	Patrick J. Stewart.
Ward 5 . . .	James F. Tonery.
	John J. Ryan.
	Michael J. Trinity.
	Martin J. Whalen.
	George P. Riordan.
	Martin E. Sullivan.
	John J. Shaughnessey.
	Nicholas Sasseville.
Ward 6 . . .	Horace Marshall.
	Almus W. Morse.
	Samuel Couch.
	Andrew B. Bunton.
Ward 7 . . .	Hanson R. Armstrong.
Ward 8 . . .	Gottlieb Graf.
	George Ed. Quimby.
	Dennis F. Scannell.
	Edwin L. Tinkham.
	Arthur W. Dinsmore.
Ward 9 . . .	Louis A. Dozois.
	August Filion.
	Peter Gunderman.
	Henry I. Lemay.
	Omer Janelle.
	Hugh F. Lynch.
	Thomas F. Kohler.
Ward 10 . .	John A. Kane.
	Frank P. Newman.
	William E. Simpson.
	Frank A. Emerson
Mason	Benjamin F. March.
Merrimack . . .	James C. F. Hodgman.
Milford . . .	Frederick W. Sawyer.
	William N. Robinson.
	George H. Needham.
Mont Vernon . .	William H. Kendall.

Nashua—

Ward 1 . . .	Fred C. Lund.
	Andrew J. Tuck.
Ward 2 . . .	Eugene W. Duncklee.
	Frank T. Lewis.
Ward 3 . . .	John P. Lampron.
	Michael H. Buckley.
	Thomas E. Ingham.
Ward 4 . . .	Charles S. Bussell.
Ward 5 . . .	Timothy P. Shea.
Ward 6 . . .	Charles M. Spalding.
Ward 7 . . .	Charles H. Morse.
	Herbert C. Lintott.
	Enoch Shenton.
Ward 8 . . .	Charles S. Collins.
	George P. Hills.
	John T. Sullivan.
Ward 9 . . .	John M. Earley.
	James H. Moran.
	Joseph A. Desmarais.
	Fereol Dionne.
New Boston . . .	James N. McLane.
New Ipswich . .	Frederick W. Jones.
Pelham	William H. Peabody.
Peterborough . .	Arthur H. Miller.*
	Ezra M. Smith.
Sharon	John F. Fitzgerald.
Temple . . .	DeWitt C. Bragdon.
Weare	Horace O. Chase.
Wilton	Samuel J. Sheldon.

CHESHIRE COUNTY.

Alstead . . .	George H. P. Ware.
Chesterfield . . .	Fred J. Harris.
Dublin	Clifford Gowing.
Fitzwilliam . . .	Henry C. Tenney.
Gilsum	Robert Polzer.
Harrisville . . .	Bernard F. Bemis.
Hinsdale . . .	Frank H. Fuller.
	Henry C. Holland.

Jaffrey . . . . Myron S. Cutler.
Clark M. Pierce.
Keene—
Ward 1 . . . William E. Maloney.
Milan F. Jones.
Ward 2 . . . Herbert E. Fay.
Warren B. Fitch.*
Ward 3 . . . Alfred T. Batchelder.
George E. Whitney.
Ward 4 . . . Windsor H. Goodnow.
Ward 5 . . . John J. Donovan.
Marlborough . . . Cyrus S. Moors.
Marlow . . . . Perley E. Fox.
Nelson . . . . Fred A. Scott.
Richmond . . . Frank Amidon.
Rindge . . . . Henry W. Fletcher.
Stoddard . . . Charles H. Merrill.
Swanzey . . . Chester L Lane.
Troy . . . . William J. Boyden.
Walpole . . . Ira W. Ramsay.
George E. Sherman.
Westmoreland . . Forrest W. Hall.
Winchester . . . Franklin P. Kellom.
La Fell Dickinson.

SULLIVAN COUNTY.

Acworth . . . Henry A. Clark.
Charlestown . . . Frank W. Hamlin.
Claremont . . . Hiram G. Sherman.
Charles H. Long.
John W. Jewett.
Frank P. Huntley.
Ira F. Chandler.
Cornish . . . Winston Churchill.
Grantham . . . Harry G. Walker.
Langdon . . . Charles M. Lufkin.
Newport . . . Frederick W. Aiken.
Charles H. Matthews.
William F. Richards.

Plainfield	.	.	.	Frank W. True.
Springfield	.	.	.	Elwin F. Philbrick.
Sunapee	.	.	.	Charles L. Russell.
Unity	.	.	.	French J. Straw.
Washington	.	.	.	Sumner N. Ball.

GRAFTON COUNTY.

Alexandria	.	.	.	Alvertus N. McMurphey.
Ashland	.	.	.	John H. Morrill.
Bath	.	.	.	George E. Davenport.
Bethlehem	.	.	.	John Pierce, Jr.
Bristol	.	.	.	David M. Calley.
Campton	.	.	.	Jason C. Little.
Canaan	.	.	.	Horatio B. Gates.
Enfield	.	.	.	Walter S. Dorothy.
				Edwin F. Foster.
Franconia	.	.	.	Ivory H. Glover.
Grafton	.	.	.	George B. Kimball.
Hanover	.	.	.	Albert Pinneo.
				Hamilton T. Howe.
Haverhill	.	.	.	William F. Whitcher.
				Daniel E. Carr.
				Edwin Bertram Pike.
Hebron	.	.	.	George B. Barnard.
Holderness	.	.	.	John H. Evans, Jr.
Lebanon	.	.	.	Harry M. Cheney.
				John Goold.
				John B. Pike.
				Charles B. Comings.
Lincoln	.	.	.	James E. Henry.
Lisbon	.	.	.	Edgar O. Crossman.
				William J. B. Stanley.
Littleton	.	.	.	Daniel C. Remich.
				William H. Mitchell.
				William H. Blake.
Lyme	.	.	.	Sidney A. Converse.
Monroe	.	.	.	Oscar Frazer.
Orange	.	.	.	James F. King.
Orford	.	.	.	Ezra C. Chase.

Piermont	. . .	Edwin R. Celley.
Plymouth	. . .	Charles J. Gould.
		Moses A. Ferrin.
Rumney	. . .	Ai S. Russell.
Thornton	. . .	Frank L. Houston.
Warren	. . .	William P. Goodrich.
Wentworth	. . .	Hiram M. Bowen.
Woodstock	. . .	Ernest L. Bell.

COÖS COUNTY.

Berlin—		
Ward 1	.	George Caird.
		John Stewart.
		Patrick J. Smyth.
Ward 2	. . .	Herbert I. Goss.
		Joseph A. Vaillancourt.
		George E. Kent.
Ward 3	. . .	George E. Hutchins.
		Evan A. Notterstead.
Carroll	. . . .	Stephen F. Gallagher.
Clarksville	. . .	James C. Gathercole.
Colebrook	. . .	Elisha P. Hicks.
		George W. Martin.
Columbia	. . .	Charles S. Jordan.
Dalton	. . . .	Frank B. Tillotson.
Dummer	. . .	James G. Hamlin.
Errol	. . . .	William A. Bragg.
Gorham	. . .	Jesse F. Libby.
Jefferson	. . .	Philip C. Plaisted.
Lancaster	. . .	Ezra Mitchell.
		William P. Buckley.
		Thomas S. Ellis.
Milan	. . . .	Almon A. Trafton.
Northumberland	. .	Fred W. McDonald.
		Frank N. Piper.
Pittsburg	. . .	William A. Smith.
Shelburne	. . .	John C. Wilson.
Stark	. . . .	Patrick J. O'Connor.
Stewartstown	. .	Martin R. Harriman.

Stratford	.	.	.	Henry E. Lennon.
Whitefield	.	.	.	George W. Darling.
				Bernard A. Babcock.

The clerk then called the House to order and stated that the first business before the House was the election of a temporary presiding officer.

On motion of Mr. Whitcher of Haverhill, William F. Nason of Dover was elected temporary presiding officer, and was escorted to the chair by a committee of two, appointed by the clerk, consisting of Messrs. Whitcher of Haverhill and Mathes of Dover.

On motion of Mr. Sawyer of Milford, the House proceeded to the election of a Speaker by ballot. The temporary presiding officer appointed Messrs. Barrett of Dover and Ahern of Concord as a committee to receive, sort, and count the votes. Mr. Ahern, for the committee, reported the following result of the ballot:

Whole number of votes cast	.	.	.	381
Necessary for a choice	.	.	.	192
Frederic E. Small had	.	.	.	128
Harry M. Cheney had	.	.	.	253

and Harry M. Cheney, having a majority of all the votes cast, was declared duly elected Speaker.

The Speaker was conducted to the chair by a committee of three, appointed by the temporary presiding officer, consisting of Messrs. Mitchell of Littleton, Small of Rochester, and French of Moultonborough, and addressed the House as follows:

Gentlemen of the House:

To be elected Speaker of the popular branch of the General Court of our state is a compliment most highly appreciated by every man called to the position. I assure you that I deem my election to be an honor of such great degree that I am unable to give adequate expression to my feelings of grati-

---

*Those marked with an asterisk were not present. Mr. Straw of Manchester appeared and qualified January 8. Messrs. Place of Middleton and Whittemore of Dover appeared and qualified January 13. Mr. Fontaine of Allenstown appeared and qualified January 20. Messrs. Miller of Peterborough, Fitch of Keene, and Langley of Wilmot, were delayed by sickness and appeared and qualified later. (See Index.)

tude for the favor conferred. I can only speak to you the very common words, " I thank you," accompanied by my assurance that, though common, the words are intended to include every imaginable expression of genuine appreciation. I trust that I comprehend the dignity and the responsibility of the position, and frankly confess the doubting of my ability to approximate the requirements of the Chair.

I assume its duties free from every obligation save that of serving New Hampshire, as duty and conscience oblige us all. I acknowledge it to be my duty to enforce and execute your expressed wishes, and in so far as I may attempt to perform the duties of the office in that spirit, your good will and support is due me. I do not permit myself to doubt that it will be given. Remembering that we have mutual obligations, let us do in a manly fashion whatever is expected of us, and conclude the business of the session as speedily as possible. I await the pleasure of the House.

On motion of Mr. Ahern of Concord,—

Resolved, That the Speaker be authorized to cast one ballot for James M. Cooper of Concord, for clerk, and one ballot for Harrie M. Young of Manchester, for assistant clerk, of the House of Representatives for the ensuing two years.

The vote was so cast, and James M. Cooper and Harrie M. Young were declared duly elected clerk and assistant clerk, respectively, for the ensuing two years.

James M. Cooper and Harrie M. Young then appeared and were duly qualified by taking the oath as clerk and assistant clerk respectively.

HENRY E. BROCK,
Clerk for 1901–1903.

On motion of Mr. Small of Rochester,—

Resolved, That the Speaker be authorized to cast one ballot for John K. Law of New London, for sergeant-at-arms, and one ballot for Warren W. Lovejoy of Littleton, Horatio W. Longa of Manchester, Martin L. Piper of Auburn, and John Young of Rochester, for doorkeepers of the House of Representatives for the ensuing two years.

On motion of Mr. Donahue of Manchester,—

Resolved, That a committee of ten, one from each county, be appointed by the Chair to select a chaplain to serve during the present session of the Legislature.

On motion of Mr. Whitcher of Haverhill,—

Resolved, That the Speaker of the House is hereby authorized to appoint the following messengers and pages of the House : A warden and an assistant warden, who shall have charge of the cloak-room corridor ; two messengers, who shall be under the joint direction of the sergeant-at-arms and the state librarian, and whose first duty shall be to answer calls of members for books, documents, and papers in the custody of the state librarian, and be responsible for their return, and distribute the mail coming to the House ; also six pages in attendance upon the House, one of whom is to be known as the Speaker's page.

On motion of Mr. Remich of Littleton,—

Resolved, That the Honorable Senate be informed that the House of Representatives has organized by the election of Harry M. Cheney as Speaker, James M. Cooper as clerk, Harrie M. Young as assistant clerk, and John K. Law as sergeant-at-arms, and is now ready to proceed with the business of the session.

MESSAGE FROM THE SENATE.

A message from the Honorable Senate, by its clerk, announced that the Senate had adopted the following resolution :

Resolved, That the House of Representatives be informed that the Senate, having assembled, has organized by the choice of Hon. Charles W. Hoitt as President, Thomas F. Clifford as clerk, Louis A. Thorp as assistant clerk, William H. Weston as sergeant-at-arms, Herbert A. McElwain as messenger, Hiram E. Currier as doorkeeper, and is now ready to proceed with the business of the session.

The message also announced that the Senate had adopted the following resolution :

Resolved, That a message be sent to the House of Representatives that from an examination of the returns of votes there appear to be vacancies in Senatorial Districts Nos. 6

and 24; that Elmer S. Tilton and Harry W. Daniell are the two constitutional candidates in District No. 6; that Calvin Page and Ira C. Seymour are the two constitutional candidates in District No. 24; and that the Senate is ready to meet the House in convention at such time as the House may suggest, for the purpose of filling the vacancies in the Senate, agreeable to the provisions of the constitution.

On motion of Mr. Batchelder of Keene,—

Resolved, That the Judiciary Committee and the Committee on Railroads, when appointed, be authorized to each employ a person to act as clerk and stenographer of the respective committees.

On motion of Mr. Remich of Littleton,—

Resolved, That the sergeant-at-arms of the House be instructed to procure and furnish to each member of the House and officers thereof, during the session, two daily newspapers, each member and officer to choose the papers he desires to have, and to indicate the same to the sergeant-at-arms forthwith.

On motion of Mr. Ahern of Concord,—

Resolved, That the rules of the House of the last session be adopted as the rules of the present session, unless otherwise ordered.

On motion of Mr. Remich of Littleton,—

Resolved, That a new house committee be established, to be known as the Committee on Feeble-minded School.

The Speaker named as a committee to select a chaplain to serve during the present session of the Legislature the following gentlemen: Messrs. Donahue of Manchester, Newton of Portsmouth, Wallace of Rochester, Chase of Laconia, Beacham of Wolfeborough, Hutchinson of Pittsfield, Kellom of Winchester, Hamlin of Charlestown, Dorothy of Enfield, and Libby of Gorham.

On motion of Mr. Whitcher of Haverhill,—

Resolved, That the drawing of seats be made a special order for this afternoon at 2 o'clock.

On motion of Mr. Collins of Nashua,—

Resolved, That unless otherwise ordered, the hours of assembling of the House be 11 o'clock in the forenoon and 2 o'clock in the afternoon.

On motion of Mr. Batchelder of Keene,—

Resolved, That the Honorable Senate be notified that the House of Representatives will be ready to meet the Senate in joint convention, for the purpose of canvassing the votes for Governor and Councilors, for the election of a commissary-general, agreeably to the provisions of the constitution, and for the purpose of filling vacancies in Senatorial Districts Nos. 6 and 24, at 3 o'clock this afternoon.

On motion of Mr. Sawyer of Milford,—

Resolved, That a committee of five, consisting of the Speaker and four members, be appointed by the Chair to report on the subject of proper rules of procedure in this House, and that they, with such members as the Senate may join, be a Committee on Joint Rules of the Senate and House of Representatives.

On motion of Mr. French of Moultonborough, at 12.32 the House adjourned.

AFTERNOON.

The House met at 2 o'clock.

SPECIAL ORDER.

Mr. Howe of Hanover called for the special order, it being the drawing of seats.

On motion of Mr. Whitcher of Haverhill,—

Resolved, That Messrs. Batchelder of Keene, French of Moultonborough, Small of Rochester, and Ahern of Concord be given a selection of seats before the drawing of the same takes place.

The above named gentlemen having selected seats, on motion of Mr. Batchelder of Keene,—

Resolved, That the clerk be authorized to draw seats for all members absent from the House at the time of the drawing.

The House then proceeded with the drawing of seats.

MESSAGE FROM THE SENATE.

A message from the Honorable Senate, by its clerk, announced that the Senate had adopted the following resolution, in the adoption of which it asked the concurrence of the House of Representatives :

Resolved by the Senate, the House of Representatives concurring, That the joint rules of the last Legislature be the joint rules of this Legislature until otherwise ordered.

The resolution was concurred in on motion of Mr. Severance of Exeter.

The message also announced that the Honorable Senate concurred with the House of Representatives in the adoption of the following resolution :

Resolved, That a committee of five, consisting of the Speaker and four members, be appointed by the Chair to report on the subject of proper rules of procedure in this House, and that they, with such members as the Senate may join, be a committee on joint rules of the Senate and House of Representatives, and the Senate has joined as members of said committee, on the part of the Senate, the President and Senator Bickford of District No. 17.

IN CONVENTION.

The Honorable Senate then came in and, the two branches being in convention, the Honorable Secretary of State appeared and laid before the convention the returns of the votes for Governor and Councilors cast in the last election.

On motion of Senator Neal of District No. 12,—

Resolved, That the votes for Governor and Councilors be referred to a committee, consisting of one on the part of the Senate and two on the part of the House, to examine, compare, and count the same, and report thereon.

The chairman named as such committee Senator Neal of District No. 12, and Messrs. Sheehan of Manchester and Bussell of Nashua.

On motion of Senator Bickford of District No. 17,—

Resolved, That the convention proceed to the election of a commissary-general for the ensuing two years.

On motion of Senator Stillings of District No. 10,—

Resolved, That the clerk of the House be instructed to cast one ballot for Colonel William A. Barron of Carroll, for commissary-general for the ensuing two years.

The ballot was so cast, and Colonel William A. Barron of Carroll, having a majority of all the votes cast, was declared duly elected commissary-general for the period prescribed by the constitution and by-laws of the state.

On motion of Senator Lightbody of District No. 16,—

Resolved, That a committee of three be appointed by the Chair to wait upon Colonel William A. Barron and inform him of his election as commissary-general.

The chairman named as such committee Senator Lightbody of District No. 16, and Messrs. Churchill of Cornish and Jones of Franklin.

On motion of Senator Burnell of District No. 5,—

Resolved, That a committee of five be appointed by the Chair to wait upon His Excellency Chester B. Jordan, Governor, and inform him that a quorum of each branch of the Legislature has assembled and completed its organization, and is ready to receive any communication he may be pleased to make.

The chairman named as such committee Senators Burnell of District No. 5 and Tolles of District No. 20, and Messrs. Dorothy of Enfield, Worcester of Rochester, and Rogers of Tilton.

Senator Burnell, for the committee, subsequently reported that they had attended to that duty and that His Excellency the Governor was present in person to answer for himself.

His Excellency Governor Jordan then appeared and briefly addressed the convention.

On motion of Senator Bickford of District No. 17,—

Resolved, That the convention proceed to fill the vacancy existing in Senatorial District No. 6.

The chairman announced that the constitutional candidates were Elmer S. Tilton of Laconia, Republican, and Harry W. Daniell of Franklin, Democrat.

The chairman appointed as tellers Mr. Mitchell of Littleton and Senator Foley of District No. 18.

The result of the ballot was as follows:

Whole number of votes cast	312
Necessary for a choice	157
Harry W. Daniell had	100
Elmer S. Tilton had	212

and Elmer S. Tilton, having a majority of all the votes cast, was declared elected Senator from District No. 6 for the ensuing two years.

On motion of Senator Marvin of District No. 8,—

Resolved, That the convention proceed to fill the vacancy existing in Senatorial District No. 24.

The chairman announced that the constitutional candidates were Calvin Page of Portsmouth, Democrat, and Ira C. Seymour of Portsmouth, Independent Labor.

The result of the ballot was as follows:

Whole number of votes cast . . .	303
Necessary for a choice	152
Ira C. Seymour had	43
Calvin Page had	260

and Calvin Page, having a majority of all the votes cast, was declared duly elected Senator from District No. 24 for the ensuing two years.

REPORT OF COMMITTEE.

Senator Neal, for the joint committee, to whom were referred the returns of the votes cast for Governor and Councilors at the last biennial election, reported that they had examined, compared, and counted the same with the following result:

FOR GOVERNOR.

Whole number of votes cast . . .	79,173
Necessary for a choice	39,587
Nahum J. Bachelder had . . .	42,115
Henry F. Hollis had	33,844
John C. Berry had	1,621
George Howie had	57
Michael H. O'Neil had	1,057
Alonzo Elliott had	468
Scattering	11

and Nahum J. Bachelder, having a majority of all the votes cast, is elected Governor for the ensuing two years.

FOR COUNCILORS.

District No. 1.

Whole number of votes cast . . .	15,836
Necessary for a choice	7,919
James Frank Seavey had . . .	8,932
Charles A. Morse had	6,607
John P. M. Brown had	297

and James Frank Seavey, having a majority of all the votes cast, is elected Councilor for the ensuing two years.

District No. 2.

Whole number of votes cast . . .	14,577
Necessary for a choice	7,289
Alfred A. Collins had	8,296
Alliston L. Partridge had . . .	6,117
John N. Bradford had	164

and Alfred A. Collins, having a majority of all the votes cast, is elected Councilor for the ensuing two years.

District No. 3.

Whole number of votes cast . . .	13,249
Necessary for a choice	6,625
Frank E. Kaley had	7,517
Frank A. Dearborn had	5,549
Charles Osborne had	183

and Frank E. Kaley, having a majority of all the votes cast, is elected Councilor for the ensuing two years.

District No. 4.

Whole number of votes cast . . .	16,259
Necessary for a choice	8,130
Seth M. Richards had	9,688
Horace K. Martin had	6,245
Arthur W. Kidder had	325
All others had	1

and Seth M. Richards, having a majority of all the votes cast, is elected Councilor for the ensuing two years.

District No. 5.

Whole number of votes cast	.	.	.	15,033
Necessary for a choice	.	.	.	7,517
Alpheus Crosby Kennett had	.	.	.	8,916
Leonard M. Knight had	.	.	.	5,863
Henry O. Jackson had	.	.	.	248
All others had	.	.	.	.	6

and Alpheus Crosby Kennett, having a majority of all the votes cast, is elected Councilor for the ensuing two years.

On motion of Senator Marvin of District No. 8, the report was accepted and declaration made accordingly.

On motion of Mr. Hoyt of Sandwich,—

Resolved, That a committee of five be appointed by the Chair to wait upon the Hon. Nahum J. Bachelder and inform him officially of his election as Governor of the state of New Hampshire, and that the Senate and House of Representatives are ready to receive any communication from His Excellency at such time as he may desire.

The chairman named as such committee Messrs. Hoyt of Sandwich, Pike of Lebanon, and Huntley of Claremont, and Senators Fellows of District No. 11 and Tolles of District No. 20.

On motion of Mr. Collins of Nashua,—

Resolved, That a committee of three be appointed by the Chair to wait upon James Frank Seavey, Alfred A. Collins, Frank E. Kaley, Seth M. Richards, and Alpheus Crosby Kennett, and inform them of their election to the Honorable Council.

The chairman named as such committee Messrs. Collins of Nashua and Lennon of Stratford, and Senator Cooper of District No. 7.

On motion of Senator Keyes of District No. 2, the convention rose.

HOUSE.

On motion of Mr. Remich of Littleton,—

Resolved, That the clerk of the House be instructed to procure as soon as possible 2,200 copies of the Legislative

Manual, in substantially the same form as in 1901, in morocco binding, for the use of the House and Senate and the Executive Department.

On motion of Mr. Whitcher of Haverhill, at 4.34 the House adjourned.

***

THURSDAY, JANUARY 8, 1903.

The House met at 11 o'clock.

Prayer was offered by Rev. Joel B. Slocum of Concord.

LEAVES OF ABSENCE.

Mr. Henry of Lincoln was granted leave of absence for three weeks on account of urgent business.

Mr. Fitch of Keene was granted leave of absence for two weeks on account of sickness.

REPORT OF COMMITTEE.

Mr. Donahue, for the committee appointed to select a chaplain for the House of Representatives, reported the following resolution and recommended its adoption:

Resolved, That Rev. William H. Getchell of Laconia be elected chaplain for the ensuing two years.

The resolution was adopted.

On motion of Mr. Howe of Hanover,—

Resolved, That the Honorable Senate be notified that the House of Representatives is ready to meet the Senate in joint convention for the purpose of receiving His Excellency the Governor, and any communication he may he pleased to make, and for the transaction of such other business as may properly come before such convention.

On motion of Mr. Rogers of Tilton,—

Resolved, That the Speaker be authorized to appoint a committee of ten members, consisting of one from each county, on a new apportionment for the assessment of public taxes.

On motion of Mr. Severance of Exeter,—

Resolved, That the House take a recess subject to the call of the Speaker.

The House having re-assembled,

IN CONVENTION.

REPORTS OF COMMITTEES.

The Honorable Senate then came in and, the two branches being in convention, Mr. Hoyt of Sandwich, for the committee appointed by the Chair to wait upon the Hon. Nahum J. Bachelder and inform him officially of his election as Governor of the state of New Hampshire, reported that they had attended to that duty; that the Governor-elect had accepted said office, and would meet the Senate and House of Representatives in convention at the earliest convenient time to take the oath of office and make such communication as he might deem proper.

The report was accepted.

Mr. Collins of Nashua, for the committee appointed to inform the Honorable Councilors of their election, reported that the committee had attended to its duty, and had notified the gentlemen of their election.

The report was accepted.

The Chair appointed Senator Keyes of District No. 2, and Messrs. Foye of Portsmouth and Graves of Andover, as a committee to escort the Governor and Governor-elect to the House of Representatives.

The Governor, Governor-elect, and the Honorable Council then came in, and the Hon. Nahum J. Bachelder, Governor-elect, then took and subscribed the oath of office and the oaths of allegiance before the President of the Senate and in the presence of both branches of the Legislature, whereupon the Hon. Charles W. Hoitt, President of the Senate, made proclamation as follows:

Nahum J. Bachelder, having been duly elected Governor of New Hampshire, accepted the office, and taken the oaths prescribed by the constitution, I do therefore declare and proclaim His Excellency Nahum J. Bachelder, Governor of the state of New Hampshire, to hold the office during the period prescribed by the constitution and laws of the state, and I present Your Excellency with a copy of the constitution of the state as a guide in the discharge of your official duties.

His Excellency then read the following message:

Members of the Legislature:

In attempting to comply with the time-honored custom which requires a governor upon his inauguration to address the General Court regarding the matters of state which it will have to consider, I shall avoid, as far as practicable, specific recommendations, and content myself with a brief statement of what information I have, and of the *principles* which I believe should govern us in the performance of the duties which we have assumed.

STATE FINANCES.

The report of the state treasurer discloses a highly satisfactory condition of the state finances. The total funded debt June 1, 1902, was $839,200. Of this amount $3,700 was overdue, and $450,000, the balance of the municipal war loan of 1872, maturing between January 1, 1903, and January 1, 1905. The overdue bond of 1873 of $500, library bonds to the amount of $175,000, due July 1, 1911, and $75,000 due July 1, 1913, and Agricultural College loan bonds amounting to $135,000, due July 1, 1913, make up the total. Other liabilities of the state are various trust funds amounting to $813,574.37, a school fund of $14,825, and two small items, making $1,669,071.30.

To offset these liabilities there were cash on hand, $575,-615.12, securities from the Thompson estate, $329,443.76, and due from railroad corporations $7,580.06, a total of $912,-638.94. The balance, $756,432.36, was the net indebtedness of the state.

The state tax of $425,000, which has already been voted for the years 1902 and 1903, with the other revenues from corporations and miscellaneous sources will yield sufficient surplus above the regular expenses to meet the obligations that mature on and before January 1, 1905, and from that time until July 1, 1911, no part of the debt will become due. The ordinary revenues of the state from sources other than the direct tax are about $250,000 annually, and the current expenses besides interest are about $525,000. The interest charges after the debt that matures January 1, 1903, is paid, may be reckoned at $50,000 more, making $575,000.

It therefore appears that with due regard for the taxpayers

and a consequent avoidance of extravagant appropriation to which the treasury surplus is always a temptation, the state tax can be reduced $100,000, leaving that amount to be distributed to the cities and towns in addition to what they now receive from the collections of the state treasurer from corporations, and relieving to that extent the burdens of local taxation which are the heaviest that our people have to bear. At different times the state has accepted trust funds, interest on which it has obligated itself to pay perpetually to the institutions designated as beneficiaries. The largest of these is the Benjamin Thompson fund for the benefit of the New Hampshire College of Agriculture and the Mechanic Arts, which was originally $363.823.32, and has been, and is to be, increased by the state until January 30, 1910, when it will amount to $797,181.67, on which four per cent. interest, or $31,887.27, must be paid to the institution annually. Other trust funds will on that date (January 30, 1910) bring the total amount to nearly a million dollars, involving an annual interest charge of $40,000. It has been suggested that in order to prepare for this payment, the state tax should be left as it is, $425,000, and from the surplus it will yield we should accumulate a sinking fund, the interest on which will meet that upon the trust funds. This involves the taxation of the present to pay the debts of the future, and the embarkment of the state in the banking business,—that is, the investment and management of large sums of money, which I think should be avoided. If we pay as we go, and while we are going cancel all war debts and other obligations incurred to meet emergencies, leaving to those who will succeed us to provide for their expenses, we shall do our whole duty in that regard. As suggested, it is to be constantly considered that the state tax cannot be reduced nor a sinking fund provided unless appropriations are rigidly kept within the limits of wise economy. The calls for state aid are very many and very urgent, and they multiply each year. They are all made upon the plea that the public good demands them, and they should be carefully scrutinized and responded to, to such an extent as will return to the people of the state as a whole value received for the money appropriated.

It is always to be considered that hearings upon petitions for appropriations from the state treasury are *ex parte*. Those who hope to profit by such grants are often the only ones to appear. The many who pay the taxes are too busily engaged in earning and saving money with which to meet the demands of tax collectors to present their opinions to the Legislature, but it is clearly our duty to constantly bear in mind that we are the servants of the masses, that what they cannot afford they should not be compelled to pay for by any act of ours. In the past the state expenditures have not been on a niggardly scale. They have been profuse. In my judgment they should not exceed in the near future those of the last two years, and if I can prevent it, they shall not. The argument that we are getting out of debt, that our revenues from the taxation of railroads, insurance, telegraph, and telephone companies is steadily increasing, and that we can therefore afford what we could not last year, is more specious than sound.

It is true that the corporation taxes are constantly increased and that the interest charge disappears as the war debt is cancelled, but these changes should be for the benefit of the great body of taxpayers rather than the favored few. In restricting ourselves to expenditures that are just and necessary, it is not enough that we refuse to authorize obligations in support of new undertakings which are presented in the name of education, charity, and material progress, but which are of questionable promise. If there are offices that can be dispensed with without injury to the public, they should be abolished. If there are projects and plans which have secured state approval and have proved to be too costly, they should be abandoned. It is no part of our duty to drive home entering wedges that have been set into the state treasury.

SAVINGS BANKS.

The savings banks that withstood the storms of 1893 and 1894 are steadily recovering from the depression of that period, and are now on safe ground. The amount due their depositors increased from $57,078.433.15 in 1901 to $60,249,862.29 in 1902, a gain of $3,171,429.14, and their

assets from $66,846,692.53 to $70,725,954.79, a gain of
$3,879,262.26. With this margin of guaranty they are more
than solvent, and with their conservative investment policy,
which seeks safety rather than high rates of interest, they
merit the confidence which they command among those who
intrust their savings to their management. Thirty-one banks
were in process of liquidation January 30, 1900. The as-
signees have made final distribution of the assets of thirteen
of these to stockholders and closed their accounts. Four
others have paid dividends since June 30, 1902, and will
soon be taken from the list. The aggregate dividends to
depositors have ranged from 60 to 100 per cent., averaging
about 80 per cent. To the average shortage of 20 per cent. must
be added interest since the institutions were closed, but even
with this the loss is much smaller than was apprehended. The
failure of these banks has left localities without savings-bank
accommodations and this, with other considerations, has
induced some national banks to open accounts with depositors to whom a small rate of interest is paid, thus doing
a savings-bank business. It is charged that deposits, while
legally taxable to the owners as money in hand, escape the
taxation which those in savings banks are compelled to
bear and are therefore unjustly favored, and it is also claimed
that this growing practice, in places where there are sound
savings banks, diverts business which they were chartered to
do and have a right to. It is suggested that the national banks
should be required to make returns which will disclose to the
local assessors the ownership of the interest-bearing deposits
that they may be taxed at the local rates, which would un-
doubtedly result in their withdrawal and investment elsewhere.

In the brief time since the subject was called to my attention
I have been unable to satisfy myself that this is advisable
unless it be so extended as to include all deposits that are
taxable under our laws, but I ask for it your careful consideration, as it deeply affects the savings-bank interests,
which it is the true policy of the state to protect.

The building and loan associations, which have assets
amounting to $1,740,116.64, and 28,867 shares outstanding,
are apparently sound and successful.

RAILROADS.

The steam railroads of New Hampshire appear to be permanently fixed in three great systems, all of which have tide-water terminals in other states and far-reaching western connections.

Of the 1,190 miles of line, 1,038 miles are operated by the Boston & Maine Railroad, 100 miles by the Maine Central, and 52 miles by the Grand Trunk. The consolidations by which this grouping has been effected, and earnings have been distributed over great systems, have been of great advantage to our people, especially those of sparsely settled sections, who have accommodations and rates that could not have been afforded them if the roads had not been united and were obliged to bear the expense and depend upon the earnings of independent operation. I am not aware that the corporations in control of these roads are refusing or neglecting to perform their duty to the public, that there is any demand for an extension of the existing lines, or that any radical changes in the laws relating to steam railways are needed or will be asked for.

Since January 1, 1902, the electric track mileage has increased from 138 to 226 miles and the capitalization of these enterprises from $2,964,339 to $5,659,083. A beginning has been made upon about twenty miles more, and there are charters covering about 150 miles of line that have not been used. Such expansion of development and opportunity evideuces the soundness of the street railway policy which is formulated in our statutes and faithfully carried out by our authorities to whom has been committed the execution of those laws.

MANUFACTURES.

Manufacturing constitutes the chief industry of New Hampshire, with $88,943,325 invested, employing 76,667 wage-earners in 1901, to whom was paid in wages and salaries $30,160,446, and marketing a product to the value of $111,933,030, an increase of $8,503,477 over the previous year. In the enactment of laws bearing upon this great industry, consideration should be given to the rights of capital as well as the rights of labor. There should also be careful study of the effect of proposed legislation upon the welfare of the people engaged in various industries and professions established around manufacturing plants constituting our thrifty cities and villages. The state of New Hampshire, in common with other states, has established a Bureau of Labor for the investigation of conditions existing between capital and labor. The report recently issued by the bureau will give the result of its investigations in various important matters.

AGRICULTURE.

The 29,324 farms valued, including equipment, at $85,842,-096, furnish employment to 38,782 people, or twenty-one per cent. of the population of the state, while as many more people are directly dependent upon agriculture for support. This industry is only second in value to manufacturing, and is entitled to greater consideration by the legislature than its relative magnitude would indicate. It is not expected that you will discriminate in favor of this or any other industry, but it is important that no unjust burdens be placed upon the farmers of the state in taxation or otherwise by the enactment of laws having for their object the public welfare. Recent changes in agriculture require a better knowledge of the science in order to make the industry profitable, and you will doubtless consider the means of imparting this special knowledge as important as any educational work. This is the chief function of the State Board of Agriculture, an important state department, and also of the Dairymen's association and Horticultural society, voluntary associations given state aid. The Grange is a vigorous organization of 25,000 members without state aid that is exerting an influence of great value for better farming methods and increased intelligence and culture among the rural people. There are many reasons for protecting and promoting agriculture in legislative matters so far as is consistent with other state interests.

FISH AND GAME.

The fish and game interests have become an important factor in the state's development, and the rigid enforcement of wise laws is essential, although it may seem to infringe upon property rights of individual owners. The legislation reducing the number of fish hatcheries was in the right direction, and the general closing of public waters against fishing through the ice is looked upon with favor by true sportsmen and those having the advancement of the fish and game interests of the state at heart. The 70,000 acres of water in New Hampshire afford an opportunity for producing a vast quantity of food material and unlimited sporting facilities under wise legislative action. The marked increase in deer and their frequent appearance are evidence of the practical working of wise laws protecting them. I call your attention to the importance of the fish and game interests of the state.

Forestry.

If New Hampshire is to retain her supremacy as a summer resort state, it is essential that practical means be employed for the preservation and extension of our existing forest area. The work undertaken thus far has been chiefly directed to securing a more rational treatment of the forest cover by the larger landowners and lumbering concerns, and to promoting public sentiment in favor of forest preservation. It is claimed that the time has arrived for affirmative action on the part of the state through its forestry commission by coöperating with landowners, both to secure needed restrictions in the harvesting of the timber crop now standing, and to take steps to reclaim with forest growth many areas which are now naked or unproductive. It is also suggested that as preliminary to future work in scientific forestry, and as a measure calculated to stimulate an immediate wider interest in the attractiveness of our mountain forests, the completion of the topographic survey in those sections is a matter of no small importance. This work was begun by the general government many years ago, but was never completed because other states, by coöperating to share the expense of the work, have secured the first claim upon the services of the field workers. You will give due consideration to these and other proposed means of promoting the forestry interests, constantly bearing in mind the peculiar importance of forest preservation to various industries of the state, and wisely discriminating between extravagant measures and those that will probably yield a cash return commensurate with the expense involved.

ROADS.

The building and maintenance of roads that will adequately meet the reasonable requirements of our citizens and visitors, is important in the progress and development of New Hampshire. The state has made annual appropriations for mountain roads and has built a section of stone road near the coast. With these exceptions the roads of the state have been constructed and repaired under local authority and with funds provided by local taxation. The mileage of roads is given as 15,582, forty-seven towns having over one hundred miles each, and one town, three hundred miles. You will have submitted for your consideration various plans for providing state aid for roads in rural towns and for the construction of roads between populous sections of the state. The importance of good roads to the development of the summer industry, and their value to residents of the state, suggest a liberal policy in dealing with the subject. Thus far the money appropriated by the state has been with reference to no fixed system but in response to demands from various localities. To whatever extent the financial credit of the state is involved in securing better roads, action should be based upon a recognition of the interests of the rural towns as well as of populous centers, and should require the payment of a just proportion of the cost of the roads by the taxpayers of the locality where roads are constructed, and by the abutting landowners whose property is enhanced. This involves a fixed state policy in place of the uncertain policy heretofore prevailing. The expense involved in the execution of such a policy, and the advantages to be derived by the people of the state therefrom, are the factors to be considered in legislating upon this matter, to which I invite your attention.

THE SUMMER INDUSTRY.

The peculiar advantages of New Hampshire as a health and pleasure resort render a consideration of the subject a matter

of importance. Eight million dollars annually expended in
the state by summer tourists and three million dollars already
expended here by people from outside the state in building,
equipping, and adorning summer homes, generally replacing
decaying structures, yield a revenue to a large number of people, while the presence of summer visitors adds a charm to
rural life through increased social and mental recreation. The
summer industry is not of a nature to require state supervision or control, yet the work of the various departments is
closely connected with it. Whatever contributes to giving
wider publicity to the healthful conditions and scenic attractions of the state, to more plentiful fish and game, and extended forest cover, to better roads and more attractive road-
sides, to the health and safety of rural life, will aid in the development of this important industry. An intelligent presentation of the advantages of New Hampshire as a health and
pleasure resort at the St. Louis Exposition, at moderate cost,
would be useful in more widely extending the fame of our
state in this respect.

STATE BOARD OF HEALTH.

The work of the State Board of Health is so well known that
little need be said of it at this time. During the existence of
the board, and largely through its efforts, important sanitary
laws have been enacted, efficient local boards of health have
been established, the public educated to a greater degree than
ever before in the restriction and prevention of many diseases,
in the dangers of unsanitary environment, in the evils of contaminated water supplies, and on many other subjects inti-
mately connected with public health. The board has large
executive authority in the management of epidemic diseases,
and in this respect has has been of material aid to many towns.
Its indirect sanitary supervision of our summer-resort localities is an especially valuable work. In addition to its duties
as a State Board of Health, the board also has charge of the
registration of vital statistics, and in 1889 was constituted a
Board of Commissioners of Lunacy ; it renders, therefore,
three reports to the Legislature, containing the details of the
work in these several departments.

INSURANCE.

One hundred and thirteen fire insurance companies are authorized by the insurance department to do business in New Hampshire. The entire business transacted by these companies.in the state for the year ending December 31, 1901, was $111,581,480.96, upon which premiums amounting to $875,-364.92 were paid. Twenty-four life insurance companies during the same period collected premiums to the amount of $1,556,680.95, and paid losses amounting to $723,688,17. Eight fidelity and surety and seventeen casualty companies wrote policies amounting to $29,392,117, upon which premiums were received amounting to $149,826.15, and losses were paid amounting to $49,835.42. Thirty-five fraternal beneficiary associations received in assessments $382,627.88, and paid in losses $341,448.54. The entire amount of premiums and assessments received by all authorized companies and associations for the business year ending December 31, 1901, was $3,583,438.78. The entire amount paid the state treasurer by all authorized companies for fees and taxes for the same period was $65,033.35. The companies authorized to do business here include some of the best in the country and good risks can find ample protection.

NATIONAL GUARD.

The National Guard consists of one brigade of two twelve-company regiments of infantry, one four-gun light battery, one troop of cavalry, a signal corps, and a hospital corps. The present strength of the force is one hundred and ten commissioned officers and one thousand two hundred and forty-four enlisted men. The state camp ground, the arsenal, and the regimental stables are in excellent condition. It is reported that two regimental mess halls are needed to replace those built years ago and now in poor condition. The rigid discipline enforced in all matters pertaining to the National Guard has resulted in a degree of efficiency in military tactics that reflects great credit upon those in command, and must be pleasing to the people of the state.

EDUCATION.

The educational department of the state government has been given increased responsibilities in recent years by the enactment of laws bearing upon education and imposing new duties upon the department. The enforcement of the truancy law, the designation of high schools and academies entitled to receive tuition from towns under the act of 1901, and determining the apportionment of money appropriated for the support of schools in towns entitled to state aid under the act of 1899, enable the department to exert an influence for the cause of education heretofore unknown in the state. That such legislative action has been wise is manifested in the longer school year and increased average attendance. The rural educational facilities have been broadened with no injury or injustice to New Hampshire's general educational facilities.

STATE PRISON, INDUSTRIAL SCHOOL, NORMAL SCHOOL, STATE HOSPITAL, AND SCHOOL FOR FEEBLE-MINDED CHILDREN.

You will be furnished with the reports of those in charge of the State Prison, the State Hospital, the Normal School, the Industrial School, and the School for Feeble-minded Children, which will inform you of the work, condition, and wants of these institutions, all of which the state is under obligation to sustain without niggardliness and without prodigality. So far as I can learn they are well managed and there is no reason for changing the laws which govern their operation. Their financial needs, if any, should be carefully investigated and intelligently provided for.

DARTMOUTH COLLEGE.

Dartmouth college provides for the higher education of New Hampshire, apart from that given by the Agricultural college, the academies, the high schools, and the Normal school, and, of the students in Dartmouth, one hundred and eighty-eight from New Hampshire are in the academic department. The cost to the college of education per man, as calculated by the officers, is $250 a year, which would make the cost of educating the New Hampshire contingent $47,000. Deduct from this sum the amount received from tuition paid by them, and from scholarship moneys the income of which is devoted to New Hampshire students, and the balance of cost of educating New Hampshire men above receipts is $27,055, which is paid from the income of invested funds.

The state of New Hampshire has established a policy in higher education that is exceedingly liberal. It requires towns to pay high school tuition for resident students who attend approved high schools elsewhere; it contributes liberally to the support of the Agricultural college in order that students may have special instruction at reasonable rates; it maintains the Normal school that teachers may obtain proper education and training; and while the Agricultural college and the Normal school are state institutions under state control, as Dartmouth is not, it seems just and consistent that, as New Hampshire is freed by this college from supporting a similar institution of its own, it should to some extent contribute to Dartmouth's expenses when its income from other sources is insufficient.

AGRICULTURAL COLLEGE.

The Agricultural college derives its chief financial support from the national government, receiving annually therefrom $25,000 for instruction, and $15,000 for the support of the experiment station connected. Under the acts of congress making these appropriations, the management of the institution is vested in the state through a board of trustees, and the state by annual appropriation and the interest on trust funds contributes about $10,000 to its maintenance. In 1910 the income from the Benjamin Thompson trust fund will be available, amounting to $31,887.27 annually. The studies taught in this college are those relating to agriculture and the mechanic arts and those pertaining to the various industries connected therewith, yet the prominent object in view in the establishment of the institution through the enactment of laws by congress, and by the action of those who have made bequests for its support, was the advancement of agriculture by educating and training men in this great science. A committee will visit the college, where it will be learned that the state, in proportion to its wealth, has been liberal in providing the buildings forming the basis of a magnificent institution dedicated primarily to the cause of agriculture. I urge upon you to become familiar with the conditions and needs of this college, and to take such action as will make the institution especially influential in promoting agriculture and successful along the line contemplated by its founder and benefactors.

AUTOMOBILES.

There is a widespread, earnest, and just feeling that some restrictions or regulations should be put upon the use of our public highways by automobiles. These vehicles have come to us by the evolution of the age and are to be accepted as improvements; but when recklessly used, as they often are, they are unquestionably a menace to life and property and a terror to our citizens, who have built, and are entitled to the use of, roads and streets from which they are debarred by fear of meeting these machines. While no one would close our thoroughfares against such carriages, some reasonable legislation which will compel their owners to respect the rights of others is desirable. I commend the subject to your careful consideration.

LIQUOR LAWS.

The people of this state have been very generally forced by observation and experience to the conclusion that our statutes relating to the sale of intoxicating beverages have failed, in our larger cities and towns, to accomplish the purposes for which they were enacted, and there is therefore a very widespread demand for a change in these laws. No subject has been more thoroughly considered or is better understood by the people than this, and no local question was more prominently an issue in the recent election which resulted in our assignment to the positions we occupy, in which we are the servants of the people who are individually as interested as any of us, and collectively wiser than all of us, in the matter. Most of you have come here commissioned by your constituents to bring about changes in our statutes which will make them more effective in restraining and regulating the traffic in intoxicants, and thereby lessen, so far as it is possible, the manifold evils of intemperance. I shall gladly coöperate with you in what you may do in obedience to this mandate, by approving any well-considered enactment in which is formulated the judgment of the good citizens of the state.

LABOR LEGISLATION.

Much of the prosperity of New Hampshire has been due to the amicable relations that have generally existed between capital and labor, which have worked together to promote their mutual interests. Some differences have arisen between wage-workers and their employers which have caused temporary suspensions of production, but we have been free from the prolonged and destructive labor wars that have paralyzed industry, skill, and enterprise, making capital unprofitable and impoverishing labor, elsewhere. This is to be credited to the intelligence and fairness of both parties, and is full of promise for the future, in which only the optimist can fail to see disastrous possibilities unless there is a spirit of justice and concession, which is lacking in some sections of the country. We must hereafter depend mainly, as we have so successfully done heretofore, upon the character of our people to save us from such evils.

Nevertheless something has been, and more doubtless can be, effected by legislation, and whatever will reduce the hours of labor or otherwise safeguard our workers without crippling employers and impairing their ability to furnish work and pay wages, or unnecessarily abridging the right of every man of sound mind to work when, where, and upon what terms he pleases, should be enacted.

Located as we are, far away from the bases of manufacturing supplies and the principal markets for manufactured products, and therefore at a disadvantage as compared with others, it is not to be expected that we can lead the way in making laws to limit the time people shall labor or in instituting other desirable reforms. If we keep abreast of, or very close to, those more favorably situated, it is all that can reasonably be demanded. We have thus far pursued a conservative course and the result proves it to have been a wise one. We have not only had comparative exemption from strikes and lock-outs, but our wage-workers are as well paid, and in every way as well treated, as those engaged in the same lines anywhere. Factory operatives especially, who seek to better their condition, do not leave New Hampshire and go to other states; they come here when they can find openings. These facts are so well known and appreciated that there is little disagreement between the great majority of our wage-workers and broad-minded, fair-dealing employers. That a few unreasonable and over-greedy capitalists and professional agitators, who live by stirring up strife, stand in the way of a peaceable and satisfactory solution of the labor problem here, by the enactment of such laws as will be for the good of all concerned, is not to be denied, but, with these ignored as they should be, the great mass of our employed and employers can, I believe, be trusted to meet upon common and safe ground, and I do not apprehend that you will have serious difficulty in making the statutes conform to the wishes of both.

In conclusion, allow me to assure you of my earnest coöperation in all legislative matters having for their object the welfare of the people of New Hampshire. In our deliberations we should constantly be cognizant of the fact that we represent the people by whose suffrage we occupy our various positions, and to whom we must make return of our stewardship when our duties have ended. I think we understand that the interest of the people will be best served, and the honor and dignity of the state best maintained by an economical administration and the enactment of but few laws. It will be well to bear in mind the fact that there is more to be feared from too much than from too little legislation. I am confident that all legislative matters coming before you will receive careful attention, and that you will reach such wise conclusions as will redound to your credit and the welfare of the good people of the state of New Hampshire.

On motion of Senator Bickford of District No. 17,—

Resolved, That the message of His Excellency the Governor be laid on the table, and that the clerk of the House be directed to procure the usual number of printed copies.

On motion of Senator Stillings of District No. 10, the convention rose.

HOUSE.

On motion of Mr. Severance of Exeter,—

Resolved, That when the House adjourns this morning it adjourn to meet to-morrow morning at 9 o'clock, and when the House adjourns to-morrow morning it adjourn to meet Monday evening at 8 o'clock.

Mr. Straw of Manchester, having been duly qualified by His Excellency the Governor, appeared and took his seat as a member of the House.

On motion of Mr. Collins of Nashua, at 12.36 the House adjourned.

FRIDAY, JANUARY 9, 1903.

The House met at 9 o'clock, according to adjournment.

NOTICES OF BILLS.

By Mr. Willis of Concord, An act reviving and continuing the charter of the Warner & Kearsarge Road Company and amendments to said charter.

By Mr. Willis of Concord, An act to regulate the sale of merchandise in bulk.

By Mr. Willis of Concord, An act to regulate the speed and operation of automobiles and motor vehicles on streets and highways.

By Mr. Willis of Concord, An act in amendment of the charter of the city of Concord creating the office of city comptroller.

By Mr. Mitchell of Littleton, An act relating to the completion of the topographical survey.

By Mr. Smith of Peterborough, An act to amend chapter 282 of the Public Statutes, entitled " Common jails and prisoners therein."

By Mr. Smith of Peterborough, An act to amend section 1 chapter 185 of the Pamphlet Laws of 1901, entitled "An act authorizing the Hillsborough county convention to raise money for the building and repairing of court houses."

By Mr. Hoyt of Sandwich, Joint resolution in favor of the Sandwich Notch road in the town of Sandwich.

In accordance with a resolution adopted at the morning session, January 7, the Speaker announced the following appointments:

Warden of Cloak Room.—George H. Brigham of Nashua.

Assistant Warden of Cloak Room.—Donald P. Upton of Manchester.

Library Messengers.—Charles S. Ford of Lebanon, Merritt C. Huse of Concord.

Speaker's Page.—Joseph Glennon of Concord.

Pages of the House.—James Laughlin of Dover, Earl C. Gordon of Canaan, Ralph Clement of Moultonborough, Temple Grey of Whitefield, Robert P. Conant of Portsmouth.

On motion of Mr. Woodman of Concord, at 9.03 the House adjourned.

MONDAY, JANUARY 12, 1903.

The House met at 8 o'clock in the evening, according to adjournment.

LEAVE OF ABSENCE.

Mr. Hamlin of Charlestown was granted leave of absence for Tuesday, January 13, on account of important business.

NOTICES OF BILLS.

By Mr. Rogers of Tilton, An act to establish a new apportionment for the assessment of public taxes.

By Mr. Cavanaugh of Manchester, An act in relation to the salary of the state reporter.

By Mr. Small of Rochester, An act in amendment of section 1, chapter 138, of the Public Statutes, relating to homestead right.

By Mr. Small of Rochester, An act in amendment of section 15, chapter 93, of the Public Statutes, relating to scholars.

By Mr. Taggart of Manchester, An act authorizing the Manchester Mills to increase its capital stock.

By Mr. Woodman of Concord, An act in amendment of section 26, chapter 79, of the Laws of 1901, for the better protection of grey squirrel.

By Mr. Howe of Hanover, An act to regulate the speed and operation of automobiles and motor vehicles on highways.

By Mr. Quimby of Manchester, An act to incorporate the Manchester & Milford Electric Railway Company.

By Mr. Woodman of Concord, An act in amendment of the charter of the city of Concord, relating to the assessment of taxes.

By Mr. Filion of Manchester, An act to incorporate the Manchester & Derry Electric Railway Company.

By Mr. Bartlett of Manchester, An act to incorporate the Nashua, Manchester & Concord Railway Company.

By Mr. Roby of Concord, An act authorizing the Concord & Montreal Railroad, lessor, to acquire the Concord Street Railway and other property, to issue stock and bonds to pay therefor and authorizing a physical connection of the Manchester Street Railway with the electric branches of the Concord & Montreal Railroad.

By Mr. Jones of Franklin, An act in amendment of chapter 112 of the Public Statutes, establishing local option in the sale of intoxicating liquors.

By Mr. Ellis of Lancaster, Joint resolution making an appropriation for necessary repairs upon the buildings erected by the state for the New Hampshire Veterans' Association at the grounds at The Weirs.

By Mr. Mitchell of Littleton, An act to provide for a more economical and practical expenditure of moneys appropriated by the state for the construction and improvement of highways.

By Mr. Remich of Littleton, An act to amend chapter 243 of the Laws of 1901, creating the Grafton Improvement, Manufacturing and Power Co.

By Mr. Remich of Littleton, An act to promote cleanliness and to protect the public from the disease commonly known as consumption.

By Mr. Remich of Littleton, An act to amend sections 15, 16, and 17 of chapter 112 of the Public Statutes, relating to the sale of spirituous and malt liquors.

By Mr. Remich of Littleton, An act to incorporate the Littleton, Franconia & Bethlehem Electric Railroad Co.

By Mr. Mitchell of Littleton, Joint resolution in favor of screening the outlet of Forest lake.

The Speaker announced the following

STANDING COMMITTEES OF THE HOUSE.

On Agriculture.—Hoyt of Sandwich, Converse of Lyme, Mathews of Concord, Ramsay of Walpole, Gerrish of Nottingham, Ball of Washington, Farley of Amherst, Pattee of Goffstown, Center of Litchfield, Felker of Madbury, Chase of Weare, Potter of Gilford, Gathercole of Clarksville.

On Agricultural College.—Edgerly of Tuftonborough, Bragdon of Temple, True of Plainfield, Harriman of Stewartstown, Hodgman of Merrimack, Chase of Stratham, Critchett of Concord, Langley of Durham, Connell of Hudson, Boyden of Troy, Barr of Bedford, Peabody of Pelham, McMurphey of Alexandria.

On Appropriations.—Wallace of Rochester, Dow of Conway, Foye of Portsmouth, Collins of Nashua, Smith of Exeter, Pike of Haverhill, Quimby of Meredith, Wright of Manchester. McDonald of Northumberland, Ahern of Concord, Huntley of Claremont, Davenport of Bath, Dickinson of Winchester.

On Asylum for Insane.—Crossman of Lisbon, Bunton (A. B.) of Manchester, White of Bow, Goodnow of Keene, Carr of Haverhill, Shepard of Concord, March of Mason, Kent of Newmarket, Corson of Raymond, Greene of Madison, Newman of Manchester, Sanborn of Loudon, Sasseville of Manchester.

On Banks.—Sawyer of Milford, Yeaton of Portsmouth, Bunton (A. S.) of Manchester, Fay of Keene, Payne of Portsmouth, Etter of Somersworth, Beacham of Wolfeborough, McDonald of Manchester, Ellis of Lancaster, Hill (E. J.) of Concord, Kellom of Winchester, Morrill of Ashland, Walker of Pittsfield.

On Claims.—Hamlin of Charlestown, Mathes of Dover, Smith of Center Harbor, Preston of Auburn, French of Moultonborough, Little of Salisbury, Kimball of Grafton, Chase of Orford, Tinkham of Manchester, Donagan of Concord,

Brown of Greenville, Morse of Nashua, Babcock of White-field.

On County Affairs.—Ward of Hillsborough, Eaton of Goffstown, Messer of New London, Hubbard of Candia, Johnson of Manchester, Fletcher of Rindge, Hamlin of Dummer, Frazer of Monroe, Walker of Grantham, Bergeron of Rochester, Philbrick of Effingham, Litchfield of Danbury, Prescott of Laconia.

On Education.—Fox of Marlow, Jones of New Ipswich, Kimball of Concord, Fifield of Conway, Pinkham of Alton, Pierce of Bethlehem, Emerson of Hampstead, Miller of Peterborough, Lennon of Stratford, Andrews of Somersworth, Stewart of Manchester, Spalding of Nashua, Badger of Newington.

On Elections.—Taggart of Manchester, Matthews of Newport, Hardy of Derry, Abbott of Ossipee, Holt of Lyndeborough, Trafton of Milan, Place of Middleton, Worthley of Hooksett, Rogers of Tilton, Bemis of Harrisville, Barnard of Hebron, Gould of Bennington, Dionne of Nashua.

On Feeble-Minded School.—Howe of Hanover, Symonds of Concord, Hayes of Dover, Foss of Pembroke, Blake of Littleton, Couch of Manchester, Tenney of Fitzwilliam, Bickford of Northwood, Cochran of Windham, Hills of Nashua, Shattuck of Brookline, Fitzgerald of Sharon, Lynch of Manchester.

On Fisheries and Game.—Goold of Lebanon, Roby of Concord, Newton of Portsmouth, Sherman of Claremont, Tuttle of Farmington, Sargent of Belmont, Burnell of Conway, Nelson of Portsmouth, Carpenter of Manchester, Hicks of Colebrook, Sullivan of Nashua, Merrill of Stoddard, Bowen of Wentworth.

On Forestry.—Churchill of Cornish, Pike of Lebanon, McDonald of Northumberland, Burbank of Webster, Pike of Haverhill, Needham of Milford, McLane of New Boston, Weeks of Chatham, Howe of Barrington, Harris of Chesterfield, Sheldon of Wilton, Duntley of Greenland, Langley of Wilmot.

On Incorporations.—Preston of Henniker, Farrell of Manchester, Matson of Concord, Stevens of Bartlett, Davis of

Laconia, Chase of Newfields, Nyberg of Manchester, Holland of Hinsdale, Vaillancourt of Berlin, Ingham of Nashua, King of Orange, Jones of New Durham, Woodbury of Antrim.

On Industrial School.—Sheehan of Manchester, Jewett of Claremont, Pinneo of Hanover, Wentworth of Somersworth, Moors of Marlborough, Gunderman of Manchester, Lane of Hampton, Kendall of Mont Vernon, Sawyer of Atkinson, Morse of Bradford, Lampron of Nashua, Plaisted of Jefferson, Cogan of Portsmouth.

On Insurance.—Donahue of Manchester, Barrett of Dover, Tuck of Nashua, Willis of Concord, Barr of Manchester, Shute of Derry, Lewis of Nashua, Lane of Swanzey, Aiken of Newport, Russell of Rumney, Chase of Laconia, Graves of Andover, Hutchins of Berlin.

On Judiciary.—Batchelder of Keene, Nason of Dover, Remich of Littleton, Mitchell of Littleton, Buckley of Lancaster, Cavanaugh of Manchester, Whittemore of Dover, Scammon of Exeter, Goss of Berlin, Woodman of Concord, Whitcher of Haverhill, Phillips of Franklin, Small of Rochester.

On Labor.—Worcester of Rochester, Adams of Franklin, Armstrong of Manchester, Crowell of Londonderry, Calley of Bristol, Blake of Wakefield, Whitaker of Hillsborough, Straw of Unity, Amidon of Richmond, Mason of Tilton, Tripp of Epsom, Gallagher of Carroll, Farley of Hollis.

On Liquor Laws.—Batchelder of Keene, Nason of Dover, Remich of Littleton, Mitchell of Littleton, Buckley of Lancaster, Cavanaugh of Manchester, Whittemore of Dover, Scammon of Exeter, Goss of Berlin, Woodman of Concord, Whitcher of Haverhill, Phillips of Franklin, Small of Rochester.

On Manufactures.—Ela of Warner, Whitney of Keene, Davis of Franklin, York of Farmington, Darbe of Danville, Townsend of Milton, Henry of Lincoln, Graf of Manchester, Ware of Hancock, Clough of Gilmanton, Morse of Manchester, Earley of Nashua, Kane of Manchester.

On Mileage.—Edwards of Laconia, Pollard of Tamworth, Durgin of Concord, Philbrick of Springfield, Houston of

Thornton, Wilson of Shelburne, Abbott of Manchester, Edgerly of Epping, Dow of Seabrook, Boutin of Somersworth, Shaughnessey of Manchester, Jones of Keene, Moran of Nashua.

On Military Affairs.—Roby of Concord, Smith of Dover, Bunten of Dunbarton, Lintott of Nashua, Tobie of Francestown, Quimby of Kingston, Duncklee of Nashua, White of Deerfield, Kent of Berlin, Chandler of Claremont, Riordan of Manchester, Putnam of Greenfield, Evans of Holderness.

On National Affairs.—Hill (A. W.) of Concord, Davis of Lee, Quimby of Manchester, Shepard of Concord, Little of Campton, Filion of Manchester, Abbott of Salem, Jordan of Columbia, Fitch of Keene, Clark of Acworth, Pridham of Newcastle, Sleeper of Plaistow, Tonery of Manchester.

On Normal School.—Gould of Plymouth, Marshall of Manchester, Cutler of Jaffrey, Fontaine of Allenstown, Morse of Chester, Crocker of Rochester, Sanborn of Sanbornton, Brown of Rye, Bartlett of Manchester, Buckley of Nashua, Langmaid of Chichester, Craine of Deering, O'Connor of Stark.

On Public Health.—Mitchell of Lancaster, Chase of Orford, Adams of Franklin, Bell of Woodstock, Hill (A. W.) of Concord, McDonald of Manchester, McCrillis of Rochester, Gordon of Salem, Kennedy of Concord, Maloney of Keene, Sullivan of Nashua, Young of Sandown, Morin of Franklin.

On Public Improvements.—Collins of Nashua, Richards of Newport, Blaisdell of Portsmouth, Emerson of Concord, Churchill of Cornish, Fuller of Hinsdale, Filion of Manchester, Goodrich of Warren, Caird of Berlin, Simpson of Manchester, Warren of Rochester, Drake of Freedom, Pillsbury of Sutton.

On Railroads.—French of Moultonborough, Harris of Boscawen, Crossman of Lisbon, Dorothy of Enfield, Kimball of Laconia, Long of Claremont, Hall of Westmoreland, Morgan of Manchester, Ahern of Concord, Bussell of Nashua, Jewell of Dover, Haines of Newmarket, Martin of Colebrook.

On Retrenchment and Reform.—Morrill of New Hampton, Brown of Hampton Falls, Ware of Alstead, Scott of Nelson, Dozois of Manchester, Smith of Pittsburg, Lemay of Manchester, Adams of Portsmouth, Libby of Dover, Trinity of

Manchester, Stewart of Berlin, Kohler of Manchester, Fecteau of Laconia.

On Revision of Statutes.—Bartlett of Derry, Smith of Peterborough, Demers of Somersworth, Britton of Wolfeborough, Tallant of Pembroke, Ramsdell of Dover, Shenton of Nashua, Straw of Manchester, Ferrin of Plymouth, Gowing of Dublin, Libby of Gorham, Jones of Franklin, Lufkin of Langdon.

On Roads, Bridges, and Canals.—Foye of Portsmouth, Fisk of Hopkinton, Trickey of Jackson, Foster of Enfield, Morrill of New Hampton, Bell of Woodstock, Robinson of Milford, Brown of Fremont, Russell of Sunapee, Bragg of Errol, Harrity of Rollinsford, Sherman of Walpole, Dinsmore of Manchester.

On Soldiers' Home.—Severance of Exeter, Hull of Laconia, Warner of North Hampton, Aldrich of Pembroke, Comings of Lebanon, Bunce of Dover, Twombly of Hill, Davis of Concord, Sanborn of Northfield, Littlefield of Albany, Hoitt of Barnstead, Glover of Franconia, Couhig of Portsmouth.

On State Prison.—Nowell of Exeter, Edwards of Laconia, Cate of Concord, George of Newton, Gates of Canaan, Chase of Manchester, Piper of Northumberland, Lund of Nashua, Scannell of Manchester, Murnane of Somersworth, Hutchins of Pittsfield, Donovan of Keene, Ryan of Manchester.

On Towns.—Darling of Whitefield, Pierce of Jaffrey, Stanley of Lisbon, Pollard of Tamworth, Swain of South Hampton, Tillotson of Dalton, Emerson of Manchester, Polzer of Gilsum, Beck of Canterbury, Caverly of Strafford, Shea of Nashua, Janelle of Manchester, Notterstead of Berlin.

On Unfinished Business.—Mathes of Dover, Hull of Laconia, Symonds of Concord, Abbott of Manchester, Fellows of Brentwood, Dubuc of Manchester, Darrah of Manchester, Wesley of Dover, Sullivan of Manchester, Desmarais of Nashua, Whalen of Manchester, Smyth of Berlin, Celley of Piermont.

Special Committee on Apportionment.—Tallant of Pembroke, Wallace of Rochester, Straw of Manchester, Hardy of Derry, Beacham of Wolfeborough, Ellis of Lancaster, Kellom of Winchester, Rogers of Tilton, Huntley of Claremont, Davenport of Bath.

On Rules.—Speaker, Batchelder of Keene, Remich of Littleton, Nason of Dover, Small of Rochester.

On Journal of the House.—Speaker, Buckley of Lancaster, Drake of Freedom.

JOINT STANDING COMMITTEES.

On Engrossed Bills.—Willis of Concord, Converse of Lyme.

On State Library.—Whitcher of Haverhill, Hayes of Dover, Libby of Gorham.

On State House and State House Yard.—Lintott of Nashua, Fellows of Brentwood, Hill (E. J.) of Concord.

On motion of Mr. Howe of Hanover, at 8.20 the House adjourned.

TUESDAY, JANUARY 13, 1903.

The House met at 11 o'clock.

Prayer was offered by the chaplain.

BILLS INTRODUCED.

The following bills were severally introduced, read twice, and referred as follows:

By Mr. Cavanaugh of Manchester, An act in relation to the salary of the state reporter.   To the Committee on Judiciary.

By Mr. Remich of Littleton, An act to promote cleanliness and to protect the public from the disease commonly known as consumption.   To the Committee on Public Health.

The following bill was introduced and read a first time:

By Mr. Remich of Littleton, An act to amend sections 15, 16, and 17 of chapter 112 of the Public Statutes, relating to the sale of spirituous and malt liquors.

The question being, Shall the bill be read a second time, on a *viva voce* vote, the bill was refused a second reading.

Mr. Remich of Littleton called for a division.

(Discussion ensued.)

Mr. Remich withdrew his call for a division and on a *viva voce* vote the bill was given a second reading and referred to the Committee on Liquor Laws.

The following bill was introduced, read twice, and referred as follows:

By Mr. Howe of Hanover, An act to regulate the speed and operation of automobiles and motor vehicles on highways. To the Committee on Judiciary.

The following bill was introduced, and on motion of Mr. Ahern of Concord, the rules were suspended, the bill read a first and second time by its title and laid upon the table to be printed:

By Mr. Jones of Franklin, An act in amendment of chapter 112 of the Public Statutes, establishing local option in the sale of intoxicating liquors.

The following bill was introduced, read twice, and referred as follows:

By Mr. Willis of Concord, An act to regulate the speed and operation of automobiles and motor vehicles on streets and highways.   To the Committee on Judiciary.

The following bill was introduced and on motion of Mr. Remich of Littleton, the rules were suspended, the bill read a first and second time by its title and referred as follows:

By Mr. Remich of Littleton, An act to amend chapter 243 of the Laws of 1901, creating the Grafton Improvement, Manufacturing and Power Company.   To the Committee on Judiciary.

The following bill was introduced, read twice, and referred as follows:

By Mr. Smith of Peterborough, An act in amendment of chapter 282 of the Public Statutes, entitled " Common jails and prisoners therein." To the Committee on Revision of Statutes.

The following bill was introduced and on motion of Mr. Ahern of Concord, the rules were suspended, the bill read a first and second time by its title, and referred to a special committee consisting of the Concord delegation:

By Mr. Willis of Concord, An act in amendment of the charter of the city of Concord creating the office of city comptroller.

The following bill was introduced and on motion of Mr. Remich of Littleton, the rules were suspended, the bill read a first and second time by its title, and referred as follows:

By Mr. Remich of Littleton, An act to incorporate the Littleton, Franconia and Bethlehem Electric Railroad Company. To the Committee on Railroads.

The following bills were severally introduced, read twice, and referred as follows:

By Mr. Taggart of Manchester, An act authorizing the Manchester Mills to increase its capital stock. To the Committee on Judiciary.

By Mr. Roby of Concord, An act authorizing the Concord & Montreal Railroad, lessor, to acquire the Concord Street Railway and other property, to issue stock and bonds to pay therefor and authorizing a physical connection of the Manchester Street Railway with the electric branches of the Concord & Montreal Railroad. To the Committee on Railroads.

By Mr. Willis of Concord, An act reviving and continuing the charter of the Warner & Kearsarge Road Company, and amendments to said charter. To the Committee on Judiciary.

The following bill was introduced, and on motion of Mr. Rogers of Tilton, the rules were suspended, the bill read a first and second time by its title, and referred as follows:

By Mr. Rogers of Tilton, An act to establish a new apportionment for the assessment of public taxes. To the special Committee on Apportionment.

The following bill was introduced, read twice, and referred as follows:

By Mr. Willis of Concord, An act to regulate the sale of merchandise in bulk. To the Committee on Judiciary.

The following joint resolutions were severally introduced, read twice, and referred as follows:

By Mr. Hoyt of Sandwich, Joint resolution in favor of the Sandwich Notch road in the town of Sandwich. To the Committee on Roads, Bridges, and Canals.

By Mr. Mitchell of Littleton, Joint resolution relating to the completion of the topographical survey. To the Committee on Forestry.

By Mr. Mitchell of Littleton, Joint resolution in favor of screening the outlet of Forest lake. To the Committee on Fisheries and Game.

NOTICES OF BILLS.

By Mr. Bussell of Nashua, An act to allow the city of Nashua to appropriate money for the celebration of its semi-centennial.

By Mr. Crossman of Lisbon, An act including the town of Lyman among deer hunting towns.

By Mr. Crossman of Lisbon, An act in favor of Oren Clough of Lisbon.

By Mr. Crossman of Lisbon, An act protecting sportsmen during deer season.

By Mr. Crossman of Lisbon, An act amending the present medical practice law of New Hampshire.

By Mr. Remich of Littleton, Joint resolution in favor of the Forest Lake road in the towns of Whitefield and Dalton.

By Mr. Remich of Littleton, An act to encourage the use of wide tires on certain vehicles constructed before January 1, 1900, and now in use in New Hampshire.

By Mr. Howe of Barrington, An act to provide for the better enforcement of the liquor laws.

By Mr. Tenney of Fitzwilliam, An act in amendment of, and in addition to, section 3, chapter 105 of the Laws of 1901, in relation to political caucuses and conventions.

By Mr. Tenney of Fitzwilliam, An act to regulate the speed and operation of automobiles and motor vehicles on highways.

By Mr. Emerson of Hampstead, An act to incorporate the Hampstead & Haverhill Street Railway Company.

By Mr. Langley of Durham, An act to incorporate the Dover & Durham Street Railway Company.

By Mr. Pridham of Newcastle, An act to incorporate the Portsmouth & Newcastle Street Railway Company.

By Mr. Severance of Exeter, An act to regulate the speed and operation of automobiles and motor vehicles on the public highways.

By Mr. Remich of Littleton, Joint resolution to provide for completing the painting and decorating of the walls of the state library building.

By Mr. Remich of Littleton, Joint resolution favoring the

establishment of a national forest reserve in the White Mountain region.

By Mr. Tallant of Pembroke, An act relative to the enlargement of the state library building.

By Mr. Lane of Hampton, An act for the protection of clams in Hampton river.

By Mr. Goss of Berlin, An act to provide for the holding of library institutes.

By Mr. Warner of North Hampton, An act to incorporate the North Hampton Street Railway Company.

By Mr. Badger of Newington, An act to incorporate the Portsmouth & Newington Street Railway Company.

By Mr. Severance of Exeter, An act to amend section 33 of chapter 2 of the Public Statutes, relating to the construction of certain statutes.

By Mr. Buckley of Lancaster, An act to abolish the board of library commissioners.

By Mr. Churchill of Cornish, An act to regulate the speed and operation of automobiles and motor vehicles on highways.

By Mr. Ahern of Concord, An act to establish traveling libraries.

By Mr. Kimball of Concord, Joint resolution in favor of the New Hampshire State Hospital.

By Mr. Hoyt of Sandwich, An act providing a seal for the State Board of Agriculture.

By Mr. Bartlett of Derry, An act to incorporate the Derry Savings Bank of Derry.

By Mr. Bartlett of Derry, An act to incorporate the Derry & Salem Street Railway Company.

By Mr. Bartlett of Derry, An act relating to the salary of the judge of probate for the county of Rockingham.

By Mr. Adams of Portsmouth, An act to provide for the continuous operation of cars upon the Portsmouth & Exeter Street Railway and the Portsmouth Electric Railway, owned and operated by the Boston & Maine Railroad.

By Mr. Brown of Greenville, An act to establish the police court of Greenville.

By Mr. Whitcher of Haverhill, An act repealing chapter

200 of the Laws of 1899, and amending chapter 207 of the Laws of 1895.

By Mr. Brown of Greenville, An act to incorporate the Greenville Electric Light, Power and Heat Company.

By Mr. Whitcher of Haverhill, Joint resolution in favor of the North and South road, so called, in the town of Benton.

By Mr. Whittemore of Dover, An act in amendment of the charter of the city of Dover, creating a board of police commissioners for said city, and fixing the salaries of the officers in the police department.

By Mr. Whittemore of Dover, An act to incorporate the New Hampshire Genealogical Society.

On motion of Mr. Woodman of Concord,—

Resolved, That the use of Representatives' Hall be granted to the Democrats of the Legislature Wednesday, January 14, directly after adjournment of the morning session, for the purpose of holding a caucus.

On motion of Mr. Remich of Littleton,—

Resolved, That the Committee on Appropriations are hereby requested to make early investigation of the state finances with a view to the reduction of the state tax, and report by bill or otherwise.

On motion of Mr. Whitcher of Haverhill,—

Resolved, That the use of Representatives' Hall be granted to the State Board of Associated Charities for a public meeting on the evening of Tuesday, February 3.

On motion of Mr. Bell of Woodstock,—

Resolved, That prayers be offered in the House five minutes before the hour fixed for the first session each day, and that His Excellency the Governor, the Council, and the Honorable Senate be informed thereof, and be invited to attend.

On motion of Mr. Morgan of Manchester,—

Resolved, by the House of Representatives, the Senate concurring, That a committee of three on the part of the House be appointed to confer with a like committee on the part of the Senate, to make assignment of rooms to the various committees and employees of both branches of the Legislature.

The Speaker named as such committee Messrs. Morgan of Manchester, Darling of Whitefield, and Drake of Freedom.

On motion of Mr. Small of Rochester,—

Resolved, That the use of Representatives' Hall be granted the Republican members for Wednesday evening, January 14, for the purpose of nominating a United States Senator and state officers.

The Speaker named as permanent tellers of the House :

Division 1, Mr. Nelson of Portsmouth.
Division 2, Mr. Bussell of Nashua.
Division 3, Mr. Barrett of Dover.
Division 4, Mr. French of Moultonborough.
Division 5, Mr. Gould of Plymouth.

On motion of Mr. Mitchell of Littleton, at 12.10 the House adjourned.

AFTERNOON.

The House met at 2 o'clock.

NOTICES OF BILLS.

By Mr. Sheehan of Manchester, An act to repeal the charter and franchises of the Massabesic Horse Railroad Company.

By Mr. Chase of Manchester, An act to incorporate the Uncanoonuc Incline Railway and Development Company.

By Mr. Chandler of Claremont, An act to extend the charter for the building of the Claremont Street Railway.

By Mr. Harrity of Rollinsford, An act to unite the school districts of the town of Rollinsford.

By Mr. Piper of Northumberland, An act to prevent telephone, telegraph, electric light and power companies from cutting down or injuring trees within the limits of the highway.

By Mr. Farley of Hollis, An act to incorporate the Nashua & Hollis Electric Railroad Company.

By Mr. Hoyt of Sandwich, An act for the better preservation of highways and accommodating public travel.

By Mr. Haines of Newmarket, An act in amendment of an act approved March 26, 1895, entitled "An act in amendment of an act incorporating the Newmarket Manufacturing Company," approved June 12, 1823, and an act in amendment thereof, approved July 7, 1881.

By Mr. Sawyer of Milford, An act relating to negotiable instruments, being an act to establish a law uniform with the laws of other states on that subject.

By Mr. Vaillancourt of Berlin, An act regulating the charges for passenger service on railways in this state, and to provide for the sale of mileage books.

By Mr. Vaillancourt of Berlin, An act relating to probate bonds and to the liability of sureties thereunder.

By Mr. Sherman of Claremont, An act to close Crescent lake, formerly known as Cold pond, in the towns of Unity and Acworth to ice fishing.

By Mr. Shute of Derry, An act requiring goods made in whole or part by convict labor to be so stamped.

By Mr. Shute of Derry, An act regulating fares on electric roads.

By Mr. Cutler of Jaffrey, An act to amend fish and game laws, to prevent fishing through the ice in waters of this state by non-residents of the state.

By Mr. Cutler of Jaffrey, An act to amend fish and game laws, shortening the open season for partridge and grouse.

By Mr. Smith of Dover, An act authorizing the city of Dover to exempt from taxation the property of the Hayes hospital.

By Mr. Howe of Hanover, An act relating to the counting of votes at biennial elections.

By Mr. Fellows of Brentwood, An act to incorporate the Epping, Brentwood & Kingston Street Railway Company.

Messrs. Place of Middleton and Whittemore of Dover, having been duly qualified by His Excellency the Governor, appeared and took their seats as members of the House.

On motion of Mr. Ahern of Concord, at 2.05 the House adjourned.

WEDNESDAY, JANUARY 14, 1903.

The House met at 11 o'clock.

Prayer was offered by the chaplain.

PETITION PRESENTED AND REFERRED.

By Mr. Darling of Whitefield, Petition of James J. Parks for a seat in the House of Representatives. To the Committee on Elections.

REPORTS OF COMMITTEES.

Mr. Roby, for the special committee of the Concord delegation, to whom was referred An act in amendment of the charter of the city of Concord, creating the office of city comptroller, having considered the same, report the same with the following resolution:

Resolved, That it is inexpedient to legislate.

The report was accepted and the resolution adopted.

Mr. Nason, for the Committee on Judiciary, to whom was referred An act authorizing the Manchester Mills to increase its capital stock, having considered the same, report the same with the following suggestion: That the object sought in the bill cannot be had under the Public Statutes, and suggest its reference to the Committee on Incorporations.

The report was accepted and the bill referred to the Committee on Incorporations.

Mr. Remich, for the Committee on Judiciary, to whom was referred An act to amend chapter 243 of the laws of 1901, creating the Grafton Improvement, Manufacturing and Power Company, having considered the same, report the same with the following resolution:

Resolved, That the objects sought in said bill cannot be obtained under the general law.

The report was accepted, the resolution adopted, and the bill referred to the Committee on Incorporations.

BILLS, ETC., INTRODUCED.

The following bill was introduced, read twice, and referred as follows:

By Mr. Ahern of Concord, An act to establish traveling libraries. To the Committee on State Library.

The following joint resolution was introduced, read twice, and on motion of Mr. Remich of Littleton, the rules were suspended and the joint resolution put upon its third reading and passage at the present time :

By Mr. Remich of Littleton, Joint resolution favoring the establishment of a national forest reserve in the White Mountain region.

The reading having commenced, the further reading of the joint resolution was dispensed with on motion of Mr. Ahern of Concord, and the joint resolution was passed and sent to the Senate for concurrence.

The following bills were severally introduced, read twice, and referred as follows :

By Mr. Chase of Manchester, An act to incorporate the Uncanoonuc Incline Railway and . Development Company. To the Committee on Railroads.

By Mr. Harrity of Rollinsford, An act to unite the school districts of the town of Rollinsford. To the Committee on Education.

By Mr. Tallant of Pembroke, An act relative to the enlargement of the state library building. To the Committee on State Library.

By Mr. Whitcher of Haverhill, An act to repeal chapter 200 of the Laws of 1899, entitled ''An act to amend chapter 207 of the Laws of 1895, relating to the police court of Haverhill.'' To the Committee on Judiciary.

By Mr. Howe of Hanover, An act relating to the counting of votes at biennial elections. To the Committee on Revision of Statutes.

By Mr. Haines of Newmarket, An act in amendment of an act, approved March 26, 1895, entitled ''An act in amendment of an act incorporating the Newmarket Manufacturing Company,'' approved June 12, 1823, and an act in amendment thereof, approved July 7, 1881. To the Committee on Judiciary.

By Mr. Small of Rochester, An act in amendment of section 15 of chapter 93 of the Public Statutes as amended in 1901, relating to scholars. To the Committee on Judiciary.

By Mr. Farley of Hollis, An act to incorporate the Nashua & Hollis Electric Railroad Company. To the Committee on Railroads.

By Mr. Whittemore of Dover, An act to incorporate the New Hampshire Genealogical Society. To the Committee on Judiciary.

By Mr. Smith of Dover, An act authorizing the city of Dover to exempt from taxation the property of the Hayes Hospital. To the Committee on Judiciary.

By Mr. Buckley of Lancaster, An act to abolish the board of library commissioners. To the Committee on State Library.

By Mr. Whittemore of Dover, An act in amendment of the charter of the city of Dover, creating a board of police commissioners for said city, and fixing the salaries of the officers in the police department. To the Committee on Judiciary.

By Mr. Goss of Berlin, An act to provide for the holding of library institutes. To the Committee on State Library.

By Mr. Remich of Littleton, An act to encourage the use of wide tires on certain vehicles constructed before January 1, 1900, and now in use in New Hampshire. To the Committee on Agriculture.

By Mr. Remich of Littleton, Joint resolution to provide for completing the painting and decorating of the walls of the state library building. To the Committee on State Library.

By Mr. Remich of Littleton, Joint resolution in favor of the Forest Lake road, in the towns of Whitefield and Dalton. To the Committee on Roads, Bridges, and Canals.

By Mr. Kimball of Concord, Joint resolution in favor of the New Hampshire State Hospital. To the Committee on Asylum for Insane.

By Mr. Severance of Exeter, An act to amend section 33 of chapter 2 of the Public Statutes, relating to the construction of certain statutes. To the Committee on Liquor Laws.

By Mr. Howe of Barrington, An act to provide for the better enforcement of the liquor laws. To the Committee on Liquor Laws.

By Mr. Sherman of Claremont, An act to close Crescent lake, formerly known as Cold pond, in the towns of Unity and Acworth, to ice fishing. To the Committee on Fisheries and Game.

By Mr. Crossman of Lisbon, An act in favor of Oren Clough of Lisbon. To the Committee on Claims.

By Mr. Crossman of Lisbon, An act protecting sportsmen during deer season. To the Committee on Fisheries and Game.

By Mr. Churchill of Cornish, An act to regulate the speed and operation of automobiles and motor vehicles on highways. To the Committee on Judiciary.

By Mr. Piper of Northumberland, An act to prevent telegraph, telephone, electric light and power companies from cutting down or injuring trees within the limits of the highway. To the Committee on Judiciary.

By Mr. Smith of Peterborough, An act in amendment of section 1, chapter 185, Laws of 1901, entitled "An act authorizing the Hillsborough county convention to raise money for the building and repairing of court houses." To the Committee on Revision of Statutes.

By Mr. Whitcher of Haverhill, Joint resolution for the repair of the North and South road, so called, in the town of Benton. To the Committee on Roads, Bridges, and Canals.

By Mr. Tenney of Fitzwilliam, An act in amendment of, and in addition to, section 3, chapter 105 of the Laws of 1901, in relation to political caucuses and conventions. To the Committee on Judiciary.

By Mr. Tenney of Fitzwilliam, An act to regulate the speed and operation of automobiles and motor vehicles on highways. To the Committee on Judiciary.

MESSAGE FROM THE SENATE.

A message from the Honorable Senate, by its clerk, announced that the Senate concur with the House of Representatives in the passage of the following concurrent resolution:

Resolved, by the House of Representatives, the Senate concurring, That a committee of three on the part of the House be appointed to confer with a like committee on the part of the Senate, to make assignment of rooms to the various committees and employees of both branches of the Legislature.

The President has named as members of such committee, on the part of the Senate, Senators Burnell of District No. 5, Marvin of District No. 8, and Richmond of District No. 23.

The message also announced that the Senate has adopted the following resolution :

Resolved, That the Senate accept the invitation to attend prayers, extended by the House of Representatives.

The message further announced that the Senate concur with the House of Representatives in the passage of the following joint resolution :

Joint resolution favoring the establishment of a national forest reserve in the White Mountain region.

NOTICES OF BILLS.

By Mr. Yeaton of Portsmouth, An act to regulate the traffic in intoxicating liquors.

By Mr. Donovan of Keene, An act in relation to licensing dogs kept for breeding purposes.

By Mr. Churchill of Cornish, An act to amend section 4 of chapter 96 of the Laws of 1901, and section 6 of chapter 92 of the Public Statutes, relating to courses of study.

By Mr. Buckley of Lancaster, An act relating to persons employed under and by virtue of an act of congress relating to the surveys of the geological survey of the United States.

By Mr. Buckley of Lancaster, An act to abolish capital punishment.

By Mr. Mitchell of Lancaster, An act to establish a state sanatorium for consumptives.

By Mr. Howe of Hanover, An act in amendment of chapter 23 of the Laws of 1901, entitled "An act to establish a laboratory of hygiene."

By Mr. Whittemore of Dover, An act to establish a state normal school.

By Mr. Rogers of Tilton, An act to amend an act to establish a corporation by the name of the Trustees of the New Hampshire Conference Seminary and the New Hampshire Female College, approved December 29, 1852, and other acts amending the same.

By Mr. Scammon of Exeter, An act in amendment of chapter 51 of the Public Statutes, relating to cemeteries.

By Mr. Fox of Marlow, An act to extend the charter of the Keene, Marlow & Newport Electric Railway Company.

By Mr. Dow of Conway, Joint resolution in favor of the Hurricane Mountain road, so called, in the towns of Conway and Chatham.

By Mr. Scammon of Exeter, An act to permit executors and administrators to resign.

By Mr. Howe of Barrington, Joint resolution in favor of highways and bridges in the town of Barrington.

By Mr. Barrett of Dover, An act to amend the charter of the Concord, Dover & Rochester Street Railway.

By Mr. Chase of Laconia, An act to incorporate the Winnipiseogee Valley Street Railway.

By Mr. Fifield of Conway, An act to amend chapter 92 of the Public Statutes, relating to duties of school boards.

By Mr. Morrill of New Hampton, An act to include the town of New Hampton among deer-hunting towns.

By Mr. Trickey of Jackson, Joint resolution in favor of the Pinkham Notch road, so called, in the town of Jackson.

By Mr. Ramsdell of Dover, An act to prohibit the sitting of justices of police courts in certain cases.

By Mr. Lynch of Manchester, An act to amend section 14, chapter 180, Public Statutes, regulating the hours of labor for women and minors in manufacturing or mechanical establishments.

By Mr. Riordan of Manchester, An act to enable the city of Manchester to appropriate money toward the armory rent of Camp Derwin, No. 184, Spanish American War Veterans.

By Mr. Gould of Plymouth, An act to amend chapter 95 of the Public Statutes relating to normal school.

By Mr. Hoyt of Sandwich, An act to encourage the planting and perpetuation of forests.

By Mr. Hoyt of Sandwich, An act to incorporate the Ashland, Sandwich & Wolfeborough Railway Company.

By Mr. Roby of Concord, An act to amend chapter 76 of the Laws of 1897, in relation to hawkers and peddlers.

By Mr. Brown of Fremont, An act to incorporate the Chester, Fremont & Brentwood Street Railway Company.

By Mr. Gunderman of Manchester, An act to open the ponds and lakes of the state for ice fishing for one month in the year.

By Mr. Matson of Concord, An act to regulate the sale of intoxicating liquors.

By Mr. Morrill of Ashland, Joint resolution in favor of raising Squam bridge in Holderness and Little Squam bridge in Ashland, and of improving navigation in Squam lake and connecting waters.

By Mr. Tuck of Nashua, Joint resolution for the preservation of the records and files of the probate court of the county of Hillsborough.

By Mr. Little of Campton, Joint resolution for the repair of highways and bridges in the town of Campton.

By Mr. Whitcher of Haverhill, Joint resolution for construction of a road in the town of Benton from the Tunnel Stream road, so called, to High Street road, so called, in said town.

By Mr. Whitcher of Haverhill, An act to amend chapter 69 of the Laws of 1901, being an act to protect the Ammonoosuc river in Carroll, Bethlehem, Littleton, Lisbon, and Bath, and its tributaries from pollution by sawdust and other waste.

By Mr. Whitcher of Haverhill, An act to establish a police court in Haverhill.

By Mr. French of Moultonborough, Joint resolution in favor of highways laid out agreeably to chapter 70 of Public Statutes of New Hampshire.

By Mr. French of Moultonborough, An act to amend sections 1-3 and 4, chapter 72 of Public Statutes, relating to discontinuance of highways.

On motion of Mr. Remich of Littleton,—

Resolved, That the National American Woman's Suffrage Association be given the use of Representatives' Hall for Wednesday evenings, February 11 and 25.

On motion of Mr. Remich of Littleton,—

Resolved, That the committee appointed to assign committee rooms be instructed to investigate for the purpose of ascertaining whether they can obtain suitable rooms for committee purposes from private owners in case the rooms belonging to the state are insufficient in number and size to accommodate all of the committees properly, and to secure such rooms as they think necessary.

On motion of Mr. French of Moultonborough, at 12.35 the House adjourned.

AFTERNOON.

The House met at 2 o'clock.

NOTICES OF BILLS.

By Mr. French of Moultonborough, An act to legalize the biennial election of the town of Conway, held November 4, 1902.

By Mr. Ramsay of Walpole, An act in amendment of the charter of the Walpole Electric Light and Power Company.

By Mr. Sherman of Walpole, An act to incorporate the Walpole Water and Sewer Company.

By Mr. McMurphey of Alexandria, Joint resolution providing for an appropriation for the repair of the Sugar Loaf road, so called, in Alexandria.

By Mr. Crossman of Lisbon, An act to amend Laws of 1901, chapter 79, section 16, with reference to the protection of deer.

By Mr. Crossman of Lisbon, An act amending section 11 of chapter 63 of the Session Laws of 1897, entitled " Practice of Medicine."

By Mr. Lennon of Stratford, An act to amend section 4, chapter 159 of the Public Statutes relating to railroad grade crossings.

(Mr. Nason of Dover in the chair.)

BILLS, ETC., INTRODUCED.

Mr. Cheney of Lebanon called for the unfinished business of the morning session, it being the introduction of bills, and the following bills and joint resolutions were severally introduced, read twice, and referred as follows :

By Mr. Ramsay of Walpole, An act in amendment of the charter of the Walpole Electric Light and Power Company. To the Committee on Judiciary.

By Mr. Bartlett of Derry, An act to incorporate the Derry Savings Bank of Derry. To the Committee on Banks.

By Mr. Cutler of Jaffrey, An act to amend an act in the fish and game laws. To the Committee on Fisheries and Game.

By Mr. Cutler of Jaffrey, An act to prevent fishing through the ice and transporting the same out of the state by non-residents. To the Committee on Fisheries and Game.

By Mr. Ramsdell of Dover, An act to prohibit the sitting of justices of police courts in certain cases. To the Committee on Judiciary.

By Mr. Gould of Plymouth, An act to amend chapter 95 of the Public Statutes relating to normal school. To the Committee on Normal School.

By Mr. Hoyt of Sandwich, An act providing a seal for the State Board of Agriculture. To the Committee on Agriculture.

By Mr. Sherman of Walpole, An act to incorporate the Walpole Water and Sewer Company. To the Committee on Judiciary.

By Mr. Crossman of Lisbon, An act to amend Laws of 1901, chapter 79, section 16, with reference to the protection of deer. To the Committee on Fisheries and Game.

By Mr. Crossman of Lisbon, An act amending section 11, chapter 63 of the Session Laws of 1897, entitled " Practice of Medicine." To the Committee on Judiciary.

By Mr. Howe of Barrington. Joint resolution in favor of highways and bridges in town of Barrington. To the Committee on Roads, Bridges, and Canals.

By Mr. Tuck of Nashua, Joint resolution for the preservation of the records and files of the probate court of the county of Hillsborough. To the Committee on Appropriations.

By Mr. Little of Campton, Joint resolution for the repairs of highways and bridges in the town of Campton. To the Committee on Roads, Bridges, and Canals.

By Mr. Churchill of Cornish, An act to amend section 4 of chapter 96 of the Laws of 1901, and section 6 of chapter 92 of the Public Statutes, relating to courses of study. To the Committee on Education.

By Mr. Mitchell of Lancaster, An act to establish a state

sanatorium for consumptives. To the Committee on Public Health.

The following bill was introduced, and on motion of Mr. Ahern of Concord, the rules were suspended and the bill read a first and second time by its title:

By Mr. Chase of Laconia, An act to incorporate the Winnipiseogee Valley Street Railway. The bill was referred to the Committee on Railroads.

COMMITTEE REPORT.

By unanimous consent of the House, Mr. Cavanaugh of Manchester, for the Committee on Judiciary, to whom was referred An act in amendment of an act approved March 26, 1895, entitled "An act in amendment of an act incorporating the Newmarket Manufacturing Company," approved June 12, 1823, and an act in amendment thereof, approved July 7, 1881, having considered the same, report the same with the following resolution:

Resolved, That the bill be referred to the Committee on Incorporations, as the objects sought by the bill cannot be attained under the general laws.

The report was accepted, the resolution adopted, and the bill referred to the Committee on Incorporations.

NOTICES OF BILLS.

By Mr. Prescott of Laconia, An act in amendment of chapter 262 of the Public Statutes relating to coroners and coroners' inquests.

By Mr. Sawyer of Milford, An act to amend chapter 92, Public Statutes, relating to school boards.

By Mr. Plaisted of Jefferson, An act in amendment of an act, entitled "An act to provide for the survey, location, and construction of the Jefferson rotch Road, in Jefferson, Low and Burbank's Grant, Crawford's Purchase, and Bean's Purchase," approved March 22, 1901.

By Mr. Pierce of Bethlehem, An act providing for the construction of certain sections of road and the completion of a line of public highways inaugurated by the state in the north regions of the White Mountains.

By Mr. Andrews of Somersworth, An act to amend chapter 93, in relation to scholars.

By Mr. Howe of Hanover, An act to amend chapter 60, section 3, Statute Laws of 1891, relating to dog licenses.

By Mr. Libby of Gorham, An act to amend the prohibitory law by permitting local option.

On motion of Mr. Wallace of Rochester, at 2.55 the House adjourned.

THURSDAY, JANUARY 15, 1903.

The House met at 11 o'clock.

Prayer was offered by the chaplain.

On motion of Mr. French of Moultonborough,—

Resolved, That the Speaker be authorized to appoint a messenger, whose duties shall be to assist in the telephone service of this House, and in such other service as he may be directed.

PETITIONS PRESENTED AND REFERRED.

By Mr. Darrah of Manchester, Petition of Herbert N. Davison for a seat in the House of Representatives. To the Committee on Elections.

By Mr. Nelson of Portsmouth, Petition of John W. Weeks of Greenland for a seat in the House of Representatives. To the Committee on Elections.

REPORTS OF COMMITTEES.

Mr. Whittemore of Dover, for the Committee on Judiciary, to whom was referred An act in amendment of the charter of the city of Dover, creating a board of police commisioners for said city, and fixing the salaries of the officers in the police department, having considered the same, report the same with the following resolution :

Resolved, That the bill ought to pass.

The report was accepted, the resolution adopted, and the bill laid upon the table to be printed. On motion of Mr.

Whittemore of Dover, the rules were suspended and the printing of the bill dispensed with. The bill was then ordered to a third reading. On motion of Mr. Nason of Dover, the rules were further suspended and the bill read a third time and passed and sent to the Senate for concurrence.

(Mr. Small of Rochester in the chair.)

Mr. Mitchell of Littleton, for the Committee on Judiciary, to whom was referred An act in relation to the salary of the state reporter, having considered the same, report the same with the following resolution:

Resolved, That the bill ought to pass.

The report was accepted, the resolution adopted, and the bill referred to the Committee on Appropriations.

Mr. Libby of Gorham, for the Committee on Revision of Statutes, to whom was referred An act in amendment of chapter 282 of the Public Statutes, entitled " Common jails and prisoners therein," having considered the same, report the same with the following resolution:

Resolved, That the bill ought to pass.

The report was accepted, and the question being upon the adoption of the resolution reported by the committee, on motion of Mr. Cavanaugh of Manchester, the bill was re-committed to the Committee on Revision of Statutes.

Mr. Nason of Dover, for the Committee on Judiciary, to whom was referred An act to incorporate the Walpole Water and Sewer Co., having considered the same, report the same with the following suggestion:

That the object to be attained by the bill cannot be had under the general laws.

The report was accepted, the suggestion adopted, and the bill referred to the Committee on Incorporations.

Mr. Woodman of Concord, for the Committee on Judiciary, to whom was referred An act in amendment of the charter of the Walpole Electric Light and Power Company, having considered the same, report the same with the following resolution:

Resolved, Object asked for cannot be granted under the general laws.

The report was accepted, the resolution adopted, and the bill referred to the Committee on Incorporations.

Mr. Ingham of Nashua, for the Committee on Incorporations, to whom was referred An act in amendment of an act approved March 26, 1895, entitled, "An act in amendment of an act incorporating the Newmarket Manufacturing Co.," approved June 12, 1823, and an act in amendment thereof approved July 7, 1881, having considered the same, report the same with the recommendation that the bill ought to pass.

Mr. Shenton of Nashua, for the Committee on Revision of Statutes, to whom was referred An act in amendment of section 1, chapter 185, Laws of 1901, entitled "An act authorizing the Hillsborough County Convention to raise money for building and repairing of court houses," having considered the same, report the same with the following resolution:

Resolved, That the bill ought to pass.

The reports were severally accepted, the resolutions reported by the committees adopted, and the bills laid upon the table to be printed.

Mr. Bell of Woodstock, for the Committee on Public Health, to whom was referred Joint resolution to promote cleanliness and to protect the public from the disease commonly known as consumption, having considered the same, report the same with the following resolution:

Resolved, That the bill ought to pass, with the following amendment: Strike out the word "fifty" in section 5, and insert the word " ten." The section, as amended, to read as follows:

SECT. 5. Any person violating the provisions of this act shall be punished by a fine not exceeding ten dollars.

The report was accepted, the amendment adopted, and the joint resolution laid upon the table to be printed.

Mr. Mitchell of Littleton, for the Committee on Judiciary, to whom was referred An act to regulate the sale of merchandise in bulk, having considered the same, report the same with the following resolution:

Resolved, That it is inexpedient to legislate.

The report was accepted and the resolution reported by the committee adopted.

Mr. Whittemore of Dover, for the Committee on Judiciary, to whom was referred An act to incorporate the New Hampshire Genealogical Society, having considered the same, report the same with the following suggestion:

That the objects to be accomplished under this act cannot be had under the general laws, and recommend that the same be referred to the Committee on Incorporations.

The report was accepted, the recommendation adopted, and the bill referred to the Committee on Incorporations.

Mr. Ingham of Nashua, for the Committee on Incorporations, to whom was referred An act authorizing the Manchester Mills to increase its capital stock, having considered the same, report the same with the recommendation that the bill ought to pass.

The report was accepted, the recommendation adopted, and the bill laid upon the table to be printed. On motion of Mr. Taggart of Manchester, the rules were suspended, the printing dispensed with and the bill ordered to a third reading. Upon motion of the same gentleman the rules were further suspended, the bill read a third time and passed and sent to the Senate for concurrence.

Mr. Morgan of Manchester, for the Committee on Conference, to whom was referred the assignment of rooms to the various committees and employees of both branches of the Legislature, reported with the following resolution:

Resolved, That the assignment of rooms to the standing committees of the House and the joint standing committees of the Senate and House be as follows:

On Agriculture, office of the secretary of the board of agriculture.

On Agricultural College, office of the secretary of the board of agriculture.

On Apportionment, office of state treasurer.

On Appropriations, room 5.

On Asylum for Insane, room 6.

On Banks, bank commissioners' office.

On Claims, room 7.

On County Affairs, room 8.

On Education, office of the superintendent of public instruction.

On Elections, room 4.

On Feeble-Minded School, room 10.

On Fisheries and Game, state library.

On Forestry, room 7.

On Incorporations, room 9.

On Industrial School, room 10.

On Insurance, insurance commissioner's office.

On Journal of the House, Representatives' Hall.

On Judiciary, room 1.

On Labor, labor commissioner's office.

On Liquor Laws, room 1.

On Manufactures, room 9.

On Mileage, room 10.

On Military Affairs, adjutant-general's office.

On National Affairs, state library.

On Normal School, room 10.

On Public Health, room 2.

On Public Improvements, room 4.

On Railroads, office of state board of charities and Union hall.

On Retrenchment and Reform, room 10.

On Revision of Statutes, room 5.

On Roads, Bridges, and Canals, room 8.

On Rules, Representatives' Hall.

On Soldiers' Home, room 10.

On State Prison, room 8.

On Towns, room 7.

On Unfinished Business, room 10.

On Engrossed Bills, office of the secretary of state.

On State House and State House Yard, state library.

On State Library, state library.

BILLS, ETC., INTRODUCED.

The following bill was introduced and on motion of Mr. Mitchell of Littleton, the rules were suspended, the bill read a first and second time by its title, and laid upon the table to be printed :

By Mr. Pierce of Bethlehem, An act providing for the construction of certain sections of roads and the completion of a line of public highways already inaugurated by the state in the north regions of the White Mountains.

The following bill was introduced and on motion of Mr. Remich of Littleton, the rules were suspended, the bill read a first and second time by its title, and laid upon the table to be printed:

By Mr. Mitchell of Littleton, An act to provide for a more economical and practical expenditure of money appropriated by the state for the construction and repairs of highways.

The following bill was introduced and on motion of Mr. Whitcher of Haverhill, the rules were suspended and the bill read a first and second time by its title, and laid upon the table to be printed:

By Mr. Plaisted of Jefferson, An act in amendment of an act entitled "An act to provide for the survey, location and construction of the Jefferson Notch road, in Jefferson, Low & Burbank's Grant, Crawford's Purchase, and Bean's Purchase," approved March 2ₔ, 1901.

The following bills were severally introduced, read twice, and referred as follows:

By Mr. Gunderman of Manchester, An act to open the ponds and lakes of the state for ice fishing for one month in the year. To the Committee on Fisheries and Game.

By Mr. Buckley of Lancaster, An act to abolish capital punishment. To the Committee on Judiciary.

By Mr. Rogers of Tilton, An act to amend an act to establish a corporation by the name of the Trustees of the New Hampshire Conference Seminary and the New Hampshire Female College, approved December 29, 1852, and other acts amending the same. To the Committee on Judiciary.

By Mr. Whitcher of Haverhill, An act to establish a police court in the town of Haverhill. To the Committee on Judiciary.

By Mr. Buckley of Lancaster, An act relating to persons employed under and by virtue of an act of congress relating to the surveys of the geological survey of the United States. To the Committee on Judiciary.

By Mr. Whitcher of Haverhill, An act to amend chapter 69 of the Laws of 1901, entitled "An act to protect the Ammonoosuc river in Carroll, Bethlehem, Littleton, Lisbon, and Bath, and its tributaries, from pollution by sawdust and other waste." To the Committee on Judiciary.

By Mr. Donovan of Keene, An act in relation to licensing dogs kept for breeding purposes. To the Committee on Judiciary.

By Mr. Howe of Hanover, An act to amend chapter 60, section 3 of the Statute Laws of 1891, relating to dog licenses. To the Committee on Revision of Statutes.

By Mr. Adams of Portsmouth, An act to provide for the continuous operation of cars upon the Portsmouth & Exeter street railway, and the Portsmouth electric railway, owned and operated by the Boston & Maine Railroad. To the Committee on Railroads.

By Mr. French of Moultonborough, An act to legalize the biennial election of the town of Conway, held November 4, 1902. To the Committee on Elections.

By Mr. Fifield of Conway, An act to amend chapter 92 of the Public Statutes, relating to duties of school boards. To the Committee on Education.

By Mr. Fox of Marlow, An act to extend the time of the charter of the Keene, Marlow & Newport Electric Railway Company. To the Committee on Railroads.

By Mr. Prescott of Laconia, An act in amendment of chapter 262 of the Public Statutes, relating to coroners and coroners' inquests. To the Committee on Revision of Statutes.

By Mr. Chandler of Claremont, An act to extend the charter for the building of the Claremont Street Railway. To the Committee on Railroads.

By Mr. Andrews of Somersworth, An act to amend chapter 93, in relation to scholars. To the Committee on Education.

By Mr. Barrett of Dover, An act to amend the charter of the Concord, Dover & Rochester Street Railway. To the Committee on Railroads.

By Mr. Small of Rochester, An act in amendment of section 1 of chapter 138 of the Public Statutes, relating to homestead right. To the Committee on Revision of Statutes.

By Mr. Howe of Hanover, An act in amendment of chapter

23 of the Laws of 1901, entitled " An act to establish a laboratory of hygiene." To the Committee on Public Health.

By Mr. Dow of Conway, Joint resolution in favor of the Hurricane Mountain road, so called, in the towns of Conway and Chatham. To the Committee on Roads, Bridges, and Canals.

By Mr. Trickey of Jackson, Joint resolution in favor of the Pinkham Notch road, so called, in Jackson. To the Committee on Roads, Bridges, and Canals.

By Mr. Ellis of Lancaster, Joint resolution making appropriation for repairs on buildings erected by the state for the New Hampshire Veterans' Association at The Weirs. To the Committee on Public Improvements.

By Mr. Morrill of Ashland, Joint resolution in favor of raising Squam bridge in Ashland and of improving navigation in Squam lake and connecting waters. To the Committee on Roads, Bridges, and Canals.

By Mr. Morrill of New Hampton, Joint resolution in amendment of section 16, chapter 97, Laws of 1901, entitled " An act to revise the fish and game laws of the state." To the Committee on Fisheries and Game.

The following bill was introduced, and on motion of Mr. Riordan of Manchester, the rules were suspended, the bill read a first and second time by its title, and referred to a special committee consisting of the Manchester delegation:

By Mr. Riordan of Manchester, An act to enable the city of Manchester to appropriate money toward the armory rent of Camp Derwin, No. 184, Spanish American War Veterans.

BILL FORWARDED.

An act in amendment of chapter 112 of the Public Statutes, establishing local option in the sale of intoxicating liquors.

Taken from the table and referred to the Committee on Liquor Laws.

NOTICES OF BILLS.

By Mr. Goss of Berlin, An act confirming and legalizing the organization and acts of the Berlin Street Railway.

By Mr. Bussell of Nashua, An act to authorize the Governor, with consent of the Council, to cause the original maps and surveys by the town proprietors of the state to be mounted and preserved.

By Mr. Whittemore of Dover, An act in amendment of section 9, chapter 105 of the laws passed January session, 1901, relating to political caucuses and conventions.

By Mr. Merrill of Stoddard, Joint resolution in favor of the stage road in the town of Stoddard.

By Mr. Merrill of Stoddard, An act to provide for a bounty on hedgehogs.

By Mr. Woodman of Concord, An act in amendment of chapter 7 of the Public Statutes, relating to the state house and yard.

Mr. Fay of Keene, An act in amendment of section 19, chapter 57 of the Public Statutes, relating to the annual invoice of polls and taxable property.

By Mr. Russell of Rumney, Joint resolution in favor of the highways in the towns of Rumney and Ellsworth.

By Mr. Symth of Berlin, An act regulating the examination and licensing of engineers and firemen.

By Mr. George of Newton, Joint resolution in favor of the County Pond road in the towns of Newton and Kingston.

By Mr. Libby of Gorham, An act in amendment of section 3, chapter 209 of the Public Statutes, relating to exemptions from serving as jurors.

By Mr. Libby of Gorham, An act relating to agreed lines between adjoining owners.

By Mr. Fitzgerald of Sharon, Joint resolution for aid in keeping in repair the road in Sharon from the brick schoolhouse to the Peterborough line on the McCoy road.

By Mr. King of Orange, Joint resolution in favor of Mountain road in the town of Orange.

By Mr. Whitcher of Haverhill, An act to change the name of the Dodge's Falls Dam & Manufacturing Company to " Ryegate Paper Co."

By Mr. Newton of Portsmouth, An act to prevent the destruction of fish in the Piscataqua river and its tributaries.

By Mr. Filion of Manchester, An act enabling the city of Manchester to establish, maintain, and operate an electric lighting plant, and to borrow money to pay for the same.

By Mr. Kent of Berlin, Joint resolution to appropriate the sum of three hundred dollars for the purpose of turning Silver stream into Success pond, in the township of Success, and to screen the outlet of said pond.

By Mr. Barr of Manchester, An act to provide suitable armory quarters for the National Guard at Manchester.

By Mr. Smith of Peterborough, An act in amendment of sections 4, 5, and 9 of chapter 85 of the Public Statutes, entitled " Support of County Paupers."

By Mr. Smith of Peterborough, An act in amendment of section 1, chapter 83 of the Public Statutes, entitled " Settlement of paupers."

By Mr. Pike of Haverhill, Joint resolution to provide for a forest examination of the White Mountain region.

By Mr. Donovan of Keene, An act in amendment of section 3 of chapter 60 of the Session Laws of 1901.

By Mr. Willis of Concord, An act to amend chapter 149 of the Public Statutes by repealing sections 5 and 7 and enacting substitutes in place thereof.

By Mr. Barrett of Dover, An act to amend section 17, chapter 286 of the Public Statutes, fixing the salary of the judge of probate for Strafford county.

By Mr. Ward of Hillsborough, An act amending chapter 43 of the Public Statutes by repealing section 5 thereof, relating to the choice and duties of selectmen, and creating a substitute.

By Mr. Stevens of Bartlett, Joint resolution in favor of the highway leading from the Willey house in Hart's Location to the west line of Bartlett.

By Mr. Donovan of Keene, An act to incorporate the Universal Health and Accident Association.

By Mr. Donovan of Keene, An act in amendment of chapter 236 of the Session Laws of 1901.

By Mr. Willis of Concord, An act to amend the charter of the New England and Louisiana Land Company.

By Mr. Hoyt of Sandwich, An act in amendment of chapter 121, Laws of 1901, relating to the protection of public rights in New Hampshire.

By Mr. Smith of Peterborough, An act in amendment of

section 1, chapter 31 of the Laws of 1897, entitled "An act in amendment of section 6 of chapter 83 of the Public Statutes, in relation to the settlement of paupers."

On motion of Mr. Churchill of Cornish,—

Resolved, That the state treasurer be requested to communicate, for the information of the House, a statement of the receipts and disbursements of the treasury department, from June 1 to December 31, 1902.

(The Speaker in the chair.)

On motion of Mr. Barrett of Dover,—

Resolved, That when the House adjourns this morning it be to meet to-morrow morning at 9 o'clock, and when it adjourns to-morrow morning it be to meet on Monday evening at 8 o'clock.

In accordance with the resolution authorizing the Speaker to appoint a messenger to assist in the telephone service and to render such other service as may be directed, the Speaker appointed Edward J. Bouvier of Swanzey.

LEAVES OF ABSENCE.

Mr. Piper of Northumberland was granted leave of absence until Monday on account of previous important engagements.

Messrs. Harriman of Stewartstown, Hicks of Colebrook, Gathercole of Clarksville, Smith of Pittsburg, and Wilson of Shelburne, were granted leave of absence for the balance of the week.

On motion of Mr. Barrett of Dover, at 12.28 the House adjourned.

FRIDAY, JANUARY 16, 1903.

The House met at 9 o'clock according to adjournment, being called to order by Mr. William J. Ahern of Concord, and the following communication was read by the clerk :

CONCORD, January 15, 1903.

Mr. William J. Ahern, Concord, N. H.

DEAR SIR :—I shall be unable to be present at the morning

session of the House on Friday morning, January 16, 1903.
Will you please preside at that session?

Yours truly,

HARRY M. CHENEY,

Speaker.

COMMITTEE REPORT.

Mr. Woodman of Concord, for the Committee on Judiciary, to whom was referred An act reviving and continuing the charter of the Warner & Kearsarge Road Company and amendment to said charter, having considered the same, are of the opinion that the object sought cannot be obtained under the general law; therefore report with the recommendation that the same be referred to the Committee on Incorporations.

The report was accepted, the resolution adopted, and the bill referred to the Committee on Incorporations.

BILLS, ETC., INTRODUCED.

The following bills and joint resolution were severally introduced, read twice, and referred as follows:

By Mr. Donovan of Keene, An act in amendment of section 3 of chapter 60 of Session Laws of 1891. To the Committee on Judiciary.

By Mr. Goss of Berlin, An act confirming and legalizing the organization and acts of the Berlin Street Railway. To the Committee on Railroads.

By Mr. Willis of Concord, An act to amend chapter 149 of the Public Statutes by repealing sections 5 and 7 and enacting substitutes in place thereof. To the Committee on Judiciary.

By Mr. Willis of Concord, An act to amend the charter of the New England and Louisiana Land Company. To the Committee on Judiciary.

By Mr. George of Newton, Joint resolution in favor of the County Pond road in the towns of Newton and Kingston. To the Committee on Roads, Bridges, and Canals.

NOTICES OF BILLS.

By Mr. Hoyt of Sandwich, An act to amend chapter 95 of the Public Statutes, relating to the trustees of the State Normal School.

By Mr. Barrett of Dover, An act to amend section 7, chapter 169 of the Public Statutes, relating to insurance agents.

By Mr. Bragdon of Temple, Joint resolution in favor of the Miller Park mountain road in the towns of Temple and Peterborough.

By Mr. Davis of Concord, Joint resolution appropriating a sum of money to erect a monument at Vicksburg, Miss.

By Mr. Willis of Concord, An act to amend the charter of the N. H. Health and Accident Insurance Company.

LEAVE OF ABSENCE.

Mr. Houston of Thornton was granted leave of absence on account of sickness.

On motion of Mr. Kennedy of Concord, at 9.09 the House adjourned.

_____

MONDAY, JANUARY 19, 1903.

The House met at 8 o'clock in the evening, according to adjournment, being called to order by Mr. Frederic T. Woodman of Concord, and the following communication was read by the clerk:

CONCORD, January 16, 1903.

Mr. Frederic T. Woodman, Concord, N. H.

DEAR SIR:—I shall be unable to be present at the evening session on Monday, January 19, 1903. Will you kindly preside at that session and oblige me by so doing?

Yours truly,

HARRY M. CHENEY,

Speaker.

BILLS, ETC., INTRODUCED.

The following bills and joint resolutions were severally introduced, read twice, and referred as follows:

By Mr. Roby of Concord, An act to amend chapter 76 of the Laws of 1897, in relation to hawkers and peddlers. To he Committee on Judiciary.

By Mr. French of Moultonborough, An act in amendment of sections 1, 3, and 4 of chapter 72 of the Public Statutes, relating to the discontinuance of highways. To the Committee on Judiciary.

By Mr. French of Moultonborough, Joint resolution in favor of highways laid out under the provisions of chapter 70 of the Public Statutes.

By Mr. Stevens of Bartlett, Joint resolution in favor of the highway leading from the Willey house in Hart's Location to the west line of Bartlett.

Severally to the Committee on Roads, Bridges, and Canals.

By Mr. Hoyt of Sandwich, An act to amend chapter 95 of the Public Statutes, relating to the trustees of the State Normal School. To the Committee on Normal School.

By Mr. Woodman of Concord, An act in amendment of chapter 7 of the Public Statutes, relating to the state house and yard. To the Committee on State House and State House Yard.

By Mr. Willis of Concord, An act to amend the charter of the N. H. Health and Accident Insurance Company. To the Committee on Insurance.

STATE TREASURER'S REPORT.

STATE OF NEW HAMPSHIRE.

OFFICE OF STATE TREASURER.

CONCORD, January 16, 1903.

Hon. Harry M. Cheney, Speaker of the House of Representatives:

SIR :—Agreeably to a resolution of the House, adopted January 15, 1903, I have the honor to transmit herewith an abstract of the transactions of the treasury department from June 1, 1902, to December 31, 1902, both dates inclusive, accompanied by a certificate of the accountant and committee of the Honorable Council, of the result of a special audit of the treasurer's accounts for the above named period :

The cash and cash items on hand June 1, 1902, amounted to $575,615.12

RECEIPTS TO JANUARY 1, 1903.

Savings bank tax,	$362,628.99
Interest on deposits,	3,687.45
State tax, 1902,	376,764.69

6

Railroad tax, 1902,	$394,893.65
Expenses railroad commissioners,	7,580.06
Insurance tax (home stock companies),	14,850.00
Telegraph tax, 1902,	2,523.00
Telephone tax, 1902,	6,867.78
Fees, secretary of state,	1,260.40
Fees, insurance department,	1,132.00
Escheated estates,	1,162.15
Fines and forfeitures,	781.00
Charter fees,	245.00
Soldiers' Home,	2,304.26
Miscellaneous revenue	32.00
Total receipts,	$1,176,712.43
	$1,752,327.55

DISBURSEMENTS.

Governor's salary,	$1,500.00
Secretary of state,	2,250.00
Deputy secretary of state,	900.00
State treasurer,	1,875.00
Deputy state treasurer,	900.00
Adjutant-General,	1,125.00
Superintendent public instruction,	1,875.00
Librarian and assistants,	3,745.00
Warden of state prison,	1,500.00
Chaplain of state prison,	600.00
Janitor of state house,	487.50
Attorney-general,	1,875.00
Law reporter,	750.00
Secretary board of equalization,	450.00
Indexing records (secretary),	750 00
Secretary board of agriculture,	1,125.00
Insurance commissioner,	1,500.00
Clerical expenses, treasury department,	750.00
Clerk adjutant-general's department,	375.00
Clerk superintendent public instruction,	750.00
Clerk insurance department,	750.00

Clerk bank commissioners,	$562.50
Secretary forestry commission,	750 00
Labor commissioner,	1,125.00
Watchmen at state house,	975.00
Honorable council,	1,158.60
Justices of supreme court,	13,650.00
Clerk of supreme court,	375.00
Messenger of supreme court,	53.00
Justices of superior court,	13,650.00
Judges of probate,	5,850.00
Registers of probate,	6,037.50
Secretary board of charities and correction,	750.00
Clerk board of charities and correction,	450.00
Historian,	38.17
State house,	2,712.14
State printing,	5,312.53
State library,	4,775.99
Library commissioners,	76.60
Trustees of state library (expenses),	90.05
Commissioners of pharmacy,	372.81
Commissioners of lunacy,	11,769.13
Board of agriculture,	1,110.48
Board of equalization,	651.75
Board of charities and correction,	374 06
Board of health,	2,841.04
Bank commissioners,	5,567.80
Railroad commissioners,	5,244.65
Fish commissioners,	4,468.30
Game detectives,	341.43
Contagious diseases (cattle),	2,847.13
Bounty on wild animals,	223.50
Incidentals,	2,441.35
Indexing records (registrar),	1,299.87
Indexing province records,	1,047.60
Deaf and dumb,	2,235.51
Blind,	1,333.33
Idiotic and feeble-minded,	454.70
Normal school,	11,250.00
Trustees normal school (expenses),	127.56

State truant officer,	$237.26
Industrial school,	4,500.00
Indigent insane,	4,500.00
Convict insane,	4,090.03
Twenty year patients,	3,131.35
Soldiers' Home,	8.805.65
Agricultural college,	25,500.00
Interest, Agricultural college fund,	2,400.00
Interest on Fiske legacy,	527.57
Interest on H. Smith trust fund,	200 00
Auditing printers' accounts,	300.00
State prison,	1,121.86
Auditing treasurer's accounts,	200.00
Prison library,	259.95
Dartmouth college,	15,000.00
N. H. Historical society,	500.00
N. H. Horticultural society,	300.00
Compiling financial statistics,	200.00
Lighting Weirs channel,	188.15
Contingent fund,	407.29
Steamboat inspector,	5.00
Labor bureau,	797.92
Forestry commission,	80.35
Public printing commission,	581.80
Australian ballot,	2,685.42
Constitutional convention,	24,712.56
White Mountain roads,	21,302.37
Highways to public waters,	898.94
Protection of public rights,	1,204.38
N. H. National Guard,	24,096.61
Rifle ranges,	600.00
Justices of court (expenses),	952.82
Teachers' institutes,	1,033.49
Epidemic fund,	670.61
Sanatorium for consumptives,	176.73
Laboratory of hygiene,	2,334.25
School for feeble-minded,	14,161.62
Bonds,	72,500 00
Coupons and interest on registered bonds,	34,945.00

Probate commission,	$80.75
Legislative manuals,	147.50
Railroad tax,	210,592.74
Savings bank tax,	292,450.83
Insurance tax,	9,801.98
School fund,	18,504.37
High school tuition,	3,469.48
Abatement of state tax,	1,810.50
Literary fund,	28,901.50
Total disbursements,	$982,095.21
Cash and cash items on hand,	770,232.34
	$1,752,327.55

Yours very respectfully,

SOLON A. CARTER,
State Treasurer.

CONCORD, N. H., Dec. 31, 1902.

To His Excellency the Governor and Honorable Council :

An examination and audit of accounts of the state treasurer for the seven months from May 31 to December 31, 1902, has been made by the committee of the Honorable Council and accountant, and the result is herewith submitted.

All the revenue for the seven months has been credited to the state, and all disbursements have been made in accordance with the statutes, and vouchers are on file for the same.

We find all books and accounts carefully and accurately kept, and everything pertaining to the office reflects great credit on the treasurer and his assistants.

But little more income can be expected before October next, when corporation taxes will be due ; meantime, disbursements to towns, the running expenses of the state, including expenses of the legislature, three-quarters of a year's salaries of all state and court officers, interest on bonded debt, and redemption of maturing bonds will very largely reduce the cash balance.

Cash on hand May 31, 1902,	$575,615.12	
Receipts for seven months ending Dec. 31, 1902,	1,176,712.43	
		$1,752,327.55

Disbursements, May 31 to Dec.
31, 1902, $982,095.21
Cash on hand Dec. 31, 1902,   770,232.34
———————— $1,752,327.55

The Benjamin Thompson fund
in hands of the treasurer at
original appraisal is $329.443.76
Other assets in hands of the treas-
urer are:
Income and liquidations of the
Benjamin Thompson estate,
from May 31 to Dec. 31, 1902,   20,161.77
State prison account (balance),   940.84
Deposits of railroad corporations
to secure land damages,   372.50
Deposit of boulevard commis-
sioners to secure land damages,   33.00
Balance of literary fund,   624.27
Spanish war gratuity (balance),   699.08
Arrearages of savings bank tax
(1900),   4,455.00
Treasurer's cash balance, Dec.
31, 1902,   770,232.34
———————— $1,126,962.56

R. N. CHAMBERLIN,
CHARLES H. HERSEY,
Committee of the Council.

IRA CROSS,
Accountant.

On motion of Mr. Churchill of Cornish, the report was laid
upon the table and the usual number of copies ordered
printed.

NOTICES OF BILLS.

By Mr. Roby of Concord, Joint resolution in favor of screening the outlet of Penacook lake in the city of Concord.

By Mr. Roby of Concord, An act to amend the charter of
the New Hampshire Odd Fellows' Widows' and Orphans'
Home, approved August 15, 1883.

By Mr. Whitaker of Hillsborough, Joint resolution for the erection of a statue of President Franklin Pierce.

By Mr. Pollard of Tamworth, An act to extend the time for the location, construction, and completion of the railroad of the Moosilauke Railroad Company.

By Mr. Brown of Greenville, An act to enable the town of Greenville to acquire, own, and operate an electric power and lighting plant.

By Mr. French of Moultonborough, Joint resolution in favor of placing and maintaining buoys and lights in Lake Winnipesaukee and adjacent waters.

By Mr. Hull of Laconia, Joint resolution in favor of placing and maintaining buoys and lights in Lake Winnipesaukee and adjacent waters.

By Mr. Churchill of Cornish, An act in amendment of chapter 44 of the Laws of 1893, relating to the powers and duties of the forestry commission with respect to public parks.

By Mr. Kimball of Laconia, An act relating to life, fidelity, casualty, and other forms of insurance, and providing certain conditions and stipulations relating to insurance and insurance contracts.

By Mr. Edwards of Laconia, Joint resolution for an appropriation for the construction of a screen across the outlet of Lake Winnisquam at East Tilton in the county of Belknap.

By Mr. Cavanaugh of Manchester, An act to prohibit the further employment of convict labor of certain kinds at the State Industrial School.

By Mr. Hull of Laconia, Joint resolution for an appropriation to complete the screen at the outlet of Lake Winnipesaukee in the city of Laconia.

By Mr. Quimby of Meredith, An act to annex a certain island in Lake Winnipesaukee, now owned and occupied by George W. Sherwell, being one of the group of islands known as the Aunt Dolly island, to the town of Meredith.

By Mr. Edwards of Laconia, An act to amend chapter 241 of the Session Laws of 1893, entitled "An act to establish the city of Laconia," and repealing chapter 200 of the Laws of 1901, entitled "An act to amend chapter 241 of the Session Laws of 1893, entitled 'An act to establish the city of Laconia.' "

By Mr. Philbrick of Effingham, An act to legalize the biennial election of the town of Effingham, held November 4, 1902.

By Mr. Drake of Freedom, An act to amend the charter of the Ossipee Valley Railroad Company.

By Mr. Dow of Conway, An act to incorporate the North Conway Savings Bank at North Conway.

By Mr. Blake of Littleton, An act to regulate the selling, procuring, furnishing, or giving away of spirituous liquors by clubs, associations, or individuals.

By Mr. Whitcher of Haverhill, An act to provide for obtaining the testimony of non-resident directors, officers, and agents of New Hampshire corporations and for the production of corporate books, records, and papers.

By Mr. Collins of Nashua, An act to provide for the care and support of the dependent insane by the state.

By Mr. Remich of Littleton, An act to amend section 3 of chapter 110 of the Public Statutes, relating to pestilential diseases.

By Mr. Remich of Littleton, An act to amend section 14 of chapter 169 of the Public Statutes, as amended in section 1 of chapter 67, Laws of 1901, also section 13 of chapter 167 of the Public Statutes, relating to insurance commissioner, also section 1 of chapter 54, Laws of 1891, relating to foreign insurance companies and agents.

By Mr. Remich of Littleton, An act authorizing towns and cities to vote money for the construction or maintenance of public gymnasiums, amusement rooms, bath houses, working men's clubs, hospitals, and district nursing associations.

LEAVE OF ABSENCE.

Mr. Glover of Franconia was granted leave of absence on account of sickness.

On motion of Mr. Emerson of Concord, at 8.33 the House adjourned.

TUESDAY, JANUARY 20, 1903.

The House met at 11 o'clock.

Prayer was offered by the chaplain.

PETITION PRESENTED AND REFERRED.

By Mr. Hutchins of Pittsfield, For an appropriation for the Granite State Deaf Mute Mission. To the Committee on Appropriations.

COMMITTEE REPORTS.

Mr. Bell of Woodstock, for the Committee on Public Health, to whom was referred An act in amendment of chapter 23 of the Laws of 1901, entitled "An act to establish a laboratory of hygiene," having considered the same, report the same with the following resolution :

Resolved, That the bill be reported favorably and recommended for passage.

The report was accepted, the resolution adopted, and the bill laid upon the table to be printed.

Mr. Bell of Woodstock, for the Committee on Public Health, to whom was referred An act to establish a State Sanatorium for Consumptives, having considered the same, report the same with the following resolution :

Resolved, That the bill be favorably reported and recommended for passage.

The report was accepted, the resolution adopted, and the bill laid upon the table to be printed.

BILLS, ETC., INTRODUCED.

The following bill was introduced, and on motion of Mr. Edwards of Laconia, the rules were suspended and the bill read a first and second time by its title and referred to a special committee consisting of the Laconia delegation.

By Mr. Edwards of Laconia, An act to amend chapter 241 of the Session Laws of 1893, entitled "An act to establish the city of Laconia," and repealing chapter 200 of the Laws of 1901, entitled "An act to amend chapter 241 of the Session Laws of 1893, entitled 'An act to establish the city of Laconia.' "

The following bill was introduced and read twice :

By Mr. Bussell of Nashua, An act to allow the city of Nashua to appropriate money for the celebration of its semi-centennial.

On motion of Mr. Bussell of Nashua, the rules were suspended, and reference to committee dispensed with. The bill·was then laid upon the table to be printed. On motion of the same gentleman the rules were suspended and the printing of the bill dispensed with. The bill was then ordered to a third reading. On motion of the same gentleman the rules were further suspended and the bill read a third time and passed and sent to the Senate for concurrence.

The following bills and joint resolutions were severally introduced, read twice, and referred as follows :

By Mr. Remich of Littleton, An act to amend section 3 of chapter 110 of the Public Statutes, relating to pestilential diseases. To the Committee on Public Health

By Mr. Vaillancourt of Berlin, An act regulating the charges for passenger service on railways in this state, and to provide for the sale of mileage books. To the Committee on Railroads.

By Mr. Davis of Concord, Joint resolution appropriating money to be expended for a monument at Vicksburg, Miss.

By Mr. Whitcher of Haverhill, An act to change the name of Dodge's Falls Dam & Manufacturing Company to " Ryegate Paper Company."

By Mr. Roby of Concord, An act to amend the charter of the New Hampshire Odd Fellows' Widows' and Orphans' Home, approved August 15, 1883.

By Mr. Remich of Littleton, An act authorizing towns and cities to vote money for the construction or maintenance of public gymnasiums, amusement rooms, bath houses, working men's clubs, hospitals, and district nursing associations.

By Mr. Vaillancourt of Berlin, An act relating to probate bonds and to the liability of sureties thereunder.

Severally to the Committee on Judiciary.

By Mr. Pike of Haverhill, Joint resolution to provide for a forest examination of the White Mountain region. To the Committee on Forestry.

By Mr. Roby of Concord, Joint resolution in favor of screening the outlet to Penacook lake, in the city of Concord. To the Committee on Fisheries and Game.

By Mr. Russell of Rumney, Joint resolution in favor of the highways in the towns of Rumney and Ellsworth.

By Mr. French of Moultonborough, Joint resolution in favor of placing and maintaining buoys and lights in Lake Winnipesaukee and adjacent waters.

By Mr. Fitzgerald of Sharon, Joint resolution for aid in keeping in repair the road in Sharon from the brick schoolhouse to the Peterborough line on the McCoy road.

Severally to the Committee on Roads, Bridges, and Canals.

By Mr. Ward of Hillsborough, An act amending chapter 43 of the Public Statutes. To the Committee on Revision of Statutes.

By Mr. Collins of Nashua, An act to provide for the care and support of the dependent insane by the state. To the Committee on Asylum for Insane.

By Mr. Blake of Littleton, An act to regulate the selling, procuring, furnishing, or giving away of spirituous liquors by clubs, associations, or individuals. To the Committee on Liquor Laws.

By Mr. Barr of Manchester, An act to provide suitable armory quarters for the National Guard at Manchester. To the Committee on Military Affairs.

By Mr. Donovan of Keene, An act to incorporate the Universal Health and Accident Insurance Company.

By Mr. Donovan of Keene, An act in amendment of chapter 236 of the Session Laws of 1901.

By Mr. Barrett of Dover, An act to amend section 7, chapter 169 of the Public Statutes, relating to insurance agents.

Severally to the Committee on Insurance.

By Mr. Philbrick of Effingham, An act to legalize the biennial election of the town of Effingham, held November 4, 1902. To the Committee on Elections.

By Mr. Sheehan of Manchester, An act to repeal the charter of the Massabesic Horse Railroad Company. To the Committee on Railroads.

By Mr. Whitaker of Hillsborough, Joint resolution for the erection of a statue of President Franklin Pierce. To the Committee on Public Improvements.

By Mr. Lynch of Manchester, An act in amendment of section 14, chapter 180, Public Statutes, regulating the hours of labor for women and minors in manufacturing or mechanical establishments. To the Committee on Labor.

NOTICES OF BILLS.

By Mr. Stanley of Lisbon, An act to incorporate the First Free Baptist church of Franconia.

By Mr. Woodman of Concord, An act providing for the purchase of a bond for the deputy state treasurer.

By Mr. Bell of Woodstock, Joint resolution in favor of the Warren road in the town of Woodstock.

By Mr. Howe of Hanover, An act in amendment of chapter 2555, Laws of 1861, entitled " An act to incorporate the Alpha Delta Phi Society."

By Mr. Bell of Woodstock, Joint resolution in favor of the Kinsman Notch, or Lost River road, in the town of Woodstock.

By Mr. Bussell of Nashua, An act relating to salary of associate justice of police court of Nashua, in case of vacancy in office of justice.

By Mr. Goss of Berlin, An act in amendment of the charter of the city of Berlin.

By Mr. Jones of New Ipswich, An act to incorporate the New Ipswich, Greenville & Wilton Electric Railway Company.

By Mr. Mitchell of Littleton, An act in amendment of section 1, chapter 119, Public Statutes, relating to the inspection and licensing of boats, their engineers, and pilots.

By Mr. O'Connor of Stark, Joint resolution for the appropriation of five hundred dollars for the repairing of the highways and bridges in the town of Stark.

By Mr. Bussell of Nashua, An act to amend the Public Statutes, section 5, chapter 37 of the Laws of 1895, relating to the fee of bail commissioners.

By Mr. Fox of Marlow, An act in amendment of section 27,

chapter 154 of the Public Statutes, relating to the calling of proprietors' meetings.

By Mr. Martin of Colebrook, An act to prevent the deposit of sawdust and other waste in the Mohawk river in Colebrook.

By Mr. Beacham of Wolfeborough, An act to amend chapter 183 of Session Laws of 1897, entitled " An act to authorize the Village Fire Precinct of Wolfeborough to construct and maintain an electric plant."

By Mr. Lennon of Stratford, An act to amend section 13, chapter 269 of the Public Statutes, relating to the sale of deadly poisons.

By Mr. Ball of Washington, An act to screen the outlets of Ashuelot and Millen lakes in the town of Washington.

By Mr. Goodrich of Warren, An act to incorporate the Warren Water and Light Company.

By Mr. Phillips of Franklin, An act to amend section 1 of chapter 46 of the Session Laws of 1895, relating to annual enumeration of school children.

By Mr. Ahern of Concord, An act relating to savings banks.

By Mr. Jones of Franklin, An act in amendment of section 16, chapter 220 of the Public Statutes, relating to attachments.

By Mr. Tuttle of Farmington, An act concerning savings banks.

By Mr. Bragg of Errol, An act to aid in the reconstruction of the Magalloway road in Errol on a practicable route.

By Mr. Whitney of Keene, An act to amend section 1, chapter 259 of the Laws of 1893, being an act to exempt certain property of the Keene Young Men's Christian Association.

By Mr. Cavanaugh of Manchester, An act to incorporate the Sons of Veterans' Memorial Hall Association.

By Mr. Prescott of Laconia, An act to amend section 54, chapter 78 of the fish and game laws of New Hampshire.

By Mr. Shute of Derry, An act to incorporate the Nutfield Loan and Trust Company.

By Mr. Warren of Rochester, An act in amendment of sections 14 and 20, chapter 180 of the Public Statutes, relating to the hours of labor.

By Mr. Cavanaugh of Manchester, An act in amendment of chapter 114 of the Session Laws of 1901, entitled "An act to regulate and limit the investments of savings banks."

By Mr. Cavanaugh of Manchester, An act in amendment of chapter 64 of the Public Statutes, relating to taxation of railroads, and telegraph, and telephone lines.

By Mr. Roby of Concord, Joint resolution for lighting the lighthouse on Loon island in Sunapee lake, repairing the cable connected therewith, improving the light service, placing and maintaining buoys on said lake, and removing obstructions to navigation in said lake.

By Mr. Nyberg of Manchester, An act to incorporate the Bellman club of Manchester, N. H.

By Mr. Whitcher of Haverhill, An act to change the time of holding probate courts in Grafton county.

By Mr. Whitcher of Haverhill, Joint resolution in favor of William J. Patch.

By Mr. Sheehan of Manchester, An act to incorporate the Manchester Fire Insurance Company of New Hampshire.

By Mr. Kohler of Manchester, An act in amendment of chapter 11, Laws of 1899, entitled " An act relating to holidays."

By Mr. Badger of Newington, An act to repeal chapter 671 of the Laws of 1842, approved June 22, 1842, annexing the farm of Richard Pickering to the town of Portsmouth for school purposes.

By Mr. Remich of Littleton, An act to provide a stenographer for the House and Senate, for the publication of a journal of the Senate and House, and a calendar.

By Mr. Remich of Littleton, An act to authorize the town of Littleton to establish, maintain, and operate a water and electric light plant.

By Mr. Hoyt of Sandwich, An act to prohibit the deposit of sawdust, shavings, or other refuse in Bearcamp river and tributaries, east of Bearcamp pond in the town of Sandwich.

By Mr. Britton of Wolfeborough, An act in amendment of chapter 202 of the Laws of 1889, entitled " An act to establish water-works in the town of Wolfeborough," as amended by chapter 191 of the Laws of 1891.

By Mr. Britton of Wolfeborough, An act to repeal section 2 of chapter 152 of the Public Statutes.

By Mr. Barrett of Dover, An act in relation to the salary of the judge for probate for Strafford county.

On motion of Mr. Ahern of Concord,—

Resolved, That the afternoon sessions of the House hereafter be held commencing at 3 o'clock instead of 2 o'clock as now in vogue.

On motion of Mr. Hoyt of Sandwich,—

Resolved, That the use of Representatives' Hall be granted to the Farmers' Council for meetings Wednesday evenings, January 21 and 28.

On motion of Mr. Small of Rochester,—

Resolved, That the House now proceed by a *viva voce* vote, in accordance with the provisions of the Laws of the United States, to the choice of a Senator from New Hampshire in the United States Senate, for the full term of six years, from March 4, 1903.

VOTE FOR UNITED STATES SENATOR.

Pursuant to the preceding resolution, the House proceeded by a *viva voce* vote to the choice of a Senator from New Hampshire in the United States Senate, for the full term of six years, beginning March 4, 1903, with the following result:

One hundred and sixteen gentlemen, namely, Messrs. Sawyer of Atkinson, Edgerly of Epping, Duntley, Pridham, Badger, Haines, Sleeper, Cogan, Couhig, Corson, Young, Libby of Dover, Jewell, Wesley, Felker, Jones of New Durham, Warren, Small, Harrity, Murnane, Boutin, Andrews, Caverly, Hoitt of Barnstead, Potter, Clough, Fecteau, Prescott, Chase of Laconia, Rogers, Philbrick of Effingham, Drake, Greene, Graves, Beck, Langmaid, Hill, E. J., of Concord, Ahern, Donagan, Litchfield, Tripp, Jones of Franklin, Sanborn of Loudon, Hutchins of Pittsfield, Walker of Pittsfield, Pillsbury, Woodbury, Barr of Bedford, Shattuck, Craine, Putnam, Brown of Greenville, Ware of Hancock, Farley of Hollis, Connell, Center, Stewart of Manchester, Tonery, Ryan, Trinity, Riordan, Sullivan of Manchester, Shaughnessey, Sasseville, Morse of Manchester,

Dinsmore, Janelle, Kohler, Lynch, Kane, Newman, Simpson, Lampron, Buckley of Nashua, Ingham, Bussell, Shea, Spalding, Morse of Nashua, Hills of Nashua, Sullivan of Nashua, Earley, Moran of Nashua, Peabody, Fitzgerald, Sheldon, Bemis, Maloney, Jones of Keene, Donovan, Merrill, Boyden, Sherman of Walpole, Kellom, Dickinson, McMurphey, Morrill of Ashland, Davenport, Barnard, Evans, King, Celley, Russell of Rumney, Bowen, Stewart of Berlin, Smyth, Hutchins of Berlin, Notterstead, Gallagher, Gathercole, Martin, Bragg, Plaisted, O'Connor, Lennon, and Babcock, named John M. Mitchell.

Two hundred and twenty-one gentlemen, namely, Messrs. Preston of Auburn, Fellows, Hubbard, Morse of Chester, White of Deerfield, Hardy, Bartlett of Derry, Shute, Scammon, Severance, Smith of Exeter, Brown of Fremont, Lane of Hampton, Brown of Hampton Falls, Quimby of Kingston, Crowell, Chase of Newfields, George, Warner, Bickford, Gerrish, Payne, Blaisdell, Foye, Nelson, Yeaton, Adams of Portsmouth, Newton, Brown of Rye, Abbott of Salem, Swain, Chase of Stratham, Cochran, Howe of Barrington, Ramsdell, Nason, Whittemore, Bunce, Smith of Dover, Barrett, Langley of Durham, York, Tuttle, Davis of Lee, Place, McCrillis, Crocker, Worcester, Wallace, Etter, Wentworth, Demers, Sargent, Smith of Center Harbor, Davis of Laconia, Hull, Edwards, Kimball of Laconia, Quimby of Meredith, Morrill of New Hampton, Sanborn of Sanbornton, Stevens, Weeks, Fifield, Dow of Conway, Burnell, Trickey, French, Abbott of Ossipee, Hoyt of Sandwich, Pollard, Edgerly of Tuftonborough, Blake of Wakefield, Beacham, Britton, Fontaine, Harris of Boscawen, White of Bow, Symonds, Cate, Shepard, Kennedy, Willis, Matson, Hill, A. W., of Concord, Roby, Woodman, Kimball of Concord, Emerson of Concord, Davis of Concord, Critchett, Mathews of Concord, Bunten of Dunbarton, Phillips, Adams of Franklin, Davis of Franklin, Preston of Henniker, Twombly, Worthley, Messer, Sanborn of Northfield, Tallant, Aldrich, Foss, Little of Salisbury, Farley of Amherst, Tobie, Pattee, Eaton, Whitaker, Ward, Holt, Cavanaugh, Nyberg, Abbott of Manchester, Chase of Manchester, Donahue, Bartlett of

Manchester, Taggart, Sheehan, Bunton, A. S., of Manchester, Farrell, Johnson. Straw of Manchester, McDonald of Manchester, Wright, Barr of Manchester, Dubuc, Carpenter, Morgan, Darrah, Marshall, Couch, Bunton, A. B., of Manchester, Armstrong, Tinkham, Graf, Quimby of Manchester, Scannell, Dozois, Gunderman, Filion, Lemay, Emerson of Manchester, March, Hodgman, Sawyer of Milford, Robinson, Needham, Kendall, Lund, Tuck, Duncklee, Lewis, Lintott, Shenton, Collins, McLane, Jones of New Ipswich, Ware of Alstead, Harris of Chesterfield, Gowing, Tenney, Fuller, Cutler, Pierce of Jaffrey, Batchelder, Whitney, Goodnow, Moors, Fox, Scott, Amidon, Lane of Swanzey, Hall, Clark, Churchill, Ball, Pierce of Bethlehem, Calley, Little of Campton, Dorothy, Foster, Kimball of Grafton, Pinneo, Howe of Hanover, Whitcher, Carr, Pike, Cheney, Goold of Lebanon, Pike of Lebanon, Comings, Crossman, Stanley, Remich, Mitchell of Littleton, Blake of Littleton, Converse, Frazer, Chase of Orford, Gould of Plymouth, Ferrin, Goodrich, Bell, Caird, Goss, Vaillancourt, Kent of Berlin, Hicks, Jordan, Hamlin of Dummer, Mitchell of Lancaster, Buckley of Lancaster, Ellis, Trafton, McDonald of Northumberland, Piper, Smith of Pittsburg, Harriman, and Darling, named Jacob H. Gallinger.

Jacob H. Gallinger being named as the choice of a majority of the members of the House, and having received a majority of the votes cast, it was ordered that the name of Jacob H. Gallinger be entered upon the journal of the House of Representatives as the choice of a majority of its members for Senator of the United States from the state of New Hampshire, for the full term of six years from the fourth day of March, 1903.

On motion of Mr. Sawyer of Milford,—

Resolved, That the Honorable Senate be notified that the House of Representatives will be ready to meet the Senate in joint convention at 12 o'clock noon, to-morrow, January 21, for the purpose of proceeding to the election of a United States Senator for the full term of six years from March 4, 1903, according to the law, and for the election of a secretary of state and state treasurer.

MESSAGE FROM THE SENATE.

A message from the Honorable Senate, by its clerk, announced that the President has named as members of the Joint Standing Committees of the Senate and House of Representatives, on the part of the Senate, the following senators:

On Engrossed Bills.—Senators Burnell of District No. 5 and Keyes of District No. 2.

On State Library.—Senator Stillings of District No. 10.

On State House and State House Yard.—Senator Fellows of District No. 11.

On motion of Mr. Whittemore of Dover,—

Resolved, That the use of Representatives' Hall be granted to the New Hampshire Library Association on Tuesday evening, February 10, for holding a state meeting.

LEAVES OF ABSENCE.

Mr. Mathes of Dover was granted leave of absence until Wednesday, January 21, on account of death in his family.

Mr. Cochran of Windham was granted leave of absence for the rest of the week on account of sickness in his family.

The Speaker announced that the morning train over the Claremont division of the Boston & Maine road was delayed by a wreck, and that the members traveling thereon would seem to have a good excuse for being absent.

Mr. Fontaine of Allenstown, having been duly qualified by His Excellency the Governor, appeared and took his seat as a member of the House of Representatives.

On motion of Mr. Ahern of Concord, at 12.55 the House adjourned.

AFTERNOON.

The House met at 3 o'clock.

BILLS, ETC., INTRODUCED.

Mr. Ahern of Concord called for the unfinished business of the morning session, it being the introduction of bills, and the following bills and joint resolutions were severally introduced, read twice, and referred as follows:

By Mr. Brown of Greenville, An act to enable the town of Greenville to acquire, own, and operate an electric power and lighting plant.

By Mr. Severance of Exeter, An act to regulate the speed and operation of automobiles and motor vehicles on the public hi. hways.

By Mr. Mitchell of Littleton, An act in amendment of section 1, chapter 119, Public Statutes, relating to the inspection and licensing of boats, their engineers and pilots.

By Mr. Whitcher of Haverhill, An act to provide for obtaining the testimony of non-resident directors, officers, and agents of New Hampshire corporations, and the production of corporate books, records, and papers.

Severally to the Committee on Judiciary.

The following bill was introduced, and on motion of Mr. French of Moultonborough, the rules were suspended and the bill read a first and second time by its title:

By Mr. Chase of Laconia, An act to incorporate the Winnipiseogee Valley Street Railway. The bill was referred to the Committee on Railroads.

The following joint resolution was introduced, read twice, and referred as follows:

By Mr. Edwards of Laconia, Joint resolution for an appropriation for the construction of a screen across the outlet of Lake Winnisquam at East Tilton, in the county of Belknap. To the Committee on Fisheries and Game.

NOTICES OF BILLS.

By Mr. Whittemore of Dover, An act to authorize the Dover & Eliot Street Railway and the Eliot Bridge Company to transfer their properties and franchises to the Berwick, Eliot & York Street Railway.

By Mr. Adams of Portsmouth, An act for the protection of employees.

By Mr. Jordan of Columbia, An act to legalize and confirm the selectmen's warrant for and the votes and proceedings thereunder at the biennial election and meeting in the town of Columbia, held in said town on the fourth day of November, A. D. 1902.

By Mr. Collins of Nashua, An act in amendment of section 11, chapter 79 of the Session Laws of 1901, relating to the fish and game commissioners.

By Mr. Sherman of Claremont, An act in relation to milk tickets.

By Mr. Center of Litchfield, An act to incorporate the Goff's Falls, Litchfield & Hudson Street Railway.

By Mr. Edgerly of Tuftonborough, An act annexing certain islands in Lake Winnipesaukee to the town of Tuftonborough.

By Mr. Messer of New London, An act in amendment of the charter of the Colby academy, providing for filling vacancies and election of members.

By Mr. Mitchell of Littleton, An act in amendment of the charter of the Wells River bridge, and authorizing the Concord & Montreal Railroad to hold stock therein.

By Mr. Smith of Dover, An act allowing compensation to majors of battalions in the National Guard in certain cases.

By Mr. Cavanaugh of Manchester, An act regulating the holding of political caucuses and conventions, and providing for substitutes in case of vacancies in the positions of delegates to conventions.

By Mr. Straw of Manchester, An act to protect milk dealers and consumers against the unlawful use and destruction of milk cans and other receptacles.

By Mr. Crossman of Lisbon, An act to enlarge the powers of the Lisbon fire district.

By Mr. Dorothy of Enfield, An act to establish water-works in Enfield fire district, in the town of Enfield.

On motion of Mr. Dow of Conway, at 3.30 the House adjourned.

WEDNESDAY, JANUARY 21, 1903.

The House met at 11 o'clock.

Prayer was offered by the chaplain.

On motion of Mr. Phillips of Franklin,—

Resolved, That a special committee of three be appointed by the Speaker to confer with Mr. N. M. Colby, the owner of the Webster birthplace, as to the terms and conditions on which he will transfer the title to said farm and buildings to the state, and report the same to this House.

The Speaker subsequently named as members of such committee Messrs. Phillips of Franklin, Burbank of Webster, and Graves of Andover.

MESSAGE FROM THE GOVERNOR.

STATE OF NEW HAMPSHIRE.

COUNCIL CHAMBER, January 21, 1903.

To the House of Representatives:

I hereby transmit the following reports:

Of the Secretary of State.

Of the State Treasurer.

Of the Adjutant-General.

Of the Insurance Commissioner.

Of the Bank Commissioners.

Of the Commissioner of Labor.

Of the Registrar of Vital Statistics.

Of the Attorney-General.

Of the Superintendent of Public Instruction.

Of the State Normal School.

Of the State Board of Health.

Of the Commission to Consider the Question of a State Sanatorium for Consumptives.

Of the Trustees of the School for the Feeble-minded.

Of the Forestry Commission.

Of the State Library.

Of the Commissioners of Lunacy.

Of the Board of Equalization.

Of the Commission to ascertain and exactly determine the position of each New Hampshire Regiment in the Siege of Vicksburg.

Of the Fish and Game Commission.

Of the Industrial School.

Of the Board of Charities and Correction.

Of the State Hospital.

Of the Cattle Commission.

NAHUM J. BACHELDER,
Governor.

The above mentioned reports were referred as follows:

Report of the Secretary of State, to the Committee on Incorporations.

Report of the State Treasurer, to the Committee on Appropriations.

Report of the Adjutant-General, to the Committee on Military Affairs.

Report of the Insurance Commissioner, to the Committee on Insurance.

Report of the Bank Commissioners, to the Committee on Banks.

Report of the Commissioner of Labor, to the Committee on Labor.

Report of the Registrar of Vital Statistics, to the Committee on Public Health.

Report of the Attorney-General, to the Committee on Judiciary.

Report of the Superintendent of Public Instruction, to the Committee on Education.

Report of the Trustees of the State Normal School, to the Committee on Normal School.

Report of the State Board of Health, to the Committee on Public Health.

Report of the Commission to Consider the Question of a State Sanatorium for Consumptives, to the Committee on Public Health.

Report of the Trustees of the School for Feeble-minded, to the Committee on Feeble-minded School.

Report of the Forestry Commission, to the Committee on Forestry.

Report of the Trustees of the State Library, to the Committee on State Library.

Report of the Commissioners of Lunacy, to the Committee on Public Health.

Report of the Board of Equalization, to the Committee on Appropriations.

Report of the Commission to ascertain and exactly determine the position of each New Hampshire regiment in the Siege of Vicksburg, to the Committee on Appropriations.

Report of the Fish and Game Commission, to the Committee on Fisheries and Game.

Report of the Trustees of the Industrial School, to the Committee on Industrial School.

Report of the Board of Charities and Correction, to the Committee on Public Health.

Report of the State Hospital, to the Committee on Asylum for the Insane.

Report of the Cattle Commission, to the Committee on Agriculture.

On motion of Mr. Libby of Gorham,—

Resolved, That the clerk of the House be and hereby is instructed immediately to request from the secretary of the convention of 1902 to revise the constitution, that he transmit to the House certified copies of the resolutions of said convention relating to the subjects of passes and trusts, and to report the same to the House as soon as they are received by him.

PETITIONS PRESENTED AND REFERRED.

By Mr. Woodman of Concord, Petition of Henry K. Mason of Wilmot for a seat in the House of Representatives. To the Committee on Elections.

By Mr. Warner of North Hampton, Petition of Seaside District Sunday School Union, regarding liquor legislation. To the Committee on Liquor Laws.

COMMITTEE REPORTS.

Mr. Ahern of Concord, for the Committee on Railroads, to whom was referred An act authorizing the Concord & Montreal Railroad, lessor, to acquire the Concord Street Railway and other property, to issue stock and bonds to pay therefor, and authorizing a physical connection of the Manchester Street Railway with electric branches of the Concord & Montreal Railroad, having considered the same, report the same with the following resolution :

Resolved, That the bill ought to pass.

The report was accepted, the resolution adopted, and the bill laid upon the table to be printed.

Mr. Whitcher of Haverhill, for the Committee on Judiciary, to whom was referred An act to provide for obtaining of testimony of non-resident officers and agents of New Hampshire corporations and the production of corporate books, records, and papers, having considered the same, report the same with the following resolution :

Resolved, That the bill ought to pass.

The report was accepted, the resolution adopted, and the bill laid upon the table to be printed.

Mr. Whittemore of Dover, for the Committee on Judiciary, to whom was referred An act authorizing the city of Dover to exempt from taxation the property of the Hayes Hospital, having considered the same, report the same with the following resolution :

Resolved, That the bill ought to pass.

The report was accepted, the resolution adopted, and the bill laid upon the table to be printed.

Mr. Straw of Manchester, for the Committee on Revision of Statutes, to whom was referred An act amending chapter 43 of the Public Statutes by repealing section 5 thereof, relating to the choice and duties of selectmen, and creating a substitute, having considered the same, report the same with the following resolution :

Resolved, That this committee report upon this bill favorably and recommend its passage.

The report was accepted, the resolution adopted, and the bill laid upon the table to be printed.

Mr. Cavanaugh of Manchester, for the Committee on Judiciary, to whom was referred Joint resolution for the preservation of the records and files of the probate court of the county of Hillsborough, having considered the same, report the same with the following resolution :

Resolved, That it is inexpedient to legislate.

The report was accepted and the resolution adopted.

Mr. Whitcher of Haverhill, for the Committee on Judiciary, to whom was referred An act to repeal chapter 200 of the Laws of 1899, relating to the police court of Haverhill, having considered the same, report the same with the following resolution :

Resolved, That the bill ought to pass.

The report was accepted, the resolution adopted, and the bill laid upon the table to be printed. On motion of Mr. Whitcher of Haverhill, the rules were suspended and the printing of the bill dispensed with. The bill was then ordered to a third reading. On motion of the same gentleman, the rules were further suspended and the bill read a third time and passed and sent to the Senate for concurrence.

Mr. Phillips of Franklin, for the Committee on Judiciary, to whom was referred An act appropriating money to be expended for a monument at Vicksburg, Miss., having considered the same, report the same with the following resolution :

Resolved, That the bill be referred to the Committee on Appropriations.

The report was accepted, the resolution adopted, and the bill referred to the Committee on Appropriations.

Mr. Whitcher of Haverhill, for the Committee on Judiciary, to whom was referred An act to establish a police court in the town of Haverhill, having considered the same, report the same with the following resolution :

Resolved, That the bill ought to pass.

The report was accepted, the resolution adopted, and the bill laid upon the table to be printed. On motion of Mr. Whitcher of Haverhill, the rules were suspended and the printing of the bill dispensed with. The bill was then ordered to a third reading. On motion of the same gentleman the rules were further suspended and the bill read a third time and passed and sent to the Senate for concurrence.

Mr. Woodman of Concord, for the Committee on Judiciary, to whom was referred An act to prohibit the sitting of justices of police courts in certain cases, having considered the same, report the same with the following resolution :

Resolved, That it is inexpedient to legislate.

The report was accepted and the resolution adopted.

Mr. Hull of Laconia, for the special committee consisting of the Laconia delegation, to whom was referred An act to amend chapter 241 of the Session Laws of 1893, entitled " An act to establish the city of Laconia," and repealing chapter 200 of the Laws of 1901, entitled " An act to amend chapter

241 of the Session Laws of 1893, entitled 'An act to establish the city of Laconia,'" having considered the same, report the same with the following resolution:

Resolved, That the bill ought to pass.

The report was accepted, and the question being upon the adoption of the resolution reported by the committee, on motion of Mr. Small of Rochester, the bill was recommitted to the special committee consisting of the Laconia delegation.

Mr. Whitcher of Haverhill, for the Committee on Judiciary, to whom was referred An act to amend chapter 69 of the Laws of 1901, entitled "An act to protect the Ammonoosuc river in Carroll, Bethlehem, Littleton, Lisbon, and Bath, and its tributaries, from pollution by sawdust and other waste," having considered the same, report the same with the following resolution:

Resolved, That the same ought to pass.

The report was accepted, the resolution adopted, and the bill laid upon the table to be printed. On motion of Mr. Whitcher of Haverhill, the rules were suspended and the printing of the bill dispensed with. The bill was then ordered to a third reading. On motion of the same gentleman, the rules were further suspended and the bill read a third time and passed and sent to the Senate for concurrence.

Mr. Woodman of Concord, for the Committee on Judiciary, to whom was referred An act to amend the charter of the New Hampshire Odd Fellows' Widows' and Orphans' Home, approved August 15, 1883, having considered the same, report the same with the following resolution:

Resolved, That the bill ought to pass.

The report was accepted, the resolution adopted, and the bill laid upon the table to be printed. On motion of Mr. Small of Rochester, the rules were suspended and the printing of the bill dispensed with. The bill was then ordered to a third reading. On motion of the same gentleman, the rules were further suspended and the bill read a third time and passed and sent to the Senate for concurrence.

Mr. Whitcher of Haverhill, for the Committee on Judiciary, to whom was referred An act to change the name of Dodge's Falls Dam & Manufacturing Company to " Ryegate Paper

Company," having considered the same, report the same with the following resolution :

Resolved, That the same ought to pass.

The report was accepted, the resolution adopted, and the bill laid upon the table to be printed. On motion of Mr. Whitcher of Haverhill, the rules were suspended and the printing of the bill dispensed with. The bill was then ordered to a third reading. On motion of the same gentleman, the rules were further suspended and the bill read a third time and passed and sent to the Senate for concurrence.

Mr. Converse of Lyme, for the Committee on Agriculture, to whom was referred An act providing a seal for the state board of agriculture, having considered the same, report the same with the following resolution :

Resolved, That the bill ought to pass.

The report was accepted, the resolution adopted, and the bill laid upon the table to be printed. On motion of Mr. Hoyt of Sandwich, the rules were suspended and the printing of the bill dispensed with. The bill was then ordered to a third reading. On motion of the same gentleman, the rules were further suspended and the bill read a third time and passed and sent to the Senate for concurrence.

Mr. Buckley of Lancaster, for the Committee on Judiciary, to whom was referred An act relating to persons employed under and by virtue of an act of congress relating to the surveys of the geological survey of the United States, having considered the same, report the same with the following resolution :

Resolved, That the bill ought to pass.

The report was accepted, the resolution adopted, and the bill laid upon the table to be printed. On motion of Mr. Batchelder of Keene, the rules were suspended and the printing of the bill dispensed with. The bill was then ordered to a third reading. On motion of the same gentleman, the rules were further suspended and the bill read a third time and passed and sent to the Senate for concurrence.

Mr. Mitchell of Littleton, for the Committee on Judiciary, to whom was referred An act amending section 11 of chapter 63 of Session Laws of 1897, entitled " Practice of medicine," having considered the same, report the same with the following resolution :

Resolved, That the bill ought to pass after being amended by striking out all of section 1 of said bill after the word " employees " in the fourth line of said section. The report was accepted, the amendment adopted, and the bill laid upon the table to be printed. On motion of Mr. Crossman of Lisbon, the rules were suspended and the printing of the bill dispensed with. The bill was then ordered to a third reading. On motion of the same gentleman, the rules were further suspended and the bill read a third time and passed and sent to the Senate for concurrence.

Mr. Converse of Lyme, for the Committee on Engrossed Bills. reported that they had examined a joint resolution with the following title and found it correctly engrossed :

Joint resolution favoring the establishment of a national forest reserve in the White Mountain region.

The report was accepted.

MESSAGE FROM THE SENATE.

A message from the Honorable Senate, by its clerk, announced that the Senate concur with the House of Representatives in the passage of the following entitled bill :

An act authorizing the Manchester Mills to increase its capital stock.

The message also announced that the Senate has adopted the following resolution :

Resolved, That the House of Representatives be notified that the Senate will be ready to meet the House of Representatives in convention at 12 o'clock. noon, for the purpose of proceeding to the election of a United States Senator for the term of six years from March 4, 1903. according to the law, and for the election of a secretary of state and state treasurer.

The message further announced that the Senate has passed a bill with the following title, in the passage of which it asks the concurrence of the House of Representatives :

An act to amend section 1 of an act of June, 1814, incorporating the Congregational Society of Durham.

Read a first and second time and referred to the Committee on Judiciary.

The following bills were severally introduced, read twice, and referred as follows:

By Mr. Whitcher of Haverhill, An act to amend chapter 79 of the Laws of 1889, entitled "An act to amend chapter 184 of the Public Statutes, relating to the times and places of holding courts of probate within and for the county of Grafton." To the Committee on Judiciary.

By Mr. Cavanaugh of Manchester, An act to incorporate the Sons of Veterans' Memorial Hall Association. To the Committee on Judiciary.

By Mr. Lennon of Stratford, An act to amend section 13, chapter 269, Public Statutes, relating to the sale of deadly poisons. To the Committee on Public Health.

The following bill was introduced, and on motion of Mr. French of Moultonborough, the rules were suspended and the bill read a first and second time by its title:

By Mr. Pridham of Newcastle, An act to incorporate the Portsmouth & Newcastle Street Railway Company. The bill was then referred to the Committee on Railroads.

The following bill was introduced, and on motion of Mr. Goss of Berlin, the rules were suspended and the bill read a first and second time by its title and referred to a special committee consisting of the delegation from the city of Berlin:

By Mr. Goss of Berlin, An act in amendment of the charter of the city of Berlin.

On motion of Mr. French of Moultonborough, the rules were suspended and the first and second reading of bills by their titles made in order, and the following bills and joint resolutions were severally introduced, read twice by title, and referred as follows:

By Mr. Edgerley of Tuftonborough, An act annexing certain islands in Lake Winnipesaukee to the town of Tuftonborough. To the Committee on Judiciary.

By Mr. Whittemore of Dover, An act in amendment of section 9, chapter 105 of the laws passed January session, 1901, relating to political caucuses and conventions. To the Committee on Judiciary.

By Mr. Churchill of Cornish, An act in amendment of chapter 44 of the Laws of 1893, relating to the powers and duties of the forestry commission with respect to public parks. To the Committee on Forestry.

By Mr. Sawyer of Milford, An act to amend chapter 92, Public Statutes, relating to school boards. To the Committee on Education.

By Mr. Bartlett of Derry, An act relating to the salary of the judge of probate for the county of Rockingham. To the Committee on Judiciary.

By Mr. Roby of Concord, Joint resolution for lighting the lighthouse on Loon island in Sunapee lake, repairing the cable connected therewith, improving the light service, placing and maintaining buoys on said lake, and removing obstructions to navigation in said lake. To the Committee on Public Improvements.

By Mr. Remich of Littleton, An act to provide a stenographer for the House and Senate; for the publication of a Journal of the Senate and House, and a calendar. To the Committee on Judiciary.

By Mr. Smith of Dover, An act allowing compensation to majors of battalions in the National Guard in certain cases. To the Committee on Military Affairs.

By Mr. Jordan of Columbia, An act to legalize and confirm the selectmen's warrant for and the votes and proceedings thereunder at the biennial election and meeting in the town of Columbia held in said town the fourth day of November, A. D. 1902. To the Committee on Elections.

By Mr. Hull of Laconia, Joint resolution for an appropriation to complete the screen at the outlet of Lake Winnipesaukee in the city of Laconia. To the Committee on Fisheries and Game.

By Mr. Smith of Peterborough, An act in amendment of section 1, chapter 31 of the Laws of 1897, entitled "An act in amendment of section 6 of chapter 83 of the Public Statutes, in relation to the settlement of paupers." To the Committee on Revision of Statutes.

By Mr. Stanley of Lisbon, An act to incorporate the First Free Baptist church of Franconia. To the Committee on Judiciary.

By Mr. Scammon of Exeter, An act in amendment of chapter 51 of the Public Statutes, relating to cemeteries. To the Committee on Judiciary.

On motion of Mr. Small of Rochester, the further reading of bills was suspended in order that the House might meet the Senate in joint convention according to the resolution adopted at the morning session, January 20.

IN CONVENTION.

The two branches of the Legislature, having met in joint convention at 12 o'clock, noon, agreeably to the laws of the United States, the journal of the Senate, containing its proceedings in the choice of a United States Senator on Tuesday, January 20, 1903, was read by the clerk of the Senate; and the journal of the House, containing its proceedings in the choice of a United States Senator on Tuesday, January 20, 1903, was read by the clerk of the House; and it appearing that Jacob H. Gallinger had received a majority of all the votes cast in each branch of the Legislature, the chairman made declaration as follows:

Jacob H. Gallinger having been named as the choice of a majority of the members, and having a majority of all the votes cast in each branch of the Legislature, is declared elected to represent the state of New Hampshire in the Senate of the United States, for the full term of six years, beginning on the fourth day of March, 1903, and ending on the fourth day of March, 1909.

On motion of Senator Burnell of District No. 5,—

Resolved, That a committee of three be appointed by the Chair to notify Hon. Jacob H. Gallinger of his election as United States Senator, and request his acceptance of the office; also to notify His Excellency the Governor of Mr. Gallinger's election as Senator to represent the state in the Congress of the United States, for the full term of six years, from the fourth day of March, 1903.

The chairman named as such committee Senator Burnell of District No. 5, and Messrs. Kimball of Concord and Jewell of Dover.

On motion of Mr. Small of Rochester, and by unanimous consent, the clerk of the House was authorized to cast one ballot for Edward N. Pearson for secretary of state.

The ballot was so cast, and Edward N. Pearson, having a majority of all the votes cast, was declared duly elected secretary of state for the ensuing two years.

On motion of Senator Page of District No. 24, and by unanimous consent, the clerk of the House was authorized to cast one ballot for Solon A. Carter for state treasurer.

The ballot was so cast, and Solon A. Carter, having a majority of all the votes cast, was declared duly elected state treasurer for the ensuing two years.

On motion of Mr. Barr of Manchester,—

Resolved, That a committee of three be appointed by the Chair to notify the secretary of state and state treasurer of their election.

The chairman named as such committee Mr. Barr of Manchester, Senator Thompson of District No. 22, and Mr. Bemis of Harrisville.

On motion of Senator Bickford of District No. 17, the convention then rose.

HOUSE.

LEAVES OF ABSENCE.

Messrs. Houston of Thornton, Nowell of Exeter, and Mason of Tilton were granted leave of absence for the balance of the week on account of sickness.

BILLS, ETC., INTRODUCED.

(Mr. Small of Rochester in the Chair.)

The reading of bills and joint resolutions was then resumed, the following being severally introduced, read twice by title, and referred as follows:

By Mr. Fox of Marlow, An act in amendment of section 27, chapter 154 of the Public Statutes, relating to the calling of proprietors' meetings. To the Committee on Revision of Statutes.

By Mr. Bussell of Nashua, An act to authorize the Governor, with the consent of the Council, to cause the original maps and surveys by the town proprietors of New Hampshire to be mounted and preserved. To the Committee on State Library.

By Mr. Howe of Hanover, An act in amendment of section 2, chapter 2555, Laws of 1861, entitled "An act to incorporate the Alpha Delta Phi Society." To the Committee on Judiciary.

By Mr. Jones of Franklin, An act in amendment of section 16, chapter 220 of the Public Statutes, relating to attachments. To the Committee on Judiciary.

By Mr. Barrett of Dover, An act in relation to the salary of the judge of probate for Strafford county. To the Committee on Judiciary.

By Mr. Bussell of Nashua, An act to amend the Public Statutes, section 5, chapter 37 of the Laws of 1895, relating to the fee of bail commissioner. To the Committee on Revision of Statutes.

By Mr. Beacham of Wolfeborough, An act to amend chapter 183 of Session Laws of 1897, entitled "An act to authorize the village fire precinct of Wolfeborough to construct and maintain an electric plant." To the Committee on Judiciary.

By Mr. Shute of Derry, An act to incorporate the Nutfield Loan and Trust Company. To the Committee on Banks.

By Mr. Dorothy of Enfield, An act to establish waterworks in Enfield Village fire district, in the town of Enfield. To the Committee on Judiciary.

By Mr. Phillips of Franklin, An act to amend section 1 of chapter 46, Session Laws of 1895, relating to annual enumeration of school children. To the Committee on Education.

By Mr. Scammon of Exeter, An act to permit executors and administrators to resign. To the Committee on Judiciary.

By Mr. Collins of Nashua, An act in amendment of section 2, chapter 79 of the Session Laws of 1901, relating to the fish and game commissioners. To the Committee on Fisheries and Game.

By Mr. Sherman of Claremont, An act in relation to milk tickets. To the Committee on Public Health.

8

By Mr. Bussell of Nashua, An act relating to salary of associate justice of police court of Nashua in case of vacancy in office of justice.   To the Committee on Judiciary.

By Mr. Whitney of Keene, An act to amend section 1, chapter 259 of the Laws of 1893, "An act to exempt certain property of the Keene Young Men's Christian Association." To the Committee on Judiciary.

By Mr. Woodman of Concord, An act providing for the purchase of a bond for the deputy state treasurer.   To the Committee on Judiciary.

By Mr. Quimby of Meredith, An act to annex a certain island in Lake Winnipesaukee now owned and occupied by George W. Sherwell, being one of the group of islands known as the Aunt Dolly islands, to the town of Meredith. To the Committee on Judiciary.

By Mr. O'Connor of Stark, Joint resolution for the appropriation of $500 for the repairing of the highways and bridges in the town of Stark.   To the Committee on Roads, Bridges, and Canals.

By Mr. Babcock of Whitefield, Joint resolution in favor of the Forest lake road, running from the Bethlehem road to the northerly side of said lake.   To the Committee on Roads, Bridges, and Canals.

By Mr. Fay of Keene, An act in amendment of section 19, chapter 57 of the Public Statutes, relating to the annual invoice of polls and taxable property.   To the Committee on Banks.

By Mr. Britton of Wolfeborough, An act in amendment of chapter 202 of the Laws of 1889, entitled "An act to establish water-works in the town of Wolfeborough," as amended by chapter 191 of the Laws of 1891.   To the Committee on Judiciary.

By Mr. Smith of Peterborough, An act in amendment of sections 4, 5 and 9 of chapter 85 of the Public Statutes, entitled "Support of county paupers."   To the Committee on Revision of Statutes.

By Mr. Smith of Peterborough, An act in amendment of section 1, chapter 83 of the Public Statutes, entitled "Settlement of paupers."   To the Committee on Revision of Statutes.

By Mr. Whitcher of Haverhill, Joint resolution in favor of William J. Patch.   To the Committee on Claims.

By Mr. Bell of Woodstock, Joint resolution in favor of the Warren road in the town of Woodstock.   To the Committee on Roads, Bridges, and Canals.

By Mr. Bell of Woodstock, Joint resolution in favor of the Kinsman Notch or Lost River road in the town of Woodstock.   To the Committee on Roads, Bridges, and Canals.

By Mr. Yeaton of Portsmouth, An act to regulate the traffic in intoxicating liquors.   To the Committee on Liquor Laws.

By Mr. Warner of North Hampton, An act to incorporate the North Hampton Street Railway Company.   To the Committee on Railroads.

By Mr. Filion of Manchester, An act enabling the city of Manchester to build and operate an electric lighting plant for the purpose of lighting its streets and public buildings.   To a special committee consisting of the Manchester delegation, on motion of Mr. Filion of Manchester.

By Mr. Badger of Newington, An act to incorporate the Portsmouth & Newington Street Railway Company.   To the Committee on Railroads.

By Mr. Sheehan of Manchester, An act to incorporate the Manchester Fire Insurance Company of New Hampshire.   To the Committee on Insurance.

By Mr. Kohler of Manchester, An act in amendment of chapter 11, Laws of 1889, entitled " An act relating to holidays."   To the Committee on Revision of Statutes.

By Mr. Ahern of Concord, An act relating to savings banks. To the Committee on Banks.

By Mr. Remich of Littleton, An act to amend section 14 of chapter 169 of the Public Statutes, as amended in section 1, chapter 67, Laws of 1901 ; also section 13 of chapter 167 of the Public Statutes, relating to insurance commissioner ; also section 1, chapter 54, Laws of 1891, relating to foreign insurance companies and agents.   To the Committee on Insurance.

By Mr. Bragg of Errol, An act to aid in the reconstruction of the Magalloway road in Errol, on a practicable route.   To the Committee on Roads, Bridges, and Canals.

By Mr. Crossman of Lisbon, An act to enlarge the powers of the Lisbon fire district. To the Committee on Judiciary.

BILLS FORWARDED.

By Mr. Mitchell of Littleton, An act to provide for a more economical and practical expenditure of money appropriated by the state for the construction and repairs of highways.

By Mr. Pierce of Bethlehem, An act providing for the construction of certain sections of roads and the completion of a line of public highways already inaugurated by the state in the north regions of the White Mountains.

By Mr. Plaisted of Jefferson, An act in amendment of "An act to provide for the survey, location, and construction of the Jefferson Notch road in Jefferson, Low and Burbank's Grant, Crawford's Purchase and Bean's Purchase," approved March 22, 1901.

Severally taken from the table and referred to the Committee on Roads, Bridges, and Canals.

By Mr. Haines of Newmarket, An act in amendment of an act approved March 26, 1895, entitled "An act in amendment of an act incorporating the Newmarket Manufacturing Company," approved June 12, 1823, and an act in amendment thereof, approved July 7, 1881.

By Mr. Smith of Peterborough, An act in amendment of section 1, chapter 185, Laws of 1901, entitled " An act authorizing the Hillsborough county convention to raise money for the building and repairing of court houses."

By Mr. Remich of Littleton, An act to promote cleanliness and to protect the public from the disease commonly known as consumption.

Severally taken from the table and ordered to a third reading.

MESSAGE FROM THE SENATE.

A message from the Honorable Senate, by its clerk, announced that the Senate concurs with the House of Representatives in the passage of the following entitled bill:

An act in amendment of the charter of the city of Dover, creating a board of police commissioners for said city, and fixing the salaries of the officers in the police department.

NOTICES OF BILLS.

By Mr. Smith of Pittsburg, Joint resolution in favor of highway in the town of Pittsburg.

By Mr. Hall of Westmoreland, An act in addition to chapter 58 of the Public Statutes, relating to the appraisal of taxable real estate.

By Mr. Mitchell of Littleton, Joint resolution in favor of Charles H. Roberts.

By Mr. Davenport of Bath, An act for the permanent improvement of the highways of the state.

By Mr. Davenport of Bath, An act for the better protection of deer.

By Mr. Morrill of Ashland, Joint resolution in favor of maintaining buoys and placing lights in Squam lake.

By Mr. Scammon of Exeter, Joint resolution to appropriate a sum of money to pay Arthur W. Dudley a balance due him for money expended and labor performed in making surveys for the state.

By Mr. Scammon of Exeter, An act in amendment of the charter of the Exeter Gas Light Company.

By Mr. Scammon of Exeter, Joint resolution in favor of Thomas Leavitt of Exeter, N. H.

By Mr. Scammon of Exeter, Joint resolution in favor of Horace S. Cummings.

By Mr. Scammon of Exeter, Joint resolution relating to a state highway between Massachusetts state line and Fort Point, in Newcastle, N. H.

By Mr. Scammon of Exeter, An act to amend section 1, chapter 184, of the Public Statutes, relative to the time and places for holding courts of probate, repealing chapter 29 of the Session Laws of 1901.

By Mr. Chase of Stratham, An act to legalize and confirm the warrant for, and the votes and proceedings at, the biennial election and meeting in Stratham, held the fourth day of November, 1902.

By Mr. Hutchins of Pittsfield, An act to authorize the town of Pittsfield to construct and maintain an electric light plant for lighting, heat, or power purposes.

By Mr. Goss of Berlin, An act to incorporate the Caledonia Power Company.

By Mr. Goss of Berlin, An act to incorporate the Peabody River Improvement Company.

By Mr. Gould of Plymouth, An act to legalize town meetings in Dorchester for years 1896, 1897, 1898, 1899, and 1900.

By Mr. Abbott of Manchester, An act in relation to the practice of Christian Science, faith cure, or mind healing, in cases of illness.

By Mr. Houston of Thornton, Joint resolution for an appropriation for the Sandwich Notch road, in the town of Thornton.

By Mr. Buckley of Lancaster, Joint resolution appropriating money to aid Dartmouth college in educating New Hampshire students.

By Mr. Whitcher of Haverhill, An act for the promotion of horticulture.

By Mr. Littlefield of Albany, Joint resolution for maintenance and repair of highways in the town of Albany for the years 1903 and 1904.

By Mr. Tobie of Francestown, Joint resolution providing for repairs upon the Crotchett Mountain road, so called, in the town of Francestown.

By Mr. Goodrich of Warren, Joint resolution in favor of that portion of the mountain road in the town of Warren leading from North Woodstock to Breezy Point.

By Mr. Babcock of Whitefield, Joint resolution in favor of the Forest lake road which leads from the Bethlehem road to the northerly side of said lake.

By Mr. Holland of Hinsdale, An act to incorporate the Connecticut River Power Company of New Hampshire.

By Mr. Gathercole of Clarksville, Joint resolution for the appropriation of $200 for the repairing of the Pond road, so called, in the town of Clarksville.

By Mr. Buckley of Lancaster, An act to amend chapter 179 of the Public Statutes, relating to guardians of insane persons and spendthrifts.

By Mr. Smith of Peterborough, An act to reimburse the town or county for aid furnished paupers.

By Mr. Russell of Sunapee, Joint resolution in favor of a new highway in the town of Sunapee.

By Mr. Remich of Littleton, An act to regulate the practice of pharmacy and the sale of spirituous and malt liquors for medicinal, mechanical, scientific, and sacramental purposes.

By Mr. Fay of Keene, An act relating to the salary of the register of probate for the county of Cheshire.

By Mr. Cutler of Jaffrey, An act to prohibit speculation or combination against the public good.

By Mr. Cutler of Jaffrey, An act to amend section 28 of chapter 112 of the Public Statutes, relating to the sale of spirituous liquor.

By Mr. Remich of Littleton, An act to provide for the sale of the stocks, bonds, and other securities in the state treasury, which represent the Benjamin Thompson fund, and the disposal of the avails thereof.

By Mr. Brown of Fremont, An act repealing chapter 83 of the Public Statutes, relating to the settlement of paupers.

By Mr. Morrill of Ashland, An act to amend section 16, chapter 79, Laws of 1901, so as to permit deer hunting in the town of Ashland.

By Mr. Remich of Littleton, An act to amend section 10 of chapter 169 of the Public Statutes, relating to insurance companies combining to fix and control rates.

By Mr. Goold of Lebanon, Joint resolution for the screening of Pleasant lake in the town of New London, and asking for an appropriation for the same.

By Mr. Goold of Lebanon, Joint resolution for the screening of Highland lake in the town of Andover, and asking for an appropriation for the same.

By Mr. Goold of Lebanon, An act to prohibit the dumping of sawdust and other waste into the waters of Blood brook, in the towns of Lebanon and Plainfield.

By Mr. Remich of Littleton, An act to provide for the forfeiture of the charters of insurance companies, and the revocation of their licenses to do business in New Hampshire.

By Mr. Kellom of Winchester, An act relating to the setting off by the Legislature of territory of one town or city on to that of another town or city.

By Mr. Goold of Lebanon, An act to prohibit the dumping of sawdust and other waste into the waters of Mink brook, in the town of Hanover.

By Mr. Bowen of Wentworth, Joint resolution in favor of Sand road, in the town of Wentworth.

By Mr. Goold of Lebanon, Joint resolution for the screening of Tewksbury pond, in the town of Grafton, and asking for an appropriation for the same.

By Mr. Britton of Wolfeborough, An act to incorporate the First Congregational church of Wolfeborough.

By Mr. Fay of Keene, An act relating to books of deposit issued by savings banks when lost, destroyed, or assigned.

By Mr. Couch of Manchester, An act in amendment of chapter 202 of the Laws of the State of New Hampshire, passed at the January session, 1893, entitled "An act in relation to the city of Manchester, establishing a board of police commissioners for said city."

By Mr. Couch of Manchester, An act in amendment of so much of chapter 264 of the Laws of the State of New Hampshire, passed at the January session, 1893, as relates to the establishing of a board of street and park commissioners for the city of Manchester.

By Mr. Couch of Manchester, An act establishing a permanent board of assessors for the city of Manchester.

By Mr. Caird of Berlin, An act in relation to the insurance of children under ten years of age.

By Mr. Blaisdell of Portsmouth, An act to authorize the city of Portsmouth to raise money and issue bonds for a new high schoolhouse.

By Mr. Riordan of Manchester, An act in amendment of chapter 59, Laws of 1891, entitled "An act in amendment of chapter 7 of the Laws of 1883, entitled 'An act in relation to the exemption of disabled soldiers and sailors of the late war from the payment of poll tax.'"

By Mr. Bell of Woodstock, An act to amend chapter 63 of the Laws of 1897, relating to the so-called "counter prescribing," by druggists or registered pharmacists, of drugs and medicines without the prescription of a regularly qualified physician.

By Mr. True of Plainfield, An act to put a bounty on foxes.

On motion of Mr. Bell of Woodstock, at 1.15 the House adjourned.

AFTERNOON.

The House met at 3 o'clock.

THIRD READINGS.

An act to promote cleanliness and to protect the public from the disease commonly known as consumption.

An act in amendment of an act, approved March 26, 1895, entitled "An act in amendment of an act incorporating the Newmarket Manufacturing Company," approved June 12, 1823, and An act in amendment thereof, approved July 7, 1881.

An act in amendment of section 1, chapter 185, Laws of 1901, entitled "An act authorizing the Hillsborough county convention to raise money for the building and repairing of court houses."

Severally read a third time, passed, and sent to the Senate for concurrence.

NOTICES OF BILLS.

By Mr. Barnard of Hebron, Joint resolution for the appropriation of $200 for the repairing of the highway running around Newfound lake in the town of Hebron.

By Mr. Davis of Concord, An act amending section 4, chapter 40 of the Public Statutes, relating to towns.

By Mr. Tuck of Nashua, An act for the better regulation of the business of fire insurance and to increase the public revenue.

By Mr. Donahue of Manchester, Joint resolution in favor of the Industrial School.

By Mr. Ware of Hancock, Joint resolution for the screening of the outlet of Nubanusett lake, in the towns of Hancock and Nelson.

By Mr. Woodman of Concord, An act fixing office hours in state and county offices.

By Mr. Etter of Somersworth, An act in relation to the salary of the register of probate for Strafford county.

By Mr. Harriman of Stewartstown, Joint resolution for the appropriation of $500 for the repairing of the highway from Little Diamond pond to Diamond pond, in the town of Stewartstown.

By Mr. Yeaton of Portsmouth, An act to prevent discrimination in rates by express companies.

By Mr. Yeaton of Portsmouth, An act to amend the charter of the Portsmouth Savings Bank.

By Mr. Nelson of Portsmouth, An act to provide for the distribution of fines imposed in certain cases by police courts.

By Mr. Churchill of Cornish, An act to provide, in common with the state of Vermont, for the building and maintenance of free bridges across the Connecticut river.

By Mr. Chase of Newfields, An act to protect striped bass in the waters of the Piscataqua river.

By Mr. Brown of Fremont, An act to amend chapter 110 of the Public Statutes, in relation to smallpox.

By Mr. Yeaton of Portsmouth, An act to fix the form of life insurance policies, and to establish cash surrender values.

By Mr. Ware of Hancock, Joint resolution in favor of the Nelson road, so called, in the towns of Hancock, Harrisville, and Nelson.

By Mr. Tuttle of Farmington, Joint resolution for screening the outlet of Merry Meeting lake in the town of New Durham.

By Mr. Cutler of Jaffrey, An act to prohibit fishing on Sunday.

On motion of Mr. Ahern of Concord, the rules were suspended and business in order to-morrow morning at 11 o'clock was made in order at the present time.

BILLS, ETC., INTRODUCED.

(Mr. Nason of Dover in the chair.)

On motion of Mr. Ahern of Concord, the rules were suspended and the first and second reading of bills by their titles made in order, and the following bills and joint resolutions were severally introduced, read twice by title, and referred as follows:

By Mr. Gathercole of Clarksville, Joint resolution for the

appropriation of $200 for the repairing of the Pond road, so called, in the town of Clarksville. To the Committee on Roads, Bridges, and Canals.

By Mr. Littlefield of Albany, Joint resolution for maintenance and repair of highways in the town of Albany for the years 1903-1904. To the Committee on Roads, Bridges, and Canals.

By Mr. Tobie of Francestown, Joint resolution providing for repairs upon the Crotchett Mountain road, so called, in the town of Francestown. To the Committee on Roads, Bridges, and Canals.

By Mr. Straw of Manchester, An act to protect milk dealers and consumers against the unlawful use and destruction of milk cans and other receptacles. To the Committee on Agriculture.

By Mr. Adams of Portsmouth, An act for the protection of employees. To the Committee on Judiciary.

By Mr. Hoyt of Sandwich, An act to prohibit the deposit of sawdust, shavings, or other refuse in Bearcamp river and tributaries east of Bearcamp pond, in the town of Sandwich. To the Committee on Judiciary.

By Mr. Scammon of Exeter, An act to amend.section 1, chapter 184 of the Public Statutes, relative to the times and places for holding courts of probate, repealing chapter 29 of the Session Laws of 1901. To the Committee on Judiciary.

By Mr. Hall of Westmoreland, An act in addition to chapter 58 of the Public Statutes, relating to the appraisal of taxable real estate. To the Committee on Judiciary.

By Mr. Chase of Stratham, An act to legalize and confirm the warrant for, and the votes and proceedings at, the biennial election and meeting in Stratham, held the fourth day of November, 1902. To the Committee on Elections.

By Mr. Morrill of Ashland, An act to amend section 16, chapter 79, Laws of 1901, so as to permit deer hunting in the town of Ashland. To the Committee on Fisheries and Game.

By Mr. Harriman of Stewartstown, Joint resolution for the appropriation of $500 for the repairing of the highway from Little Diamond pond to Diamond pond, in the town of Stewartstown. To the Committee on Roads, Bridges, and Canals.

By Mr. Tuck of Nashua, An act for the better regulation of the business of fire insurance and to increase the public revenue. To the Committee on Insurance.

By Mr. Mitchell of Littleton, An act in amendment of the charter of the Wells River bridge, and authorizing the Concord & Montreal Railroad to hold stock therein. To the Committee on Railroads.

By Mr. Smyth of Berlin, An act regulating the examining and licensing of engineers and firemen. To the Committee on Judiciary.

By Mr. Smith of Pittsburg, Joint resolution in favor of highway in the town of Pittsburg. To the Committee on Roads, Bridges, and Canals.

By Mr. Gould of Plymouth, An act to legalize the town meetings in Dorchester for years 1896, 1897, 1898, 1899, and 1900. To the Committee on Elections.

By Mr. Goodrich of Warren, Joint resolution in favor of that portion of the Mountain road in the town of Warren leading from North Woodstock to Breezy Point. To the Committee on Roads, Bridges, and Canals.

By Mr. Messer of New London, An act in amendment of the charter of the Colby academy, providing for filling vacancies and election of members. To the Committee on Judiciary.

By Mr. Russell of Sunapee, Joint resolution in favor of a new highway in the town of Sunapee. To the Committee on Roads, Bridges, and Canals.

By Mr. Woodman of Concord, An act fixing office hours in state and county offices. To the Committee on Judiciary.

By Mr. Chase of Newfields, An act to protect striped bass in the waters of the Piscataqua river. To the Committee on Fisheries and Game.

By Mr. Morrill of Ashland, Joint resolution in favor of maintaining buoys and placing lights in Squam lake. To the Committee on Public Improvements.

By Mr. Kent of Berlin, Joint resolution to appropriate the sum of $300 for the purpose of turning Silver stream into Success pond, in the township of Success, and to screen the outlet to said pond. To the Committee on Fisheries and Game.

By Mr. Kellom of Winchester, An act relating to the setting off by the Legislature of territory of one town or city on to that of another town or city. To the Committee on Towns.

By Mr. Buckley of Lancaster, An act to amend chapter 179 of the Public Statutes, relating to guardians of insane persons and spendthrifts. To the Committee on Judiciary.

By Mr. Etter of Somersworth, An act in relation to the salary of the register of probate for Strafford county. To the Committee on Judiciary.

By Mr. Tuttle of Farmington, An act concerning savings banks. To the Committee on Banks.

By Mr. Remich of Littleton, An act to regulate the practice of pharmacy, and the sale of spirituous and malt liquors for medicinal, mechanical, scientific, and sacramental purposes. To the Committee on Liquor Laws.

By Mr. Goss of Berlin, An act to incorporate the Caledonia Power Company. To the Committee on Judiciary.

The following bill was introduced, read twice by title, and on motion of Mr. Whittemore of Dover, laid upon the table to be printed:

By Mr. Whittemore of Dover, An act to establish a state normal school.

(The Speaker in the chair.)

NOTICES OF BILLS.

By Mr. Gould of Plymouth, Joint resolution appropriating $1,000 for a monument to be erected at Hackensack, N. J., in memory of Gen. Enoch Poor.

By Mr. Chase of Manchester, An act to regulate the operation of the insurance companies, corporations, associations, individuals, and insurance agencies in the state of New Hampshire, and prohibiting the payment of any commission, compensation, or valuable consideration to any but legally authorized resident agents, and providing the penalty for violations of this act.

By Mr. Darling of Whitefield, An act to amend the charter of Brown's Lumber Company of Whitefield, approved July 1, 1874.

By Mr. Messer of New London, Joint resolution to authorize the appropriation and expenditure of $100 for the repair of highway leading from Lakeside to Soonipi park in the town of New London.

On motion of Mr. Sheehan of Manchester, at 4 o'clock the House adjourned.

THURSDAY, JANUARY 22, 1903.

The House met at 11 o'clock.

Prayer was offered by the chaplain.

COMMITTEE REPORTS.

Mr. Richards of Newport, for the Committee on Public Improvements, to whom was referred Joint resolution making appropriation for repairs on buildings erected by the state for the New Hampshire Veterans' Association at The Weirs, having considered the same, report the same with the following resolution :

Resolved, That the joint resolution ought to pass.

The report was accepted, the resolution adopted, and the joint resolution laid upon the table to be printed, and then referred to the Committee on Appropriations.

Mr. Churchill of Cornish, for the Committee on Forestry, to whom was referred Joint resolution to provide for a forest examination of the White Mountain region, having considered the same, report the same with the following resolution :

Resolved, That the joint resolution ought to pass.

The report was accepted, the resolution adopted, and the joint resolution laid upon the table to be printed, and then referred to the Committee on Appropriations.

Mr. Whitcher of Haverhill, for the Joint Committee on State Library, to whom was referred an act to establish traveling libraries, having considered the same, report the same with the following resolution :

Resolved, That it is inexpedient to legislate.

The report was accepted and the resolution adopted.

Mr. Whitcher of Haverhill, for the Joint Committee on State Library, to whom was referred an act relative to the enlargement of the state library building, having considered the same, report the same with the following resolution :

Resolved, That the bill ought to pass.

The report was accepted, the resolution adopted, and the bill laid upon the table to be printed, and then referred to the Committee on Appropriations.

Mr. Whitcher of Haverhill, for the Joint Committee on State Library, to whom was referred an act to abolish the board of library commissioners, having considered the same, report the same with the following resolution :

Resolved, That the bill ought to pass.

The report was accepted, the resolution adopted, and the bill laid upon the table to be printed.

Mr. Crocker of Rochester, for the Committee on Normal School, to whom was referred an act to amend chapter 95 of the Public Statutes, relating to the trustees of the State Normal School, having considered the same, report the same with the following resolution :

Resolved, That the bill ought to pass.

The report was accepted, the resolution adopted, and the bill laid upon the table to be printed.

Mr. Batchelder of Keene, for the Committee on Judiciary, to whom was referred an act relating to probate bonds and to the liability of sureties thereunder, having considered the same, report the same with the following resolution :

Resolved, That it is inexpedient to legislate.

The report was accepted and the resolution adopted.

Mr. Hull of Laconia, for the special committee consisting of the delegation from the city of Laconia, to whom was referred An act to amend chapter 241 of the Session Laws of 1893, entitled " An act to establish the city of Laconia," and repealing chapter 200 of the Laws of 1901, entitled "An act to amend chapter 241 of the Session Laws of 1893, entitled 'An act to establish the city of Laconia,' " having considered the same, report the same with the following resolution :

Resolved, That the bill ought to pass.

The report was accepted, the resolution adopted, and the bill laid upon the table to be printed.

The Speaker, for the Committee on Rules, made the follow-

ing report, recommending the following changes in the rules
of the House:

Strike out the words " on Asylum for Insane " and insert in
the place thereof " on State Hospital."

And recommend the establishment of a standing committee
to be known as the " Committee on Feeble-Minded School."
It shall be the duty of the Committee on Feeble-Minded
School to examine the rules and government of the institution
and all matters of general interest connected therewith, and all
such matters as may be referred to it.

The report was accepted.

MESSAGE FROM THE SENATE.

A message from the Honorable Senate, by its clerk, announced that the Senate concurs with the House of Representatives in the passage of the following entitled bill:

An act authorizing the Manchester Mills to increase its
capital stock.

The message also announced that the Senate concurs with
the House of Representatives in the passage of the following
bill, with amendment, in the passage of which amendment it
asks the concurrence of the House of Representatives:

An act to allow the city of Nashua to appropriate money
for the celebration of its semi-centennial.

Amend section 1 by striking out the words, " a sum not
exceeding one thousand dollars ($1,000) " in the second line
of said section, and insert in lieu thereof the words, " such
sum as the city council may determine."

On motion of Mr. Bussell of Nashua, the amendment was
concurred in.

BILLS, ETC., INTRODUCED.

The introduction of bills being in order, Mr. French of
Moultonborough moved that the rules of the House be suspended so that the first and second readings of bills by their
titles be in order.

Mr. Lennon of Stratford offered an amendment that only
bills of a private or local nature should be read by their titles,
all other bills to be read in full.

The question being upon the adoption of the amendment offered by Mr. Lennon,

(Discussion ensued.)

On a *viva voce* vote, the amendment offered by Mr. Lennon was not adopted.

The main question being put, on a *viva voce* vote the motion offered by Mr. French prevailed and the following bills and joint resolutions were severally introduced, read twice by title, and referred as follows:

By Mr. Bartlett of Manchester, An act to incorporate the Nashua, Manchester & Concord Railway Company. To the Committee on Railroads.

By Mr. Goold of Lebanon, Joint resolution in favor of appropriating money for screening the outlet of Tewksbury pond in the town of Grafton. To the Committee on Fisheries and Game.

By Mr. Goold of Lebanon, Joint resolution for appropriating money for screening the outlet of Highland lake in the town of Andover. To the Committee on Fisheries and Game.

By Mr. Goold of Lebanon, Joint resolution appropriating money for screening the outlet of Pleasant pond in New London. To the Committee on Fisheries and Game.

By Mr. Mitchell of Littleton, Joint resolution in favor of Charles H. Roberts. To the Committee on Claims.

By Mr. Bragdon of Temple, Joint resolution in aid of Miller Park Mountain road, so called, situated in the towns of Temple and Peterborough. To the Committee on Roads, Bridges, and Canals.

By Mr. Chase of Manchester, An act to regulate the operation of the insurance companies, corporations, associations, individuals, and insurance agencies in the state of New Hampshire, and prohibiting the payment of any commission, compensation, or valuable consideration, to any but legally authorized resident agents, and providing the penalty for violations of this act. To the Committee on Insurance.

By Mr. Davis of Concord, An act amending section 4, chapter 40 of the Public Statutes, relating to towns. To the Committee on Judiciary.

9

By Mr. Holland of Hinsdale, An act to incorporate the Connecticut River Power Company of New Hampshire. To the Committee on Judiciary.

By Mr. Cutler of Jaffrey, An act to prohibit fishing on Sunday. To the Committee on Fisheries and Game.

By Mr. Cutler of Jaffrey, An act to annul section 8 of chapter 112 of the Public Statutes, relating to the sale of spirituous liquors. To the Committee on Liquor Laws.

By Mr. Darling of Whitefield, An act to amend the charter of Brown's Lumber Company of Whitefield, approved July 1, 1874. To the Committee on Judiciary.

By Mr. Smith of Peterborough, An act to reimburse the town or county for aid furnished paupers. To the Committee on Judiciary.

By Mr. Scammon of Exeter, Joint resolution to appropriate a sum of money to pay Arthur W. Dudley a balance due him for money expended and labor performed in making surveys for the state. To the Committee on Claims.

By Mr. Whittemore of Dover, An act to authorize the Dover & Eliot Street Railway and the Eliot Bridge Company to transfer their properties and franchises to the Berwick, Eliot & York Street Railway. To the Committee on Railroads.

(Mr. Whitcher of Haverhill in the chair.)

By Mr. Bartlett of Derry, An act to incorporate the Derry & Salem Street Railway Company. To the Committee on Railroads.

By Mr. Tuttle of Farmington, Joint resolution for screening the outlet of Merry Meeting lake in the town of New Durham. To the Committee on Fisheries and Game.

By Mr. Hutchins of Pittsfield, An act to authorize the town of Pittsfield to construct and maintain an electric plant for lighting, heat, or power purposes. To the Committee on Judiciary.

By Mr. Hoyt of Sandwich, An act for the better preservation of highways and accommodating public travel. To the Committee on Agriculture.

By Mr. Blaisdell of Portsmouth, An act to authorize the

city of Portsmouth to raise money and issue bonds for a new high schoolhouse. On motion of Mr. Blaisdell of Portsmouth, to a special committee consisting of the Portsmouth delegation.

By Mr. Goold of Lebanon, An act to prohibit the pollution of the waters of Mink brook, in the town of Hanover, from sawdust and other waste. To the Committee on Judiciary.

By Mr. Pollard of Tamworth, An act to extend the time for the location, construction, and completion of the railroad of the Moosilauke Railroad Company. To the Committee on Railroads.

By Mr. King of Orange, Joint resolution in favor of Mountain road in the town of Orange. To the Committee on Roads, Bridges, and Canals.

By Mr. Shute of Derry, An act requiring goods made in whole or part by convict labor to be so stamped. To the Committee on Labor.

By Mr. Shute of Derry, An act regulating fares on electric roads. To the Committee on Railroads.

By Mr. Cutler of Jaffrey, An act to prohibit speculation or combination against the public good. To the Committee on Judiciary.

By Mr. Fellows of Brentwood, An act to incorporate the Epping, Brentwood & Kingston Street Railway. To the Committee on Railroads.

By Mr. Whitcher of Haverhill, An act for the promotion of horticulture. To the Committee on Agriculture.

By Mr. Bowen of Wentworth, Joint resolution in favor of Sand road in the town of Wentworth. To the Committee on Roads, Bridges, and Canals.

By Mr. Emerson of Hampstead, An act to incorporate the Hampstead & Haverhill Railway Company. To the Committee on Railroads.

By Mr. Goold of Lebanon, An act to prohibit the pollution of the waters of Blood brook, so called, in the towns of Lebanon and Plainfield. To the Committee on Judiciary.

By Mr. Brown of Fremont, An act in relation to town and county paupers. To the Committee on Judiciary.

By Mr. Brown of Fremont, An act in amendment of chapter 110 of the Public Statutes, relating to smallpox. To the Committee on Revision of Statutes.

By Mr. Libby of Gorham, An act in amendment of section 3, chapter 209 of the Public Statutes, relating to exemptions from serving as jurors. To the Committee on Revision of Statutes.

By Mr. Libby of Gorham, An act relating to agreed lines between adjoining owners. To the Committee on Judiciary.

By Mr. McMurphey of Alexandria, Joint resolution in favor of the Sugar Loaf road in the town of Alexandria. To the Committee on Roads, Bridges, and Canals.

By Mr. Hoyt of Sandwich, An act in amendment of chapter 121, Laws of 1901, relating to the protection of public rights in New Hampshire. To the Committee on Revision of Statutes.

By Mr. Badger of Newington, An act to repeal an act of the Legislature of 1842, entitled "An act to annex Richard Pickering of Newington to School District No. 1 in Portsmouth," approved June 22, 1842. To the Committee on Education.

BILLS FORWARDED.

(The Speaker in the chair.)

An act to establish a state sanatorium for consumptives.

An act in amendment of chapter 23 of the Laws of 1901, entitled "An act to establish a Laboratory of Hygiene."

Severally taken from the table and referred to the Committee on Appropriations.

An act authorizing the Concord & Montreal Railroad, lessor, to acquire the Concord Street Railway and other property, to issue stock and bonds to pay therefor, and authorizing a physical connection of the Manchester Street Railway with the electric branches of the Concord & Montreal Railroad.

Taken from the table and ordered to a third reading.

NOTICES OF BILLS.

By Mr. Buckley of Lancaster, An act to authorize the town of Lancaster to acquire property for the protection of the sources of water supply.

By Mr. Fletcher of Rindge, An act relating to the assessment of poll taxes.

By Mr. Sheehan of Manchester, An act in amendment of section 1 of chapter 67, Laws of 1899, relating to expenses of judges of the Supreme Court.

By Mr. Ball of Washington, Joint resolution relating to screening the outlets of Ashuelot and Millen lakes in the town of Washington.

By Mr. Sheehan of Manchester, An act in amendment of "An act to incorporate the North Conway & Mount Kearsarge Railroad," passed June session, 1883, and all subsequent acts relating to the same.

By Mr. Goss of Berlin, An act in amendment of section 4, chapter 206 of the Laws of 1897, being "An act to incorporate the Bethlehem Electric Light Company."

By Mr. Libby of Gorham, An act to incorporate the Maynesboro Fire Insurance Company.

By Mr. Libby of Gorham, An act to amend section 2 of chapter 121 of the Laws of 1895, relating to bounty on bears.

By Mr. Wallace of Rochester, An act to incorporate the Omicron Deuteron Charge of the Theta Delta Chi Fraternity.

By Mr. Goodnow of Keene, An act to incorporate the Keene Trust Company.

By Mr. Emerson of Hampstead, Joint resolution for the repair of the stage road in Hampstead.

By Mr. Carr of Haverhill, An act to exempt from taxation real estate reservations of the Appalachian Mountain Club.

By Mr. Kennedy of Concord, An act extending the liability of railroads for injuries to employees.

By Mr. Hicks of Colebrook, An act requiring the discharge of personal property mortgages after payment.

By Mr. Barrett of Dover, An act in reference to the duties of county commissioner.

By Mr. Goss of Berlin, An act to incorporate the Peabody River Improvement Company.

By Mr. Blaisdell of Portsmouth, An act to ratify the lease of the Portsmouth & Exeter Street Railway Company to the Exeter, Hampton & Amesbury Street Railway Company.

By Mr. Blaisdell of Portsmouth, An act to ratify the lease of the Seabrook & Hampton Beach Street Railway Company to the Exeter, Hampton & Amesbury Street Railway Company.

By Mr. Blaisdell of Portsmouth, An act to authorize the Hudson, Pelham & Salem Electric Railway to take a lease of the railway and property of the Lowell & Pelham Street Railway Company.

By Mr. Center of Litchfield, An act to incorporate The Goff's Falls, Litchfield & Hudson Street Railway Company.

By Mr. Clough of Gilmanton, Joint resolution for an appropriation for screening Crystal lake in Gilmanton.

By Mr. Nelson of Portsmouth, An act to provide for the distribution of fines imposed by police courts in certain cases.

By Mr. Cate of Concord, An act in amendment of chapter 82 of the Laws of 1897.

By Mr. Morse of Manchester, An act to make the mayor of Manchester chairman of the board of street and park commissioners.

By Mr. Blaisdell of Portsmouth, An act to authorize the Hudson, Pelham & Salem Electric Railway Company to take a lease of the railway and property of the Lawrence & Methuen Street Railway Company.

By Mr. Blaisdell of Portsmouth, An act to authorize the Hudson, Pelham & Salem Electric Railway Company to take a lease of the railway and property of the Haverhill & Southern New Hampshire Street Railway Company.

By Mr. Blaisdell of Portsmouth, An act concerning the New Hampshire Traction Company.

By Mr. Blaisdell of Portsmouth, An act to ratify the lease of the Haverhill, Plaistow & Newton Street Railway Company to the Exeter, Hampton & Amesbury Street Railway Company.

By Mr. Clough of Gilmanton, An act to prohibit fishing through the ice on Crystal lake in the town of Gilmanton.

By Mr. Warren of Rochester, An act to provide for the better equipment of cars for the transportation of lumber and wood.

By Mr. Phillips of Franklin, An act requiring state certification of teachers of public schools.

By Mr. Morse of Manchester, An act to prohibit the city of Manchester from making a contract for a longer term than two years.

By Mr. Gordon of Salem, Joint resolution in favor of an appropriation for highways in the town of Salem.

By Mr. Nason of Dover, An act to amend chapter 96 of the Session Laws of 1901, relating to high schools.

By Mr. Scammon of Exeter, An act to enable the Hedding Camp Meeting Association to fund its indebtedness.

By Mr. Clough of Gilmanton, An act to incorporate a village improvement society at Gilmanton Iron Works.

By Mr. Pike of Haverhill, Joint resolution to provide a nursery for the growth and distribution of forest seedling trees within the state at cost.

By Mr. Jewell of Dover, An act to incorporate the Dover Loan and Banking Company.

By Mr. Jewell of Dover, An act to protect resident life insurance agents and managers from competition with non-resident life agents and managers, and to prohibit the sale of deceptive speculative life insurance in this state.

By Mr. Ahern of Concord, An act in amendment of chapter 86 of the Public Statutes, in relation to state aid to indigent deaf and dumb, blind, and feeble-minded persons.

By Mr. Scott of Nelson, An act to change the name of the body of water formerly called Munsonville pond, lying in the towns of Nelson and Stoddard.

By Mr. Willis of Concord, An act to regulate the traffic in intoxicating liquors.

By Mr. Darling of Whitefield, An act to aid in constructing a highway around the east end of Forest lake in Whitefield.

By Mr. Kimball of Concord, An act to amend chapter 94 of the Public Statutes, in relation to the superintendent of public instruction.

By Mr. Fifield of Conway, An act relating to the salary of the judge of probate of the county of Carroll.

By Mr. Marshall of Manchester, An act in amendment of

chapter 202 of the Public Statutes, relative to bills and promissory notes.

By Mr. Fox of Marlow, An act in amendment of sections 15 and 23 of chapter 112 of the Public Statutes, relating to the enforcement of the provisions of said chapter.

By Mr. Stevens of Bartlett, Joint resolution in favor of the new road on the north side of the Saco river, in the town of Bartlett.

By Mr. Chase of Weare, An act to incorporate the Goffstown & Henniker Electric Railway Company.

By Mr. Hoyt of Sandwich, An act to amend the charter of the Ashland & Asquam Electric Railway Company.

By Mr. Nelson of Portsmouth, An act to amend the charter of the North Shore Water Company.

By Mr. Kimball of Concord, An act amending chapter 92 of the Public Statutes, relating to school boards.

By Mr. Place of Middleton, An act severing the homestead farm of Hiram H. Stevens from the school district of the town of Middleton, and annexing the same to the town of Wakefield, for school purposes.

By Mr. Carpenter of Manchester, An act to prohibit all ice fishing, except in certain specified lakes.

By Mr. Shute of Derry, An act in relation to mileage books.

By Mr. Farley of Hollis, Joint resolution in favor of the road leading from Patch's Corner to the Amherst line, in the town of Hollis.

By Mr. Jewell of Dover, An act to establish a state aid road fund to be subject to the disposal of the Governor and Council, to aid such towns and places as are unable to keep the roads and bridges in their town or place in suitable repair.

By Mr. Blaisdell of Portsmouth, An act to ratify the lease of the Dover, Somersworth & Rochester Street Railway Company to the Exeter, Hampton & Amesbury Street Railway Company.

By Mr. McDonald of Northumberland, Joint resolution to aid in repairing the Nash Stream road in Stratford.

On motion of Mr. French of Moultonborough, at 12.15 the House adjourned.

AFTERNOON.

The House met at 3 o'clock.

MESSAGE FROM THE SENATE.

A message from the Honorable Senate, by its clerk, announced that the Senate concurs with the House of Representatives in the passage of the following entitled bills:

An act amending section 11 of chapter 63 of the Session Laws of 1897, entitled "Practice of medicine."

An act to repeal chapter 200 of the Laws of 1899, entitled "An act to amend chapter 207 of the Laws of 1895, relating to the police court of Haverhill."

The message also announced that the Senate has passed a bill with the following title, in the passage of which it asks the concurrence of the House of Representatives:

An act to change the name of the Woman's Auxiliary to the City Missionary Society of Manchester.

Read a first and second time and referred to the Committee on Judiciary.

THIRD READING.

An act authorizing the Concord & Montreal Railroad, lessor, to acquire the Concord Street Railway and other property, to issue stock and bonds to pay therefor and authorizing a physical connection of the Manchester Street Railway with the electric branches of the Concord & Montreal Railroad.

Read a third time and passed, and sent to the Senate for concurrence.

On motion of Mr. Yeaton of Portsmouth,—

Resolved, that the clerk of the House be instructed to procure 700 printed copies of House Bill No. 130, entitled " An act to regulate the traffic in intoxicating liquors," now before that committee for consideration.

On motion of Mr. Cavanaugh of Manchester,—

Resolved, that when the House adjourns this afternoon, it be to meet at 9.30 o'clock Friday morning, and when it adjourns Friday morning it be to meet at 8 o'clock Monday evening.

By Mr. Barrett of Dover, An act to incorporate the Prudential Fire Insurance Company.

By Mr. Scott of Nelson, Joint resolution to aid in repairing the highway around Granite lake, so called, lying in the towns of Nelson and Stoddard.

By Mr. Tallant of Pembroke, An act relative to the issue of bonds, coupon notes, and other evidences of indebtedness of street railway companies.

By Mr. Marshall of Manchester, An act in relation to the term of office of the chief engineer and assistant engineers of the Manchester fire department.

By Mr. Donahue of Manchester, An act relating to salaries of county commissioners for Hillsborough county.

By Mr. Sheldon of Wilton, An act in relation to the trapping of fur-bearing animals.

By Mr. Sheldon of Wilton, An act relating to the use of bait or scent for the purpose of trapping foxes.

By Mr. White of Deerfield, An act to incorporate the Manchester, Candia & Deerfield Street Railway Company.

By Mr. Scammon of Exeter, An act relating to the province records of New Hampshire.

By Mr. Barr of Manchester, An act to regulate the appointment of insurance agents.

By Mr. Woodman of Concord, An act to provide for taking depositions outside this state, and depositions within this state for use in other states.

By Mr. Woodman of Concord, An act authorizing the Concord & Montreal Railroad, lessor, to vote on all stock owned by it in other corporations.

By Mr. Kellom of Winchester, An act providing for tax exemption in homesteads owned by soldiers' widows.

By Mr. Sawyer of Milford, Joint resolution in favor of John M. Stanyan, for soldiers' pay and bounty.

By Mr. Hill, A. W., of Concord, An act in relation to the salary of the judge of probate for Merrimack county.

By Mr. Mitchell of Littleton, An act to prevent trespassing on railroad tracks.

By Mr. Bunten of Dunbarton, An act to extend the street electric railway from Goffstown to the town of Dunbarton.

By Mr. Tuck of Nashua, An act to amend section 12, chapter 59 of the militia law of 1895.

By Mr. Badger of Newington, An act in relation to the re-demption of rebates by railroad companies.

By Mr. Yeaton of Portsmouth, An act to regulate telephone and telegraph companies.

On motion of Mr. Whitcher of Haverhill, the rules were suspended and business in order to-morrow morning at 11 o'clock was made in order at the present time.

COMMITTEE REPORTS.

Mr. Andrews of Somersworth, for the Committee on Education, to whom was referred An act to unite the school districts of the town of Rollinsford, having considered the same, report the same with the following resolution :

Resolved, That the bill ought to pass.

The report was accepted, the resolution adopted and the bill laid upon the table to be printed.

Mr. Andrews of Somersworth, for the Committee on Education, to whom was referred An act to amend chapter 92 of the Public Statutes, relating to duties of school boards, having considered the same, report the same with the following resolution :

Resolved, That the committee recommend that the bill pass.

The report was accepted, the resolution adopted and the bill laid upon the table to be printed.

Mr. Andrews of Somersworth, for the Committee on Education, to whom was referred An act to amend chapter 93, in relation to scholars, having considered the same, report the same with the following resolution :

Resolved, That it is the recommendation of the committee that the bill pass.

The report was accepted, the resolution adopted, and the bill laid upon the table to be printed.

Mr. Matson of Concord, for the Committee on Incorporations, to whom was referred An act reviving and continuing the charter of the Warner & Kearsarge Road Company, and amendments to said charter, having considered the same, report the same with the following resolution :

Resolved, That the bill ought to pass.

The report was accepted, the resolution adopted, and the bill laid upon the table to be printed.

Mr. Goold of Lebanon, for the Committee on Fisheries and Game, to whom was referred An act in amendment of section 11, chapter 79 of the Session Laws of 1901, relating to the fish and game commissioners, having considered the same, report the same with the following resolution :

Resolved, That the bill ought to pass.

The report was accepted, the resolution adopted, and the bill laid upon the table to be printed, and then referred to the Committee on Appropriations.

Mr. Bartlett of Derry, for the Committee on Revision of Statutes, to whom was referred An act relating to the counting of votes at biennial elections, having considered the same, report the same in a new draft.

The report was accepted, and the bill in its new draft read a first time and ordered to a second reading.

Mr. Long of Claremont, for the Committee on Railroads, to whom was referred An act to extend the charter for the building of the Claremont Street Railway, having considered the same, report the same with the following resolution :

Resolved, That the bill ought to pass.

The report was accepted, the resolution adopted, and the bill laid upon the table to be printed. On motion of Mr. French of Moultonborough, the rules were suspended and the printing of the bill dispensed with. The bill was then ordered to a third reading. On motion of the same gentleman, the rules were further suspended, and the bill read a third time and passed, and sent to the Senate for concurrence.

Mr. Converse of Lyme, for the Committee on Engrossed Bills, reported that they had examined bills with the following titles and found them correctly engrossed :

An act in amendment of the charter of the city of Dover, creating a board of police commissioners for said city, and fixing the salaries of the officers of the police department.

An act authorizing the Manchester Mills to increase its capital stock.

BILLS, ETC., INTRODUCED.

On motion of Mr. Ahern of Concord, the rules were further suspended, and the first and second readings of bills by their titles made in order, and the following bills and joint resolutions were severally introduced, read twice by title, and referred as follows:

By Mr. Place of Middleton, An act severing the homestead farm of Hiram H. Stevens from the school district of the town of Middleton, and annexing the same to the town of Wakefield, for school purposes. To the Committee on Education.

By Mr. Houston of Thornton, Joint resolution for an appropriation for the Sandwich Notch road in the town of Thornton. To the Committee on Roads, Bridges, and Canals.

By Mr. Wallace of Rochester, An act to incorporate the Omicron Deuteron Charge of the Theta Delti Chi. To the Committee on Judiciary.

By Mr. Goss of Berlin, An act in amendment of section 4 of chapter 206 of the Laws of 1897, being "An act to incorporate the Bethlehem Electric Light Company." To the Committee on Judiciary.

By Mr. Fifield of Conway, An act relating to the salary of the judge of probate for the county of Carroll. To the Committee on Judiciary.

By Mr. Nelson of Portsmouth, An act to provide for the distribution of fines imposed by police courts in certain cases. To the Committee on Judiciary.

By Mr. Clough of Gilmanton, Joint resolution for an appropriation for screening Crystal lake in Gilmanton. To the Committee on Fisheries and Game.

By Mr. Goss of Berlin, An act to incorporate the Peabody River Improvement Company. To the Committee on Judiciary.

By Mr. Carpenter of Manchester, An act to prohibit all ice fishing, except in certain specified waters. To the Committee on Fisheries and Game.

By Mr. Barrett of Dover, An act in reference to the duties

of county commissioners. To the Committee on County Affairs.

By Mr. Farley of Hollis, Joint resolution in favor of the road leading from Patch's Corner to the Amherst line in the town of Hollis. To the Committee on Roads, Bridges, and Canals.

By Mr. Hicks of Colebrook, An act requiring the discharge of personal property mortgages after payment. To the Committee on Judiciary.

By Mr. Caird of Berlin, An act relating to the insurance of children under ten years of age. To the Committee on Insurance.

By Mr. Sheehan of Manchester, An act in amendment of "An act to incorporate the North Conway & Mount Kearsarge Railroad," passed June session, 1883, and all subsequent acts relating to the same. To the Committee on Railroads.

By Mr. Center of Litchfield, An act to incorporate the Goff's Falls, Litchfield & Hudson Street Railway Company. To the Committee on Railroads.

By Mr. Langley of Durham, An act to incorporate the Dover & Durham Street Railway Company. To the Committee on Railroads.

By Mr. Yeaton of Portsmouth, An act to prevent discrimination in rates by express companies. To the Committee on Railroads.

By Mr. Shute of Derry, An act in relation to mileage books. To the Committee on Railroads.

By Mr. Sawyer of Milford, An act relating to negotiable instruments, being an act to establish a law uniform with the laws of other states on that subject. To the Committee on Judiciary.

By Mr. Sheldon of Wilton, An act in relation to the trapping of fur-bearing animals. To the Committee on Fisheries and Game.

By Mr. Ahern of Concord, An act in amendment of chapter 86 of the Public Statutes, in relation to state aid to indigent deaf and dumb, blind, and feeble-minded persons. To the Committee on Judiciary.

By Mr. Sheldon of Wilton, An act relating to the use of bait, or scent, for the purpose of trapping foxes. To the Committee on Fisheries and Game.

By Mr. Marshall of Manchester, An act in amendment of chapter 202 of the Public Statutes, relative to bills and notes. To the Committee on Judiciary.

By Mr. Lane of Hampton, An act to prevent and regulate the digging or taking clams in or near Hampton river. To the Committee on Fisheries and Game.

By Mr. Scammon of Exeter, Joint resolution in favor of Horace S. Cummings. To the Committee on Claims.

By Mr. Clough of Gilmanton, An act to prohibit fishing through the ice on Crystal lake in the town of Gilmanton. To the Committee on Fisheries and Game.

By Mr. Scott of Nelson, An act to change the name of the body of water formerly called Munsonville pond, lying in the towns of Nelson and Stoddard. To the Committee on Fisheries and Game.

By Mr. Emerson of Hampstead, Joint resolution for the repair of the stage road in Hampstead. To the Committee on Roads, Bridges, and Canals.

By Mr. Sheehan of Manchester, An act in amendment of section 1, chapter 67, Laws of 1899, relating to expenses of judges of the Supreme Court. To the Committee on Judiciary.

By Mr. Ball of Washington, Joint resolution relating to screening the outlets of Ashuelot and Millen lakes in the town of Washington. To the Committee on Fisheries and Game.

By Mr. Gould of Plymouth, Joint resolution appropriating $1,000 for a monument to be erected at Hackensack, N. J., in memory of General Enoch Poor. To the Committee on Judiciary.

By Mr. Libby of Gorham, An act to amend section 2 of chapter 191 of the Laws of 1895, relating to bounty on bears. To the Committee on Fisheries and Game.

By Mr. Libby of Gorham, An act to incorporate the Maynesboro Fire Insurance Company. To the Committee on Insurance.

By Mr. Messer of New London, Joint resolution to authorize the appropriation and expenditure of one hundred dollars to repair the highway leading from Lakeside to Soonipi park in New London.   To the Committee on Roads, Bridges and Canals.

By Mr. Carr of Haverhill, An act to exempt from taxation real estate reservations of the Appalachian Mountain Club. To the Committee on Judiciary.

NOTICES OF BILLS.

By Mr. Caird of Berlin, An act to establish and create an employers' liability act.

By Mr. Hill, A. W., of Concord, An act relating to the salary of the solicitor for the county of Merrimack.

By Mr. Lynch of Manchester, An act to establish and create an inspector of factories for the state of New Hampshire.

On motion of Mr. Goold of Lebanon, at 4 o'clock the House adjourned.

FRIDAY, JANUARY 23, 1903.

The House met at 9.30 o'clock, according to adjournment.

PETITION PRESENTED AND REFERRED.

By Mr. Gould of Plymouth, Petition of the New Hampshire Society of the Sons of the American Revolution for an appropriation for a statue for General Enoch Poor at Hackensack, N. J.   To the Committee on Judiciary.

COMMITTEE REPORT.

Mr. Ahern of Concord, for the Committee on Appropriations, to whom was referred An act in relation to the salary of the state reporter, having considered the same, report the same with the following resolution:

Resolved, That the bill ought to pass.

The report was accepted, the resolution adopted, and the bill laid upon the table to be printed.

BILLS, ETC., INTRODUCED.

The introduction of bills being in order, on motion of Mr.

Ahern of Concord, the rules were suspended and the first and second reading of bills, by their titles, made in order. The following bills and joint resolutions were severally introduced, read twice by title, and referred as follows:

By Mr. Nyberg of Manchester, An act to incorporate the Bellman club of Manchester, N. H. To the Committee on Judiciary.

By Mr. Couch of Manchester, An act establishing a permanent board of assessors for the city of Manchester. To a special committee consisting of the Manchester delegation, on motion of Mr. Couch of Manchester.

By Mr. Couch of Manchester, An act in amendment of chapter 202 of the Laws of the State of New Hampshire, passed at the January session, 1893, entitled "An act in relation to the city of Manchester, establishing a board of police commissioners for said city." To a special committee consisting of the Manchester delegation, on motion of Mr. Couch of Manchester.

By Mr. Couch of Manchester, An act in amendment of so much of chapter 264 of the Laws of the State of New Hampshire, passed at the January session, 1893, as relates to the establishing of a board of street and park commissioners for the city of Manchester. To a special committee consisting of the Manchester delegation, on motion of Mr. Couch of Manchester.

By Mr. Hill, A. W., of Concord, An act in relation to the salary of the judge of probate for Merrimack county. To the Committee on Judiciary.

By Mr. Woodman of Concord, An act authorizing the Concord & Montreal Railroad, lessor, to vote on all stock owned by it in other corporations. To the Committee on Railroads.

By Mr. Yeaton of Portsmouth, An act to regulate telephone and telegraph companies. To the Committee on Railroads.

By Mr. Tuck of Nashua, An act to amend section 12, chapter 59 of the Militia Law of 1895. To the Committee on Military Affairs.

By Mr. Cavanaugh of Manchester, An act to prohibit the further employment of convict labor of certain kinds at the State Industrial School. To the Committee on Judiciary.

10

By Mr. Stevens of Bartlett, Joint resolution in favor of the new road on the north side of Saco river in the town of Bartlett. To the Committee on Roads, Bridges, and Canals.

By Mr. Pike of Haverhill, Joint resolution to provide a nursery for the growth and distribution of forest seedling trees within the state at cost. To the Committee on Forestry.

By Mr. Tallant of Pembroke, An act relative to the issue of bonds, coupon notes, and other evidences of indebtedness of street railway companies. To the Committee on Railroads.

By Mr. Woodman of Concord, An act to provide for taking depositions outside this state, and depositions within this state for use in other states. To the Committee on Judiciary.

By Mr. Hill, A. W., of Concord, An act relating to the salary of the solicitor for the county of Merrimack. To the Committee on Judiciary.

SECOND READING.

An act in amendment of chapter 78 of the Laws of 1897, relating to biennial elections.

Read a second time and laid upon the table to be printed.

NOTICES OF BILLS.

By Mr. Farrell of Manchester, An act in amendment of section 16, chapter 79 of the Laws of 1901, relating to the taking of deer.

By Mr. Ryan of Manchester, An act for the regulation of bake-shops and candy factories, and to improve their sanitary condition.

By Mr. Ahern of Concord, An act to authorize the city of Concord to appropriate money for the celebration of its semi-centennial.

By Mr. Willis of Concord, An act relating to domestic life insurance companies.

By Mr. French of Moultonborough, An act to amend the charter of the Meredith & Ossipee Electric Railway Company.

By Mr. Janelle of Manchester, An act to amend paragraph 2 of section 20 of chapter 245 of the Public Statutes, relating to exemptions from trustee process.

By Mr. Caird of Berlin, An act to amend chapter 141 of the Public Statutes, relating to the liens of mechanics and others.

By Mr. Tinkham of Manchester, An act to regulate the traffic of spirituous liquors.

By Mr. Remich of Littleton, Joint resolution in favor of the New Hampshire Feeble-Minded School.

By Mr. Ela of Warner, An act to incorporate the Kearsarge Mountain Electric Railway Company.

By Mr. Hodgman of Merrimack, Joint resolution to encourage the breeding and exhibiting of thoroughbred farm animals.

On motion of Mr. Donahue of Manchester, at 9.55 the House adjourned.

MONDAY, JANUARY 26, 1903.

The House met at 8 o'clock, according to adjournment.

LEAVES OF ABSENCE.

Mr. Stanley of Lisbon was granted leave of absence for a few days on account of sickness.

The Committee on Agriculture were granted leave of absence for Tuesday, January 27, for the purpose of visiting the New Hampshire College of Agriculture and the Mechanic Arts.

NOTICES OF BILLS.

By Mr. Ellis of Lancaster, An act to authorize the town of Lancaster to acquire property for the protection of its water supply.

By Mr. Mitchell of Lancaster, An act to authorize the town of Lancaster to exempt certain property from taxation and to ratify its doings in the same.

By Mr. Kennedy of Concord, An act in amendment of chapter 89, Session Laws of 1897, relating to passenger, freight, and railroad police.

By Mr. Batchelder of Keene, Joint resolution appropriating money to complete the payment of expenses of the recent constitutional convention.

By Mr. Goss of Berlin, Joint resolution in aid of changing and repairing the Dixville Notch road in Dixville.

By Mr. Kimball of Concord, An act in amendment of section 16 of chapter 150 of the Public Statutes, relating to annual returns of corporations.

By Mr. Langley of Durham, Joint resolution in favor of the Durham Point road in the town of Durham in this state.

By Mr. Langley of Durham, An act amending the charter of the Newmarket Electric Light, Power, and Heat Company.

By Mr. Libby of Dover, An act to amend section 1, chapter 64 of the Public Statutes, relating to the taxation of railroads.

By Mr. Woodman of Concord, An act to establish the salary of the justice of the police court of Concord.

By Mr. Walker, of Grantham, Joint resolution to reimburse the town of Grantham for quarantine expenses.

By Mr. Smith of Peterborough, An act authorizing the town of Peterborough to exempt from taxation the improvements or new buildings to be erected on the Tarbell block lot.

By Mr. Barrett of Dover, An act to provide for and regulate the inspection and care of steam boilers and all steam generating apparatus, and thereby prevent the loss of life and property.

By Mr. Davis of Lee, Joint resolution in aid of the public highways in the town of Lee, N. H.

By Mr. Felker of Madbury, Joint resolution in aid of the public highways of the town of Madbury, N. H.

By Mr. Woodman of Concord, Joint resolution in relation to the New Hampshire reports.

By Mr. Woodman of Concord, An act providing for the appointment of guardians for minors in certain cases.

By Mr. Edwards of Laconia, An act to abolish the board of public works of the city of Laconia.

By Mr. Donovan of Keene, An act to change the homesteads of Albert E. Snow, Hiram Blake, Carey & Faulkner, and Fred S. Roundy from the town school district of Keene and Swanzey to the Union school district of the city of Keene.

By Mr. Polzer of Gilsum, Joint resolution in favor of the main road in the town of Gilsum.

By Mr. Worcester of Rochester, An act to regulate the rates of fare to be charged by street railway companies for the transportation of pupils of the public schools.

By Mr. Smith of Dover, An act to provide equitable process after judgment in certain cases.

By Mr. Calley of Bristol, An act to amend section 1, chapter 96, Laws of 1901, relating to high schools.

By Mr. Calley of Bristol, Joint resolution in favor of the further construction and repair of the road and bridle path leading to Mt. Cardigan.

By Mr. Bowen of Wentworth, An act in amendment of chapter 79, Laws of 1901, relating to the fish and game laws of the state.

By Mr. Brown of Fremont, Joint resolution in favor of the Pawtuckaway mountain road in the town of Deerfield.

By Mr. Hill, A. W., of Concord, An act to incorporate the Capital Investment Company.

By Mr. Barnard of Hebron, Joint resolution in favor of the repairs of highways in the town of Groton.

By Mr. Kennedy of Concord, An act to extend and regulate the liability of employers to make compensation for personal injuries suffered by employees.

By Mr. Lynch of Manchester, An act relating to catching shiners in Squog river, so called.

By Mr. Shepard of Concord, An act to prohibit the manufacture of malt and spirituous liquors.

By Mr. Kennedy of Concord, An act in amendment of section 34 of chapter 43 of the Public Statutes, in regard to the ncompatibility of certain town officers.

By Mr. Barr of Manchester, An act amending section 12 of chapter 125 of the Public Statutes, relating to weights and measures.

By Mr. Barr of Manchester, An act in relation to attempted suicide.

By Mr. Morgan of Manchester, An act to confirm, revive, and continue the charter of the Manchester City Fire Insurance Company.

By Mr. Filion of Manchester, An act to incorporate the Queen City Social Club of Manchester, N. H.

By Mr. Abbott of Manchester, An act incorporating Manchester Aerie, No. 290, Fraternal Order of Eagles.

By Mr. Remich of Littleton, An act to amend chapter 164, Laws of 1895, to enable the Littleton village district to acquire and maintain water-works and an electric light plant.

By Mr. Remich of Littleton, An act to repeal chapter 85 of the Laws of 1899, amending chapter 167 of the Public Statutes, in relation to the insurance commissioner.

By Mr. Remich of Littleton, An act to amend sections 14, 15 and 16 of chapter 168 of the Public Statutes, entitled "Insurance companies and agents."

By Mr. Remich of Littleton, Joint resolution to provide for the sale of the securities in the state treasury known as the Benjamin Thompson securities.

By Mr. Remich of Littleton, Joint resolution appropriating money for the support of the New Hampshire School for Feeble-Minded Children, necessary school buildings and a water supply.

By Mr. Churchill of Cornish, An act to provide for the representation of the state of New Hampshire and the exhibition of its resources and attractions at the Louisiana Purchase Exposition at St. Louis in 1904.

By Mr. Chandler of Claremont, An act authorizing the Claremont Railway and Lighting Company to construct and maintain as a part of its system an electric railway and lights in the town of Cornish and an electric railway in the town of Newport, and the acquirement by contract of the property and franchises of the Newport Electric Light Company.

By Mr. Drake of Freedom, Joint resolution in favor of the main highway between Center Ossipee village and Effingham Falls.

By Mr. Chase of Manchester, An act in amendment of chapter 168, Public Statutes, in relation to insurance companies and agents.

By Mr. Ahern of Concord, An act relating to foreign corporations doing business in this state.

By Mr. Newton of Portsmouth, An act to prevent the pollution of the Piscataqua river and its tributaries.

By Mr. Prescott of Laconia, An act in amendment of section 20 of chapter 245 of the Public Statutes, relating to exemptions from the trustee process.

By Mr. French of Moultonborough, Joint resolution to amend section 8, chapter 171, Public Statutes, relating to life insurance.

By Mr. Darling of Whitefield, An act relating to the production and preservation of ornamental and shade trees in the highways.

By Mr. Worthley of Hooksett, An act to amend section 1 of chapter 54, Laws of 1891, relating to foreign insurance companies and agents.

By Mr. Fecteau of Laconia, An act to amend chapter 241 of the Session Laws of 1893, as amended by chapter 278 of the Session Laws of 1901.

By Mr. Ferrin of Plymouth, Joint resolution appropriating $500 for the repair of highways in the town of Dorchester.

By Mr. French of Moultonborough, An act to amend section 5 of chapter 286 of the Public Statutes, as amended by chapter 56 of the Laws of 1901, relating to the salaries and compensation of certain officers.

By Mr. French of Moultonborough, An act in relation to the appointment of guardians over insane persons.

By Mr. French of Moultonborough, An act to incorporate the Swift River Railroad Company.

By Mr. Davis of Concord, An act in amendment of the charter of the city of Concord, providing for the election of overseers of the poor.

By Mr. Davis of Concord, An act in amendment of the charter of the city of Concord, authorizing the establishment of precincts within said city for the collection of garbage.

By Mr. Smyth of Berlin, An act to regulate state and municipal contracts.

By Mr. Frazer of Monroe, An act concerning the settlement of paupers.

By Mr. Frazer of Monroe, An act to create a bridge commission.

By Mr. Taggart of Manchester, An act to amend section 1, chapter 169 of the Public Statutes, relating to foreign insurance companies.

By Mr. Worthley of Hooksett, An act prohibiting the manufacture and sale of cigarettes.

By Mr. Worthley of Hooksett, An act equalizing and regulating toll and charges of telephone companies.

By Mr. Willis of Concord, An act to change the name of the N. H. Health and Accident Insurance Company.

By Mr. Willis of Concord, An act to incorporate the Northern Transportation and Transfer Company.

By Mr. Fecteau of Laconia, An act to incorporate the Mt. Belknap Railroad.

By Mr. Blake of Littleton, An act in amendment of the act relating to the terms of the superior court in Grafton county.

By Mr. Mitchell of Littleton, An act explanatory of the powers of the courts in reference to the fees of commissioners in certain cases.

By Mr. Buckley of Lancaster, An act to punish embezzlement by executors, administrators, guardians, and trustees.

By Mr. Buckley of Lancaster, Joint resolution in favor of James J. Parks of Carroll.

By Mr. Woodman of Concord, An act to facilitate the settlement of the estates of deceased persons.

By Mr. Woodman of Concord, Joint resolution in favor of a highway in the town of Newbury.

By Mr. Woodman of Concord, An act severing the homestead of David A. Welch from the town district of the city of Concord and annexing the same to the Union School District of said Concord.

By Mr. Barrett of Dover, An act in amendment of the charter of Pembroke Academy, increasing the number of trustees.

By Mr. Bunce of Dover, An act in amendment of the charter of the city of Dover, creating a board of street and park commissioners for said city.

By Mr. Pike of Haverhill, Joint resolution to appropriate money to screen the outlet of Armington pond, so called, in the town of Piermont.

By Mr. French of Moultonborough, An act in relation to the appointment of guardians over insane persons.

By Mr. Kendall of Mont Vernon, An act in relation to the diseases of domestic animals.

By Mr. Brown of Greenville, An act to establish water-works in the town of Greenville.

By Mr. Fontaine of Allenstown, An act to provide for the support of indigent consumptive patients in Pembroke Sanatorium.

By Mr. Etter of Somersworth, Joint resolution to appropriate $400 to repair road leading from Forest Glade cemetery to Diamond Corner in city of Somersworth.

By Mr. McCrillis of Rochester, Joint resolution to appropriate a sum of money to repair the River road near North Rochester.

By Mr. Crocker of Rochester, Joint resolution to appropriate a sum not exceeding $500, to be expended on Blue Job mountain road in Strafford.

By Mr. Goold of Lebanon, An act to protect the waters of Plowmeadow brook in the towns of Plainfield and Cornish.

By Mr. Nelson of Portsmouth, An act to protect the public from extortion.

By Mr. Connell of Hudson, An act authorizing the town of Hudson to construct water-works and establish an electric light plant.

By Mr. Connell of Hudson, An act in amendment of chapter 33, Laws of 1893, entitled " An act to regulate the compensation for cattle killed by order of cattle commissioners."

By Mr. Connell of Hudson, Joint resolution for an appropriation to compensate for destruction of animals affected with the foot and mouth disease and other losses occasioned by said disease.

By Mr. Connell of Hudson, An act in amendment and in addition to chapter 113 of the Public Statutes, entitled "Diseases of domestic animals."

By Mr. Notterstead of Berlin, An act in amendment of section 21 of chapter 180 of the Public Statutes.

By Mr. Jones of Franklin, An act to prohibit the taking of

fish from the waters of Morrill's pond, a natural pond in Canterbury.

By Mr. Remich of Littleton, Joint resolution providing for the erection of an elevator, or elevators, in the state house for the use of the members of the Senate, House of Representatives, state officers, and employees.

By Mr. Graves of Andover, An act to protect the lives of freight brakemen, being an amendment of chapter 39, section 1 of the Statutes of 1893.

By Mr. Libby of Gorham, Joint resolution for the repair of highways in the town of Randolph.

By Mr. Bragg of Errol, An act in amendment of Laws of 1901, chapter 79, sections 16 and 57, being an act entitled " An act to revise the fish and game laws of the state."

By Mr. Couch of Manchester, An act requiring the use of the label of the International Typographical Union upon all printed matter of the state.

By Mr. Young of Sandown, An act to amend and extend the charter of the Manchester & Haverhill Street Railway.

By Mr. Ahern of Concord, An act to authorize the managers of the New Hampshire Soldiers' Home to provide an adequate supply of water for said home.

By Mr. Tuck of Nashua, An act to amend section 1 of chapter 21 of the Laws of 1895, entitled " An act to amend section 6 of chapter 184, entitled ' Times and places of holding courts of probate.' "

By Mr. Bussell of Nashua, An act authorizing the city of Nashua to issue bonds.

By Mr. Bussell of Nashua, An act to enable Nashua to issue bonds to erect high school buildings, and exempt same from taxation.

By Mr. Bussell of Nashua, An act for the construction of state highways up the Merrimack valley, and in other sections of the state.

By Mr. Bussell of Nashua, An act in amendment of the charter of the city of Nashua, relating to the appointment of police commissioners, and to the collection of fines and costs.

By Mr. Bussell of Nashua, An act authorizing the city of

Nashua to exempt the Highland Spring Sanatorium Company from taxation.

By Mr. Bussell of Nashua, An act to amend the charter of the city of Nashua, changing the time of holding the municipal election for said city.

By Mr. Sawyer of Milford, An act authorizing the state treasurer to transfer certain sums of money to the literary fund for schools.

By Mr. Sawyer of Milford, An act in addition to chapter 153, Public Statutes, creating section 20 of said chapter.

By Mr. Ferrin of Plymouth, An act to amend section 52 of chapter 79, Laws of 1901.

By Mr. Donahue of Manchester, An act in amendment of chapter 134 of the Public Statutes, relating to the practice of dentistry.

By Mr. Woodman of Concord, An act in amendment of chapter 265, section 1, Public Statutes, relating to the abandonment of children.

By Mr. Woodman of Concord, An act in amendment of chapter 91, section 8, Laws of 1897, relating to the duties of the State Board of Charities and Correction.

By Mr. Donagan of Concord, An act regulating the sale of intoxicating liquors.

By Mr. Gould of Plymouth, An act relating to taking shiners or red fins from waters of the state for bait.

By Mr. Cavanaugh of Manchester, An act to change the name of the Manchester Heating and Lighting Company.

By Mr. Shaughnessey of Manchester, An act in relation to street railway terminals.

By Mr. Woodman of Concord, Joint resolution granting Little island in Bradford pond to Lawrence E. Harris.

By Mr. Woodman of Concord, An act to save counties the expense of jury trials in certain cases.

By Mr. Morrill of Ashland, An act to incorporate the New Hampshire Beneficiary Union.

By Mr. Russell of Sunapee, An act to prevent the pollution of the water in Ledge pond in the town of Sunapee.

By Mr. Littlefield of Albany, Joint resolution in favor of highways in the town of Albany.

By Mr. Newton of Portsmouth, An act relative to the state arsenal at Portsmouth.

By Mr. Darling of Whitefield, An act to aid in constructing a highway around the east end of Forest lake in Whitefield.

By Mr. Kimball of Laconia, An act to amend chapter 169 of the Public Statutes, chapter 64 of the Laws of 1899, and chapter 67 of the Laws of 1901, relating to the taxation of insurance companies.

By Mr. Kimball of Laconia, An act relating to contracts by casualty and employers' liability insurance companies.

By Mr. Kimball of Laconia, An act relating to the investments of foreign fire, life, casualty and other insurance companies.

By Mr. Woodman of Concord, An act in amendment of the charter of the Contoocook River Navigation and Improvement Company.

By Mr. Woodman of Concord, An act in amendment of section 15, chapter 141 of the Public Statutes, relating to liens.

By Mr. Bartlett of Derry, An act to amend the charter of the Derry Electric Light Co.

By Mr. Sleeper of Plaistow, Joint resolution for an appropriation for repair of highway in Plaistow, N. H., leading from Atkinson Depot to the Haverhill line.

By Mr. Scammon of Exeter, An act relating to telephone, telegraph, and electric light companies.

By Mr. Yeaton of Portsmouth, An act to amend the charter of the city of Portsmouth, in relation to assessors of taxes.

By Mr. Yeaton of Portsmouth, An act to amend the charter of the city of Portsmouth, in relation to street commissioner.

By Mr. Wentworth of Somersworth, An act to establish an electric lighting, heating, and power plant in the city of Somersworth.

By Mr. Townsend of Milton, An act to incorporate the Milton Mills & Union Electric Street Railway Company.

By Mr. Blaisdell of Portsmouth, An act to authorize the Portsmouth & Exeter Street Railway Company to construct a branch from Stratham through Newfields and Newmarket.

By Mr. Blaisdell of Portsmouth, An act authorizing the

Portsmouth, Kittery & York Street Railway to keep and maintain a ferry on Piscataqua river and for other purposes.

By Mr. Blaisdell of Portsmouth, An act to ratify the location and construction of the Hudson, Pelham & Salem Electric Railway and all of its branches.

By Mr. Lane of Hampton, An act to authorize the town of Hampton to elect one or three road agents at the March election, 1903, and subsequent elections.

By Mr. Kimball of Concord, An act in amendment of chapter 171 of the Public Statutes, in relation to life insurance.

By Mr. Scammon of Exeter, An act to repeal section 13 of chapter 133 of the Public Statutes of New Hampshire, and all laws which protect smelts in tide water in New Hampshire.

BILLS, ETC., INTRODUCED.

On motion of Mr. Ahern of Concord, the rules were suspended and business in order to-morrow morning at 11 o'clock was made in order at the present time.

On motion of Mr. Woodman of Concord, the rules were further suspended and the reading of bills a first and second time by their titles made in order. The following bills and joint resolutions were severally introduced, read twice by title, and referred as follows:

By Mr. Mitchell of Littleton, An act to prevent trespassing on railroad tracks. To the Committee on Railroads.

By Mr. Woodman of Concord, An act in amendment of section 26, chapter 79 of the Laws of 1901, for the better protection of gray squirrel. To the Committee on Fisheries and Game.

By Mr. Ahern of Concord, An act to authorize the city of Concord to appropriate money for the celebration of its semicentennial. To a special committee consisting of the Concord delegation, on motion of Mr. Ahern of Concord.

By Mr. Farrell of Manchester, An act in amendment of section 16, chapter 79 of the Laws of 1901, relating to the taking of deer. To the Committee on Fisheries and Game.

By Mr. Donahue of Manchester, An act in amendment of section 20 of chapter 27 of the Public Statutes, entitled "County commissioners." To the Committee on County Affairs.

By Mr. Donahue of Manchester, Joint resolution appropriating nine thousand dollars for additions and repairs to the Industrial School. To the Committee on Industrial School.

By Mr. Young of Sandown, An act to amend and extend the charter of the Manchester & Haverhill Street Railway. To the Committee on Railroads.

By Mr. Barnard of Hebron, Joint resolution for the appropriation of $200 for the repairing of the highway running around Newfound lake in Hebron. To the Committee on Roads, Bridges, and Canals.

By Mr. Drake of Freedom, An act to amend the charter of the Ossipee Valley Railroad Company. To the Committee on Railroads.

By Mr. Remich of Littleton, Joint resolution in favor of the New Hampshire School for Feeble-Minded Children. To the Committee on Feeble-Minded School.

By Mr. Tinkham of Manchester, An act to regulate the traffic of spirituous liquors. To the Committee on Liquor Laws.

By Mr. Connell of Hudson, Joint resolution for an appropriation to compensate for destruction of animals affected with the foot and mouth disease and other losses occasioned bysaid disease.

By Mr. Darling of Whitefield, An act relating to the protecting and preservation of ornamental and shade trees in the highways.

By Mr. Connell of Hudson, An act in amendment of chapter 33, Laws of 1893, entitled "An act to regulate the compensation for cattle killed by order of the cattle commissioners."

By Mr. Connell of Hudson, An act in amendment and in addition to chapter 113 of the Public Statutes, entitled "Diseases of domestic animals."

Severally to the Committee on Agriculture.

By Mr. Calley of Bristol, An act to amend section 1, chapter 96, Laws of 1901, relating to high schools.

By Mr. Woodman of Concord, An act severing the homestead of David Welch from the town district of the city of Concord and annexing the same to the Union School District of said Concord.

Severally to the Committee on Education.

By Mr. Davenport of Bath, An act for the better protection of deer.

By Mr. Jones of Franklin, An act to prohibit the taking of fish from the waters of Morrill's pond, a natural pond in Canterbury.

By Mr. Bowen of Wentworth, An act in amendment of chapter 79, Laws of 1901, relating to the fish and game laws of the state.

Severally to the Committee on Fisheries and Game.

By Mr. Taggart of Manchester, An act to amend section 7, chapter 169, of the Public Statutes, relating to foreign life insurance companies.

By Mr. Chase of Manchester, An act in amendment of chapter 168, Public Statutes, in relation to insurance companies and agents.

By Mr. Barrett of Dover, An act to incorporate the Prudential Fire Insurance Company.

By Mr. Morgan of Manchester, An act to confirm, revive, and continue the charter of the Manchester City Fire Insurance Company.

Severally to the Committee on Insurance.

By Mr. Kimball of Concord, An act in amendment of section 16 of chapter 150 of the Public Statutes, relating to annual returns of corporations.

By Mr. Cate of Concord, An act in amendment of chapter 82 of the Laws of 1897.

By Mr. Scammon of Exeter, An act relating to the province records of New Hampshire.

By Mr. Woodman of Concord, An act in amendment of chapter 285, section 1, Public Statutes, relating to the abandonment of children.

By Mr. Barr of Manchester, An act amending section 12 of chapter 125 of the Public Statutes, relating to weights and measures.

By Mr. Kennedy of Concord, An act in amendment of section 34 of chapter 43 of the Public Statutes, in regard to the incompatibility of certain town officers.

Severally to the Committee on Revision of Statutes.

By Mr. McDonald of Northumberland, Joint resolution to aid in repairing the Nash stream road in Stratford.

By Mr. Goss of Berlin, Joint resolution in aid of changing and repairing the Dixville Notch road in Dixville.

By Mr. Littlefield of Albany, Joint resolution in favor of highways in the town of Albany.

By Mr. Barnard of Hebron, Joint resolution in favor of the repair of highways in the town of Groton.

By Mr. Ferrin of Plymouth, Joint resolution appropriating five hundred dollars for the repair of highways in the town of Dorchester.

By Mr. Etter of Somersworth, Joint resolution to appropriate four hundred dollars to repair road leading from Forest Glade cemetery to Diamond Corner in city of Somersworth.

By Mr. Calley of Bristol, Joint resolution in favor of the further construction and repair of the road and bridle path leading to Mount Cardigan in the town of Alexandria.

By Mr. Crocker of Rochester, Joint resolution to appropriate a sum not exceeding five hundred dollars to be expended on Blue Job mountain road in Strafford.

By Mr. Woodman of Concord, Joint resolution in favor of a highway in the town of Newbury.

By Mr. Langley of Durham, Joint resolution in favor of the Durham Point road in the town of Durham in this state.

By Mr. Brown of Fremont, Joint resolution in favor of the Pawtuckaway mountain road in the town of Deerfield.

By Mr. Libby of Gorham, Joint resolution for the repair of highways in the town of Randolph.

By Mr. McCrillis of Rochester, Joint resolution to appropriate a sum of money to repair the River road near North Rochester.

By Mr. Scammon of Exeter, Joint resolution relating to a state highway between Massachusetts state line and Fort Point, in Newcastle, N. H.

By Mr. Darling of Whitefield, An act to aid in constructing a highway around the east end of Forest lake, in Whitefield, N. H.

Severally to the Committee on Roads, Bridges, and Canals.

By Mr. Fontaine of Allenstown, Joint resolution to provide

for the care of indigent consumptive patients at the Pembroke Sanatorium. To the Committee on Public Health.

By Mr. Notterstead of Berlin, An act in amendment of section 21 of chapter 180 of the Public Statutes.

By Mr. Couch of Manchester, An act requiring the use of the label of the International Typographical Union upon all printed matter of the state.

Severally to the Committee on Labor.

By Mr. Fecteau of Laconia, An act to incorporate the Mt. Belknap Railroad.

By Mr. Kennedy of Concord, An act extending the liability of railroads for injuries to employees.

By Mr. Blaisdell of Portsmouth, An act to ratify the lease of the Haverhill, Plaistow & Newton Street Railway Company to the Exeter, Hampton & Amesbury Street Railway Company.

By Mr. Worthley of Hooksett, An act equalizing and regulating tolls and charges of telephone companies.

By Mr. Blaisdell of Portsmouth, An act concerning the New Hampshire Traction Company.

By Mr. Worcester of Rochester, An act in regard to the rates of fare to be charged by street railway companies for the transportation of pupils of the public schools.

By Mr. Blaisdell of Portsmouth, An act to authorize the Hudson, Pelham & Salem Electric Railway Company to take a lease of the railway and property of the Lawrence & Methuen Street Railway Company.

By Mr. Blaisdell of Portsmouth, An act to ratify the lease of the Portsmouth & Exeter Street Railway Company to the Exeter, Hampton & Amesbury Street Railway Company.

By Mr. Blaisdell of Portsmouth, An act to ratify the lease of the Seabrook & Hampton Beach Street Railway Company to the Exeter, Hampton & Amesbury Street Railway Company.

By Mr. Blaisdell of Portsmouth, An act to authorize the Hudson, Pelham & Salem Electric Railway Company to take a lease of the railway and property of the Lowell & Pelham Street Railway Company.

By Mr. Blaisdell of Portsmouth, An act to ratify the lease

11

of the Dover, Somersworth & Rochester Street Railway Company to the Exeter, Hampton & Amesbury Street Railway Company.

By Mr. Graves of Andover, An act to protect the lives of freight brakemen, being an amendment of chapter 39, section 1 of the Statutes of 1893.

By Mr. Kennedy of Concord, An act in amendment of chapter 89, Session Laws of 1897, relating to passenger, freight, and railroad police.

By Mr. Blaisdell of Portsmouth, An act to authorize the Hudson, Pelham & Salem Electric Railway Company to take a lease of the railway and property of the Haverhill & Southern New Hampshire Street Railway Company.

By Mr. French of Moultonborough, An act to incorporate the Swift River Railroad Company.

Severally to the Committee on Railroads.

By Mr. French of Moultonborough, An act in relation to the appointment of guardians over insane persons.

By Mr. French of Moultonborough, An act to amend section 5, chapter 286 of the Public Statutes, as amended by chapter 56 of the Laws of 1901, relating to the salaries and compensation of certain officers.

By Mr. Woodman of Concord, An act in amendment of the charter of the Contoocook River Navigation and Improvement Company.

By Mr. Churchill of Cornish, An act to provide, in common with the state of Vermont, for the acquisition, building and maintenance of free bridges across the Connecticut river.

By Mr. Mitchell of Lancaster, An act to authorize the town of Lancaster to exempt certain property from taxation and to ratify its doings in the same.

By Mr. Caird of Berlin, An act to create and establish an employers' liability act.

By Mr. Worthley of Hooksett, An act prohibiting the manufacture and sale of cigarettes.

By Mr. Buckley of Lancaster, An act to punish embezzlement by executors, administrators, guardians, and trustees.

By Mr. Woodman of Concord, An act providing for the appointment of guardians for minors in certain cases.

By Mr. Batchelder of Keene, Joint resolution appropriating money to complete the payment of expenses of the recent constitutional convention.

By Mr. Fay of Keene, An act in amendment of chapter 114, Session Laws of 1901, entitled "An act to regulate and limit the investments of savings banks."

By Mr. Hill, A. W., of Concord, An act to incorporate the Capital Investment Company.

By Mr. Barr of Manchester, An act in relation to attempted suicide.

By Mr. Bussell of Nashua, An act authorizing the city of Nashua to exempt the Highland Spring Sanatorium Company from taxation.

By Mr. Barrett of Dover, An act to provide for and regulate the inspection and care of steam boilers and all steam generating apparatus and thereby prevent the loss of life and property.

By Mr. Buckley of Lancaster, Joint resolution appropriating money to aid Dartmouth college in the education of New Hampshire students.

By Mr. Ellis of Lancaster, An act to authorize the town of Lancaster to acquire property for the protection of its water supply.

By Mr. Kennedy of Concord, An act to extend and regulate the liability of employers to make compensation for personal injuries suffered by employees.

By Mr. Caird of Berlin, An act to amend chapter 141 of the Public Statutes, relating to the liens of mechanics and others.

By Mr. Connell of Hudson, An act authorizing the town of Hudson to construct water-works and establish an electric light plant.

By Mr. Woodman of Concord, An act to save counties the expense of jury trials in certain cases.

By Mr. Morrill of Ashland, An act to incorporate the New Hampshire Beneficiary Union.

By Mr. Scammon of Exeter, An act in amendment of the charter of the Exeter Gas Light Company.

By Mr. Scammon of Exeter, An act to enable the Hedding Camp Meeting Association to fund its indebtedness.

By Mr. Woodman of Concord, An act in amendment of chapter 91, section 8, Laws of 1897, relating to the duties of the State Board of Charities and Correction.

Severally to the Committee on Judiciary.

By Mr. Davis of Concord, An act in amendment of the charter of the city of Concord, providing for the election of overseers of the poor.

To a special committee consisting of the Concord delegation, on motion of Mr. Ahern of Concord.

By Mr. Libby of Gorham, An act to amend the prohibitory law by permitting local option. To the Committee on Liquor Laws.

On motion of Mr. Ahern of Concord, the order by which the following entitled bill, "An act to amend the prohibitory law by permitting local option," was referred to the Committee on Liquor Laws, was vacated, and the bill laid upon the table to be printed and then be referred to that committee.

On motion of Mr. Remich of Littleton,—

Resolved, That all bills now before the Committee on Liquor Laws, and which have not been printed, be recalled from that committee, laid upon the table to be printed, and be then referred back to the committee in question.

On motion of Mr. Drake of Freedom, at 9.55 the House adjourned.

TUESDAY, JANUARY 27, 1903.

The House met at 11 o'clock.

Prayer was offered by the chaplain.

Mr. Fitch of Keene, having been duly qualified by His Excellency the Governor, appeared and took his seat as a member of the House of Representatives.

LEAVES OF ABSENCE.

Mr. Bartlett of Derry was granted leave of absence on account of sickness.

Mr. Jewett of Claremont was granted an indefinite leave of absence on account of sickness.

Mr. Cochran of Windham was granted leave of absence for the balance of the week on account of serious illness in his family.

The Nashua delegation was granted leave of absence for Wednesday afternoon, January 28, for the purpose of visiting the Industrial School.

The Committee on Feeble-Minded School were granted leave of absence for Wednesday, January 28, in order to visit that institution.

PETITION PRESENTED AND REFERRED.

By Mr. Fifield of Conway, Petition of George Allard and others to be disannexed from the town of Madison and annexed to the town of Conway. To the Committee on Towns.

COMMITTEE REPORTS.

Mr. Morgan of Manchester, for the Committee on Railroads, to whom was referred An act to repeal the charter of the Massabesic Horse Railroad Company, having considered the same, report the same with the following resolution :

Resolved, That the bill ought to pass.

The report was accepted, the resolution adopted, and the bill laid upon the table to be printed.

Mr. Bartlett of Derry, for the Committee on Revision of Statutes, to whom was referred An act in amendment of section 1 of chapter 138 of the Public Statutes, relating to homestead rights, having considered the same, report the same with the following resolution :

Resolved, That it is inexpedient to legislate.

The report was accepted and the resolution adopted.

Mr. Goss of Berlin, for the Committee on Judiciary, reported the following entitled bill, "An act in amendment of chapter 78 of the Laws of 1901, entitled, 'An act providing for a judiciary system consisting of two courts,'" with the resolution that the bill ought to pass.

The report was accepted and the bill read a first time and ordered to a second reading.

Mr. Willis of Concord, for the Committee on Engrossed Bills, reported that they had examined bills with the following titles and found them correctly engrossed :

An act amending section 11 of chapter 63 of the Session Laws of 1897, entitled " Practice of medicine."

An act to repeal chapter 200 of the Laws of 1899, entitled " An act to amend chapter 207 of the Laws of 1895, relating to the police court of Haverhill."

An act to allow the city of Nashua to appropriate money for the celebration of its semi-centennial.

BILLS, ETC., INTRODUCED.

On motion of Mr. French of Moultonborough, the rules were suspended and the reading of bills a first and second time by their titles made in order. The following bills and joint resolutions were severally introduced, read twice by title, and referred as follows :

(Mr. Cavanaugh of Manchester in the chair.)

By Mr. Smith of Peterborough, An act authorizing the town of Peterborough to exempt from taxation the improvements or new buildings to be erected on the Tarbell block lot.

By Mr. Scammon of Exeter, An act relating to telephone, telegraph, and electric light companies.

By Mr. Cavanaugh of Manchester, An act to change the name of the Manchester Heating and Lighting Company of Manchester, N. H.

By Mr. Cavanaugh of Manchester, An act regulating the holding of political caucuses and conventions and providing for substitution in case of vacancies in the position of delegates to conventions.

By Mr. Ryan of Manchester, An act for the regulation of bake shops and candy factories and to improve their sanitary condition.

By Mr. Fecteau of Laconia, An act in amendment of the charter of the city of Laconia.

By Mr. Yeaton of Portsmouth, An act to amend the charter of the city of Portsmouth in relation to street commissioner.

By Mr. Bussell of Nashua, An act to enable the city of Nashua to issue bonds to erect high school buildings and exempt same from taxation.

By Mr. Bussell of Nashua, An act in amendment of the charter of the city of Nashua, relating to the appointment of police commissioners and to the collections of fines and costs.

By Mr. Nelson of Portsmouth, An act to amend the charter of the North Shore Water Company.

By Mr. Brown of Greenville, An act to establish water-works in the town of Greenville.

By Mr. Martin of Colebrook, An act to prevent the deposit of sawdust and other waste in the Mohawk river in Colebrook.

By Mr. Prescott of Laconia, An act in amendment of section 30, chapter 245 of the Public Statutes, relating to exemptions from the trustee process.

By Mr. Goodrich of Warren, An act to incorporate the Warren Water and Light Company.

By Mr. Bussell of Nashua, An act authorizing the city of Nashua to issue bonds.

By Mr. Fay of Keene, An act relating to the salary of the register of probate for the county of Cheshire.

By Mr. Ahern of Concord, An act relating to foreign corporations doing business in this state.

By Mr. Donahue of Manchester, An act in amendment of chapter 134 of the Public Statutes, relating to the practice of dentistry.

Severally to the Committee on Judiciary.

By Mr. Nason of Dover, An act to amend chapter 96 of the Session Laws of 1901, relating to high schools.

By Mr. Kimball of Concord, An act amending chapter 92 of the Public Statutes, in relation to school boards.

By Mr. Kimball of Concord, An act to amend chapter 94 of the Public Statutes, in relation to the superintendent of public instruction.

Severally to the Committee on Education.

By Mr. Wentworth of Somersworth, An act to establish an electric lighting, heating, and power plant in the city of Som-

ersworth.   To a special committee consisting of the Somersworth delegation, on motion of Mr. Andrews of Somersworth.

By Mr. Woodman of Concord, An act to establish the salary
of the justice of police court of Concord.   To a special committee consisting of the Concord delegation, on motion of Mr.
Ahern of Concord.

By Mr. Morse of Manchester, An act to amend chapter 264
of the Session Laws of 1893, entitled "An act to establish a
board of street and park commissioners for the city of Manchester, and authorizing said city to issue bonds for certain
purposes."   To a special committee consisting of the Manchester delegation, on motion of Mr. Morse of Manchester.

By Mr. Yeaton of Portsmouth, An act to fix the form of life
insurance policies, and to establish cash surrender values.

By Mr. Willis of Concord, An act to change the name of the
New Hampshire Health and Accident Insurance Company.

By Mr. Kimball of Laconia, An act to amend chapter 169
of the Public Statutes, chapter 64 of the Laws of 1899, and
chapter 67 of the Laws of 1901, relating to the taxation of
insurance companies.

By Mr. Worthley of Hooksett, An act to amend section 1,
chapter 54 of the Laws of 1891, relating to foreign insurance
companies and agents.

By Mr. Kimball of Laconia, An act relating to the investments of foreign fire, life, casualty, and other insurance companies.

By Mr. Kimball of Laconia, An act relating to contracts by
casualty and employers' liability insurance companies.

By Mr. Jewell of Dover, An act to protect resident life insurance agents and managers from competition with non-resident
life insurance agents and managers, and to prohibit the sale of
deceptive life insurance in this state.

By Mr. Barr of Manchester, An act to regulate the appointment of insurance agents.

By Mr. Willis of Concord, An act relating to domestic life
insurance companies.

Severally to the Committee on Insurance.

(The Speaker in the chair.)

By Mr. Bunce of Dover, An act in amendment of the charter of the city of Dover in regard to a board of street and park commissioners for said city. To a special committee consisting of the Dover delegation, on motion of Mr. Whittemore of Dover.

By Mr. Churchill of Cornish, An act to provide for the representation of the state of New Hampshire and the exhibition of its products and attractions at the Louisiana Purchase Exposition at St. Louis in 1904.

By Mr. Jewell of Dover, An act to establish a state aid fund to be subject to the disposal of the Governor and Council to aid such towns and villages as are unable to keep the roads and bridges in their towns in suitable repair.

Severally to the Committee on Public Improvements.

By Mr. Lane of Hampton, An act to allow the town of Hampton to readopt chapter 29 of the Laws of 1893, in relation to the repair of highways.

By Mr. Tuck of Nashua, An act to amend section 1, chapter 21 of the Laws of 1895, entitled "An act to amend section 6 of chapter 184 of the Public Statutes, entitled ' Times and places of holding courts of probate.' "

By Mr. Riordan of Manchester, An act in amendment of chapter 59 of the Laws of 1891, entitled "An act in amendment of chapter 7 of the Laws of 1883, entitled 'An act in relation to the exemption of disabled soldiers and sailors of the late war to payment of poll tax.' "

By Mr. Janelle of Manchester, An act to amend paragraph 2 of section 20 of chapter 245 of the Public Statutes, relating to exemption from trustee process.

Severally to the Committee on Revision of Statutes.

By Mr. Ahern of Concord, An act to authorize the managers of the New Hampshire Soldiers' Home to procure an adequate supply of water for the use of said home. To the Committee on Soldiers' Home.

By Mr. Cavanaugh of Manchester, An act in amendment of clauses 12 and 14, section 1 of the act entitled "An act to regulate and limit the investments of savings banks," approved March 22, 1901.

By Mr. Goodnow of Keene, An act to incorporate the Keene Trust Company.

By Mr. Fay of Keene, An act relating to books of deposit issued by savings banks when lost, destroyed, or worn.

By Mr. Jewell of Dover, An act to incorporate the Dover Loan and Banking Company.

By Mr. Yeaton of Portsmouth, An act amending the charter of the Portsmouth Savings Bank.

By Mr. Fay of Keene, An act in amendment of chapter 114, Session Laws of 1901, entitled "An act to regulate and limit the investments of savings banks."

Severally to the Committee on Banks.

By Mr. Prescott of Laconia, An act to amend sections 54 and 58, chapter 78 of fish and game laws.

By Mr. Gould of Plymouth, An act relating to taking shiners or red fins from the waters of the state for bait.

By Mr. Ferrin of Plymouth, An act in amendment of section 52, chapter 79 of the Laws of 1901.

By Mr. Bragg of Errol, An act in amendment of Laws of 1901, chapter 79, sections 16 and 57, being an act entitled "An act to revise the fish and game laws of the state."

By Mr. Scammon of Exeter, An act to repeal section 13, chapter 133 of the Public Statutes of New Hampshire, and all laws which protect smelts in tide water in New Hampshire.

By Mr. Merrill of Stoddard, An act to provide for a bounty on hedgehogs.

Severally to the Committee on Fisheries and Game.

By Mr. Shaughnessey of Manchester, An act in relation to street railway terminals.

By Mr. White of Deerfield, An act to incorporate the Manchester, Candia & Deerfield Street Railway Company.

By Mr. French of Moultonborough, An act in amendment of the charter of the Meredith & Ossipee Electric Railway Company.

By Mr. Jones of New Ipswich, An act to incorporate the New Ipswich, Greenfield & Wilton Electric Railway Company.

By Mr. Warren of Rochester, An act to provide for the better equipment of cars for the transportation of lumber and wood.

By Mr. Chandler of Claremont, An act authorizing the

Claremont Railway and Lighting Company to construct and maintain as a part of its system an electric railway and lights in the town of Cornish and an electric railway in the town of Newport and the acquirement by contract of the property and franchises of the Newport Electric Light Company.

By Mr. Willis of Concord, An act to incorporate the Northern Transportation and Transfer Company.

By Mr. Blaisdell of Portsmouth, An act to ratify the location and construction of the Hudson, Pelham & Salem Electric Railway and all its branches.

By Mr. Blaisdell of Portsmouth, An act authorizing the Portsmouth, Kittery & York Street Railway to keep and maintain a ferry in Piscataqua river and for other purposes.

By Mr. Blaisdell of Portsmouth, An act to authorize the Portsmouth & Exeter Street Railway Company to construct a branch from Stratham through Newfields and Newmarket.

By Mr. Ela of Warner, An act to incorporate the Kearsarge Mountain Electric Railway Company.

By Mr. Brown of Fremont, An act to incorporate the Chester, Fremont & Brentwood Street Railway Company.

Severally to the Committee on Railroads.

By Mr. Warren of Rochester, An act amending section 14 and section 20 of chapter 180 of the Public Statutes, relating to the hours of labor.   To the Committee on Labor.

By Mr. Bell of Woodstock, An act to amend chapter 63 of the Laws of 1897, restricting the so-called "counter prescribing" by druggists or registered pharmacists of drugs and medicines not under the prescription of a regularly qualified physician.   To the Committee on Public Health.

By Mr. White of Sandwich, An act to encourage the planting and perpetuation of forests.   To the Committee on Forestry.

By Mr. True of Plainfield, An act to establish a bounty on foxes.   To the Committee on Agriculture.

By Mr. Marshall of Manchester, An act in relation to the term of office of the chief engineer and assistant engineers of the fire department of the city of Manchester.   To a special committee consisting of the Manchester delegation, on motion of Mr. Taggart of Manchester.

By Mr. Phillips of Franklin, An act requiring state certification of teachers of public schools. On motion of Mr. Phillips of Franklin, the rules were suspended and the bill laid upon the table to be printed before reference to committee.

By Mr. Willis of Concord, An act to regulate the traffic in intoxicating liquors.

By Mr. Fox of Marlow, An act in amendment of sections 15 and 23 of chapter 112 of the Public Statutes, relating to the enforcement of the provisions of said chapter.

Severally to the Committee on Liquor Laws.

On motion of Mr. Ahern of Concord, the reference was rescinded and both bills laid upon the table to be printed and then referred to the Committee on Liquor Laws.

By Mr. Shepard of Concord, An act to prohibit the manufacture of malt and spirituous liquors. To the Committee on Liquor Laws.

On motion of Mr. Remich of Littleton, the reference was rescinded and the bill was laid upon the table to be printed and then referred to the Committee on Liquor Laws.

By Mr. Woodman of Concord, Joint resolution granting Little island in Bradford pond to Lawrence E. Davis.

By Mr. Remich of Littleton, Joint resolution to provide for the sale of securities in the state treasurer's office, known as the Benjamin Thompson securities.

By Mr. Woodman of Concord, Joint resolution in relation to the New Hampshire Reports.

By Mr. Newton of Portsmouth, Joint resolution relating to the state arsenal at Portsmouth.

Severally to the Committee on Judiciary.

By Mr. Pike of Haverhill, Joint resolution to appropriate money for screening the outlet of Armington pond, so called, in the town of Piermont.

By Mr. Ware of Hancock, Joint resolution in favor of screening the outlet of Nubanuset lake, in the towns of Hancock and Nelson.

Severally to the Committee on Fisheries and Game.

By Mr. Prescott of Grantham, Joint resolution to reimburse the town of Grantham for quarantine expenses.

By Mr. Sawyer of Milford, Joint resolution in favor of John M. Stanyan for soldier's pay and bounty.

By Mr. Buckley of Lancaster, Joint resolution in favor of James J. Parks of Carroll.

Severally to the Committee on Claims.

By Mr. Sawyer of Milford, An act in addition to chapter 153 of the Public Statutes, creating section 20 of said chapter. To the Committee on Revision of Statutes.

By Mr. Remich of Littleton, Joint resolution providing for the erection of an elevator or elevators in the state house for the use of members of the Senate, House of Representatives, state officers, employees, and the public.   To the Committee on State House and State House Yard.

By Mr. Remich of Littleton, Joint resolution appropriating money for the support of the New Hampshire School for Feeble-Minded Children, necessary school buildings, and to provide for a suitable water supply.   To the Committee on Feeble-Minded School.

By Mr. Drake of Freedom, Joint resolution in favor of the main highway between Centre Ossipee village and Effingham Falls.

By Mr. Felker of Madbury, Joint resolution in aid of the highways of the town of Madbury.

By Mr. Davis of Lee, Joint resolution in aid of the highways of the town of Lee.

By Mr. Gordon of Salem, Joint resolution in favor of highways in the town of Salem.

By Mr. Ware of Hancock, Joint resolution in favor of the Nelson road, so called, in the towns of Hancock, Harrisville, and Nelson.

By Mr. Sleeper of Plaistow, Joint resolution for an appropriation for repair of highway in Plaistow, N. H., leading from Atkinson Depot to the Haverhill line.

Severally to the Committee on Roads, Bridges and Canals.

BILLS FORWARDED.

An act to establish a state normal school.

Taken from the table and referred to the Committee on Appropriations.   The Speaker subsequently recalled the bill by unanimous consent of the House and referred it to the Committee on Normal School, as the bill had been printed before reference to committee.

An act to unite the school districts of the town of Rollinsford.

An act in amendment of chapter 78 of the Laws of 1897, relating to biennial elections.

An act to authorize the city of Dover to exempt from taxation the property of the Hayes Hospital.

An act to abolish the board of library commissioners.

An act to amend chapter 92 of the Public Statutes, relating to duties of school boards.

An act reviving and continuing the charter of the Warner and Kearsarge Road Company and amendments to said charter.

An act to amend chapter 93, in relation to scholars.

An act to amend chapter 95 of the Public Statutes, relating to the trustees of the State Normal School.

An act to provide for obtaining the testimony of non-resident directors, officers, and agents of New Hampshire corporations and the production of corporate books, records, and papers.

An act in relation to the salary of the state reporter.

An act amending chapter 43 of the Public Statutes, by repealing section 5 thereof, relating to the choice and duties of selectmen, and creating a substitute.

An act to amend chapter 241 of the Session Laws of 1893, entitled " An act to establish the city of Laconia," and repealing chapter 200 of the Laws of 1901, entitled "An act to amend chapter 241 of the Session Laws of 1893, entitled 'An act to establish the city of Laconia.' "

Severally taken from the table and ordered to a third reading.

On motion of Mr. Fisk of Hopkinton, at 12.55 the House adjourned.

AFTERNOON.

The House met at 3 o'clock.

THIRD READINGS.

An act to unite the school districts of the town of Rollinsford.

An act in amendment of chapter 78 of the Laws of 1897, relating to biennial elections.

An act authorizing the city of Dover to exempt from taxation the property of the Hayes Hospital.

An act to abolish the board of library commissioners.

An act to amend chapter 92 of the Public Statutes, relating to duties of school boards.

An act reviving and continuing the charter of the Warner and Kearsarge Road Company and amendments to said charter.

An act to amend chapter 93, in relation to scholars.

An act to amend chapter 95 of the Public Statutes, relating to the trustees of the State Normal School.

An act to provide for obtaining the testimony of non-resident directors, officers, and agents of New Hampshire corporations and the production of corporate books, records, and papers.

An act in relation to the salary of the state reporter.

Severally read a third time and passed and sent to the Senate for concurrence.

An act amending chapter 43 of the Public Statutes, by repealing section 5 thereof, relating to the choice and duties of selectmen, and creating a substitute.

Read a third time.

The question being,

Shall the bill pass?

Mr. Shute of Derry moved that the bill be indefinitely postponed.

(Discussion ensued.)

Mr. Shute withdrew his motion, and on motion of Mr. Ahern of Concord, the bill was recommitted to the Committee on Revision of Statutes.

An act to amend chapter 241 of the Session Laws of 1893, entitled "An act to establish the city of Laconia," and repealing chapter 200 of the Laws of 1901, entitled "An act to amend chapter 241 of the Session Laws of 1893, entitled 'An act to establish the city of Laconia.'"

The third reading having commenced, Mr. Small of Rochester moved that the bill be indefinitely postponed. Mr. French of Moultonborough moved that the bill be laid upon the table. On a *viva voce* vote the motion of Mr. French prevailed. Mr. Small of Rochester called for a division.

(Discussion ensued.)

Mr. French of Moultonborough raised the point of order that the motion was not debatable.

The Speaker ruled that the point of order was well taken.

A division being had, 116 gentlemen voted in the affirmative and 105 gentlemen in the negative, and the motion of Mr. Small of Rochester prevailed and the bill was laid upon the table.

Mr. Libby of Gorham offered the following motion:

That the rules of the House be so far suspended that the following entitled bill, "An act authorizing the Concord & Montreal Railroad, lessor, to acquire the Concord Street Railway and other property, to issue stock and bonds to pay therefor, and authorizing a physical connection of the Manchester Street Railway with the electric branches of the Concord & Montreal Railroad," be recalled from the Senate, to which it had been sent for concurrence, for further consideration by the House.

(Discussion ensued.)

Mr. French of Moultonborough called for a division.

(Discussion ensued.)

Mr. Remich of Littleton moved that the motion of Mr. Libby of Gorham be divided into two parts: a. That the rules of the House be suspended to permit of a reconsideration of the vote whereby the bill was passed after the expiration of the time limit for such motion of reconsideration; b. That the bill be recalled from the Senate.

(Discussion ensued.)

Mr. Ahern of Concord moved that the motion of Mr. Libby of Gorham be laid upon the table.

(Discussion ensued.)

Mr. Whitcher of Haverhill raised the point of order that a motion to lay upon the table was not debatable.

The Speaker ruled that the point of order was well taken.

The question being upon the motion of Mr. Ahern of Concord, on a *viva voce* vote the motion did not prevail.

Mr. Ahern of Concord called for a division.

A division being had, 69 gentlemen voted in the affirmative and 142 gentlemen in the negative, and the motion did not prevail.

Mr. Nason of Dover moved that the clerk of the House be requested to inquire of the clerk of the Senate the status of the bill in the Senate.

(Discussion ensued.)

On a *viva voce* vote the motion did not prevail.

Mr. Remich of Littleton moved that the bill be recalled from the Senate.

On a *viva voce* vote the motion prevailed.

Mr. French of Moultonborough called for a yea and nay vote.

The roll was called with the following result:

YEAS, 150.

ROCKINGHAM COUNTY. Sawyer of Atkinson, Fellows, Morse of Chester, Edgerly of Epping, Emerson of Hampstead, Lane of Hampton, Quimby of Kingston, Pridham, Warner, Sleeper, Yeaton, Adams of Portsmouth, Gordon.

STRAFFORD COUNTY. Howe of Barrington, York, Davis of Lee, Place, Crocker, Warren, Small, Etter, Wentworth, Demers, Caverly.

BELKNAP COUNTY. Hoitt of Barnstead, Smith of Center Harbor, Clough, Hull, Prescott, Chase of Laconia, Morrill of New Hampton, Sanborn of Sanbornton.

CARROLL COUNTY. Littlefield, Weeks, Fifield, Philbrick of Effingham, Green, Abbott of Ossipee, Hoyt of Sandwich.

MERRIMACK COUNTY. Graves, White of Bow, Morse of Bradford, Beck, Langmaid, Shepard, Willis, Donagan, Litchfield, Bunten of Dunbarton, Tripp, Phillips, Jones of Franklin, Sanborn of Loudon, Little of Salisbury, Burbank.

HILLSBOROUGH COUNTY. Shattuck, Craine, Tobie, Eaton,

12

Putnam, Brown of Greenville, Ware of Hancock, Ward, Cavanaugh, Nyberg, Abbott of Manchester, Bunton, A. S., of Manchester, Farrell, Johnson, Straw of Manchester, Stewart of Manchester, Tonery, Whalen, Riordan, Shaughnessey, Morse of Manchester, Couch, Tinkham, Dozois, Janelle, Filion, Lynch, Kane, Newman, Simpson, Sawyer of Milford, Robinson, Needham, Duncklee, Spalding, Lintott, Sullivan of Nashua, McLane, Jones of New Ipswich, Smith of Peterborough, Fitzgerald, Sheldon.

CHESHIRE COUNTY. Gowing, Tenney, Polzer, Fuller, Holland, Pierce of Jaffrey, Fay, Fitch, Whitney, Donovan, Moors, Fox, Scott, Fletcher, Merrill, Sherman of Walpole, Kellom.

SULLIVAN COUNTY. Clark, Chandler, Huntley, Philbrick of Springfield, Russell of Sunapee, Straw of Unity.

GRAFTON COUNTY. Davenport, Pierce of Bethlehem, Calley, Foster, Kimball of Grafton, Pinneo, Carr, Pike of Haverhill, Evans, Henry, Remich, Blake of Littleton, Frazer, Ferrin, Russell of Rumney, Bowen.

Coös COUNTY. Caird, Stewart of Berlin, Smyth, Notterstead, Jordan, Tillotson, Hamlin of Dummer, Bragg, Libby of Gorham, Ellis, McDonald of Northumberland, Piper, Smith of Pittsburg, Lennon.

NAYS, 82.

ROCKINGHAM COUNTY. Severance, Brown of Fremont, George, Bickford, Foye, Nelson.

STRAFFORD COUNTY. Mathes, Jewell, Nason, Bunce, Barrett, Tuttle, Felker, Townsend, Worcester.

BELKNAP COUNTY. Davis of Laconia, Fecteau, Edwards, Kimball of Laconia, Quimby of Meredith, Rogers, Mason.

CARROLL COUNTY. Stevens, Dow of Conway, Burnell, Drake, Trickey, French, Pollard, Blake of Wakefield.

MERRIMACK COUNTY. Harris of Boscawen, Durgin, Cate, Kennedy, Matson, Hill, A. W., of Concord, Roby, Woodman, Kimball of Concord, Emerson of Concord, Ahern, Aldrich.

HILLSBOROUGH COUNTY. Gould of Bennington, Bartlett of Manchester, Taggart, Wright, Barr of Manchester, Carpenter, Morgan, Armstrong, Emerson of Manchester, Tuck.

CHESHIRE COUNTY. Harris of Chesterfield, Batchelder, Lane of Swanzey, Hall.

SULLIVAN COUNTY. Sherman of Claremont, Long, Churchill.

GRAFTON COUNTY. Morrill of Ashland, Dorothy, Glover, Howe of Hanover, Whitcher, Goold of Lebanon, Pike of Lebanon, Comings, Crossman, Mitchell of Littleton, King, Chase of Orford, Celley, Gould of Plymouth, Houston, Bell.

COÖS COUNTY. Goss, Hutchins of Berlin, Gallagher, Martin, Buckley of Lancaster, Wilson, Babcock.

And less than two thirds of the members having voted, and less than two thirds of those voting having voted in the affirmative, the motion did not prevail.

BILLS, ETC., INTRODUCED.

Mr. Ahern of Concord called for the unfinished business of the morning session, it being the introduction of bills, and the following bills and joint resolutions were severally introduced, read twice, and referred as follows:

By Mr. Newton of Portsmouth, An act to prevent the pollution of the Piscataqua river and its tributaries.

By Mr. Lynch of Manchester, An act relating to catching shiners in Squog river, so called.

Severally to the Committee on Fisheries and Game.

By Mr. Hodgman of Merrimack, Joint resolution to encourage the breeding and exhibition of thoroughbred farm animals.

By Mr. Kendall of Mont Vernon, An act to amend section 1 of chapter 33 of the Laws of 1893, relating to the diseases of domestic animals.

Severally to the Committee on Agriculture.

By Mr. Lynch of Manchester, An act to create and establish an inspector of factories.

By Mr. Blake of Littleton, An act in amendment of the act relating to the terms of the superior court in Grafton county.

By Mr. Abbott of Manchester, An act in relation to the practice of Christian Science, faith cure, or mind healing in cases of illness.

By Mr. Frazer of Munroe, An act in relation to the settlement of paupers.

By Mr. Nelson of Portsmouth, An act to protect the public from extortion.

By Mr. Smith of Dover, An act to provide equitable process after judgment in certain cases.

By Mr. Barrett of Dover, An act in amendment of the charter of Pembroke Academy, increasing the number of trustees.

By Mr. Woodman of Concord, An act to facilitate the settlement of the estates of deceased persons.

By Mr. Mitchell of Littleton, An act explanatory of the powers of the courts in reference to the fees of commissioners in certain cases.

By Mr. Yeaton of Portsmouth, An act to amend the charter of the city of Portsmouth in relation to the assessors of taxes.

Severally to the Committee on Judiciary.

By Mr. Townsend of Milton, An act to incorporate the Milton Mills and Union Electric Railway Company.

By Mr. Hoyt of Sandwich, An act to amend the charter of the Ashland and Asquam Electric Railway Company.

By Mr. Libby of Dover, An act to amend section 1 of chapter 64 of the Public Statutes.

By Mr. Hoyt of Sandwich, An act to incorporate the Ashland, Sandwich & Wolfeborough Railway Company.

Severally to the Committee on Railroads.

By Mr. Woodman of Concord, An act in amendment of section 13, chapter 141 of the Public Statutes, relating to liens.   To the Committee on Revision of Statutes.

By Mr. Dow of Conway, An act to incorporate the North Conway Savings Bank at North Conway.   To the Committee on Banks.

By Mr. Davenport of Bath, An act for the permanent improvement of the highways of the state.   To the Committee on Public Improvements.

By Mr. Donovan of Keene, An act to change the homesteads of the following :   Carey & Faulkner, Fred L. Roundy, Albert E. Snow, and Hiram Blake from the town school districts of Swanzey and the city of Keene to the Union school district of Keene.   To the Committee on Education.

By Mr. French of Moultonborough, An act to amend section 8, chapter 171 of the Public Statutes, relating to life insurance.

By Mr. Kimball of Concord, An act in amendment of chapter 171 of the Public Statutes, relating to life insurance.

Severally to the Committee on Insurance.

By Mr. Scott of Nelson, Joint resolution to aid in repairing the highway around Granite lake, so called, lying in the towns of Nelson and Stoddard.

By Mr. Polzer of Gilsum, Joint resolution in favor of the main road in the town of Gilsum.

By Mr. Davis of Concord, An act in amendment of the charter of the city of Concord, authorizing the establishment of precincts within said city for the collection of garbage. To a special committee consisting of the Concord delegation, on motion of Mr. Ahern of Concord.

On motion of Mr. Sherman of Claremont, at 5 o'clock the House adjourned.

WEDNESDAY, JANUARY 28, 1903.

The House met at 11 o'clock.

Prayer was offered by the chaplain.

LEAVES OF ABSENCE.

The Sullivan county delegation was granted leave of absence for Friday, January 30, for the purpose of visiting the Sullivan county farm.

Mr. Pinkham of Alton was granted an indefinite leave of absence on account of sickness.

COMMITTEE REPORTS.

Mr. Bussell of Nashua, for the Committee on Railroads, to whom was referred An act to extend the time of the charter of the Keene, Marlow & Newport Electric Railway Company, having considered the same, report the same with the following resolution :

Resolved, That the bill ought to pass.

The report was accepted, the resolution adopted, and the bill laid upon the table to be printed. On motion of Mr. French of Moultonborough, the rules were suspended and the printing of the bill dispensed with. The bill was then ordered to a third reading. On motion of the same gentleman, the rules were further suspended and the bill put upon its third reading and passed and sent to the Senate for concurrence.

Mr. Cavanaugh of Manchester, for the Committee on Judiciary, to whom was referred An act relating to the salary of the register of probate for the county of Cheshire, having considered the same, report the same with the following resolution :

Resolved, That the bill ought to pass.

The report was accepted, and the bill laid upon the table to be printed, and then referred to the Committee on Appropriations.

Mr. Buckley of Lancaster, for the Committee on Judiciary, to whom was referred An act to amend chapter 179 of the Public Statutes, relating to guardians of insane persons and spendthrifts, having considered the same, report the same with the following resolution :

Resolved, That the bill ought to pass.

Mr. Whittemore of Dover, for the Committee on Judiciary, to whom was referred An act in amendment of section nine (9), chapter one hundred five (105) of the Laws passed January session, 1901, relating to political caucuses and conventions, having considered the same, report the same with the following resolution :

Resolved, That the bill ought to pass.

Mr. Sanborn of Loudon, for the Committee on State Hospital, to whom was referred Joint resolution in favor of the state hospital, having considered the same, report the same with the following resolution :

Resolved, That the joint resolution ought to pass.

Mr. Whitcher of Haverhill, for the Committee on Judiciary, to whom was referred An act in amendment of the charter of the Colby Academy, providing for filling vacancies and election of members, having considered the same, report the same with the following resolution :

Resolved, That the bill ought to pass.

Mr. Andrews of Somersworth, for the Committee on Education, to whom was referred An act to amend section 4 of chapter 96 of the Laws of 1901, and section 6 of chapter 92 of the Public Statutes, relating to courses of study, having considered the same, report the same with the following resolution :

Resolved, That the committee recommend its passage.

Mr. Andrews of Somersworth, for the Committee on Education, to whom was referred An act to amend chapter 92, Public Statutes, relating to school boards, having considered the same, report the same with the following resolution :

Resolved, That the bill ought to pass.

Mr. Ingham of Nashua, for the Committee on Incorporations, to whom was referred An act to incorporate the Walpole Water and Sewer Co., having considered the same, report the same with the following resolution :

Resolved, That the bill ought to pass.

Mr. Ingham of Nashua, for the Committee on Incorporations, to whom was referred An act in amendment of the charter of the Walpole Electric Light and Power Company, having considered the same, report the same with the following resolution :

Resolved, That the bill ought to pass.

Mr. Ingham of Nashua, for the Committee on Incorporations, to whom was referred An act to incorporate the New Hampshire Genealogical Society, having considered the same, report the same with the following resolution :

Resolved, That the bill ought to pass.

Mr. Whitcher of Haverhill, for the Committee on Judiciary, to whom was referred An act to amend "An act to establish a corporation by the name of the trustees of the New Hampshire Conference Seminary and the New Hampshire Female College," approved December 29, 1852, and other acts amending the same, having considered the same, report the same with the following resolution :

Resolved, That the bill ought to pass.

Mr. Scammon of Exeter, for the Committee on Judiciary, to whom was referred An act in amendment of the charter of the

Exeter Gas Light Company, having considered the same, report the same with the following resolution :

Resolved, That the bill ought to pass.

The reports were severally accepted and the bills and joint resolution laid upon the table to be printed.

Mr. Woodman of Concord, for the Committee on Judiciary, to whom was referred An act to incorporate the Caledonia Power Company, having considered the same, report the same with the following resolution :

Resolved, That the object sought cannot be attained under the general law.

The report was accepted and the bill referred to the Committee on Incorporations.

Mr. Whitcher of Haverhill, for the Committee on Judiciary, to whom was referred An act to amend chapter 76 of the Laws of 1897, in relation to hawkers and peddlers, having considered the same, report the same with the following resolution :

Resolved, That it is inexpedient to legislate.

The report was accepted and the resolution adopted.

Mr. Cavanaugh of Manchester, for the Committee on Judiciary, to whom was referred An act in amendment of sections 1, 3, and 4 of chapter 72 of the Public Statutes, relating to the discontinuance of highways, having considered the same, report the same with the following resolution :

Resolved, That the bill ought to pass.

Mr. Mitchell of Littleton, for the Committee on Judiciary, to whom was referred An act to incorporate the First Free Baptist Church of Franconia, having considered the same, report the same with the following resolution :

Resolved, That it ought to pass.

The reports were severally accepted and the bills laid upon the table to be printed.

Mr. Ingham of Nashua, for the Committee on Incorporations, to whom was referred An act to amend chapter 243 of the Laws of 1901, creating the Grafton Improvement, Manufacturing and Power Company, having considered the same, report the same with the following resolution :

Resolved, That the bill ought to pass with the following

amendment: Amend section 5 by striking out the words "Waterford Bridge, so-called," in the sixth line in said section, and inserting in place thereof the words "the point where the lower Waterford Bridge used to stand."

Amend section 8 by adding the following at the end thereof: "but not in any such manner as to obstruct the full and free use of said river as a public highway."

Strike out section 9.

The report was accepted, the amendments reported by the committee adopted, and the bill laid upon the table to be printed.

Mr. Cavanaugh of Manchester, for the Committee on Judiciary, to whom was referred An act to prevent telegraph, electric light and power companies from cutting down or injuring trees within the limits of the highway, having considered the same, report the same with the following resolution:

Resolved, That it is inexpedient to legislate.

The report was accepted, and the question being upon the adoption of the resolution reported by the committee,

(Discussion ensued.)

On a *viva voce* vote the resolution was adopted.

MESSAGE FROM THE SENATE.

A message from the Honorable Senate, by its clerk, announced that the Senate concurs with the House of Representatives in the passage of the following entitled bills:

An act to establish a police court in the town of Haverhill.

An act to change the name of Dodge's Falls Dam and Manufacturing company to "Ryegate Paper Company."

The message also announced that the Senate had passed bills with the following titles, in the passage of which it asks the concurrence of the House of Representatives:

An act in amendment of section 14 of chapter 264 of the Public Statutes, relating to offences against the police of towns.

Read a first and second time and referred to the Committee on Judiciary.

An act in amendment of section 128, chapter 59 of the Laws of 1895, entitled "An act to revise and amend title 13 of the Public Statutes, relating to militia."

Read a first and second time and referred to the Committee on Military Affairs.

SECOND READING.

An act in amendment of chapter 78 of the Laws of 1901, entitled "An act providing for a judiciary system consisting of two courts."

Read a second time and ordered to a third reading.

Mr. Small of Rochester moved that the following entitled bill, An act to amend chapter 241 of the Session Laws of 1893, entitled "An act to establish the city of Laconia," and repealing chapter 200 of the Laws of 1901, entitled "An act to amend chapter 241 of the Session Laws of 1893, entitled 'An act to establish the city of Laconia,'" be taken from the table.

The question being upon the pending motion of Mr. Small of Rochester, that the bill be indefinitely postponed,

(Discussion ensued.)

Mr. Small of Rochester withdrew his motion.

Mr. Hoyt of Sandwich moved that the rules be suspended and the bill put back upon its second reading for purposes of amendment.

(Discussion ensued.)

Mr. Hoyt of Sandwich withdrew his motion.

Mr. Remich of Littleton moved that the bill be referred to the Committee on Judiciary.

Mr. Barrett of Dover moved to amend the motion of Mr. Remich of Littleton by adding, " for amendment and public hearing, the committee to give notice when said hearing will be held."

The question being upon the adoption of the amendment offered by Mr. Barrett of Dover,

(Discussion ensued.)

On a *viva voce* vote the amendment was lost.

The question being upon the motion offered by Mr. Remich of Littleton, on a *viva voce* vote the motion prevailed, and the bill was referred to the Committee on Judiciary.

On motion of Mr. Richards of Newport, at 12 o'clock the House adjourned.

AFTERNOON.

The House met at 2 o'clock.

LEAVES OF ABSENCE.

Mr. Fontaine of Allenstown was granted leave of absence for three weeks on account of sickness.

Mr. Abbott of Salem was granted leave of absence for the balance of the week on account of illness.

THIRD READING.

An act in amendment of chapter 78 of the Laws of 1901, entitled "An act providing for a judiciary system consisting of two courts."

Read a third time and passed and sent to the Senate for concurrence.

MESSAGE FROM THE SENATE.

A message from the Honorable Senate, by its clerk, announced that the Senate concurs with the House of Representatives in the passage of the following entitled bills:

An act to extend the charter for the building of the Claremont Street Railway.

An act to promote cleanliness and to protect the public from the disease commonly known as consumption.

An act authorizing the Concord & Montreal Railroad, lessor, to acquire the Concord Street Railway and other property, to issue stock and bonds to pay therefor, and authorizing a physical connection of the Manchester Street Railway with the electric branches of the Concord & Montreal Railroad.

The message also announced that the Senate has passed a bill with the following title, in the passage of which it asks the concurrence of the House of Representatives:

An act in amendment of the charter of the Salem Water-Works Company, and legalizing and confirming the acts of said corporation in relation thereto.

Read a first and second time and referred to the Committee on Judiciary.

COMMITTEE REPORT.

On motion of Mr. Nason of Dover, the rules were so far

suspended as to permit of the following report being received at this time :

Mr. Woodman of Concord, for the Committee on Judiciary, to whom was referred An act to amend chapter 241 of the Session Laws of 1893, entitled "An act to establish the city of Laconia," and repealing chapter 200 of the Laws of 1901, entitled "An act to amend chapter 241 of the Session Laws of 1893, entitled 'An act to establish the city of Laconia,'" having considered the same, report the same with the following resolution :

Resolved, That the proposed amendment would not change the condition of the bill.

The report was accepted and the resolution adopted.

The question being,

Shall the bill be read a third time?

Mr. Small of Rochester moved that the bill be laid upon the table until to-morrow morning for the purposes of amendment. On a *viva voce* vote the motion prevailed.

On motion of Mr. Sasseville of Manchester, at 3.11 the House adjourned.

THURSDAY, JANUARY 29, 1903.

The House met at 11 o'clock.

Prayer was offered by the chaplain.

LEAVES OF ABSENCE.

Messrs. Hicks of Colebrook, Harriman of Stewartstown, and Gathercole of Clarksville were granted leave of absence for Friday, January 30.

NOTICE OF RECONSIDERATION.

Mr. Hodgman of Merrimack gave notice that on to-morrow, or some subsequent day, he would move to reconsider the vote whereby the following entitled bill, An act in amendment of chapter 78 of the Laws of 1901, entitled " An act providing for a judiciary system, consisting of two courts," was passed.

COMMITTEE REPORTS.

Mr. Woodman of Concord, for the Committee on Judiciary,

to whom was referred Joint resolution relating to the state arsenal at Portsmouth, having considered the same, report the same with the following resolution :

Resolved, That it is inexpedient to legislate because the object sought by the bill is provided for under the existing law.

Mr. Mitchell of Littleton, for the Committee on Judiciary, to whom was referred An act to prohibit the pollution of the waters of Blood brook, so-called, in the towns of Lebanon and Plainfield, having considered the same, report the same with the following resolution :

Resolved, That it is inexpedient to legislate.

Mr. Mitchell of Littleton, for the Committee on Judiciary, to whom was referred An act to prohibit the pollution of the waters of Mink brook, in the town of Hanover, from sawdust and other waste, having considered the same, report the same with the following resolution :

Resolved, That it is inexpedient to legislate.

Mr. Woodman of Concord, for the Committee on Judiciary, to whom was referred An act in amendment of the charter of the city of Nashua, relating to the appointment of police commissioners and to the collection of fines and costs, having considered the same, report the same with the following resolution :

Resolved, That it is inexpedient to legislate.

The reports were severally accepted and the resolutions adopted.

Mr. Foye of Portsmouth, for the Committee on Roads, Bridges, and Canals, to whom was referred Joint resolution in favor of raising Squam bridge in Holderness and Little Squam bridge in Ashland, and of improving navigation in Squam lake and connecting waters, having considered the same, report the same with the following resolution :

Resolved. That the joint resolution be referred to the Committee on Public Improvements.

The report was accepted and the joint resolution referred to the Committee on Public Improvements.

Mr. Churchill of Cornish, for the Committee on Forestry, to whom was referred An act to encourage the planting and perpetuation of forests, having considered the same, report the same with the following resolution :

Resolved, That the bill ought to pass.

Mr. Churchill of Cornish, for the Committee on Forestry, to whom was referred An act in amendment of chapter 44 of the Laws of 1893, relating to the powers and duties of the Forestry Commission with respect to public parks, having considered the same, report the same with the following resolution :

Resolved, That the bill ought to pass.

The reports were severally accepted and the bills laid upon the table to be printed.

Mr. Woodman of Concord, for the Committee on Judiciary, to whom was referred An act authorizing the city of Nashua to issue bonds, having considered the same, report the same with the following resolution :

Resolved, That it is inexpedient to legislate.

The report was accepted and the resolution adopted.

Mr. Wallace of Rochester, for the Committee on Appropriations, to whom was referred Joint resolution appropriating money to be expended for a monument at Vicksburg, Miss., having considered the same, report the same with the following resolution :

Resolved, That it ought to pass.

The report was accepted and the joint resolution ordered to a third reading.

(Mr. Nason of Dover in the chair.)

Mr. Bunton, A. S., of Manchester, for the Committee on Banks, to whom was referred An act concerning savings banks, having considered the same, report the same with the following resolution :

Resolved, That it is inexpedient to legislate.

Mr. Andrews of Somersworth, for the Committee on Education, to whom was referred An act to amend section 1, chapter 96, Laws of 1901, relating to high schools, having considered the same, report the same with the following resolution :

Resolved, That it is inexpedient to legislate.

Mr. Bunton, A. S., of Manchester, for the Committee on Banks, to whom was referred An act relating to savings banks, having considered the same, report the same with the following resolution :

Resolved, That it is inexpedient to legislate.

Mr. Woodman of Concord, for the Committee on Judiciary, to whom was referred An act in amendment of section 20, chapter 245 of the Public Statutes, relating to exemptions from the trustee process, having considered the same, report the same with the following resolution :

Resolved, That it is inexpedient to legislate.

Mr. Batchelder of Keene, for the Committee on Judiciary, to whom was referred An act in relation to the appointment of guardians over insane persons, having considered the same, report the same with the following resolution :

Resolved, That it is inexpedient to legislate.

Mr. Cavanaugh of Manchester, for the Committee on Judiciary, to whom was referred An act to create and establish an employers' liability act, having considered the same, report the same with the following resolution :

Resolved, That it is inexpedient to legislate.

Mr. Buckley of Lancaster, for the Committee on Judiciary, to whom was referred An act in relation to attempted suicide, having considered the same, report the same with the following resolution :

Resolved, That it is inexpedient to legislate.

The reports were severally accepted and the resolutions adopted.

Mr. Roby of Concord, for the Committee on Military Affairs, to whom was referred An act to amend section 12, chapter 59 of the Militia Laws of 1895, having considered the same, report the same with the following resolution :

Resolved, That the bill ought to pass.

Mr. Scammon of Exeter, for the Committee on Judiciary, to whom was referred An act to permit executors and administrators to resign, having considered the same, report the same with the following resolution :

Resolved, That the bill ought to pass.

Mr. Woodman of Concord, for the Committee on Judiciary, to whom was referred An act to amend the charter of the North Shore Water Company, having considered the same, report the same with the following resolution :

Resolved, That the bill ought to pass.

Mr. Newton of Portsmouth, for the special committee consisting of the Portsmouth delegation, to whom was referred An act to authorize the city of Portsmouth to raise money and issue bonds for a new high schoolhouse, having considered the same, report the same with the following resolution :

Resolved, That the bill ought to pass.

Mr. Buckley of Lancaster, for the Committee on Judiciary, to whom was referred An act to authorize the town of Lancaster to exempt certain property from taxation and to ratify its doings in the same, having considered the same, report the same with the following resolution :   .

Resolved, That the bill ought to pass.

Mr. Whitcher of Haverhill, for the Committee on State Library, to whom was referred An act to provide for the holding of library institutes, having considered the same, report the same with the following resolution :

Resolved, That the bill ought to pass.

The reports were severally accepted and the bills laid upon the table to be printed.

Mr. Whitcher of Haverhill, for the Committee on State Library, to whom was referred An act to authorize the Governor with the consent of the Council to cause the original maps and surveys by the town proprietors of New Hampshire to be mounted and preserved, having considered the same, report the same with the following resolution :

Resolved, That the bill ought to pass.

Mr. Batchelder of Keene, for the Committee on Judiciary, to whom was referred Joint resolution appropriating money to complete the payment of expenses of the recent constitutional convention, having considered the same, report the same with the following resolution :

Resolved, That the joint resolution ought to pass.

The reports were severally accepted, and the bills and joint resolution laid upon the table to be printed and then referred to the Committee on Appropriations.

Mr. Willis of Concord, for the special committee consisting of the Concord delegation, to whom was referred An act in amendment of the charter of the city of Concord, authorizing the establishment of precincts within said city for the collection of garbage, having considered the same, report the same with the following resolution :

Resolved, That the bill ought to pass.

The report was accepted and the bill laid upon the table to be printed. On motion of Mr. Ahern of Concord, the rules were suspended and the printing of the bill dispensed with. The bill was then ordered to a third reading. On motion of the same gentleman the rules were further suspended and the bill read a third time and passed and sent to the Senate for concurrence.

Mr. Whitcher of Haverhill, for the Committee on Judiciary, to whom was referred An act to amend chapter 79 of the Laws of 1899, entitled "An act to amend chapter 184 of the Public Statutes, relating to the times and places of holding courts of probate within and for the county of Grafton," having considered the same, report the same with the following resolution :

Resolved, That the bill ought to pass.

The report was accepted and the bill laid upon the table to be printed. On motion of Mr. Whitcher of Haverhill, the rules were suspended and the printing of the bill dispensed with. The bill was then ordered to a third reading. On motion of the same gentleman, the rules were further suspended and the bill read a third time and passed and sent to the Senate for concurrence.

Mr. Woodman of Concord, for the Committee on Judiciary, to whom was referred An act relating to salary of associate justice of police court of Nashua, in case of vacancy in office of justice, having considered the same, report the same with the following resolution :

Resolved, That the bill ought to pass.

The report was accepted and the bill laid upon the table to be printed. On motion of Mr. Bussell of Nashua, the rules were suspended and the printing of the bill dispensed with.

The bill was then ordered to a third reading. On motion of the same gentleman, the rules were further suspended and the bill read a third time and passed and sent to the Senate for concurrence.

Mr. Small of Rochester, for the Committee on Judiciary, to whom was referred An act to amend chapter 183 of the Session Laws of 1897, entitled "An act to authorize the village fire precinct of Wolfeborough to construct and maintain an electric plant," having considered the same, report the same with the following resolution :

Resolved, That the bill ought to pass.

The report was accepted and the bill laid upon the table to be printed. On motion of Mr. Small of Rochester, the rules were suspended and the printing of the bill dispensed with. The bill was then ordered to a third reading. On motion of the same gentleman, the rules were further suspended and the bill read a third time and passed and sent to the Senate for concurrence.

Mr. Willis of Concord, for the special committee consisting of the Concord delegation, to whom was referred An act in amendment of the charter of the city of Concord, providing for the election of overseers of the poor, having considered the same, report the same with the following resolution :

Resolved, That the bill ought to pass.

The report was accepted and the bill laid upon the table to be printed. On motion of Mr. Woodman of Concord, the rules were suspended and the printing of the bill dispensed with. The bill was then ordered to a third reading. On motion of the same gentleman, the rules were further suspended and the bill read a third time and passed and sent to the Senate for concurrence.

Mr. Willis of Concord, for the special committee consisting of the Concord delegation, to whom was referred An act to authorize the city of Concord to appropriate money for the celebration of its semi-centennial, having considered the same, report the same with the following resolution :

Resolved, That the bill ought to pass.

The report was accepted and the bill laid upon the table to be printed. On motion of Mr. Ahern of Concord, the rules were suspended and the printing of the bill was dispensed with. The bill was then ordered to a third reading. On motion of the same gentleman, the rules were further suspended and the bill read a third time and passed and sent to the Senate for concurrence.

Mr. Buckley of Lancaster, for the Committee on Judiciary, to whom was referred Joint resolution appropriating money to aid Dartmouth College in the education of New Hampshire students, having considered the same, report the same with the following resolution :

Resolved, That the joint resolution ought to pass.

The report was accepted and the joint resolution laid upon the table to be printed and then referred to the Committee on Appropriations.

Mr. Cavanaugh of Manchester, for the Committee on Judiciary, to whom was referred An act to incorporate the Sons of Veterans' Memorial Hall Association, having considered the same, report the same with the following resolution :

Resolved, That the object sought cannot be attained under the general law, and that the bill be referred to the Committee on Incorporations.

The report was accepted and the bill referred to the Committee on Incorporations.

Mr. Pike of Haverhill, for the Committee on Appropriations, to whom was referred An act in amendment of section 11, chapter 79 of the Session Laws of 1901, relating to the fish and game commissioners, having considered the same, report the same with the following resolution :

Resolved, That the bill ought to pass.

The report was accepted and the bill ordered to a third reading.

Mr. Small of Rochester, for the Committee on Judiciary, to whom was referred An act in amendment of section 15 of chapter 93 of the Public Statutes as amended in 1901, relating to scholars, having considered the same, report the same with the following resolution :

Resolved, That the bill be reported in a new draft with the recommendation that the bill in new draft ought to pass.

The report was accepted and the bill in its new draft read

a first time and ordered to a second reading. On motion of
Mr. Small of Rochester, the rules were suspended and the bill
read a second time and ordered to a third reading. On motion
of the same gentleman, the rules were further suspended and
the bill read a third time and passed and sent to the Senate
for concurrence.

Mr. Willis of Concord, for the special committee consisting of the Concord delegation, to whom was referred An act
to establish the salary of the justice of the police court of Concord, having considered the same, report the same with the
following resolution :

Resolved, That the bill ought to pass in a new draft.

The report was accepted and the bill in its new draft read
a first time and ordered to a second reading. On motion of
Mr. Woodman of Concord, the rules were suspended and the
bill read a second time and ordered to a third reading. On
motion of the same gentleman, the rules were further suspended and the bill read a third time and passed and sent
to the Senate for concurrence.

Mr. Whitcher of Haverhill, for the Joint Committee on
State Library, to whom was referred Joint resolution to provide for completing the painting and decorating of the walls
of the state library building, having considered the same, report the same with the following amendment, and the recommendation that the joint resolution as amended ought to pass :

Strike out the words "seven hundred and fifty" in the
seventh line and insert the words "twelve hundred," so that
the joint resolution as amended shall read : The governor and
the trustees of the state library, as custodians of the state
library building, are hereby authorized and instructed to cause
the walls of the judges' suite, the art gallery, the clerk of
court's room, and the smoking room in said building to be
painted and decorated in a proper manner, and the governor
is hereby authorized to draw his warrant for a sum not exceeding twelve hundred dollars, to pay the expenses incurred
in carrying into effect this resolution, upon any money in the
treasury not otherwise appropriated.

The report was accepted and the question being upon the
adoption of the resolution reported by the committee, on a

viva voce vote the resolution was not adopted.   Mr. Whitcher of Haverhill called for a division.   A division being had, the vote was declared to be manifestly in the affirmative and the resolution was adopted.   The bill was then laid upon the table to be printed, and then referred to the Committee on Appropriations.

(The Speaker in the chair.)

Mr. Jewell of Dover, for the Committee on Railroads, to whom was referred An act to extend the time for the location, construction, and completion of the railroad of the Moosilauke Railroad Company, having considered the same, report the same with the following resolution :

Resolved, That it ought to pass.

The report was accepted and the bill laid upon the table to be printed.   On motion of Mr. French of Moultonborough, the rules were suspended and the printing of the bill dispensed with.   The bill was then ordered to a third reading.   On motion of the same gentleman, the rules were further suspended and the bill read a third time and passed and sent to the Senate for concurrence.

Mr. Roby of Concord, for the Committee on Military Affairs, to whom was referred An act in amendment of section 128, chapter 59 of the Laws of 1895, entitled " An act to revise and amend Title 13 of the Public Statutes, relating to militia," having considered the same, report the same with the following resolution :

Resolved, That the bill ought to pass.

The report was accepted and the bill referred to the Committee on Appropriations.

Mr. Woodman of Concord, for the Committee on Judiciary, to whom was referred An act in relation to the practice of Christian Science, faith cure, or mind healing in cases of illness, having considered the same, report the same with the following resolution :

Resolved, That it is inexpedient to legislate.

The report was accepted, and the question being upon the adoption of the resolution reported by the committee, Mr.

Abbott of Manchester moved that the bill be recommitted to the Committee on Judiciary for a hearing.

(Discussion ensued.)

On a *viva voce* vote the motion prevailed.   Mr. Ahern of Concord called for a division.

(Discussion ensued.)

A division being had, 70 gentlemen voted in the affirmative and 194 gentlemen in the negative, and the resolution reported by the committee was adopted.

Mr. Converse of Lyme, for the Committee on Engrossed Bills, reported that they had examined bills with the following titles, and found them correctly engrossed :

An act authorizing the Concord & Montreal Railroad, lessor, to acquire the Concord Street Railway and other property, to issue stock and bonds to pay therefor, and authorizing a physical connection of the Manchester Street Railway with the electric branches of the Concord & Montreal Railroad.

An act to extend the charter for the building of the Claremont Street Railway.

An act to promote cleanliness, and to protect the public from the disease commonly known as consumption.

An act to change the name of Dodge's Falls Dam and Manufacturing Company to Ryegate Paper Company.

An act to establish a police court in the town of Haverhill.

On motion of Mr. Small of Rochester, An act to amend chapter 241 of the Session Laws of 1893, entitled "An act to establish the city of Laconia," and repealing chapter 200 of the Laws of 1901, entitled "An act to amend chapter 241 of the Session Laws of 1893, entitled 'An act to establish the city of Laconia,'" was taken from the table.

The question being,

Shall the bill be read a third time?

(Discussion ensued.)

Mr. Small of Rochester moved that the bill be indefinitely postponed.

(Discussion ensued.)

Mr. Remich of Littleton called for a yea and nay vote.

The roll was called with the following result:

YEAS, 117.

ROCKINGHAM COUNTY.   Sawyer of Atkinson, Pridham, Badger, Sleeper, Cogan, Adams of Portsmouth, Couhig, Corson, Dow of Seabrook.

STRAFFORD COUNTY.   Libby of Dover, Jewell,, Wesley, Felker, Warren, Small, Bergeron, Harrity, Murnane, Boutin, Andrews, Caverly.

BELKNAP COUNTY.   Potter, Clough, Fecteau, Prescott, Rogers, Mason.

CARROLL COUNTY.   Philbrick of Effingham, Greene.

MERRIMACK COUNTY.   Graves, Morse of Bradford, Beck, Langmaid, Hill, E. J., of Concord, Ahern, Donagan, Litchfield, Tripp, Morin of Franklin, Jones of Franklin, Twombly, Hutchins of Pittsfield, Walker of Pittsfield, Pillsbury.

HILLSBOROUGH COUNTY.   Woodbury, Barr of Bedford, Shattuck, Craine, Putnam, Brown of Greenville, Ware of Hancock, Farley of Hollis, Connell, Stewart of Manchester, Tonery, Ryan, Trinity, Riordan, Shaughnessey, Sasseville, Morse of Manchester, Dinsmore, Dozois, Janelle, Kohler, Lynch, Kane, Newman, Lampron, Buckley of Nashua, Ingham, Bussell, Shea, Spalding, Sullivan of Nashua, Moran of Nashua, Peabody, Fitzgerald, Chase of Weare, Sheldon.

CHESHIRE COUNTY.   Ware of Alstead, Bemis, Maloney, Jones of Keene, Donovan, Merrill, Boyden, Sherman of Walpole, Hall, Kellom, Dickinson.

SULLIVAN COUNTY.   Hamlin of Charlestown, Sherman of Claremont, Chandler, Huntley, Walker of Grantham, Lufkin, Philbrick of Springfield, Russell of Sunapee.

GRAFTON COUNTY.   McMurphey, Morrill of Ashland, Davenport, Gates, Barnard, Evans, Frazer, King, Celley, Russell of Rumney, Bowen.

COÖS COUNTY.   Smyth, Gallagher, Gathercole, Bragg, Libby of Gorham, O'Connor, Lennon.

NAYS, 204.

ROCKINGHAM COUNTY.   Preston of Auburn, Fellows, Hubbard, Morse of Chester, Darbe, White of Deerfield, Hardy,

Shute, Edgerly of Epping, Nowell, Scammon, Severance, Smith of Exeter, Brown of Fremont, Emerson of Hampstead, Lane of Hampton, Brown of Hampton Falls, Quimby of Kingston, Crowell, George, Warner, Bickford, Gerrish, Payne, Blaisdell, Foye, Nelson, Yeaton, Newton, Brown of Rye, Gordon, Swain.

STRAFFORD COUNTY. Howe of Barrington, Mathes, Ramsdell, Nason, Whittemore, Smith of Dover, Barrett, Langley of Durham, York, Tuttle, Davis of Lee, Place, Worcester, Wallace, Etter, Wentworth, Demers.

BELKNAP COUNTY. Sargent, Smith of Center Harbor, Davis of Laconia, Hull, Edwards, Kimball of Laconia, Quimby of Meredith, Morrill of New Hampton, Sanborn of Sanbornton.

CARROLL COUNTY. Littlefield, Stevens, Weeks, Fifield, Dow of Conway, Trickey, French, Hoyt of Sandwich, Pollard, Edgerly of Tuftonborough, Blake of Wakefield, Beacham.

MERRIMACK COUNTY. Harris of Boscawen, White of Bow, Durgin, Symonds, Shepard, Kennedy, Willis, Matson, Hill, A. W., of Concord, Roby, Woodman, Kimball of Concord, Emerson of Concord, Davis of Concord, Critchett, Mathews of Concord, Bunten of Dunbarton, Phillips, Adams of Franklin, Davis of Franklin, Preston of Henniker, Worthley, Messer, Sanborn of Northfield, Tallant, Aldrich, Foss, Ela, Burbank.

HILLSBOROUGH COUNTY. Gould of Bennington, Eaton, Whitaker, Ward, Holt, Cavanaugh, Nyberg, Abbott of Manchester, Chase of Manchester, Donahue, Bartlett of Manchester, Taggart, Bunton, A. S., of Manchester, Farrell, Johnson, McDonald of Manchester, Wright, Barr of Manchester, Dubuc, Morgan, Darrah, Marshall, Couch, Bunton, A. B., of Manchester, Armstrong, Tinkham, Graf, Quimby of Manchester, Scannell, Gunderman, Filion, Lemay, Emerson of Manchester, Simpson, Hodgman, Sawyer of Milford, Robinson, Needham, Kendall, Tuck, Duncklee, Lewis, Lintott, Shenton, McLane, Jones of New Ipswich, Smith of Peterborough, Bragdon.

CHESHIRE COUNTY. Harris of Chesterfield, Gowing, Tenney, Fuller, Holland, Cutler, Pierce of Jaffrey, Fay, Fitch,

Batchelder, Goodnow, Moors, Fox, Scott, Fletcher, Lane of Swanzey, Ramsay.

SULLIVAN COUNTY.   Clark, Long, Churchill, Aiken, Matthews of Newport, Richards, True, Straw of Unity, Ball.

GRAFTON COUNTY.   Pierce of Bethlehem, Calley, Little of Campton, Dorothy, Foster, Kimball of Grafton, Pinneo, Howe of Hanover, Whitcher, Carr, Pike of Haverhill, Goold of Lebanon, Comings, Crossman, Remich, Blake of Littleton, Converse, Chase of Orford, Gould of Plymouth, Ferrin, Honston, Goodrich.

Coös COUNTY.   Goss, Kent of Berlin, Hicks, Buckley of Lancaster, Ellis, Smith of Pittsburg, Wilson, Harriman, Darling.

And the motion to indefinitely postpone was lost.

Mr. Nason of Dover offered the following amendment:

Amend the bill by striking out lines 82 to 87 inclusive and substituting the following:

Ward 6, as hereby constituted, shall contain all the territory of ward 1 as heretofore constituted in the original city charter.

On a *viva voce* vote the amendment was adopted.   The bill was then ordered to a third reading.   On motion of Mr. Nason of Dover, the rules were suspended and the bill put upon its third reading.   The reading having commenced, on motion of Mr. Remich of Littleton, the rules were further suspended and the bill read a third time by its title, passed, and sent to the Senate for concurrence.

On motion of Mr. Remich of Littleton,—

Resolved, That the use of Representatives' hall be granted to the Committee on Liquor Laws on Tuesday evening, February 10, for a public meeting.

On motion of Mr. Ahern of Concord,—

Resolved, That the sergeant-at-arms be authorized to provide transportation for the Committee on Feeble-Minded School to visit the Massachusetts School for Feeble-Minded at Waltham.

On motion of Mr. Richards of Newport,—

Resolved, That the use of Representatives' hall on Wednesday evening, February 4, be granted to the Committee on

Public Improvements for the purpose of holding a good roads meeting to be addressed by Mr. Dodge, the director of Public Roads Inquiries of Department of Agriculture in Washington, and Col. W. H. Moore, president of the National Good Roads Association.

On motion of Mr. Warren of Rochester,—

Resolved, That when the House adjourns this afternoon it be to meet at 9.30 Friday morning, and when the House adjourns Friday morning it be to meet at 8 o'clock Monday evening.

NOTICE OF RECONSIDERATION.

Mr. Bussell of Nashua gave notice that on to-morrow, or some subsequent day, he would move to reconsider the vote whereby the report of the committee was accepted on the following entitled bill, "An act authorizing the city of Nashua to issue bonds."

MESSAGE FROM THE SENATE.

A message from the Honorable Senate, by its clerk, announced that the Senate concurs with the House of Representatives in the passage of the following entitled bills:

An act to abolish the board of library commissioners.

An act to amend chapter 92 of the Public Statutes, relating to duties of school boards.

An act to amend chapter 95 of the Public Statutes, relating to the trustees of the State Normal School.

Mr. Remich of Littleton offered the following resolution:

Resolved, That the House of Representatives require the opinion of the Supreme Court upon the following questions, viz.:

First.   Did His Excellency George A. Ramsdell have legal authority under the constitution and laws of the State of New Hampshire to make and execute the following appointment and agreement in behalf of the state:

MEMORANDUM OF AN APPOINTMENT AND AGREEMENT, made this eleventh day of May, A. D. 1897, by and between the State of New Hampshire by the Honorable George A. Ramsdell, its Governor, on the one part, and Horace S. Cummings,

of Washington, in the District of Columbia, on the other part,
WITNESSETH:

That the said State of New Hampshire in consideration of
the things to be done by said Horace S. Cummings as hereinafter set forth, hath appointed, and by these presents doth appoint, said Horace S. Cummings its agent and attorney, to
present, prosecute, and recover before the Congress, any Department, the Court of Claims, or the Supreme Court of the
United States, any claim or claims of said State against the
United States, for costs, charges, and expenses properly incurred by said State for enrolling, subsisting, clothing, arming,
equipping, paying, and transporting the troops of said State,
employed in aiding to suppress the insurrection against the
United States between the years 1861 and 1865, both inclusive, under an Act of Congress entitled "An Act to indemnify
the States for expenses incurred by them in defense of the
United States," approved July 27th, 1861. And said Horace
S. Cummings shall have and receive for his legal services in
and about said matter, a sum equal to fifteen per cent. of the
entire sum collected, payable only out of any sums that may
be collected hereunder, and without any liability on the part
of the State for expenses in connection therewith.

And in consideration of the premises said Horace S. Cummings agrees to undertake the presentation and prosecution of
said claims at the compensation above stated and without any
liability on behalf of the State for his expenses in connection
therewith.

IN WITNESS WHEREOF said State of New Hampshire has
caused these presents to be signed by the said George A.
Ramsdell, its Governor, and its seal to be hereto affixed and
said Horace S. Cummings has hereunto set his hand and seal,
the day and year first above written.

THE STATE OF NEW HAMPSHIRE,
        By
    GEORGE A. RAMSDELL, *Governor*.
(Seal of State.)
    HORACE S. CUMMINGS.

Second, Is the State under legal obligation to pay Horace

S. Cummings fifteen per cent. of the entire sum collected by virtue of said contract?

Resolved, That the Speaker of the House of Representatives for and in its behalf be and hereby is directed to present said questions to the Supreme Court with a request for a decision at as early a date as is compatible with a careful consideration of the important questions involved.

The question being upon the adoption of the resolution,

(Discussion ensued.)

On a *viva voce* vote the resolution was adopted.

LEAVES OF ABSENCE.

Mr. Cutler of Jaffrey was granted leave of absence for the balance of the week on account of urgent business.

The Committee on Soldiers' Home were granted leave of absence for Friday, February 6, for the purpose of visiting the Soldiers' Home at Tilton.

On motion of Mr. Nyberg of Manchester, at 1.20 the House adjourned.

AFTERNOON.

The House met at 3 o'clock.

MESSAGE FROM THE SENATE.

A message from the Honorable Senate, by its clerk, announced that the Senate concurs with the House of Representatives in the passage of the following entitled bills:

An act to amend chapter 241 of the Session Laws of 1893, entitled "An act to establish the city of Laconia," and repealing chapter 200 of the Laws of 1901, entitled "An act to amend chapter 241 of the Session Laws of 1893, entitled 'An act to establish the city of Laconia.'"

An act in amendment of chapter 78 of the Laws of 1901, entitled "An act providing for a judiciary system consisting of two courts."

The message also announced that the Senate has passed the following bills and joint resolution, in the passage of which it asks the concurrence of the House of Representatives:

An act in relation to bail in criminal cases.

Read a first and second time and referred to the Committee on Judiciary.

Joint resolution in relation to a fish hatching house at Laconia.

Read a first and second time and referred to the Committee on Judiciary.

THIRD READINGS.

An act in amendment of section 11, chapter 79 of the Session Laws of 1901, relating to the fish and game commissioners.

Read a third time and passed and sent to the Senate for concurrence.

Joint resolution appropriating money to be expended for a monument at Vicksburg, Miss.

Read a third time.

The question being,

Shall the bill pass?

(Discussion ensued.)

On a *viva voce* vote the bill passed and was sent to the Senate for concurrence.

On motion of Mr. Cate of Concord,—

Resolved, That the following entitled bill, "An act in amendment of chapter 82 of the Laws of 1897," be recalled from the Committee on Revision of Statutes and referred to the Committee on Judiciary.

NOTICE OF RECONSIDERATION.

Mr. Goold of Lebanon gave notice that on to-morrow, or some subsequent day, he would move a reconsideration of the vote whereby the report of the committee on the following entitled bill, "An act to prohibit the pollution of the waters of Blood brook, so called, in the towns of Lebanon and Plainfield," was adopted.

LEAVES OF ABSENCE.

The Committee on Normal School were granted leave of absence for Tuesday, February 3, for the purpose of visiting the Normal School.

The Committee on Feeble-Minded School were granted leave of absence for Tuesday, February 3, for the purpose of visiting the School for Feeble-Minded at Waltham, Mass.

On motion of Mr. Pierce of Bethlehem, at 3.16 the House adjourned.

FRIDAY, JANUARY 30, 1903.

The House met at 9.30 o'clock, according to adjournment.

COMMITTEE REPORTS.

Mr. Roby of Concord, for the Committee on Fisheries and Game, to whom was referred An act in amendment of section 26, chapter 79 of the Laws of 1901, for better protection of gray squirrels, having considered the same, report the same with the following resolution:

Resolved, That the bill ought to pass.

Mr. Goold of Lebanon, for the Committee on Fisheries and Game, to whom was referred An act to amend sections 54 and 58, chapter 78 of the fish and game laws, having considered the same, report the same with the following resolution:

Resolved, That the bill ought to pass.

The reports were severally accepted and the bills laid upon the table to be printed.

Mr. Willis of Concord, for the Committee on Engrossed Bills, reported that they had examined a bill with the following title and found it correctly engrossed:

An act to amend chapter 241 of the Session Laws of 1893, entitled "An act to establish the city of Laconia," and repealing chapter 200 of the Laws of 1901, entitled "An act to amend chapter 241 of the Session Laws of 1893, entitled 'An act to establish the city of Laconia.'"

The report was accepted.

On motion of Mr. Brown of Fremont, at 9.35 the House adjourned.

MONDAY, FEBRUARY 2, 1903.

The House met at 8 o'clock in the evening, according to adjournment, being called to order by Mr. James E. French of Moultonborough, and the following communication was read by the clerk:

CONCORD, January 30, 1903.

Mr. James E. French, Moultonborough, N. H.

Dear Sir:—I shall be unable to be present at the session on Monday evening, February 2. Will you kindly preside for me and greatly oblige,

Yours very truly,
HARRY M. CHENEY,
Speaker.

LEAVE OF ABSENCE.

Mr. Woodman of Concord was granted leave of absence for the balance of the week on account of illness.

On motion of Mr. Ahern of Concord, at 8.02 the House adjourned.

TUESDAY, FEBRUARY 3, 1903.

The House met at 11 o'clock.

Prayer was offered by the chaplain.

PETITION PRESENTED AND REFERRED.

By Mr. Sargent of Belmont, Petition of the Belknap Association of Free Baptist churches, for the suppression of the liquor traffic. To the Committee on Liquor Laws.

COMMITTEE REPORTS.

Mr. Roby of Concord, for the Committee on Fisheries and Game, to whom was referred An act to amend section 2 of chapter 121 of the Laws of 1895, relating to bounty on bears, having considered the same, report the same with the following resolution:

Resolved, That it is inexpedient to legislate.

Mr. Libby of Gorham, for the Committee on Revision of Statutes, to whom was referred An act in amendment of chapter 110 of the Public Statutes, relating to smallpox, having considered the same, report the same with the following resolution :

Resolved, That it is inexpedient to legislate.

Mr. Roby of Concord, for the Committee on Fisheries and Game, to whom was referred An act to prohibit fishing on Sunday, having considered the same, report the same with the following resolution :

Resolved, That it is inexpedient to legislate.

The reports were severally accepted and the resolutions adopted.

Mr. Dow of Conway, for the Committee on Appropriations, to whom was referred Joint resolution to provide for a forest examination of the White Mountain region, having considered the same, report same with the following resolution :

Resolved, That the joint resolution ought to pass.

The report was accepted and the joint resolution ordered to a third reading.

Mr. Mitchell of Littleton, for the Committee on Judiciary, to whom was referred An act to authorize the town of Pittsfield to construct and maintain an electric plant for lighting, heat, or power purposes, having considered the same, report the same with the following resolution :

Resolved, That the object sought cannot be attained under the general law, and recommend that the bill be referred to the Committee on Incorporations.

The report was accepted and the bill referred to the Committee on Incorporations.

Mr. Mitchell of Littleton, for the Committee on Judiciary, to whom was referred An act to enlarge the powers of the Lisbon fire district, having considered the same, report the same with the following resolution :

Resolved, That the bill be reported favorably in a new draft and amended title, entitled " An act to establish the Lisbon village district," and that the same ought to pass.

The report was accepted and the bill in its new draft and with amended title read a first time and ordered to a second reading. On motion of Mr. Crossman of Lisbon, the rules were suspended and the bill read a second time by its title and laid upon the table to be printed. On motion of the same gentleman, the rules were further suspended and the printing of the bill dispensed with. The bill was then ordered to a third reading. On motion of the same gentleman, the rules were still further suspended and the bill read a third time by its title and passed and sent to the Senate for concurrence.

Mr. Morgan of Manchester, for the Committee on Railroads, to whom was referred An act confirming and legalizing the organization and acts of the Berlin Street Railway, having considered the same, report the same with the following resolution:

Resolved, That it ought to pass.

The report was accepted, and the bill laid upon the table to be printed. On motion of Mr. Goss of Berlin, the rules were suspended and the printing of the bill dispensed with. The bill was then ordered to a third reading. On motion of the same gentleman, the rules were further suspended and the bill read a third time and passed and sent to the Senate for concurrence.

Mr. Harris of Boscawen, for the Committee on Railroads, to whom was referred An act in amendment of the charter of the Wells River Bridge, and authorizing the Concord & Montreal railroad to hold stock therein, having considered the same, report the same with the following resolution:

Resolved, That it ought to pass.

The report was accepted, and the bill laid upon the table to be printed. On motion of Mr. Whitcher of Haverhill, the rules were suspended and the printing of the bill dispensed with. The bill was then ordered to a third reading. On motion of the same gentleman, the rules were further suspended and the bill read a third time and passed and sent to the Senate for concurrence.

Mr. Converse of Lyme, for the Committee on Engrossed Bills, reported that they had examined bills with the following titles and found them correctly engrossed:

An act to abolish the board of library commissioners.

An act to amend chapter 92 of the Public Statutes, relating to duties of school boards.

14

An act to amend chapter 95 of the Public Statutes, relating to the trustees of the State Normal School.

An act in amendment of chapter 78 of the Laws of 1901, entitled "An act providing for a judiciary system consisting of two courts."

The report was accepted.

BILLS, ETC., FORWARDED.

An act to amend chapter 92, Public Statutes, relating to school boards.

An act in amendment of the charter of the Colby Academy, providing for filling vacancies and election of members.

Joint resolution in favor of the New Hampshire State Hospital.

An act to incorporate the First Free Baptist church of Franconia.

An act to amend chapter 179 of the Public Statutes, relating to guardians of insane persons and spendthrifts.

An act to amend "An act to establish a corporation by the name of the trustees of the New Hampshire Conference Seminary and the New Hampshire Female College," approved December 29, 1852, and other acts amending the same.

An act in amendment of sections 1, 3, and 4 of chapter 72 of the Public Statutes, relating to the discontinuance of highways.

An act in amendment of the charter of the Walpole Electric Light and Power Company.

An act to repeal the charter of the Massabesic Horse Railroad Company.

An act to incorporate the Walpole Water and Sewer Company.

An act to encourage the planting and perpetuation of forests.

An act to authorize the town of Lancaster to exempt certain property from taxation and to ratify its doings in the same.

An act in amendment of the charter of the Exeter Gas Light Company.

An act to permit executors and administrators to resign.

An act to provide for the holding of library institutes.

An act to amend sections 54 and 58, chapter 78 of the fish and game laws.

An act to amend the charter of the North Shore Water Company.

An act to amend section 12, chapter 59 of the militia law of 1895.

Severally taken from the table and ordered to a third reading.

An act requiring state certification of teachers of public schools.

Taken from the table and referred to the Committee on Education.

An act to authorize the city of Portsmouth to raise money and issue bonds for a new high schoolhouse.

Taken from the table and ordered to a third reading.. On motion of Mr. Cogan of Portsmouth, the rules were suspended and the bill read a third time and passed and sent to the Senate for concurrence.

An act in amendment of chapter 44 of the Laws of 1893, relating to the powers and duties of the forestry commission with respect to public parks.

Taken from the table and ordered to a third reading. On motion of Mr. Churchill of Cornish, the rules were suspended and the bill read a third time and passed and sent to the Senate for concurrence.

An act to amend section 4 of chapter 96 of the Laws of 1901, and section 6 of chapter 92 of the Public Statutes, relating to courses of study.

Taken from the table and ordered to a third reading. On motion of Mr. Churchill of Cornish, the rules were suspended and the bill read a third time and passed and sent to the Senate for concurrence.

An act in amendment of section 26, chapter 79 of the Laws of 1901, for the better protection of gray squirrel.

Taken from the table and the question being,

Shall the bill be read a third time?

On a *viva voce* vote the bill was refused a third reading.

Mr. Ahern of Concord called for a division and, a division pending, moved that the bill be laid upon the table.

On a *viva voce* vote the motion prevailed.

An act in amendment of section 9, chapter 105 of the laws passed January session, 1901, relating to political caucuses and conventions.

Taken from the table and ordered to a third reading. Mr. Whittemore of Dover moved that the rules be suspended and the bill be read a third time at the present time and placed upon its passage. The question being upon the adoption of the motion,

(Discussion ensued.)

On a *viva voce* vote the motion prevailed and the bill was read a third time and passed and sent to the Senate for concurrence.

An act to amend chapter 243 of the Laws of 1901, creating the Grafton Improvement, Manufacturing and Power Company.

Taken from the table, and on motion of Mr. Buckley of Lancaster, laid upon the table.

LEAVES OF ABSENCE.

Mr. Small of Rochester was granted leave of absence for the day for the purpose of visiting the State Normal School at Plymouth.

Mr. Kohler of Manchester was granted leave of absence for the day on account of important business.

On motion of Mr. Buckley of Lancaster, the following entitled bill, "An act to amend chapter 243 of the Laws of 1901, creating the Grafton Improvement, Manufacturing and Power Company," was taken from the table. Mr. Buckley of Lancaster offered the following amendment:

Amend the bill by adding at the end of line 16 of section 5, the following words, viz.:

Provided, however, that the structures authorized by this act shall in no case be of such a character as to infringe the public right to a highway in said river as free and convenient as would be afforded by the river in its natural condition.

The amendment was adopted and the bill ordered to a third reading.

On motion of Mr. Remich of Littleton,—

Resolved, That the Committee on Liquor Laws be given the use of Representatives' hall for Tuesday evening, February 17.

Mr. Miller of Peterborough, having been duly qualified by His Excellency the Governor, appeared and took his seat as a member of the House of Representatives.

On motion of Mr. Wallace of Rochester, at 12 o'clock the House adjourned.

AFTERNOON.

The House met at 3 o'clock.

THIRD READINGS.

An act to amend chapter 243 of the Laws of 1901, creating the Grafton Improvement, Manufacturing and Power Company.

The third reading having commenced, on motion of Mr. Remich of Littleton, the bill was laid upon the table.

An act in amendment of the charter of the Walpole Electric Light and Power Company.

The third reading having begun, on motion of Mr. Whitcher of Haverhill, the rules were suspended and the bill put back upon its second reading for amendment.

Mr. Whitcher of Haverhill offered the following amendment:

Amend by adding after the words, " Cold river," wherever they occur in section 4, the following : " and its tributaries."

The amendment was adopted and the bill ordered to a third reading. On motion of Mr. Whitcher of Haverhill, the rules were suspended and the bill read a third time and passed and sent to the Senate for concurrence.

An act to amend section 12, chapter 59 of the militia law of 1895.

Read a third time.

The question being,

Shall the bill pass?

Mr. Buckley of Lancaster moved that the bill be indefinitely postponed.

(Discussion ensued.)

On a *viva voce* vote the motion prevailed and the bill was indefinitely postponed.

An act to provide for the holding of library institutes.

The third reading having commenced, on motion of Mr. Ahern of Concord, the rules were suspended and the bill put back upon its second reading and referred to the Committee on Appropriations.

An act to amend sections 54 and 58, chapter 78 of the fish and game laws.

An act to amend the charter of the North Shore Water Company.

An act to permit executors and administrators to resign.

An act to incorporate the First Free Baptist church of Franconia.

An act to amend chapter 179 of the Public Statutes, relating to guardians of insane persons and spendthrifts.

An act to amend "An act to establish a corporation by the name of the trustees of the New Hampshire Conference Seminary and the New Hampshire Female College," approved December 29, 1852, and other acts amending the same.

An act in amendment of the charter of the Colby Academy, providing for filling vacancies and election of members.

An act to incorporate the Walpole Water and Sewer Company.

An act in amendment of the charter of the Exeter Gas Light Company.

An act to authorize the town of Lancaster to exempt certain property from taxation and to ratify its doings in the same.

An act to repeal the charter of the Massabesic Horse Railroad Company.

Severally read a third time and passed and sent to the Senate for concurrence.

An act to encourage the planting and perpetuation of forests.

Read a third time.

The question being,

Shall the bill pass?

On a *viva voce* vote the bill was refused a passage.

Mr. Remich of Littleton called for a division.

(Discussion ensued.)

Mr. Remich withdrew his call for a division and on a *viva voce* vote the bill passed and was sent to the Senate for concurrence.

An act in amendment of sections 1, 3, and 4 of chapter 72 of the Public Statutes, relating to the discontinuance of highways.

An act to amend chapter 92, Public Statutes, relating to school boards.

Joint resolution to provide for a forest examination of the White Mountain region.

Severally read a third time and passed and sent to the Senate for concurrence.

Joint resolution in favor of the New Hampshire State Hospital.

The third reading having commenced, on motion of Mr. Ahern of Concord, the rules were suspended and the joint resolution put back upon its second reading and referred to the Committee on Appropriations.

MESSAGE FROM THE SENATE.

A message from the Honorable Senate, by its clerk, announced that the Senate concurs with the House of Representatives in the passage of the following entitled bill:

An act to amend chapter 69 of the Laws of 1901, entitled "An act to protect the Ammonoosuc river in Carroll, Bethlehem, Littleton, Lisbon, and Bath, and its tributaries, from pollution by sawdust and other waste."

The message also announced that the Senate has passed a bill with the following title, in the passage of which it asks the concurrence of the House of Representatives:

An act to authorize the state board of agriculture to appoint a state nursery inspector, and to provide for the protection of trees and shrubs from injurious insects and diseases.

Read a first and second time and referred to the Committee on Agriculture.

LEAVES OF ABSENCE.

The Coös county delegation were granted leave of absence for Thursday and Friday, February 5 and 6, for the purpose of visiting the county farm.

The Belknap county delegation were granted leave of absence for Friday, February 6, for the purpose of visiting the county farm.

On motion of Mr. Blake of Wakefield, at 4.45 the House adjourned.

WEDNESDAY, FEBRUARY 4, 1903.

The House met at 11 o'clock.

Prayer was offered by the chaplain.

LEAVE OF ABSENCE.

Mr. Fitch of Keene was granted leave of absence for the balance of the week on account of sickness.

PETITION PRESENTED AND REFERRED.

By Mr. Harris of Boscawen, Petition of Boscawen Lodge, No. 127, I. O. G. T., against the enactment of a license law. To the Committee on Liquor Laws.

COMMITTEE REPORTS.

Mr. Goold of Lebanon, for the Committee on Fisheries and Game, to whom was referred Joint resolution appropriating money for screening the outlet of Highland lake in the town of Andover, having considered the same, report the same with the following resolution :

Resolved, That the joint resolution ought to pass.

The report was accepted, and the joint resolution laid upon the table to be printed, and then referred to the Committee on Appropriations.

Mr. Goold of Lebanon, for the Committee on Fisheries and Game, to whom was referred Joint resolution in relation to a fish hatching house at Laconia, having considered the same, report the same with the following resolution :

Resolved, That the joint resolution ought to pass.

The report was accepted, and the joint resolution referred to the Committee on Appropriations.

Mr. Hamlin of Charlestown, for the Committee on Claims,

to whom was referred Joint resolution to appropriate a sum of money to pay Arthur W. Dudley a balance due him for money expended and labor performed in making surveys for the state, having considered the same, report the same with the following resolution:

Resolved, That the joint resolution ought to pass.

The report was accepted, and the joint resolution laid upon the table to be printed, and then referred to the Committee on Appropriations.

Mr. Rogers of Tilton, for the Committee on Elections, to whom was referred An act to legalize and confirm the selectmen's warrant for and the votes and proceedings thereunder at the biennial election and meeting in the town of Columbia, held in said town on the fourth day of November, A. D. 1902, having considered the same, report the same with the following resolution:

Resolved, That the bill ought to pass.

The report was accepted, and the bill laid upon the table to be printed. On motion of Mr. Taggart of Manchester, the rules were suspended and the printing of the bill dispensed with. The bill was then ordered to a third reading. On motion of the same gentleman, the rules were further suspended and the bill read a third time and passed and sent to the Senate for concurrence.

Mr. Dionne of Nashua, for the Committee on Elections, to whom was referred An act to legalize the biennial election of the town of Conway, held November 4, 1902, having considered the same, report the same with the following resolution:

Resolved, That the bill ought to pass.

The report was accepted, and the bill laid upon the table to be printed. On motion of Mr. French of Moultonborough, the rules were suspended and the printing of the bill dispensed with. The bill was then ordered to a third reading. On motion of the same gentleman, the rules were further suspended and the bill read a third time and passed and sent to the Senate for concurrence.

Mr. Tallant of Pembroke, for the Committee on Revision of Statutes, to whom was referred An act amending chapter

43 of the Public Statutes by repealing section 5 thereof, relating to the choice and duties of selectmen, and creating a substitute, having considered the same, report the same with the following resolution:

Resolved, That it is inexpedient to legislate.

Mr. Andrews of Somersworth, for the Committee on Education, to whom was referred An act to change the homesteads of the following: Carey and Faulkner, Fred L. Roundy, Albert E. Snow, and Hiram Blake from the town school districts of Swanzey and the city of Keene, to the Union school district of Keene, having considered the same, report the same with the following resolution:

Resolved, That it is inexpedient to legislate.

Mr. Bell of Woodstock, for the Committee on Public Health, to whom was referred An act to amend section 13, chapter 269, Public Statutes, relating to the sale of deadly poison, having considered the same, report the same with the following resolution:

Resolved, That it is inexpedient to legislate.

The reports were severally accepted and the resolutions adopted.

Mr. Goold of Lebanon, for the Committee on Fisheries and Game, to whom was referred Joint resolution in favor of screening the outlet of Forest lake, having considered the same, report the same with the following resolution:

Resolved, That the joint resolution ought to pass.

Mr. Goold of Lebanon, for the Committee on Fisheries and Game, to whom was referred Joint resolution to appropriate money for the screening of Armington pond, so called, in the town of Piermont, having considered the same, report the same with the following resolution:

Resolved, That the joint resolution ought to pass.

Mr. Goold of Lebanon, for the Committee on Fisheries and Game, to whom was referred Joint resolution for an appropriation for screening Crystal lake in Gilmanton, having considered the same, report the same with the following resolution:

Resolved, That the joint resolution ought to pass.

Mr. Goold of Lebanon, for the Committee on Fisheries and

Game, to whom was referred Joint resolution appropriating money for screening the outlet of Pleasant pond in New London, having considered the same, report the same with the following resolution :

Resolved, That the joint resolution ought to pass.

Mr. Goold of Lebanon, for the Committee on Fisheries and Game, to whom was referred Joint resolution in favor of appropriating money for screening the outlet of Tewksbury's pond in the town of Grafton, having considered the same, report the same with the following resolution :

Resolved, That the joint resolution ought to pass.

The reports were severally accepted, and the joint resolutions laid upon the table to be printed and then referred to the Committee on Appropriations.

Mr. Goss of Berlin, for the Committee on Judiciary, to whom was referred An act in amendment of section 4 of chapter 206 of the Laws of 1897, being "An act to incorporate the Bethlehem Electric Light Company," having considered the same, report the same with the following resolution :

Resolved, That the bill ought to pass.

Mr. Bell of Woodstock, for the Committee on Public Health, to whom was referred An act in relation to milk tickets, having considered the same, report the same with the following resolution :

Resolved, That the bill ought to pass.

Mr. Andrews of Somersworth, for the Committee on Education, to whom was referred An act amending chapter 92 of the Public Statutes, in relation to school boards, having considered the same, report the same with the following resolution :

Resolved, That the bill ought to pass.

Mr. Andrews of Somersworth, for the Committee on Education, to whom was referred An act to amend chapter 96 of the Session Laws of 1901, relating to high schools, having considered the same, report the same with the following resolution :

Resolved, That the bill ought to pass.

Mr. Whittemore of Dover, for the Committee on Judiciary, to whom was referred An act in relation to the salary of the judge of probate for Strafford county, having considered the same, report the same with the following resolution :

Resolved, That the bill ought to pass.

Mr. Hamlin of Charlestown, for the Committee on Claims, to whom was referred Joint resolution in favor of William J. Patch, having considered the same, report the same with the following resolution :

Resolved, That the joint resolution ought to pass.

Mr. Goold of Lebanon, for the Committee on Fisheries and Game, to whom was referred Joint resolution in favor of screening the outlet to Penacook lake in the city of Concord, having considered the same, report the same with the following resolution :

Resolved, That the joint resolution ought to pass.

The reports were severally accepted, and the bills and joint resolutions laid upon the table to be printed, and then referred to the Committee on Appropriations.

Mr. Cavanaugh of Manchester, for the Committee on Judiciary, to whom was referred An act to prohibit speculation or combination against the public good, having considered the same, report the same with the following resolution :

Resolved, That it is inexpedient to legislate.

The report was accepted and the resolution adopted.

Mr. Demers of Somersworth, for the Committee on Revision of Statutes, to whom was referred An act in amendment of section 3, chapter 209 of the Public Statutes, relating to exemptions from serving as jurors, having considered the same, report the same with the following resolution :

Resolved, That it ought to pass in a new draft.

The report was accepted, and the bill in its new draft read a first time and ordered to a second reading.

Mr. Sawyer of Milford, for the Committee on Banks, to whom was referred An act to incorporate the Derry Savings Bank of Derry, having considered the same, report the same with the following resolution :

Resolved, That the bill ought to pass in new draft.

The report was accepted, and the bill in its new draft read a first time and ordered to a second reading.

Mr. Bunton, A. S., of Manchester, for the Committee on

Banks, to whom was referred An act amending the charter of the Portsmouth Savings Bank, having considered the same, report the same with the following resolution :

Resolved, That the bill ought to pass in new draft.

The report was accepted, and the bill in its new draft read a first time and ordered to a second reading.

Mr. Abbott of Ossipee, for the Committee on Elections, to whom was referred An act to legalize the town meetings in Dorchester for the years 1896, 1897, 1898, 1899, and 1900, having considered the same, report the same with the following resolution :

Resolved, That the bill ought to pass.

The report was accepted, and the bill laid upon the table to be printed.   On motion of Mr. Taggart of Manchester, the rules were suspended and the printing of the bill dispensed with.   The bill was then ordered to a third reading.   On motion of the same gentleman, the rules were further suspended and the bill read a third time and passed and sent to the Senate for concurrence.

Mr. Holt of Lyndeborough, for the Committee on Elections, to whom was referred An act to legalize and confirm the warrant for and the votes and proceedings at the biennial election and meeting in Stratham, held the fourth day of November, 1902, having considered the same, report the same with the following resolution :

Resolved, That the bill ought to pass.

The report was accepted, and the bill laid upon the table to be printed.   On motion of Mr. French of Moultonborough, the rules were suspended and the printing of the bill dispensed with.   The bill was then ordered to a third reading. On motion of the same gentleman, the rules were further suspended and the bill read a third time and passed and sent to the Senate for concurrence.

Mr. Worthley of Hooksett, for the Committee on Elections, to whom was referred An act to legalize the biennial election of the town of Effingham, held November 4, 1902, having considered the same, report the same with the following resolution :

Resolved, That the bill ought to pass.

The report was accepted, and the bill laid upon the table to be printed. On motion of Mr. French of Moultonborough, the rules were suspended and the printing of the bill dispensed with. The bill was then ordered to a third reading. On motion of the same gentleman, the rules were further suspended and the bill read a third time and passed and sent to the Senate for concurrence.

Mr. Andrews of Somersworth, for the Committee on Education, to whom was referred An act to repeal an act of the legislature of 1842, entitled "An act to annex Richard Pickering of Newington to school district No. 1, in Portsmouth," approved June 22, 1842, having considered the same, report the same with the following resolution:

Resolved, That the bill ought to pass.

The report was accepted, and the bill laid upon the table to be printed. On motion of Mr. Badger of Newington, the rules were suspended and the printing of the bill dispensed with. The bill was then ordered to a third reading. On motion of the same gentleman, the rules were further suspended and the bill read a third time and passed and sent to the Senate for concurrence.

Mr. Mitchell of Littleton, for the Committee on Judiciary, to whom was referred An act to exempt from taxation real estate reservations of the Appalachian Mountain Club, having considered the same, report the same with the following amendment:

Strike out the words " or hereafter acquired " in the first line of section 1, and recommend that the bill as amended ought to pass.

The report was accepted, the amendment adopted, and the bill laid upon the table to be printed.

Mr. Trickey of Jackson, for the Committee on Roads, Bridges, and Canals, to whom was referred Joint resolution in favor of placing and maintaining buoys and lights in Lake Winnipesaukee and adjacent waters, having considered the same, report the same with the recommendation that the joint resolution be referred to the Committee on Public Improvements.

The report was accepted, and the joint resolution referred to the Committee on Public Improvements.

Mr. Churchill of Cornish, for the Committee on Public Improvements, to whom was referred An act to provide for the representation of the state of New Hampshire and the exhibition of its products and attractions at the Louisiana Purchase Exposition at St. Louis in 1904, having considered the same, report the same with the following amendment, and the recommendation that the bill as amended ought to pass

In section 4, lines 2 and 3, strike out the words " at a salary not exceeding one hundred dollars per month," and insert the words " with a salary."   And in line 4 insert after the word " and" the words " he shall be allowed," so that said section shall read:

SECT. 4.   The board is authorized to appoint one executive commissioner with a salary, and he shall be allowed expenses of travel actually incurred for such months as the board may deem such services necessary, payable monthly out of the appropriation hereafter made; and said executive commissioner shall be authorized and required to assume and exercise, subject to the supervision of the board, all such powers as may be necessary to secure a creditable display of the interests and attractions of the state at said exposition; he shall be the executive agent of the board and shall devote his whole time to the solicitation, collection, and disposition of objects sent under the authority of the state, and shall aid all persons desiring to make private exhibits.   He shall report to the board at such intervals as the board may direct and hold his office at their pleasure.

The report was accepted, the amendment adopted, and the bill laid upon the table to be printed, and then be referred to the Committee on Appropriations.

BILL FORWARDED.

An act to incorporate the New Hampshire Genealogical Society.

Taken from the table and ordered to a third reading.

On motion of Mr. Ahern of Concord,—

Resolved, That the Honorable Senate be requested to return

to the House of Representatives the following entitled bill:
"An act in amendment of section 15 of chapter 93 of the
Public Statutes, as amended in 1901, relating to scholars."

Mr. Goold of Lebanon moved that the vote whereby the
resolution "inexpedient to legislate," reported by the Committee on Judiciary on the following entitled bill, "An act
to prohibit the pollution of the waters of Blood brook, so
called, in the towns of Lebanon and Plainfield," was adopted,
be reconsidered.

The question being upon the adoption of the motion,

(Discussion ensued.)

On a *viva voce* vote the motion prevailed and the vote was
reconsidered.

The question being upon the adoption of the resolution reported by the committee, Mr. Goold of Lebanon moved that
the bill be recommitted to the Committee on Judiciary.

(Discussion ensued.)

On a *viva voce* vote the motion prevailed and the bill was
recommitted to the Committee on Judiciary.

On motion of Mr. Ahern of Concord, the following entitled
bill, "An act in amendment of section 26, chapter 79 of the
Laws of 1901, for the better protection of gray squirrel," was
taken from the table.

Mr. Ahern withdrew his call for a division.

(Discussion ensued.)

Mr. Hoyt of Sandwich moved that the bill be indefinitely
postponed and on a *viva voce* vote the motion prevailed.

On motion of Mr. Mathes of Dover, at 12.12 the House
adjourned.

AFTERNOON.

The House met at 3 o'clock.

On motion of Mr. Whitcher of Haverhill,—

Resolved, That the vote whereby the use of Representatives'
hall was granted for Tuesday evening, February 10, to the
New Hampshire Library Association for a public meeting, be
rescinded.

On motion of Mr. Whitcher of Haverhill,—

Resolved, That the use of Representatives' hall be granted for Tuesday evening, February 10, to the Committee on Liquor Laws for a public hearing.

On motion of Mr. Remich of Littleton, the House took a recess of 30 minutes.

(After recess.)

THIRD READING.

An act to incorporate the New Hampshire Genealogical Society.

Read a third time and passed and sent to the Senate for concurrence.

MESSAGE FROM THE SENATE.

A message from the Honorable Senate by its clerk announced that the Senate has granted the request of the House of Representatives asking that the following entitled bill be returned: "An act in amendment of section 15 of chapter 93 of the Public Statutes, as amended in 1901, relating to scholars."

Mr. Bussell of Nashua moved that the vote whereby the resolution "inexpedient to legislate," reported by the Committee on Judiciary on the following entitled bill, "An act authorizing the city of Nashua to issue bonds," was adopted, be reconsidered.

On a *viva voce* vote the motion prevailed.

On motion of Mr. Bussell of Nashua, the bill was recommitted to the Committee on Judiciary.

On motion of Mr. Hoyt of Sandwich, the following entitled bill, "An act in amendment of the charter of the city of Laconia," was recalled from the Committee on Judiciary and referred to a special committee consisting of the delegation from the city of Laconia.

COMMITTEE REPORTS.

On motion of Mr. Remich of Littleton, the rules were suspended and business in order to-morrow morning at 11 o'clock was made in order at the present time.

15

Mr. Churchill of Cornish, for the Committee on Forestry, to whom was referred An act to provide a nursery for the growth and distribution of forest seedling trees within the state at cost, having considered the same, report the same with the following resolution :

Resolved, That the bill ought to pass.

Mr. Drake of Freedom, for the Committee on Public Improvements, to whom was referred Joint resolution for lighting the lighthouse on Loon island in Sunapee lake, repairing the cable connected therewith, improving the light service, placing and maintaining buoys on said lake, and removing obstructions to navigation in said lake, having considered the same, report the same with the following resolution :

Resolved, That the joint resolution ought to pass.

Mr. Crocker of Rochester, for the Committee on Normal School, to whom was referred An act to amend chapter 95 of the Public Statutes, relating to Normal School, having considered the same, report the same with the following resolution :

Resolved, That the bill ought to pass.

Mr. Foye of Portsmouth, for the Committee on Roads, Bridges, and Canals, to whom was referred Joint resolution relating to a state highway between Massachusetts state line and Fort Point in New Castle, N. H., having considered the same, report the same with the following resolution :

Resolved, That the joint resolution ought to pass.

The reports were severally accepted, and the bills and joint resolutions laid upon the table to be printed, and then referred to the Committee on Appropriations.

Mr. Buckley of Lancaster, for the Committee on Judiciary, to whom was referred An act to provide equitable process after judgment in certain cases, having considered the same, report the same with the following resolution :

Resolved, That it is inexpedient to legislate.

Mr. Bunton, A. S., of Manchester, for the Committee on Banks, to whom was referred An act to incorporate the North Conway Savings Bank at North Conway, having considered the same, report the same with the following resolution :

Resolved, That it is inexpedient to legislate.

Mr. Hamlin of Charlestown, for the Committee on Claims, to whom was referred Joint resolution to reimburse the town of Grantham for quarantine expenses, having considered the same, report the same with the following resolution:

Resolved, That it is inexpedient to legislate.

The reports were severally accepted and the resolutions adopted.

Mr. Woodman of Concord, for the Committee on Judiciary, to whom was referred An act to incorporate the Warren Water and Light Company, having considered the same, report the same with the following resolution:

Resolved, That the object sought cannot be attained under the general law and recommend that the bill be referred to the Committee on Incorporations.

The report was accepted and the bill referred to the Committee on Incorporations.

Mr. Goold of Lebanon, for the Committee on Fisheries and Game, to whom was referred Joint resolution for an appropriation for the construction of a screen across the outlet of Lake Winnisquam at East Tilton, in the county of Belknap, having considered the same, report the same with the following amendment, and the recommendation that the joint resolution as amended ought to pass:

Amend by inserting after the word "appropriated" in the second line of section 1, the words "in addition to the sum appropriated session of 1901," so that said section shall read: "SECTION 1. That the sum of fifteen hundred dollars be, and the same is hereby, appropriated, in addition to the sum appropriated session of 1901, for the purpose of constructing a screen across the outlet of Lake Winnisquam at East Tilton, in the county of Belknap, to prevent the escape from the waters of said lake of salmon and other fish propagated and placed in said lake, said appropriation to be expended, and said screen constructed, during the year 1903, and the work and expenditure under this resolution to be done under the direction and supervision of the fish and game commissioners of the state of New Hampshire, whose bills for expense and cost of construction of said screen are to be audited by the

Governor and Council, and said amount so appropriated to be paid and expended out of any money in the treasury not otherwise expended."

The report was accepted, the amendment adopted, and the joint resolution laid upon the table to be printed and then referred to the Committee on Appropriations.

Mr. Foye of Portsmouth, for the Committee on Roads, Bridges, and Canals, to whom was referred An act in amendment of "An act to provide for the survey, location, and construction of the Jefferson Notch road in Jefferson, Low and Burbank's Grant, Crawford's Purchase, and Bean's Purchase," approved March 22, 1901, having considered the same, report the same with the following resolution :

Resolved, That the bill ought to pass.

The report was accepted and the bill referred to the Committee on Appropriations.

Mr. Woodman of Concord, for the Committee on Judiciary, to whom was referred An act to enable the town of Greenville to acquire, own, and operate an electric power and lighting plant, having considered the same, report the same with the following resolution :

Resolved, That the bill ought to pass.

The report was accepted and the bill laid upon the table to be printed.

Mr. Buckley of Lancaster, for the Committee on Judiciary, to whom was referred An act to authorize the town of Lancaster to acquire property for the protection of its water supply, having considered the same, report the same with the following resolution :

Resolved, That the bill ought to pass.

The report was accepted and the bill laid upon the table to be printed. On motion of Mr. Buckley of Lancaster, the rules were suspended and the printing of the bill dispensed with. The bill was then ordeied to a third reading. On motion of the same gentleman, the rules were further suspended and the bill read a third time and passed and sent to the Senate for concurrence.

Mr. Foye of Portsmouth, for the Committee on Roads, Bridges, and Canals, to whom was referred An act providing for the construction of certain sections of roads and the completion of a line of public highways already inaugurated by the state in the central regions of the White Mountains, having considered the same, report the same in a new draft and recommend the passage of the bill in the new draft.

The report was accepted, and on motion of Mr. Ahern of Concord, the rules were suspended and the bill in its new draft read a first time by its title. It was then ordered to a second reading. On motion of the same gentleman, the rules were further suspended and the bill read a second time by its title. The bill was then laid upon the table to be printed and then referred to the Committee on Appropriations.

Mr. Davenport of Bath, for the Committee on Appropriations, to whom was referred An act in amendment of chapter 23 of the Laws of 1901, entitled "An act to establish a laboratory of hygiene," having considered the same, report the same in a new draft with the following resolution :

Resolved, That the bill in a new draft ought to pass.

The report was accepted and the bill in its new draft read a first time and ordered to a second reading.

Mr. Tallant of Pembroke, for the Special Committee on Apportionment, to whom was referred An act to establish a new apportionment for the assessment of public taxes, having considered the same, report the same with the following resolution :

Resolved, That the bill ought to pass.

The report was accepted and the bill laid upon the table to be printed.

Mr. Buckley of Lancaster, for the Committee on Judiciary, to whom was referred An act to punish embezzlement by executors, administrators, guardians, and trustees, having considered the same, report the same with the following resolution :

Resolved, That the bill be reported in a new draft with the recommendation that it ought to pass.

The report was accepted and the bill in its new draft read a first time and ordered to a second reading.

Mr. Woodman of Concord, for the Committee on Judiciary, to whom was referred An act in amendment of the charter of the Salem Water-Works Company, and legalizing and confirming the acts of said corporation in relation thereto, having considered the same, report the same with the following resolution :

Resolved, That the bill ought to pass.

The report was accepted and the bill laid upon the table to be printed.

Mr. Whittemore of Dover, for the special committee consisting of the Dover delegation, to whom was referred An act in amendment of the charter of the city of Dover, creating a board of street and park commissioners for said city, having considered the same, report the same in a new draft with the following resolution :

Resolved, That the bill in new draft ought to pass.

The report was accepted, and the reading of the bill in its new draft having commenced, on motion of Mr. Whittemore of Dover, the rules were suspended and the bill read a first time by its title.   The bill was then ordered to a second reading.

Mr. Converse of Lyme, for the Committee on Engrossed Bills, reported that they had examined bills with the following titles and found them correctly engrossed :

An act to amend chapter 69 of the Laws of 1901, entitled "An act to protect the Ammonoosuc river in Carroll, Bethlehem, Littleton, Lisbon, and Bath, and its tributaries from pollution by sawdust and other waste."

An act in relation to the salary of the state reporter.

The report was accepted.

On motion of Mr. Emerson of Concord, at 4.03 the House adjourned.

THURSDAY, FEBRUARY 5, 1903.

The House met at 11 o'clock.

Prayer was offered by the chaplain.

LEAVE OF ABSENCE.

Mr. Bragg of Errol was granted leave of absence until Monday, February 16, on account of important business.

PETITIONS PRESENTED AND REFERRED.

By Mr. Moors of Marlborough, Petition of the Weare Monthly Meeting of Friends, asking for the maintenance of the prohibitory law.

By Mr. Moors of Marlborough, Petition of the Sullivan County Association of Congregational Ministers, not to legalize the sale of intoxicating liquors as a beverage.

By Mr. Moors of Marlborough, Petition of the Pittsfield Free Baptist Church, Pittsfield, N. H., for the maintenance of the prohibitory law with amendments for better enforcement.

By Mr. Moors of Marlborough, Petition of the New Hampshire Christian Endeavor Union, representing 454 societies, against legalized saloons under any form of license.

By Mr. Cutler of Jaffrey, Petition of the New Hampshire Evangelical Sunday-school Association, representing 50,000, against licensed saloons.

By Mr. Cutler of Jaffrey, Petition of the New Hampshire Baptist Convention, representing 87 churches and 9,413 members, praying for the maintenance of the prohibitory law with necessary amendments to facilitate its better enforcement.

By Mr. Cutler of Jaffrey, Petition of the First Baptist Church, enrollment 580, against any form of legalized saloons.

By Mr. Cutler of Jaffrey, Petition of the State New Hampshire Woman's Christian Temperance Union and 84 local unions, representing 2,900 members, asking for the maintenance of the prohibitory law with amendments thereto to aid in its better enforcement.

By Mr. Kellom of Winchester, Petition of the Woman's Christian Temperance Union of Winchester, N. H., to retain the present prohibitory law with amendments.

Severally to the Committee on Liquor Laws.

COMMITTEE REPORTS.

Mr. Woodman of Concord, for the Committee on Judiciary, to whom was referred An act in amendment of chapter 82 of the Laws of 1897, having considered the same, report the same with the following resolution :

Resolved, That the bill ought to pass.

Mr. Cavanaugh of Manchester, for the Committee on Judiciary, to whom was referred An act in addition to chapter 58 of the Public Statutes, relating to the appraisal of taxable real estate, having considered the same, report the same with the following resolution:

Resolved, That the bill ought to pass.

Mr. Demers of Somersworth, for the Committee on Revision of Statutes, to whom was referred An act in amendment of section 1, chapter 83 of the Public Statutes, entitled " Settlement of paupers," having considered the same, report the same with the following resolution:

Resolved, That the bill ought to pass.

Mr. Demers of Somersworth, for the Committee on Revision of Statutes, to whom was referred An act in amendment of section 1, chapter 31 of the Laws of 1897, entitled "An act in amendment of section 6 of chapter 83 of the Public Statutes, in relation to the settlement of paupers," having considered the same, report the same with the following resolution:

Resolved, That the bill ought to pass.

Mr. Mitchell of Littleton, for the Committee on Judiciary, to whom was referred An act to provide for taking depositions outside this state, and depositions within this state for use in other states, having considered the same, report the same with the following resolution:

Resolved, That the bill ought to pass.

The reports were severally accepted and the bills laid upon the table to be printed.

Mr. Sheehan of Manchester, for the Committee on Industrial School, to whom was referred Joint resolution appropriating nine thousand dollars for additions and repairs to the Industrial School, having considered the same, report the same with the following resolution:

Resolved, That it ought to pass.

Mr. Buckley of Lancaster, for the Committee on Judiciary, to whom was referred An act in amendment of section 1, chapter 67, Laws of 1899, relating to expenses of judges of the supreme court, having considered the same, report the same with the following resolution:

Resolved, That the bill ought to pass.

The reports were severally accepted and the bill and joint resolution laid upon the table to be printed and then referred to the Committee on Appropriations.

Mr. Hoyt of Sandwich, for the Committee on Agriculture, to whom was referred An act to authorize the state board of agriculture to appoint a state nursery inspector and to provide for the protection of trees and shrubs from injurious insects and diseases, having considered the same, report the same with the following amendment and with the recommendation that the bill as amended ought to pass:

Amend section 6 by adding at the close of said section the words, "The cost of said inspection shall not exceed $300 annually."

The report was accepted, the amendment adopted, and the bill laid upon the table to be printed. On motion of Mr Hoyt of Sandwich, the rules were suspended and the printing of the bill dispensed with. The bill was then referred to the Committee on Appropriations.

Mr. Cavanaugh of Manchester, for the Committee on Judiciary, to whom was referred An act authorizing the town of Hudson to construct water-works and establish an electric light plant, having considered the same, report the same with the following resolution:

Resolved, That the bill ought to pass.

The report was accepted and the bill laid upon the table to be printed. On motion of Mr. Connell of Hudson, the rules were suspended and the printing of the bill dispensed with. The bill was then ordered to a third reading. On motion of the same gentleman, the rules were further suspended and the bill read a third time and passed and sent to the Senate for concurrence.

Mr. Hoyt of Sandwich, for the Committee on Agriculture, to whom was referred An act to establish a bounty on foxes, having considered the same, report the same with the following resolution:

Resolved, That it is inexpedient to legislate.

The report was accepted and the resolution adopted.

Mr. Nason of Dover, for the Committee on Judiciary, to whom was referred An act to amend the charter of the city of

Portsmouth, in relation to street commissioner, having considered the same, report the same with the following resolution :

Resolved, That the bill be referred to a special committee consisting of the Portsmouth delegation.

The report was accepted and the bill referred to a special committee consisting of the delegation from the city of Portsmouth.

Mr. Scammon of Exeter, for the Committee on Judiciary, to whom was referred An act in relation to the salary of the judge of probate for Merrimack county, having considered the same, report the same with the following resolution :

Resolved, That the bill be reported in a new draft and recommend that the bill in new draft ought to pass.

The report was accepted and the bill in its new draft read a first time and ordered to a second reading.

Mr. Nason of Dover, for the Committee on Judiciary, to whom was referred An act to amend the charter of the city of Portsmouth, in relation to the assessors of taxes, having considered the same, report the same with the following resolution :

Resolved, That the bill be referred to a special committee consisting of the Portsmouth delegation.

The report was accepted and the bill referred to a special committee consisting of the delegation from the city of Portsmouth.

Mr. Buckley of Lancaster, for the Committee on Judiciary, to whom was referred An act to establish water-works in Enfield village fire district in the town of Enfield, having considered the same, report the same with the following resolution :

Resolved, That the bill be reported in a new draft and recommend that the bill in new draft ought to pass.

The report was accepted, and on motion of Mr. Remich of Littleton, the rules were suspended and the bill in its new draft read a first time by its title and ordered to a second reading. On motion of the same gentleman, the rules were suspended and the bill read a second time by its title and laid upon the table to be printed. On motion of the same gentleman, the rules were further suspended and the printing of the bill dispensed with. The bill was then ordered to a third reading. On motion of the same gentleman, the rules were suspended and the bill read a third time by its title and passed and sent to the Senate for concurrence.

Mr. French of Moultonborough, for the Committee on Railroads, to whom was referred An act to amend section 1 of chapter 64 of the Public Statutes, having considered the same, report the same with the following resolution:

Resolved, That it be indefinitely postponed.

The report was accepted and the resolution adopted.

Mr. Scammon of Exeter, for the Committee on Judiciary, to whom was referred An act relating to the salary of the judge of probate for the county of Rockingham, having considered the same, report the same with the following resolution:

Resolved, That the bill be reported in a new draft and recommend that the bill in new draft ought to pass.

The report was accepted and the bill in its new draft read a first time and ordered to a second reading.

Mr. Kimball of Laconia, for the Committee on Railroads, to whom was referred An act in amendment of "An act to incorporate the North Conway & Mount Kearsarge Railroad," passed June session, 1883, and all subsequent acts relating to the same, having considered the same, report the same with the following resolution:

Resolved, That it ought to pass.

The report was accepted and the bill laid upon the table to be printed. On motion of Mr. French of Moultonborough, the rules were suspended and the printing of the bill dispensed with. The bill was then ordered to a third reading. On motion of the same gentleman, the rules were further suspended and the bill read a third time and passed and sent to the Senate for concurrence.

Mr. Martin of Colebrook, for the Committee on Railroads, to whom was referred An act to incorporate the Portsmouth & Newcastle Street Railway Company, having considered the same, report the same with the following amendments and with the recommendation that said bill as amended ought to pass:

Amend section 1 by inserting after the word " through " in the eleventh line of said section the following : " through Pleasant street, Marcy street and Newcastle avenue in."

Further amend section 1 by striking out the words " some convenient point" in the twelfth and thirteenth lines of said section, and insert in place thereof the words, " a point in the highway near Green's restaurant." Amend section 2 by striking out all after the word " provisions " in line 11 of said section, and adding after the said word " provisions" the words " of the general laws."

So that said sections 1 and 2 as amended will read as follows :

SECTION 1. That Edwin D. Rand, Albert W. Hanscom, Thaddeus Talton, Howard M. Curtis, and James W. Pridham, their associates, successors, and assigns, are hereby made a corporation by the name of " Portsmouth and Newcastle Street Railway Company," with power to construct, maintain, and operate a railway with convenient branches, connections, sidings, poles, wires, turnouts, and switches from some convenient point in the town of Portsmouth, beginning at a spike in the ground at the track of the Portsmouth Electric Railway on Market square, thence in and through Pleasant street, Marcy street, and Newcastle avenue in said city of Portsmouth and through and in the town of Newcastle to a point in the highway near Green's restaurant in the town of Newcastle ; and in said towns said street railway may be constructed upon and over such highways and lands as may be necessary ; and may acquire by purchase or otherwise any property of bridge corporations or others met with in its course, and may carry on the business of said corporation, or others, as may be needful for the operation of the said railway ; and may also construct and maintain suitable buildings, dams, water and other motors, engines, electric and other machinery for the generation of electricity or other motive power, except steam, for the operation of said railway.

SECT. 2. The capital stock of said corporation shall not exceed seventy-five thousand dollars, and shall be divided into shares of a par value of one hundred dollars each ; but said company may issue capital stock and bonds to such an amount only as may be necessary to construct and equip said railway, including the amount required to provide motive power for the operation thereof; and its bonded and other indebtedness shall at no time exceed the amount of its capital stock actually paid in. The amount of capital stock and bonds to be so issued from time to time shall be determined and issued in accordance with the provisions of the general laws.

The report was accepted, the amendments adopted, and the bill laid upon the table to be printed. On motion of Mr. French of Moultonborough, the rules were suspended and the printing of the bill dispensed with. The bill was then ordered to a third reading. On motion of the same gentleman, the rules were further suspended and the bill read a third time and passed and sent to the Senate for concurrence.

Mr. Morgan of Manchester, for the Committee on Railroads, to whom was referred An act to incorporate the Uncanoonuc Incline Railway and Development Company, having considered the same, report the same with the following amendments, and with the recommendation that said bill, as amended, ought to pass:

Amend section 1 of said bill by striking out the words "lighting purposes" in the sixteenth line of said section and inserting in place thereof the words: "for furnishing lights on its own premises only; all said power and lights are to be used in said town of Goffstown."

Amend section 13 of said bill by adding after the last word thereof the following: "but shall be void and inoperative as to all parts of said railway not constructed and ready for operation within two years from its passage."

The report was accepted, the amendments adopted, and the bill laid upon the table to be printed. Mr. French of Moultonborough moved that the rules be suspended and the printing of the bill dispensed with.

The question being upon the adoption of the motion,

(Discussion ensued.)

Mr. French withdrew his motion and the bill was laid upon the table to be printed.

Mr. French of Moultonborough, for the Committee on Rail-

roads, to whom was referred An act to incorporate the Littleton, Franconia & Bethlehem Electric Railroad Company,
having considered the same, report the same with the following amendments, and with the recommendation that said bill,
as amended, ought to pass :

Amend section 1 by striking out after the word " Littleton "
in the thirteenth line thereof the following words : " to the top
of Mt. Agassiz in the town of Bethlehem, and through the village of Bethlehem to a point near and opposite the Maplewood
farm buildings in said Bethlehem, with a branch railway from
some convenient point in Bethlehem, between Littleton and
the village of Bethlehem, on the line of said railway."

Further amend the same section by inserting after the words
" in Franconia " in the twentieth line of said section the following words : " provided that said railway shall not approach
nearer to Bethlehem village than Edward E. Bishop's house in
said Bethlehem, except upon the following conditions : Said
railway corporation may construct, maintain, and operate a
branch railway from some convenient point on its line aforesaid, to the top of Mt. Agassiz in the town of Bethlehem, and
through the village of Bethlehem to a point near and opposite the Maplewood farm buildings in said Bethlehem, *provided*
that said town of Bethlehem, at a meeting of its legal voters,
the warrant for which shall contain a proper article upon this
subject, shall vote to give its consent to the construction, maintenance and operation of such branch railway, and not otherwise."

So that said section 1 as amended shall read as follows :

SECTION 1. Oscar C. Hatch, William H. Mitchell, Albert
S. Batchellor, James W. Remick, Henry F. Green, Charles
F. Eastman, Frank P. Bond, Fred H. English, Frederick G.
Chutter, James H. Bailey, Elmore Whipple, Wilbur Parker,
Daniel C. Remich, Irving C. Renfrew, George W. McGregor,
George A. Edson, William J. Beattie, Edward H. Gould,
Robert Tuttle, Cortes F. Nutting, George F. Abbott, Irving
B. Andrews, George N. Turner, and Frank H. Abbott, their
associates, successors, and assigns, are hereby made a body
corporate by the name of the Littleton, Franconia and Bethle-
hem Street Railway, with the power to construct, maintain,

and operate over and across such lands as may be necessary
and in such public highways as may be necessary, a railway
with convenient single or double tracks, spur tracks, sidings,
turnouts and switches from some convenient point in the town
of Littleton, through Bethlehem, Lisbon, and Franconia, to
the Lafayette House in Franconia, provided that said railway
shall not approach nearer to Bethlehem village than Edward
E. Bishop's house in said Bethlehem, except upon the following conditions: Said railway corporation may construct,
maintain, and operate a branch railway from some convenient
point on its line aforesaid, to the top of Mt. Agassiz in the
town of Bethlehem, and through the village of Bethlehem, to
a point near and opposite the Maplewood farm buildings in
said Bethlehem, *provided* that said town of Bethlehem, at a
meeting of its legal voters, the warrant for which shall contain a proper article upon the subject, shall vote to give its
consent to the construction, maintenance, and operation of
such branch railway, and not otherwise, and may also acquire,
purchase, construct, and maintain suitable buildings, dams,
water-powers, water-motors, engines, electric, and other machinery, or electric or steam plants for the generation of electricity or other motive power, except steam, for the operation
of said railway, with full power to furnish any of said towns,
or their citizens, now without electric lighting plants, with
electric lights, heat, or power, and to furnish any of said towns,
or their citizens now having electric light plants, with lights,
heat, and power, provided said corporation shall hereafter acquire such plant, or plants, by agreement with their owners.

Amend section 12 by adding after the last word of said section the following words: " but shall be void and inoperative
as to all parts of said railway not constructed and ready for
operation within two years from its passage; " so that said
section as amended shall read as follows:

SECT. 12. This act shall take effect upon its passage, but
shall be void and inoperative as to all parts of said railway
not constructed and ready for operation within two years from
its passage.

. The report was accepted, the amendments adopted, and the
bill laid upon the table to be printed. On motion of Mr.

French of Moultonborough, the rules were suspended and the printing of the bill dispensed with. The bill was then ordered to a third reading. On motion of the same gentleman, the rules were further suspended and the bill read a third time and passed and sent to the Senate for concurrence.

Mr. Willis of Concord, for the Committee on Engrossed Bills, reported that they had examined a bill with the following title and found it correctly engrossed:

An act providing a seal for the state board of agriculture.

Mr. Goss of Berlin, for the Committee on Judiciary, reported the following entitled bill, "An act relative to the salary for the register of probate for Coös county," with the recommendation that the bill ought to pass.

Mr. Scammon of Exeter, for the Committee on Judiciary, reported the following entitled bill, "An act in relation to the town of Newmarket and the Newmarket water-works," with the recommendation that the bill ought to pass.

Mr. Wallace of Rochester, for the Committee on Appropriations, reported the following joint resolution, " Joint resolution in favor of the Granite State Deaf Mute Mission," with the recommendation that the joint resolution ought to pass.

Mr. Foye of Portsmouth, for the Committee on Roads, Bridges, and Canals, reported the following joint resolution, " Joint resolution in favor of an appropriation for the repair of the Mayhue turnpike and Point road, so called, in the town of Bridgewater," with the recommendation that the joint resolution ought to pass.

Mr. Goold of Lebanon, for the Committee on Fisheries and Game, reported the following entitled bill, "An act to change the name of Station lake in the town of Springfield," with the recommendation that the bill ought to pass.

Mr. Donahue of Manchester, for the Committee on Insurance, reported the following entitled bill, "An act relating to domestic insurance companies," with the recommendation that the bill ought to pass.

The reports were severally accepted and the bills and joint resolutions read a first time and ordered to a second reading.

SECOND READINGS.

An act in amendment of section 3, chapter 209 of the Public Statutes, relating to exemptions from serving as jurors.

An act to punish embezzlement by executors, administrators, guardians, and trustees.

An act in amendment of chapter 23 of the Laws of 1901, entitled "An act to establish a laboratory of hygiene."

Severally read a second time and laid upon the table to be printed.

An act amending the charter of the Portsmouth Savings Bank.

Read a second time and laid upon the table to be printed. Mr. Yeaton of Portsmouth moved that the rules be suspended and the printing dispensed with and the bill put upon its third reading and final passage at the present time.

The question being upon the adoption of the motion,

(Discussion ensued.)

Mr. Yeaton withdrew his motion and the bill was laid upon the table to be printed.

An act to incorporate the Derry Savings Bank of Derry.

Before the second reading began, Mr. Shute of Derry moved that the bill be recommitted to the Committee on Banks. On a *viva voce* vote the motion did not prevail, and the bill was read a second time and laid upon the table to be printed.

An act in amendment of the charter of the city of Dover, creating a board of street and park commissioners for said city.

The second reading having commenced, on motion of Mr. Whittemore of Dover, the rules were suspended and the bill read a second time by its title and laid upon the table to be printed. On motion of the same gentleman, the rules were suspended and the printing of the bill was dispensed with. The bill was then ordered to a third reading. On motion of the same gentleman, the rules were further suspended and the bill read a third time and passed and sent to the Senate for concurrence.

16

On motion of Mr. Ahern of Concord,—

Resolved, That the following entitled bill, "An act severing the homestead of David A. Welch from the town district of the city of Concord and annexing the same to the Union School District of said Concord," be recalled from the Committee on Education and referred to a special committee consisting of the delegation from the city of Concord.

On motion of Mr. Cavanaugh of Manchester,—

Resolved, That the following entitled bill, "An act in amendment of section 20 of chapter 27 of the Public Statutes, entitled ' County commissioners,' " be recalled from the Committee on County Affairs and referred to a special committee consisting of the delegation from Hillsborough county.

MESSAGE FROM THE SENATE.

A message from the Honorable Senate, by its clerk, announced that the Senate has passed bills with the following titles, in the passage of which it asks the concurrence of the House of Representatives:

An act in amendment of chapter 171 of the Public Statutes, relating to life insurance.

Read a first and second time and referred to the Committee on Insurance.

An act in amendment of chapter 192 of the Public Statutes, relating to insolvent estates.

Read a first and second time and referred to the Committee on Revision of Statutes.

The message also announced that the Senate concurs with the House of Representatives in the passage of the following entitled bills:

An act in relation to the salary of the State Reporter.

An act providing a seal for the State Board of Agriculture.

An act in amendment of section 11, chapter 79 of the Session Laws of 1901, relating to the fish and game commissioners.

An act in amendment of the charter of the city of Concord, authorizing the establishment of precincts within said city for the collection of garbage.

An act to authorize the city of Portsmouth to raise money and issue bonds for a new high schoolhouse.

An act to authorize the city of Concord to appropriate money for the celebration of its semi-centennial.

Mr. Center of Litchfield offered the following resolution :

Resolved, That the sergeant-at-arms be instructed to procure printed copies of the rules of the House and distribute the same to the members immediately.

The question being upon the adoption of the resolution,

(Discussion ensued.)

On motion of Mr. French of Moultonborough, the resolution was laid upon the table.

On motion of Mr. Donagan of Concord, at 12.22 the House adjourned.

AFTERNOON.

The House met at 3 o'clock.

On motion of Mr. French of Moultonborough, the rules were suspended and reports of committees and bills for second reading in order for to-morrow morning at 11 o'clock were made in order at this time.

COMMITTEE REPORTS.

Mr. Woodman of Concord, for the Committee on Judiciary, to whom was referred An act to provide, in common with the state of Vermont, for the acquisition, building, and maintenance of free bridges across the Connecticut river, having considered the same, report the same with the following resolution :

Resolved, That the bill ought to pass.

Mr. Hamlin of Charlestown, for the Committee on Claims, to whom was referred Joint resolution in favor of John M. Stanyan for soldier's pay and bounty, having considered the same, report the same with the following resolution

Resolved, That the joint resolution ought to pass.

The reports were severally accepted and the bill and joint resolution laid upon the table to be printed and then referred to the Committee on Appropriations.

Mr. Demers of Somersworth, for the Committee on Revision of Statutes, to whom was referred An act to amend section 1 of chapter 21 of the Laws of 1895, entitled "An act to amend section 6 of chapter 184 of the Public Statutes, entitled ' Times and places of holding courts of probate,'" having considered the same, report the same with the following resolution :

Resolved, That it is inexpedient to legislate.

Mr. Demers of Somersworth, for the Committee on Revision of Statutes, to whom was referred An act in amendment of chapter 262 of the Public Statutes, relating to coroners and coroners' inquests, having considered the same, report the same with the following resolution :

Resolved, That it is inexpedient to legislate.

The reports were severally accepted and the resolutions adopted.

Mr. Demers of Somersworth, for the Committee on Revision of Statutes, to whom was referred An act in amendment of section 27, chapter 154 of the Public Statutes, relating to the calling of proprietors' meetings, having considered the same, report the same with the following resolution :

Resolved, That the bill ought to pass.

Mr. Nelson of Portsmouth, for the Committee on Fisheries and Game, to whom was referred An act to provide for a bounty on hedgehogs, having considered the same, report the same with the following resolution :

Resolved, That the bill ought to pass.

The reports were severally accepted and the bills laid upon the table to be printed.

SECOND READINGS.

An act relating to domestic insurance companies.

Joint resolution in favor of the Granite State Deaf Mute Mission.

An act in relation to the salary of the judge of probate for Merrimack county.

An act relative to the salary of the register of probate for Coös county.

Joint resolution in favor of an appropriation for the repair of the Mayhue turnpike and Point road, so called, in the town of Bridgewater.

An act to change the name of Station lake in the town of Springfield.

Severally read a second time and laid upon the table to be printed.

An act in relation to the town of Newmarket and the Newmarket water-works.

Read a second time and laid upon the table to be printed. On motion of Mr. Scammon of Exeter, the rules were suspended and the printing dispensed with. The bill was then ordered to a third reading. On motion of the same gentleman, the rules were further suspended and the bill read a third time and passed and sent to the Senate for concurrence.

On motion of Mr. Hill, E. J., of Concord,—

Resolved, That the following entitled bill, "An act amending the charter of the Portsmouth Savings Bank," be recalled from the printer and recommitted to the Committee on Banks for a hearing.

On motion of Mr. Ahern of Concord,—

Resolved, That when the House adjourns this afternoon it be to meet at 9.30 o'clock Friday morning, and when it adjourns Friday morning it be to meet at 8 o'clock Monday evening.

MESSAGE FROM THE SENATE.

A message from the Honorable Senate, by its clerk, announced that the Senate concurs with the House of Representatives in the passage of the following entitled bills:

An act relating to salary of associate justice of police court of Nashua, in case of vacancy in office of justice.

An act to amend chapter 79 of the Laws of 1899, entitled "An act to amend chapter 184 of the Public Statutes, relating to the times and places of holding courts of probate within and for the county of Grafton."

An act reviving and continuing the charter of the Warner and Kearsarge Road Company, and amendments to said charter.

An act to amend chapter 183 of the Session Laws of 1897, entitled "An act to authorize the village fire precinct of Wolfeborough to construct and maintain an electric plant."

The message also announced that the Senate concurs with the House of Representatives in the passage of the following joint resolution :

Joint resolution appropriating money to be expended for a monument at Vicksburg, Miss.

The message further announced that the Senate has passed a bill with the following title, in the passage of which it asks the concurrence of the House of Representatives :

An act to revive, renew, and amend the charter of the Knights of Pythias Building Association of Manchester.

Read a first and second time and referred to the Committee on Judiciary.

On motion of Mr. Burnell of Conway, at 3.20 the House adjourned.

FRIDAY, FEBRUARY 6, 1903.

The House met at 9.30 o'clock, according to adjournment, being called to order by Mr. William J. Ahern of Concord, and the following communication was read by the clerk :

CONCORD, February 5, 1903.

Mr. William J. Ahern, Concord, N. H.

DEAR SIR : Will you kindly preside at the morning session of the House on Friday, February 6, 1903, as I shall be unable to be present?

Yours truly,

HARRY M. CHENEY,

Speaker.

SECOND READING.

An act relating to the salary of the judge of probate for the county of Rockingham.

Read a second time and laid upon the table to be printed.

On motion of Mr. Babcock of Whitefield, at 9.32 the House adjourned.

MONDAY, FEBRUARY 9, 1903.

The House met at 8 o'clock in the evening, according to adjournment, being called to order by Mr. James E. French of Moultonborough, and the following communication was read by the clerk:

CONCORD, February 9, 1903.

Mr. James E. French, Moultonborough, N. H.

DEAR SIR: Will you kindly preside at the session of the House to-night, as I shall not be present?

Yours truly,

HARRY M. CHENEY,
Speaker.

On motion of Mr. Pollard of Tamworth, at 8.01 the House adjourned.

TUESDAY, FEBRUARY 10, 1903.

The House met at 11 o'clock.

Prayer was offered by the chaplain.

LEAVE OF ABSENCE.

Mr. Morin of Franklin was granted leave of absence for a week on account of sickness in his family.

COMMITTEE REPORT.

Mr. Willis of Concord, for the Committee on Engrossed Bills, reported that they had examined bills with the following titles and a joint resolution and found them correctly engrossed:

An act to authorize the city of Concord to appropriate money for the celebration of its semi-centennial.

An act to authorize the city of Portsmouth to raise money and issue bonds for a new high schoolhouse.

An act in amendment of the charter of the city of Concord, authorizing the establishment of precincts within said city for the collecting of garbage.

An act in amendment of section 11, chapter 79 of the Session Laws of 1901, relating to the fish and game commissioners.

An act to amend "An act to establish a corporation by the name of trustees of the N. H. Conference Seminary and the N. H. Female College," approved December 29, 1852, and other acts amending the same.

An act to amend chapter 183 of Session Laws of 1897, entitled "An act to authorize the village fire precinct of Wolfeborough to construct and maintain an electric plant."

An act relating to salary of associate justice of police court of Nashua, in case of vacancy in office of justice.

An act to amend chapter 79 of the Laws of 1899, entitled "An act to amend chapter 184 of the Public Statutes, relating to the times and places of holding courts of probate within and for the county of Grafton."

An act reviving and continuing the charter of the Warner & Kearsarge Road Company, and amendments to said charter.

Joint resolution appropriating money to be expended for a monument at Vicksburg, Miss.

BILLS FORWARDED.

An act to incorporate the Uncanoonuc Incline Railway and Development Company.

Taken from the table and on motion of Mr. Eaton of Goffstown, recommitted to the Committee on Railroads.

An act to exempt from taxation real estate reservations of the Appalachian Mountain Club.

Taken from the table. Mr. Hoyt of Sandwich offered the following amendment:

Amend section 1 by adding at the close of said section the following words: "when a majority of the legal voters of the town where said real estate is located shall so vote at any annual March meeting."

The question being upon the adoption of the amendment,

(Discussion ensued.)

On motion of Mr. Remich of Littleton, the bill and amendment were laid upon the table.

Joint resolution in favor of an appropriation for the repair of the Mayhue turnpike and Point road, so called, in the town of Bridgewater.

Taken from the table and referred to the Committee on Appropriations.

An act to amend chapter 96 of the Session Laws of 1901, relating to high schools.

Taken from the table and on motion of Mr. Fox of Marlow, recommitted to the Committee on Education.

An act in amendment of section 1, chapter 31 of the Laws of 1897, entitled "An act in amendment of section 6 of chapter 83 of the Public Statutes, in relation to the settlement of paupers."

Taken from the table and on motion of Mr. Ahern of Concord, laid upon the table.

An act amending chapter 93 of the Public Statutes, in relation to school boards.

An act in amendment of section 3, chapter 209 of the Public Statutes, relating to exemptions from serving as jurors.

An act in amendment of section 27, chapter 154 of the Public Statutes, relating to the calling of proprietors' meetings.

An act in amendment of chapter 82 of the Laws of 1897.

An act to provide for taking depositions outside this state and depositions within this state for use in other states.

An act in amendment of the charter of the Salem Water-Works Company, and legalizing and confirming the acts of said corporation in relation thereto.

An act in amendment of section 4 of chapter 206 of the Laws of 1897, being "An act to incorporate the Bethlehem Electric Light Company."

An act to incorporate the Derry Savings Bank of Derry.

An act to enable the town of Greenville to acquire, own, and operate an electric power and lighting plant.

An act to establish a new apportionment for the assessment of public taxes.

An act in relation to milk tickets.

Severally taken from the table and ordered to a third reading.

An act in amendment of section 1, chapter 83 of the Public Statutes, entitled " Settlement of paupers."

Taken from the table and on motion of Mr. Ahern of Concord, laid upon the table.

On motion of Mr. Scammon of Exeter, at 11.18 the House adjourned.

AFTERNOON.

The House met at 3 o'clock.

LEAVE OF ABSENCE.

Mr. March of Mason was granted leave of absence for two weeks on account of serious illness.

THIRD READINGS.

An act in amendment of chapter 82 of the Laws of 1897.

Read a third time and passed.   On motion of Mr. Scammon of Exeter, the title was amended by substituting therefor "An act in amendment of chapter 82 of the Laws of 1897, concerning the preservation and inspection of ballots."   The bill was then sent to the Senate for concurrence.

An act to establish a new apportionment for the assessment of public taxes.

The third reading being in order, Mr. Ahern of Concord moved that the rules be suspended and the bill read a third time by its title.

The question being upon the adoption of the motion,

(Discussion ensued.)

On a *viva voce* vote the motion prevailed and the bill was read a third time by its title and passed and sent to the Senate for concurrence.

An act in amendment of section 3, chapter 209 of the Public Statutes, relating to exemptions from serving as jurors.

An act in amendment of section 27, chapter 154 of the Public Statutes, relating to the calling of proprietors' meetings.

An act to provide for taking depositions outside this state and depositions within this state for use in other states.

An act to incorporate the Derry Savings Bank of Derry.

An act to enable the town of Greenville to acquire, own, and operate an electric power and lighting plant.

An act amending chapter 92 of the Public Statutes, in relation to school boards.

An act in amendment of section 4 of chapter 206 of the Laws of 1897, being "An act to incorporate the Bethlehem Electric Light Company."

Severally read a third time and passed and sent to the Senate for concurrence.

An act in amendment of the charter of the Salem Water-Works Company, and legalizing and confirming the acts of said corporation in relation thereto.

Read a third time and passed and sent to the secretary of state to be engrossed.

An act in relation to milk tickets.

Read a third time.

The question being,

Shall the bill pass?

On motion of Mr. Ahern of Concord, the bill was laid upon the table.

On motion of Mr. Jones of New Ipswich,—

Resolved, That the House extend its sympathies to Mr. Benjamin F. March of Mason, one of the members, now unable to be present, on account of sickness and a surgical operation recently performed, which revealed an incurable disease.

On motion of Mr. Hoyt of Sandwich,—

Resolved, That the following entitled bill, "An act to exempt from taxation real estate reservations of the Appalachian Mountain Club," be taken from the table and made the special order for Wednesday afternoon, February 11, at 3 o'clock.

MESSAGE FROM THE SENATE.

A message from the Honorable Senate, by its clerk, announced that the Senate concurs with the House of Representatives in the passage of the following entitled bills and joint resolutions:

An act authorizing the city of Dover to exempt from taxation the property of the Hayes hospital.

An act in amendment of sections 1, 3, and 4 of chapter 72 of the Public Statutes, relating to the discontinuance of highways.

An act to amend chapter 179 of the Public Statutes, relating to guardians of insane persons and spendthrifts.

An act in amendment of the charter of the Colby Academy, providing for filling vacancies and election of members.

An act in amendment of the charter of the city of Concord, providing for the election of overseers of the poor.

An act to amend the charter of the North Shore Water Company.

An act in amendment of the charter of the Walpole Electric Light and Power Company.

An act in relation to the town of Newmarket and the Newmarket water-works.

The message also announced that the Senate concurs with the House of Representatives in the passage of the following entitled bill with amended title, in the passage of which amendment it asks the concurrence of the House of Representatives :

Amend the title to the bill by inserting after the figures "93" the following, "of the Public Statutes," so that the title as amended shall read

"An act to amend chapter 93 of the Public Statutes, in relation to scholars."

On a *viva voce* vote the amendment to the title was concurred in and the bill sent to the secretary of state to be engrossed.

The message further announced that the Senate has passed a bill with the following title, in the passage of which it asks the concurrence of the House of Representatives :

An act to amend chapter 93, section 15 of the Public Statutes, as amended by chapter 61 of the Session Laws of 1901, relating to scholars.

Read a first and second time and on motion of Mr. Donahue of Manchester, laid upon the table.

The message further announced that the Senate concurs

with the House of Representatives in the passage of the follow-ing entitled bill with amendment, in the passage of which amendment it asks the concurrence of the House of Representatives:

An act to incorporate the Walpole Water and Sewer Co.

Amend section 3, by inserting in the seventh line, after the word "Walpole," the following words, viz.: "excepting that part of said town which lies northerly of a line drawn from the southwest corner of the town of Langdon, near Table Rock, so called, on Fall mountain, to the east end of the present stone arch bridge of the Boston & Maine Railroad Company across the Connecticut River at Bellows Falls, Vermont."

On motion of Mr. French of Moultonborough, the amendment was concurred in and the bill sent to the secretary of state to be engrossed.

Agreeably to a resolution adopted at the morning session, Wednesday, January 21, instructing the clerk to request the secretary of the convention of 1902 to revise the constitution to transmit to the House certified copies of the resolutions of said convention relating to the subjects of passes and trusts, and to report the same to the House, the clerk submitted the following:

CONCORD, N. H., February 3, 1903.

Mr. J. M. Cooper, Clerk of the House of Representatives, Concord, N. H.

SIR: Enclosed herewith please find a certified copy of the amendment to the Constitution, as passed by the recent Convention to Revise the Constitution, pertaining to the regulation and control of trusts. Also a certified copy of the resolution introduced by Mr. Leach of Franklin, on the subject of free passes, and a transcript of my journal relating thereto.

Very respectfully yours,

T. H. MADIGAN, JR.,

Secretary of the Convention to Revise the Constitution.

On motion of Mr. Chandler of Concord, the various resolutions on the subject of free passes, together with the substitute resolution of Mr. Leach of Franklin, were recalled from the committee of the whole.

The question was upon the adoption of the resolution offered by Mr. Leach of Franklin:

Resolved, That the committee report to the convention in favor of the indefinite postponement of all proposed amendments relating to free passes with the recommendation that the legislature consider the subject and enact such legislation, if any, as in their opinion the public good may require.

The yeas and nays were ordered taken upon the question and 221 gentlemen having voted in the affirmative and 101 in the negative, the motion prevailed.

I hereby certify that the above is a true copy of the record.

T. H. MADIGAN, JR.,
Secretary of the Convention of 1902 to Revise the Constitution.

TRUSTS.

Article 82 of the constitution is amended by adding the following: Free and fair competition in the trades and industries is an inherent and essential right of the people and should be protected against all monopolies and conspiracies which tend to hinder or destroy it. The size and functions of all corporations should be so limited and regulated as to prohibit fictitious capitalization, and provision should be made for the supervision and government thereof:

Therefore, all just power possessed by the state is hereby granted to the general court to enact laws to prevent the operations within the state of all persons and associations, and all trusts and corporations, foreign or domestic, and the officers thereof, who endeavor to raise the price of any article of commerce or to destroy free and fair competition in the trades and industries through combination, conspiracy, monopoly, or any other unfair means; to control and regulate the acts of all persons, associations, corporations, trusts and officials doing business within the state; to prevent fictitious capitalization; and to authorize civil and criminal proceedings in respect to all the wrongs herein declared against.

I hereby certify that the above is a true copy of the record.

T. H. MADIGAN, JR.,
Secretary of the Convention of 1902 to Revise the Constitution.

Mr. Small of Rochester moved that the resolutions be referred to the Committee on Judiciary.   The question being upon the adoption of the motion,

(Discussion ensued.)

Mr. French of Moultonborough moved that the resolutions be indefinitely postponed, and on a *viva voce* vote the motion prevailed.   Mr. Small of Rochester called for a division.   A division being had, 145 gentlemen voted in the affirmative and 45 gentlemen voted in the negative and, no quorum having voted, the House stood adjourned.

WEDNESDAY, FEBRUARY 11, 1903.

The House met at 11 o'clock.
Prayer was offered by the chaplain.

LEAVE OF ABSENCE.

Mr. Britton of Wolfeborough was granted leave of absence for the balance of the week on account of the illness of his father.

PETITIONS PRESENTED AND REFERRED.

By Mr. Cutler of Jaffrey, Petition of 814 women of Manchester, outside of the W. C. T. U., many mothers of boys, protesting against the repeal of the prohibitory law.

By Mr. Cutler of Jaffrey, Petition of the Hollis Association of Congregational Ministers, protesting against legalizing the saloon in New Hampshire. .

By Mr. Cutler of Jaffrey, Petition of Rev. J. B. Lemon of Manchester and 110 ministers, petitioning against any law looking toward license or local option.

Severally to the Committee on Liquor Laws.

COMMITTEE REPORTS.

Mr. Bemis of Harrisville, for the Committee on Elections, to whom was referred the petition of Henry K. Mason of Wilmot for a seat in this House, having considered the same, report the same with the following resolution :

Resolved, That the said Henry K. Mason is entitled to the seat in this House now held by Warren F. Langley.

Mr. Taggart of Manchester, for the Committee on Elections, to whom was referred the petition of Herbert N. Davison of Manchester for a seat in this House now held by Park J. Stewart, having considered the same, report the same with the following resolution:

Resolved, That the petitioner has not complied with the law requiring a contestant to give to the sitting member a notice in writing with the reasons for contesting the election, and therefore recommend that the said Davison have leave to withdraw.

Mr. Abbott of Ossipee, for the Committee on Elections, to whom was referred the petition of John W. Weeks of Greenland for a seat in this House, having considered the same, report the same with the following resolution:

Resolved, That the petitioner have leave to withdraw.

Mr. Taggart of Manchester, for the Committee on Elections, to whom was referred the petition of James J. Parks of Carroll for a seat in this House, having considered the same, report the same with the following resolution:

Resolved, That the petitioner have leave to withdraw.

Mr. Donahue of Manchester, for the Committee on Insurance, to whom was referred An act to change the name of the New Hampshire Health and Accident Insurance Company, having considered the same, report the same with the following resolution:

Resolved, That it is inexpedient to legislate, as the subject matter has been covered by a bill introduced by the committee.

Mr. Converse of Lyme, for the Committee on Agriculture, to whom was referred An act in amendment of and in addition to chapter 113 of the Public Statutes, entitled " Diseases of domestic animals," having considered the same, report the same with the following resolution:

Resolved, That it is inexpedient to legislate.

Mr. Hoyt of Sandwich, for the Committee on Agriculture, to whom was referred Joint resolution for an appropriation to compensate for destruction of animals affected with foot and mouth disease, and losses occasioned by said disease, having considered the same, report the same with the following resolution :

Resolved, That it is inexpedient to legislate.

Mr. Goold of Lebanon, for the Committee on Fisheries and Game, to whom was referred An act to prevent and regulate the digging or taking clams in or near Hampton river, having considered the same, report the same with the following resolution :

Resolved, That it is inexpedient to legislate.

Mr. Donahue of Manchester, for the Committee on Insurance, to whom was referred An act relating to domestic life insurance companies, having considered the same, report the same with the following resolution :

Resolved, That it is inexpedient to legislate, as the subject matter has been covered by a bill introduced by the committee.

Mr. Goold of Lebanon, for the Committee on Fisheries and Game, to whom was referred An act to protect striped bass in the waters of the Piscataqua river, having considered the same, report the same with the following resolution :

Resolved, That it is inexpedient to legislate.

Mr. Tallant of Pembroke, for the Committee on Revision of Statutes, to whom was referred An act in amendment of chapter 282 of the Public Statutes, entitled " Common jails and prisoners therein," having considered the same, report the same with the following resolution :

Resolved, That it is inexpedient to legislate.

The reports were severally accepted and the resolutions reported by the committees adopted.

Mr. Woodman of Concord, for the Committee on Judiciary, to whom was referred An act to annex a certain island in Lake Winnipesaukee, now owned and occupied by Geo. W. Sherwell, being one of the group of islands known as the Aunt Dolly islands, to the town of Meredith, having considered the same, report the same with the following resolution :

Resolved, That the bill ought to pass.

Mr. Goold of Lebanon, for the Committee on Fisheries and Game, to whom was referred An act to prevent the pollution of the Piscataqua river and its tributaries, having considered the same, report the same with the following resolution :

17

Resolved, That the bill ought to pass.

The reports were severally accepted and the bills laid upon the table to be printed.

Mr. Woodman of Concord, for the Committee on Judiciary, to whom was referred An act authorizing the town of Peterborough to exempt from taxation the improvements or new buildings to be erected on the Tarbell block lot, having considered the same, report the same with the following amendment and with the resolution that the bill, as amended, ought to pass:

Amend by inserting between the words " from " and " taxation " in the second line the word " local," so that said bill as amended shall read: " That the town of Peterborough be and hereby is authorized to exempt from local taxation the improvements or new buildings to be erected on the Tarbell block lot, on the corner of Main and Grove streets in said town, for a term not exceeding ten years, the limit of the same to be fixed by a vote of the said town at its annual town meeting."

The report was accepted, the amendment adopted, and the bill laid upon the table to be printed.

Mr. Goold of Lebanon, for the Committee on Fisheries and Game, to whom was referred An act for screening the outlet of Merry Meeting lake in the town of New Durham, having considered the same, report the same with the following resolution:

Resolved, That the bill ought to pass.

The report was accepted and the bill laid upon the table to be printed and then referred to the Committee on Appropriations.

Mr. Bunton, A. S., of Manchester, for the special committee consisting of the delegation from the city of Manchester, to whom was referred An act to enable the city of Manchester to appropriate money toward the armory rent of Camp Derwin, No. 184, Spanish-American War Veterans, having considered the same, report the same with the following resolution:

Resolved, That the bill ought to pass.

The report was accepted and the bill laid upon the table to

be printed.   On motion of Mr. Cavanaugh of Manchester, the rules were suspended and the printing of the bill dispensed with.   The bill was then ordered to a third reading.   On motion of the same gentleman, the rules were further suspended and the bill read a third time and passed and sent to the Senate for concurrence.

Mr. Goold of Lebanon, for the Committee on Fisheries and Game, to whom was referred An act to change the name of the body of water formerly called Munsonville pond, lying in the towns of Nelson and Stoddard, having considered the same, report the same with the following resolution :

Resolved, That the bill ought to pass.

The report was accepted and the bill laid upon the table to be printed.   On motion of Mr. Scott of Nelson, the rules were suspended and the printing of the bill dispensed with.   The bill was then ordered to a third reading.   On motion of the same gentleman, the rules were further suspended and the bill read a third time and passed and sent to the Senate for concurrence.

Mr. Smith of Peterborough, for the Committee on Revision of Statutes, to whom was referred An act to amend chapter 60, section 3 of the Statute Laws of 1891, relating to dog licenses, having considered the same, report the same in a new draft with the following resolution :

Resolved, That the bill in the new draft ought to pass.

The report was accepted and the bill in its new draft read a first time and ordered to a second reading.

Mr. Stewart of Berlin, for the special committee consisting of the delegation from the city of Berlin, to whom was referred An act in amendmment of the charter of the city of Berlin, having considered the same, report the same with the following resolution :

Resolved, That the bill be reported in a new draft with the recommendation that the bill in its new draft ought to pass.

The report was accepted, and the reading of the bill in its new draft having commenced, Mr. Stewart of Berlin moved that the rules be suspended and the bill read a first time by its title.   The question being upon the adoption of the motion,

(Discussion ensued.)

On a *viva voce* vote the motion did not prevail.

(Discussion ensued.)

Mr. Stewart withdrew his motion, and the bill was read a first time and ordered to a second reading. On motion of Mr. Goss of Berlin, the rules were suspended and the bill read a second time by its title. The bill was then laid upon the table to be printed. On motion of the same gentleman, the rules were suspended and the printing of the bill dispensed with. The bill was then ordered to a third reading. On motion of the same gentleman, the rules were further suspended and the bill read a third time by its title and passed and sent to the Senate for concurrence.

Mr. Donahue of Manchester, for the Committee on Insurance, reported the following entitled bill, "An act to change the name of the New Hampshire Health and Accident Insurance Company and to further define its powers and duties," with the resolution that the bill ought to pass.

The report was accepted and Mr. Willis of Concord moved that the rules be suspended and the bill read a first and second time by its title and laid upon the table to be printed. The question being upon the adoption of the motion,

(Discussion ensued.)

On a *viva voce* vote the motion prevailed, the rules were suspended, and the bill read a first and second time by its title and laid upon the table to be printed.

Mr. Bell of Woodstock, for the Committee on Public Health, reported the following entitled bill, "An act to prohibit the use of arsenic in embalming human bodies," with the resolution that the bill ought to pass.

The report was accepted and the bill read a first time and ordered to a second reading.

Mr. Bell of Woodstock, for the Committee on Public Health, reported the following entitled bill, "An act in relation to smallpox," with the resolution that the bill ought to pass.

The report was accepted and the bill read a first time and ordered to a second reading.

Mr. Bell of Woodstock, for the Committee on Public Health, reported the following entitled bill, "An act to enable the state board of health to prevent contaminated water being furnished for domestic consumption," with the resolution that the bill ought to pass.

The report was accepted and the bill read a first time and ordered to a second reading.

Mr. Morgan of Manchester, for the Committee on Railroads, reported the following entitled bill, "An act to authorize the Connecticut River Railroad Company to acquire stock of the Vermont Valley Railroad," with the resolution that the bill ought to pass.

The report was accepted and the bill read a first time and ordered to a second reading.

Mr. French of Moultonborough, for the Committee on Railroads, reported the following entitled bill, "An act in relation to reports and increase of stocks and bonds of corporations owning stock in railways," with the resolution that the bill ought to pass.

The report was accepted and the bill read a first time and ordered to a second reading.

Mr. Hamlin of Charlestown, for the Committee on Claims, to whom was referred Joint resolution in favor of Charles H. Roberts, having considered the same, report the same in a new draft, with the annexed statement of facts, which is hereby made the report of your said committee, and with the recommendation that said joint resolution, in the new draft, ought to pass.

> FRANK W. HAMLIN,
> GEORGE F. MATHES,
> EDGAR W. SMITH,
> ALBERT E. PRESTON,
> JAMES E. FRENCH,
> GEORGE B. KIMBALL,
> THOMAS R. LITTLE,
> E. C. CHASE,
> E. L. TINKHAM,
> JAS. J. DONAGAN,
> ROBERT BROWN, JR.,
> CHARLES H. MORSE,
> BERNARD A. BABCOCK,
> *Committee on Claims.*

FACTS FOUND IN THE CHARLES H. ROBERTS CASE.

This case as presented to your committee offers four points for consideration:

First: Did Mr. Charles H. Roberts have an appointment from the state to collect certain claims against the United States?

Second: Under this appointment did he make collections for the state, and to what amount?

Third: Has he received any compensation therefor?

Fourth: What is a reasonable compensation?

Your committee find that this claimant, Charles H. Roberts, who had previously collected large sums from the United States for the state (see state treasurer's report), was on the 22d day of April, 1884, recognized as the agent of the state for the collection of certain other claims. The official vote of the Governor and Council, showing his authority, is as follows:

"STATE OF NEW HAMPSHIRE.
"OFFICE OF THE SECRETARY OF STATE.
"CONCORD, April 28, 1884.

" *Col. Charles H. Roberts.*

"DEAR SIR: At a meeting of the Governor and Council held April 22d inst., it was voted that 'Charles H. Roberts is hereby recognized as the agent of the state of New Hampshire for the prosecution of the claims against the United States for payment of interest on money expended on account of recruiting, clothing, arming and transporting troops, raised for the suppression of the Rebellion, and for the refunding of the direct tax collected from the state; and in case he succeeds in making any or all of such collections, he is to be paid a reasonable compensation, otherwise, to receive nothing.'

"Yours truly,
"A. B. THOMPSON,
" *Secretary of State.*"

Mr. Roberts was before the committee in person and by counsel; he also submitted a written statement as to his services, and we had letters before us from ex-Governor David

H. Goodell, Hon. John A. Spalding, and Hon. Grosvenor A. Curtice, who were members of Governor Hale's Council at the time the above mentioned agreement was made. These letters are as follows:

"ANTRIM, N. H., Jan. 23, 1903.

" *Col. C. H. Roberts.*

"DEAR SIR: Your letter of yesterday is received. I am surprised to learn that you have never received any compensation for your services in securing money for the state of New Hampshire from the U. S. government, in accordance with the agreement made with you by the Governor and Council in 1884.

"Unless some explanation can be made, which I know nothing of, I sincerely hope the state will, without further delay, make you suitable compensation.

" Truly yours,

"D. H. GOODELL."

NASHUA, N. H., Jan. 19th, 1903.

"MY DEAR ROBERTS:

" In response to your letter of recent date regarding agreement of Governor Hale's Council with you, would say, that I was a member of that Council and know that the whole matter was carefully considered. It was not thought that the U. S. government, having the direct tax money in the treasury, would return it to the state, or that the interest upon our war claim would be allowed.

" This being the situation, the Governor and Council were unwilling to obligate the state to pay any expense unless collections were actually made. Hence, the agreement provided that you should take all the risks.

" I understand that after the direct tax money had been received by the state, Governor Ramsdell entered into a contract with other parties in the matter of interest. Why he should have done so I cannot tell. I hope the legislature will place a liberal construction upon the words ' reasonable compensation,' and pay you well for your services. I am sure you are entitled to it.

" Very truly,

"J. A. SPALDING."

" CONTOOCOOK, N. H., Jan. 22d, 1903.

" *Col. C. H. Roberts.*

" My Dear Sir : Referring to yours of some days ago, I remember in your appointment by Governor Hale as state agent no compensation was agreed upon, but that it should be reasonable.

" I was surprised to learn that you had not received that compensation. I was also surprised to learn that a subsequent administration had appointed another agent for apparently the same purpose. It would seem to me that the sums of money recovered by the state in 1891–'94 should have settled any question as to your competency and as to whether you had attended to your duties or not.

" Your claim is a modest one and should be settled without haggling. Anything I can do to further your interests I shall be glad to do.

" Yours very truly,

"G. A. CURTICE."

It appears that the whole matter was carefully considered ; that the claim of the state against the United States was considered of such a doubtful nature that they were unwilling in any way to obligate the state to pay anything, either for services or expenses, unless collections should be made. This proposition was accepted by Mr. Roberts, and, as he stated, he immediately proceeded to Washington and commenced his labors in the direction of procuring friendly legislation. It appears that at this time a bill was before congress for the refunding of the direct tax, and also bills before the committees of both Houses, which, had they been enacted, would have opened up the matter of payment of interest to the states.

On March 2d, 1891, the act for the refunding of the direct tax finally passed congress and became a law. Under its provisions the state of New Hampshire received one hundred and eighty-five thousand six hundred and forty-five dollars and sixty-seven cents ($185,645.67), being the full amount of its claim. About $181,000 was received in the year 1891, and the last payment in 1894. For his services, which extended over a period of six years, and for his expenses in securing the refunding of the tax, amounting to $185,645.67, Mr. Roberts has never been paid anything. (See state treasurer's reports for 1902.)

In this connection we may state that we had before us a letter from Hon. Hiram A. Tuttle, who was governor of the state when this money was received into the state treasury. His letter is as follows:

"PITTSFIELD, N. H., Nov. 26.

"MY DEAR COL. ROBERTS:

"I want to say to you that I was greatly surprised to learn to-day that you had not been paid for your services as agent of the state in the matter of refunding of the direct tax. The money was received when I was governor of the state, and had you made your claim at that time it would have been paid, or if legislative action was needed, I should have recommended such action. There is no question in my mind but that you should be paid a reasonable compensation for that service, also for what you did and was prepared to do in the collection of interest, paid by New Hampshire upon money borrowed to pay the cost of raising troops. The fact that Governor Ramsdell, without your knowledge and without attempting to annul your contract, made an agreement with other parties, ought not to affect your rights or weaken your claim against the state for what your contract was worth to you.

"I shall be glad to be of service to you, and you are at liberty to make such use of this letter as you may think best.

"Most truly yours,

"H. A. TUTTLE."

Mr. Roberts made no claim for compensation when this money was turned over to the state, for the reason that the question of interest was still pending.

As to the matter of interest upon the money expended in raising troops, it appears that the state of New York took a similar claim before the Court of Claims; that the whole matter was finally taken before the Supreme Court of the United States, where in the year 1896 the case was decided in favor of New York. The justice promulgating the decision used the following language :

" We are of the opinion that the claim of the state for money paid on account of interest is not one against the United States for interest as such, but it is a claim for costs, charges, and expenses properly incurred and paid by the state in aid of the general government and is embraced by the act of congress declaring that the states would be indemnified by the general government for money so expended." (See 160 U. S. Reports, 624.)

This decision settled the law for all the states having similar claims. Mr. Roberts states that during his stay in Washington in the winter of 1896–'97 he informed himself as to the necessary steps to be taken to bring the claim for interest before the Court of Claims and the accounting officers of the treasury ; that he came to Concord in June, 1897, for the purpose of preparing the claim for presentation, when he learned for the first time that Governor Ramsdell had entered into a contract with other parties to collect the interest claim, but that he has never been notified that his services as agent were no longer required, nor of any attempt to cancel or annul his contract.

Your committee have no reason to doubt that Mr. Roberts had, under the terms of his contract, full authority to proceed in the collection of the interest ; the money expended by the state being the money borrowed and upon which interest was paid ; and it would seem that he is entitled to an equitable consideration for what he did in preparing himself to prosecute that part of the claim ; but we believe the sum for which he asks to be no more than a " reasonable compensation " for his services in connection with the refunding of the direct tax money.

In brief, the committee find,—

First : That the said Charles H. Roberts did have an appointment from the state to collect certain claims.

Second : Under this appointment that he did make collections for the state amounting to $185,645.67, and

Third : That he has not received any compensation therefor, and

Fourth: That the amount he asks for is no more than a reasonable compensation.

The reading of the report having been begun, on motion of Mr. French of Moultonborough, the rules were suspended and the further reading of the report dispensed with. The report was then accepted and the joint resolution in its new draft read a first time and ordered to a second reading.

Mr. Woodman of Concord, for the Committee on Judiciary, reported the following entitled bill, "An act to amend an act passed at the January session, 1903, entitled 'An act to amend chapter 241 of the Session Laws of 1893, entitled "An act to establish the city of Laconia,"' and repealing chapter 200 of the Laws of 1901, entitled 'An act to amend chapter 241 of the Session Laws of 1893, entitled "An act to establish the city of Laconia,"'" with the resolution that the bill ought to pass.

The report was accepted and on motion of Mr. Remich of Littleton, the rules were suspended and the bill read a first time by its title. The bill was then ordered to a second reading. On motion of the same gentleman, the rules were suspended and the bill read a second time by its title.

Mr. Small of Rochester offered the following amendment:

Amend by striking out all of said bill except the last line of the enacting clause, and substitute in place thereof the following:

Be it enacted by the Senate and House of Representatives in General Court convened:

SECTION 1. Amend chapter 241 of the Session Laws of 1893 as follows:

"Strike out all of sections 2 and 3 as amended, and insert in place thereof the following:

"'SECT. 2. The said city of Laconia is hereby divided into four wards, which shall be constituted as follows, viz.:

"'Ward No. 1 shall include all that part of said city which constituted Ward No. 6 under the original charter of the city of Laconia.

"'Ward No. 2 shall include all that part of said city bounded westerly by a line commencing on the easterly shore of Round bay or Lake Opechee where the northwesterly boundary of Ward No. 2 as constituted under the original charter of said city commenced; thence southerly by the easterly shore of Round bay or Lake Opechee and the easterly shore of the Winnipesaukee river to a point on the easterly shore of said river in the center of Main street; thence southerly through the center of Main street to a point opposite the center of Union avenue; thence northerly through the center of Union avenue to a point opposite the center of Baldwin street; thence southeasterly through the center of Baldwin street to Baldwin-street extension; thence following the direction of the center line of said Baldwin-street extension to the Gilford town line; thence easterly and northerly by said Gilford town line and the southerly line of Ward No. 1, as herein established, to the point of beginning.

" 'Ward No. 3 shall include all that part of said city which was included in Wards Nos. 1 and 3 as constituted in said original charter, and all that part of Ward No. 4 as constituted in said original charter lying on the westerly side of the Winnipesaukee river.

" 'Ward No. 4 shall include all that part of said city not embraced in the three before mentioned wards.

" 'SECT. 3. Said Wards Nos. 1, 2, and 4 shall elect two representatives, and Ward No. 3 one representative, to the general court until such time when their constitutional rights shall entitle any of said wards to a greater number.'

" It is hereby declared to be the intention and purpose of this section to restore and establish said wards as they were established under chapter 200 of the Session Laws of 1901."

SECT. 2. All ward and city officials who were holding office in said city on the 26th day of January, 1903, shall be continued therein, or restored thereto, and shall hereafter exercise the functions and perform the duties of said offices as formerly until their successors are duly elected and qualified; and said successors shall be chosen, and shall qualify and exercise the functions and perform the duties prescribed by said original charter of said city as amended and existing on said 26th day of January, 1903.

It is hereby declared to be the intention and purpose of this section to restore and establish the various ward and city offices of said city and the incumbents of said offices as they were established under the charter of said city as amended and existing on the 26th day of January, 1903.

SECT. 3. All acts and parts of acts inconsistent with this act are hereby repealed, and this act shall take effect on and after its passage.

So that the bill as amended will read as follows:

Be it enacted by the Senate and House of Representatives in General Court convened:

SECTION 1. Amend chapter 241 of the Session Laws of 1893 as follows:

" Strike out all of sections 2 and 3 as amended, and insert in place thereof the following:

" 'SECT. 2. The said city of Laconia is hereby divided into four wards, which shall be constituted as follows, viz.:

" 'Ward No. 1 shall include all that part of said city which constituted Ward No. 6 under the original charter of the city of Laconia.

" 'Ward No. 2 shall include all that part of said city bounded westerly by a line commencing on the easterly shore of Round bay or Lake Opechee where the northwesterly boundary of Ward No. 2 as constituted under the original charter of said city commenced; thence southerly by the easterly shore of Round bay or Lake Opechee and the easterly shore of the Winnipesaukee river to a point on the easterly shore of said river in the center of Main street; thence southerly through the center of Main street to a point opposite the center of Union avenue; thence northerly through the center of Union avenue to a point opposite the center of Baldwin street; thence southeasterly through the center of Baldwin street to Baldwin-street extension; thence following the direction of the center line of said Baldwin-street extension to the Gilford town line; thence easterly and northerly by said Gilford town line and the southerly line of Ward No. 1, as herein established, to the point of beginning.

" 'Ward No. 3 shall include all that part of said city which was included in Wards Nos. 1 and 3 as constituted in said original charter, and all that part of Ward No. 4 as constituted in said original charter lying on the westerly side of the Winnipesaukee river.

" 'Ward No. 4 shall include all that part of said city not embraced in the three before mentioned wards.

" 'SECT. 3. Said Wards Nos. 1, 2, and 4 shall elect two representatives, and Ward No. 3 one representative, to the general court until such time when their constitutional rights shall entitle any of said wards to a greater number.'

" It is hereby declared to be the intention and purpose of this section to restore and establish said wards as they were established under chapter 200 of the Session Laws of 1901."

SECT. 2. All ward and city officials who were holding office in said city on the 26th day of January, 1903, shall be continued therein, or restored thereto, and shall hereafter exercise the functions and perform the duties of said offices as formerly until their successors are duly elected and qualified; and said successors shall be chosen, and shall qualify and exercise the functions and perform the duties prescribed by said original charter of said city as amended and existing on said 26th day of January, 1903.

It is hereby declared to be the intention and purpose of this section to restore and establish the various ward and city offices of said city and the incumbents of said offices as they were established under the charter of said city as amended and existing on the 26th day of January, 1903.

SECT. 3. All acts and parts of acts inconsistent with this act are hereby repealed, and this act shall take effect on and after its passage.

The reading of the amendment having commenced, on motion of Mr. Remich of Littleton, the rules were suspended and the further reading dispensed with.

The question being upon the adoption of the amendment, Mr. Ahern of Concord moved that both reports be laid upon the table and printed.

(Discussion ensued.)

Mr. Remich of Littleton raised the point of order that a motion to lay upon the table was not debatable.

The Speaker ruled that the point of order was well taken.

Mr. Nason of Dover raised the point of order that there was no report to be printed.

The Speaker ruled that the point of order was well taken.

Mr. Ahern of Concord withdrew his motion and moved that the bill and amendment be laid upon the table.

On a *viva voce* vote the motion prevailed.

Mr. Remich of Littleton called for a division. The counting having begun Mr. Remich withdrew his call.

On motion of Mr. Whitcher of Haverhill, the bill and amendment were laid upon the table and made the special order for Thursday, February 12, at 11 o'clock.

BILLS FORWARDED.

An act to provide for a bounty on hedgehogs.

An act relating to the salary of the judge of probate for the county of Rockingham.

Severally taken from the table and referred to the Committee on Appropriations.

An act to punish embezzlement by executors, administrators, guardians, and trustees.

An act in addition to chapter 58 of the Public Statutes, relating to the appraisal of taxable real estate.

An act in amendment of chapter 23 of the Laws of 1901, entitled "An act to establish a laboratory of hygiene."

An act to change the name of Station lake in the town of Springfield.

An act relating to domestic insurance companies.

Joint resolution in favor of the Granite State Deaf Mute Mission.

Severally taken from the table and ordered to a third reading.

UNFINISHED BUSINESS.

Mr. Small of Rochester called for the unfinished business, it being the consideration of the resolutions regarding free passes and trusts adopted by the constitutional convention of

1902. The question pending being, Shall the resolutions be indefinitely postponed?

(Discussion ensued.)

Mr. Small of Rochester called for a yea and nay vote. The roll was called with the following result:

YEAS, 191.

ROCKINGHAM COUNTY. Fellows, Hubbard, Morse of Chester, Darbe, White of Deerfield, Hardy, Nowell, Scammon, Severance, Smith of Exeter, Brown of Fremont, Duntley, Emerson of Hampstead, Lane of Hampton, Brown of Hampton Falls, Quimby of Kingston, Crowell, Chase of Newfields, George, Warner, Bickford, Payne, Blaisdell, Foye, Nelson, Yeaton, Newton, Brown of Rye, Abbott of Salem, Gordon, Young, Swain, Chase of Stratham, Cochran.

STRAFFORD COUNTY. Mathes, Ramsdell, Nason, Whittemore, Bunce, Barrett, Hayes, Langley of Durham, York, Tuttle, Davis of Lee, Place, McCrillis, Crocker, Worcester, Wallace, Harrity, Etter, Wentworth, Demers, Murnane.

BELKNAP COUNTY. Sargent, Smith of Centre Harbor, Davis of Laconia, Hull of Laconia, Edwards, Quimby of Meredith, Morrill of New Hampton, Sanborn of Sanbornton.

CARROLL COUNTY. Littlefield, Stevens, Weeks, Fifield, Dow of Conway, Burnell, Drake, Trickey, French, Abbott of Ossipee, Hoyt of Sandwich, Pollard, Edgerly of Tuftonborough, Blake of Wakefield, Beacham.

MERRIMACK COUNTY. Harris of Boscawen, Morse of Bradford, Durgin, Symonds, Shepard, Matson, Woodman, Emerson of Concord, Critchett, Hill, E. J., of Concord, Bunten of Dunbarton, Preston of Henniker, Twombly, Worthley, Messer, Tallant, Aldrich, Foss, Little of Salisbury, Ela, Burbank.

HILLSBOROUGH COUNTY. Farley of Amherst, Tobie, Pattee, Whitaker, Cavanaugh, Nyberg, Donahue, Bartlett of Manchester, Taggart, Sheehan, Bunton, A. S., of Manchester, Farrell, Johnson, Wright, Barr of Manchester, Carpenter, Morgan, Armstrong, Tinkham, Quimby of Manchester, Gunderman, Emerson of Manchester, Needham, Kendall, Lund,

Tuck, Lewis, Ingham, Bussell, Spalding, Shenton, McLane, Jones of New Ipswich, Bragdon.

CHESHIRE COUNTY. Gowing, Tenney, Bemis, Fuller, Fay, Fitch, Batchelder, Whitney, Moors, Fox, Ramsay, Hall.

SULLIVAN COUNTY. Clark, Hamlin of Charlestown, Sherman of Claremont, Long, Churchill, Aiken, Richards, True, Philbrick of Springfield, Russell of Sunapee, Straw of Unity, Ball.

GRAFTON COUNTY. Pierce of Bethlehem, Little of Campton, Gates, Dorothy, Foster, Glover, Kimball of Grafton, Howe of Hanover, Whitcher, Carr, Pike of Haverhill, Goold of Lebanon, Pike of Lebanon, Comings, Crossman, Stanley, Mitchell of Littleton, Blake of Littleton, Chase of Orford, Ferrin, Houston, Goodrich.

COÖS COUNTY. Goss, Kent of Berlin, Hutchins of Berlin, Hicks, Tillotson, Buckley of Lancaster, Ellis, Trafton, McDonald of Northumberland, Piper, Smith of Pittsburg, Wilson.

NAYS, 140.

ROCKINGHAM COUNTY. Shute, Pridham, Badger, Haines, Gerrish, Sleeper, Cogan, Adams of Portsmouth, Corson, Dow of Seabrook.

STRAFFORD COUNTY. Howe of Barrington, Libby of Dover, Jewell, Wesley, Felker, Warren, Small, Bergeron, Boutin, Caverly.

BELKNAP COUNTY. Potter, Clough, Fecteau, Prescott, Rogers, Mason.

CARROLL COUNTY. Philbrick of Effingham, Greene.

MERRIMACK COUNTY. Graves, Beck, Langmaid, Kennedy, Willis, Kimball of Concord, Davis of Concord, Mathews of Concord, Ahern, Donagan, Litchfield, Tripp, Jones of Franklin, Adams of Franklin, Davis of Franklin, Fisk, Sanborn of Loudon, Sanborn of Northfield, Hutchins of Pittsfield, Walker of Pittsfield, Pillsbury.

HILLSBOROUGH COUNTY. Barr of Bedford, Gould of Bennington, Shattuck, Craine, Putnam, Brown of Greenville, Ware of Hancock, Ward, Farley of Hollis, Connell, Center, Chase of Manchester, Stewart of Manchester, Tonnery, Ryan,

18

Riordan, Sullivan of Manchester, Shaughnessey, Sasseville, Marshall, Morse of Manchester, Couch, Bunton, A. B., of Manchester, Graf, Dinsmore, Dozois, Janelle. Kohler, Filion, Lemay, Kane, Newman, Simpson, Duncklee, Lampron, Buckley of Nashua, Shea, Lintott, Sullivan of Nashua, Earley, Desmarais, Peabody, Smith of Peterborough, Fitzgerald, Chase of Weare, Sheldon.

CHESHIRE COUNTY. Ware of Alstead, Polzer, Holland, Cutler, Maloney, Jones of Keene, Goodnow, Donovan, Scott, Amidon, Fletcher, Merrill, Lane of Swanzey, Boyden, Sherman of Walpole, Kellom, Dickinson.

SULLIVAN COUNTY. Chandler, Huntley, Walker of Grantham, Lufkin.

GRAFTON COUNTY. McMurphey, Morrill of Ashland, Davenport, Calley, Pinneo, Barnard, Evans, Henry, Remich, Converse, Frazer, King, Celley, Gould of Plymouth. Russell of Rumney.

COÖS COUNTY. Caird, Stewart of Berlin, Smyth, Gathercole, Martin, Hamlin of Dummer, O'Connor, Harriman, Lennon, Babcock.

On motion of Mr. Fay of Keene,—

Resolved, That the following entitled bill, "An act in amendment of section 19, chapter 57 of the Public Statutes, relating to the annual invoice of polls and taxable property," be recalled from the Committee on Banks and be laid upon the table to be printed, and then recommitted to the Committee on Banks.

On motion of Mr. Bunton, A. B., of Manchester, at 12.38 the House adjourned.

AFTERNOON.

The House met at 3 o'clock.

LEAVES OF ABSENCE.

Mr. Stanley of Lisbon was granted leave of absence for next week on account of important business.

Mr. Preston of Auburn was granted leave of absence on account of death in his family.

THIRD READINGS.

An act to punish embezzlement by executors, administrators, guardians, and trustees.

An act in addition to chapter 58 of the Public Statutes, relating to the appraisal of taxable real estate.

An act in amendment of chapter 23 of the Laws of 1901, entitled " An act to establish a laboratory of hygiene."

An act to change the name of Station lake in the town of Springfield.

An act relating to domestic insurance companies.

Joint resolution in favor of the Granite State Deaf Mute Mission.

Severally read a third time and passed and sent to the Senate for concurrence.

SPECIAL ORDER.

Mr. Hoyt of Sandwich called for the special order, it being " An act to exempt from taxation real estate reservations of the Appalachian Mountain Club."

The question being upon the adoption of an amendment offered by Mr. Hoyt of Sandwich,

(Discussion ensued.)

On a *viva voce* vote the amendment was not adopted. Mr. Hoyt of Sandwich called for a division. The counting having begun, Mr. Hoyt withdrew his call.

Mr. Buckley of Lancaster offered the following amendment:

Amend by adding at the end of section 2 the following words: " but this act may be altered, amended, or repealed whenever the public good may require."

The question being upon the adoption of the amendment,

(Discussion ensued.)

On a *viva voce* vote the amendment was not adopted. The bill was then ordered to a third reading. On motion of Mr. Whitcher of Haverhill, the rules were suspended and the bill read a third time and passed and sent to the Senate for concurrence.

On motion of Mr. Severance of Exeter, the following entitled bill, " An act in relation to milk tickets," was taken from the table.

The question being,

Shall the bill pass?

(Discussion ensued.)

On a *viva voce* vote the bill passed and was sent to the Senate for concurrence.

On motion of Mr. Donahue of Manchester, at 4.15 the House adjourned.

THURSDAY, FEBRUARY 12, 1903.

The House met at 11 o'clock.

Prayer was offered by the chaplain.

LEAVES OF ABSENCE.

Mr. Libby of Gorham was granted leave of absence until Monday, February 16, on account of important business.

Mr. Glover of Franconia was granted leave of absence for a few days next week on account of town business.

Mr. Boyden of Troy was granted leave of absence for the balance of the week on account of sickness.

COMMITTEE REPORTS.

Mr. Drake of Freedom, for the Committee on Public Improvements, to whom was referred Joint resolution in favor of raising Squam bridge in Holderness, and Little Squam bridge in Ashland, and of improving navigation in Squam lake and connecting waters, having considered the same, report the same with the following resolution :

Resolved, That the joint resolution ought to pass.

Mr. Bickford of Northwood, for the Committee on Feeble-Minded School, to whom was referred Joint resolution in favor of the New Hampshire school for feeble-minded children, having considered the same, report the same with the following resolution :

Resolved, That the joint resolution ought to pass.

Mr. Drake of Freedom, for the Committee on Public Improvements, to whom was referred Joint resolution in favor of maintaining buoys and placing lights in Squam lake, having considered the same, report the same with the following resolution :

Resolved, That the joint resolution ought to pass.

The reports were severally accepted and the joint resolutions laid upon the table to be printed, and then referred to the Committee on Appropriations.

Mr. Woodman of Concord, for the Committee on Judiciary, to whom was referred An act amending section 4, chapter 40 of the Public Statutes, relating to towns, having considered the same, report the same with the following resolution :

Resolved, That the bill ought to pass.

Mr. Whitcher of Haverhill, for the Committee on Judiciary, to whom was referred An act in amendment of section 2, chapter 2555, Laws of 1861, entitled "An act to incorporate the Alpha Delta Thi Society," having considered the same, report the same with the following resolution :

Resolved, That the bill ought to pass.

The reports were severally accepted and the bills laid upon the table to be printed.

Mr. Prescott of Laconia, for the Committee on County Affairs, to whom was referred An act in reference to the duties of county commissioners, having considered the same, report the same with the following resolution :

Resolved, That it is inexpedient to legislate.

Mr. Demers of Somersworth, for the Committee on Revision of Statutes, to whom was referred An act amending section 12 of chapter 125 of the Public Statutes, relating to weights and measures, having considered the same, report the same with the following resolution :

Resolved, That it is inexpedient to legislate.

Mr. Demers of Somersworth, for the Committee on Revision of Statutes, to whom was referred An act relating to the province records of New Hampshire, having considered the same, report the same with the following resolution :

Resolved, That it is inexpedient to legislate.

Mr. Woodman of Concord, for the Committee on Judiciary, to whom was referred An act to prevent the deposit of sawdust and other waste in the Mohawk river in Colebrook, having considered the same, report the same with the following resolution :

Resolved, That it is inexpedient to legislate.

Mr. Roby of Concord, for the Committee on Fisheries and Game, to whom was referred An act to repeal section 13, chapter 133 of Public Statutes of New Hampshire, and all laws which protect smelts in tide water in New Hampshire, having considered the same, report the same with the following resolution :

Resolved, That it is inexpedient to legislate.

Mr. Demers of Somersworth, for the Committee on Revision of Statutes, to whom was referred An act in amendment of chapter 11, Laws of 1899, entitled "An act relating to holidays," having considered the same, report the same with the following resolution :

Resolved, That it is inexpedient to legislate.

Mr. Demers of Somersworth, for the Committee on Revision of Statutes, to whom was referred An act in amendment of chapter 265, section 1, Public Statutes, relating to the abandonment of children, having considered the same, report the same with the following resolution :

Resolved, That it is inexpedient to legislate.

The reports were severally accepted and the resolutions reported by the committees adopted.

Mr. Buckley of Lancaster, for the Committee on Judiciary, to whom was referred An act in amendment of the act relating to the terms of the superior court in Grafton county, having considered the same, report the same with the following amendment and with the resolution that the bill as amended ought to pass :

Amend section 1 of said bill by adding at the end thereof the following words : " It is provided, however, that nothing in this act or in the act of which this act is an amendment shall affect the rights of parties under the rules of court heretofore prescribed, or which may hereafter be prescribed by the court relative to continuances of actions."

THURSDAY, FEBRUARY 12, 1903.

The report was accepted, the amendment adopted, and the bill laid upon the table to be printed.

Mr. Demers of Somersworth, for the Committee on Revision of Statutes, to whom was referred An act to allow the town of Hampton to re-adopt chapter 29, Laws of 1893, in relation to the repair of highways, having considered the same, report the same with the following resolution :

Resolved, That it is inexpedient to legislate.

The report was accepted.

The question being upon the adoption of the resolution reported by the committee,

(Discussion ensued.)

On a *viva voce* vote the resolution was not adopted. The bill was then laid upon the table to be printed. On motion of Mr. Brown of Hampton Falls, the rules were suspended and the printing of the bill dispensed with. The bill was then ordered to a third reading. On motion of the same gentleman, the rules were further suspended and the bill read a third time and passed and sent to the Senate for concurrence.

Mr. Andrews of Somersworth, for the Committee on Education, to whom was referred An act severing the homestead farm of Hiram H. Stevens from the school district of the town of Middleton, and annexing the same to the town of Wakefield for school purposes, having considered the same, report the same in a new draft with the following resolution :

Resolved, That the bill in its new draft ought to pass.

The report was accepted and the bill in its new draft read a first time and ordered to a second reading. On motion of Mr. Blake of Wakefield, the rules were suspended and the bill read a second time and laid upon the table to be printed. On motion of the same gentleman, the rules were suspended and the printing of the bill dispensed with. The bill was then ordered to a third reading. On motion of the same gentleman, the rules were further suspended, and the bill read a third time and passed and sent to the Senate for concurrence.

Mr. Andrews of Somersworth, for the Committee on Education, to whom was referred An act to amend chapter 94 of the Public Statutes, in relation to the Superintendent of Public

Instruction, having considered the same, report the same in a new draft with the following resolution :

Resolved, That the bill in its new draft ought to pass.

The report was accepted and the bill in its new draft read a first time and ordered to a second reading.

Mr. Martin of Colebrook, for the Committee on Railroads, to whom was referred An act in relation to the issue of bonds, coupon notes, and other evidences of indebtedness of street railway companies, having considered the same, report the same in a new draft and with the following resolution :

Resolved, That the bill in new draft ought to pass.

The report was accepted and the bill in its new draft read a first time and ordered to a second reading.

Mr. Severance of Exeter, for the Committee on Soldiers' Home, reported the following joint resolution, " Joint resolution in favor of New Hampshire Soldiers' Home," with the resolution that the joint resolution ought to pass.

The report was accepted and the joint resolution read a first time and ordered to a second reading.

Mr. Roby of Concord, for the Committee on Military Affairs, reported the following joint resolution, " Joint resolution appropriating money to be expended for the preservation of the muster rolls," with the resolution that the joint resolution ought to pass.

The report was accepted and the joint resolution read a first time and ordered to a second reading.

Mr. Hamlin of Charlestown, for the Committee on Claims, to whom was referred An act in favor of Oren Clough of Lisbon, having considered the same, report the same in a new draft with the following resolution :

Resolved, That the said bill in its new draft ought to pass.

The report was accepted and the bill in its new draft read a first time and ordered to a second reading.

SECOND READINGS.

Joint resolution in favor of Charles H. Roberts.

Read a second time and laid upon the table to be printed and then referred to the Committee on Appropriations. On motion of Mr. French of Moultonborough, the report of the

Committee on Claims with reference to this joint resolution was ordered printed with the joint resolution.

An act to amend chapter 60, section 3, of the Statute Laws of 1891, relating to dog licenses.

An act to enable the State Board of Health to prevent contaminated water being furnished for domestic consumption.

An act in relation to smallpox.

An act to prohibit the use of arsenic in embalming human bodies.

An act in relation to reports and increase of stock and bonds of corporations owning stock in railways.

An act to authorize the Connecticut River Railroad Company to acquire stock of the Vermont Valley Railroad.

Severally read a second time and laid upon the table to be printed.

SPECIAL ORDER.

Mr. Whitcher of Haverhill called for the special order, it being the consideration of An act to amend an act, passed at the January session, 1903, entitled "An act to amend chapter 241 of the Session Laws of 1893, entitled ' An act to establish the city of Laconia,' " and repealing chapter 200 of the Laws of 1901, entitled "An act to amend chapter 241 of the Session Laws of 1893, entitled 'An act to establish the city of Laconia.' "

The question being,

Shall the amendment offered by Mr. Small of Rochester be adopted?

(Discussion ensued.)

Mr. Donovan of Keene moved that the bill and amendment be read in full.

The question being upon the adoption of the motion offered by Mr. Donovan,

(Discussion ensued.)

On a *viva voce* vote the motion offered by Mr. Donovan did not prevail.

The question being upon the adoption of the amendment offered by Mr. Small,

(Discussion ensued.)

Mr. Whitcher of Haverhill moved the previous question.
The question being,
Shall the main question be now put?

(Discussion ensued.)

On a *viva voce* vote the motion of Mr. Whitcher prevailed.

Mr. Ahern of Concord called for a division. A division being had, 179 gentlemen voted in the affirmative and 125 gentlemen voted in the negative, and the previous question was ordered put.

The question being upon the adoption of the amendment offered by Mr. Small of Rochester, on a *viva voce* vote the amendment was not adopted.

Mr. Small of Rochester demanded a yea and nay vote. The roll was called with the following result:

YEAS, 127.

ROCKINGHAM COUNTY. Sawyer of Atkinson, Edgerly of Epping, Pridham, Badger, Haines, Warner, Sleeper, Cogan, Adams of Portsmouth, Couhig, Corson, Young, Dow of Seabrook, Swain.

STRAFFORD COUNTY. Libby of Dover, Jewell, Wesley, Felker, Jones of New Durham, Warren, Small, Bergeron, Harrity, Murnane, Andrews, Caverly.

BELKNAP COUNTY. Hoitt of Barnstead, Potter, Clough, Fecteau, Prescott, Rogers, Mason.

CARROLL COUNTY. Philbrick of Effingham, Drake, Greene.

MERRIMACK COUNTY. Graves, Morse of Bradford, Beck, Langmaid, Durgin, Mathews of Concord, Ahern, Donagan, Tripp, Jones of Franklin, Sanborn of Loudon, Sanborn of Northfield, Hutchins of Pittsfield, Walker of Pittsfield, Little of Salisbury, Pillsbury.

HILLSBOROUGH COUNTY. Barr of Bedford, Gould of Bennington, Shattuck, Craine, Putnam, Brown of Greenville, Ware of Hancock, Farley of Hollis, Connell, Center, Holt, Stewart of Manchester, Tonery, Ryan, Riordan, Sullivan of

Manchester, Shaughnessey, Sasseville, Morse of Manchester, Dinsmore, Dozois, Gunderman, Janelle, Kohler, Lynch, Kane, Newman, Simpson, Lampron, Buckley of Nashua, Ingham, Bussell, Shea, Spalding, Dionne, Peabody, Smith of Peterborough, Fitzgerald, Chase of Weare, Sheldon.

CHESHIRE COUNTY. Bemis, Jones of Keene, Donovan, Scott, Amidon, Sherman of Walpole, Hall.

SULLIVAN COUNTY. Clark, Sherman of Claremont, Chandler, Walker of Grantham, Lufkin, Philbrick of Springfield, Russell of Sunapee, Straw of Unity, Ball.

GRAFTON COUNTY. McMurphey, Morrill of Ashland, Davenport, Glover, Pinneo, Barnard, Evans, Frazer, King, Celley, Russell of Rumney, Bowen.

COÖS COUNTY. Caird, Smyth, Gallagher, Gathercole, Piper, O'Connor, Harriman.

NAYS, 198.

ROCKINGHAM COUNTY. Fellows, Hubbard, Morse of Chester, Darbe, White of Deerfield, Hardy, Shute, Nowell, Scammon, Severance, Smith of Exeter, Brown of Fremont, Duntley, Lane of Hampton, Brown of Hampton Falls, Quimby of Kingston, Crowell, Chase of Newfields, George, Gerrish, Payne, Blaisdell, Foye, Nelson, Yeaton, Newton, Brown of Rye, Abbott of Salem, Chase of Stratham, Cochran.

STRAFFORD COUNTY. Howe of Barrington, Mathes, Ramsdell, Nason, Whittemore, Bunce, Smith of Dover, Barrett, Langley of Durham, Tuttle, Davis of Lee, Place, McCrillis, Worcester, Wallace, Etter, Wentworth, Demers.

BELKNAP COUNTY. Sargent, Smith of Center Harbor, Davis of Laconia, Hull of Laconia, Edwards, Kimball of Laconia, Quimby of Meredith, Morrill of New Hampton, Sanborn of Sanbornton.

CARROLL COUNTY. Littlefield, Stevens, Weeks, Fifield, Dow of Conway, Burnell, Trickey, French, Abbott of Ossipee, Hoyt of Sandwich, Pollard, Edgerly of Tuftonborough, Blake of Wakefield.

MERRIMACK COUNTY. Harris of Boscawen, White of Bow, Shepard, Kennedy, Willis, Matson, Hill, A. W., of

Concord, Roby, Woodman, Kimball of Concord, Emerson of Concord, Davis of Concord, Critchett, Bunten of Dunbarton, Phillips, Adams of Franklin, Davis of Franklin, Preston of Henniker, Twombly, Worthley, Fisk, Messer, Tallant, Aldrich, Ela, Burbank.

Hillsborough County. Farley of Amherst, Tobie, Pattee, Whitaker, Ward, Cavanaugh, Nyberg, Chase of Manchester, Donahue, Bartlett of Manchester, Taggart, Sheehan, Bunton, A. S., of Manchester, Farrell, Johnson, Wright, Barr of Manchester, Dubuc, Carpenter, Morgan, Marshall, Bunton, A. B., of Manchester, Armstrong, Tinkham, Graf, Scannell, Filion, Lemay, Emerson of Manchester, Hodgman, Sawyer of Milford, Robinson, Needham, Kendall, Tuck, Duncklee, Lewis, Lintott, Shenton, Hills of Nashua, McLane, Jones of New Ipswich, Miller, Bragdon.

Cheshire County. Ware of Alstead, Gowing, Tenney, Fuller, Holland, Cutler, Fay, Fitch, Batchelder, Whitney, Goodnow, Moors, Fox, Fletcher, Lane of Swanzey, Ramsay.

Sullivan County. Hamlin of Charlestown, Long, Churchill, Aiken, Matthews of Newport, Richards, True.

Grafton County. Pierce of Bethlehem, Calley, Little of Campton, Gates, Dorothy, Foster, Kimball of Grafton, Howe of Hanover, Whitcher, Carr, Pike of Haverhill, Goold of Lebanon, Pike of Lebanon, Comings, Crossman, Remich, Mitchell of Littleton, Blake of Littleton, Converse, Chase of Orford, Gould of Plymouth, Ferrin, Houston, Goodrich, Bell.

Coös County. Goss, Kent of Berlin, Hutchins of Berlin, Hicks, Hamlin of Dummer, Buckley of Lancaster, Ellis, McDonald of Northumberland, Smith of Pittsburg, Wilson.

The question being,

Shall the bill be read a third time?

On a *viva voce* vote the bill was ordered to a third reading.

Mr. Small of Rochester called for a division. The counting having begun, Mr. Small withdrew his call and the bill was ordered to a third reading.

On motion of Mr. Nason of Dover, the bill was laid upon the table and made the special order for Tuesday, February 17, at 3 o'clock.

On motion of Mr. Goold of Lebanon, the following entitled bill, "An act to prevent the pollution of the Piscataqua river and its tributaries," was recalled from the printer and recommitted to the Committee on Fisheries and Game.

LEAVES OF ABSENCE.

The Rockingham county delegation were granted leave of absence for Friday, February 13, for the purpose of visiting their county farm.

The Carroll county delegation were granted leave of absence for Friday, February 13, for the purpose of visiting their county farm.

On motion of Mr. Morrill of Ashland, at 12.40 the House adjourned.

AFTERNOON.

The House met at 3 o'clock.

On motion of Mr. Taggart of Manchester, the rules were suspended and business in order to-morrow morning at 11 o'clock was made in order at the present time.

SECOND READINGS.

An act in favor of Oren Clough of Lisbon.

Joint resolution appropriating money to be expended for the preservation of the muster rolls.

Joint resolution in favor of the New Hampshire Soldiers' Home.

Severally read a second time, laid upon the table to be printed and then referred to the Committee on Appropriations.

An act to amend chapter 94 of the Public Statutes, in relation to the superintendent of public instruction.

Read a second time and laid upon the table to be printed.

An act relative to the issue of bonds, coupon notes, and other evidences of indebtedness of street railway companies.

Read a second time and laid upon the table to be printed. On motion of Mr. French of Moultonborough, the rules were suspended and the printing of the bill dispensed with. The bill was then ordered to a third reading. On motion of the same gentleman, the rules were further suspended and the bill read a third time and passed. On motion of Mr. French of Moultonborough, the title of the bill was amended by adding after the word " railway " the words " or other railroad," so that said title as amended shall read, " An act relative to the issue of bonds, coupon notes, and other evidences of indebtedness of street railway or other railroad companies." The bill was then sent to the Senate for concurrence.

On motion of Mr. Churchill of Cornish,—

Resolved, That when the House adjourn this afternoon it be to meet at 9.30 Friday morning, and when it adjourn Friday morning it be to meet at 8 o'clock Monday evening.

LEAVE OF ABSENCE.

Mr. Russell of Sunapee was granted leave of absence until Wednesday, February 18, on account of town business.

On motion of Mr. Tuck of Nashua, at 3.12 the House adjourned.

FRIDAY, FEBRUARY 13, 1903.

The House met at 9.30 according to adjournment, being called to order by Mr. Winston Churchill of Cornish, and the following communication was read by the clerk:

CONCORD, February 12, 1903.

Mr. Winston Churchill, Cornish, N. H.

DEAR SIR: I shall be unable to be present at the morning session on Friday, February 13, 1903. Will you kindly preside for me, and oblige

Yours truly,

HARRY M. CHENEY,

Speaker.

MESSAGE FROM THE GOVERNOR.

STATE OF NEW HAMPSHIRE.

COUNCIL CHAMBER, February 13, 1903.

To the House of Representatives:

I hereby transmit the following reports:

Of the Railroad Commissioners.

Of the Soldiers' Home.

Of the State Prison.

Of the Boulevard Commissioners.

NAHUM J. BACHELDER,
Governor.

The above mentioned reports were referred as follows:

Report of the Railroad Commissioners to the Committee on Railroads.

Report of the Soldiers' Home to the Committee on Soldiers' Home.

Report of the State Prison to the Committee on State Prison.

Report of the Boulevard Commissioners to the Committee on Public Improvements.

COMMITTEE REPORTS.

Mr. Demers of Somersworth, for the Committee on Revision of Statutes, to whom was referred An act in amendment of chapter 192 of the Public Statutes, relating to insolvent estates, having considered the same, report the same with the following resolution:

Resolved, That the bill ought to pass.

The report was accepted and the bill laid upon the table to be printed.

Mr. Willis of Concord, for the Committee on Engrossed Bills, reported that they had examined bills with the following titles and found them correctly engrossed:

An act in relation to the town of Newmarket and the Newmarket water-works.

An act in amendment of sections 1, 3, and 4 of chapter 72 of the Public Statutes, relating to the discontinuance of highways.

An act authorizing the city of Dover to exempt from taxation the property of the Hayes hospital.

An act in amendment of the charter of the city of Concord, providing for the election of overseers of the poor.

An act in amendment of the charter of the Colby academy, providing for filling vacancies and election of members.

An act to amend chapter 179 of the Public Statutes, relating to guardians of insane persons and spendthrifts.

An act in amendment of the charter of the Walpole Electric Light and Power Company.

An act to incorporate the Walpole Water and Sewer Company.

An act to amend the charter of the North Shore Water Company.

An act to amend chapter 93 of the Public Statutes, in relation to scholars.

An act in amendment of the charter of the Salem Water-Works Company, and legalizing and confirming the acts of said corporation in relation thereto.

On motion of Mr. Ahern of Concord, at 9.33 the House adjourned.

_____

MONDAY, FEBRUARY 16, 1903.

The House met at 8 o'clock in the evening.

LEAVES OF ABSENCE.

Mr. Merrill of Stoddard was granted leave of absence for the balance of the week.

Mr. Tenney of Fitzwilliam was granted leave of absence for the balance of the week on account of sickness.

On motion of Mr. True of Plainfield, at 8.01 the House adjourned.

_____

TUESDAY, FEBRUARY 17, 1903.

The House met at 11 o'clock.

COMMITTEE REPORTS.

Mr. Mitchell of Littleton, for the Committee on Judiciary, to whom was referred An act relating to negotiable instruments, being an act to establish a law uniform with the laws of other states on that subject, having considered the same, report the same with the following resolution:

Resolved, That it is inexpedient to legislate.

Mr. Woodman of Concord, for the Committee on Judiciary, to whom was referred An act in amendment of chapter 202 of the Public Statutes, relative to bills and notes, having considered the same, report the same with the following resolution:

Resolved, That it is inexpedient to legislate.

Mr. Buckley of Lancaster, for the Committee on Judiciary, to whom was referred Joint resolution granting Little island in Bradford pond to Lawrence E. Davis, having considered the same, report the same with the following resolution:

Resolved, That it is inexpedient to legislate.

Mr. Buckley of Lancaster, for the Committee on Judiciary, to whom was referred An act to incorporate the Capital Investment Company, having considered the same, report the same with the following resolution:

Resolved, That it is inexpedient to legislate because the object sought can be achieved under the general laws.

Mr. Mitchell of Littleton, for the Committee on Judiciary, to whom was referred An act regulating the examining and licensing of engineers and firemen, having considered the same, report the same with the following resolution:

Resolved, That it is inexpedient to legislate.

Mr. Mitchell of Littleton, for the Committee on Judiciary, to whom was referred An act requiring the discharge of personal property mortgages after payment, having considered the same, report the same with the following resolution:

Resolved, That it is inexpedient to legislate.

Mr. Buckley of Lancaster, for the Committee on Judiciary, to whom was referred An act in relation to town and county paupers, having considered the same, report the same with the following resolution:

Resolved, That it is inexpedient to legislate because a bill covering the same subject matter has already been reported favorably.

The reports were severally accepted and the resolutions reported by the committees adopted.

19

Mr. Mitchell of Littleton, for the Committee on Judiciary, to whom was referred An act to amend the charter of Brown's Lumber Company of Whitefield, approved July 1, 1874, having considered the same, report the same with the following resolution :

Resolved, That the bill ought to pass.

Mr. Mitchell of Littleton, for the Committee on Judiciary, to whom was referred An act explanatory of the powers of the courts in reference to the fees of commissioners in certain cases, having considered the same, report the same with the following resolution :

Resolved, That the bill ought to pass.

Mr. Mitchell of Littleton, for the Committee on Judiciary, to whom was referred An act to amend the charter of the New England and Louisiana Land Company, having considered the same, report the same with the following resolution :

Resolved, That the bill ought to pass.

The reports were severally accepted and the bills laid upon the table to be printed.

Mr. Mitchell of Littleton, for the Committee on Judiciary, to whom was referred An act in amendment of chapter 86 of the Public Statutes, in relation to state aid to indigent deaf and dumb, blind, and feeble-minded persons, having considered the same, report the same with the following resolution :

Resolved, That the bill ought to pass.

Mr. Woodman of Concord, for the Committee on Judiciary, to whom was referred An act providing for the purchase of a bond for the deputy state treasurer, having considered the same, report the same with the following resolution :

Resolved, That the bill ought to pass.

The reports were severally accepted and the bills laid upon the table to be printed and then referred to the Committee on Appropriations.

Mr. Woodman of Concord, for the Committee on Judiciary, to whom was referred An act relating to the salary of the solicitor for the county of Merrimack, having considered the same, report the same with the following resolution :

Resolved, That the bill ought to pass.

The report was accepted and on motion of Mr. Ahern of

Concord, the bill was referred to a special committee consisting of the delegation from the county of Merrimack.

Mr. Remich of Littleton, for the Committee on Judiciary, to whom was referred An act to provide a stenographer for the House and Senate; for the publication of a journal of the Senate and House, and a calendar, having considered the same, report the same in a new draft with the following resolution:

Resolved, That the bill in a new draft ought to pass.

The report was accepted and the bill in its new draft read a first time and ordered to a second reading.

Mr. Remich of Littleton, for the Committee on Judiciary, to whom was referred An act in relation to the settlement of paupers, having considered the same, report the same with the following amendment and with the resolution that the bill as amended ought to pass:

Amend the bill by adding after the word "charges" at the end of section 1 the following: "This act shall in no way change the status of soldiers and their families as provided in chapter 116, Laws of 1901, except that the expenses incurred by reason of said act shall be paid by the county."

The report was accepted, the amendment adopted, and the bill laid upon the table to be printed.

Mr. Mitchell of Littleton, for the Committee on Judiciary, to whom was referred An act in amendment of section 1 of chapter 119, Public Statutes, relating to the inspection and licensing of boats, their engineers and pilots, having considered the same, report the same in a new draft with the following resolution:

Resolved, That the bill in its new draft ought to pass.

The report was accepted. The reading of the bill in its new draft having commenced, on motion of Mr. Mitchell of Littleton, the rules were suspended and the bill in its new draft read a first time by its title. The bill was then ordered to a second reading. On motion of the same gentleman, the rules were further suspended and the bill read a second time by its title and laid upon the table to be printed.

Mr. Buckley of Lancaster, for the Committee on Judiciary, reported the following entitled bill, "An act authorizing the

Mt. Pleasant Hotel Company to increase its capital stock,"
with the resolution that the bill ought to pass.

The report was accepted and the bill read a first time and
ordered to a second reading

BILLS FORWARDED.

An act authorizing the town of Peterborough to exempt
from taxation the improvements or new buildings to be erected
on the Tarbell block lot.

An act to annex a certain island in Lake Winnipesaukee,
now owned and occupied by George W. Sherwell, being one
of the group of islands known as the Aunt Dolly islands, to
the town of Meredith.

An act to change the name of the New Hampshire Health
and Accident Insurance Company, and to further define its
powers and privileges.

An act to amend chapter 94 of the Public Statutes, in relation to the superintendent of public instruction.

An act in amendment of the act relating to the terms of the
superior court in Grafton county.

An act to prohibit the use of arsenic in embalming human
bodies.

An act to authorize the Connecticut River Railroad Company to acquire stock of the Vermont Valley Railroad.

An act amending section 4, chapter 40 of the Public Statutes, relating to towns.

An act in amendment of section 2, chapter 2555, Laws of
1861, entitled "An act to incorporate the Alpha Delta Thi
Society."

An act in relation to reports and increase of stock and bonds
of corporations owning stock in railways.

An act to enable the state board of health to prevent contaminated water being furnished for domestic consumption.

An act in relation to smallpox.

An act in amendment of chapter 192 of the Public Statutes,
relating to insolvent estates.

Severally taken from the table and ordered to a third reading.

An act to amend chapter 60, section 3 of the Statute Laws
of 1891, relating to dog licenses.

Taken from the table.   Mr. Howe of Hanover offered the following amendment:

Amend section 3 by inserting the word " one " in the second line in place of the word " two," and by striking out the word " five " in the third line and inserting in place thereof the word " three," so that said section, as amended, shall read:

SECT. 3.   The fee for every license for a year shall be one dollar for a male or spayed female dog and three dollars for a female dog.

The question being upon the adoption of the amendment,

(Discussion ensued.)

On motion of Mr. Remich of Littleton the bill and amendment were laid upon the table.

Mr. Remich of Littleton offered as a substitute for the resolution introduced by him and adopted at the morning session of Thursday, January 29, in relation to the claim of Horace S. Cummings, the following resolution:

Resolved, That the House of Representatives requests the opinion of the supreme court upon the following, namely:

First.   Did His Excellency George A. Ramsdell, Governor of New Hampshire, have authority to make and execute the following appointment and agreement in behalf of this state or otherwise:

AGREEMENT.

MEMORANDUM OF AN APPOINTMENT AND AGREEMENT, made this eleventh day of May, A. D. 1897, by and between the State of New Hampshire by the Honorable George A. Ramsdell, its Governor, on the one part, and Horace S. Cummings of Washington, in the District of Columbia, on the other part, WITNESSETH:

That the said State of New Hampshire in consideration of the things to be done by said Horace S. Cummings as hereinafter set forth, hath appointed, and by these presents doth appoint, said Horace S. Cummings, its agent and attorney, to present, prosecute, and recover before the Congress, any Department, the Court of Claims, or the Supreme Court of the United States, any claim or claims of said State against the United States, for costs, charges, and expenses properly incurred by said state for enrolling, subsisting, clothing, supplying, arming, equipping, paying, and transporting the troops of said State, employed in aiding to suppress the insurrection against the United States between the years 1861 and 1865, both inclusive, under an Act of Congress, entitled "An Act to indemnify the States for expenses incurred by them in defense of the United States," approved July 27th, 1861. And said Horace S. Cummings shall have and receive for his legal services in and about said matter, a sum equal to fifteen per cent. of the entire sum collected, payable only out of any sums that may be collected hereunder, and without any liability on the part of the State for expenses in connection therewith.

And in consideration of the premises said Horace S. Cummings agrees to undertake the presentation and prosecution of said claims at the compensation above stated and without any liability on behalf of the State for his expenses in connection therewith.

IN WITNESS WHEREOF said State of New Hampshire has caused these presents to be signed by the said George A. Ramsdell, its Governor, and its seal to be hereto affixed and said Horace S. Cummings has hereunto set his hand and seal, the day and year first above written.

THE STATE OF NEW HAMPSHIRE,

By

GEO. A. RAMSDELL, *Governor.*

(Seal of State.)

HORACE S. CUMMINGS.

1. The foregoing agreement and appointment was duly executed and delivered to said Cummings at the date thereof.

2. Said Cummings thereupon entered on the work of prosecuting the claim mentioned in said agreement before the Honorable the Secretary of the Department of the Treasury of the United States, the Court of Claims, and the Congress of the United States.

3. The claim against the United States accrued to the state of New Hampshire between the years 1861 and 1864, and by

the statutes of the United States at the date of the agreement aforesaid had become barred by the Statute of Limitation of the United States so that no judgment against the United States thereon could be obtained in any court of the United States.

But not being a stale claim, it could be and was audited, allowed and paid by the treasury department, under laws existing at the time Cummings's contract was made.

The accounting officers of the Department of the Treasury claimed that said claim could not be audited because it was a stale claim and such proceedings were had as is set forth in Vol. 36, Ct. of Claims Reports.

4. The Treasurer of the State of New Hampshire in the year 1864 considered said claim as worthless, and the same was in the year 1865 carried to the deficiency account.

Said Cummings prosecuted the work of collecting said claims before the Department of the Treasury, and the Court of Claims, which resulted in the auditing of said claim on behalf of the state of New Hampshire in the amount of $108,373.52 ; and thereafter the Congress of the United States appropriated said sum on said audit, and the Secretary of the Treasury issued a warrant of the United States, payable to the order of the Governor of the state of New Hampshire for said sum and delivered the same to said Cummings as the agent of said state.

Immediately upon the receipt of said warrant said Cummings transmitted by mail said warrant to the Governor of the state of New Hampshire, inclosing therewith a copy of said agreement and appointment and requested the Governor to forward to him his check for the amount of fees due him as said agent in accordance with the terms of said agreement and appointment.

The Governor did not comply with the request of said Cummings, but thereafter, to wit, on March 4, 1902, turned the said $108,372.52 into the treasury of said state of New Hampshire, where it was on the date aforesaid entered upon the books of the state and commingled with other moneys of the state and has since been used and disposed of for state purposes.

Said Cummings protested that the moneys representing the fees aforesaid were not the proper moneys of the state of New Hampshire, but belonged to him by virtue of his contract of agreement and appointment; but said moneys have never been paid to said Cummings.

Second. Is said Cummings entitled to receive from the state fifteen per centum of the amount so collected and paid into the state treasury?

Resolved, That the Speaker of the House of Representatives, for and in its behalf, be and hereby is directed to present said questions to the Supreme Court with a request for its decision at as early a date as is compatible with a careful consideration of the important questions involved.

The question being upon the adoption of the resolution,

(Discussion ensued.)

On a *viva voce* vote the resolution was adopted.

LEAVE OF ABSENCE.

Mr. Wentworth of Somersworth was granted leave of absence for the balance of the week on account of death in his family.

On motion of Mr. Trickey of Jackson, at 11.57 the House adjourned.

AFTERNOON.

The House met at 3 o'clock.

LEAVE OF ABSENCE.

Mr. Ela of Warner was granted leave of absence for Wednesday and Thursday, February 18 and 19, on account of important business.

THIRD READINGS.

An act in amendment of chapter 192 of the Public Statutes, relating to insolvent estates.

Read a third time and passed, and sent to the secretary of state to be engrossed.

An act to amend chapter 94 of the Public Statutes, in relation to the superintendent of public instruction.

An act in amendment of the act relating to the terms of the superior court in Grafton county.

An act to authorize the Connecticut River Railroad Company to acquire stock of the Vermont Valley Railroad.

An act amending section 4, chapter 40 of the Public Statutes, relating to towns.

An act in amendment of section 2, chapter 2555, Laws of 1861, entitled "An act to incorporate the Alpha Delta Thi Society."

An act in relation to reports and increase of stocks and bonds of corporations owning stock in railways.

An act to enable the state board of health to prevent contaminated water being furnished for domestic consumption.

An act in relation to smallpox.

An act authorizing the town of Peterborough to exempt from taxation the improvements or new buildings to be erected on the Tarbell block lot.

An act to annex a certain island in Lake Winnipesaukee, now owned and occupied by George W. Sherwell, being one of the group of islands known as the Aunt Dolly islands, to the town of Meredith.

Severally read a third time and passed and sent to the Senate for concurrence.

An act to prohibit the use of arsenic in embalming human bodies.

The third reading being in order, on motion of Mr. Eaton of Goffstown, the rules were suspended and the bill placed back upon its second reading and recommitted to the Committee on Public Health.

An act to change the name of the New Hampshire Health and Accident Insurance Company, and to further define its powers and privileges.

The third reading having commenced, on motion of Mr. Small of Rochester the rules were suspended and the bill read a third time by its title and passed and sent to the Senate for concurrence.

SPECIAL ORDER.

Mr. Nason of Dover called for the special order, it being the following entitled bill: An act to amend an act passed at the January session, 1903, entitled "An act to amend chapter 241 of the session Laws of 1893, entitled 'An act to establish the city of Laconia,'" and repealing chapter 200 of the Laws of 1901, entitled "An act to amend chapter 241 of the Session Laws of 1893, entitled 'An act to establish the city of Laconia.'"

On motion of Mr. Nason of Dover, the bill was laid upon the table and made the special order for Wednesday, Feb-18, at 3 o'clock.

On motion of Mr. Messer of New London, at 3.28 the House adjourned.

WEDNESDAY, February 18, 1903.

The House met at 11 o'clock.

Mr. Mason of Wilmot, having been qualified by His Excellency the Governor, appeared and took his seat as a member of the House of Representatives.

PETITIONS PRESENTED AND REFERRED.

By Mr. Cutler of Jaffrey, Petition of the Granite State Lodge of Good Templars not to enact a license law.

By Mr. Cutler of Jaffrey, Petition of the Belknap Women's Christian Temperance Union, representing 162 members, for the retention of the prohibitory law, with amendments.

By Mr. Cutler of Jaffrey, Petition of the Congregational church and Sunday-school of Hampstead for the maintenance of the prohibitory law.

Severally to the Committee on Liquor Laws.

COMMITTEE REPORTS.

Mr. Woodman of Concord, for the Committee on Judiciary, to whom was referred An act in amendment of chapter 51 of the Public Statutes, relating to cemeteries, having considered the same, report the same with the following resolution:

Resolved, That the bill ought to pass.

Mr. Woodman of Concord, for the Committee on Judiciary,

to whom was referred An act providing for the appointment of guardians for minors in certain cases, having considered the same, report the same with the following resolution :

Resolved, That the bill ought to pass.

Mr. Scammon of Exeter, for the Committee on Judiciary, to whom was referred An act to enable the Hedding Camp-meeting Association to fund its indebtedness, having considered the same, report the same with the following resolution :

Resolved, That the bill ought to pass.

Mr. Woodman of Concord, for the Committee on Judiciary, to whom was referred An act to incorporate the Omicron Deuteron Charge of the Theta Delta Chi, having considered the same, report the same with the following resolution :

Resolved, That the bill ought to pass.

Mr. Woodman of Concord, for the Committee on Judiciary, to whom was referred An act to amend section 1 of an act of June, 1814, incorporating the Congregational Society in Durham, having considered the same, report the same with the following resolution :

Resolved, That the bill ought to pass.

Mr. Demers of Somersworth, for the Committee on Revision of Statutes, to whom was referred An act in amendment of section 34 of chapter 43 of the Public Statutes, in regard to the incompatibility of certain town offices, having considered the same, report the same with the following resolution :

Resolved, That the bill ought to pass.

Mr. Woodman of Concord, for the Committee on Judiciary, to whom was referred An act in relation to bail in criminal cases, having considered the same, report the same with the following resolution :

Resolved, That the bill ought to pass.

Mr. Woodman of Concord, for the Committee on Judiciary, to whom was referred An act to change the name of the Women's Auxiliary to the City Missionary Society of Manchester, having considered the same, report the same with the following resolution :

Resolved, That the bill ought to pass.

Mr. Woodman of Concord, for the Committee on Judiciary, to whom was referred An act to revive, renew, and amend the charter of the Knights of Pythias Building Association of Manchester, having considered the same, report the same with the following resolution :

Resolved, That the bill ought to pass.

Mr. Woodman of Concord, for the Committee on Judiciary, to whom was referred An act in amendment of section 14 of chapter 264 of the Public Statutes, relating to offenses against the police of towns, having considered the same, report the same with the following resolution :

Resolved, That the bill ought to pass.

Mr. Woodman of Concord, for the Committee on Judiciary, to whom was referred An act in amendment of chapter 91, section 8, Laws of 1897, relating to the duties of the State Board of Charities and Correction, having considered the same, report the same with the following resolution :

Resolved, That the bill ought to pass.

Mr. Mitchell of Littleton, for the Committee on Judiciary, to whom was referred An act relating to agreed lines between adjoining owners, having considered the same, report the same with the following resolution :

Resolved, That the bill ought to pass.

The reports were severally accepted and the bills laid upon the table to be printed.

Mr. Smith of Peterborough, for the Committee on Revision of Statutes, to whom was referred An act in amendment of sections 4, 5, and 9 of chapter 85 of the Public Statutes, entitled "Support of county paupers," having considered the same, report the same with the following amendment and with the resolution that the bill as amended ought to pass.

Amend section 5 as follows : strike out the word "five" in the third line of said section and insert in place thereof the word "ten."

The report was accepted, the amendment adopted, and the bill laid upon the table to be printed.

Mr. Small of Rochester, for the Committee on Judiciary, to whom was referred An act in relation to the salary of the register of probate for Strafford county, having considered the same, report the same with the following resolution :

Resolved, That the bill ought to pass.

The report was accepted and the bill laid upon the table to be printed and then referred to the Committee on Appropriations.

Mr. Remich of Littleton, for the Committee on Judiciary, to whom was referred An act in amendment of section 3 of chapter 60 of Session Laws of 1891, having considered the same, report the same with the following resolution :

Resolved, That the bill be indefinitely postponed because a bill covering the same subject has been reported favorably by the Committee on Revision of Statutes.

Mr. Demers of Somersworth, for the Committee on Revision of Statutes, to whom was referred An act in amendment of section 16 of chapter 150 of the Public Statutes, relating to annual returns of corporations, having considered the same, report the same with the following resolution :

Resolved, That it is inexpedient to legislate.

Mr. Willis of Concord, for the Committee on Insurance, to whom was referred An act in amendment of chapter 168, Public Statutes, in relation to insurance companies and agents, having considered the same, report the same with the following resolution :

Resolved, That it is inexpedient to legislate.

Mr. Woodman of Concord, for the Committee on Judiciary, to whom was referred An act to provide for the distribution of fines imposed by police courts in certain cases, having considered the same, report the same with the following resolution :

Resolved, That it is inexpedient to legislate.

Mr. Donahue of Manchester, for the Committee on Insurance, to whom was referred An act to regulate the appointment of insurance agents, having considered the same, report the same with the following resolution :

Resolved, That it is inexpedient to legislate.

Mr. Remich of Littleton, for the Committee on Judiciary, to whom was referred An act to prohibit the deposit of sawdust, shavings, or other refuse in Bearcamp river and tributaries, east of Bearcamp pond, in the town of Sandwich, having considered the same, report the same with the following resolution :

Resolved, That it is inexpedient to legislate.

Mr. Woodman of Concord, for the Committee on Judiciary, to whom was referred An act to protect the public from extortion, having considered the same, report the same with the following resolution :

Resolved, That it is inexpedient to legislate.

Mr. Barrett of Dover, for the Committee on Insurance, to whom was referred An act to regulate the operation of the insurance companies, corporations, associations, individuals, and insurance agencies in the state of New Hampshire, and prohibiting the payment of any commission, compensation, or valuable consideration to any but legally authorized resident agents, and providing the penalty for violations of this act, having considered the same, report the same with the following resolution :

Resolved, That it is inexpedient to legislate.

Mr. Woodman of Concord, for the Committee on Judiciary, to whom was referred An act to amend chapter 141 of the Public Statutes, relating to the liens of mechanics and others, having considered the same, report the same with the following resolution :

Resolved, That it is inexpedient to legislate.

Mr. Woodman of Concord, for the Committee on Judiciary, to whom was referred An act to amend section 5, chapter 286, of the Public Statutes, as amended by chapter 56, relating to the salaries and compensation of certain officers, having considered the same, report the same with the following resolution :

Resolved, That it is inexpedient to legislate.

Mr. Woodman of Concord, for the Committee on Judiciary, to whom was referred An act in amendment of section 16, chapter 220 of the Public Statutes, relating to attachments, having considered the same, report the same with the following resolution :

Resolved, That it is inexpedient to legislate.

Mr. Foye of Portsmouth, for the Committee on Roads, Bridges, and Canals, to whom was referred Joint resolution in favor of the Kinsman Notch or Lost River road in the town of Woodstock, having considered the same, report the same with the following resolution :

Resolved, That it is inexpedient to legislate, the subject matter having been included in a bill in a new draft.

Mr. Foye of Portsmouth, for the Committee on Roads, Bridges, and Canals, to whom was referred Joint resolution in favor of the highway in the town of Pittsburg, having considered the same, report the same with the following resolution :

Resolved, That it is inexpedient to legislate, the subject having been included in a bill in a new draft.

Mr. Foye of Portsmouth, for the Committee on Roads, Bridges, and Canals, to whom was referred Joint resolution for maintenance and repair of highways in the town of Albany for the years 1902 and 1904, having considered the same, report the same with the following resolution ·

Resolved, That it is inexpedient to legislate, the subject matter having been included in a bill in a new draft.

Mr. Foye of Portsmouth, for the Committee on Roads, Bridges, and Canals, to whom was referred Joint resolution for the appropriation of $500 for the repairing of the highway from Little Diamond pond to Diamond pond in the town of Stewartstown, having considered the same, report the same with the following resolution :

Resolved, That it is inexpedient to legislate, the subject matter having been included in a bill in a new draft.

Mr. Foye of Portsmouth, for the Committee on Roads, Bridges, and Canals, to whom was referred An act in favor of that portion of the mountain road in the town of Warren leading from North Woodstock to Breezy Point, having considered the same, report the same with the following resolution :

Resolved, That it is inexpedient to legislate, the subject matter having been included in a bill in a new draft.

Mr. Foye of Portsmouth, for the Committee on Roads, Bridges, and Canals, to whom was referred An act in favor of the Sugar Loaf road in the town of Alexandria, having considered the same, report the same with the following resolution :

Resolved, That it is inexpedient to legislate, the subject matter having been included in a bill in a new draft.

Mr. Foye of Portsmouth, for the Committee on Roads, Bridges, and Canals, to whom was referred Joint resolution in favor of a new highway in the town of Sunapee, having considered the same, report the same with the following resolution:

Resolved, That it is inexpedient to legislate, the subject matter having been included in a bill in a new draft.

Mr. Foye of Portsmouth, for the Committee on Roads, Bridges, and Canals, to whom was referred Joint resolution in aid of Miller Park Mountain road, so called, situated in the towns of Temple and Peterborough, having considered the same, report the same with the following resolution:

Resolved, That it is inexpedient to legislate, the subject matter having been included in a bill in a new draft.

Mr. Foye of Portsmouth, for the Committee on Roads, Bridges, and Canals, to whom was referred Joint resolution to authorize the appropriation and expenditure of one hundred dollars to repair the highway leading from Lakeside to Soonipi park in New London, having considered the same, report the same with the following resolution:

Resolved, That it is inexpedient to legislate, the subject matter having been included in a bill in a new draft.

Mr. Foye of Portsmouth, for the Committee on Roads, Bridges, and Canals, to whom was referred Joint resolution in favor of the further construction and repair of the road and bridle path leading to Mt. Cardigan in the town of Alexandria, having considered the same, report the same with the following resolution:

Resolved, That it is inexpedient to legislate, the subject matter having been included in a bill in a new draft.

Mr. Foye of Portsmouth, for the Committee on Roads, Bridges, and Canals, to whom was referred Joint resolution in favor of the Sandwich Notch road in the town of Thornton, having considered the same, report the same with the following resolution:

Resolved, That it is inexpedient to legislate, the subject matter having been included in a bill in a new draft.

Mr. Foye of Portsmouth, for the Committee on Roads, Bridges, and Canals, to whom was referred Joint resolution in favor of the new road on the north side of Saco river in the town of Bartlett, having considered the same, report the same with the following resolution :

Resolved, That it is inexpedient to legislate, the subject matter having been included in a bill in a new draft.

Mr. Foye of Portsmouth, for the Committee on Roads, Bridges, and Canals, to whom was referred Joint resolution to aid in repairing the Nash Stream road in Stratford, having considered the same, report the same with the following resolution :

Resolved, That it is inexpedient to legislate, the subject matter having been included in a bill in a new draft.

Mr. Foye of Portsmouth, for the Committee on Roads, Bridges, and Canals, to whom was referred Joint resolution to aid in constructing a highway around the east end of Forest lake in Whitefield, having considered the same, report the same with the following resolution :

Resolved, That it is inexpedient to legislate, the subject matter having been included in a bill in a new draft.

Mr. Foye of Portsmouth, for the Committee on Roads, Bridges, and Canals, to whom was referred Joint resolution in favor of highways in the town of Albany, having considered the same, report the same with the following resolution :

Resolved, That it is inexpedient to legislate, the subject matter having been included in a bill in a new draft.

Mr. Foye of Portsmouth, for the Committee on Roads, Bridges, and Canals, to whom was referred Joint resolution in favor of a highway in the town of Newbury, having considered the same, report the same with the following resolution :

Resolved, That it is inexpedient to legislate, the subject matter having been included in a bill in a new draft.

Mr. Foye of Portsmouth, for the Committee on Roads, Bridges, and Canals, to whom was referred Joint resolution for the repairs of highways in the town of Randolph, having considered the same, report the same with the following resolution :

Resolved, That it is inexpedient to legislate, the subject matter having been included in a bill in a new draft.

20

Mr. Foye of Portsmouth, for the Committee on Roads, Bridges, and Canals, to whom was referred Joint resolution in favor of the highways in the town of Groton, having considered the same, report the same with the following resolution :

Resolved, That it is inexpedient to legislate, the subject matter having been included in a bill in a new draft.

Mr. Foye of Portsmouth, for the Committee on Roads, Bridges, and Canals, to whom was referred Joint resolution appropriating five hundred dollars for the repair of highways in the town of Dorchester, having considered the same, report the same with the following resolution :

Resolved, That it is inexpedient to legislate, the subject matter having been included in a bill in a new draft.

Mr. Foye of Portsmouth, for the Committee on Roads, Bridges, and Canals, to whom was referred Joint resolution in favor of the Sandwich Notch road, in the town of Sandwich, having considered the same, report the same with the following resolution :

Resolved, That it is inexpedient to legislate, the subject matter having been included in a bill in a new draft.

Mr. Foye of Portsmouth, for the Committee on Roads, Bridges, and Canals, to whom was referred Joint resolution for the repairs of the North and South roads, so called, in the town of Benton, having considered the same, report the same with the following resolution :

Resolved, That it is inexpedient to legislate, the subject matter having been included in a bill in a new draft.

Mr. Foye of Portsmouth, for the Committee on Roads, Bridges, and Canals, to whom was referred Joint resolution in favor of the Forest Lake road in the towns of Whitefield and Dalton, having considered the same, report the same with the following resolution :

Resolved, That it is inexpedient to legislate, the subject matter having been included in a bill in a new draft.

Mr. Foye of Portsmouth, for the Committee on Roads, Bridges, and Canals, to whom was referred Joint resolution for the repairs of highways and bridges in the town of Campton, having considered the same, report the same with the following resolution :

Resolved, That it is inexpedient to legislate, the subject matter having been included in a bill in a new draft.

Mr. Foye of Portsmouth, for the Committee on Roads, Bridges, and Canals, to whom was referred Joint resolution in favor of the Hurricane Mountain road, so called, in the towns of Conway and Chatham, having considered the same, report the same with the following resolution:

Resolved, That it is inexpedient to legislate, the subject matter having been included in a bill in a new draft.

Mr. Foye of Portsmouth, for the Committee on Roads, Bridges, and Canals, to whom was referred Joint resolution in favor of the Pinkham Notch road, so called, in Jackson, having considered the same, report the same with the following resolution:

Resolved, That it is inexpedient to legislate, the subject matter having been included in a bill in a new draft.

Mr. Foye of Portsmouth, for the Committee on Roads, Bridges, and Canals, to whom was referred Joint resolution in favor of the County Pond road in the towns of Newton and Kingston, having considered the same, report the same with the following resolution:

Resolved, That it is inexpedient to legislate, the subject matter having been included in a bill in a new draft.

Mr. Foye of Portsmouth, for the Committee on Roads, Bridges, and Canals, to whom was referred Joint resolution in favor of highways laid out under the provisions of chapter 70 of the Public Statutes, having considered the same, report the same with the following resolution:

Resolved, That it is inexpedient to legislate, the subject matter having been included in a bill in a new draft.

Mr. Foye of Portsmouth, for the Committee on Roads, Bridges, and Canals, to whom was referred Joint resolution in favor of the highway leading from the Willey house in Hart's Location to the west line of Bartlett, having considered the same, report the same with the following resolution:

Resolved, That it is inexpedient to legislate, the subject matter having been included in a bill in a new draft.

Mr. Foye of Portsmouth, for the Committee on Roads, Bridges, and Canals, to whom was referred Joint resolution in favor of the highways in the towns of Rumney and Ellsworth, having considered the same, report the same with the following resolution:

Resolved, That it is inexpedient to legislate, the subject matter having been included in a bill in a new draft.

Mr. Foye of Portsmouth, for the Committee on Roads, Bridges, and Canals, to whom was referred Joint resolution in favor of the Forest Lake road running from Bethlehem road to the northerly side of said lake, having considered the same, report the same with the following resolution:

Resolved, That it is inexpedient to legislate, the subject matter having been included in a bill in a new draft.

Mr. Foye of Portsmouth, for the Committee on Roads, Bridges, and Canals, to whom was referred An act in favor of the Warren road in the town of Woodstock, having considered the same, report the same with the following resolution:

Resolved, That it is inexpedient to legislate, the subject matter having been included in a bill in a new draft.

The reports were severally accepted and the resolutions reported by the committees adopted.

Mr. Pike of Haverhill, for the Committee on Appropriations, to whom was referred Joint resolution to provide for completing the painting and decorating of the walls of the state library building, having considered the same, report the same with the following resolution:

Resolved, That the joint resolution ought to pass with the following amendment: Amend the seventh line by striking out the words "twelve hundred" and inserting the words "one thousand," so that the joint resolution as amended shall read:

"The governor and the trustees of the state library as custodians of the state library building are hereby authorized and instructed to cause the walls of the judges' suite, the art gallery, the clerk of court's room, and the smoking room in said building to be painted and decorated in a proper manner, and the governor is hereby authorized to draw his warrant for a sum not exceeding one thousand dollars, to pay the expenses incurred in carrying into effect this resolution, upon any money in the treasury not otherwise appropriated."

The report was accepted, the amendment adopted, and the joint resolution ordered to a third reading.

Mr. Dickinson of Winchester, for the Committee on Appropriations, to whom was referred Joint resolution appropriating money to aid Dartmouth College in the education of New Hampshire students, having considered the same, report the same with the following resolution :

Resolved, That the joint resolution ought to pass.

Mr. Ahern of Concord, for the Committee on Appropriations, to whom was referred Joint resolution appropriating money to complete the payment of expenses of the recent constitutional convention, having considered the same, report the same with the following resolution :

Resolved, That the joint resolution ought to pass.

Mr. Wallace of Rochester, for the Committee on Appropriations, to whom was referred Joint resolution in favor of the New Hampshire State Hospital, having considered the same, report the same with the following resolution :

Resolved, That the joint resolution ought to pass.

Mr. Foye of Portsmouth, for the Committee on Appropriations, to whom was referred An act to authorize the governor with the consent of the council to cause the original maps and surveys by the town proprietors of New Hampshire to be mounted and preserved, having considered the same, report the same with the following resolution :

Resolved, That the bill ought to pass.

The reports were severally accepted and the joint resolutions and bill ordered to a third reading.

Mr. Whittemore of Dover, for the Committee on Judiciary, to whom was referred An act to reimburse the town or county for aid furnished paupers, having considered the same, report the same in new draft with the following resolution :

Resolved, That the bill in new draft ought to pass.

Mr. Woodman of Concord, for the Committee on Judiciary, to whom was referred An act fixing office hours in state and county offices, having considered the same, report the same in new draft with the following resolution :

Resolved, That the bill in new draft ought to pass.

The reports were severally accepted and the bills in their

new drafts read a first time and ordered to a second reading.

Mr. Trickey of Jackson, for the Committee on Roads, Bridges, and Canals, to whom was referred An act to provide for a more economical and practical expenditure of money appropriated by the state for the construction and repairs of highways, having considered the same, report the same in a new draft with the following resolution :

Resolved, That the bill in a new draft ought to pass.

The report was accepted. On motion of Mr. Ahern of Concord, the rules were suspended and the bill in its new draft read a first time by its title. It was then ordered to a second reading. On motion of the same gentleman, the rules were suspended and the bill read a second time by its title. It was then laid upon the table to be printed. On motion of the same gentleman, the rules were further suspended, the printing of the bill dispensed with, and the bill referred to the Committee on Appropriations.

Mr. Barr of Manchester, for the Committee on Insurance, to whom was referred An act to incorporate the Maynesboro Fire Insurance Company, having considered the same, report the same with the following amendment, and the resolution that the bill as amended ought to pass

Amend section 2 by adding after the word " security," " The principal office of the company shall be in Berlin, N. H. The majority of the directors shall be citizens of New Hampshire, and no person shall be qualified as a director who does not hold, in his own right, one thousand dollars in par value of the capital stock," so that section 2 as amended shall read :

Sect. 2. Said corporation shall have a capital stock of fifty thousand dollars divided into shares of one hundred dollars each, with liberty to increase the capital stock to five hundred thousand dollars ; and may acquire and hold real estate for its own use to the value of twenty-five thousand dollars, exclusive of such real estate as may be taken for debt or may be held for collateral security. The principal office of the company shall be in Berlin, N. H. The majority of the directors shall be citizens of New Hampshire, and no person shall be qualified as a director who does not hold, in his own right, one thousand dollars in par value of the capital stock.

The report was accepted and the question being upon the adoption of the amendment reported by the committee, Mr. Goss of Berlin offered the following amendment to the amendment:

Amend section 2 by striking out the word "five" in the third line of said section and inserting the word "two" in place thereof, so that said section as amended shall read:

SECT. 2   Said corporation shall have a capital stock of fifty thousand dollars, divided into shares of one hundred dollars each, with liberty to increase the capital stock to two hundred thousand dollars; and may acquire and hold real estate for its own use to the value of twenty-five thousand dollars, exclusive of such real estate as may be taken for debt or may be held for collateral security. The principal office of the company shall be in Berlin, N. H. The majority of the directors shall be citizens of New Hampshire, and no person shall be qualified as a director who does not hold, in his own right, one thousand dollars in par value of the capital stock.

The question being upon the adoption of the amendment offered by Mr. Goss,

(Discussion ensued.)

On a *viva voce* vote the amendment offered by Mr. Goss was adopted.

The question being upon the adoption of the amendment reported by the committee, on a *viva voce* vote the amendment was adopted. The bill was then laid upon the table to be printed.

Mr. Aiken of Newport, for the Committee on Insurance, to whom was referred An act to incorporate the Manchester Fire Insurance Company of New Hampshire, having considered the same, report the same with the following amendment and with the resolution that the bill as amended ought to pass:

Amend section 2 by adding after the word "security," "The principal office of the company shall be in Manchester, N. H. The majority of the directors shall be citizens of New Hampshire, and no person shall be qualified as a director who does not hold, in his own right, one thousand dollars in par value of the capital stock," so that section 2 as amended shall read :

SECT. 2. Said corporation shall have a capital stock of fifty thousand dollars, divided into shares of one hundred dollars each, with liberty to increase the capital stock to five hundred thousand dollars; and may acquire and hold real estate, for its own use, to the value of twenty-five thousand dollars, exclusive of such real estate as may be taken for debt or may be held for collateral security. The principal office of the company shall be in Manchester, N. H. The majority of the directors shall be citizens of New Hampshire, and no person shall be qualified as a director who does not hold, in his own right, one thousand dollars in par value of the capital stock.

The report was accepted. The question being upon the adoption of the amendment, Mr. Sheehan offered the following amendment to the amendment :

Amend section 2 by striking out the words "five hundred thousand" where they occur in said section and inserting the words "two hundred and fifty thousand" in place thereof, so that said section as amended shall read :

SECT. 2. Said corporation shall have a capital stock of fifty thousand dollars, divided into shares of one hundred dollars each, with liberty to increase the capital stock to two hundred and fifty thousand dollars; and may acquire and hold real estate for its own use to the value of twenty-five thousand dollars, exclusive of such real estate as may be taken for debts or may be held for collateral security. The principal office of the company shall be in Manchester, N. H. The majority of the directors shall be citizens of New Hampshire, and no person shall be qualified as a director who does not hold, in his own right, one thousand dollars in par value of the capital stock.

On a *viva voce* vote the amendment offered by Mr. Sheehan was adopted.

The question being upon the adoption of the amendment reported by the committee, on a *viva voce* vote the amendment was adopted. The bill was then laid upon the table to be printed.

Mr. Demers of Somersworth, for the Committee on Revision of Statutes, to whom was referred An act to amend the Public Statutes, section 5, chapter 37 of the Laws of 1895, relating to the fee of bail commissioner, having considered the same, report the same with the following resolution:

Resolved, That it is inexpedient to legislate.

The report was accepted and the question being upon the adoption of the resolution reported by the committee,

(Discussion ensued.)

On motion of Mr. Bussell of Nashua, the bill was recommitted to the Committee on Revision of Statutes.

Mr. Scammon of Exeter, for the Committee on Judiciary, to whom was referred An act to amend section 1, chapter 184 of the Public Statutes, relative to the times and places for holding courts of probate, repealing chapter 29 of the Session Laws of 1901, having considered the same, report the same in a new draft and with the resolution that the bill in new draft ought to pass.

The report was accepted. On motion of Mr. Scammon of Exeter, the rules were suspended and the bill in its new draft read a first time by its title. The bill was then ordered to a second reading. On motion of the same gentleman, the rules were suspended and the bill read a second time by its title. The bill was then laid upon the table to be printed. On motion of the same gentleman, the rules were suspended and the printing of the bill dispensed with. The bill was then ordered to a third reading. On motion of the same gentleman, the rules were further suspended and the bill read a third time by its title and passed and sent to the Senate for concurrence.

Mr. Bragg of Errol, for the Committee on Roads, Bridges, and Canals, to whom was referred Joint resolution to aid in the reconstruction of the Magalloway road in Errol on a practicable route, having considered the same, report the same with the following resolution:

Resolved, That the joint resolution ought to pass.

The report was accepted and the joint resolution laid upon the table to be printed. On motion of Mr. Ahern of Concord, the rules were suspended, the printing of the joint resolution dispensed with, and the joint resolution referred to the Committee on Appropriations.

Mr. Brown of Fremont, for the Committee on Roads, Bridges, and Canals, to whom was referred Joint resolution in aid of changing and repairing the Dixville Notch road in Dixville, having considered the same, report the same with the following resolution :

Resolved, That the joint resolution ought to pass.

The report was accepted and the joint resolution laid upon the table to be printed. On motion of Mr. Ahern of Concord, the rules were suspended, the printing of the joint resolution dispensed with, and the joint resolution referred to the Committee on Appropriations.

Mr. Wright of Manchester, for the Committee on Appropriations, to whom was referred Joint resolution making appropriations for repairs on buildings erected by the state for the New Hampshire Veterans' Association at The Weirs, having considered the same, report the same with the following resolution :

Resolved, That the joint resolution ought to pass.

The report was accepted and the joint resolution ordered to a third reading. On motion of Mr. Ahern of Concord, the rules were suspended and the joint resolution read a third time and passed and sent to the Senate for concurrence.

Mr. Whitcher of Haverhill, for the Committee on Judiciary, to whom was referred Joint resolution appropriating one thousand dollars for a monument to be erected at Hackensack, New Jersey, in memory of Gen. Enoch Poor, having considered the same, report the same with the following resolution :

Resolved, That the joint resolution be referred to the Committee on Appropriations.

The report was accepted and the joint resolution referred to the Committee on Appropriations.

Mr. Small of Rochester, for the Committee on Judiciary, to whom was referred An act in amendment of chapter 202 of the Laws of 1889, entitled " An act to establish water-works in the town of Wolfeborough, as amended by chapter 191 of the Laws of 1891," having considered the same, report the same with the following resolution :

Resolved, That the bill ought to pass.

The report was accepted and the bill laid upon the table to

be printed.   On motion of Mr. Small of Rochester, the rules were suspended and the printing of the bill dispensed with. The bill was then ordered to a third reading.   On motion of the same gentleman, the rules were further suspended and the bill read a third time and passed and sent to the Senate for concurrence.

Mr. Converse of Lyme, for the Committee on Agriculture, to whom was referred An act to encourage the use of wide tires on certain vehicles constructed before January 1, 1900, and now in use in New Hampshire, having considered the same, report the same with the following resolution :

Resolved, That it is inexpedient to legislate.

The report was accepted.   The question being upon the adoption of the resolution reported by the committee,

(Discussion ensued.)

On motion of Mr. Whitcher of Haverhill, the bill and report were laid upon the table.

On motion of Mr. Remich of Littleton, the bill and report were subsequently taken from the table and laid upon the table to be printed.

Mr. Converse of Lyme, for the Committee on Engrossed Bills, reported that they had examined bills with the following titles and found them correctly engrossed :

An act to establish the salary of the justice of the police court of Concord.

An act in amendment of chapter 192 of the Public Statutes, relating to insolvent estates.

The report was accepted.

Mr. Bunton, A. S., of Manchester, for the Committee on Banks, reported the following entitled bill, "An act in amendment of section 1 of chapter 3 of the Laws of 1893, fixing the salary of the clerk of the board of bank commissioners," with the resolution that the bill ought to pass.

The report was accepted and the bill read a first time and ordered to a second reading.

Mr. Bunton, A. S., of Manchester, for the Committee on Banks, reported the following entitled bill, "An act in amendment of section 4 of chapter 162 of the Public Statutes, fixing the salaries of the members of the board of bank commissioners," with the resolution that the bill ought to pass.

The report was accepted and the bill read a first time and ordered to a second reading.

Mr. Andrews of Somersworth, for the Committee on Education, reported the following entitled bill, "An act to equalize school privileges in the town of Littleton," with the resolution that the bill ought to pass.

The report was accepted. On motion of Mr. Mitchell of Littleton, the rules were suspended and the bill read a first time by its title. It was then ordered to a second reading. On motion of the same gentleman, the rules were suspended and the bill read a second time by its title. The bill was then laid upon the table to be printed. On motion of the same gentleman, the rules were further suspended and the printing of the bill dispensed with. The bill was then ordered to a third reading. On motion of the same gentleman, the rules were suspended and the bill read a third time by its title and passed and sent to the Senate for concurrence.

Mr. Goss of Berlin, for the Committee on Judiciary, reported the following entitled bill, "An act in amendment of chapter 215, Laws of 1895, entitled 'An act to confirm the organization of the Androscoggin Hospital Association,'" with the resolution that the bill ought to pass.

The report was accepted. On motion of Mr. Whitcher of Haverhill, the rules were suspended and the bill read a first time by its title. The bill was then ordered to a second reading.

SECOND READINGS.

An act authorizing the Mt. Pleasant Hotel Company to increase its capital stock.

An act to provide for the daily publication of the journal of the Senate and House of Representatives.

Severally read a second time and laid upon the table to be printed.

MESSAGE FROM THE SENATE.

A message from the Honorable Senate, by its clerk, announced that the Senate concurs with the House of Representatives in the passage of the following entitled bill:

An act to incorporate the Littleton, Franconia, and Bethlehem Electric Railway Company.

The message also announced that the Senate has passed bills with the following titles, in the passage of which it asks the concurrence of the House of Representatives:

An act in amendment of the charter of the Plymouth Guaranty Savings Bank.

Read a first and second time and referred to the Committee on Banks.

An act amending the charter of the Nashua Light, Heat, and Power Company of Nashua.

Read a first and second time and referred to the Committee on Judiciary.

The message further announced that the Senate concurs with the House of Representatives in the passage of the following bill, with amendments, in the passage of which amendments it asks the concurrence of the House of Representatives:

An act to provide for obtaining the testimony of nonresident directors, officers, and agents of New Hampshire corporations and the production of corporate books, records, and papers.

Amend section 4 of said act by adding at the end thereof the words: "Provided said witness shall be summoned to come from another state into this state, he shall be paid double fees for his travel and attendance."

Amend by striking out section 5 and substitute in place thereof the following:

"SECT. 5. If any such director, officer, or agent shall wilfully neglect, or refuse to appear, produce books, records, or papers, or testify, or give his deposition as required by such order, or summons, the superior court, in its discretion upon notice and hearing, may thereupon appoint a receiver to manage and control such corporation until the reasonable and just orders of the court shall be complied with, and when such orders shall have been complied with, such receiver shall be discharged."

Mr. Remich of Littleton moved that the House concur

with the Honorable Senate in its amendments.   The question being upon the adoption of the motion,

(Discussion ensued.)

Mr. Smith of Peterborough moved that the bill and amendments be laid upon the table.

(Discussion ensued.)

Mr. Small of Rochester raised the point of order that a motion to lay upon the table was not debatable.

The Speaker ruled that the point of order was well taken.

Mr. Ahern of Concord moved to amend the motion of Mr. Smith of Peterborough by inserting after the word "table" the words " to be printed."   Mr. Smith accepted the amendment, and on a *viva voce* vote the motion of Mr. Smith was adopted and the bill and amendments laid upon the table to be printed.

On motion of Mr. Nason of Dover, the rules were suspended and business in order this afternoon at 3 o'clock was made in order at 12 o'clock.

SPECIAL ORDER.

Mr. Nason of Dover called for the special order, it being An act to amend an act passed at the January session, 1903, entitled "An act to amend chapter 241 of the Session Laws of 1893, entitled 'An act to establish the city of Laconia,'" and repealing chapter 200 of the Laws of 1901, entitled "An act to amend chapter 241 of the Session Laws of 1893, entitled 'An act to establish the city of Laconia.'"

The third reading being in order, Mr. Libby of Gorham moved that the rules be suspended and the bill put back upon its second reading for amendment.   On a *viva voce* vote the motion did not prevail.   Mr. Libby of Gorham called for a division. A division being had, 74 gentlemen voted in the affirmative and 163 gentlemen voted in the negative and the motion did not prevail.   On motion of Mr. Whitcher of Haverhill, the rules were suspended and the bill read a third time by its title.

The question being,

Shall the bill pass?

(Discussion ensued.)

Mr. Small of Rochester moved that the bill be laid upon the table until after the March election. On a *viva voce* vote the motion did not prevail. Mr. Small of Rochester called for a division. A division being had, 91 gentlemen voted in the affirmative and 154 gentlemen in the negative and the motion did not prevail.

Mr. Remich of Littleton moved the previous question.

The question being,

Shall the main question be now put?

On a *viva voce* vote the motion was adopted.

The question being,

Shall the bill pass?

On a *viva voce* vote the bill passed and was sent to the Senate for concurrence.

On motion of Mr. Ahern of Concord, the following entitled bill, "An act in amendment of section 15 of chapter 93 of the Public Statutes, as amended in 1901, relating to scholars," which was recalled from the Honorable Senate, was referred to the Committee on Appropriations.

On motion of Mr. Donahue of Manchester, the following entitled bill, "An act to amend chapter 93, section 15 of the Public Statutes, as amended by chapter 61 of the Session Laws of 1901, relating to scholars," was taken from the table and referred to the Committee on Education.

NOTICE OF RECONSIDERATION.

Mr. Sawyer of Milford gave notice that on to-morrow, or some subsequent day, he would move to reconsider the vote whereby the report of the Committee on Judiciary that " it is inexpedient to legislate" on the following entitled bill, "An act relating to negotiable instruments, being an act to establish a law uniform with the laws of other states on that subject," was adopted.

On motion of Mr. Whitcher of Haverhill, at 1.11 the House adjourned.

AFTERNOON.

The House met at 3 o'clock.

LEAVE OF ABSENCE.

Mr. Barnard of Hebron was granted leave of absence for the balance of the week on account of town business.

THIRD READINGS.

(Mr. Nason of Dover in the chair.)

An act to authorize the Governor, with the consent of the Council, to cause the original maps and surveys by the town proprietors of New Hampshire to be mounted and preserved.

Joint resolution appropriating money to complete the payment of expenses of the recent constitutional convention.

Joint resolution appropriating money to aid Dartmouth college in the education of New Hampshire students.

Joint resolution in favor of the New Hampshire State Hospital.

Joint resolution to provide for completing the painting and decorating of the walls of the state library building.

Severally read a third time and passed and sent to the Senate for concurrence.

On motion of Mr. Buckley of Lancaster, at 3.06 the House adjourned.

THURSDAY, FEBRUARY 19, 1903.

The House met at 11 o'clock.

Prayer was offered by the chaplain.

COMMITTEE REPORTS.

Mr. Donahue of Manchester, for the Committee on Insurance, to whom was referred An act to protect resident life insurance agents and managers from competition with nonresident agents and managers and to prohibit the sale of deceptive life insurance in this state, having considered the same, report the same with the following resolution :

Resolved, That it is inexpedient to legislate.

Mr. Demers of Somersworth, for the Committee on Revision of Statutes, to whom was referred An act to amend paragraph 2 of section 20 of chapter 245 of the Public Statutes, relating to exemption from trustee process, having considered the same, report the same with the following resolution :

Resolved, That it is inexpedient to legislate.

The reports were severally accepted and the resolutions reported by the committees adopted.

Mr. Crocker of Rochester, for the Committee on Normal School, to whom was referred An act to establish a state normal school, having considered the same, report the same with the following resolution :

Resolved, That the bill ought to pass.

The report was accepted and the bill referred to the Committee on Appropriations.

Mr. Smith of Exeter, for the Committee on Appropriations, to whom was referred Joint resolution in favor of Charles H. Roberts, having considered the same, report the same with the following resolution :

Resolved, That the joint resolution ought to pass.

The report was accepted and the joint resolution ordered to a third reading.

Mr. Demers of Somersworth, for the Committee on Revision of Statutes, to whom was referred An act in addition to chapter 153, Public Statutes, creating section 20 of said chapter, having considered the same, report the same with the following resolution :

Resolved, That the bill ought to pass.

The report was accepted and the bill laid upon the table to be printed.

Mr. Chase of Weare, for the Committee on Agriculture, to whom was referred Joint resolution to encourage the breeding and exhibiting of thoroughbred farm animals, having considered the same, report the same in new draft, with the following resolution

21

Resolved, That the joint resolution in its new draft ought to pass.

The report was accepted and the joint resolution in its new draft read a first time and ordered to a second reading.

Mr. Nason of Dover, for the Committee on Judiciary, reported the following entitled bill, "An act to amend section 2, chapter 179 of the Public Statutes, relating to the appointment of guardians of insane persons," with the resolution that the bill ought to pass.

The report was accepted and the bill read a first time and ordered to a second reading.

Mr. Edgerly of Tuftonborough, for the Committee on Agricultural College, reported the following joint resolution, "Joint resolution for an appropriation for the benefit of the New Hampshire College of Agriculture and Mechanic Arts," with the resolution that the joint resolution ought to pass.

The report was accepted and the joint resolution read a first time and ordered to a second reading.

Mr. Nelson of Portsmouth, for the Committee on Fisheries and Game, reported the following entitled bill, "An act to amend section 10, chapter 79 of the Session Laws of 1901, relating to the duties of the fish and game commissioners," with the resolution that the bill ought to pass.

The report was accepted and the bill read a first time and ordered to a second reading.

Mr. Ahern of Concord, for the Committee on Appropriations, reported the following joint resolution, "Joint resolution in favor of John K. Law and others," with the resolution that the joint resolution ought to pass.

The report was accepted and the joint resolution read a first time and ordered to a second reading.

SECOND READINGS.

An act in amendment of section 4 of chapter 162 of the Public Statutes, fixing the salaries of the members of the board of bank commissioners.

An act in amendment of section 1 of chapter 3 of the Laws of 1893, fixing the salary of the clerk of the board of bank commissioners.

Severally read a second time and laid upon the table to

be printed and then referred to the Committee on Appropriations.

An act fixing office hours in state and county offices.

An act to reimburse the town or county for aid furnished paupers.

An act in amendment of chapter 215, Laws of 1895, entitled "An act to confirm the organization of the Androscoggin Hospital Association."

Severally read a second time and laid upon the table to be printed.

BILLS FORWARDED.

An act in amendment of section 1, chapter 119, Public Statutes, relating to the inspection and licensing of boats, their engineers and pilots.

Taken from the table and referred to the Committee on Appropriations.

An act explanatory of the powers of the courts in reference to the fees of commissioners in certain cases.

An act to amend the charter of the New England and Louisiana Land Company.

An act to amend the charter of Brown's Lumber Company of Whitefield, approved July 1, 1874.

An act in relation to the settlement of paupers.

Severally taken from the table and ordered to a third reading.

MESSAGE FROM THE SENATE.

A message from the Honorable Senate, by its clerk, announced that the Senate concurs with the House of Representatives in the passage of the following entitled bills and joint resolutions:

An act in amendment of chapter 23 of the Laws of 1901, entitled "An act to establish a laboratory of hygiene."

An act to legalize the biennial election of the town of Conway, held November 4, 1902.

An act to amend the charter of the New Hampshire Odd Fellows' Widows' and Orphans' Home, approved August 15, 1883.

An act to establish water-works in Enfield village fire district, in the town of Enfield.

An act to establish the Lisbon village district.

An act to legalize and confirm the selectmen's warrant for, and the votes and proceedings thereunder at, the biennial election and meeting in the town of Columbia, held in said town on the fourth day of November, A. D. 1902.

An act in amendment of chapter 44 of the Laws of 1893, relating to the powers and duties of the Forestry Commission with respect to public parks.

An act to legalize and confirm the warrant for, and the votes and proceedings at, the biennial election and meeting in Stratham, held the fourth day of November, 1902.

An act to legalize the town meetings in Dorchester for years 1896, 1897, 1898, 1899, and 1900.

An act to repeal an act of the legislature of 1842, entitled "An act to annex Richard Pickering of Newington to school district No. 1 in Portsmouth," approved June 22, 1842.

An act in amendment of "An act to incorporate the North Conway and Mount Kearsarge Railroad," passed June session 1883, and all subsequent acts relating to the same.

An act to change the name of the body of water formerly called Munsonville pond, lying in the towns of Nelson and Stoddard.

An act to authorize the town of Lancaster to exempt certain property from taxation and to ratify its doings in the same.

An act in amendment of the charter of the city of Dover, creating a board of street and park commissioners for said city.

An act to legalize the biennial election of the town of Effingham, held November 4th, 1902.

An act to change the name of Station lake in the town of Springfield.

Joint resolution to provide for a forest examination of the White Mountain region.

Joint resolution in favor of the Granite State Deaf Mute Mission.

An act confirming and legalizing the organization and acts of the Berlin Street Railway.

An act in amendment of the charter of the Wells River bridge, and authorizing the Concord and Montreal Railroad to hold stock therein.

An act to extend the time for the location, construction, and completion of the railroad of the Moosilauke Railroad Company.

An act to authorize the town of Lancaster to acquire property for the protection of its water supply.

The message also announced that the Senate concurs with the House of Representatives in the passage of the following entitled bill, in Senate new draft, in the passage of which it asks the concurrence of the House of Representatives:

An act in amendment of an act approved March 26, 1895, entitled "An act in amendment of an act incorporating the Newmarket Manufacturing Company," approved June 12, 1823, and an act in amendment thereof, approved July 7, 1881.

Read a first and second time and referred to the Committee on Judiciary.

The message also announced that the Senate concurs with the House of Representatives in the passage of the following bill, with amendments, in the passage of which amendments it asks the concurrence of the House of Representatives:

An act to amend sections 54 and 58, chapter 78 of the fish and game laws.

Amend section 1 of the bill by striking out the number " 78 " and inserting in place thereof the number " 79."

Also amend by striking out the present title and inserting in place thereof the following:

"An act to amend section 54 and 58 of chapter 79 of the Laws of 1901, relating to the fish and game laws of the state."

On motion of Mr. Goold of Lebanon, the amendments were concurred in and the bill sent to the secretary of state to be engrossed.

The message further announced that the Senate has passed a bill with the following title, in the passage of which it asks the concurrence of the House of Representatives:

An act to incorporate the Ossipee Water and Electric Company.

On motion of Mr. Nason of Dover, the rules were suspended and the bill read a first time by its title. The bill was then read a second time and referred to the Committee on Judiciary.

On motion of Mr. Sawyer of Milford, the vote whereby the resolution, " That it is inexpedient to legislate," reported by the Committee on Judiciary on the following entitled bill, "An act relating to negotiable instruments, being an act to establish a law uniform with the laws of other states on that subject," was adopted was reconsidered.

The question being upon the adoption of the resolution reported by the committee,

(Discussion ensued.)

On motion of Mr. Sawyer of Milford the bill and report were laid upon the table and the bill was ordered to be printed.

On motion of Mr. Armstrong of Manchester, at 11.40 the House adjourned.

AFTERNOON.

The House met at 3 o'clock.

THIRD READINGS.

An act explanatory of the powers of the courts in reference to the fees of commissioners in certain cases.

An act to amend the charter of the New England and Louisiana Land Company.

An act to amend the charter of Brown's Lumber Company of Whitefield, approved July 1, 1874.

An act in relation to the settlement of paupers.

Severally read a third time and passed and sent to the Senate for concurrence.

MESSAGE FROM THE SENATE.

A message from the Honorable Senate, by its clerk, announced that the Senate concurs with the House of Representatives in the passage of the following entitled bills :

An act to incorporate the New Hampshire Genealogical Society.

An act in amendment of the charter of the city of Berlin.

An act in amendment of section 27, chapter 154 of the Public Statutes, relating to the calling of proprietors' meetings.

An act in addition to chapter 58 of the Public Statutes, relating to the appraisal of taxable real estate.

An act in amendment of section 3, chapter 209 of the Public Statutes, relating to exemptions from serving as jurors.

An act in amendment of section 4 of chapter 206 of the Laws of 1897, being an act to incorporate the Bethlehem Electric Light Company.

An act relative to the issue of bonds, coupon notes, and other evidences of indebtedness of street railway or other railroad companies.

An act to provide for taking depositions outside this state, and depositions within this state for use in other states.

An act authorizing the town of Hudson to construct waterworks and establish an electric light plant.

An act to punish embezzlement by executors, administrators, guardians, and trustees.

An act relating to domestic insurance companies.

An act to amend an act passed at the January session, 1903, entitled "An act to amend chapter 241 of the Session Laws of 1893, entitled 'An act to establish the city of Laconia,'" and repealing chapter 200 of the Laws of 1901, entitled "An act to amend chapter 241 of the Session Laws of 1893, entitled 'An act to establish the city of Laconia.'"

On motion of Mr. Rogers of Tilton,—

Resolved, That the use of Representatives' hall be granted for Wednesday evening, March 4, for a meeting to discuss the anti-woman suffrage question.

On motion of Mr. French of Moultonborough, the rules were suspended and business in order to-morrow morning at 11 o'clock was made in order at the present time.

COMMITTEE REPORTS.

Mr. Quimby of Meredith, for the Committee on Appropriations, to whom was referred An act in amendment of chapter 86 of the Public Statutes, in relation to state aid to indigent deaf and dumb, blind, and feeble-minded persons, having considered the same, report the same with the following resolution :

Resolved, That it ought to pass.

The report was accepted and the bill ordered to a third reading. On motion of Mr. Ahern of Concord, the rules were suspended and the bill read a third time and passed and sent to the Senate for concurrence.

Mr. Andrews of Somersworth, for the Committee on Education, to whom was referred An act to amend section 1 of chapter 46, Session Laws of 1895, relating to annual enumeration of school children, having considered the same, report the same in a new draft and with the following resolution :

Resolved, That the bill in new draft ought to pass.

The report was accepted and the bill in its new draft read a first time and ordered to a second reading.

Mr. Severance of Exeter, for the Committee on Soldiers' Home, to whom was referred An act to authorize the managers of the New Hampshire Soldiers' Home to procure an adequate supply of water for the use of said home, having considered the same, report the same in a new draft and with the following resolution :

Resolved, That the bill in new draft ought to pass.

The report was accepted and the bill in its new draft read a first time and ordered to a second reading.

Mr. Riordan of Manchester, for the Committee on Military Affairs, to whom was referred An act to provide suitable armory quarters for the National Guard at Manchester, having considered the same, report the same with the following resolution :

Resolved, That the bill ought to pass.

The report was accepted and the bill referred to the Committee on Appropriations.

Mr. Taggart of Manchester, for the Committee on Elections, reported the following entitled bill, "An act in amendment of sections 2 and 3, chapter 42 of the Public Statutes, relating to government of town meetings," with the resolution that the bill ought to pass.

The report was accepted and the bill read a first time and ordered to a second reading.

Mr. Ingham of Nashua, for the Committee on Incorporations, reported the following entitled bill, "An act amending the charter of the Newmarket Electric Light, Power and Heat Company," with the resolution that the bill ought to pass.

The report was accepted and the bill read a first time and ordered to a second reading.

Mr. Pike of Haverhill, for the Committee on Appropriations, to whom was referred An act providing for the purchase of a bond for the deputy state treasurer, having considered the same, report the same with the following resolution:

Resolved, That the bill ought to pass.

The report was accepted and the bill ordered to a third reading.

Mr. Newton of Portsmouth, for the special committee consisting of the delegation from the city of Portsmouth, to whom was referred An act to amend the charter of the city of Portsmouth, in relation to the assessors of taxes, having considered the same, report the same with the following resolution:

Resolved, That it is inexpedient to legislate.

The report was accepted and the resolution adopted.

Mr. Wallace of Rochester, for the Committee on Appropriations, to whom was referred An act to provide for a more economical and practical expenditure of money appropriated by the state for the construction and repair of highways, having considered the same, report the same in a new draft and with the following resolution:

Resolved, That the bill in new draft ought to pass.

The report was accepted. On motion of Mr. Pike of Haverhill, the rules were suspended and the bill in its new draft read a first time by its title. The bill was then ordered to a second reading. On motion of the same gentleman, the rules were suspended and the bill read a second time by its title. The bill was then laid upon the table to be printed.

Mr. Newton of Portsmouth, for the special committee consisting of the delegation from the city of Portsmouth, to whom was referred An act to amend the charter of the city of Portsmouth, in relation to street commissioner, having considered the same, report the same in a new draft with amended title and with the following resolution:

Resolved, That the bill in a new draft and with amended title ought to pass.

The report was accepted. On motion of Mr. Remich of Littleton, the rules were suspended and the bill in its new draft read a first time by its title. The bill was then ordered to a second reading. On motion of the same gentleman, the rules were suspended and the bill read a second time by its title. The bill was then laid upon the table to be printed.

SECOND READINGS.

An act to amend section 2, chapter 179 of the Public Statutes, relating to the appointment of guardians of insane persons.

Joint resolution in favor of John K. Law and others.

Severally read a second time and laid upon the table to be printed.

An act to amend section 10, chapter 79 of the Session Laws of 1901, relative to the duties of the fish and game commissioners.

Joint resolution for an appropriation for the benefit of the New Hampshire College of Agriculture and the Mechanic Arts.

Joint resolution to encourage the breeding and exhibiting of thoroughbred farm animals.

Severally read a second time and laid upon the table to be printed and then referred to the Committee on Appropriations.

On motion of Mr. Morgan of Manchester,—

Resolved, That when the House adjourns this afternoon it be to meet to-morrow morning at 9.30 o'clock, and when it adjourns to-morrow morning it be to meet Monday evening at 8 o'clock.

LEAVE OF ABSENCE.

Mr. Pinneo of Hanover was granted leave of absence for a few days on account of town business.

On motion of Mr. Foster of Enfield, at 3.36 the House adjourned.

FRIDAY, FEBRUARY 20, 1903.

The House met at 9.30 o'clock, according to adjournment.

COMMITTEE REPORT.

Mr. Willis of Concord, for the Committee on Engrossed Bills, reported that they had examined and found correctly engrossed the following entitled bill:

An act to amend an act passed at the January session, 1903, entitled "An act to amend chapter 241 of the Session Laws of 1893, entitled 'An act to establish the city of Laconia,'" and repealing chapter 200 of the Laws of 1901, entitled "An act to amend chapter 241 of the Session Laws of 1893, entitled 'An act to establish the city of Laconia.'"

The report was accepted.

SECOND READINGS.

On motion of Mr. French of Moultonborough, the rules were suspended and the second reading of bills by their titles made in order.

An act to amend section 1 of chapter 46, Session Laws of 1895, relating to annual enumeration of school children.

An act in amendment of sections 2 and 3, chapter 42 of the Public Statutes, relating to government of town meetings.

An act amending the charter of the Newmarket Electric Light, Power and Heat Company.

Severally read a second time by their titles and laid upon the table to be printed.

An act to authorize the managers of the New Hampshire Soldiers' Home to procure an adequate supply of water for the use of said home.

Read a second time by its title and laid upon the table to be printed and then referred to the Committee on Appropriations.

On motion of Mr. Ellis of Lancaster, at 9.32 the House adjourned.

MONDAY, FEBRUARY 23, 1903.

The House met at 8 o'clock in the evening, according to adjournment, being called to order by Mr. James E. French of Moultonborough, and the following communication was read by the clerk:

CONCORD, February 23, 1903.

Mr. James E. French, Moultonborough, N. H.

DEAR SIR: I shall be unable to be present at the evening session on Monday, Feb. 23, 1903. Will you kindly preside for me, and oblige

Yours truly,
HARRY M. CHENEY,
Speaker.

On motion of Mr. Stevens of Bartlett, at 8.01 the House adjourned.

TUESDAY, FEBRUARY 24, 1903.

The House met at 11 o'clock.

Prayer was offered by the chaplain.

LEAVES OF ABSENCE.

Mr. Lynch of Manchester was granted leave of absence for a few days on account of sickness.

Mr. Scott of Nelson was granted leave of absence for the balance of the week on account of sickness in his family.

COMMITTEE REPORTS.

Mr. Bussell of Nashua, for the Committee on Railroads, to whom was referred An act to incorporate the Nashua and Hollis Electric Railroad Company, having considered the same, report the same in a new draft with the following resolution:

Resolved, That the bill in its new draft ought to pass.

The report was accepted and the reading of the bill in its

new draft having commenced, on motion of Mr. French of Moultonborough, the rules were suspended and the bill read a first time by its title. The bill was then ordered to a second reading. On motion of the same gentleman, the rules were suspended and the bill read a second time by its title. The bill was then laid upon the table to be printed. On motion of the same gentleman, the rules were suspended and the printing of the bill dispensed with. The bill was then ordered to a third reading. On motion of the same gentleman, the rules were further suspended and the bill read a third time by its title and passed and sent to the Senate for concurrence.

Mr. Smith of Peterborough, for the Committee on Revision of Statutes, to whom was referred An act in amendment of chapter 59 of the Laws of 1891, entitled " An act in amendment of chapter 7 of the Laws of 1883, entitled ' An act in relation to the exemption of disabled soldiers and sailors of the late war from the payment of poll tax,'" having considered the same, report the same in a new draft and with a new title and with the resolution that the bill in the new draft and new title ought to pass.

The report was accepted and the bill in its new draft read a first time and ordered to a second reading.

Mr. Edwards of Laconia, for the Committee on Mileage, reported the following resolution :

Resolved, That each member and officer of the House be allowed the number of miles set opposite his name in the accompanying list, and that the clerk be instructed to make the mileage roll of the House of Representatives in accordance therewith.

The report was accepted, the resolution adopted, and on motion of Mr. French of Moultonborough, the resolution and accompanying list were laid upon the table to be printed.

BILLS FORWARDED.

An act to amend section 10 of chapter 79 of the Session Laws of 1901, relative to the duties of the fish and game commissioners.

An act to provide for the daily publication of the journals of the Senate and House of Representatives.

Severally taken from the table and referred to the Committee on Appropriations.

An act to enable the Hedding Campmeeting Association to fund its indebtedness.

Taken from the table and ordered to a third reading. On motion of Mr. Small of Rochester, the rules were suspended and the bill read a third time and passed and sent to the Senate for concurrence.

Joint resolution in favor of John K. Law and others.

Taken from the table and ordered to a third reading. On motion of Mr. French of Moultonborough, the rules were suspended and the joint resolution read a third time and passed and sent to the Senate for concurrence.

An act in amendment of chapter 51 of the Public Statutes, relating to cemeteries.

An act relating to agreed lines between adjoining owners.

An act to incorporate the Omicron Deuteron Charge of the Theta Delta Chi.

An act to provide for a more economical and practical expenditure of money appropriated by the state for the construction and repair of highways.

An act in amendment of chapter 215, Laws of 1895, entitled " An act to confirm the organization of the Androscoggin Hospital Association."

An act in amendment of section 34 of chapter 43 of the Public Statutes, in regard to the incompatibility of certain town officers.

An act in addition to chapter 153, Public Statutes, creating section 20 of said chapter.

An act to amend section 1 of chapter 46, Session Laws of 1895, relating to annual enumeration of school children.

An act fixing office hours in state and county offices.

An act amending the charter of the Newmarket Electric Light, Power and Heat Company.

An act in amendment of sections 2 and 3, chapter 42 of the Public Statutes, relating to government of town meetings.

An act to incorporate the Maynesboro Fire Insurance Company.

An act providing for the appointment of guardians for minors in certain cases.

An act to reimburse the town or county for aid furnished paupers.

An act to incorporate the Manchester Fire Insurance Company of New Hampshire.

An act to amend section 2, chapter 179 of the Public Statutes, relating to the appointment of guardians of insane persons.

An act in amendment of section 14 of chapter 264 of the Public Statutes, relating to offenses against the police of towns.

An act to change the name of the Woman's Auxiliary to the City Missionary Society of Manchester.

An act authorizing the Mt. Pleasant Hotel Company to increase its capital stock.

An act in amendment of sections 4, 5, and 9 of chapter 85 of the Public Statutes, entitled "Support of county paupers."

An act in amendment of chapter 91, section 8, Laws of 1897, relating to the duties of the State Board of Charities and Correction.

An act to revive, renew, and amend the charter of the Knights of Pythias Building Association of Manchester.

An act to amend section 1 of an act of June, 1814, incorporating the Congregational Society in Durham.

An act in relation to bail in criminal cases.

Severally taken from the table and ordered to a third reading.

An act relating to negotiable instruments, being an act to establish a law uniform with the laws of other states on that subject.

Taken from the table. The question being upon the adoption of the resolution reported by the Committee on Judiciary that it is inexpedient to legislate,

(Discussion ensued.)

On motion of Mr. Libby of Gorham, the bill was laid upon the table.

On motion of Mr. Hoyt of Sandwich, the following entitled

bill, "An act to encourage the use of wide tires on certain vehicles constructed before January 1, 1900, and now in use in New Hampshire," was taken from the table. The question being upon the adoption of the resolution reported by the Committee on Agriculture that it is inexpedient to legislate,

(Discussion ensued.)

Mr. Ahern of Concord moved the previous question.
The question being,
Shall the main question be now put?
On a *viva voce* vote the motion prevailed.

The question being upon the adoption of the resolution reported by the committee, on a *viva voce* vote the resolution was not adopted. Mr. Hoyt of Sandwich called for a division. The counting having begun, the vote was declared to be manifestly in the negative, and the resolution reported by the committee was not adopted. The bill was then ordered to a third reading. On motion of Mr. Remich of Littleton, the rules were suspended and the bill read a third time and passed and sent to the Senate for concurrence.

Mr. Smith of Peterborough moved that the following entitled bill, "An act in relation to the settlement of paupers," be recalled from the Senate.
The question being upon the adoption of the motion,

(Discussion ensued.)

On a *viva voce* vote, the motion prevailed.

On motion of Mr. French of Moultonborough, the following entitled bill, "An act to provide for obtaining the testimony of non-resident directors, officers, and agents of New Hampshire corporations, and the production of corporate books, records, and papers," was taken from the table and made the special order for this afternoon at 3 o'clock.

On motion of Mr. Remich of Littleton,—
Resolved, That the use of Representatives' hall be granted to the Woman's Suffrage Association for Thursday evening, March 5, 1903.

On motion of Mr. Davis of Concord, at 12.30 the House adjourned.

AFTERNOON.

The House met at 3 o'clock.

LEAVE OF ABSENCE.

Mr. Swain of South Hampton was granted leave of absence on account of sickness.

THIRD READINGS.

An act in amendment of sections 2 and 3, chapter 42 of the Public Statutes, relating to government of town meetings.

Read a third time.

The question being,

Shall the bill pass?

(Discussion ensued.)

On motion of Mr. Ahern of Concord, the bill was laid upon the table.

An act to change the name of the Woman's Auxiliary to the City Missionary Society of Manchester.

An act to revive, renew and amend the charter of the Knights of Pythias Building Association of Manchester.

An act in amendment of section 14 of chapter 264 of the Public Statutes, relating to offenses against the police of towns.

An act in relation to bail in criminal cases.

Severally read a third time and passed and sent to the secretary of state to be engrossed.

An act to provide for a more economical and practical expenditure of money appropriated by the state for the construction and repair of highways.

The third reading being in order, on motion of Mr. Small of Rochester, the rules were suspended and the bill read a third time by its title. The bill was then passed and sent to the Senate for concurrence.

(Mr. Small of Rochester in the chair.)

An act in amendment of chapter 91, section 8, Laws of 1897, relating to the duties of the state board of charities and correction.

22

An act to amend section 2, chapter 179 of the Public Statutes, relating to the appointment of guardians of insane persons.

An act in amendment of chapter 215, Laws of 1895, entitled "An act to confirm the organization of the Androscoggin Hospital Association."

An act in amendment of section 34 of chapter 43 of the Public Statutes, in regard to the incompatibility of certain town officers.

An act in addition to chapter 153, Public Statutes, creating section 30 of said chapter.

An act to amend section 1 of chapter 46, Session Laws of 1895, relating to annual enumeration of school children.

An act amending the charter of the Newmarket Electric Light, Power and Heat Company.

An act to incorporate the Maynesboro Fire Insurance Company.

An act providing for the appointment of guardians for minors in certain cases.

An act to reimburse the town or county for aid furnished paupers.

An act relating to agreed lines between adjoining owners.

An act to incorporate the Omicron Deuteron Charge of the Theta Delta Chi.

An act authorizing the Mt. Pleasant Hotel Company to increase its capital stock.

An act in amendment of chapter 51 of the Public Statutes, relating to cemeteries.

An act providing for the purchase of a bond for the deputy state treasurer.

Severally read a third time and passed and sent to the Senate for concurrence.

An act to incorporate the Manchester Fire Insurance Company of New Hampshire.

The third reading being in order, on motion of Mr. Whittemore of Dover, the rules were suspended and the bill read a third time by its title. The bill was then passed and sent to the Senate for concurrence.

An act to amend section 1 of an act of June, 1814, incorporating the Congregational Society in Durham.

Read a third time and passed and sent to the secretary of state to be engrossed.

An act fixing office hours in state and county offices.

The third reading being in order, on motion of Mr. Buckley of Lancaster, the rules were suspended and the bill placed back upon its second reading for purposes of amendment. On motion of the same gentleman, the bill was laid upon the table.

An act in amendment of sections 4, 5, and 9 of chapter 85 of the Public Statutes, entitled " Support of county paupers."

Read a third time.

The question being,

Shall the bill pass?

On motion of Mr. Smith of Peterborough, the bill was laid upon the table.

MESSAGE FROM THE SENATE.

(The Speaker in the chair.)

A message from the Honorable Senate, by its clerk, announced that the Senate concurs with the House of Representatives in the passage of the following bill, with amendment, in the passage of which amendment it asks the concurrence of the House of Representatives:

An act in amendment of chapter 82 of the Laws of 1897, concerning the preservation and inspection of ballots.

Amend section 1 by striking out in the first line the figures " 17 " and insert in place thereof the figure " 1 " so that section 1 shall read: "Amend section 1 by striking out all of said section and inserting the following :"

On motion of Mr. Ahern of Concord, the amendment was concurred in and the bill sent to the secretary of state to be engrossed.

The message also announced that the Senate has passed the following entitled bills, in the passage of which it asks the concurrence of the House of Representatives:

An act to exempt certain property of the Manchester Young Men's Christian Association from taxation.

An act in relation to state officials, commissioners, trustees, or other persons having control of public funds.

Severally read a first and second time and referred to the Committee on Judiciary.

SPECIAL ORDER.

Mr. French of Moultonborough called for the special order, it being An act to provide for obtaining the testimony of non-resident directors, officers, and agents of New Hampshire corporations and the production of corporate books, records, and papers.

The question being upon the adoption of the motion of Mr. Remich of Littleton, that the House concur in the amendments sent down by the Honorable Senate,

(Discussion ensued.)

Mr. Small of Rochester moved to lay the bill and amendments upon the table and upon this question demanded a yea and nay vote. The roll was called with the following result :

YEAS, 95.

ROCKINGHAM COUNTY. Shute, Edgerly of Epping, Smith of Exeter, Brown of Fremont, Lane of Hampton, Pridham, Badger, Warner, Sleeper, Adams of Portsmouth, Corson, Gordon.

STRAFFORD COUNTY. Howe of Barrington, Libby of Dover, Jewell, Langley, Tuttle, Felker, McCrillis, Warren, Small, Caverly.

BELKNAP COUNTY. Smith of Center Harbor, Potter, Clough, Chase of Laconia.

CARROLL COUNTY. Littlefield, Philbrick of Effingham.

MERRIMACK COUNTY. Graves, Morse of Bradford, Beck, Durgin, Cate, Willis, Davis of Concord, Mathews of Concord, Hill, E. J., of Concord, Donagan, Litchfield, Morin of Franklin, Jones of Franklin, Davis of Franklin, Sanborn of Loudon.

HILLSBOROUGH COUNTY. Gould of Bennington, Shattuck,

Putnam, Brown of Greenville, Ware of Hancock, Connell, Cavanaugh, Wright, Dubuc, Carpenter, Darrah, Ryan, Trinity, Riordan, Shaughnessey, Couch, Bunton, A. B., of Manchester, Dinsmore, Janelle, Kohler, Filion, Kane, Needham, Desmarais, Peabody, Miller, Smith of Peterborough, Fitzgerald, Chase of Weare, Sheldon.

CHESHIRE COUNTY. Gowing, Pierce of Jaffrey, Jones of Keene, Fitch, Donovan, Moors, Fox, Amidon, Merrill, Sherman of Walpole, Dickinson.

SULLIVAN COUNTY. Huntley.

GRAFTON COUNTY. McMurphey, Davenport, Converse, Russell of Rumney, Bowen.

Coös COUNTY. Stewart of Berlin, Smyth, Gathercole, Bragg, Smith of Pittsburg.

NAYS, 180.

ROCKINGHAM COUNTY. Sawyer of Atkinson, Fellows, Morse of Chester, White of Deerfield, Nowell, Scammon, Severance, Emerson of Hampstead, Brown of Hampton Falls, Quimby of Kingston, George, Gerrish, Foye, Nelson, Yeaton, Newton, Chase of Stratham.

STRAFFORD COUNTY. Mathes, Nason, Whittemore, Barrett, Davis of Lee, Crocker, Worcester, Wentworth, Demers.

BELKNAP COUNTY. Pinkham, Edwards, Kimball of Laconia, Quimby of Meredith, Morrill of New Hampton, Sanborn of Sanbornton, Rogers, Mason.

CARROLL COUNTY. Stevens, Weeks, Fifield, Dow of Conway, Drake, Trickey, Greene, French, Abbott of Ossipee, Hoyt of Sandwich, Pollard, Blake of Wakefield, Beacham.

MERRIMACK COUNTY. White of Bow, Symonds, Shepard, Kennedy, Roby, Woodman, Kimball of Concord, Emerson of Concord, Ahern, Bunten of Dunbarton, Preston of Henniker, Twombly, Worthley, Messer, Sanborn of Northfield, Tallant, Burbank, Mason.

HILLSBOROUGH COUNTY. Pattee, Eaton, Ward, Holt, Nyberg, Abbott of Manchester, Chase of Manchester, Donahue, Bartlett of Manchester, Taggart, Sheehan, Bunton, A. S., of Manchester, Johnson, McDonald of Manchester, Barr of Manchester, Morgan, Stewart of Manchester, Tonery,

Whalen, Sullivan of Manchester, Armstrong, Tinkham, Graf, Quimby of Manchester, Scannell, Dozois, Gunderman, Lemay, Newman, Hodgman, Sawyer of Milford, Lund, Tuck, Duncklee, Lewis, Ingham, Bussell, Shenton, Collins, McLane, Jones of New Ipswich, Bragdon.

CHESHIRE COUNTY. Ware of Alstead, Harris of Chesterfield, Tenney, Bemis, Holland, Cutler, Fay, Batchelder, Whitney, Fletcher, Lane of Swanzey, Ramsay, Hall.

SULLIVAN COUNTY. Clark, Hamlin of Charlestown, Sherman of Claremont, Long, Churchill, Walker of Grantham, Aiken, Matthews of Newport, Richards, True, Philbrick of Springfield, Russell of Sunapee, Straw of Unity, Ball.

GRAFTON COUNTY. Morrill of Ashland, Pierce of Bethlehem, Calley, Little of Campton, Gates, Dorothy, Foster, Glover, Kimball of Grafton, Whitcher, Carr, Pike of Haverhill, Evans, Goold of Lebanon, Pike of Lebanon, Comings, Crossman, Stanley, Remich, Mitchell of Littleton, Blake of Littleton, Frazer, Chase of Orford, Gould of Plymouth, Ferrin, Houston, Bell.

Coös COUNTY. Goss, Vaillancourt, Hutchins of Berlin, Gallagher, Hicks, Martin, Tillotson, Libby of Gorham, Mitchell of Lancaster, Buckley of Lancaster, Ellis, Trafton, McDonald of Northumberland, Wilson, O'Connor, Harriman, Lennon, Darling, Babcock.

And the motion to lay upon the table did not prevail.

Mr. Ahern of Concord moved the previous question.

The question being,

Shall the main question be now put ?

(Discussion ensued.)

Mr. Small of Rochester moved that the House do now adjourn and upon this question demanded a yea and nay vote. The roll was called with the following result:

YEAS, 71.

ROCKINGHAM COUNTY. Shute, Brown of Fremont, Lane of Hampton, Pridham, Badger, Warner, Sleeper, Adams of Portsmouth, Corson, Gordon.

STRAFFORD COUNTY. Howe of Barrington, Langley, Tuttle, Felker, Warren, Small, Caverly.

Belknap County. Potter, Clough, Chase of Laconia.

Merrimack County. Beck, Durgin, Kennedy, Willis, Davis of Concord, Mathews of Concord, Donagan, Davis of Franklin.

Hillsborough County. Gould of Bennington, Shattuck, Putnam, Ware of Hancock, Cavanaugh, Wright, Dubuc, Carpenter, Darrah, Ryan, Trinity, Riordan, Shaughnessey, Dinsmore, Janelle, Kohler, Filion, Kane, Needham, Peabody, Miller, Smith of Peterborough, Fitzgerald, Chase of Weare, Sheldon.

Cheshire County. Pierce of Jaffrey, Jones of Keene, Fitch, Donovan, Merrill, Ramsay, Dickinson.

Sullivan County. Lufkin, Straw of Unity.

Grafton County. McMurphey, Foster, Converse, Russell of Rumney, Bowen.

Coös County. Stewart of Berlin, Smyth, Trafton, O'Connor.

Nays, 190.

Rockingham County. Sawyer of Atkinson, Fellows, Morse of Chester, White of Deerfield, Edgerly of Epping, Nowell, Scammon, Severance, Smith of Exeter, Emerson of Hampstead, Brown of Hampton Falls, Quimby of Kingston, George, Gerrish, Foye, Nelson, Yeaton, Newton, Brown of Rye, Chase of Stratham.

Strafford County. Mathes. Libby of Dover, Jewell, Nason, Whittemore, Barrett, Davis of Lee, McCrillis, Crocker, Worcester, Wentworth, Demers.

Belknap County. Pinkham, Smith of Center Harbor, Fecteau, Edwards, Kimball of Laconia, Quimby of Meredith, Morrill of New Hampton, Sanborn of Sanbornton, Rogers, Mason.

Carroll County. Littlefield, Stevens, Weeks, Fifield, Dow of Conway, Burnell, Drake, Trickey, Greene, French, Abbott of Ossipee, Hoyt of Sandwich, Pollard, Blake of Wakefield, Beacham.

Merrimack County. White of Bow, Morse of Bradford, Symonds, Cate, Shepard, Roby, Woodman, Emerson of Concord, Hill, E. J., of Concord, Ahern, Bunten of Dunbarton,

Morin of Franklin, Preston of Henniker, Twombly, Worthley, Messer, Sanborn of Northfield, Tallant, Burbank, Mason.

HILLSBOROUGH COUNTY. Farley of Amherst, Pattee, Eaton, Ward, Connell, Holt, Nyberg, Abbott of Manchester, Donahue, Bartlett of Manchester, Taggart, Sheehan, Bunton, A. S., of Manchester, Johnson, McDonald of Manchester, Barr of Manchester, Morgan, Stewart of Manchester, Tonery, Sullivan of Manchester, Couch, Bunton, A. B., of Manchester, Armstrong, Graf, Quimby of Manchester, Scannell, Dozois, Gunderman, Lemay, Newman, Hodgman, Sawyer of Milford, Lund, Tuck, Duncklee, Lewis, Ingham, Bussell, Shenton, Collins, McLane, Jones of New Ipswich, Bragdon.

CHESHIRE COUNTY. Ware of Alstead, Harris of Chesterfield, Tenney, Bemis, Holland, Cutler, Fay, Batchelder, Whitney, Moors, Fox, Fletcher, Lane of Swanzey, Sherman of Walpole, Hall.

SULLIVAN COUNTY. Clark, Hamlin of Charlestown, Sherman of Claremont, Long, Churchill, Walker of Grantham, Aiken, Matthews of Newport, Richards, True, Philbrick of Springfield, Russell of Sunapee, Ball.

GRAFTON COUNTY. Morrill of Ashland, Pierce of Bethlehem, Dorothy, Glover, Kimball of Grafton, Whitcher, Carr, Pike of Haverhill, Evans, Goold of Lebanon, Pike of Lebanon, Comings, Crossman, Stanley, Remich, Mitchell of Littleton, Blake of Littleton, Frazer, Gould of Plymouth, Ferrin, Houston, Bell.

COÖS COUNTY. Goss, Vaillancourt, Hutchins of Berlin, Gallagher, Gathercole, Hicks, Martin, Tillotson, Libby of Gorham, Mitchell of Lancaster, Buckley of Lancaster, Ellis, McDonald of Northumberland, Smith of Pittsburg, Wilson, Harriman, Lennon, Darling, Babcock.

And the motion to adjourn did not prevail.

The question being,

Shall the main question be now put ?

Mr. Ahern of Concord called for a division.

(Discussion ensued.)

On motion of Mr. Whitcher of Haverhill, at 5.45 the House adjourned.

WEDNESDAY, FEBRUARY 25, 1903.

The House met at 11 o'clock.

Prayer was offered by the chaplain.

COMMITTEE REPORTS.

Mr. Andrews of Somersworth, for the Committee on Education, to whom was referred An act to amend chapter 93, section 15 of the Public Statutes, as amended by chapter 61 of the Session Laws of 1901, relating to scholars, having considered the same, report the same with the following resolution:

Resolved, That it is inexpedient to legislate.

Mr. Quimby of Meredith, for the Committee on Appropriations, to whom was referred An act to establish a state normal school, having considered the same, report the same with the following resolution:

Resolved, That it is inexpedient to legislate.

Mr. Dow of Conway, for the Committee on Appropriations, to whom was referred An act in favor of Oren Clough of Lisbon, having considered the same, report the same with the following resolution:

Resolved, That it is inexpedient to legislate.

Mr. Ingham of Nashua, for the Committee on Incorporations, to whom was referred An act to authorize the town of Pittsfield to construct and maintain an electric plant for lighting, heat, and power purposes, having considered the same, report the same with the following resolution:

Resolved, That it is inexpedient to legislate.

Mr. Demers of Somersworth, for the Committee on Revision of Statutes, to whom was referred An act to amend the Public Statutes, section 5, chapter 37 of the Laws of 1895, relating to the fee of bail commissioner, having considered the same, report the same with the following resolution:

Resolved, That it is inexpedient to legislate.

The reports were severally accepted and the resolutions reported by the committees adopted.

Mr. Woodman of Concord, for the Committee on Judiciary, to whom was referred An act to incorporate the Connecticut

River Power Company of New Hampshire, having considered the same, find that the object sought cannot be attained under the general law, and therefore report the bill with the recommendation that it be referred to the Committee on Incorporations.

The report was accepted and the bill referred to the Committee on Incorporations.

Mr. Wallace of Rochester, for the Committee on Appropriations, to whom was referred An act relative to the salary of the judge of probate for the county of Rockingham, having considered the same, report the same with the following resolution :

Resolved, That the bill ought to pass.

Mr. McDonald of Northumberland, for the Committee on Appropriations, to whom was referred An act in relation to the salary of the judge of probate for Merrimack county, having considered the same, report the same with the following resolution :

Resolved, That the bill ought to pass.

Mr. Pike of Haverhill, for the Committee on Appropriations, to whom was referred An act to amend chapter 95 of the Public Statutes, relating to normal school, having considered the same, report the same with the following resolution :

Resolved, That the bill ought to pass.

The reports were severally accepted and the bills ordered to a third reading.

Mr. Bunton, A. S., of Manchester, for the Committee on Banks, to whom was referred An act relating to books of deposit issued by savings banks, when lost, destroyed, or assigned, having considered the same, report the same with the following resolution :

Resolved, That the bill ought to pass.

The report was accepted and the bill laid upon the table to be printed.

Mr. Huntley of Claremont, for the Committee on Appropriations, to whom was referred An act relative to the salary of the judge of probate for Strafford county, having considered the same, report the same with the following amendment and with the resolution that the bill as amended ought to pass :

Amend by striking out the words "one thousand" and inserting in place thereof the words "eight hundred."

The report was accepted, the amendment adopted, and the bill ordered to a third reading.

Mr. Wright of Manchester, for the Committee on Appropriations, to whom was referred An act relating to the salary of the register of probate for the county of Cheshire, having considered the same, report the same with the following amendment and with the resolution that the bill as amended ought to pass.

Amend by striking out the word "seven" and inserting in the place thereof the word "six."

The report was accepted, the amendment adopted, and the bill ordered to a third reading.

Mr. Foye of Portsmouth, for the Committee on Appropriations, to whom was referred An act relative to the salary of the register of probate for Coös county, having considered the same, report the same with the following amendment and with the resolution that the bill as amended ought to pass.

Amend by striking out the word "eight" and inserting in place thereof the word "seven."

The report was accepted, the amendment adopted, and the bill ordered to a third reading.

Mr. Davenport of Bath, for the Committee on Appropriations, to whom was referred An act in relation to the salary of the register of probate for Strafford county, having considered the same, report the same with the following amendment and with the resolution that the bill as amended ought to pass.

Amend by striking out the word "twelve" and inserting in place thereof the word "ten."

The report was accepted, the amendment adopted, and the bill ordered to a third reading.

Mr. Whittemore of Dover, for the Committee on Judiciary, to whom was referred An act in amendment of an act approved March 26, 1895, entitled "An act in amendment of an act incorporating the Newmarket Manufacturing Company, approved June 12, 1823, and an act in amendment thereof, approved July 7, 1881," having considered the same, report the same with the following resolution :

Resolved, That the bill ought to pass.

The report was accepted and the bill laid upon the table to be printed. On motion of Mr. Whittemore of Dover, the rules were suspended and the printing of the bill dispensed with. The bill was then ordered to a third reading. On motion of the same gentleman, the rules were further suspended and the bill read a third time and passed and sent to the secretary of state to be engrossed.

Mr. Willis of Concord, for the Committee on Engrossed Bills, reported that they had examined and found correctly engrossed the following entitled bills and joint resolutions:

An act to change the name of Station lake in the town of Springfield.

An act to legalize the biennial election of the town of Conway, held November 4, 1902.

An act to extend the time for the location, construction, and completion of the railroad of the Moosilauke Railroad Company.

An act to amend the charter of the New Hampshire Odd Fellows' Widows' and Orphans' Home, approved August 15, 1883.

An act in addition to chapter 58 of the Public Statutes, relating to the appraisal of taxable real estate.

An act in amendment of chapter 23 of the Laws of 1901, entitled "An act to establish a laboratory of hygiene."

An act relative to the issue of bonds, coupon notes, and other evidences of indebtedness of street railway or other railroad companies.

An act in amendment of the charter of the city of Berlin.

An act to amend sections 54 and 58 of chapter 79 of the Laws of 1901, relating to the fish and game laws of the state.

An act in amendment of section 4 of chapter 206 of the Laws of 1897, being "An act to incorporate the Bethlehem Electric Light Company."

An act in amendment of section 27, chapter 154 of the Public Statutes, relating to the calling of proprietors' meetings.

An act authorizing the town of Hudson to construct waterworks and establish an electric light plant.

An act to legalize and confirm the selectmen's warrant for,

and the votes and proceedings thereunder at, the biennial election and meeting in the town of Columbia, held in said town on the 4th day of November, A. D. 1902.

Joint resolution in favor of the Granite State Deaf Mute Mission.

Joint resolution to provide for a forest examination of the White Mountain region.

An act to legalize town meetings in Dorchester for the years 1896, 1897, 1898, 1899, and 1900.

An act to legalize and confirm the warrant for, and the votes and proceedings at, the biennial election and meeting in Stratham, held the 4th day of November, 1902.

An act in amendment of the charter of the Wells River bridge, and authorizing the Concord & Montreal Railroad to hold stock therein.

An act to legalize the biennial election of the town of Effingham, held November 4th, 1902.

An act to change the name of the body of water formerly called Munsonville pond.

An act to repeal an act of the legislature of 1842, entitled "An act to annex Richard Pickering of Newington to school district No. 1 in Portsmouth," approved June 22, 1842.

An act to authorize the town of Lancaster to acquire property for the protection of its water supply.

An act to provide for taking depositions outside this state, and depositions within this state for use in other states.

An act to punish embezzlement by executors, administrators, guardians, and trustees.

An act in amendment of the charter of the city of Dover, creating a board of street and park commissioners for said city.

An act to incorporate the New Hampshire Genealogical Society.

An act to establish the Lisbon village district.

An act in amendment of an act to incorporate the North Conway & Mount Kearsarge Railroad, passed June session, 1883, and all subsequent acts relating to the same.

An act to establish water-works in Enfield village fire district, in the town of Enfield.

An act relating to domestic insurance companies.

An act confirming and legalizing the organization and acts of the Berlin Street Railway.

An act to authorize the town of Lancaster to exempt certain property from taxation, and to ratify its doings in the same.

An act to incorporate the Littleton, Franconia & Bethlehem Electric Railway Company.

An act in amendment of chapter 44 of the Laws of 1893, relating to the powers and duties of the forestry commission with respect to public parks.

An act in amendment of section 3, chapter 209 of the Public Statutes, relating to exemptions from serving as jurors.

The report was accepted.

Mr. Morgan of Manchester, for the Committee on Railroads, to whom was referred An act to incorporate the Uncanoonuc Incline Railway and Development Company, having considered the same, report the same in a new draft with the following resolution :

Resolved, That the bill in the new draft ought to pass.

The report was accepted. On motion of Mr. French of Moultonborough, the rules were suspended, and the bill in new draft read a first time by its title. The bill was then ordered to a second reading.

Mr. Bickford of Northwood, for the Committee on Feeble-Minded School, to whom was referred Joint resolution appropriating money for the support of the New Hampshire School for Feeble-Minded Children, necessary buildings, and to provide a suitable water supply, having considered the same, report the same with the following resolution :

Resolved, That the joint resolution ought to pass.

The report was accepted and the joint resolution laid upon the table to be printed and then referred to the Committee on Appropriations. On motion of Mr. Ahern of Concord, the rules were suspended, and the printing of the joint resolution dispensed with. It was then referred to the Committee on Appropriations.

Mr. Ingham of Nashua, for the Committee on Incorporations, reported the following entitled bill, " An act to incorporate the Pittsfield Light and Power Company," with the resolution that the bill ought to pass.

The report was accepted and the reading of the bill having commenced, on motion of Mr. Preston of Henniker, the rules were suspended, and the bill read a first time by its title. The bill was then ordered to a second reading. On motion of the same gentleman, the rules were suspended and the bill read a second time by its title. The bill was then laid upon the table to be printed. On motion of the same gentleman, the rules were suspended and the printing of the bill dispensed with. The bill was then ordered to a third reading. On motion of the same gentleman, the rules were further suspended and the bill read a third time by its title and passed and sent to the Senate for concurrence.

Mr. Whittemore of Dover, for the Committee on Judiciary, reported the following entitled bill, " An act to change the name of the South Congregational Society of Newmarket, N. H., now located in Newfields, N. H.," with the resolution that the bill ought to pass.

The report was accepted and the bill read a first time and ordered to a second reading. On motion of Mr. Whittemore of Dover, the rules were suspended and the bill read a second time. The bill was then laid upon the table to be printed. On motion of the same gentleman, the rules were suspended and the printing of the bill dispensed with. The bill was then ordered to a third reading. On motion of the same gentleman, the rules were further suspended and the bill read a third time and passed and sent to the Senate for concurrence.

Mr. Roby of Concord, for the Committee on Fisheries and Game, reported the following joint resolution, " Joint resolution for screening the outlet to Center pond in the town of Stoddard," with the resolution that the joint resolution ought to pass.

The report was accepted and the joint resolution read a first time and ordered to a second reading.

SECOND READING.

An act to exempt soldiers and sailors of the Spanish-American War from paying a poll tax.

Read a second time and laid upon the table to be printed.

BILL FORWARDED.

An act to amend the charter of the city of Portsmouth, in relation to a board of public works.

Taken from the table and ordered to a third reading.

UNFINISHED BUSINESS.

Mr. Ahern of Concord called for the unfinished business, it being An act to provide for obtaining the testimony of non-resident directors, officers, and agents of New Hampshire corporations and the production of corporate books, records, and papers.

The question being,

Shall the main question be now put?

On a *viva voce* vote the motion prevailed.

The question being,

Shall the House concur in the amendments sent down by the Honorable Senate?

Mr. Small of Rochester demanded a yea and nay vote. The roll was called with the following result:

YEAS, 253.

ROCKINGHAM COUNTY. Sawyer of Atkinson, Fellows, Hubbard, Morse of Chester, White of Deerfield, Hardy, Shute, Edgerly of Epping, Nowell, Scammon, Severance, Brown of Fremont, Emerson of Hampstead, Brown of Hampton Falls, Quimby of Kingston, Crowell, Chase of Newfields, Haines, George, Warner, Bickford, Gerrish, Payne, Blaisdell, Foye, Nelson, Cogan, Corson, Brown of Rye, Gordon, Young, Chase of Stratham, Cochran.

STRAFFORD COUNTY. Mathes, Libby of Dover, Jewell, Nason, Whittemore, Bunce, Smith of Dover, Barrett, Hayes, Wesley, York, Davis of Lee, Place, McCrillis, Crocker, Worcester, Wallace, Etter, Wentworth, Demers.

BELKNAP COUNTY. Pinkham, Smith of Centre Harbor, Davis of Laconia, Hull, Edwards, Kimball of Laconia, Quimby of Meredith, Morrill of New Hampton, Sanborn of Sanbornton, Rogers.

CARROLL COUNTY. Littlefield, Stevens, Weeks, Fifield,

Dow of Conway, Philbrick of Effingham, Drake, Trickey, Greene, French, Abbott of Ossipee, Pollard, Edgerly of Tuftonborough, Blake of Wakefield, Beacham.

MERRIMACK COUNTY. Morse of Bradford, Durgin, Symonds, Cate, Shepard, Matson, Hill, A. W.. of Concord, Woodman, Kimball of Concord, Emerson of Concord, Critchett, Hill, E. J., of Concord, Ahern, Bunten of Dunbarton, Tripp, Phillips, Adams of Franklin, Preston of Henniker, Twombly, Worthley, Fisk, Messer, Sanborn of Northfield, Tallant, Aldrich, Foss, Walker of Pittsfield, Little of Salisbury, Pillsbury, Ela, Burbank, Mason.

HILLSBOROUGH COUNTY. Tobie, Pattee, Eaton, Whitaker, Ward, Connell, Center, Holt, Nyberg, Abbott of Manchester, Chase of Manchester, Donahue, Sheehan, Farrell, Straw of Manchester, Barr of Manchester, Morgan, Stewart of Manchester, Whalen, Sullivan of Manchester, Marshall, Morse of Manchester, Bunton, A. B., of Manchester, Armstrong, Tinkham, Graf, Quimby of Manchester, Scannell, Dozois, Gunderman, Lemay, Newman, Emerson of Manchester, Hodgman, Sawyer of Milford, Needham, Kendall, Lund, Tuck, Duncklee, Lampron, Buckley of Nashua, Ingham, Bussell, Spalding, Lintott, Morse of Nashua, Collins, Hills of Nashua, Sullivan of Nashua, Desmarais, Dionne, McLane, Jones of New Ipswich, Bragdon.

CHESHIRE COUNTY. Ware of Alstead, Harris of Chesterfield, Tenney, Polzer, Bemis, Fuller, Holland, Cutler, Fay, Batchelder, Whitney, Moors, Scott, Fletcher, Lane of Swanzey, Boyden, Ramsay, Sherman of Walpole, Hall, Dickinson.

SULLIVAN COUNTY. Clark, Hamlin of Charlestown, Chandler, Long, Churchill, Walker of Grantham, Aiken, Matthews of Newport, Richards, True, Philbrick of Springfield, Russell of Sunapee, Straw of Unity, Ball.

GRAFTON COUNTY. Morrill of Ashland, Davenport, Pierce of Bethlehem, Calley, Little of Campton, Gates, Dorothy, Foster, Glover, Whitcher, Carr, Pike of Haverhill, Evans, Pike of Lebanon, Comings, Crossman, Stanley, Remich, Mitchell of Littleton, Blake of Littleton, Converse, Frazer, King, Chase of Orford, Celley, Gould of Plymouth. Ferrin, Houston, Goodrich, Bell.

23

Coös County. Stewart of Berlin, Goss, Vaillancourt, Kent of Berlin, Hutchins of Berlin, Gallagher, Gathercole, Hicks, Martin, Jordan, Tillotson, Hamlin of Dummer, Bragg, Libby of Gorham, Buckley of Lancaster, Ellis, Trafton, Piper, Smith of Pittsburg, Wilson, Harriman, Lennon, Darling, Babcock.

Nays, 79.

Rockingham County. Duntley, Lane of Hampton, Pridham, Badger, Sleeper, Adams of Portsmouth.

Strafford County. Howe of Barrington, Langley, Tuttle, Felker, Jones of New Durham, Warren, Small, Boutin.

Belknap County. Hoitt of Barnstead, Potter, Clough, Prescott.

Merrimack County. Graves, White of Bow, Beck, Langmaid, Kennedy, Willis, Davis of Concord, Donagan, Litchfield, Morin of Franklin, Jones of Franklin, Davis of Franklin, Sanborn of Loudon, Hutchins of Pittsfield.

Hillsborough County. Woodbury, Barr of Bedford, Gould of Bennington, Shattuck, Craine, Putnam, Brown of Greenville, Ware of Hancock, Farley of Hollis, Cavanaugh, Wright, Dubuc, Tonery, Ryan, Riordan, Sasseville, Couch, Janelle, Kohler, Filion, Kane, Simpson, Peabody, Miller, Smith of Peterborough, Fitzgerald, Chase of Weare, Sheldon.

Cheshire County. Gowing, Pierce of Jaffrey, Maloney, Jones of Keene, Fitch, Donovan, Fox, Amidon, Merrill, Kellom.

Sullivan County. Huntley, Lufkin.

Grafton County. McMurphey, Barnard, Russell of Rumney, Bowen.

Coös County. Smyth, Plaisted, O'Connor, and the House concurred in the amendments sent down by the Honorable Senate. The bill was then sent to the secretary of state to be engrossed.

MESSAGE FROM THE SENATE.

A message from the Honorable Senate, by its clerk, announced that the Senate concurs with the House of Representatives in the passage of the following entitled bills and joint resolutions:

An act in amendment of chapter 202 of the Laws of 1889, entitled " An act to establish water-works in the town of Wolfeborough," as amended by chapter 191 of the Laws of 1891.

An act to exempt from taxation real estate reservations of the Appalachian Mountain Club.

Joint resolution to provide for completing the painting and decorating of the walls of the state library building.

Joint resolution making appropriation for repairs on buildings erected by the state for the New Hampshire Veterans' Association at The Weirs.

Joint resolution appropriating money to complete the payment of expenses of the recent constitutional convention.

An act to amend section 1, chapter 184 of the Public Statutes, relative to the times and places for holding courts of probate, repealing chapter 29 of the Session Laws of 1901.

An act to unite the school districts of the town of Rollinsford.

An act to enable the city of Manchester to appropriate money toward the armory rent of Camp Derwin, No. 184, Spanish-American War Veterans.

An act amending chapter 92 of the Public Statutes, in relation to school boards.

An act to permit executors and administrators to resign.

An act to equalize school privileges in the town of Littleton.

An act in amendment of the act relating to the terms of the superior court in Grafton county.

An act to repeal the charter of the Massabesic Horse Railroad Company.

An act to amend chapter 94 of the Public Statutes, in relation to the superintendent of public instruction.

An act in amendment of section 2, chapter 2555, Laws of 1861, entitled " An act to incorporate the Alpha Delta Thi Society."

An act to amend section 4 of chapter 96 of the Laws of 1901, and section 6 of chapter 92 of the Public Statutes, relating to courses of study.

On motion of Mr. Comings of Lebanon, at 12.25 the House adjourned.

AFTERNOON.

The House met at 3 o'clock.

LEAVE OF ABSENCE.

The Committee on Fisheries and Game was granted leave of absence for Thursday, February 26, for the purpose of visiting the fish hatchery at Colebrook.

THIRD READINGS.

An act to amend the charter of the city of Portsmouth, in relation to a board of public works.

The third reading being in order, on motion of Mr. Cogan of Portsmouth, the rules were suspended and the bill placed back upon its second reading and recommitted to the special committee consisting of the delegation from the city of Portsmouth.

An act to amend chapter 95 of the Public Statutes, relating to normal school.

An act relative to the salary of the register of probate for Coös county.

An act relating to the salary of the register of probate for the county of Cheshire.

An act in relation to the salary of the judge of probate for Merrimack county.

An act in relation to the salary of the register of probate for Strafford county.

An act in relation to the salary of the judge of probate for Strafford county.

An act relating to the salary of the judge of probate for the county of Rockingham.

Severally read a third time and passed and sent to the Senate for concurrence.

MESSAGE FROM THE SENATE.

A message from the Honorable Senate, by its clerk, announced that the Senate concurs with the House of Representatives in the passage of the following bill, with amendment, in the passage of which amendment it asks the concurrence of the House of Representatives:

An act to enable the state board of health to prevent contaminated water being furnished for domestic consumption.

Amend section one by striking out in line seven the words " and the directors of corporations" and inserting in their place the words " or corporation official or agent"; and in line eight inserting between the words " fine " and " not " the words " of not less than one hundred dollars and."

On motion of Mr. Remich of Littleton, the amendment was concurred in.

The message also announced that the Senate concurs with the House of Representatives in the passage of the following bill, with amendment, in the passage of which amendment it asks the concurrence of the House of Representatives:

An act to change the name of the New Hampshire Health and Accident Insurance Company and to further define its powers and privileges.

Amend by striking out the words " New Hampshire" in the second line of section 1 and inserting instead the words " State Security," so that said section as amended shall read:

SECTION 1. The name of the New Hampshire Health and Accident Insurance Company is hereby changed to State Security Life and Accident Company, hereinafter called the Company.

On motion of Mr. Ahern of Concord, the amendment was concurred in.

The message further announced that the Senate has passed a bill with the following title and joint resolution, in the passage of which it asks the concurrence of the House of Representatives:

An act to incorporate the Jackson Water-Works Company.

On motion of Mr. Ahern of Concord, the rules were suspended and the bill read a first time by its title. The bill was then read a second time and referred to the Committee on Judiciary.

Joint resolution in favor of Arthur E. Clarke.

Read a first and second time and referred to the Committee on Claims.

COMMUNICATION FROM THE SUPREME COURT.

The Speaker submitted the following communication from the supreme court:

STATE OF NEW HAMPSHIRE.

HOUSE OF REPRESENTATIVES.

CONCORD, February 18, 1903.

MR. A. J. SHURTLEFF,
Clerk of the Supreme Court,
Concord, N. H.

DEAR SIR: At the morning session of the House of Representatives, Tuesday, February 18, 1903, the enclosed resolutions and inquiries were unanimously adopted, the same to be considered by the Supreme Court to be a substitute for the resolutions and inquiries previously adopted by the House and recently transmitted by me to the Court.

In accordance with the terms of the resolutions I transmit the same to you, with the request that you lay the same before the Court.

Yours very truly,
HARRY M. CHENEY.
Speaker.

Resolved, That the House of Representatives requests the opinion of the Supreme Court upon the following, namely:

First—Did His Excellency George A. Ramsdell, Governor of New Hampshire, have authority to make and execute the following appointment and agreement in behalf of this state or otherwise?

AGREEMENT.

MEMORANDUM OF AN APPOINTMENT AND AGREEMENT, made this eleventh day of May, A. D. 1897, by and between the State of New Hampshire by the Honorable George A. Ramsdell, its Governor, on the one part, and Horace S. Cummings, of Washington, in the District of Columbia, on the other part, WITNESSETH:

That the said State of New Hampshire in consideration of the things to be done by said Horace S. Cummings as hereinafter set forth, hath appointed, and by these presents doth appoint, said Horace S. Cummings, its agent and attorney, to present, prosecute, and recover before the Congress, any Department, the Court of Claims, or the Supreme Court of the United States, any claim or claims of said State against the United States, for costs, charges, and expenses properly incurred by said State for enrolling, subsisting, clothing, supplying, arming, equipping, paying and transporting the troops of said State, employed in aiding to suppress the insurrection against the United States between the years 1861 and 1865, both inclusive, under an Act of Congress entitled "An Act to indemnify the States for expenses incurred by them in defense of the United States," approved July 27th, 1861. And said Horace S. Cummings shall have and receive for his legal services in and about said matter, a sum equal to fifteen per cent. of the entire sum collected, payable only out of any sums that may be collected hereunder, and without any liability on the part of the State for expenses in connection therewith.

And in consideration of the premises said Horace S. Cummings agrees to undertake the presentation and prosecution of said claims at the compensation above stated and without any liability on behalf of the State for his expenses in connection therewith.

IN WITNESS WHEREOF said State of New Hampshire has caused these presents to be signed by the said George A. Ramsdell, its Governor, and its seal to be hereto affixed, and said Horace S. Cummings has hereunto set his hand and seal, the day and year first above written.

THE STATE OF NEW HAMPSHIRE.
By GEO. A. RAMSDELL,
(Seal of State.) *Governor.*
HORACE S. CUMMINGS.

1. The foregoing agreement and appointment was duly executed and delivered to said Cummings at the date thereof.

2. Said Cummings thereupon entered on the work of prosecuting the claim mentioned in said agreement before the Honorable, the Secretary of the Department of the Treasury of the United States, the Court of Claims and the Congress of the United States.

3. The claim against the United States accrued to the State of New Hampshire between the years 1861 and 1864, and by the Statute of the United States at the date of the agreement aforesaid had become barred by the Statute of Limitation of the United States so that no judgment against the United States thereon could be obtained in any court of the United States.

But not being a stale claim, it could be and was audited, allowed, and paid by the Treasury Department, under laws existing at the time Cummings's contract was made.

The accounting officers of the Department of the Treasury claimed that said claim could not be audited because it was a stale claim, and such proceedings were had as is set forth in Vol. 36, Ct. of Claims Reports.

4. The Treasurer of the State of New Hampshire in the year 1864 considered said claim as worthless, and the same was in the year 1865 carried to the deficiency account.

Said Cummings prosecuted the work of collecting said claims before the Department of the Treasury and the Court of Claims, which resulted in the auditing of said claim on behalf of the State of New Hampshire in the amount of $108,-372.52; and thereafter the Congress of the United States appropriated said sum on said audit, and the Secretary of the Treasury issued a warrant of the United States, payable to the order of the Governor of the State of New Hampshire, for said sum and delivered the same to said Cummings as the agent of said State.

Immediately upon the receipt of said warrant said Cummings transmitted by mail said warrant to the Governor of the state of New Hampshire, inclosing therewith a copy of said agreement and appointment and requested the Governor to forward to him his check for the amount of fees due him as said agent in accordance with the terms of said agreement and appointment.

The Governor did not comply with the request of said Cummings, but thereafter, to wit, on March 4, 1902, turned the said $108,372.52 into the treasury of said State of New Hampshire, where it was on the date aforesaid entered upon the books of the state and commingled with other moneys of the state and has since been used and disposed of for state purposes.

Said Cummings protested that the moneys representing the fees aforesaid were not the proper moneys of the State of New Hampshire, but belonged to him by virtue of his contract of agreement and appointment; but said moneys have never been paid to said Cummings.

Second—Is said Cummings entitled to receive from the state fifteen per centum of the amount so collected and paid in to the State Treasury?

Resolved, That the Speaker of the House of Representatives, for and in its behalf, be and hereby is directed to present said questions to the Supreme Court with a request for its decision at as early a date as is compatible with a careful consideration of the important questions involved.

To the House of Representatives:

In answer to the foregoing resolution the undersigned, the justices of the Supreme Court, respectfully submit their opinions upon the questions therein contained.

As the claimant can not sue the state under the contract of May 11, 1897, to which the resolution relates, and as no money can be paid him except by direction of the legislature, Const., Part II, Art. 55 (56); P. S., *c.* 16, *s.* 4; *c.* 20, *s.* 1, it might be argued that the legality of that agreement was unimportant, and that the only question for the legislature to determine was one of expediency, upon which our opinion could not be constitutionally required. Const., Part II, Art. 73 (74). But assuming that it is the policy of the House to provide for the liquidation of this claim, if it was legally incurred, we have considered the questions submitted as though they had arisen in an authorized suit. The fact that no suit can be maintained against the state affords the legislature a proper occasion for requiring our advice as to the legal validity of the contract in question.

By *s.* 3, *c.* 2479, Laws of 1861, the Governor, with the advice and consent of the Council, was "authorized and empowered to negotiate, adjust, and settle all questions, accounts, matters, and things, between this state and the United States, in any way growing out of . . . any contracts or expenditures which may be made for the public defense or the payment of troops." The Governor and Council at the date of the appointment in question, this act being still in force, were therefore expressly authorized to negotiate, adjust, and settle any accounts or claims of this character then existing in favor of the state against the general government. That there were such claims appears to have been then contended and is now established. The power so conferred, by necessary implication, included authority to do whatever was reasonably necessary for its proper and efficient execution. It is not to be supposed the legislature understood the Governor and Council would, or could, personally perform all the services incident to the proper investigation, proof, and prosecution of such claims by the state. Such matters are commonly conducted by persons having special training, experience, and skill. The appointment of suitable persons to represent the state in the prosecution of its claim before the appropriate tribunals must, therefore, have been understood to have been embraced within the general terms by which power in the matter was conferred upon the executive. Evidence in support of this conclusion is furnished by c. 4076, Laws of 1865, in which the Governor and Council were empowered " to pay the authorized agent or agents employed by the state in prosecuting the claims of said state against the United States." No other statutory provision in the matter being found, this act appears to be a legislative recognition of the legal employment of "agents" for the purpose named under the act first cited. We therefore conclude that the Governor and Council had authority, May 11, 1897, to appoint Mr. Cummings to prosecute the claim of the state in the matter in question before the proper tribunals. The authority to employ agents and other persons necessarily implies the power to contract with them for their compensation according to the method usual in matters of the kind. *Bohonon* v. *Railroad*, 70 N. H. 526. There is nothing in the facts submitted to us establishing as matter of law that the provisions made were out of the usual course or improperly induced. A contract between private individuals in which the compensation was contingent upon success might be claimed to be void as against good morals and public policy. *Edgerly* v. *Hale*, 71 N. H. 138, 150; *Butler* v. *Legro*, 62 N. H. 350. But the legislature can determine for itself what public policy requires or permits to be done in the prosecution of claims in favor of the state. *Davis* v. *Commonwealth*, 164 Mass. 141. If there are reasons why the state should refuse to recognize and comply with the agreement made in 1897 by his Excellency Gov. Ramsdell, legal ground therefor is not to be found in absence of power in the executive to make the appointment and agreement in question or in any objection arising as matter of law upon the facts stated to us. We therefore upon these facts answer in the affirmative both questions submitted, whether under the provision of the constitution requiring the Governor and Council "from time to time to hold a council for ordering and directing the affairs of the state, according to the laws of the land," Const., Part II, Art. 61, or under any power constitutionally inherent in the executive, in the absence of legislation, authority exists for the action taken in 1897 has not been considered.

FRANK N. PARSONS.
WM. M. CHASE.
REUBEN E. WALKER.
JAMES W. REMICK.
GEORGE H. BINGHAM.

February 25, 1903.

On motion of Mr. Remich of Littleton, the communication was laid upon the table to be printed.

Mr. Remich of Littleton moved that the Honorable Senate be requested to return to the House for further consideration the following entitled bill, "An act to establish a new apportionment for the assessment of public taxes."

The question being upon the adoption of the motion,

(Discussion ensued.)

On a *viva voce* vote the motion prevailed.

On motion of Mr. Buckley of Lancaster, the following entitled bill, "An act fixing office hours in state and county offices," was taken from the table.

Mr. Buckley of Lancaster, offered the following amendment:

Amend section 1 by striking out in the first line the words "and county," so that said section as amended shall read as follows:

SECTION 1. All state offices and departments may be closed on legal holidays and on Saturday afternoons throughout the year if not incompatible with public business.

On a *viva voce* vote the amendment was adopted. The bill was then ordered to a third reading. On motion of Mr. Buckley of Lancaster, the rules were suspended and the bill read a third time and passed. On motion of Mr. Buckley of Lancaster, the title was amended by striking out the words "and county." The bill was then sent to the Senate for concurrence.

On motion of Mr. Jones of New Ipswich,—

Resolved, That the Speaker be authorized to appoint a committee to draft resolutions on the death of the late Mr. Benjamin F. March, member of the House of Representatives from the town of Mason ; and, be it further

Resolved, That, out of respect for the memory of Mr. March, the House do now adjourn.

The Speaker named as such committee Messrs. Jones of New Ipswich, Crossman of Lisbon, and Brown of Greenville.

At 4.05 the House was declared adjourned.

THURSDAY, FEBRUARY 26, 1903.

The House met at 11 o'clock.

Prayer was offered by the chaplain.

LEAVE OF ABSENCE.

Mr. Notterstead of Berlin was granted leave of absence on account of sickness in his family.

COMMITTEE REPORTS.

Mr. Collins of Nashua, for the Committee on Appropriations, to whom was referred An act to establish a state sanatorium for consumptives, having considered the same, report the same with the following resolution :

Resolved, That the bill ought to pass.

The report was accepted and the bill ordered to a third reading.

Mr. Kimball of Laconia, for the Committee on Railroads, to whom was referred An act to incorporate the Portsmouth & Newington Street Railway Company, having considered the same, report the same with the following resolution :

Resolved, That it is inexpedient to legislate.

The report was accepted. The question being upon the adoption of the resolution reported by the committee,

(Discussion ensued.)

On a *viva voce* vote the resolution was not adopted. The bill was then laid upon the table to be printed. On motion of Mr. Badger of Newington, the rules were suspended and the printing of the bill dispensed with.

The question being,

Shall the bill be read a third time?

(Discussion ensued.)

Mr. Ahern of Concord moved that the bill be laid upon the table. On a *viva voce* vote the motion did not prevail.

The question being,

Shall the bill be read a third time?

On a *viva voce* vote the bill was ordered to a third reading.

Mr. Badger of Newington moved that the rules be suspended and the bill read a third time by its title and put upon its passage at the present time. On this question, Mr. Bussell of Nashua demanded a yea and nay vote.

(Discussion ensued.)

Mr. Badger of Newington withdrew his motion. The third reading having commenced, Mr. Bussell of Nashua moved that the rules be suspended and the bill read a third time by its title. The question being upon the adoption of the motion,

(Discussion ensued.)

Mr. French of Moultonborough moved that the bill be laid upon the table. Upon a *viva voce* vote the motion did not prevail.

The question being upon the motion of Mr. Bussell of Nashua, on a *viva voce* vote the motion prevailed. Mr. French of Moultonborough called for a yea and nay vote.

(Discussion ensued.)

Mr. Ahern of Concord moved that the bill be recommitted to the Committee on Railroads.

(Discussion ensued.)

On a *viva voce* vote the motion prevailed and the bill was recommitted to the Committee on Railroads.

Mr. Converse of Lyme, for the Committee on Engrossed Bills, reported that they had examined and found correctly engrossed the following entitled bills and joint resolutions:

An act amending chapter 92 of the Public Statutes, in relation to school boards.

An act to amend section 4 of chapter 96 of the Laws of 1901, and section 6 of chapter 92 of the Public Statutes, relating to courses of study.

An act to repeal the charter of the Massabesic Horse Railroad Company.

An act to permit executors and administrators to resign.

An act to amend chapter 94 of the Public Statutes, in relation to the superintendent of public instruction.

An act in amendment of chapter 82 of the Laws of 1897.

An act in amendment of the act relating to the terms of the superior court in Grafton county.

An act to equalize school privileges in the town of Littleton.

An act to enable the city of Manchester to appropriate money toward the armory rent of Camp Derwin, No. 184, Spanish-American War Veterans.

An act to unite the school districts of the town of Rollinsford.

An act in amendment of section 2, chapter 2555, Laws of 1861, entitled "An act to incorporate the Alpha Delta Phi Society."

An act to amend section 1, chapter 184 of the Public Statutes, relative to the times and places for holding courts of probate, repealing chapter 29 of the Session Laws of 1901.

An act to amend section 1 of an act of June, 1814, incorporating the Congregational Society in Durham.

An act to change the name of the Woman's Auxiliary to the City Missionary Society of Manchester.

An act in amendment of section 14 of chapter 264 of the Public Statutes, relating to offenses against the police of towns.

An act in relation to bail in criminal cases.

An act to revive, renew, and amend the charter of the Knights of Pythias Building Association of Manchester.

Joint resolution in favor of Charles H. Roberts.

An act to provide for obtaining the testimony of non-resident directors, officers, and agents of New Hampshire corporations, and the production of corporate books, records, and papers.

The report was accepted.

Mr. Bunton, A. S., of Manchester, for the Committee on Banks, to whom was referred An act to incorporate the Nutfield Loan and Trust Company, having considered the same, report the same with the following resolution:

Resolved, That it is inexpedient to legislate.

Mr. Bunton, A. S., of Manchester, for the Committee on Banks, to whom was referred An act in amendment of the charter of the Plymouth Guaranty Savings Bank, having considered the same, report the same with the following resolution:

Resolved, That it is inexpedient to legislate.

Mr. Pike of Haverhill, for the Committee on Appropriations, to whom was referred An act in amendment of section 1, chapter 119, Public Statutes, relating to the inspection and licensing of boats, their engineers and pilots, having considered the same, report the same with the following resolution:

Resolved, That it is inexpedient to legislate.

Mr. Lintott of Nashua, for the Committee on State House and State House Yard, to whom was referred An act in amendment of chapter 7 of the Public Statutes, relating to the state house and yard, having considered the same, report the same with the following resolution:

Resolved, That it is inexpedient to legislate.

The reports were severally accepted and the resolutions reported by the committees adopted.

Mr. Foye of Portsmouth, for the Committee on Appropriations, to whom was referred Joint resolution to provide a nursery for the growth and distribution of forest seedling trees within the state at cost, having considered the same, report the same with the following resolution :

Resolved, That the joint resolution ought to pass.

Mr. Dickinson of Winchester, for the Committee on Appropriations, to whom was referred Joint resolution appropriating a sum of money to pay Arthur W. Dudley a balance due him for money expended and labor performed in making surveys for the state, having considered the same, report the same with the following resolution :

Resolved, That the joint resolution ought to pass.

The reports were severally accepted and the joint resolutions ordered to a third reading.

Mr. Sanborn of Loudon, for the Committee on State Hospital, to whom was referred An act to provide for the care and support of the dependent insane by the state, having considered the same, report the same with the following resolution :

Resolved, That the bill ought to pass.

The report was accepted and the bill laid upon the table to be printed.

Mr. Wallace of Rochester, for the Committee on Appropriations, to whom was referred An act to authorize the state board of agriculture to appoint a state nursery inspector and to provide for the protection of trees and shrubs from injurious insects and diseases, having considered the same, report the same with the following amendment and with the following resolution :

Resolved, That the bill as amended ought to pass.

Amend by adding the following :

Sect. 8. This act shall take effect upon its passage.

The report was accepted, the amendment adopted, and the bill ordered to a third reading.

Mr. Pike of Haverhill, for the Committee on Appropriations, to whom was referred Joint resolution in favor of raising Squam bridge in Holderness and Little Squam bridge in Ashland, and of improving navigation in Squam lake and connecting waters, having considered the same, report the same with the following amendment and with the following resolution :

Resolved, That the joint resolution as amended ought to pass.

Amend by striking out all after the enacting clause and substituting the following :

That the sum of four thousand dollars ($4,000.00) be and hereby is appropriated for the purpose of raising said Squam bridge and said Little Squam bridge not less than three feet and suitably grading the approaches to the same ; for the purpose of dredging the outlet of said Squam lake and Little Squam lake and otherwise improving the navigation in said lakes and the outlets thereof; said sum to be expended under the direction of the Governor and Council when it is shown to the satisfaction of the Governor and Council that said work will be completed without further demand upon the state.

The report was accepted, the amendment adopted, and the joint resolution ordered to a third reading.

Mr. Huntley of Claremont, for the Committee on Appropriations, to whom was referred an act relative to the enlargement of the state library building, having considered the same, report the same with the following amendment and with the resolution that the bill as amended ought to pass :

Amend by striking out the words " one thousand " and inserting in place thereof the words " two hundred and fifty."

The report was accepted, the amendment adopted, and the bill ordered to a third reading.

Mr. Wright of Manchester, for the Committee on Appropriations, to whom was referred An act to provide for a bounty on hedgehogs, having considered the same, report the same with the following resolution

Resolved, That the bill ought to pass.

The report was accepted and the bill ordered to a third reading. On motion of Mr. Merrill of Stoddard, the rules

24

were suspended and the bill read a third time and passed and sent to the Senate for concurrence.

Mr. Woodman of Concord, for the Committee on Judiciary, to whom was referred An act to incorporate the Ossipee Water and Electric Company, having considered the same, report the same with the following resolution:

Resolved, That the bill ought to pass.

The report was accepted and the bill laid upon the table to be printed.

Mr. French of Moultonborough, for the Committee on Railroads, to whom was referred An act to incorporate the Hampstead & Haverhill Street Railway Company, having considered the same, report the same in a new draft with the following resolution:

Resolved, That the bill in new draft ought to pass.

The report was accepted and on motion of Mr. French of Moultonborough, the rules were suspended and the bill in its new draft read a first time by its title. The bill was then ordered to a second reading. On motion of the same gentleman, the rules were suspended and the bill read a second time by its title. The bill was then laid upon the table to be printed. On motion of the same gentleman, the rules were suspended and the printing of the bill dispensed with. The bill was then ordered to a third reading. On motion of the same gentleman, the rules were further suspended and the bill read a third time by its title and passed and sent to the Senate for concurrence.

Mr. Crossman of Lisbon, for the Committee on Railroads, to whom was referred An act to incorporate the Epping, Brentwood & Kingston Street Railway, having considered the same, report the same in a new draft with the following resolution:

Resolved, That the bill in new draft ought to pass.

The report was accepted and on motion of Mr. French of Moultonborough, the rules were suspended and the bill in its new draft read a first time by its title. The bill was then ordered to a second reading. On motion of the same gentleman, the rules were suspended and the bill read a second time by its title. The bill was then laid upon the table to be printed. On motion of the same gentleman, the rules were suspended and the printing of the bill dispensed with. The bill was then ordered to a third reading. On motion of the same gentleman, the rules were further suspended and the bill read a third time by its title and passed and sent to the Senate for concurrence.

Mr. Haines of Newmarket, for the Committee on Railroads, to whom was referred An act to incorporate the Goff's Falls, Litchfield & Hudson Street Railway Company, having considered the same, report the same in a new draft with the following resolution :

Resolved, That the bill in new draft ought to pass.

The report was accepted and on motion of Mr. French of Moultonborough, the rules were suspended and the bill in its new draft read a first time by its title. The bill was then ordered to a second reading. On motion of the same gentleman, the rules were suspended and the bill read a second time by its title. The bill was then laid upon the table to be printed. On motion of the same gentleman, the rules were suspended and the printing of the bill dispensed with. The bill was then ordered to a third reading. On motion of the same gentleman, the rules were further suspended and the bill read a third time by its title and passed and sent to the Senate for concurrence.

Mr. Bussell of Nashua, for the Committee on Railroads, to whom was referred An act to incorporate the Chester, Fremont & Brentwood Street Railway Company, having considered the same, report the same in a new draft with the following resolution :

Resolved, That the bill in new draft ought to pass.

The report was accepted and on motion of Mr. French of Moultonborough, the rules were suspended and the bill in its new draft read a first time by its title. The bill was then ordered to a second reading. On motion of the same gentleman, the rules were suspended and the bill read a second time by its title. The bill was then laid upon the table to be printed. On motion of the same gentleman, the rules were suspended and the printing of the bill dispensed with. The bill was then ordered to a third reading. On motion of the same gentleman, the rules were further suspended and the bill read a third time by its title and passed and sent to the Senate for concurrence.

Mr. Converse of Lyme, for the Committee on Agriculture, to whom was referred An act for the promotion of horticulture, having considered the same, report the same in a new draft with the following resolution:

Resolved, That the bill in its new draft ought to pass.

The report was accepted and the bill in its new draft read a first time and ordered to a second reading. On motion of Mr. Hoyt of Sandwich, the rules were suspended and the bill read a second time by its title. The bill was then laid upon the table to be printed and then referred to the Committee on Appropriations.

Mr. Lintott of Nashua, for the Joint Committee on State House and State House Yard, to whom was referred Joint resolution providing for the erection of an elevator or elevators in the state house for the use of members of the Senate, House of Representatives, state officers, employees and the public, having considered the same, report the same in a new draft with the following resolution:

Resolved, That the joint resolution in new draft ought to pass.

The report was accepted and the joint resolution in its new draft read a first time and ordered to a second reading.

Mr. Pike of Haverhill, for the Committee on Appropriations, to whom was referred Joint resolution in favor of screening the outlet of Forest lake, having considered the same, report the same with the following amendment and with the resolution that the joint resolution as amended ought to pass:

Amend by striking out "$500" in the fourth line and substituting "$300," so that the joint resolution as amended shall read:

"That the fish and game commissioners be and hereby are instructed to construct suitable screens at the outlet of Forest lake, in the towns of Whitefield and Dalton, to prevent the egress of fish from said waters, and that the sum of $300 be and the same is hereby appropriated for that purpose, and the

Governor is authorized to draw his warrant for that sum out of any money in the treasury not otherwise appropriated."

The report was accepted, the amendment adopted, and the joint resolution ordered to a third reading. On motion of Mr. Remich of Littleton, the rules were suspended and the joint resolution read a third time and passed and sent to the Senate for concurrence.

Mr. Andrews of Somersworth, for the Committee on Education, to whom was referred An act requiring state certification of teachers of public schools, having considered the same, report the same with the following resolution :

Resolved, That it is inexpedient to legislate.

The report was accepted and the question being upon the adoption of the resolution reported by the committee,

(Discussion ensued).

Mr. Remich of Littleton moved that the bill and report be laid upon the table. On a *viva voce* vote the motion did not prevail.

(Discussion ensued.)

Upon a *viva voce* vote the motion of Mr. Remich was adopted and the bill and report were laid upon the table.

Mr. Ahern of Concord, for the Committee on Appropriations, reported the following entitled bill, "An act to provide for the assessment and collection of an annual state tax for the term of two years," with the resolution that the bill ought to pass.

Mr. Piper of Northumberland, for the Committee on State Prison, reported the following entitled bill, "An act in amendment of section 17 of chapter 285 of the Public Statutes, relating to the state prison," with the resolution that the bill ought to pass.

Mr. Piper of Northumberland, for the Committee on State Prison, reported the following entitled bill, "An act in relation to the administration of the state prison and to provide for necessary improvements and repairs," with the resolution that the bill ought to pass.

Mr. Mitchell of Littleton, for the Committee on Judiciary, reported the following entitled bill, "An act in amendment of chapter 119 of the Public Statutes, relating to the inspection and licensing of boats, their engineers and pilots," with the resolution that the bill ought to pass.

Mr. Woodman of Concord, for the Committee on Judiciary, reported the following entitled bill, "An act to permit the town of Gorham to exempt certain property from taxation," with the resolution that the bill ought to pass.

Mr. Buckley of Lancaster, for the Committee on Judiciary, reported the following entitled bill, "An act in amendment of section 1 of chapter 196 of the Public Statutes, relating to the descent of intestate estates," with the resolution that the bill ought to pass.

Mr. Quimby of Meredith, for the Committee on Appropriations, reported the following joint resolution, "Joint resolution in favor of the board of registration in dentistry," with the resolution that the joint resolution ought to pass.

The reports were severally accepted and the bills and joint resolution read a first time and ordered to a second reading.

Mr. Roby of Concord, for the Committee on Fisheries and Game, reported the following entitled bill, "An act to require non-residents to secure a license before hunting deer within the state of New Hampshire and providing penalties for violations of its provisions," with the resolution that the bill ought to pass.

The report was accepted. The first reading of the bill having begun, on motion of Mr. Pike of Haverhill, the rules were suspended and the bill read a first time by its title. The bill was then ordered to a second reading. On motion of the same gentleman, the rules were further suspended and the bill read a second time by its title and laid upon the table to be printed.

Mr. Hamlin of Charlestown, for the Committee on Claims, reported the following joint resolution, " Joint resolution in favor of Ella F. Densmore of Charlestown, Mary F. Lombard of Acworth, Frank G. Smith of Waltham, Mass., Eugene P. Smith of Newport, N. H., and George E. Shattuck of Hinsdale, N. H.," with the resolution that the joint resolution ought to pass.

The report was accepted and the joint resolution read a first time and ordered to a second reading. On motion of Mr.

French of Moultonborough, the rules were suspended and the second reading of the joint resolution begun. On motion of Mr. Ahern of Concord, the rules were suspended and the further reading of the joint resolution dispensed with. The joint resolution was then laid upon the table to be printed. On motion of the same gentleman, the rules were further suspended and the printing of the joint resolution dispensed with. The joint resolution was then referred to the Committee on Appropriations.

Mr. Demers of Somersworth, for the Committee on Revision of Statutes, reported the following entitled bill, "An act in amendment of chapter 262 of the Public Statutes, relating to coroners and coroners' inquests," with the resolution that the bill ought to pass.

The report was accepted, and the first reading having begun, on motion of Mr. Whitcher of Haverhill, the rules were suspended and the bill read a first time and ordered to a second reading. On motion of the same gentleman, the rules were further suspended and the bill read a second time by its title. The bill was then laid upon the table to be printed.

Mr. Batchelder of Keene, for the Committee on Judiciary, reported the following entitled bill, "An act authorizing the town of Littleton to establish or acquire a water and electric light plant," with the resolution that the bill ought to pass.

The report was accepted. On motion of Mr. Ahern of Concord, the rules were suspended and the bill read a first time by its title. The bill was then ordered to a second reading. On motion of the same gentleman, the rules were suspended and the bill read a second time by its title. The bill was then laid upon the table to be printed. On motion of the same gentleman, the rules were suspended and the printing of the bill dispensed with. The bill was then ordered to a third reading. On motion of the same gentleman, the rules were further suspended and the bill read a third time by its title and passed and sent to the Senate for concurrence.

Mr. Woodman of Concord, for the Committee on Judiciary, reported the following entitled bill, "An act to extend Union school district to include the city of Concord," with the resolution that the bill be referred to a special committee consisting of the delegation from the city of Concord and that the bill as referred ought to pass.

The report was accepted. On motion of Mr. Woodman of Concord, the rules were suspended and the bill read a first time by its title. The bill was then ordered to a second reading. . On motion of the same gentleman, the rules were further suspended and the bill read a second time by its title. The bill was then referred to a special committee consisting of the delegation from the city of Concord.

Mr. Buckley of Lancaster, for the Committee on Judiciary, reported the following entitled bill, "An act to ratify the doings of the town of Northumberland in purchasing the stock of the Northumberland Water Company," with the resolution that the bill ought to pass.

The report was accepted and the bill read a first time and ordered to a second reading.

Mr. Woodman of Concord, for the Committee on Judiciary, to whom was referred An act to incorporate the Bellman Club of Manchester, N. H., having considered the same, report the same with the following amendment, and with the resolution that the object sought cannot be obtained under the general laws, and with the recommendation that the bill and amendment be referred to the Committee on Incorporations:

Amend section 1 of said act by inserting between the seventh and eighth lines of said section the following words: " provisions for a sick benefit for its members in case of sickness, and to provide a fund, and make other," so that said section as amended shall read:

SECTION 1. That Frank Johnson, Samuel Osberg, Paul Janeson, Carl Swanson, Theodore Johnson, August Johnson, Claus O. Johnson, Ernest Turnblom, their associates and successors, be and hereby are made a body politic and corporate by the name of Bellman Club, of Manchester, N. H., for social and benevolent purposes, to have a place of meeting where discussions, readings, and lectures on instructive subjects will be held, for the benefit and social improvement of its members, and to make provisions for a sick benefit for its members in case of sickness, and to provide a fund, and make other provisions for said purposes; said fund to be accumulated and all payments from it made in accordance with the constitution and by-laws made and adopted by said corporation.

The report was accepted and the bill and amendment referred to the Committee on Incorporations.

SECOND READINGS.

Joint resolution for screening the outlet of Center pond in the town of Stoddard.

Read a second time and laid upon the table to be printed and then referred to the Committee on Appropriations.

An act to incorporate the Uncanoonuc Incline Railway and Development Company.

The second reading being in order, on motion of Mr. French of Moultonborough, the rules were suspended and the bill read a second time by its title. The bill was then laid upon the table to be printed. Mr. Sheehan of Manchester moved that the rules be suspended and the printing of the bill dispensed with. Upon this question Mr. Eaton of Goffstown called for a yea and nay vote. Mr. Sheehan withdrew his motion and the bill was laid upon the table to be printed.

MESSAGE FROM THE SENATE.

A message from the Honorable Senate, by its clerk, announced that the Senate concurs with the House of Representatives in the passage of the following bill, with amendments, in the passage of which amendments it asks the concurrence of the House of Representatives:

An act to amend chapter 92, Public Statutes, relating to school boards.

Strike out section 2 and substitute therefor:

SECT. 2. Not more than ten dollars shall be expended for the flag, flag-staff, and appliances for any one schoolhouse, and the school board shall have the same control over its preservation and display that it has over the other district property.

Also add:

SECT. 3. This act shall take effect upon its passage.

On motion of Mr. Sawyer of Milford, the amendments were concurred in. The bill was then sent to the secretary of state to be engrossed.

The message also announced that the Senate has granted the request of the House of Representatives, asking that the following entitled House bill be returned to them:

An act in relation to the settlement of paupers.

On motion of Mr. Kimball of Concord, the vote whereby the House adopted the report of the Committee on Education that it is inexpedient to legislate on the following entitled bill, "An act to amend chapter 93, section 15 of the Public Statutes, as amended by chapter 61 of the Session Laws of 1901, relating to scholars," was reconsidered. The question being upon the adoption of the resolution reported by the committee, on motion of Mr. Kimball of Concord, the bill was recommitted to the Committee on Education.

On motion of Mr. Taggart of Manchester, the following entitled bill, "An act in amendment of sections 2 and 3, chapter 42 of the Public Statutes, relating to government of town meetings," was taken from the table.

The question being,

Shall the bill pass?

(Discussion ensued.)

On a *viva voce* vote the bill passed. Mr. Smyth of Berlin demanded a yea and nay vote.

(Discussion ensued.)

On motion of Mr. Taggart of Manchester, the bill was laid upon the table.

On motion of Mr. Evans of Holderness, at 12.36 the House adjourned.

AFTERNOON.

The House met at 3 o'clock.

LEAVE OF ABSENCE.

Mr. Wallace of Rochester was granted an indefinite leave of absence on account of urgent business.

Joint resolution in favor of raising Squam bridge in Holderness and Little Squam bridge in Ashland, and of improving navigation in Squam lake and connecting waters.

An act relative to the enlargement of the state library building.

Joint resolution to appropriate a sum of money to pay Arthur W. Dudley a balance due him for money expended and labor performed in making surveys for the state.

Severally read a third time and passed and sent to the Senate for concurrence.

Joint resolution to provide a nursery for the growth and distribution of forest seedling trees within the state at cost.

Read a third time and passed and sent to the Senate for concurrence in amendments.

An act to establish a state sanatorium for consumptives.

The third reading being in order, on motion of Mr. Ahern of Concord, the rules were suspended and the bill read a third time by its title.

The question being,

Shall the bill pass?

On motion of Mr. Badger of Newington, the bill was laid upon the table.

An act to authorize the state board of agriculture to appoint a state nursery inspector and to provide for the protection of trees and shrubs from injurious insects and diseases.

The third reading having begun, on motion of Mr. French of Moultonborough, the rules were suspended and the bill read a third time by its title. The bill was then passed and sent to the secretary of state to be engrossed.

MESSAGE FROM THE SENATE.

A message from the Honorable Senate, by its clerk, announced that the Senate refuses to concur with the House of Representatives in the passage of the following entitled bill sent up from the House of Representatives:

An act to allow the town of Hampton to readopt chapter 29 in the Laws of 1893, in relation to the repair of highways.

The message also announced that the Senate concurs with

the House of Representatives in the passage of the following entitled bills and joint resolution :

An act to incorporate the Nashua & Hollis Electric Railroad Company.

An act to extend the time of the charter of the Keene, Marlow & Newport Electric Railway Company.

An act in amendment of section nine (9), chapter one hundred five (105), of the laws passed January session, 1901, relating to political caucuses and conventions.

An act to amend the charter of Brown's Lumber Company of Whitefield, approved July 1, 1874.

An act to enable the Hedding Camp Meeting Association to fund its indebtedness.

An act explanatory of the powers of the courts in reference to the fees of commissioners in certain cases.

An act to authorize the Connecticut River Railroad Company to acquire stock of the Vermont Valley Railroad.

Joint resolution appropriating money to aid Dartmouth college in the education of New Hampshire students.

The message further announced that the Senate has passed a bill with the following title in Senate new draft, in the passage of which it asks the concurrence of the House of Representatives :

An act in amendment of section 1, chapter 185, Laws 1901, entitled " An act authorizing the Hillsborough county convention to raise money for the building and repairing of court houses."

Read a first and second time and referred to the Committee on Judiciary.

The message further announced that the Senate has granted the request of the House of Representatives asking the Senate to return the following entitled bill :

An act to establish a new apportionment for the assessment of public taxes.

By unanimous consent the following entitled bill, " An act to establish a new apportionment for the assessment of public taxes," returned from the Senate, was placed back upon its second reading and recommitted to the Special Committee on Apportionment.

Mr. Ahern of Concord moved that the rules be suspended and business in order to-morrow morning at 11 o'clock be made in order at the present time. On a *viva voce* vote the motion did not prevail.

(Discussion ensued.)

On a *viva voce* vote the motion prevailed.

COMMITTEE REPORTS.

Mr. Hoyt of Sandwich, for the Committee on Agriculture, to whom was referred An act to protect milk dealers and consumers against the unlawful use and destruction of milk cans and other receptacles, having considered the same, report the same with the following resolution :

Resolved, That it is inexpedient to legislate as the subject matter appears to be covered by existing laws.

The report was accepted and the resolution adopted.

Mr. Bunton, A. S., of Manchester, for the Committee on Banks, reported the following entitled bill, " An act to change the name of the Gorham Five Cent Savings Bank," with the resolution that the bill ought to pass.

The report was accepted and the bill read a first time and ordered to a second reading.

Mr. Center of Litchfield, for the Committee on Agriculture, reported the following joint resolution, " Joint resolution in favor of the Granite State Dairymen's Association," with the resolution that the joint resolution ought to pass.

The report was accepted and the joint resolution read a first time and ordered to a second reading. On motion of Mr. Hoyt of Sandwich the rules were suspended and the joint resolution read a second time. The joint resolution was then laid upon the table to be printed and then referred to the Committee on Appropriations.

Mr. Ramsay of Walpole, for the Committee on Agriculture, reported the following entitled bill, " An act in amendment of chapter 107 of the Session Laws of 1901, relating to the inspection of milk," with the resolution that the bill ought to pass.

The report was accepted and the bill read a first time and ordered to a second reading. On motion of Mr. Hoyt of

Sandwich, the rules were suspended and the bill read a second time by its title. The bill was then laid upon the table to be printed.

SECOND READINGS.

An act to provide for the assessment and collection of an annual state tax for the term of two years.

Joint resolution in favor of the board of registration in dentistry.

An act in amendment of section 1 of chapter 196 of the Public Statutes, relating to the descent of intestate estates.

An act to permit the town of Gorham to exempt certain property from taxation.

An act to ratify the doings of the town of Northumberland in purchasing the stock of the Northumberland Water Company.

Severally read a second time and laid upon the table to be printed.

An act in amendment of section 17 of chapter 285 of the Public Statutes, relating to the state prison.

An act in amendment of chapter 119 of the Public Statutes, relating to the inspection and licensing of boats, their engineers and pilots.

An act in relation to the administration of the state prison, and to provide for necessary improvements and repairs.

Joint resolution providing for the erection of an elevator or elevators in the state house for the use of members of the Senate, House of Representatives, state officers, employees, and the public.

Severally read a second time and laid upon the table to be printed and then referred to the Committee on Appropriations.

BILLS FORWARDED.

An act relating to books of deposit issued by savings banks when lost, destroyed, or assigned.

An act to exempt soldiers and sailors of the Spanish-American War from paying a poll tax.

Severally taken from the table and ordered to a third reading.

On motion of Mr. Barr of Manchester,—

Resolved, That when the House adjourns this afternoon it be to meet to-morrow morning at 9.30 o'clock, and that when it adjourns to-morrow morning it be to meet Monday evening at 8 o'clock.

On motion of Mr. Smith of Peterborough the following entitled bill, " An act in amendment of sections 4, 5, and 9 of the Public Statutes, entitled ' Support of county paupers,' " was taken from the table. On motion of the same gentleman the rules were suspended and the bill placed back upon its second reading for the purpose of amendment.

Mr. Smith of Peterborough offered the following amendment: Strike out the word " five " in the fourth line of section 2 and insert in place thereof the word " ten."

On a *viva voce* vote the amendment was adopted. The bill was then ordered to a third reading.

On motion of Mr. Roby of Concord, at 3.36 the House adjourned.

FRIDAY, FEBRUARY 27, 1903.

The House met at 9.30 o'clock, according to adjournment.

SECOND READING. ·

An act to change the name of the Gorham Five Cent Savings Bank.

Read a second time and laid upon the table to be printed.

On motion of Mr. Stewart of Manchester, at 9.31 the House adjourned.

MONDAY, MARCH 2, 1903.

The House met at 8 o'clock in the evening, according to adjournment.

The Speaker read the following communication:

ROCHESTER, N. H., February 27, 1903.

HON. HARRY M. CHENEY,
  Speaker House of Representatives,
    Concord, New Hampshire.

SIR : In conformity to the law which prohibits one person holding a federal office and seat in the honorable body over which you have the honor to preside, I hereby resign my seat as representative from Ward five, Rochester, and desire it to take effect upon its receipt.

  Very respectfully,
   Your obedient servant,
    HORACE L. WORCESTER.

On motion of Mr. French of Moultonborough,—

Resolved, That the use of Representatives' hall be granted the Committee on Railroads for Tuesday evening, March 3, 1903, at 7 o'clock, for the purpose of a hearing on House bill No. 272, being "An act concerning the New Hampshire Traction Company," and also bills relating to the electric railways of southeastern New Hampshire, and sometimes known as the " Lovell System."

On motion of Mr. Willis of Concord,—

Resolved, That the use of Representatives' hall be given to the Concord delegation for the purpose of a hearing on House bill No. 432, on Friday evening next, March 6.

On motion of Mr. Blake of Littleton, at 8.02 the House adjourned.

TUESDAY, MARCH 3, 1903.

The House met at 11 o'clock.

Prayer was offered by the chaplain.

LEAVES OF ABSENCE.

Mr. Ryan of Manchester was granted leave of absence for a few days on account of sickness in his family.

Mr. Davis of Laconia was granted leave of absence on account of sickness.

Mr. Sherman of Claremont was granted an indefinite leave of absence on account of serious illness.

Mr. Tinkham of Manchester was granted leave of absence for the day for the purpose of attending a funeral.

Mr. Haines of Newmarket was granted an indefinite leave of absence on account of illness in his family.

COMMITTEE REPORTS.

Mr. Willis of Concord, for the Committee on Engrossed Bills, reported that they had examined and found correctly engrossed the following entitled bills and joint resolutions:

An act to enable the state board of health to prevent contaminated water being furnished for domestic consumption.

Joint resolution in favor of the New Hampshire State Hospital.

An act in amendment of chapter 202 of the Laws of 1889, entitled "An act to establish water-works in the town of Wolfeborough," as amended by chapter 191 of the Laws of 1891.

An act in amendment of an act approved March 26, 1895, entitled "An act in amendment of an act incorporating the Newmarket Manufacturing Company," approved June 12, 1823, and an act in amendment thereof, approved July 7, 1881.

Joint resolution making appropriation for repairs on buildings erected by the state for the New Hampshire Veterans' Association at The Weirs.

Joint resolution appropriating money to complete the payment of expenses of the recent constitutional convention.

An act to exempt from taxation real estate reservations of the Appalachian Mountain Club.

Joint resolution to provide for completing the painting and decorating of the walls of the state library building.

An act to change the name of the New Hampshire Health and Accident Insurance Company, and to further define its powers and privileges.

An act to incorporate the Nashua & Hollis Electric Railroad Company.

25

An act to enable the Hedding Camp Meeting Association to fund its indebtedness.

An act explanatory of the powers of the courts in reference to the fees of commissioners in certain cases.

An act to extend the time of the charter of the Keene, Marlow & Newport Electric Railway Company.

An act to authorize the Connecticut River Railroad Company to acquire stock of the Vermont Valley Railroad.

Joint resolution appropriating money to aid Dartmouth college in the education of New Hampshire students.

An act to amend the charter of Brown's Lumber Company of Whitefield, approved July 1, 1874.

An act in amendment of section 9, chapter 105 of the laws passed January session, 1901, relating to political caucuses and conventions.

An act to amend chapter 92, Public Statutes, relating to school boards.

The report was accepted.

BILLS FORWARDED.

An act in amendment of chapter 262 of the Public Statutes, relating to coroners and coroners' inquests.

An act to provide for the assessment and collection of an annual state tax for the term of two years.

An act to ratify the doings of the town of Northumberland in purchasing the stock of the Northumberland Water Company.

An act to provide for the care and support of the dependent insane by the state.

Joint resolution in favor of the board of registration in dentistry.

An act in amendment of chapter 107 of the Session Laws of 1901, relating to the inspection of milk.

An act in amendment of section 1 of chapter 196 of the Public Statutes, relating to the descent of intestate estates.

An act to change the name of the Gorham Five Cent Savings Bank.

An act to permit the town of Gorham to exempt certain property from taxation.

Severally taken from the table and ordered to a third reading.

An act to incorporate the Uncanoonuc Incline Railway and Development Company.

Taken from the table. Mr. Eaton of Goffstown offered the following amendment:

Amend the bill as follows: Strike out the words "highways and" in line 17 and insert the word "private," and insert in line 18, after the word "necessary," the following words: "with the privilege of crossing any highway and of running in and along any highway wherever private land is not available for the purpose without, in the opinion of the selectmen, causing unreasonable damage to such private land."

The question being upon the adoption of the amendment,

(Discussion ensued.)

On a *viva voce* vote the amendment was not adopted. Mr. Pattee of Goffstown called for a division. The counting having proceeded, the vote was declared to be manifestly in the negative, and the amendment was not adopted. The bill was then ordered to a third reading. On motion of Mr. Chase of Manchester, the rules were suspended and the bill put upon its third reading. The third reading having commenced, on motion of Mr. French of Moultonborough, the rules were suspended and the bill read a third time by its title. The bill was then passed and sent to the Senate for concurrence.

An act to require non-residents to secure a license before hunting deer within the state of New Hampshire and providing penalties for violation of its provisions.

Taken from the table and ordered to a third reading.

Mr. Jones of New Ipswich, for the committee who were assigned by the Speaker to draft resolutions in regard to the death of Mr. Benjamin F. March, late member of the House of Representatives from Mason, reported that they had attended to their duties and report as follows:

Mr. Benjamin F. March was born at Brookline, N. H., June 20, 1836, and died at Nashua, N. H., February 20, 1903.

At the time of his death he was a member of the board of selectmen of Mason, N. H., in which capacity he had served many years.   He had been sexton of the town for thirty-three years.

Mr. March was a member of Dunster Hill lodge, I. O. O. F., of Greenville, N. H., and also of Fruitdale grange.   He had served with honor and integrity in many of the town offices. He is survived by a wife and one adopted son.

Resolutions upon the death of Mr. Benjamin F. March:

Resolved, That this House sincerely deprecates the loss of a useful and respected member, and hereby expresses its earnest sympathy to the bereaved family in this hour of their affliction.

Resolved, That a copy of these resolutions be spread upon the journal of the House of Representatives, and that a like copy be transmitted to the family of our deceased fellow-member.

F. W. JONES,

E. O. CROSSMAN,

ROBERT BROWN, JR.,

Committee.

The report was accepted and the resolutions unanimously adopted.

Mr. Remich of Littleton offered the following resolution:

Resolved, That the Committee on Apportionment be and hereby are directed to report an apportionment bill upon a basis of valuation of New Hampshire railroad stocks such as were adopted by the apportionment committee for the year 1898, in order that the members of the House and Senate may compare the results with those contained in the bill now before the House.

The question being upon the adoption of the resolution,

(Discussion ensued.)

On a *viva voce* vote the resolution was adopted.

On motion of Mr. Ahern of Concord, the following entitled bill, "An act to establish a state sanatorium for consumptives," was taken from the table.

The question being,

Shall the bill pass?

On a *viva voce* vote the bill passed and was sent to the Senate for concurrence.

On motion of Mr. Whitney of Keene, at 12.15 the House adjourned.

AFTERNOON.

The House met at 3 o'clock.

LEAVES OF ABSENCE.

Mr. Abbott of Salem was granted leave of absence for the balance of the week on account of death in his family.

Mr. Twombly of Hill was granted leave of absence on account of sickness.

THIRD READINGS.

An act to provide for the care and support of the dependent insane by the state.

Read a third time.

The question being,

Shall the bill pass?

On a *viva voce* vote the bill passed.

Mr. Chase of Manchester called for a division.

(Discussion ensued.)

The counting having begun, Mr. Chase of Manchester withdrew his call. On a *viva voce* vote the bill passed and was sent to the Senate for concurrence.

Joint resolution in favor of the board of registration in dentistry.

An act in amendment of chapter 107 of the Session Laws of 1901, relating to the inspection of milk.

An act in amendment of section 1 of chapter 196 of the Public Statutes, relating to the descent of intestate estates.

An act to change the name of the Gorham Five Cent Savings Bank.

An act to permit the town of Gorham to exempt certain property from taxation.

An act in amendment of chapter 262 of the Public Statutes, relating to coroners and coroners' inquests.

An act to provide for the assessment and collection of an annual state tax for the term of two years.

An act to ratify the doings of the town of Northumberland in purchasing the stock of the Northumberland Water Company.

An act to exempt soldiers and sailors of the Spanish-American War from paying a poll tax.

An act in amendment of sections 4, 5, and 9 of chapter 85 of the Public Statutes, entitled " Support of county paupers."

Severally read a third time and passed and sent to the Senate for concurrence.

An act to require non-residents to secure a license before hunting deer within the state of New Hampshire, and providing penalties for violation of its provisions.

The third reading being in order, Mr. Buckley of Lancaster moved that the bill be laid upon the table. On a *viva voce* vote the motion did not prevail. Mr. Buckley of Lancaster withdrew his motion.

(Discussion ensued.)

Mr. Buckley of Lancaster moved that the bill be laid upon the table and made the special order for Wednesday, March 4, at 3 o'clock. On a *viva voce* vote the motion prevailed and the bill was laid upon the table and made the special order for Wednesday, March 4, at 3 o'clock.

MESSAGE FROM THE SENATE.

A message from the Honorable Senate, by its clerk, announced that the Senate concurs with the House of Representatives in its amendments to the following entitled Senate bill:

An act to authorize the state board of agriculture to appoint a state nursery inspector and to provide for the protection of trees and shrubs from injurious insects and diseases.

The message also announced that the Senate concurs with the House of Representatives in the passage of the following entitled bills:

An act to provide for a more economical and practical expenditure of money appropriated by the state for the construction and repairs of highways.

An act to annex a certain island in Lake Winnipesaukee, now owned and occupied by George W. Sherwell, being one of the group of islands known as the Aunt Dolly islands, to the town of Meredith.

An act to authorize the Governor with the consent of the Council to cause the original maps and surveys by the town proprietors of New Hampshire to be mounted and preserved.

An act to reimburse the town or county for aid furnished paupers.

An act authorizing the town of Peterborough to exempt from taxation the improvements or new buildings to be erected on the Tarbell block lot.

The message further announced that the Senate has passed the following entitled bills, in the passage of which it asks the concurrence of the House of Representatives:

An act in amendment of section 4 of chapter 37 of the Session Laws of 1895, entitled "An act providing for the appointment of bail commissioners for cities and towns."

An act in amendment of section 29, chapter 266 of the Public Statutes, relating to trespasses and malicious injuries.

Severally read a first and second time and referred to the Committee on Judiciary.

An act to provide for the coöperation of the state with towns and cities in the construction and repairs of highways, and for the establishment of the office of state highway engineer.

On motion of Mr. Small of Rochester, the rules were suspended and the bill read a first time by its title. The bill was then read a second time and referred to the Committee on Public Improvements.

On motion of Mr. Whitcher of Haverhill, the following entitled bill, "An act requiring state certification of teachers of public schools," was taken from the table and recommitted to the Committee on Education.

On motion of Mr. Matthews of Newport, at 4.36 the House adjourned.

WEDNESDAY, MARCH 4, 1903.

The House met at 11 o'clock.

Prayer was offered by the Rev. L. W. Phillips of Franklin.

LEAVE OF ABSENCE.

Mr. Vaillancourt of Berlin was granted leave of absence for the balance of the week on account of illness.

COMMITTEE REPORTS.

Mr. Quimby of Meredith, for the Committee on Appropriations, to whom was referred Joint resolution in favor of appropriating money for screening the outlet of Tewksbury's pond in the town of Grafton, having considered the same, report the same with the following resolution:

Resolved, That the joint resolution ought to pass.

Mr. Quimby of Meredith, for the Committee on Appropriations, to whom was referred An act for the promotion of horticulture, having considered the same, report the same with the following resolution:

Resolved, That the bill ought to pass.

Mr. Quimby of Meredith, for the Committee on Appropriations, to whom was referred Joint resolution to appropriate money for the screening of Armington pond, so called, in the town of Piermont, having considered the same, report the same with the following resolution:

Resolved, That the joint resolution ought to pass.

Mr. Quimby of Meredith, for the Committee on Appropriations, to whom was referred Joint resolution for an appropriation for screening Crystal lake in Gilmanton, having considered the same, report the same with the following resolution:

Resolved, That the joint resolution ought to pass.

Mr. Quimby of Meredith, for the Committee on Appropriations, to whom was referred Joint resolution appropriating money for screening the outlet of Highland lake in the town of Andover, having considered the same, report the same with the following resolution:

Resolved, That the joint resolution ought to pass.

Mr. Quimby of Meredith, for the Committee on Appropriations, to whom was referred Joint resolution for an appropriation for the construction of a screen across the outlet of Lake Winnisquam at East Tilton, in the county of Belknap, having considered the same, report the same with the following resolution :

Resolved, That the joint resolution ought to pass.

Mr. Quimby of Meredith, for the Committee on Appropriations, to whom was referred Joint resolution appropriating money for screening the outlet of Pleasant pond in New London, having considered the same, report the same with the following resolution :

Resolved, That the joint resolution ought to pass.

Mr. Davenport of Bath, for the Committee on Appropriations, to whom was referred An act in amendment of chapter 119, Public Statutes, relating to the inspecting and licensing of boats, their engineers and pilots, having considered the same, report the same with the following resolution :

Resolved, That the bill ought to pass.

Mr. Ahern of Concord, for the Committee on Appropriations, to whom was referred An act to provide for the daily publication of the journals of the Senate and House of Representatives, having considered the same, report the same with the following resolution :

Resolved, That the bill ought to pass.

Mr. Pike of Haverhill, for the Committee on Appropriations, to whom was referred An act to authorize the managers of the New Hampshire Soldiers' Home to procure an adequate supply of water for the use of said home, having considered the same, report the same with the following resolution :

Resolved, That the bill ought to pass.

Mr. Quimby of Meredith, for the Committee on Appropriations, to whom was referred Joint resolution in favor of screening the outlet to Penacook lake in the city of Concord, having considered the same, report the same with the following resolution :

Resolved, That the joint resolution ought to pass.

Mr. Pike of Haverhill, for the Committee on Appropriations, to whom was referred Joint resolution in favor of the New Hampshire School for Feeble-Minded Children, having considered the same, report the same with the following resolution :

Resolved, That the joint resolution ought to pass.

Mr. Huntley of Claremont, for the Committee on Appropriations, to whom was referred An act in amendment of section 17 of chapter 285 of the Public Statutes, relating to the state prison, having considered the same, report the same with the following resolution :

Resolved, That the bill ought to pass.

Mr. Quimby of Meredith, for the Committee on Appropriations, to whom was referred Joint resolution for screening the outlet of Merry Meeting lake in the town of New Durham, having considered the same, report the same with the following resolution :

Resolved, That the joint resolution ought to pass.

Mr. Quimby of Meredith, for the Committee on Appropriations, to whom was referred Joint resolution in favor of Ella F. Densmore of Charlestown, Mary F. Lombard of Acworth, Frank G. Smith of Waltham, Mass., Eugene P. Smith of Newport, and George E. Shattuck of Hinsdale, having considered the same, report the same with the following resolution :

Resolved, That the joint resolution ought to pass.

Mr. Dow of Conway, for the Committee on Appropriations, to whom was referred Joint resolution for screening the outlet to Center pond in the town of Stoddard, having considered the same, report the same with the following resolution :

Resolved, That the joint resolution ought to pass.

Mr. Quimby of Meredith, for the Committee on Appropriations, to whom was referred Joint resolution to encourage the breeding and exhibiting of thoroughbred farm animals, having considered the same, report the same with the following resolution :

Resolved, That the joint resolution ought to pass.

Mr. Quimby of Meredith, for the Committee on Appropriations, to whom was referred Joint resolution for lighting the lighthouse on Loon island in Sunapee lake, repairing the cable connected therewith, improving the light service, placing and maintaining buoys on said lake, and removing obstructions to navigation in said lake, having considered the same, report the same with the following resolution :

Resolved, That the joint resolution ought to pass.

Mr. Quimby of Meredith, for the Committee on Appropriations, to whom was referred An act to provide in common with the state of Vermont, for the acquisition, building, and maintaining of free bridges across the Connecticut river, having considered the same, report the same with the following resolution :

Resolved, That the bill ought to pass.

Mr. Quimby of Meredith, for the Committee on Appropriations, to whom was referred Joint resolution in favor of maintaining buoys and placing lights in Squam lake, having considered the same, report the same with the following resolution :

Resolved, That the joint resolution ought to pass.

Mr. Quimby of Meredith, for the Committee on Appropriations, to whom was referred Joint resolution in relation to a fish hatchery house at Laconia, having considered the same, report the same with the following resolution :

Resolved, That the joint resolution ought to pass.

The reports were severally accepted and the bills and joint resolutions ordered to a third reading.

Mr. Ingham of Nashua, for the Committee on Incorporations, to whom was referred An act to incorporate the Sons of Veterans' Memorial Hall Association, having considered the same, report the same with the following amendment and with the resolution that the bill as amended ought to pass :

Amend the bill by striking out all of section 4.

Further amend by renumbering sections 5 and 6 so that they shall be numbered sections 4 and 5.

The report was accepted, the amendments adopted, and the bill laid upon the table to be printed.

Mr. Cavanaugh of Manchester, for the Committee on Judiciary, to whom was referred An act authorizing the city of Nashua to issue bonds, having considered the same, report the same with the following resolution :

Resolved, That it is inexpedient to legislate, as the subject matter contained therein is covered by a substitute bill introduced by the committee.

Mr. Cavanaugh of Manchester, for the Committee on Judiciary, to whom was referred An act to enable the city of Nashua to issue bonds to erect high school buildings and exempt the same from taxation, having considered the same, report the same with the following resolution :

Resolved, That it is inexpedient to legislate, as the subject matter contained therein is covered by a substitute bill introduced by the committee.

Mr. Roby of Concord, for the Committee on Fisheries and Game, to whom was referred An act for the better protection of deer, having considered the same, report the same with the following resolution :

Resolved, That it is inexpedient to legislate.

Mr. Roby of Concord, for the Committee on Fisheries and Game, to whom was referred An act to prohibit the taking of fish from the waters of Morrill's pond, a natural pond in Canterbury, having considered the same, report the same with the following resolution :

Resolved, That it is inexpedient to legislate.

Mr. Roby of Concord, for the Committee on Fisheries and Game, to whom was referred An act relating to catching shiners in Squog river, so called, having considered the same, report the same with the following resolution :

Resolved, That it is inexpedient to legislate.

Mr. Roby of Concord, for the Committee on Fisheries and Game, to whom was referred An act to amend Laws 1901, chapter 79, section 16, with reference to the protection of deer, having considered the same, report the same with the following resolution :

Resolved, That it is inexpedient to legislate.

Mr. Roby of Concord, for the Committee on Fisheries and Game, to whom was referred Joint resolution amending section 16, chapter 97, Laws 1901, entitled "An act to revise the fish and game laws of the state," having considered the same, report the same with the following resolution :

Resolved, That it is inexpedient to legislate.

Mr. Bunton, A. S., of Manchester, for the Committee on Banks, to whom was referred An act in amendment of clauses 12 and 14, section 1 of an act entitled "An act to regulate and limit the investments of savings banks," approved March 22, 1901, having considered the same, report the same with the following resolution :

Resolved, That it is inexpedient to legislate.

Mr. Bunton, A. S., of Manchester, for the Committee on Banks, to whom was referred An act in amendment to chapter 114, Session Laws of 1901, entitled "An act to regulate and limit the investments of savings banks," having considered the same, report the same with the following resolution :

Resolved, That it is inexpedient to legislate.

The reports were severally accepted and the resolutions reported by the committees adopted.

Mr. Hamlin of Charlestown, for the Committee on Claims, to whom was referred Joint resolution in favor of Horace S. Cummings, having considered the same, report the same with the following amendment :

Amend said resolution by inserting after the word "interest" in the second line thereof the words " at 4%," so that the first two lines of said resolution shall read as follows :

" That the sum of sixteen thousand two hundred fifty-five dollars and eighty-seven cents and interest at 4% from February 27, 1902."

Said amendment being made, the committee report the following resolution :

Resolved, That said joint resolution as thus amended ought to pass.

Your committee also beg leave to submit the following statement :

That said claim arises under a contract made May 11, 1897, between the state of New Hampshire, by Honorable George A. Ramsdell, its Governor, and Horace S. Cummings; that while said joint resolution was pending before the committee, the following questions were raised :   (1) Whether the Governor had authority to make and execute a contract, and (2) whether Cummings is entitled to receive from the state fifteen per cent. of the amount collected and paid into the state treasury.

By resolution passed by this House February 18, 1903, the opinion of the justices of the supreme court was requested upon both the foregoing questions.

The money collected by Cummings and turned into the state treasury February 27, 1902, was $108,372.52, of which, under the contract, Cummings was entitled to $16,255.87, with interest thereon from that date.

Your committee believe that the honor and good faith of the state require that the amount which the justices of the supreme court find to be due Mr. Cummings from the state, under a contract under the seal of the state, executed by the Governor, with full authority from the legislature, should be appropriated and paid Mr. Cummings.

The report was accepted, the amendment adopted, and the joint resolution and statement of facts laid upon the table to be printed and then referred to the Committee on Appropriations.

Mr. Ingham of Nashua, for the Committee on Incorporations, to whom was referred An act to incorporate the Warren Water and Light Company, having considered the same, report the same with the following resolution:

Resolved, That the bill ought to pass.

Mr. Woodman of Concord, for the Committee on Judiciary, to whom was referred An act in relation to state officials, commissioners, trustees, or other persons having control of public funds, having considered the same, report the same with the following resolution:

Resolved, That the bill ought to pass.

Mr. Woodman of Concord, for the Committee on Judiciary, to whom was referred An act amending the charter of the Nashua Light, Heat and Power Company of Nashua, having considered the same, report the same with the following resolution:

Resolved, That the bill ought to pass.

The reports were severally accepted and the bills laid upon the table to be printed.

Mr. Woodman of Concord, for the Committee on Judiciary,

to whom was referred An act relating to the salary of the judge of probate for the county of Carroll, having considered the same, report the same with the following resolution :

Resolved, That the bill ought to pass.

Mr. Roby of Concord, for the Committee on Fisheries and Game, to whom was referred Joint resolution to appropriate the sum of three hundred dollars for the purpose of turning Silver stream into Success pond in the township of Success and to screen the outlet to said pond, having considered the same, report the same with the following resolution :

Resolved, That the joint resolution ought to pass.

The reports were severally accepted, and the bill and joint resolution laid upon the table to be printed and then referred to the Committee on Appropriations.

Mr. Woodman of Concord, for the Committee on Judiciary, to whom was referred An act to incorporate The New Hampshire Beneficiary Union, having considered the same, report the same with the following resolution :

Resolved, That the object sought cannot be attained under the general law, and recommend that the bill be referred to the Committee on Incorporations.

The report was accepted and the bill referred to the Committee on Incorporations.

Mr. Roby of Concord, for the Committee on Fisheries and Game, to whom was referred An act to prevent fishing through the ice and transporting the same out of the state by non-residents, having considered the same, report the same with the following resolution :

Resolved, That it is inexpedient to legislate.

The report was accepted. The question being upon the adoption of the resolution reported by the committee, on motion of Mr. Ahern of Concord, the bill and report were laid upon the table.

Mr. Quimby of Meredith, for the Committee on Appropriations, to whom was referred An act in amendment of section 4 of chapter 162 of the Public Statutes, fixing the salaries of the members of the board of bank commissioners, having considered the same, report the same with the following resolution :

Resolved, That the bill ought to pass.

Mr. Quimby of Meredith, for the Committee on Appropriations, to whom was referred An act in amendment of section 1 of chapter 3 of the Laws of 1893, fixing the salary of the clerk of the board of bank commissioners, having considered the same, report the same with the following resolution :

Resolved, That the bill ought to pass.

The reports were severally accepted and the bills ordered to a third reading.

Mr. Donahue of Manchester, for the Committee on Insurance, to whom was referred An act to incorporate the Prudential Fire Insurance Company, having considered the same, report the same with the following amendment and with the resolution that the bill as amended ought to pass :

Amend section 2 by striking out in the first line the word " ten " and inserting in place thereof the words " twenty-five," and striking out in line three the word " five " and inserting in place thereof the word " two," and adding after the word " dollars " at the end of said section the words, " The principal office of the company shall be in Dover, New Hampshire, and the majority of the directors shall be citizens of New Hampshire ; and no person shall be qualified as a director who does not hold, in his own right, one thousand dollars in par value of the capital stock."

So that section 2 as amended shall read as follows :

SECT. 2. Said corporation shall have a capital stock of twenty-five thousand dollars, divided into shares of fifty dollars each, with liberty to increase the sum to not exceeding two hundred thousand dollars. The principal office of the company shall be in Dover, New Hampshire, and the majority of the directors shall be citizens of New Hampshire ; and no person shall be qualified as a director who does not hold, in his own right, one thousand dollars in par value of the capital stock.

The report was accepted, the amendment adopted, and the bill laid upon the table to be printed.

Mr. French of Moultonborough, for the Committee on Railroads, reported that, agreeably to the request of the House, the Committee on Railroads return herewith the following entitled bill, "An act to incorporate the Portsmouth & Newington Street Railway Company," with a new draft of the same in the form in which electric charters have been granted the present session.

The first reading of the bill in its new draft having commenced, on motion of Mr. French of Moultonborough, the rules were suspended and the bill read a first time by its title.

The question being,

Shall the bill be read a second time?

Mr. French of Moultonborough moved that the bill be indefinitely postponed. The question being upon the adoption of the motion,

(Discussion ensued.)

On a *viva voce* vote the motion did not prevail. Mr. Nason of Dover called for a division.

(Discussion ensued.)

The counting having begun, the vote was declared manifestly in the affirmative, and the bill was indefinitely postponed.

Mr. Donahue of Manchester, for the Committee on Insurance, to whom was referred An act relating to the investments of foreign fire, life, casualty, and other insurance companies, having considered the same, report the same with the following resolution:

Resolved, That it is inexpedient to legislate.

Mr. Donahue of Manchester, for the Committee on Insurance, to whom was referred An act to amend section 8, chapter 171 of the Public Statutes, relating to life insurance, having considered the same, report the same with the following resolution:

Resolved, That it is inexpedient to legislate.

Mr. Donahue of Manchester, for the Committee on Insurance, to whom was referred An act to amend section 1, chapter 169 of the Public Statutes, relating to foreign life insurance companies, having considered the same, report the same with the following resolution:

Resolved, That it is inexpedient to legislate.

Mr. Donahue of Manchester, for the Committee on Insurance, to whom was referred An act to amend section 1, chap-

26

ter 54, Laws of 1891, relating to foreign companies and agents, having considered the same, report the same with the following resolution :

Resolved, That it is inexpedient to legislate.

Mr. Donahue of Manchester, for the Committee on Insurance, to whom was referred An act to amend chapter 169 of the Public Statutes, chapter 64 of the Laws of 1899, and chapter 67 of the Laws of 1901, relating to the taxation of insurance companies, having considered the same, report the same with the following resolution :

Resolved, That it is inexpedient to legislate.

Mr. Donahue of Manchester, for the Committee on Insurance, to whom was referred An act to amend section 7, chapter 169 of the Public Statutes, relating to insurance agents, having considered the same, report the same with the following resolution :

Resolved, That it is inexpedient to legislate.

Mr. Donahue of Manchester, for the Committee on Insurance, to whom was referred An act in amendment of chapter 171 of the Public Statutes, relating to life insurance, having considered the same, report the same with the following resolution :

Resolved, That it is inexpedient to legislate.

Mr. Bunton, A. S., of Manchester, for the special committee consisting of the delegation from the city of Manchester, to whom was referred An act in relation to the term of office of the chief engineer and assistant engineers of the fire department of the city of Manchester, having considered the same, report the same with the following resolution :

Resolved, That it is inexpedient to legislate.

Mr. Donahue of Manchester, for the Committee on Insurance, to whom was referred An act relating to the insurance of children under ten years of age, having considered the same, report the same with the following resolution :

Resolved, That it is inexpedient to legislate.

Mr. Bunton, A. S., of Manchester, for the special committee consisting of the delegation from the city of Manchester, to whom was referred An act to amend chapter 264 of the Session Laws of 1893, entitled " An act establishing a board of street and park commissioners for the city of Manchester, and authorizing said city to issue bonds for certain purposes," having considered the same, report the same with the following resolution :

Resolved, That it is inexpedient to legislate.

Mr. Bunton, A. S., of Manchester, for the special committee consisting of the delegation from the city of Manchester, to whom was referred An act in amendment of chapter 202 of the Laws of the State of New Hampshire, passed at the January session, 1893, entitled " An act in relation to the city of Manchester, establishing a board of police commissioners for said city," having considered the same, report the same with the following resolution :

Resolved, That it is inexpedient to legislate.

The reports were severally accepted and the resolutions reported by the committees were adopted.

Mr. Bunton, A. S., of Manchester, for the special committee consisting of the delegation from the city of Manchester, to whom was referred An act in amendment of the charter of the city of Manchester, establishing a board of assessors in place of the assessors provided under the chapter and laws of the state, having considered the same, report the same in a new draft and new title with the following resolution :

Resolved, That the bill in a new draft and new title ought to pass.

The report was accepted and the bill in its new draft and new title read a first time and ordered to a second reading.

Mr. Bunton, A. S., of Manchester, for the special committee consisting of the delegation from the city of Manchester, to whom was referred An act in amendment of so much of chapter 264 of the Laws of the State of New Hampshire, passed at the January session, 1893, as relates to the establishing of a board of street and park commissioners for the city of Manchester, having considered the same, report the same with the following resolution :

Resolved, That the bill ought to pass.

The report was accepted and the bill laid upon the table to be printed.

Mr. Donahue of Manchester, for the Committee on Insurance, to whom was referred An act to amend section 14 of chapter 169 of the Public Statutes, as amended in section 1, chapter 67, Laws of 1901 ; also section 13 of chapter 167 of the Public Statutes, relating to insurance commissioner ; also section 1, chapter 54, Laws of 1891, relating to foreign insurance companies and agents, having considered the same, report the same with the following resolution :

Resolved, That it is inexpedient to legislate.

The report was accepted. The question being upon the adoption of the resolution reported by the committee, on motion of Mr. Remich of Littleton, the bill and report were laid upon the table and made the special order for this afternoon at 3.30 o'clock.

Mr. Donahue of Manchester, for the Committee on Insurance, to whom was referred An act in amendment of chapter 171 of the Public Statutes, relating to life insurance, having considered the same, report the same with the following resolution :

Resolved, That it is inexpedient to legislate.

The report was accepted. The question being upon the adoption of the resolution reported by the committee, upon motion of Mr. Remich of Littleton, the bill and report were laid upon the table and made the special order for this afternoon at 4 o'clock.

Mr. Bunton, A. S., of Manchester, for a majority of the special committee consisting of the delegation from the city of Manchester, to whom was referred An act enabling the city of Manchester to build and operate an electric lighting plant for the purpose of lighting its streets and public buildings, having considered the same, report the same with the following resolution :

Resolved, That it is inexpedient to legislate.

Mr. Filion of Manchester, for a minority of the special committee consisting of the delegation from the city of Manchester, to whom was referred An act enabling the city of Manchester to build and operate an electric lighting plant for the purpose of lighting its streets and public buildings, having considered the same, report the same with the following resolution :

Resolved, That the bill ought to pass.

The reports were accepted. Mr. Filion of Manchester moved to substitute the report of the minority for that of the majority. The question being upon the adoption of the motion,

(Discussion ensued.)

Mr. Filion of Manchester moved that the bill and reports be laid upon the table and be made the special order for Thursday, March 12, at 11 o'clock. The question being upon the adoption of the motion,

(Discussion ensued.)

On a *viva voce* vote the motion was adopted and the bill and reports were laid upon the table and made the special order for Thursday, March 12, at 11 o'clock.

Mr. Darling of Whitefield, for the Committee on Towns, to whom was referred An act relating to the setting off by the legislature of territory of one town or city on to that of another town or city, having considered the same, report the same with the following amendment, and with the resolution that the bill as amended ought to pass.

Amend section 1 by striking out the word " all " in the fourth line and by adding to said section the words, " present and voting at the annual election of town or city officers," so that said section as amended shall read:

SECTION 1. No portion of the territory of any town or city shall be united with, or set off on to, another town or city unless the legislative enactment providing for such union or set-off shall be ratified by two thirds of the voters of each town or city affected present and voting at the annual election of town or city officers.

The report was accepted, the amendment adopted, and the bill laid upon the table to be printed.

On motion of Mr. Remich of Littleton, at 1 o'clock the House adjourned.

AFTERNOON.

The House met at 3 o'clock.

LEAVES OF ABSENCE.

Mr. Beck of Canterbury was granted leave of absence for Thursday, March 5, for the purpose of attending a funeral.

Mr. Andrews of Somersworth was granted leave of absence for the balance of the week on account of death in his family.

THIRD READINGS.

An act in amendment of section 4 of chapter 162 of the Public Statutes, fixing the salaries of the members of the board of bank commissioners.

An act in amendment of section 1 of chapter 3 of the Laws of 1893, fixing the salary of the clerk of the board of bank commissioners.

Joint resolution in favor of appropriating money for screening the outlet of Tewksbury's pond in the town of Grafton.

Joint resolution to appropriate money for the screening of Armington pond, so called, in the town of Piermont.

Joint resolution for an appropriation for screening Crystal lake in Gilmanton.

Joint resolution for screening the outlet of Merry Meeting lake in the town of New Durham.

Joint resolution for appropriating money for screening the outlet of Highland lake in the town of Andover.

Joint resolution appropriating money for screening the outlet of Pleasant pond in New London.

Joint resolution in favor of screening the outlet to Penacook lake in the city of Concord.

Joint resolution in favor of maintaining buoys and placing lights in Squam lake.

Joint resolution for screening the outlet to Center pond in the town of Stoddard.

Joint resolution for lighting the lighthouse on Loon island in Sunapee lake, repairing the cable connected therewith, improving the light service, placing and maintaining buoys on said lake, and removing obstructions to navigation in said lake.

Joint resolution for an appropriation for the construction of a screen across the outlet of Lake Winnisquam at East Tilton, in the county of Belknap.

An act to provide for the daily publication of the journals of the Senate and House of Representatives.

Joint resolution in favor of Ella F. Densmore of Charlestown, Mary F. Lombard of Acworth, Frank G. Smith of Waltham, Mass., Eugene P. Smith of Newport, N. H., and George E. Shattuck of Hinsdale, N. H.

An act to provide, in common with the state of Vermont, for the acquisition, building, and maintenance of free bridges across the Connecticut river.

Joint resolution to encourage the breeding and exhibiting of thoroughbred farm animals.

Joint resolution in favor of the New Hampshire School for Feeble-Minded Children.

An act in amendment of chapter 119 of the Public Statutes, relating to the inspection and licensing of boats, their engineers and pilots.

An act in amendment of section 17 of chapter 285 of the Public Statutes, relating to the state prison.

An act to authorize the managers of the New Hampshire Soldiers' Home to procure an adequate supply of water for the use of said home.

An act for the promotion of horticulture.

An act relating to books of deposit issued by savings banks, when lost, destroyed, or assigned.

Severally read a third time and passed and sent to the Senate for concurrence.

Joint resolution in relation to a fish hatching house at Laconia.

Read a third time and passed and sent to the secretary of state to be engrossed.

MESSAGE FROM THE SENATE.

A message from the Honorable Senate, by its clerk, announced that the Senate has passed the following entitled bill in the passage of which it asks the concurrence of the House of Representatives:

An act enabling the city of Concord to appropriate money for observing Memorial Day.

Read a first and second time and referred to the Committee on Judiciary.

The message also announced that the Senate concurs with the House of Representatives in the passage of the following entitled bills and joint resolutions:

An·act relative to the salary of the register of probate for Coös county.

An act relating to the salary of the register of probate for the county of Cheshire.

An act in amendment of the charter of the Exeter Gas Light Company.

An act in relation to the salary of the judge of probate for Merrimack county.

An act relating to agreed lines between adjoining owners.

An act in relation to the salary of the register of probate for Strafford county.

An act to incorporate the Manchester Fire Insurance Company of New Hampshire.

An act in relation to the salary of the judge of probate for Strafford county.

An act relating to the salary of the judge of probate for the county of Rockingham.

An act in amendment of chapter 51 of the Public Statutes, relating to cemeteries.

An act to incorporate the Derry Savings Bank of Derry.

An act in relation to smallpox.

The message also announced that the Senate refuses to concur with the House of Representatives in the passage of the following entitled bills sent up from the House of Representatives:

An act amending section 4, chapter 40 of the Public Statutes, relating to towns.

An act in amendment of section 34, chapter 43 of the Public Statutes, in regard to the incompatibility of certain town offices.

The message further announced that the Senate concurs with the House of Representatives in the passage of the following bill, with amendments, in the passage of which amendments it asks the concurrence of the House of Representatives:

An act in relation to milk tickets.

Amend section 1 of said act by inserting in the first line of said section after the word " for " the word " bread."

Amend the title of the bill by inserting the word " bread " after the word " milk."

On motion of Mr. Severance of Exeter, the amendments were concurred in and the bill sent to the secretary of state to be engrossed.

The message further announced that the Senate concurs with the House of Representatives in the passage of the following bills and joint resolution with amendments, in the passage of which amendments it asks the concurrence of the House of Representatives :

Joint resolution in favor of John K. Law and others.

Amend by adding at the end thereof the following :

" That John Demerritt be allowed the sum of thirty-three dollars and twenty cents.

" That George W. Johnson be allowed the sum of seventeen dollars and fifty cents."

On motion of Mr. Ahern of Concord, the amendment was concurred in and the joint resolution sent to the secretary of state to be engrossed.

An act to encourage the use of wide tires on certain vehicles constructed before January 1, 1900, and now in use in New Hampshire.

Strike out the word " councils " in the first line of section 1 and insert in its place the word " assessors."   Also strike out the word " highway " before the word " tax " in the third line of said section.

On motion of Mr. Remich of Littleton, the amendments were concurred in and the bill sent to the secretary of state to be engrossed.

An act authorizing the town of Littleton to establish or acquire a water and electric light plant.

Amend by adding at the end of section 3 of the bill :

" Provided, however, that entry upon and taking of property, rights, and estate, laid out and taken for the purpose of this act, shall not be postponed by reason of any failure of the parties to agree upon the compensation to be paid, or by reason of proceedings being instituted by either party for the assessment of damages as provided in this act, by the said town or district, as the case may be, but said municipal corporation may enter upon, take and occupy such property, rights, and estate by filing a bond to the satisfaction of the superior court or the clerk thereof, conditioned on the payment of all damages that may be afterwards agreed upon or allowed in any case."

On motion of Mr. Remich of Littleton, the amendment was concurred in and the bill sent to the secretary of state to be engrossed.

SPECIAL ORDER.

Mr. Buckley of Lancaster called for the special order, it being the following entitled bill, "An act to require non-residents to secure a license before hunting deer within the state of New Hampshire, and providing penalties for violation of its provisions."

On motion of Mr. Buckley of Lancaster, the rules were suspended and the bill put back upon its second reading and recommitted to the Committee on Fisheries and Game.

SPECIAL ORDER.

Mr. Remich of Littleton called for the special order, it being the following entitled bill, " An act to amend section 14 of chapter 169 of the Public Statutes, as amended in section 1, chapter 67, Laws of 1901 ; also section 13 of chapter 167 of the Public Statutes, relating to insurance commissioner ; also section 1, chapter 54, Laws of 1891, relating to foreign insurance companies and agents."

The question being upon the adoption of the resolution reported by the Committee on Insurance that it is inexpedient to legislate,

(Discussion ensued.)

Mr. Ahern of Concord moved the previous question.
The question being,
Shall the main question be now put?
On a *viva voce* vote the motion prevailed.
The question being upon the adoption of the resolution reported by the committee, on a *viva voce* vote the resolution

was adopted. Mr. Remich of Littleton demanded a yea and nay vote, but withdrew his call. Mr. Remich then called for a division. A division being had, 116 gentlemen voted in the affirmative and 67 gentlemen voted in the negative, and no quorum being present, at 5 o'clock the House was declared adjourned.

THURSDAY, MARCH 5, 1903.

The House met at 11 o'clock.

Prayer was offered by the chaplain.

LEAVE OF ABSENCE.

Mr. Howe of Barrington was granted leave of absence for the balance of the week on account of important business.

COMMITTEE REPORTS.

Mr. French of Moultonborough, for the Committee on Railroads, to whom was referred An act to incorporate the Milton Mills & Union Electric Railway Company, having considered the same, report the same with the following resolution:

Resolved, That the bill ought to pass.

The report was accepted and the bill laid upon the table to be printed. On motion of Mr. French of Moultonborough, the rules were suspended and the printing of the bill dispensed with. The bill was then ordered to a third reading. On motion of the same gentleman, the rules were suspended and the bill read a third time by its title and passed and sent to the Senate for concurrence.

Mr. Ahern of Concord, for the Committee on Appropriations, to whom was referred An act to provide suitable armory quarters for the National Guard at Manchester, having considered the same, report the same in a new draft with the resolution that the bill in new draft ought to pass.

The report was accepted and the bill in its new draft read a first time and ordered to a second reading.

Mr. Hoyt of Sandwich, for the Committee on Agriculture,

to whom was referred An act for the better preservation of highways and accommodating public travel, having considered the same, report the same with the following amendments and the recommendation that the bill as amended ought to pass.

Amend section 1 by striking out the word " shall " in the first line and inserting the word " may " in place thereof.

Amend section 2 by striking out of the third line the figures " 1903 " and inserting after the words " full payment " as found in the sixth line the words " for the first cutting."

Also amend by striking out all of sections 8 and 9, and inserting the following :

"SECT. 8. This act shall be in force only in such towns as shall by majority vote adopt the same at any legal town meeting; and any town adopting the provisions of this act may change or fix the price to be paid as provided in section 2."

The report was accepted, the amendments adopted, and the bill laid upon the table to be printed.

Mr. Foye of Portsmouth, for the Committee on Appropriations, to whom was referred An act in amendment of section 1, chapter 67, Laws of 1899, relating to expenses of judges of the supreme court, having considered the same, report the same with the following resolution :

Resolved, That the bill ought to pass.

The report was accepted and the bill ordered to a third reading.

Mr. French of Moultonborough, for the Committee on Railroads, to whom was referred An act to ratify the location and construction of the Hudson, Pelham & Salem Electric Railway and all of its branches, having considered the same, report the same with the following resolution :

Resolved, That the bill ought not to pass, the subject matter having been provided for in a substitute bill.

Mr. French of Moultonborough, for the Committee on Railroads, to whom was referred An act to authorize the Hudson, Pelham & Salem Electric Railway Company to take a lease of the railway and property of the Haverhill & Southern New Hampshire Street Railway Company, having considered the same, report the same with the following resolution :

Resolved, That the bill ought not to pass, the subject matter having been provided for in a substitute bill.

Mr. French of Moultonborough, for the Committee on Railroads, to whom was referred An act to authorize the Hudson, Pelham & Salem Electric Railway Company to take a lease of the railway and property of the Lawrence & Methuen Street Railway Company, having considered the same, report the same with the following resolution :

Resolved, That the bill ought not to pass, the subject matter having been provided for in a substitute bill.

Mr. French of Moultonborough, for the Committee on Railroads, to whom was referred An act to authorize the Hudson, Pelham & Salem Electric Railway Company to take a lease of the railway and property of the Lowell & Pelham Street Railway Company, having considered the same, report the same with the following resolution :

Resolved, That the bill ought not to pass, the subject matter having been provided for in a substitute bill.

The reports were severally accepted and the resolutions reported by the committee adopted.

Mr. French of Moultonborough, for the Committee on Railroads, reported the following entitled bill, "An act to authorize the Hudson, Pelham & Salem Electric Railway Company to take leases of the railway and property of the Haverhill & Southern New Hampshire Street Railway Company, the Lawrence & Methuen Street Railway Company and the Lowell & Pelham Street Railway Company," with the resolution that the bill ought to pass.

The report was accepted and the bill read a first time and ordered to a second reading. On motion of Mr. French of Moultonborough, the rules were suspended and the bill read a second time by its title. The bill was then laid upon the table to be printed. On motion of the same gentleman, the rules were suspended and the printing of the bill dispensed with. The bill was then ordered to a third reading. On motion of the same gentleman, the rules were further suspended and the bill read a third time by its title and passed and sent to the Senate for concurrence.

Mr. Woodman of Concord, for the Committee on Judiciary,

to whom was referred An act to incorporate the Jackson Water-Works Company, having considered the same, report the same with the following resolution :

Resolved, That the bill ought to pass.

The report was accepted and the bill laid upon the table to be printed.

Mr. Quimby of Meredith, for the Committee on Appropriations, to whom was referred Joint resolution in favor of William J. Patch, having considered the same, report the same with the following resolution :

Resolved, That the joint resolution ought to pass.

The report was accepted and the joint resolution ordered to a third reading.

Mr. Wright of Manchester, for the Committee on Appropriations, to whom was referred An act to provide for the holding of library institutes, having considered the same, report the same with the following resolution :

Resolved, That the bill ought to pass.

The report was accepted and the bill ordered to a third reading.

Mr. Bussell of Nashua, for the Committee on Railroads, to whom was referred An act to ratify the lease of the Seabrook & Hampton Beach Street Railway Company to the Exeter, Hampton & Amesbury Street Railway Company, having considered the same, report the same with the following resolution :

Resolved, That it is inexpedient to legislate.

Mr. Kimball of Laconia, for the Committee on Railroads, to whom was referred An act to ratify the lease of the Portsmouth and Exeter Street Railway Company to the Exeter, Hampton & Amesbury Street Railway Company, having considered the same, report the same with the following resolution :

Resolved, That it is inexpedient to legislate.

Mr. French of Moultonborough, for the Committee on Railroads, to whom was referred An act to ratify the lease of the Dover, Somersworth & Rochester Street Railway Company to the Exeter, Hampton & Amesbury Street Railway Company, having considered the same, report the same with the following resolution :

Resolved, That it is inexpedient to legislate.

Mr. Kimball of Laconia, for the Committee on Railroads, to whom was referred An act concerning the New Hampshire Traction Company, having considered the same, report the same with the following resolution :

Resolved, That it is inexpedient to legislate.

Mr. Martin of Colebrook, for the Committee on Railroads, to whom was referred An act to ratify the lease of the Haverhill, Plaistow & Newton Street Railway Company to the Exeter, Hampton & Amesbury Street Railway Company, having considered the same, report the same with the following resolution :

Resolved, That it is inexpedient to legislate.

Mr. Quimby of Meredith, for the Committee on Appropriations, to whom was referred An act in amendment of section 15 of chapter 93 of the Public Statutes, as amended in 1901, relating to scholars, having considered the same, report the same with the following resolution :

Resolved, That it is inexpedient to legislate.

Mr. Long of Claremont, for the Committee on Railroads, to whom was referred An act to authorize the Portsmouth & Exeter Street Railway Company to construct a branch from Stratham through Newfields and Newmarket, having considered the same, report the same with the following resolution :

Resolved, That it is inexpedient to legislate.

The reports were severally accepted and the resolutions reported by the committees adopted.

Mr. Bunton, A. S., of Manchester, for the Committee on Banks, to whom was referred An act to incorporate the Dover Loan and Banking Company, having considered the same, report the same in a new draft and new title with the following resolution :

Resolved, That the bill in a new draft and new title ought to pass.

The report was accepted and the bill in its new draft and new title read a first time and ordered to a second reading.

Mr. Quimby of Meredith, for the Committee on Appropriations, to whom was referred An act to amend section 10, chapter 79 of the Session Laws of 1901, relating to the duties of the fish and game commissioners, having considered the same, report the same with the following resolution:

Resolved, That the bill ought to pass.

The report was accepted and the bill ordered to a third reading:

Mr. Collins of Nashua, for the Committee on Appropriations, to whom was referred An act to provide for the representation of the state of New Hampshire and the exhibition of its products and attractions at the Louisiana Purchase Exhibition at St. Louis in 1904, having considered the same, report the same in a new draft with the resolution that the bill in new draft ought to pass.

The report was accepted and the bill in its new draft read a first time and ordered to a second reading.

Mr. Buckley of Lancaster, for the Committee on Judiciary, reported the following entitled bill, "An act to legalize the warrant for the town meeting to be held in the town of Franconia, on the second Tuesday of March, 1903," with the resolution that the bill ought to pass.

The report was accepted and the bill read a first time and ordered to a second reading. On motion of Mr. Glover of Franconia, the rules were suspended and the bill read a second time by its title. The bill was then laid upon the table to be printed. On motion of the same gentleman, the rules were suspended and the printing of the bill dispensed with. The bill was then ordered to a third reading. On motion of the same gentleman, the rules were further suspended and the bill read a third time by its title and passed and sent to the Senate for concurrence.

Mr. Woodman of Concord, for the Committee on Judiciary, reported the following entitled bill, "An act to legalize the annual school meeting of the town school district in the town of Franconia in the year 1902, and to legalize the acts of said district at that meeting and the subsequent acts and proceedings of the district officers elected at said meeting," with the resolution that the bill ought to pass.

The report was accepted and the bill read a first time and ordered to a second reading. On motion of Mr. Mitchell of Littleton, the rules were suspended and the bill read a second

time by its title. The bill was then laid upon the table to be
printed. On motion of the same gentleman, the rules were
suspended and the printing of the bill dispensed with. The
bill was then ordered to a third reading. On motion of the
same gentleman, the rules were further suspended and the bill
read a third time by its title and passed and sent to the Senate
for concurrence.

Mr. Cavanaugh of Manchester, for the Committee on Judiciary, reported the following entitled bill, "An act authorizing
the city of Nashua to issue bonds and to exempt the same from
taxation," with the resolution that the bill ought to pass.

The report was accepted and the bill read a first time and
ordered to a second reading. On motion of Mr. Bussell of
Nashua, the rules were suspended and the bill read a second
time by its title. The bill was then laid upon the table to be
printed. On motion of the same gentleman, the rules were
suspended and the printing of the bill dispensed with. The
bill was then ordered to a third reading. On motion of the
same gentleman, the rules were further suspended and the bill
read a third time and passed and sent to the Senate for concurrence.

Mr. Nelson of Portsmouth, for the Committee on Fisheries
and Game, reported the following entitled bill, "An act to
amend section 16 of chapter 79 of the Session Laws of 1901,
relating to the taking of deer," with the resolution that the
bill ought to pass.

The report was accepted and the bill read a first time and
ordered to a second reading.

Mr. Hall of Westmoreland, for the Committee on Railroads,
reported the following entitled bill, "An act in amendment of
section 22, chapter 27, Laws of 1895, entitled 'An act in relation to the incorporation, organization, and regulation of street
railway companies, and authorizing the use of electricity as
motive power by existing steam railroads,'" with the resolution that the bill ought to pass.

The report was accepted and the bill read a first time and
ordered to a second reading.

Mr. Bunton, A. S., of Manchester, for the Committee on
Banks, reported the following entitled bill, "An act authoriz-

27

ing the state treasurer to transfer certain sums of money to the literary fund for schools," with the resolution that the bill ought to pass.

The report was accepted and the bill read a first time and ordered to a second reading.

Mr. Hamlin of Charlestown, for the Committee on Claims, reported the following joint resolution, " Joint resolution in favor of the widow of Benjamin F. March of Mason," with the resolution that the joint resolution ought to pass.

The report was accepted and the joint resolution read a first time and ordered to a second reading.

Mr. Woodman of Concord, for the Committee on Judiciary, reported the following entitled bill, "An act relating to the salary of the judge of probate of the county of Sullivan," with the resolution that the bill ought to pass.

The report was accepted and the bill read a first time and ordered to a second reading.

Mr. Pike of Haverhill, for the Committee on Appropriations, reported the following joint resolution, " Joint resolution in favor of Horace L. Worcester," with the resolution that the joint resolution ought to pass.

The report was accepted and the joint resolution read a first time and ordered to a second reading. On motion of Mr. Ahern of Concord, the rules were suspended and the joint resolution read a second time. The joint resolution was then laid upon the table to be printed. On motion of the same gentleman, the rules were suspended and the printing of the joint resolution dispensed with. The joint resolution was then ordered to a third reading. On motion of the same gentleman, the rules were further suspended and the joint resolution read a third time and passed and sent to the Senate for concurrence.

Mr. Roby of Concord, for the Committee on Fisheries and Game, to whom was recommitted An act to require non-residents to secure a license before hunting deer within the state of New Hampshire, and providing penalties for violation of its provisions, having considered the same, report the same in a new draft with the following resolution :

Resolved, That the bill in a new draft ought to pass.

The report was accepted. On motion of Mr. Ahern of Concord, the rules were suspended and the bill in its new draft read a first time by its title. The bill was then ordered to a second reading. On motion of the same gentleman, the rules were suspended and the bill read a second time by its title. The bill was then laid upon the table to be printed.

Mr. Donahue of Manchester, for the Committee on Insurance, to whom was referred An act in amendment of chapter 171 of the Public Statutes, relating to life insurance, having considered the same, report the same with the following resolution:

Resolved, That it is inexpedient to legislate.

The report was accepted and the question being upon the adoption of the resolution reported by the committee, on motion of Mr. Donahue of Manchester, the bill was laid upon the table. On motion of the same gentleman, the bill was subsequently taken from the table. The question being upon the adoption of the resolution reported by the committee, on a *viva voce* vote the resolution was adopted.

Mr. Willis of Concord, for the Committee on Engrossed Bills, reported that they had examined, and found correctly engrossed, the following entitled bills and joint resolutions:

An act relating to the salary of the judge of probate for the county of Rockingham.

An act in relation to the salary of the judge of probate for Strafford county.

An act in relation to the salary of the judge of probate for Merrimack county.

An act in relation to the salary of the register of probate for Strafford county.

An act relating to the salary of the register of probate for the county of Cheshire.

An act relative to the salary of the register of probate for Coös county.

An act to incorporate the Derry Savings Bank of Derry.

An act in amendment of the charter of the Exeter Gas Light Company.

An act to incorporate the Manchester Fire Insurance Company of New Hampshire.

An act relating to agreed lines between adjoining owners.

An act in amendment of chapter 51 of the Public Statutes, relating to cemeteries.

An act to establish a state sanatorium for consumptives.

An act to annex a certain island in Lake Winnipesaukee, now owned and occupied by George W. Sherwell, being one of the group of islands known as the Aunt Dolly islands, to the town of Meredith.

An act to authorize the Governor with the consent of the Council to cause the original maps and surveys by the town proprietors of New Hampshire to be mounted and preserved.

An act to reimburse the town or county for aid furnished paupers.

An act authorizing the town of Peterborough to exempt from taxation the improvements or new buildings to be erected on the Tarbell block lot.

An act in relation to smallpox.

An act to authorize the state board of agriculture to appoint a state nursery inspector, and to provide for the protection of trees and shrubs from injurious insects and diseases.

An act to provide for a more economical and practical expenditure of money appropriated by the state for the construction and repair of highways.

Mr. Phillips of Franklin, for the committee appointed to confer with Mr. N. M. Colby, representing the owners of the Daniel Webster birthplace, reported that they had attended to their duty and beg leave to submit the following report:

Mr. Colby proposes to give the state the buildings and three acres of land adjoining. The buildings include the ell which was part of the original Webster homestead, and in the tract of land offered is the site of the original homestead, the only conditions of the transfer being that the state shall keep the original structure in a reasonable state of repair, and if the state ceases to hold the title to the property, it shall revert to the present owners.

The report was accepted.

Mr. Remich of Littleton offered the following resolution:

Resolved, That when the House adjourns this afternoon it adjourn to meet Friday morning at 9.30, and when it adjourns

Friday morning it adjourn to meet Monday at 3 o'clock in the afternoon; that when it adjourns Monday it adjourn to meet Wednesday afternoon at 3 o'clock; that when it adjourns Wednesday it adjourn to meet Friday at 3 o'clock in the afternoon; that when it adjourns Friday it adjourn to meet the next Monday evening at 8 o'clock.

The question being upon the adoption of the resolution, Mr. Whitcher of Haverhill moved that the rules of the House be so far suspended that when the House adjourns this afternoon, it be to meet on Friday morning at 9.30 o'clock; that when it adjourns on Friday it be to meet on Monday evening at 8 o'clock; and that when it adjourns on Monday evening it be to meet on Wednesday afternoon at 3 o'clock.

The question being upon the adoption of the motion offered by Mr. Whitcher,

(Discussion ensued.)

Mr. Remich withdrew his resolution and on a *viva voce* vote the motion of Mr. Whitcher prevailed.

SECOND READING.

An act in amendment of the charter of the city of Manchester, establishing a board of assessors in place of the assessors provided under the chapter and laws of the state.

The second reading being in order, on motion of Mr. Cavanaugh of Manchester, the rules were suspended and the bill read a second time by its title. The bill was then laid upon the table to be printed.

BILL FORWARDED.

An act to incorporate the Ossipee Water and Electric Company.

Taken from the table and ordered to a third reading. On motion of Mr. Remich of Littleton, the rules were suspended and the bill read a third time by its title and passed and sent to the secretary of state to be engrossed.

On motion of Mr. Remich of Littleton, the following entitled bill, "An act to amend chapter 243 of the Laws of 1901, creating the Grafton Improvement, Manufacturing and Power Company," was taken from the table.

On motion of the same gentleman, the rules were suspended and the bill put back upon its second reading.

Mr. Remich of Littleton offered the following amendments:

Strike out in section 5 the following words:

" Provided, however, that the structures authorized by this act shall in no case be of such a character as to infringe the public right to a highway in said river as free and convenient as would be afforded by the river in its natural condition."

And insert in place thereof:

" Provided, however, the structures authorized by this act shall in no case be of such a character as to infringe the public right of the highway for the floating of logs down said river in its natural condition."

Strike out in line 12 of section 5 the words " or rights heretofore granted or now existing in said town," and insert in place thereof the following words: " property or water rights now owned by the Dalton Power Company or its successors or assigns."

Amend section 6 by inserting in the eleventh line after the word "lease" the word "or," and by striking out in the eleventh and twelfth lines after the word "purchase" in the eleventh line the words "or take by the exercise of eminent domain or otherwise."

Strike out all of section 7 and insert the following:

" SECT. 7. If it shall become necessary at any time for such corporation to acquire any lands or water rights to enable it to build and maintain its dam or dams, works and structures, and to make and maintain its canals and slips within the limits mentioned in section 5, and it cannot agree with the owner of such land or water rights upon a price therefor, then it may file a petition in the superior court for the county of Grafton or Coös in the district in which the land and water rights lie, which petition may be filed in term or vacation, describing the particular land or water rights to be taken and praying for an assessment of the damages of the owner for such taking, and thereupon lawful process shall issue with order of notice to the owner which shall be served on the owner as required by the order, and at said term (if filed in term), or at the next term of the said court, if filed in vacation, the owner may elect a jury trial as to the assessment of damages, and his damages shall be assessed by a jury and judgment shall be entered according to the finding of the jury, and upon payment or tender to the owner by the corporation of the amount of the judgment, the corporation shall be vested with the title to the land or water right. But if the owner elects that the petition be referred to a board of referees or to the county commissioners, it shall be so referred, and they shall proceed as county commissioners proceed in hearing and determining appeals from the award of damages in laying a highway, and judgment on their report shall be final, and upon payment or tender to the owner by the corporation of the amount of the judgment, the corporation shall be vested with the title to the land or water right. But, however the damages are assessed, if the owner does not accept the amount tendered to him, it shall be deposited with the clerk of the superior court of Grafton county or Coös county, as the case may be, subject to the owner's order before the corporation shall enter upon any land taken, or use and exercise any rights, privileges, or interest taken."

The question being upon the adoption of the amendments,

(Discussion ensued.)

On a *viva voce* vote the amendments were adopted. The bill was then ordered to a third reading.

UNFINISHED BUSINESS.

Mr. Donahue of Manchester called for the unfinished business, it being the following entitled bill, " An act to amend section 14 of chapter 169 of the Public Statutes, as amended in section 1, chapter 67, Laws of 1901 ; also section 13 of chapter 167 of the Public Statutes, relating to insurance commissioner ; also section 1, chapter 54, Laws of 1891, relating to foreign insurance companies and agents.

The question being upon the adoption of the resolution reported by the Committee on Insurance that it is inexpedient to legislate, Mr. Remich of Littleton withdrew his call for a division, and on a *viva voce* vote the resolution of the committee was adopted.

On motion of Mr. Taggart of Manchester, the following entitled bill, " An act in amendment of sections 2 and 3, chapter 42 of the Public Statutes, relating to government of town meetings," was taken from the table. The question being, Shall the bill pass? and on this question Mr. Smyth of Berlin, having demanded a yea and nay vote, the roll was called with the following result:

YEAS, 251.

ROCKINGHAM COUNTY. Sawyer of Atkinson, Hubbard, White of Deerfield, Hardy, Nowell, Smith of Exeter, Duntley, Emerson of Hampstead, Brown of Hampton Falls, Quimby of Kingston, Chase of Newfields, Bickford, Payne, Blaisdell, Foye, Nelson, Yeaton, Newton, Corson, Brown of Rye, Dow of Seabrook. Chase of Stratham, Cochran.

STRAFFORD COUNTY. Mathes, Ramsdell, Libby of Dover, Nason, Bunce, Smith of Dover, Barrett, Hayes, Davis of Lee, Felker, Place, Jones of New Durham, McCrillis, Crocker, Warren, Small, Harrity, Etter, Wentworth, Demers.

BELKNAP COUNTY. Hoitt of Barnstead, Sargent, Smith of Centre Harbor, Potter, Clough, Prescott, Quimby of Meredith, Morrill of New Hampton, Sanborn of Sanbornton, Rogers, Mason.

CARROLL COUNTY. Littlefield, Stevens, Weeks, Fifield, Dow of Conway, Burnell, Philbrick of Effingham, Drake, Greene, Abbott of Ossipee, Hoyt of Sandwich, Edgerly of Tuftonborough, Blake of Wakefield, Britton.

MERRIMACK COUNTY. Fontaine, Harris of Boscawen, White of Bow, Durgin, Symonds, Cate, Kennedy, Willis, Woodman, Emerson of Concord, Davis of Concord, Critchett, Ahern, Bunten of Dunbarton, Tripp, Morin of Franklin, Adams of Franklin, Davis of Franklin, Preston of Henniker, Worthley, Fisk, Sanborn of Loudon, Messer, Sanborn of Northfield, Aldrich, Foss, Hutchins of Pittsfield, Little of Salisbury, Pillsbury, Ela, Burbank, Mason.

HILLSBOROUGH COUNTY. Farley of Amherst, Barr of Bedford, Gould of Bennington, Shattuck, Craine, Tobie, Pattee, Putnam, Ware of Hancock, Whitaker, Ward, Farley of Hollis, Connell, Center, Cavanaugh, Nyberg, Abbott of Manchester, Chase of Manchester, Donahue, Bartlett of Manchester, Taggart, Sheehan, Bunton, A. S., of Manchester, Johnson, Straw of Manchester, McDonald of Manchester, Wright, Barr of Manchester, Dubuc, Carpenter, Morgan, Darrah, Stewart of Manchester, Tonery, Trinity, Whalen, Riordan, Shaughnessey, Sasseville, Marshall, Morse of Manchester, Bunton, A. B., of Manchester, Armstrong, Tinkham, Graf, Quimby of Manchester, Scannell, Dinsmore, Dozois, Gunderman, Janelle, Kohler, Filion, Kane, Newman, Emerson of Manchester, Simpson, Hodgman, Needham, Kendall, Lund, Tuck, Duncklee, Lewis, Lampron, Buckley of Nashua, Ingham, Bussell, Shea, Spalding, Shenton, Hills of Nashua, Sullivan of Nashua, Farley, Dionne, Jones of New Ipswich, Peabody, Miller, Smith of Peterborough, Fitzgerald, Bragdon, Chase of Weare, Sheldon.

CHESHIRE COUNTY. Ware of Alstead, Harris of Chesterfield, Tenney, Cutler, Pierce of Jaffrey, Maloney, Fitch, Whitney, Goodnow, Moors, Fox, Scott, Amidon, Lane of Swanzey, Boyden, Ramsay, Sherman of Walpole, Hall.

SULLIVAN COUNTY. Clark, Hamlin of Charlestown, Long, Churchill, Walker of Grantham, Matthews of Newport, Philbrick of Springfield, Ball.

GRAFTON COUNTY. McMurphey, Morrill of Ashland, Davenport, Pierce of Bethlehem, Calley, Little of Campton, Dorothy, Foster, Glover, Kimball of Grafton, Pinneo, Howe of Hanover, Whitcher, Carr, Pike of Haverhill, Evans, Goold of Lebanon, Comings, Remich, Mitchell of Littleton, Blake of Littleton, Frazer, Ferrin, Russell of Rumney, Houston, Goodrich, Bell.

COÖS COUNTY. Caird, Goss, Hutchins of Berlin, Gallagher, Gathercole, Hicks, Martin, Jordan, Hamlin of Dummer, Bragg, Buckley of Lancaster, Ellis, O'Connor, Darling, Babcock.

NAYS, 13.

ROCKINGHAM COUNTY. Shute, Brown of Fremont, Gerrish. Adams of Portsmouth.

STRAFFORD COUNTY. Jewell, Bergeron.

MERRIMACK COUNTY. Graves, Donagan, Walker of Pittsfield.

HILLSBOROUGH COUNTY. Woodbury.

CHESHIRE COUNTY. Gowing, Kellom, Dickinson,

and the bill passed and was sent to the Senate for concurrence.

On motion of Mr. Bussell of Nashua, the order whereby the following entitled bill, "An act amending the charter of the Nashua Light, Heat and Power Company of Nashua," was laid upon the table to be printed was rescinded. The bill was then ordered to a third reading. On motion of the same gentleman, the rules were suspended and the bill read a third time by its title and passed and sent to the secretary of state to be engrossed.

By unanimous consent the vote whereby the House passed the following entitled bill, "An act in relation to the settlement of paupers," recalled from the Honorable Senate, was rescinded, the rules suspended, the bill placed back upon its second reading and recommitted to the Committee on Judiciary.

SPECIAL ORDER.

Mr. Filion of Manchester called for the special order, it being the following entitled bill, "An act enabling the city of Manchester to build and operate an electric lighting plant for the purpose of lighting its streets and public buildings."

The question being upon the adoption of the motion of Mr. Filion of Manchester, that the report of the minority of the committee be substituted for that of the majority of the committee, on motion of Mr. Filion of Manchester, the bill and reports were laid upon the table and made the special order for Thursday, March 12, at 11 o'clock.

On motion of Mr. Ahern of Concord, at 12.56 the House adjourned.

AFTERNOON.

The House met at 3 o'clock.

LEAVE OF ABSENCE.

Mr. Hicks of Colebrook was granted leave of absence for the balance of the week and for next week on account of poor health.

MESSAGE FROM THE SENATE.

A message from the Honorable Senate, by its clerk, announced that the Senate concurs with the House of Representatives in the passage of the following bill, with amendment, in the passage of which amendment it asks the concurrence of the House of Representatives:

An act to incorporate the Hampstead & Haverhill Street Railway Company.

Amend section 1 by adding in the thirteenth line after the word "Atkinson" the words " to Atkinson Depot, thence."

On motion of Mr. French of Moultonborough, the amendment was concurred in and the bill sent to the secretary of state to be engrossed.

THIRD READINGS.

Joint resolution in favor of William J. Patch.

An act to amend section 10, chapter 79 of the Session Laws of 1901, relating to the duties of the fish and game commissioners.

An act in amendment of section 1, chapter 67, Laws of 1899, relating to expenses of judges of the supreme court.

An act to provide for the holding of library institutes.

Severally read a third time and passed and sent to the Senate for concurrence.

An act to amend chapter 243 of the Laws of 1901, creating the Grafton Improvement, Manufacturing and Power Company.

The third reading being in order, on motion of Mr. Remich of Littleton, the rules were suspended and the bill read a third time by its title. The bill was then passed and sent to the Senate for concurrence.

On motion of Mr. Ahern of Concord, the rules were suspended and business in order to-morrow morning at 9.30 o'clock was made in order at the present time.

COMMITTEE REPORTS.

Mr. Donahue of Manchester, for the Committee on Insurance, to whom was referred An act to incorporate the Universal Health and Accident Insurance Company, having considered the same, report the same with the following resolution:

Resolved, That it is inexpedient to legislate.

Mr. Donahue of Manchester, for the Committee on Insurance, to whom was referred An act in amendment of chapter 236 of the Session Laws of 1901, having considered the same, report the same with the following resolution :

Resolved, That it is inexpedient to legislate.

Mr. Donahue of Manchester, for the Committee on Insurance, to whom was referred An act relating to contracts by casualty and employees' liability insurance companies, having considered the same, report the same with the following resolution :

Resolved, That it is inexpedient to legislate.

Mr. Roby of Concord, for the Committee on Fisheries and Game, to whom was referred An act in amendment of section 16, chapter 79 of the Laws of 1901, relating to the taking of deer, having considered the same, report the same with the following resolution :

Resolved, That it is inexpedient to legislate, as the object sought is already provided for by an existing bill.

Mr. Roby of Concord, for the Committee on Fisheries and Game, to whom was referred An act to amend an act in the fish and game laws, having considered the same, report the same with the following resolution :

Resolved, That it is inexpedient to legislate.

Mr. Roby of Concord, for the Committee on Fisheries and Game, to whom was referred An act to amend section 16, chapter 79, Laws of 1901, so as to permit deer hunting in the town of Ashland, having considered the same, report the same with the following resolution :

Resolved, That it is inexpedient to legislate, as the object sought is already provided for by an existing bill.

The reports were severally accepted and the resolutions reported by the committees adopted.

Mr. Pike of Haverhill, for the Committee on Appropriations, to whom was referred An act in amendment of section 128, chapter 59 of the Laws of 1895, entitled " An act to revise and amend title 13 of the Public Statutes, relating to the militia," having considered the same, report the same with the following resolution :

Resolved, That the bill ought to pass.

Mr. Quimby of Meredith, for the Committee on Appropriations, to whom was referred Joint resolution appropriating nine thousand dollars ($9,000) for additions and repairs to the industrial school, having considered the same, report the same with the following resolution:

Resolved, That the joint resolution ought to pass.

The reports were severally accepted and the bill and joint resolution ordered to a third reading.

Mr. Pike of Haverhill, for the Committee on Appropriations, to whom was referred Joint resolution in favor of the Granite State Dairymen's Association, having considered the same, report the same with the following resolution:

Resolved, That the joint resolution ought to pass.

The report was accepted and the joint resolution ordered to a third reading. On motion of Mr. Hoyt of Sandwich, the rules were suspended and the joint resolution read a third time and passed and sent to the Senate for concurrence.

Mr. Ingham of Nashua, for the Committee on Incorporations, reported the following entitled bill, "An act to amend the charter of the Bennington Water-Works Company," with the resolution that the bill ought to pass.

The report was accepted and the bill read a first time and ordered to a second reading. On motion of Mr. Ahern of Concord, the rules were suspended and the bill read a second time by its title. The bill was then laid upon the table to be printed.

Mr. Davenport of Bath, for the Committee on Appropriations, to whom was referred Joint resolution providing for the erection of an elevator or elevators in the state house for the use of members of the Senate, House of Representatives, state officers, employees, and the public, having considered the same, report the same with the following resolution:

Resolved, That it is inexpedient to legislate.

The report was accepted. The question being upon the adoption of the resolution reported by the committee, Mr. Remich of Littleton moved to lay the bill and report upon the table. On a *viva voce* vote the motion did not prevail. Mr. Remich of Littleton called for a division.

(Discussion ensued.)

Mr. Remich withdrew his call for a division, and on a *viva voce* vote the motion prevailed and the bill and report were laid upon the table.

Mr. Ingham of Nashua, for the Committee on Incorporations, to whom was referred An act to incorporate the Bellman Club of Manchester, N. H., having considered the same, report the same with the following amendment and the resolution that the bill as amended ought to pass:

Amend section 1 of said act by inserting between the seventh and eighth lines of said section the following: " provisions for a sick benefit for its members in case of sickness, and to provide a fund, and make other," so that said section as amended shall read:

SECTION 1. That Frank Johnson, Samuel Osberg, Paul Janeson, Carl Swanson, Theodore Johnson, August Johnson, Claus O. Johnson, Ernest Turnblom, their associates and successors, be and hereby are made a body politic and corporate by the name of Bellman Club, of Manchester, N. H., for social and benevolent purposes, to have a place of meeting where discussions, readings, and lectures on instructive subjects will be held, for the benefit and social improvement of its members, and to make provisions for a sick benefit for its members in case of sickness, and to provide a fund, and make other provisions for said purposes; said fund to be accumulated and all payments from it made in accordance with the constitution and by-laws made and adopted by said corporation.   •

The report was accepted, the amendment adopted, and the bill laid upon the table to be printed. Mr. Cavanaugh of Manchester moved that the rules be suspended and the printing of the bill dispensed with. On a *viva voce* vote the motion did not prevail, and the bill was laid upon the table to be printed.

Mr. Roby of Concord, for the Committee on Fisheries and Game, reported the following entitled bill, " An act in amendment of section 79 of chapter 79 of the Laws of 1901, in regard to lobster traps," with the resolution that the bill ought to pass.

The report was accepted. On motion of Mr. Remich of Littleton, the rules were suspended and the bill read a first time by its title. The bill was then ordered to a second reading. On motion of the same gentleman, the rules were further suspended and the bill read a second time by its title. The bill was then laid upon the table to be printed.

Mr. Ingham of Nashua, for the Committee on Incorporations, reported the following entitled bill, " An act to amend chapter 184 of the Laws of 1897, entitled ' An act to incorporate the Dalton Power Company, as amended by section 1, chapter 221 of the Laws of 1899,' " with the resolution that the bill ought to pass.

The report was accepted. On motion of Mr. Ahern of Concord, the rules were suspended and the bill read a first time by its title. The bill was then ordered to a second reading. On motion of the same gentleman, the rules were further suspended and the bill read a second time by its title. The bill was then laid upon the table to be printed.

SECOND READINGS.

An act to incorporate the Dover Loan and Trust Company.

The second reading being in order, on motion of Mr. Pike of Haverhill, the rules were suspended and the bill read a second time by its title. The bill was then laid upon the table to be printed.

An act to provide for the representation of the state of New Hampshire and the exhibition of its products and attractions at the Louisiana Purchase Exposition at St. Louis in 1904.

The second reading being in order, on motion of Mr. Taggart of Manchester, the rules were suspended and the bill read a second time by its title. The bill was then laid upon the table to be printed.

An act to provide suitable armory quarters for the National Guard at Manchester.

The second reading being in order, on motion of Mr. Barr of Manchester, the rules were suspended and the bill read a second time by its title. The bill was then laid upon the table to be printed.

An act authorizing the state treasurer to transfer certain sums of money to the literary fund for schools.

An act to amend section 16 of chapter 79 of the Session Laws of 1901, relating to the taking of deer.

Severally read a second time and laid upon the table to be printed.

An act in amendment of section 22, chapter 27, Laws of 1895, entitled "An act in relation to the incorporation, organization, and regulation of street railway companies, and authorizing the use of electricity as motive power by existing steam railroads."

The second reading being in order, on motion of Mr. French of Moultonborough, the rules were suspended and the bill read a second time by its title. The bill was then laid upon the table to be printed. Mr. French of Moultonborough moved that the rules be suspended and the printing of the bill be dispensed with. On a *viva voce* vote the motion did not prevail, and the bill was laid upon the table to be printed.

Joint resolution in favor of the widow of Benjamin F. March of Mason.

Read a second time and laid upon the table to be printed and then referred to the Committee on Appropriations. On motion of Mr. Ahern of Concord, the rules were suspended and the printing of the joint resolution dispensed with. The joint resolution was then referred to the Committee on Appropriations.

An act relating to the salary of the judge of probate of the county of Sullivan.

Read a second time and laid upon the table to be printed and then referred to the Committee on Appropriations.

On motion of Mr. Amidon of Richmond, at 3.36 the House adjourned.

FRIDAY, MARCH 6, 1903.

The House met at 9.30 o'clock, according to adjournment.

COMMITTEE REPORTS.

Mr. Harris of Boscawen, for the Committee on Railroads, to whom was referred An act in relation to street railway terminals, having considered the same, report the same with the following resolution :

Resolved, That it is inexpedient to legislate.

Mr. French of Moultonborough, for the Committee on Railroads, to whom was referred An act to amend the charter of the Ossipee Valley Railway Company, having considered the same, report the same with the following resolution :

Resolved, That it is inexpedient to legislate, the object sought having been provided for in another bill.

The reports were severally accepted and the resolutions adopted.

Mr. French of Moultonborough, for the Committee on Railroads, to whom was referred An act to incorporate the Swift River Railroad Company, having considered the same, report the same in a new draft with the following resolution :

Resolved, That the bill in the new draft ought to pass.

The report was accepted. On motion of Mr. French of Moultonborough, the rules were suspended and the bill in its new draft read a first time by its title. The bill was then ordered to a second reading. On motion of the same gentleman, the rules were further suspended and the bill read a second time by its title. The bill was then laid upon the table to be printed.

Mr. Drake of Freedom, for the Committee on Public Improvements, to whom was referred Joint resolution in favor of placing and maintaining buoys and lights in Lake Winnipesaukee and adjacent waters, having considered the same, report the same with the following resolution :

Resolved, That the joint resolution ought to pass

The report was accepted and the joint resolution laid upon the table to be printed and then referred to the Committee on Appropriations.

28

Mr. French of Moultonborough, for the Committee on Railroads, reported the following entitled bill, "An act to incorporate the Meredith & Ossipee Valley Railroad Company," with the resolution that the bill ought to pass.

The report was accepted. On motion of Mr. French of Moùltonborough, the rules were suspended and the bill read a first time by its title. The bill was then ordered to a second reading. On motion of the same gentleman, the rules were suspended and the bill read a second time by its title. The bill was then laid upon the table to be printed.

Mr. Drake of Freedom, for the Committee on Public Improvements, reported the following joint resolution, " Joint resolution in favor of Green's Basin in Lake Winnipesaukee," with the resolution that the joint resolution ought to pass.

The report was accepted and the joint resolution read a first time and ordered to a second reading. On motion of Mr. Remich of Littleton, the rules were suspended and the joint resolution read a second time. The joint resolution was then laid upon the table to be printed and then referred to the Committee on Appropriations.

Mr. Willis of Concord, for the Committee on Engrossed Bills, reported that they had examined, and found correctly engrossed, the following entitled bills and joint resolutions:

Joint resolution to appropriate a sum of money to pay Arthur W. Dudley a sum due him for money expended and labor performed in making surveys for the state.

An act to provide for a bounty on hedgehogs.

An act to ratify the doings of the town of Northumberland in purchasing the stock of the Northumberland Water Company.

An act relative to the enlargement of the state library building.

An act to exempt the soldiers and sailors of the Spanish-American War from paying a poll tax.

An act to incorporate the First Free Baptist church of Franconia.

An act to change the name of the Gorham Five Cents Saving Bank.

An act severing the homestead of Hiram S. Stevens from

the school district of the town of Middleton, and annexing the same to the town of Wakefield for school purposes.

An act providing for the purchase of a bond for the deputy state treasurer.

An act in relation to milk and bread tickets.

An act to change the name of the South Congregational Society in Newmarket, New Hampshire, now located in Newfields, New Hampshire.

An act to encourage the use of wide tires on certain vehicles constructed before January 1, 1900, and now in use in New Hampshire.

An act to incorporate the Goff's Falls, Litchfield & Hudson Street Railway company.

An act to enable the town of Greenville to acquire, own, and operate an electric power and lighting plant.

An act to incorporate the Ossipee Water and Electric Company.

An act to legalize the warrant for the town meeting to be held in the town of Franconia on the second Tuesday of March, 1903.

An act authorizing the town of Littleton to establish and acquire a water and electric light plant.

An act in relation to reports and increase of stock and bonds of corporations owning stock in railways.

An act in amendment of sections 4, 5, and 9 of chapter 85 of the Public Statutes, entitled " Support of county paupers."

An act to provide for the assessment and collection of an annual state tax for the term of two years.

An act in amendment of chapter 86 of the Public Statutes, in relation to state aid to indigent deaf and dumb, blind and feeble-minded persons.

An act to amend chapter 95 of the Public Statutes, relating to normal school.

An act in amendment of chapter 215, Laws of 1895, entitled "An act to confirm the organization of the Androscoggin Hospital Association."

An act in amendment to chapter 153, Public Statutes, creating section 20 of said chapter.

Joint resolution in relation to a fish hatching house at Laconia.

Joint resolution in favor of Horace L. Worcester.

Joint resolution in favor of appropriating money for screening the outlet of Pleasant pond in the town of New London.

Joint resolution for an appropriation for the construction of a screen across the outlet of Lake Winnisquam at East Tilton, in the county of Belknap.

Joint resolution for screening the outlet of Center pond in the town of Stoddard.

Joint resolution to appropriate money for the screening of Armington pond, so called, in the town of Piermont.

Joint resolution appropriating money for screening the outlet of Highland lake in the town of Andover.

Joint resolution for screening the outlet of Merry Meeting lake in the town of New Durham.

Joint resolution in favor of screening the outlet of Forest lake.

Joint resolution in favor of the board of registration in dentistry.

Joint resolution in favor of screening the outlet of Penacook lake in the city of Concord.

Joint resolution in favor of appropriating money for screening the outlet of Tewksbury's pond in the town of Grafton.

Joint resolution for an appropriation for screening Crystal lake in Gilmanton.

Joint resolution in favor of raising Squam bridge in Holderness and Little Squam bridge in Ashland, and of improving navigation in Squam lake and connecting waters.

Joint resolution in favor of John K. Law and others.

An act to permit the town of Gorham to exempt certain property from taxation.

An act to incorporate the Hampstead & Haverhill Street Railway Company.

An act in amendment of sections 2 and 3, chapter 42 of the Public Statutes, relating to government of town meetings.

An act to provide for the care and support of the dependent insane by the state.

An act amending the charter of the Nashua Light, Heat and Power Company.

The report was accepted.

On motion of Mr. Pinkham of Alton, at 9.40 the House adjourned.

MONDAY, March 9, 1903.

The House met at 8 o'clock in the evening, according to adjournment.

MESSAGE FROM THE GOVERNOR.

To the House of Representatives :

I return, with my objections, to the House in which it originated, House bill No. 49, entitled "An act to establish a state sanatorium for consumptives."

This bill appropriates $50,000 to found a state sanatorium, in which such consumptives as may be selected by a board of trustees shall be treated upon such terms as these trustees may prescribe ; mainly at the state's expense. If the bill becomes a law, it will establish as the policy of the state the theory that the state may, and should, provide medical attendance, care, and treatment for some of its citizens afflicted by a certain disease, who are not objects of charity but are as well able as their fellow-citizens who are suffering from other diseases to provide for themselves.

The statistics of mortality show that from 1884 to 1901 the deaths from tuberculosis in New Hampshire decreased from about fifteen per cent. of the whole number to less than ten per cent., and that the average for the whole period was 11.26 per cent. Is there any logical stopping place between a sanatorium for the victims of a disease of which ten people die and sanatoriums for those afflicted by maladies to which ninety people succumb? Is there any sound reason why the public should be required to maintain a home for the few consumptives that can be cured in such a home, while all other consumptives and all those stricken by other diseases are denied access to the home and at the same time taxed to support the favored few? I think not.

It is well established that a state can consistently provide education, or aid in providing education, and enforce regulations that will contribute to public health or to the general welfare of the state. I do not know that it would be justified in providing remedial treatment for people capable of self-control and susceptible of receiving instruction. I believe the state would be justified in instructing tuberculous patients in the art of treatment of the disease, and, to a limited extent in furnishing object lessons of its application, but I do not believe it would be justified in undertaking to treat tuberculosis, or any other disease, at state expense. Even if I am wrong as to the principles that should govern us in such matters, I do not think the time has come when we should inaugurate such an expensive permanent sanatorium. In considering such a subject most of us must depend mainly upon the expert testimony of the medical profession, which is divided. Eminent physicians declare that consumption is curable in our climate. Others, just as eminent, maintain that it is not. Another class, more cautious, assert that the new theories and treatment which the state is asked to approve and bear the expense of, are still in the experimental stage, which I am forced to conclude is the fact. Two, four, or six years later we shall be better informed and can act much more intelligently than we can now. All experience teaches that such an institution, once established by the state, cannot be abandoned, and I know of no evidence that one can be made self-supporting. Whether it accomplishes what its founders expect or not, it remains a constant and increasing charge upon the public. I believe that an appropriation of $50,000 for such an object this year will make necessary a larger one two years hence for construction and equipment, and the annual cost of operation will be very large ever afterwards. So far as I can ascertain, nearly all the tuberculosis sanatoriums in this country are private institutions, helped in some cases by state appropriations. Few of the states have deemed it safe to establish them permanently and make them public charges. Massachusetts has one which cost originally $175,000 and is maintained at large expense. It treats but one in five of the applicants and bars all but incipient cases. This is evidence of the demand for anything furnished at public expense at less than cost, rather than evidence of the duty of the state in providing it. Other states are waiting and inquiring before taking a step that cannot be retraced. I believe we should do the same.

The demands upon the state for financial assistance are many, urgent, and almost irresistible. At the lowest the appropriations by the present legislature will reach an aggregate unequaled in our history and appalling to those who are obliged to count the cost of public service, because to them taxes mean hard work, enforced economies and oftentimes denial to themselves of what they feel they need. We cannot with any regard for the welfare or wishes of the great body of our constituents give everything that is asked for. We must stop somewhere and it appears to me that we should stop upon ground that is safer than that upon which the bill under consideration would place us.

With these views I cannot accept any part of the responsibility of forcing such a burden upon the people of the state, who have never considered the subject generally or passed upon it in any way.

I would gladly approve a bill appropriating a reasonable sum for experimental and educational work along this line, under the direction of the state board of health, or other competent authority, in connection with any public or private institution where it can be properly carried on, but further than this I cannot go with such a doubtful and questionable project.

NAHUM J. BACHELDER,
Governor.

March 9, 1903.

The question being,

Shall the bill pass, notwithstanding the objections of His Excellency the Governor?

On motion of Mr. Ahern of Concord, the message and bill were laid upon the table and made the special order for Tuesday, March 17, at 11 o'clock.

On motion of Mr. Kennedy of Concord, at 8.06 the House adjourned.

WEDNESDAY, MARCH 11, 1903.

The House met at 3 o'clock, according to adjournment.

THIRD READINGS.

Joint resolution appropriating nine thousand dollars for additions and repairs to the industrial school.

Read a third time and passed and sent to the Senate for concurrence.

An act in amendment of section 128, chapter 59 of the Laws of 1895, entitled "An act to revise and amend title 13 of the Public Statutes, relating to militia."

Read a third time and passed and sent to the secretary of state to be engrossed.

MESSAGE FROM THE SENATE.

A message from the Honorable Senate, by its clerk, announced that the Senate concurs with the House of Representatives in the passage of the following entitled bills and joint resolutions:

An act to establish a state sanatorium for consumptives.

An act providing for the purchase of a bond for the deputy state treasurer.

An act to change the name of the South Congregational Society of Newmarket, N. H., now located in Newfields, N. H.

Joint resolution in favor of raising Squam bridge in Holderness and Little Squam bridge in Ashland, and of improving navigation in Squam lake and connecting waters.

An act to enable the town of Greenville to acquire, own, and operate an electric power and lighting plant.

An act relative to the enlargement of the state library building.

An act to amend chapter 95 of the Public Statutes, relating to normal school.

An act in amendment of chapter 86 of the Public Statutes, in relation to state aid to indigent deaf and dumb, blind, and feeble-minded persons.

An act to exempt soldiers and sailors of the Spanish-American War from paying a poll tax.

An act in addition to chapter 153, Public Statutes, creating section 20 of said chapter.

An act to incorporate the First Free Baptist church of Franconia.

An act in amendment of sections 4, 5, and 9 of chapter 85 of the Public Statutes, entitled "Support of county paupers."

An act to provide for the care and support of the dependent insane by the state.

An act in relation to reports and increase of stock and bonds of corporations owning stock in railways.

An act to provide for the assessment and collection of an annual state tax for the term of two years.

An act to change the name of the Gorham Five Cent Savings Bank.

An act to permit the town of Gorham to exempt certain property from taxation.

An act severing the homestead farm of Hiram S. Stevens from the school district of the town of Middleton and annexing the same to the town of Wakefield for school purposes.

An act in amendment of chapter 215, Laws of 1895, entitled "An act to confirm the organization of the Androscoggin Hospital Association."

An act to legalize the warrant for the town meeting to be held in the town of Franconia on the second Tuesday of March, 1903.

An act to provide for a bounty on hedgehogs.

An act to incorporate the Goff's Falls, Litchfield & Hudson Street Railway Company.

An act in amendment of sections 2 and 3, chapter 42 of the Public Statutes, relating to government of town meetings.

The message also announced that the Senate concurs with the House of Representatives in the passage of the following bill, with amendment, in the passage of which amendment it asks the concurrence of the House of Representatives:

An act to incorporate the Omicron Deuteron Charge of the Theta Delta Chi.

Amend the title of the bill by adding after the word "Chi" the word "Fraternity."

On motion of Mr. Wallace of Rochester, the amendment was concurred in and the bill sent to the secretary of state to be engrossed.

The message further announced that the Senate has passed bills with the following titles, and joint resolution, in the passage of which it asks the concurrence of the House of Representatives :

An act relating to the time required for filing notice of intention of marriage and the consent of parents to the marriage of minors.

Read a first and second time and referred to the Committee on Judiciary.

An act in amendment of sections 6 and 7 of chapter 270 of the Public Statutes, relating to lotteries, gambling, and wagers.

Read a first and second time and referred to the Committee on Judiciary.

Joint resolution authorizing the trustees of the N. H. College of Agriculture and the Mechanic Arts to permit certain real estate in Durham to be used as the site of a public library.

Read a first and second time and referred to the Committee on Agricultural College.

An act relating to highways and highway agents and street commissioners.

Read a first and second time and referred to the Committee on Public Improvements.

An act in amendment of section 56, chapter 79 of the Laws of 1901, relating to fish and game.

Read a first and second time and referred to the Committee on Fisheries and Game.

An act in amendment of sections 1, 2, and 5 of chapter 105 of the Session Laws of 1901, approved March 22, 1901, and as amended at the session of 1903.

Read a first and second time and referred to the Committee on Judiciary.

An act to amend the charter of the Newport & George's Mills Electric Railway Company.

Read a first and second time and referred to the Committee on Railroads.

On motion of Mr. Etter of Somersworth, at 3.28 the House adjourned.

THURSDAY, MARCH 12, 1903.

The House met at 11 o'clock.

Prayer was offered by the chaplain.

LEAVES OF ABSENCE.

Mr. Boyden of Troy was granted leave of absence for the balance of the week on account of illness.

Mr. Huntley of Claremont was granted leave of absence for the balance of the week on account of important business.

Mr. Critchett of Concord was granted leave of absence for the balance of the week on account of illness in his family.

PETITIONS PRESENTED AND REFERRED.

By Mr. Jones of Franklin, Petition of legal voters of the city of Franklin protesting against the enacting of any law forcing license of the liquor traffic upon any city or town without their consent.

By Mr. Remich of Littleton, Petition of Methodist ministers in northern New Hampshire against the repeal of the prohibitory law.

By Mr. Remich of Littleton, Petition of the members of the Main Street Methodist church of Nashua, N. H., in favor of maintaining the prohibitory law.

By Mr. Remich of Littleton, Petition of the Trinitarian Congregational church of Marlborough against the repeal of the prohibitory law.

By Mr. Remich of Littleton, Petition of the W. C. T. U. of Ashland against the repeal of the prohibitory law.

Severally to the Committee on Liquor Laws.

COMMITTEE REPORTS.

Mr. Woodman of Concord, for the Committee on Judiciary, to whom was referred An act annexing certain islands in Lake

Winnipesaukee to the town of Tuftonborough, having considered the same, report the same in new draft with the resolution that the bill in a new draft ought to pass.

The report was accepted and the bill in its new draft read a first time and ordered to a second reading. On motion of Mr. Edgerly of Tuftonborough, the rules were suspended and the bill read a second time. The bill was then laid upon the table to be printed. On motion of the same gentleman, the rules were suspended and the printing of the bill dispensed with. The bill was then ordered to a third reading. On motion of the same gentleman, the rules were further suspended and the bill read a third time and passed and sent to the Senate for concurrence.

Mr. French of Moultonborough, for the Committee on Railroads, to whom was referred An act to incorporate the Kearsarge Mountain Electric Railway Company, having considered the same, report the same in a new draft with the resolution that the bill in the new draft ought to pass.

The report was accepted. On motion of Mr. French of Moultonborough, the rules were suspended and the bill in its new draft read a first time by its title. The bill was then ordered to a second reading. On motion of the same gentleman, the rules were suspended and the bill read a second time by its title. The bill was then laid upon the table to be printed. On motion of the same gentleman, the rules were suspended and the printing of the bill dispensed with. The bill was then ordered to a third reading. On motion of the same gentleman, the rules were further suspended and the bill read a third time by its title and passed and sent to the Senate for concurrence.

Mr. French of Moultonborough, for the Committee on Railroads, to whom was referred An act to incorporate the New Ipswich, Greenville & Wilton Electric Railway Company, having considered the same, report the same with the following resolution:

Resolved, That the bill ought to pass.

The report was accepted and the bill laid upon the table to be printed. On motion of Mr. French of Moultonborough, the rules were suspended and the printing of the bill dispensed with. The bill was then ordered to a third reading. On motion of the same gentleman, the rules were further suspended and the bill read a third time by its title and passed and sent to the Senate for concurrence.

Mr. French of Moultonborough, for the Committee on Railroads, to whom was referred An act to incorporate the Northern Transportation and Transfer Company, having considered the same, report the same with the suggestion that the same be referred to the Committee on Judiciary.

The report was accepted and the bill referred to the Committee on Judiciary.

Mr. Batchelder of Keene, for the Committee on Judiciary, to whom was referred An act in amendment of chapter 134 of the Public Statutes, relating to the practice of dentistry, having considered the same, report the same in a new draft with the resolution that the bill in a new draft ought to pass.

The report was accepted and the bill in its new draft read a first time and ordered to a second reading.

Mr. Cavanaugh of Manchester, for the Committee on Judiciary, to whom was referred An act to change the name of the Manchester Heating and Lighting Company of Manchester, N. H., having considered the same, report the same with the following resolution:

Resolved, That the bill ought to pass.

Mr. Buckley of Lancaster, for the Committee on Judiciary, to whom was referred An act to abolish capital punishment, having considered the same, report the same with the following resolution:

Resolved, That the bill ought to pass.

The reports were severally accepted and the bills laid upon the table to be printed.

Mr. Foye of Portsmouth, for the Committee on Appropriations, to whom was referred Joint resolution in favor of New Hampshire Soldiers' Home, having considered the same, report the same with the following resolution:

Resolved, That the joint resolution ought to pass.

The report was accepted and the joint resolution ordered to a third reading.

Mr. Willis of Concord, for the Committee on Engrossed

Bills, reported that they had examined, and found correctly engrossed, the following entitled bills:

An act to incorporate the Omicron Deuteron Charge of the Theta Delta Chi Fraternity.

An act in amendment of section 128, chapter 59 of the Laws of 1895, entitled "An act to revise and amend title 13 of the Public Statutes, relating to militia."

The report was accepted.

Mr. French of Moultonborough, for the Committee on Railroads, to whom was referred An act to provide for the continuous operation of cars upon the Portsmouth & Exeter Street Railway, and the Portsmouth Electric Railway, owned and operated by the Boston & Maine Railroad, having considered the same, report the same with the following resolution:

Resolved, That it is inexpedient to legislate.

The report was accepted and the resolution adopted.

Mr. Scammon of Exeter, for the Committee on Judiciary, reported the following entitled bill, "An act to legalize and ratify the votes and proceedings at the annual meeting in Newton, holden on the tenth day of March, 1903," with the resolution that the bill ought to pass.

The report was accepted and the bill read a first time and ordered to a second reading. On motion of Mr. Scammon of Exeter, the rules were suspended and the bill read a second time by its title. The bill was then laid upon the table to be printed. On motion of the same gentleman, the rules were suspended and the printing of the bill dispensed with. The bill was then ordered to a third reading. On motion of the same gentleman, the rules were further suspended and the bill read a third time by its title and passed and sent to the Senate for concurrence.

Mr. French of Moultonborough, for the Committee on Railroads, to whom was referred An act to authorize the Dover & Eliot Street Railway and the Eliot Bridge Company to transfer their properties and franchises to the Berwick, Eliot & York Street Railway, having considered the same, report the same in a new draft with the resolution that the bill in the new draft ought to pass.

The report was accepted. On motion of Mr. French of Moultonborough, the rules were suspended and the bill in its new draft read a first time by its title. The bill was then ordered to a second reading. On motion of the same gentleman, the rules were suspended and the bill read a second time by its title. The bill was then laid upon the table to be printed. On motion of the same gentleman, the rules were suspended and the printing of the bill dispensed with. The bill was then ordered to a third reading. On motion of the same gentleman, the rules were further suspended and the bill read a third time by its title and passed and sent to the Senate for concurrence.

Mr. Morgan of Manchester, for the special committee consisting of the delegation from the County of Hillsborough, to whom was referred An act in amendment of section 20 of chapter 27 of the Public Statutes, entitled " County commissioners," having considered the same, report the same with the following amendment and the resolution that the bill as amended ought to pass :

Amend section 1 by striking out the word " five " in the fourth line and inserting in place thereof the word " four."

Further amend by striking out the word " five " in the ninth line and inserting in place thereof the word " four."

The report was accepted, the amendment adopted, and the bill laid upon the table to be printed. Mr. Morgan of Manchester moved that the rules be suspended and the printing of the bill dispensed with. The question being upon the adoption of the motion,

(Discussion ensued.)

Mr. Scammon of Exeter moved that the bill be indefinitely postponed. The question being upon the adoption of the motion,

(Discussion ensued.)

On motion of Mr. Ahern of Concord, the bill and pending motion were laid upon the table.

Mr. Woodman of Concord, for the Committee on Judiciary, reported the following entitled bill, "An act to incorporate the History Commission of Concord," with the resolution that the bill ought to pass.

The report was accepted and the bill read a first time and ordered to a second reading. Mr. Woodman of Concord moved that the rules be suspended and the bill read a second time by its title at the present time. The question being upon the adoption of the motion,

(Discussion ensued.)

On a *viva voce* vote the motion prevailed and the rules were suspended and the bill read a second time by its title. The bill was then laid upon the table to be printed. On motion of the same gentleman, the rules were suspended and the printing of the bill dispensed with. The bill was then ordered to a third reading. On motion of the same gentleman, the rules were further suspended and the bill read a third time by its title and passed and sent to the Senate for concurrence.

Mr. Remich of Littleton, for the Committee on Judiciary, reported the following entitled bill, "An act ratifying votes of the town of Littleton passed at its town meeting on the 10th day of March, 1903," with the resolution that the bill ought to pass.

The report was accepted and the bill read a first time and ordered to a second reading. On motion of Mr. Remich of Littleton, the rules were suspended and the bill read a second time by its title. The bill was then laid upon the table to be printed. On motion of the same gentleman, the rules were suspended and the printing of the bill dispensed with. The bill was then ordered to a third reading. On motion of the same gentleman, the rules were further suspended and the bill read a third time by its title and passed and sent to the Senate for concurrence.

Mr. Roby of Concord, for the Committee on Fisheries and Game, reported the following entitled bill, "An act to amend section 52 of chapter 79 of the Laws of 1901, entitled 'An act to revise the fish and game laws of the state,'" with the resolution that the bill ought to pass.

Mr. Roby of Concord, for the Committee on Fisheries and Game, reported the following entitled bill, "An act in amendment of section 59, chapter 79 of the Session Laws of 1901, relating to the taking of black bass," with the resolution that the bill ought to pass.

Mr. Foye of Portsmouth, for the Committee on Appropriations, reported the following joint resolution, "Joint resolution providing for the repairs and construction of certain state highways, certain highways in unincorporated places, and certain roads in places where such roads cannot be maintained by any local municipality," with the resolution that the joint resolution ought to pass.

Mr. Batchelder of Keene, for the Committee on Judiciary, reported the following entitled bill, "An act in amendment of section 13, chapter 59, Laws of 1895, relating to the bond of the adjutant-general," with the resolution that the bill ought to pass.

Mr. Whitcher of Haverhill, for the Committee on Judiciary, reported the following entitled bill, "An act in relation to the salary of the judge of probate for the county of Grafton," with the resolution that the bill ought to pass.

Mr. French of Moultonborough, for the Committee on Railroads, reported the following entitled bill, " An act in amendment of sections 7 and 10, chapter 27, Laws of 1895, relating to street railways," with the resolution that the bill ought to pass.

Mr. French of Moultonborough, for the Committee on Railroads, reported the following entitled bill, " An act in amendment of section 13, chapter 27, Laws of 1895, relating to street railways," with the resolution that the bill ought to pass.

Mr. Whittemore of Dover, for the Committee on Judiciary, reported the following entitled bill, " An act to authorize the town of Gilmanton to exempt certain property from taxation," with the resolution that the bill ought to pass.

The reports were severally accepted and the bills and joint resolution read a first time and ordered to a second reading.

BILLS FORWARDED.

An act to require non-residents to secure a license before hunting deer within the state of New Hampshire, and providing penalties for violation of its provisions.

An act to incorporate the Jackson Water-Works Company.

An act to incorporate the Swift River Railroad Company.

29

An act for the better preservation of highways and accommodating public travel.

An act to incorporate the Prudential Fire Insurance Company.

An act in amendment of so much of chapter 264 of the Laws of the State of New Hampshire, passed at the January session, 1893, as relates to the establishing of a board of street and park commissioners for the city of Manchester.

An act relating to the setting off by the legislature of territory of one town or city on to that of another town or city.

An act to incorporate the Sons of Veterans' Memorial Hall Association.

An act to incorporate the Meredith & Ossipee Valley Railroad Company.

An act to provide for the representation of the state of New Hampshire and the exhibition of its products and attractions at the Louisiana Purchase Exposition at St. Louis in 1904.

An act to incorporate the Warren Water and Light Company.

An act to incorporate the Bellman Club of Manchester, N. H.

An act to incorporate the Dover Loan and Trust Company.

An act in amendment of section 79 of chapter 79 of the Laws of 1901, in regard to lobster traps.

An act in relation to state officials, commissioners, trustees, or other persons having control of public funds.

An act to amend section 16 of chapter 79 of the Session Laws of 1901, relating to the taking of deer.

An act authorizing the state treasurer to transfer certain sums of money to the literary fund for schools.

An act to amend the charter of the Bennington Water-Works Company.

Severally taken from the table and ordered to a third reading.

An act in amendment of the charter of the city of Manchester, establishing board of assessors in place of the assessors provided under the chapter and laws of the state.

Taken from the table and on motion of Mr. Morse of Manchester, laid upon the table.

An act to amend chapter 184 of the Laws of 1897, entitled " An act to incorporate the Dalton Power Company," as amended by section 1, chapter 221 of the Laws of 1899.

Taken from the table and on motion of Mr. Preston of Henniker, laid upon the table.

An act in amendment of section 22, chapter 27, Laws of 1895, entitled " An act in relation to the incorporation, organization, and regulation of street railway companies and authorizing the use of electricity as motive power by existing steam railroads."

Taken from the table and on motion of Mr. White of Bow, laid upon the table.

An act to provide suitable armory quarters for the National Guard at Manchester.

Taken from the table. Mr. Whittemore of Dover moved that the bill be laid upon the table. On a *viva voce* vote the motion did not prevail. On a *viva voce* vote the bill was then ordered to a third reading.

SPECIAL ORDER.

Mr. Filion of Manchester called for the special order, it being the following entitled bill, " An act enabling the city of Manchester to build and operate an electric lighting plant for the purpose of lighting its streets and public buildings."

The question being upon the adoption of the motion of Mr. Filion of Manchester, that the report of the minority of the committee be substituted for that of the majority,

(Discussion ensued.)

Mr. Ahern of Concord moved that the bill and reports be recommitted to the special committee consisting of the delegation from the city of Manchester. The question being upon the adoption of the motion,

(Discussion ensued.)

Mr. Ahern of Concord moved that the House adjourn. On a *viva voce* vote the motion prevailed, and at 1.15 the House adjourned.

AFTERNOON.

The House met at 3 o'clock.

THIRD READINGS.

An act to require non-residents to secure a license before hunting deer within the state of New Hampshire, and providing penalties for violation of its provisions.

The third reading having commenced, on motion of Mr. Ahern of Concord, the rules were suspended and the bill read a third time by its title. The bill was then passed and sent to the Senate for concurrence.

An act to incorporate the Jackson Water-Works Company.

The third reading having commenced, on motion of Mr. French of Moultonborough, the rules were suspended and the bill read a third time by its title. The bill was then passed and sent to the secretary of state to be engrossed.

An act for the better preservation of highways and accommodating public travel.

The third reading having commenced, Mr. Small of Rochester moved that the rules be suspended and the bill read a third time by its title. The question being upon the adoption of the motion,

(Discussion ensued.)

Mr. Small of Rochester withdrew his motion. On motion of Mr. Remich of Littleton, the bill was laid upon the table.

An act in amendment of so much of chapter 264 of the Laws of the State of New Hampshire, passed at the January session, 1893, as relates to the establishing of a board of street and park commissioners for the city of Manchester.

The third reading having commenced, on motion of Mr. Small of Rochester, the rules were suspended and the bill read a third time by its title. The bill was then passed and sent to the Senate for concurrence.

An act relating to the setting off by the legislature of territory of one town or city on to that of another town or city.

Read a third time.

The question being,

Shall the bill pass?

On motion of Mr. Ahern of Concord the bill was laid upon the table.

An act to incorporate the Meredith & Ossipee Valley Railroad Company.

The third reading having commenced, on motion of Mr. French of Moultonborough, the rules were suspended and the bill read a third time by its title. The bill was then passed and sent to the Senate for concurrence.

An act to provide for the representation of the state of New Hampshire and the exhibition of its products and attractions at the Louisiana Purchase Exposition at St. Louis in 1904.

The third reading being in order, on motion of Mr. Whitcher of Haverhill, the bill was laid upon the table.

An act to incorporate the Warren Water and Light Company.

The third reading having begun, on motion of Mr. Ahern of Concord, the rules were suspended and the bill read a third time by its title. The bill was then passed and sent to the Senate for concurrence.

An act in amendment of section 79 of chapter 79 of the Laws of 1901, in regard to lobster traps.

The third reading being in order, Mr. Lane of Hampton moved that the bill be indefinitely postponed. The question being upon the adoption of the motion, on motion of Mr. Ahern of Concord the bill was laid upon the table.

An act in relation to state officials, commissioners, trustees, or other persons having control of public funds.

Read a third time and passed and sent to the secretary of state to be engrossed.

An act authorizing the state treasurer to transfer certain sums of money to the literary fund for schools.

An act to amend section 16 of chapter 79 of the Session Laws of 1901, relating to the taking of deer.

An act to amend the charter of the Bennington Water-Works Company.

An act to incorporate the Sons of Veterans' Memorial Hall Association.

An act to incorporate the Swift River Railroad Company.

An act to incorporate the Dover Loan and Trust Company.

An act to incorporate the Prudential Fire Insurance Company.

An act to incorporate the Bellman Club of Manchester, N. H.

Joint resolution in favor of the New Hampshire Soldiers' Home.

Severally read a third time and passed and sent to the Senate for concurrence.

An act to provide suitable armory quarters for the National Guard at Manchester.

Read a third time.

The question being,

Shall the bill pass?

On motion of Mr. Crossman of Lisbon, the bill was laid upon the table.

On motion of Mr. Remich of Littleton, the following joint resolution, " Joint resolution providing for the erection of an elevator or elevators in the state house for the use of members of the Senate, House of Representatives, state officers, employees, and the public," was taken from the table.

The question being upon the adoption of the resolution reported by the committee, that it is inexpedient to legislate, Mr. Remich of Littleton moved that the joint resolution be recommitted to the Committee on Appropriations. The question being upon the adoption of the motion of Mr. Remich,

(Discussion ensued.)

Mr. Lane of Hampton moved that the joint resolution be laid upon the table. On a *viva voce* vote the motion did not prevail. The question being upon the adoption of the motion of Mr. Remich, on a *viva voce* vote the motion was adopted, and the joint resolution recommitted to the Committee on Appropriations.

UNFINISHED BUSINESS.

Mr. Sheehan of Manchester called for the unfinished business, it being the following entitled bill, " An act enabling the city of Manchester to build and operate an electric lighting plant for the purpose of lighting its streets and public buildings."

The question being upon the adoption of the motion of Mr. Ahern of Concord, that the bill be recommitted to the special committee consisting of the delegation from the city of Manchester,

(Discussion ensued.)

Mr. Whitcher of Haverhill moved the previous question.

The question being,

Shall the main question be now put?

On a *viva voce* vote the previous question was ordered.

The question being upon the adoption of the motion of Mr. Ahern of Concord, on a *viva voce* vote the motion prevailed, and the bill was recommitted to the special committee consisting of the delegation from the city of Manchester.

NOTICE OF RECONSIDERATION.

Mr. Ahern of Concord gave notice that on to-morrow, or some subsequent day, he would move to reconsider the vote whereby the House passed the following entitled bill, "An act to require non-residents to secure a license before hunting deer within the state of New Hampshire, and providing penalties for violation of its provisions."

On motion of Mr. Buckley of Lancaster, the following entitled bill, "An act to amend chapter 184 of the Laws of 1897, entitled ' An act to incorporate the Dalton Power Company,' as amended by section 1, chapter 221 of the Laws of 1899," was taken from the table. On motion of the same gentleman, the bill was recommitted to the Committee on Incorporations.

On motion of Mr. Churchill of Cornish, the House took a recess of 30 minutes.

(After recess.)

MESSAGE FROM THE SENATE.

A message from the Honorable Senate, by its clerk, announced that the Senate concurs with the House of Representatives in the passage of the following entitled bills sent up from the House of Representatives:

An act to legalize the annual school meeting of the town school district in the town of Franconia in the year 1902, and to legalize the acts of said district at that meeting and the subsequent acts and proceedings of the district officers elected at said meeting.

An act authorizing the city of Nashua to issue bonds and exempt the same from taxation.

An act in amendment of chapter 119 of the Public Statutes, relating to the inspection and licensing of boats, their engineers and pilots.

An act to provide for the daily publication of the journals of the Senate and House of Representatives.

An act ratifying votes of the town of Littleton passed at its town meeting held on the 10th day of March, 1903.

An act to authorize the Hudson, Pelham & Salem Electric Railway Company to take leases of the railway and property of the Haverhill & Southern New Hampshire Street Railway Company, the Lawrence & Methuen Street Railway Company, and the Lowell & Pelham Street Railway Company.

An act authorizing the Mt. Pleasant Hotel Company to increase its capital stock.

An act to authorize the managers of the New Hampshire Soldiers' Home to procure an adequate supply of water for the use of said home.

An act amending the charter of the Newmarket Electric Light, Power, and Heat Company.

The message further announced that the Senate has passed a bill with the following title, in the passage of which it asks the concurrence of the House of Representatives :

An act to incorporate the Nutfield Loan and Trust Company.

Read a first and second time and referred to the Committee on Banks.

On motion of Mr. Hardy of Derry, at 4.20 the House adjourned.

FRIDAY, MARCH 13, 1903.

The House met at 11 o'clock.

Prayer was offered by the chaplain.

LEAVE OF ABSENCE.

Mr. Amidon of Richmond was granted leave of absence for the day on account of important business.

COMMITTEE REPORTS.

Mr. Drake of Freedom, for the Committee on Public Improvements, to whom was referred An act relating to highways and highway agents and street commissioners, having considered the same, report the same with the following resolution:

Resolved, That the bill ought to pass.

The report was accepted and the bill laid upon the table to be printed.

Mr. Goold of Lebanon, for the Committee on Fisheries and Game, to whom was referred An act to prohibit all ice fishing except in certain specified waters, having considered the same, report the same in a new draft with the following resolution:

Resolved, That the bill in new draft ought to pass.

The report was accepted and the bill in its new draft read a first time and ordered to a second reading. On motion of Mr. Remich of Littleton, the rules were suspended and the bill read a second time by its title. The bill was then laid upon the table to be printed.

Mr. Willis of Concord, for the Committee on Engrossed Bills, reported that they had examined and found correctly engrossed the following entitled bills:

An act to authorize the Hudson, Pelham & Salem Electric Railway Company to take leases of the railway and property of the Haverhill & Southern New Hampshire Street Railway Company, the Lawrence & Methuen Street Railway Company, and the Lowell & Pelham Street Railway Company.

An act authorizing the Mt. Pleasant Hotel Company to increase its capital stock.

An act to authorize the managers of the New Hampshire Soldiers' Home to procure an adequate supply of water for the use of said home.

An act amending the charter of the Newmarket Electric Light, Power, and Heat Company.

An act to legalize the annual school meeting of the town school district in the town of Franconia in the year 1902, and to legalize the acts of said district at that meeting and the subsequent acts and proceedings of the district officers elected at said meeting.

An act to provide for the daily publication of the journals of the Senate and House of Representatives.

An act in amendment of chapter 119 of the Public Statutes, relating to the inspection and licensing of boats, their engineers and pilots.

An act authorizing the city of Nashua to issue bonds and exempt the same from taxation.

An act ratifying votes of the town of Littleton passed at its town meeting held on the 10th day of March, 1903.

An act to incorporate the Jackson Water-Works Company.

An act in relation to state officials, commissioners, trustees, or other persons having control of public funds.

The report was accepted.

Mr. Davenport of Bath, for the Committee on Appropriations, to whom was referred Joint resolution in favor of Horace S. Cummings, having considered the same, report the same with the following resolution :

Resolved, That the joint resolution ought to pass.

The report was accepted and the joint resolution ordered to a third reading. On motion of Mr. Ahern of Concord, the rules were suspended and the joint resolution read a third time and passed and sent to the Senate for concurrence.

Mr. Dow of Conway, for the Committee on Appropriations, to whom was referred An act relating to the salary of the judge of probate for the county of Carroll, having considered the same, report the same with the following resolution :

Resolved, That the bill ought to pass.

The report was accepted and the bill ordered to a third reading. On motion of Mr. French of Moultonborough, the rules were suspended and the bill read a third time and passed and sent to the Senate for concurrence.

Mr. French of Moultonborough, for the Committee on Railroads, to whom was referred An act in amendment of the charter of the Meredith & Ossipee Electric Railway Company, having considered the same, report the same with the following resolution :

Resolved, That it is inexpedient to legislate, a new bill covering the same location having recently passed the House.

Mr. Batchelder of Keene, for the Committee on Judiciary,

to whom was referred An act regulating the holding of political caucuses and conventions and providing for substitutes in case of vacancies in the position of delegates to conventions, having considered the same, report the same with the following resolution :

Resolved, That it is inexpedient to legislate.

Mr. Woodman of Concord, for the Committee on Liquor Laws, to whom was referred An act to regulate the traffic in intoxicating liquor, having considered the same, report the same with the following resolution :

Resolved, That it is inexpedient to legislate, because the subject matter has been considered in a substitute bill.

Mr. French of Moultonborough, for the Committee on Railroads, to whom was referred An act equalizing and regulating tolls and charges of telephone companies, having considered the same, report the same with the following resolution :

Resolved, That it is inexpedient to legislate.

Mr. Fifield of Conway, for the Committee on Education, to whom was referred An act to amend chapter 93, section 15 of the Public Statutes, as amended by chapter 61 of the Session Laws of 1901, relating to scholars, having considered the same, report the same with the following resolution :

Resolved, That it is inexpedient to legislate.

Mr. Batchelder of Keene, for the Committee on Judiciary, to whom was referred An act to incorporate the Northern Transportation and Transfer Company, having considered the same, report the same with the following resolution :

Resolved, That it is inexpedient to legislate, the object sought being covered by the general laws.

Mr. Goold of Lebanon, for the Committee on Fisheries and Game, to whom was referred An act to open the ponds and lakes of the state for ice fishing for one month in the year, having considered the same, report the same with the following resolution :

Resolved, That it is inexpedient to legislate.

The reports were severally accepted and the resolutions reported by the committees adopted.

Mr. French of Moultonborough, for the Committee on Railroads, to whom was referred An act to amend the charter of the Newport & George's Mills Electric Railway Company, having considered the same, report the same with the following resolution :

Resolved, That the bill ought to pass.

The report was accepted and the bill laid upon the table to be printed.

Mr. Andrews of Somersworth, for the Committee on Education, to whom was referred An act to amend chapter 96 of the Session Laws of 1901, relating to high schools, having considered the same, report the same in a new draft with the following resolution :

Resolved, That the bill in a new draft ought to pass.

The report was accepted and the bill in its new draft read a first time.

The question being,

Shall the bill be read a second time?

On motion of Mr. Ahern of Concord, the bill was laid upon the table.

Mr. French of Moultonborough, for the Committee on Railroads, to whom was referred An act to incorporate the Derry & Salem Street Railway Company, having considered the same, report the same with the following resolution :

Resolved, That the bill ought to pass.

The report was accepted and the bill laid upon the table to be printed.

Mr. Smith of Exeter, for the Committee on Appropriations, to whom was referred Joint resolution for an appropriation for the benefit of the New Hampshire College of Agriculture and the Mechanic Arts, having considered the same, report the same with the following resolution :

Resolved, That the joint resolution ought to pass.

The report was accepted. The question being upon the adoption of the resolution reported by the committee, on motion of Mr. Remich of Littleton, the joint resolution was laid upon the table.

Mr. Woodman of Concord, for the Committee on Judiciary, reported the following entitled bill, "An act in amendment of Public Statutes, chapter 81, section 2, relating to telegraph,

telephone, and electric light companies," with the resolution
that the bill ought to pass.

The report was accepted and the bill read a first time and
ordered to a second reading. On motion of Mr. Batchelder of
Keene, the rules were suspended and the bill read a second
time by its title. The bill was then laid upon the table to be
printed. On motion of the same gentleman, the rules were
suspended and the printing of the bill dispensed with. The
bill was then ordered to a third reading. On motion of the
same gentleman, the rules were further suspended and the bill
read a third time by its title and passed and sent to the Senate
for concurrence.

Mr. Pike of Haverhill, for the Committee on Appropriations, reported the following entitled bill, "An act to define
the duties of the state treasurer with reference to public
funds," with the resolution that the bill ought to pass.

The report was accepted and the bill read a first time and
ordered to a second reading. On motion of Mr. Remich of
Littleton, the rules were suspended and the bill read a second
time by its title. The bill was then laid upon the table to be
printed.

Mr. Batchelder of Keene, for the Committee on Judiciary,
reported the following entitled bill, " An act in amendment of
'An act to incorporate the Society of Social Friends,' approved
June 29, 1826, 'An act to incorporate the United Fraternity,'
approved July 6, 1827, and 'An act to incorporate the Philotechnic Society of the Chandler Scientific Department of Dartmouth College,' approved July 13, 1854, and to authorize the
calling of meetings of said corporations respectively," with
the resolution that the bill ought to pass.

The report was accepted and the bill read a first time and
ordered to a second reading.

Mr. Pike of Haverhill, for the Committee on Appropriations, reported the following entitled bill, "An act to amend
sections 4 and 5 of chapter 65 of the Public Statutes, relating
to the taxation of savings banks," with the resolution that the
bill ought to pass.

The report was accepted. On motion of Mr. Pike of Haverhill, the rules were suspended and the bill read a first time by

its title. The bill was then ordered to a second reading. On motion of the same gentleman, the rules were suspended and the bill read a second time by its title. The bill was then laid upon the table to be printed.

Mr. Woodman of Concord, for the Committee on Judiciary, reported the following entitled bill, "An act to amend section 14 and section 15, chapter 286 of the Public Statutes, relating to the salaries of the judge and register of probate for Belknap county," with the resolution that the bill ought to pass.

The report was accepted and the bill read a first time and ordered to a second reading.

Mr. Libby of Gorham, for the Joint Committee on State Library, reported the following entitled bill, "An act relating to the administration of the state library," with the resolution that the bill ought to pass.

The report was accepted and the bill read a first time and ordered to a second reading. On motion of Mr. Whitcher of Haverhill, the rules were suspended and the bill read a second time by its title. The bill was then laid upon the table to be printed.

Mr. Tripp of Epsom, for the Committee on Labor, to whom was referred An act amending section 14 and section 20 of chapter 180 of the Public Statutes, relating to the hours of labor, having considered the same, report the same with the following resolution :

Resolved, That it is inexpedient to legislate, the subject matter having been covered by a bill in the hands of the committee.

The report was accepted. The question being upon the adoption of the resolution reported by the committee, on a *viva voce* vote the motion did not prevail.

(Discussion ensued.)

On motion of Mr. Cavanaugh of Manchester, the bill and report were laid upon the table.

Mr. Tripp of Epsom, for the Committee on Labor, to whom was referred An act requiring goods made in whole or part by convict labor to be so stamped, having considered the same, report the same with the following resolution :

Resolved, That it is inexpedient to legislate.

The report was accepted. The question being upon the adoption of the resolution reported by the committee,

(Discussion ensued.)

Mr. Shute of Derry called for a yea and nay vote.

(Discussion ensued.)

On motion of Mr. Ahern of Concord, the bill, report, and the call of Mr. Shute were laid upon the table.

Messrs. Batchelder of Keene, Whittemore of Dover, Mitchell of Littleton, Woodman of Concord, Goss of Berlin, Buckley of Lancaster, Scammon of Exeter, Whitcher of Haverhill, and Small of Rochester, for a majority of the Committee on Liquor Laws, to whom was referred An act to regulate the traffic in intoxicating liquor, having considered the same, report a substitute for said act with the following resolution :

Resolved, That the substitute act ought to pass.

Messrs. Remich of Littleton and Phillips of Franklin, for a minority for the Committee on Liquor Laws, to whom was referred An act to regulate the traffic in intoxicating liquor, having considered the same, report as follows :

Resolved, That it is inexpedient to legislate.

Messrs. Cavanaugh of Manchester and Nason of Dover, of the Committee on Liquor Laws, also submitted a report as follows :

To the House of Representatives :

We regret that we are not able to concur in the report of the majority of the committee. We are in favor of a modification of our liquor laws, and we believe the bill reported by the majority of the committee contains as good provisions as well might be expected in drafting new legislation, with the exception of those provisions which relate to cities. We refer to the local option feature. When this general court convened it was not contended by any one that legislation other than local option was to be had. We have not heard any reasons advanced why the cities in our state should be deprived of local government in this respect, nor any reasons assigned for forcing upon them for three years and six months the saloons, whether it be in accordance with the wishes of the people or otherwise. We are forced to the conclusion that the want of a local option feature for cities, as well as for towns, is sufficient ground to oppose that feature of the bill.

The reports were severally accepted.

Mr. Remich of Littleton moved that the report of the minority be substituted for that of the majority; that the bill and reports be laid on the table to be printed and the matter be made a special order for Tuesday next at 3 o'clock; that the clerk of the House be instructed to have the bill and reports printed at once, and also to mail a copy of the *Manchester Union* and *Concord Monitor* containing the bill to each member of the House at his home as soon as possible.

On a *viva voce* vote the motion was adopted.

Mr. Sawyer of Milford, for a majority of the Committee on Banks, to whom was referred An act in amendment of section 19, chapter 57 of the Public Statutes, relating to the annual invoice of polls and taxable property, having considered the same, report the same in new draft and amended title with the following resolution :

Resolved, That the bill in new draft ought to pass, with title amended to read as follows :

An act in amendment of section 4 of chapter 113 of the Laws of 1895, relating to the taxation of bank shares and deposits.

Mr. Fay of Keene, for a minority of the Committee on Banks, to whom was referred An act in amendment of section 19, chapter 57 of the Public Statutes, relating to the annual invoice of polls and taxable property, having considered the same, report the same in a new draft with the following resolution.

Resolved, That the bill in new draft ought to pass.

The reports were accepted.

Mr. Fay of Keene moved that the report of the minority be substituted for that of the majority of the committee and that the reports and new draft be laid upon the table to be printed.

The question being upon the adoption of the motion,

(Discussion ensued.)

Mr. Sawyer of Milford moved that the bill and accompanying reports be made the special order for Wednesday, March
18, at 3 o'clock.   On a *viva voce* vote the motion did not
prevail.
(Discussion ensued.)

On a *viva voce* vote the motion prevailed and the bill and
accompanying reports were made the special order for
Wednesday, March 18, at 3 o'clock.

SECOND READINGS.

An act in relation to the salary of the judge of probate for
the county of Grafton.

An act in amendment of chapter 134 of the Public Statutes,
relating to the practice of dentistry.

Severally read a second time and laid upon the table to be
printed and then referred to the Committee on Appropriations.

Joint resolution providing for the repairs and construction
of certain state highways, certain highways in unincorporated
places, and certain roads in places where such roads cannot
be maintained by any local municipality.

An act in amendment of section 59, chapter 79 of the Session Laws of 1901, relating to the taking of black bass.

An act in amendment of section 13, chapter 59, Laws of
1895, relating to the bond of the adjutant-general.

An act in amendment of sections 7 and 10, chapter 27,
Laws of 1895, relating to street railways.

An act to amend section 52 of chapter 79 of the Laws of
1901, entitled "An act to revise the fish and game laws of the
state."

An act to authorize the town of Gilmanton to exempt certain property from taxation.

Severally read a second time and laid upon the table to be
printed.

An act in amendment of section 13, chapter 27 of the
Pamphlet Laws of 1895, relating to street railways.

The second reading being in order, on motion of Mr.
French of Moultonborough, the rules were suspended and the

30

bill read a second time by its title.   The bill was then laid
upon the table to be printed.

On motion of Mr. Dow of Conway,—

Resolved, That when the House adjourns this afternoon it
be to meet at 8 o'clock Monday evening.

Mr. Libby of Gorham offered the following resolution :

Resolved, That the Committee on Appropriations inform
the House of the total amount of the ordinary and extraordi-
nary appropriations called for by the various bills and joint
resolutions which have been before them.

The question being upon the adoption of the resolution,

(Discussion ensued.)

Mr. Remich of Littleton offered the following amendment:

Amend by adding the words, " and that they report by
next Tuesday afternoon."

Mr. Libby of Gorham accepted the amendment and on a
viva voce vote the resolution was adopted.

On motion of Mr. Quimby of Manchester, the following
entitled bill, "An act in amendment of the charter of the city
of Manchester, establishing board of assessors in place of the
assessors provided under the chapter and laws of the state,"
was taken from the table.

Mr. Quimby of Manchester offered the following amendment :

Amend section 3 by inserting after the word " shall " in the
fifth line the words "from and after the date when this act
shall take effect"; and further amend said section by omitting
all after the word " Manchester " in the seventh line thereof,
so that said section as amended shall read as follows:

Sect. 3.   Said board of assessors shall have all power,
authority, and rights, as set forth in section 11, chapter 49 of
the Public Statutes, and all other authority and rights conferred upon assessors, and the board of assessors as now constituted shall from and after the date when this act shall take
effect cease from having any authority or rights under the law
of this state or the charter of the city of Manchester.

On a *viva voce* vote the amendment was adopted.   The bill
was then ordered to a third reading.   On motion of Mr. Shee-

han of Manchester, the rules were suspended and the bill read a third time by its title and passed and sent to the Senate for concurrence.

On motion of Mr. Goold of Lebanon, the following entitled bill, "An act in amendment of section 79 of chapter 79 of the Laws of 1901, in regard to lobster traps," was taken from the table.

The question being upon the motion of Mr. Lane of Hampton that the bill be indefinitely postponed,

(Discussion ensued.)

On a *viva voce* vote the motion did not prevail. The bill was then ordered to a third reading. On motion of Mr. Scammon of Exeter, the rules were suspended and the bill read a third time by its title and passed and sent to the Senate for concurrence.

On motion of Mr. Ahern of Concord, the following entitled bill, "An act relating to the setting off by the legislature of territory of one town or city on to that of another town or city," was taken from the table.

The question being,

Shall the bill pass?

(Discussion ensued.)

On a *viva voce* vote the bill passed and was sent to the Senate for concurrence.

On motion of Mr. Davis of Lee, at 12 :28 the House adjourned.

AFTERNOON.

The House met at 3 o'clock.

On motion of Mr. Ahern of Concord, the rules were suspended and bills in order for a second reading next Tuesday morning at 11 o'clock were made in order at the present time.

SECOND READINGS.

An act in amendment of "An act to incorporate the Society of Social Friends," approved June 29, 1826, "An act to incorporate the United Fraternity," approved July 6, 1827, and "An act to incorporate the Philotechnic Society of the Chandler

Scientific Department of Dartmouth College," approved July 13, 1854, and to authorize the calling of meetings of said corporations respectively.

Read a second time and laid upon the table to be printed.

An act to amend section 14 and section 15, chapter 286 of the Public Statutes, relating to the salaries of the judge and register of probate for Belknap county.

Read a second time and laid upon the table to be printed and then referred to the Committee on Appropriations.

On motion of Mr. French of Moultonborough, the order whereby the following entitled bill, "An act to amend the charter of the Newport & George's Mills Electric Railway Company," was ordered printed was vacated.

The question being,

Shall the bill be read a third time?

Mr. French of Moultonborough moved that the rules be suspended and the bill read a third time and put upon its passage at the present time. On a *viva voce* vote the motion did not prevail.

(Discussion ensued.)

On a *viva voce* vote the motion prevailed. The bill was then read a third time and passed and sent to the secretary of state to be engrossed.

On motion of Mr. Gates of Canaan, at 3.08 the House adjourned.

MONDAY, MARCH 16, 1903.

The House met at 8 o'clock in the evening, according to adjournment, being called to order by Mr. Frederic T. Woodman of Concord, and the following communication was read by the clerk:

CONCORD, March 16, 1903.

Mr. Frederic T. Woodman, Concord, N. H.

DEAR SIR: I shall be unable to be present at the session on Monday evening, March 16, 1903. Will you kindly preside for me and oblige,

Yours truly,

HARRY M. CHENEY,

Speaker.

On motion of Mr. Remich of Littleton,—

Resolved, That the use of Representatives' hall be granted to citizens of Concord and other cities for a public meeting for the purpose of discussing the proposed liquor law, on Wednesday evening, March 18.

On motion of Mr. Kennedy of Concord, at 8.01 the House adjourned.

TUESDAY, MARCH 17, 1903.

The House met at 11 o'clock.

Prayer was offered by the chaplain.

LEAVES OF ABSENCE.

Mr. Riordan of Manchester was granted leave of absence for the day to attend a funeral.

Mr. Holt of Lyndeborough was granted leave of absence for the week on account of illness.

COMMITTEE REPORTS.

Mr. Dow of Conway, for the Committee on Appropriations, to whom was referred Joint resolution in favor of the widow of Benjamin F. March of Mason, having considered the same, report the same with the following resolution :

Resolved, That the joint resolution ought to pass.

Mr. Smith of Exeter, for the Committee on Appropriations, to whom was referred Joint resolution in favor of.Green's basin in Lake Winnipesaukee, having considered the same, report the same with the following resolution :

Resolved, That the joint resolution ought to pass.

Mr. Davenport of Bath, for the Committee on Appropriations, to whom was referred Joint resolution in favor of placing and maintaining buoys and lights in Lake Winnipesaukee and adjacent waters, having considered the same, report the same with the following resolution :

Resolved, That the joint resolution ought to pass.

The reports were severally accepted and the joint resolutions ordered to a third reading.

Mr. French of Moultonborough, for the Committee on Railroads, to whom was referred An act authorizing the Concord & Montreal Railroad, lessor, to vote on all stock owned by it in other corporations, having considered the same, report the same with the following resolution :

Resolved, That the bill ought to pass.

The report was accepted and the bill laid upon the table to be printed.

Mr. Hoyt of Sandwich, for the Committee on Agriculture, to whom was referred An act relating to the protection and preservation of ornamental and shade trees in the highway, having considered the same, report the same in new draft with the following resolution :

Resolved, That the bill in its new draft ought to pass.

The report was accepted and the bill in its new draft read a first time and ordered to a second reading.

BILLS FORWARDED.

An act to amend section 52 of chapter 79 of the Laws of 1901, entitled "An act to revise the fish and game laws of the state."

An act in amendment of "An act to incorporate the Society of Social Friends." approved June 29, 1826, "An act to incorporate the United Fraternity," approved July 6, 1827, and "An act to incorporate the Philotechnic Society of the Chandler Scientific Department of Dartmouth College," approved July 13, 1854, and to authorize the calling of meetings of said corporations respectively.

An act in amendment of section 13, chapter 59, Laws of 1895, relating to the bond of the adjutant-general.

An act in amendment of section 59, chapter 79 of the Session Laws of 1901, relating to the taking of black bass.

An act to change the name of the Manchester Heating and Lighting Company of Manchester, N. H.

An act to authorize the town of Gilmanton to exempt certain property from taxation.

An act to define the duties of the state treasurer with reference to public funds.

An act to incorporate the Derry and Salem Street Railway Company.

An act in amendment of sections 7 and 10, chapter 27, Laws of 1895, relating to street railways.

An act to prohibit all ice fishing except in certain specified waters.

An act in amendment of section 13, chapter 27 of the Pamphlet Laws of 1895, relating to street railways.

An act to amend sections 4 and 5 of chapter 65 of the Public Statutes, relating to the taxation of savings banks.

Joint resolution providing for the repairs and construction of certain state highways, certain highways in unincorporated places and certain roads in places where such roads cannot be maintained by any local municipality.

An act relating to highways and highway agents and street commissioners.

Severally taken from the table and ordered to a third reading.

An act relating to the administration of the state library.

Taken from the table and on motion of Mr. Whitcher of Haverhill, recommitted to the joint Committee on State Library.

SPECIAL ORDER.

Mr. Ahern of Concord called for the special order, it being the following entitled bill, ''An act to establish a state sanatorium for consumptives,'' and the veto of His Excellency the Governor.

The question being,

Shall the bill pass, notwithstanding the objections of His Excellency the Governor?

(Discussion ensued.)

On motion of Mr. Ahern of Concord, at 12.40 the House took a recess until 2 o'clock.

(After recess.)

Discussion continued on the question,

Shall the bill pass, notwithstanding the objections of His Excellency the Governor?

Mr. Ahern of Concord moved the previous question.

The question being,

Shall the main question be now put?

On a *viva voce* vote the previous question was ordered.

The question being,

Shall the bill pass, notwithstanding the objections of His Excellency the Governor? the roll was called, in accordance with the requirement of the constitution of the state, with the following result:

YEAS, 193.

ROCKINGHAM COUNTY. Sawyer of Atkinson, Preston of Auburn, Hardy, Shute, Edgerly of Epping, Nowell, Scammon, Duntley, Emerson of Hampstead, Lane of Hampton, Chase of Newfields, Bickford, Payne, Blaisdell, Nelson, Yeaton, Adams of Portsmouth, Newton, Couhig, Abbott of Salem, Gordon, Young.

STRAFFORD COUNTY. Libby of Dover, Nason, Bunce, Wesley, Jones of New Durham, Crocker, Warren, Small, Harrity, Etter, Wentworth, Demers, Andrews, Caverly.

BELKNAP COUNTY. Pinkham, Clough, Davis of Laconia, Fecteau, Prescott, Morrill of New Hampton.

CARROLL COUNTY. Stevens, Weeks, Fifield, Burnell, Trickey, Greene, Abbott of Ossipee, Pollard, Blake of Wakefield, Britton.

MERRIMACK COUNTY. Fontaine, Harris of Boscawen, White of Bow, Beck, Durgin, Kennedy, Willis, Matson, Hill, A. W., of Concord, Woodman, Kimball of Concord, Emerson of Concord, Ahern, Donagan, Morin of Franklin, Jones of Franklin, Adams of Franklin, Davis of Franklin, Twombly, Worthley, Fisk, Messer, Foss, Hutchins of Pittsfield, Walker of Pittsfield, Little of Salisbury, Burbank, Mason.

HILLSBOROUGH COUNTY. Shattuck, Craine, Brown of Greenville, Cavanaugh, Nyberg, Abbott of Manchester, Sheehan, Barr of Manchester, Dubuc, Stewart of Manchester, Tonery, Ryan, Trinity, Whalen, Sullivan of Manchester, Shaughnessey, Couch, Bunton, A. B., of Manchester, Quimby of Manchester, Dinsmore, Dozois, Kohler, Lynch, Kane, Emerson of Manchester, Sawyer of Milford, Kendall, Lund,

Duncklee, Lewis, Lampron, Buckley of Nashua, Shea, Spalding, Lintott, Shenton, Earley, Moran of Nashua, Desmarais, Dionne, McLane, Jones of New Ipswich, Peabody, Miller, Fitzgerald, Chase of Weare.

CHESHIRE COUNTY. Fuller, Holland, Cutler, Fay, Batchelder, Whitney, Goodnow, Donovan, Moors, Sherman of Walpole, Kellom.

SULLIVAN COUNTY. Hamlin of Charlestown, Chandler, Long, Huntley, Churchill, Walker of Grantham, Aiken, Philbrick of Springfield, Russell of Sunapee.

GRAFTON COUNTY. Davenport, Calley, Little of Campton, Glover, Howe of Hanover, Pike of Haverhill, Barnard, Pike of Lebanon, Crossman, Stanley, Remich, Blake of Littleton, Chase of Orford, Celley, Gould of Plymouth, Russell of Rumney, Houston, Goodrich, Bowen, Bell.

COÖS COUNTY. Caird, Stewart of Berlin, Smyth, Goss, Vaillancourt, Kent of Berlin, Notterstead, Gallagher, Hicks, Martin, Jordan, Tillotson, Hamlin of Dummer, Bragg, Mitchell of Lancaster, Buckley of Lancaster, Ellis, Trafton, McDonald of Northumberland, Piper, Smith of Pittsburg, Wilson, O'Connor, Harriman, Lennon, Darling, Babcock.

NAYS, 156.

ROCKINGHAM COUNTY. Fellows, Morse of Chester, Darbe, White of Deerfield, Severance, Smith of Exeter, Brown of Fremont, Brown of Hampton Falls, Quimby of Kingston, Badger, George, Warner, Gerrish, Cogan, Corson, Chase of Stratham, Cochran.

STRAFFORD COUNTY. Mathes, Jewell, Whittemore, Smith of Dover, Langley, York, Tuttle, Davis of Lee, Felker, Place, Wallace.

BELKNAP COUNTY. Hoitt of Barnstead, Sargent, Smith of Center Harbor, Potter, Hull, Chase of Laconia, Edwards, Kimball of Laconia, Quimby of Meredith, Sanborn of Sanbornton, Rogers, Mason.

CARROLL COUNTY. Littlefield, Dow of Conway, Philbrick of Effingham, Drake, French, Hoyt of Sandwich, Edgerly of Tuftonborough.

MERRIMACK COUNTY. Langmaid, Symonds, Cate, Shepard, Davis of Concord, Critchett, Mathews of Concord, Hill, E. J., of Concord, Bunten of Dunbarton, Tripp, Phillips, Preston of Henniker, Sanborn of Loudon, Sanborn of Northfield, Tallant, Aldrich, Pillsbury, Ela.

HILLSBOROUGH COUNTY. Farley of Amherst, Gould of Bennington, Tobie, Pattee, Eaton, Putnam, Ware of Hancock, Whitaker, Ward, Farley of Hollis, Connell, Center, Chase of Manchester, Donahue, Bartlett of Manchester, Taggart, Bunton, A. S., of Manchester, Farrell, Johnson, Straw of Manchester, McDonald of Manchester, Wright, Carpenter, Morgan, Darrah, Sasseville, Marshall, Morse of Manchester, Armstrong, Tinkham, Graf, Scannell, Gunderman, Janelle, Filion, Lemay, Simpson, Hodgman, Robinson, Needham, Tuck, Ingham, Bussell, Morse of Nashua, Collins, Hills of Nashua, Smith of Peterborough, Bragdon, Sheldon.

CHESHIRE COUNTY. Ware of Alstead, Gowing, Polzer, Bemis, Pierce of Jaffrey, Maloney, Jones of Keene, Fitch, Fox, Scott, Amidon, Fletcher, Merrill, Lane of Swanzey, Ramsay, Hall, Dickinson.

SULLIVAN COUNTY. Clark, Lufkin, Matthews of Newport, Richards, True, Straw of Unity, Ball.

GRAFTON COUNTY. McMurphey, Morrill of Ashland, Pierce of Bethlehem, Gates, Foster, Kimball of Grafton, Pinneo, Whitcher, Carr, Goold of Lebanon, Comings, Henry, Mitchell of Littleton, Converse, King, Ferrin.

COÖS COUNTY. Hutchins of Berlin, Gathercole.

Mr. Foye of Portsmouth was paired with Mr. Barrett of Dover, and the House refused to pass the bill over the veto of His Excellency the Governor.

On motion of Mr. Moors of Marlborough, at 4.10 the House adjourned.

AFTERNOON.

The House was called to order in afternoon session immediately upon the adjournment of the morning session.

THIRD READINGS.

Joint resolution in favor of Green's basin in Lake Winnipesaukee.

Joint resolution in favor of placing and maintaining buoys and lights in Lake Winnipesaukee and adjacent waters.

Joint resolution in favor of the widow of Benjamin F. March of Mason.

An act to amend section 52 of chapter 79 of the Laws of 1901, entitled "An act to revise the fish and game laws of the state."

An act in amendment of "An act to incorporate the Society of Social Friends," approved June 28, 1826, "An act to incorporate the United Fraternity," approved July 6, 1827, and "An act to incorporate the Philotechnic Society of the Chandler Scientific Department of Dartmouth College," approved July 13, 1854, and to authorize the calling of meetings of said corporations respectively.

An act in amendment of section 13, chapter 59, Laws of 1895, relating to the bond of the adjutant-general.

An act in amendment of section 59, chapter 79 of the Session Laws of 1901, relating to the taking of black bass.

An act to change the name of the Manchester Heating and Lighting Company of Manchester, N. H.

An act to authorize the town of Gilmanton to exempt certain property from taxation.

An act to define the duties of the state treasurer with reference to public funds.

An act in amendment of sections 7 and 10, chapter 27, Laws of 1895, relating to street railways.

Joint resolution providing for the repairs and construction of certain state highways, certain highways in unincorporated places, and certain roads in places where such roads cannot be maintained by any local municipality.

Severally read a third time and passed and sent to the Senate for concurrence.

An act to incorporate the Derry & Salem Street Railway Company.

The third reading being in order, on motion of Mr. Scammon of Exeter, the rules were suspended and the bill read a third time by its title. The bill was then passed and sent to the Senate for concurrence.

An act to prohibit all ice fishing except in certain specified waters.

Read a third time.

The question being,

Shall the bill pass?

On a *viva voce* vote the bill was refused a passage. Mr. Goold of Lebanon called for a division.

(Discussion ensued.)

Mr. Ahern of Concord moved that the bill and call for division be laid upon the table. On a *viva voce* vote the motion did not prevail.

A division being had, 128 gentlemen voted in the affirmative and 86 gentlemen voted in the negative, and less than two thirds of the members of the House having voted, and less than two thirds of those voting having voted in the affirmative, the bill was refused a passage.

An act in amendment of section 13, chapter 27 of the Pamphlet Laws of 1895, relating to street railways.

Read a third time and passed and sent to the Senate for concurrence.

An act relating to highways and highway agents and street commissioners.

Read a third time and passed and sent to the secretary of state to be engrossed.

An act to amend sections 4 and 5 of chapter 65 of the Public Statutes, relating to the taxation of savings banks.

The third reading being in order, on motion of Mr. Whitcher of Haverhill, the bill was laid upon the table and made the special order for Wednesday, March 25, at 11 o'clock.

On motion of Mr. White of Bow, the following entitled bill, "An act in amendment of section 22, chapter 27, Laws of 1895, entitled 'An act in relation to the incorporation, organization, and regulation of street railway companies, and authorizing the use of electricity as motive power by existing steam railroads,'" was taken from the table.

The question being,

Shall the bill be read a third time?

On a *viva voce* vote the motion prevailed and the bill was ordered to a third reading.

Mr. Remich of Littleton called for the special order, it being the consideration of the following entitled bill, "An act to regulate the traffic in intoxicating liquor."

The question being upon the motion of Mr. Remich of Littleton that the report of the minority of the committee be substituted for that of the majority of the committee, on motion of Mr. Remich of Littleton, the bill and reports were laid upon the table and made the special order for Wednesday, March 18, at 11 o'clock.

Mr. Remich of Littleton offered the following resolution:

Resolved, That a committee of three be appointed by the Speaker to draft resolutions upon the death of John A. Jewett of Claremont, a member of this House, and that out of respect to his memory the House do now adjourn.

The resolution was unanimously adopted, and at 4.55 the House was declared adjourned.

WEDNESDAY, MARCH 18, 1903.

The House met at 11 o'clock.

Prayer was offered by the chaplain.

PETITIONS PRESENTED AND REFERRED.

By Mr. Ramsdell of Dover, Petition of Elisha R. Brown and 65 other citizens of Dover, protesting against the passage of any license law that does not provide for immediate local option for cities as well as towns.

By Mr. Mitchell of Lancaster, Petition of the Congregational Society of Lancaster for the defeat of the liquor bill reported by the Committee on Liquor Laws.

Severally to the Committee on Liquor Laws.

In accordance with the resolution adopted at the afternoon session, Tuesday, March 17, the Speaker named as the committee to draft resolutions upon the death of Representative Jewett of Claremont the following gentlemen: Messrs. Churchill of Cornish, Sheehan of Manchester, and Huntley of Claremont.

COMMITTEE REPORTS.

Mr. Converse of Lyme, for the Committee on Engrossed Bills, reported that they had examined, and found correctly engrossed, the following entitled bills:

An act to incorporate the Pittsfield Light and Power Company.

An act in amendment of section 1 of chapter 196 of the Public Statutes, relating to the descent of intestate estates.

An act to amend the charter of the Newport & George's Mills Electric Railway Company.

An act to legalize and ratify the votes and proceedings at the annual meeting in Newton, holden on the tenth day of March, 1903.

An act relating to highways and highway agents and street commissioners.

The report was accepted.

Mr. Remich of Littleton, for the Committee on Liquor Laws, to whom was referred An act to amend sections 15, 16, and 17 of chapter 112 of the Public Statutes, relating to the sale of spirituous and malt liquors; An act to amend section 33 of chapter 2 of the Public Statutes, relating to the construction of certain statutes; An act to provide for the better enforcement of the liquor laws; An act to regulate the selling, procuring, furnishing, or giving away of spirituous liquors by clubs, associations, or individuals; An act to regulate the practice of pharmacy, and the sale of spirituous and malt liquors for medicinal, mechanical, scientific, and sacramental purposes; An act to amend section 28 of chapter 112 of the Public Statutes, relating to the sale of spirituous liquor, having considered the same, report the same with the following resolution:

Resolved, That it is inexpedient to legislate because the committee have consolidated the same and report the same in a substitute bill.

Mr. Remich of Littleton, for the Committee on Liquor Laws, reported the following entitled bill, "An act to amend chapter 2 and 112 of the Public Statutes, and to provide for the better enforcement of the liquor laws," with the resolution that the bill ought to pass.

The report was accepted. On motion of Mr. Remich of Littleton, the rules were suspended and the bill read a first time by its title. The bill was then ordered to a second reading. On motion of the same gentleman, the rules were further suspended and the bill read a second time by its title and laid upon the table to be printed.

Mr. Donahue of Manchester, for the Committee on Insurance, to whom was referred An act to fix the form of life insurance policies and to establish cash surrender values, having considered the same, report the same with the following resolution:

Resolved, That it is inexpedient to legislate.

The report was accepted and the resolution adopted.

Mr. Churchill of Cornish, for the Committee on Public Improvements, to whom was referred An act to provide for a more economical and practical expenditure of the money appropriated by the state for the construction and repairs of highways, having considered the same, report the same in a new draft with the following resolution:

Resolved, That the bill in new draft ought to pass.

The report was accepted. On motion of Mr. French of Moultonborough, the rules were suspended and the bill in new draft read a first time by its title. The bill was then ordered to a second reading. On motion of the same gentleman, the rules were suspended and the bill read a second time by its title and referred to the Committee on Appropriations.

Mr. Burnell of Conway, for the Committee on Fisheries and Game, to whom was referred An act in amendment of section 56, chapter 79 of the Laws of 1901, relating to fish and game, having considered the same, report the same with the following resolution:

Resolved, That the bill ought to pass.

The report was accepted and the bill laid upon the table to be printed.

Mr. Farrell of Manchester, for the Committee on Incorporations, to whom was referred An act to incorporate the Caledonia Power Company, having considered the same, report the same in a new draft with the following resolution :

Resolved, That the bill in new draft ought to pass.

The report was accepted.   On motion of Mr. Goss of Berlin, the rules were suspended and the bill in new draft read a first time by its title.   The bill was then ordered to a second reading.   On motion of the same gentleman, the rules were suspended and the bill read a second time by its title.   The bill was then laid upon the table to be printed.   On motion of the same gentleman, the rules were suspended and the printing of the bill dispensed with.   The bill was then ordered to a third reading.   On motion of the same gentleman, the rules were further suspended and the bill read a third time by its title and passed and sent to the Senate for concurrence.

Mr. Remich of Littleton, for the Committee on Judiciary, to whom was referred An act to enlarge the powers of towns and cities, having considered the same, report the same in a new draft with the resolution that the bill in new draft ought to pass.

The report was accepted and the bill in new draft read a first time and ordered to a second reading.

Mr. Goss of Berlin, for the Committee on Judiciary, reported the following entitled bill, "An act to legalize and confirm the warrant for, and the votes and proceedings at, the annual election and meeting in ward three in the city of Berlin, held the tenth day of March, 1903," with the resolution that the bill ought to pass.

The report was accepted and the bill read a first time and ordered to a second reading.   On motion of Mr. Goss of Berlin, the rules were suspended and the bill read a second time.   The bill was then laid upon the table to be printed. On motion of the same gentleman, the rules were suspended and the printing of the bill dispensed with.   The bill was then ordered to a third reading.   On motion of the same gentleman, the rules were further suspended and the bill read a third time and passed and sent to the Senate for concurrence.

Mr. Batchelder of Keene, for the Committee on Judiciary, reported the following entitled bill, "An act to provide for a

revision of the General and Public Laws," with the resolution
that the bill ought to pass.

The report was accepted and the bill read a first time and
ordered to a second reading.

Mr. Churchill of Cornish, for the Committee on Forestry,
reported the following entitled bill, "An act in amendment of
chapter 98 of the Laws of 1901, relating to the duties of tree
wardens," with the resolution that the bill ought to pass.

The report was accepted and the bill read a first time and
ordered to a second reading. On motion of Mr. Churchill of
Cornish, the rules were suspended and the bill read a second
time by its title. The bill was then laid upon the table to be
printed. On motion of the same gentleman, the rules were
suspended and the printing of the bill dispensed with. The
bill was then ordered to a third reading. On motion of the same
gentleman, the rules were further suspended and the bill read
a third time by its title and passed and sent to the Senate for
concurrence.

Mr. Collins of Nashua, for the Committee on Public Improvements, reported the following entitled bill, "An act providing for a state system of highway construction and improvement and for the appointment of highway engineers," with the
resolution that the bill ought to pass.

The report was accepted. On motion of Mr. French of
Moultonborough, the rules were suspended and the bill read a
first time by its title. The bill was then ordered to a second
reading. On motion of the same gentleman, the rules were
suspended and the bill read a second time by its title and referred to the Committee on Appropriations.

SECOND READING.

An act relating to the protection and preservation of ornamental and shade trees in the highways.

Read a second time and laid upon the table to be printed.

SPECIAL ORDER.

Mr. Remich of Littleton called for the special order, it being
the consideration of the following entitled bill, "An act to regulate the traffic in intoxicating liquor."

The question being upon the adoption of the motion of Mr. Remich of Littleton, that the report of the minority of the committee be substituted for that of the majority of the committee,

(Discussion ensued.)

On motion of Mr. Remich of Littleton, at 1.45 the House took a recess until 2.30 o'clock.

(After Recess.)

Discussion was resumed upon the motion of Mr. Remich of Littleton, that the report of the minority of the committee be substituted for that of the majority of the committee.

Mr. Ahern of Concord moved the previous question.

The question being,

Shall the main question be now put?

(Discussion ensued.)

Mr. Cutler of Jaffrey moved that the House adjourn. On a *viva voce* vote the motion did not prevail.

The question being,

Shall the main question be now put?

On a *viva voce* vote the motion prevailed and the previous question was ordered.

The question being upon the motion of Mr. Remich of Littleton, that the report of the minority of the committee be substituted for that of the majority of the committee, Mr. Whitcher of Haverhill demanded a yea and nay vote and the roll was called with the following result

YEAS, 107.

ROCKINGHAM COUNTY. Sawyer of Atkinson, Fellows, Morse of Chester, Darbe, Severance, Lane of Hampton, Brown of Hampton Falls, Warner, Gerrish, Sleeper, Dow of Seabrook, Swain, Chase of Stratham.

STRAFFORD COUNTY. Howe of Barrington, Langley, York, Davis of Lee, McCrillis, Bergeron, Wentworth.

BELKNAP COUNTY. Pinkham, Smith of Center Harbor, Potter, Davis of Laconia, Quimby of Meredith, Morrill of New Hampton, Sanborn of Sanbornton, Rogers, Mason.

CARROLL COUNTY. Weeks, Fifield, Philbrick of Effingham, Pollard, Edgerly of Tuftonborough, Blake of Wakefield, Britton.

MERRIMACK COUNTY. White of Bow, Langmaid, Phillips, Adams of Franklin, Fisk, Messer, Sanborn of Northfield, Tallant, Aldrich, Little of Salisbury, Burbank, Mason.

HILLSBOROUGH COUNTY. Farley of Amherst, Whittaker, Ward, Farley of Hollis, Goodwin, Sawyer of Milford, Robinson, Needham, Kendall, Tuck, Duncklee, Shenton, Jones of New Ipswich, Smith of Peterborough, Bragdon.

CHESHIRE COUNTY. Gowing, Tenney, Cutler, Pierce of Jaffrey, Fay, Fitch, Whitney, Goodnow, Moors, Fox, Scott, Amidon, Fletcher, Lane of Swanzey, Hall, Kellom.

SULLIVAN COUNTY. Clark, True, Philbrick of Springfield, Russell of Sunapee, Straw of Unity, Ball.

GRAFTON COUNTY. McMurphey, Pierce of Bethlehem, Little of Campton, Gates, Dorothy, Foster, Glover, Pinneo, Pike of Haverhill, Barnard, Crossman, Stanley, Remich, Blake of Littleton, Converse, Frazer, Celley, Houston.

COÖS COUNTY. Hicks, Hamlin of Dummer, Smith of Pittsburg, Harriman.

NAYS, 214.

ROCKINGHAM COUNTY. Hardy, Shute, Nowell, Scammon, Brown of Fremont, Duntley, Emerson of Hampstead, Quimby of Kingston, Pridham, Chase of Newfields, Badger, George, Payne, Blaisdell, Foye, Nelson, Yeaton, Cogan, Adams of Portsmouth, Newton, Couhig, Corson, Brown of Rye, Young, Cochran.

STRAFFORD COUNTY. Mathes, Ramsdell, Libby of Dover, Jewell, Nason, Whittemore, Bunce, Smith of Dover, Hayes, Wesley, Felker, Jones of New Durham, Crocker, Warren, Small, Harrity, Etter, Boutin, Andrews, Caverly.

BELKNAP COUNTY. Clough, Hull, Fecteau, Edwards, Kimball of Laconia.

CARROLL COUNTY. Littlefield, Stevens, Dow of Conway, Drake, Trickey, Greene, French, Hoyt of Sandwich.

MERRIMACK COUNTY. Graves, Harris of Boscawen, Morse of Bradford, Beck, Durgin, Symonds, Cate, Shepard, Kennedy, Willis, Matson, Hill, A. W., of Concord, Woodman, Kimball of Concord, Emerson of Concord, Davis of Concord, Critchett, Mathews of Concord, Hill, E. J., of Concord, Ahern, Donagan, Litchfield, Bunten of Dunbarton, Morin of Franklin, Jones of Franklin, Davis of Franklin, Preston of Henniker, Twombly, Worthley, Sanborn of Loudon, Walker of Pittsfield, Pillsbury.

HILLSBOROUGH COUNTY. Barr of Bedford, Gould of Bennington, Shattuck, Craine, Eaton, Putnam, Brown of Greenville, Ware of Hancock, Connell, Cavanaugh, Nyberg, Chase of Manchester, Donahue, Bartlett of Manchester, Taggart, Sheehan, Bunton, A. S., of Manchester, Farrell, Wright, Barr of Manchester, Dubuc, Carpenter, Morgan, Darrah, Stewart of Manchester, Tonery, Ryan, Whalen, Riordan, Sullivan of Manchester, Shaughnessey, Sasseville, Marshall, Couch, Armstrong, Tinkham, Graf, Quimby of Manchester, Scannell, Dinsmore, Dozois, Gunderman, Janelle, Kohler, Filion, Lemay, Lynch, Kane, Newman, Emerson of Manchester, Simpson, Hodgman, Lewis, Lampron, Buckley of Nashua, Ingham, Bussell, Shea, Collins, Earley, Desmarais, Peabody, Miller, Fitzgerald, Chase of Weare, Sheldon.

CHESHIRE COUNTY. Ware of Alstead, Harris of Chesterfield, Polzer, Bemis, Fuller, Holland, Maloney, Jones of Keene, Batchelder, Donovan, Merrill, Ramsay, Sherman of Walpole, Dickinson.

SULLIVAN COUNTY. Hamlin of Charlestown, Chandler, Long, Huntley, Churchill, Walker of Grantham, Aiken, Matthews of Newport, Richards.

GRAFTON COUNTY. Morrill of Ashland, Davenport, Calley, Kimball of Grafton, Howe of Hanover, Whitcher, Carr, Evans, Goold of Lebanon, Pike of Lebanon, Comings, Mitchell of Littleton, King, Gould of Plymouth, Ferrin, Russell of Rumney, Goodrich.

COÖS COUNTY. Caird, Stewart of Berlin, Smyth, Goss, Vaillancourt, Kent of Berlin, Gallagher, Martin, Tillotson, Bragg, Buckley of Lancaster, Ellis, Trafton, McDonald of Northumberland, Piper, O'Connor, Darling, Babcock,

and the House refused to substitute the report of the minority of the committee for that of the majority.

The report of the majority of the committee having been accepted and the first reading of the bill being in order, on motion of Mr. Batchelder of Keene, the rules were suspended and the bill read a first time by its title. The bill was then ordered to a second reading.

On motion of Mr. Gallagher of Carroll, at 5.32 the House adjourned.

AFTERNOON.

The House was called to order in afternoon session immediately upon adjournment of the morning session.

Mr. Goodwin of Mason. having been duly elected to fill the seat of Benjamin F. March, deceased, and having duly qualified before His Excellency the Governor, appeared and took his seat as a member of the House of Representatives.

THIRD READING.

An act in amendment of section 22, chapter 27, Laws of 1895, entitled "An act in relation to the incorporation, organization, and regulation of street railway companies, and authorizing the use of electricity as motive power by existing steam railroads."

Read a third time and passed and sent to the Senate for concurrence.

SPECIAL ORDER.

Mr. Fay of Keene called for the special order, it being the consideration of the following entitled bill, "An act in amendment of section 19, chapter 57 of the Public Statutes, relating to the annual invoice of polls and taxable property."

The question being upon the motion of Mr. Fay of Keene, that the report of the minority of the committee be substituted for that of the majority, on motion of the same gentleman the bill and reports were laid upon the table and made the special order for Tuesday, March 24, at 11 o'clock.

On motion of Mr. Smith of Exeter, at 5.38 the House adjourned.

THURSDAY, MARCH 19, 1903.

The House met at 11 o'clock.

Prayer was offered by the chaplain.

MESSAGE FROM THE SENATE.

A message from the Honorable Senate, by its clerk, announced that the Senate refuses to concur with the House of Representatives in the passage of the following entitled bills and joint resolutions:

An act relating to books of deposit issued by savings banks, when lost, destroyed, or assigned.

Joint resolution to provide a nursery for the growth and distribution of forest seedling trees within the state at cost.

An act relating to persons employed under and by virtue of an act of congress relating to the surveys of the geological survey of the United States.

The message also announced that the Senate concurs with the House of Representatives in the passage of the following entitled bills and joint resolutions:

An act to legalize and ratify the votes and proceedings at the annual meeting in Newton, holden on the tenth day of March, 1903.

An act for the promotion of horticulture.

Joint resolution in favor of maintaining buoys and placing lights in Squam lake.

An act in amendment of section 4 of chapter 162 of the Public Statutes, fixing the salaries of the members of the board of bank commissioners.

An act in amendment of section 1 of chapter 3 of the Laws of 1893, fixing the salary of the clerk of the board of bank commissioners.

An act to amend section 10, chapter 79 of the Session Laws of 1901, relative to the duties of the fish and game commissioners.

An act authorizing the state treasurer to transfer certain sums of money to the literary fund for schools.

An act to amend section 10 of chapter 79 of the Session Laws of 1901, relating to the taking of deer.

Joint resolution for lighting the lighthouse on Loon island in Sunapee lake, repairing the cable connected therewith, improving the light service, placing and maintaining buoys on said lake, and removing obstructions to navigation in said lake.

Joint resolution in favor of the Granite State Dairymen's Association.

Joint resolution in favor of New Hampshire Soldiers' Home.

The message also announced that the Senate concurs with the House of Representatives in the passage of the following bill, with amendment, in the passage of which amendment it asks the concurrence of the House of Representatives:

An act in amendment of Public Statutes, chapter 81, section 2, relating to telegraph, telephone, and electric light companies.

Amend section 2 by adding the following: " provided, that the provisions of this act shall not apply to any city in which special laws relating to the subject matter of this bill are now in force," so that said section as amended shall read:

SECT. 2. All acts and parts of acts inconsistent with this act are hereby repealed, and this act shall take effect upon its passage, provided, that the provisions of this act shall not apply to any city in which special laws relating to the subject matter of this bill are now in force.

On motion of Mr. Ahern of Concord, the amendment was concurred in.

The message further announced that the Senate has passed the following entitled bills, in the passage of which it asks the concurrence of the House of Representatives:

An act in amendment of section 3 of chapter 7 of the Publi Statutes, relating to the state house and yard.

Read a first and second time and referred to the Committee on State House and State House Yard.

An act in amendment of section 14, chapter 79, Session Laws of 1901, relating to the powers of the fish and game commissioners.

Read a first and second time and referred to the Committee on Fisheries and Game.

COMMITTEE REPORTS.

Mr. Converse of Lyme, for the Committee on Engrossed Bills, reported that they had examined, and found correctly engrossed, the following entitled bills and joint resolutions:

Joint resolution in favor of the Granite State Dairymen's Association.

Joint resolution in favor of maintaining buoys and placing lights on Squam lake.

An act authorizing the state treasurer to transfer certain sums of money to the literary fund for schools.

An act to amend section 10, chapter 79 of the Session Laws of 1901, relative to duties of the fish and game commissioners.

An act for the promotion of horticulture.

An act in amendment of section 1 of chapter 3 of the Laws of 1893, fixing the salary of the clerk of the board of bank commissioners.

An act in amendment of section 4 of chapter 162 of the Public Statutes, fixing the salaries of the members of the board of bank commissioners.

Joint resolution in favor of New Hampshire Soldiers' Home.

Joint resolution for lighting the lighthouse on Loon island in Sunapee lake, repairing the cable connected therewith, improving the light service, placing and maintaining buoys on said lake, and removing obstructions to navigation in said lake.

The report was accepted.

Mr. Woodman of Concord, for the Committee on Judiciary, to whom was referred An act enabling the city of Concord to appropriate money for observing Memorial Day, having considered the same, report the same with the following resolution:

Resolved, That the bill ought to pass.

The report was accepted and the bill laid upon the table to be printed. On motion of Mr. Ahern of Concord, the rules were suspended and the printing of the bill dispensed with. The bill was then ordered to a third reading. On motion of the same gentleman, the rules were further suspended and the bill read a third time by its title and passed and sent to the secretary of state to be engrossed.

Mr. Woodman of Concord, for the Committee on Judiciary,

to whom was referred An act to establish water-works in the town of Greenville, having considered the same, report the same with the following resolution :

Resolved, That the bill ought to pass.

The report was accepted and the bill laid upon the table to be printed.

Mr. Buckley of Lancaster, for the Committee on Judiciary, to whom was referred An act to incorporate the Peabody River Improvement Company, having considered the same, report the same with amendment, and with the following resolution :

Resolved, That the bill, as amended, ought to pass.

Amend the bill by striking out the words " Jason H. Woodward, Osman W. Fernald, Fred N. Wheeler, Daniel J. Daley, and J. Fred Bell," in the first and second lines of said bill and inserting in place thereof the following: " Frank P. Thomas of Andover, Maine, James M. Lavin, Ernest McC. Macy, Jason H. Woodward, and Osman W. Fernald of Berlin, New Hampshire, and Alna B. Libby and Walter C. Libby of Gorham, New Hampshire."

The report was accepted, the amendment adopted, and the bill laid upon the table to be printed. On motion of Mr. Buckley of Lancaster, the rules were suspended and the printing of the bill dispensed with. The bill was then ordered to a third reading. On motion of the same gentleman, the rules were further suspended and the bill read a third time by its title and passed and sent to the Senate for concurrence.

Mr. Mitchell of Lancaster, for the Committee on Public Health, to whom was referred Joint resolution to provide for the care of indigent consumptive patients at the Pembroke Sanatorium, having considered the same, report the same with the following resolution :

Resolved, That it is inexpedient to legislate.

The report was accepted and the resolution adopted.

Mr. Donahue of Manchester, for the Committee on Insurance, to whom was referred An act to confirm, revive, and continue the charter of the Manchester City Fire Insurance Company, having considered the same, report the same with the following resolution :

Resolved, That it is inexpedient to legislate.

The report was accepted. The question being upon the adoption of the resolution reported by the committee, on motion of Mr. Sheehan of Manchester, the bill and report were laid upon the table.

Mr. Mitchell of Lancaster, for the Committee on Public Health, reported the following joint resolution, "Joint resolution to provide for the treatment of indigent consumptives," with the resolution that the joint resolution ought to pass.

The report was accepted and the joint resolution read a first time and ordered to a second reading. On motion of Mr. Bell of Woodstock, the rules were suspended and the joint resolution read a second time. The joint resolution was then laid upon the table to be printed and then referred to the Committee on Appropriations. On motion of the same gentleman, the rules were suspended and the printing of the joint resolution dispensed with. It was then referred to the Committee on Appropriations.

Mr. Burnell of Conway, for the Committee on Fisheries and Game, reported the following entitled bill, "An act in amendment of section 23 of chapter 79 of the Laws of 1901, in relation to fines," with the resolution that the bill ought to pass.

The report was accepted and the bill read a first time and ordered to a second reading.

Mr. Buckley of Lancaster, for the Committee on Judiciary, reported the following entitled bill, "An act to revive the charter of the Colebrook Water Company," approved February 23, 1897, with the resolution that the bill ought to pass.

The report was accepted and the bill read a first time and ordered to a second reading.

BILL FORWARDED.

An act authorizing the Concord & Montreal Railroad, lessor, to vote on all stock owned by it in other corporations.

Taken from the table and ordered to a third reading.

SECOND READINGS.

An act to provide for a revision of the General and Public Laws.

Read a second time and laid upon the table to be printed and then referred to the Committee on Appropriations.

An act to enlarge the powers of towns and cities.

Read a second time and laid upon the table to be printed.

An act to regulate the traffic in intoxicating liquor.

The second reading being in order, on motion of Mr. Batchelder of Keene, the rules were suspended and the bill read a second time by its title. Mr. Batchelder of Keene offered the following amendment:

Amend section 6 of the bill by striking out line 4 and line 5, and inserting instead thereof the following:

"Second class, to sell liquor of any kind in quantities less than five gallons to one person at one time."

The question being upon the adoption of the amendment,

(Discussion ensued.)

On motion of Mr. Remich of Littleton, at 12.05 the House took a recess until 2.30 o'clock.

(After recess.)

Discussion was resumed on the amendment offered by Mr. Batchelder of Keene. On a *viva voce* vote the amendment was adopted.

Mr. Batchelder of Keene offered the following amendment:

Amend section 7 of the bill by adding at the end of the fifth line the following words: "provided, however, that it shall be unlawful for any licensee of the first class in a no-license city or town to furnish liquor to persons other than those resorting to his house for food or lodging," so that the first paragraph of said section shall read:

"First class.—Not more than $1,000 nor less that $25 per year, and the state board of license commissioners are hereby authorized and empowered to fix the fee and restrict, define, and limit each license of the first class in their discretion, provided, however, that it shall be unlawful for any licensee of the first class in a no-license city or town to furnish liquor to persons other than those resorting to his house for food or lodging."

The question being upon the adoption of the amendment, Mr. Remich of Littleton offered the following amendment to the amendment offered by Mr. Batchelder of Keene:

Amend by striking out all after the word "however," and inserting the following: "No licensee of the first class, in a no-license city or town, shall sell or serve liquor except to *bona fide* registered guests who have resorted to his hotel for food or lodging. If the guest resorts to the hotel for food only then he must partake of and pay for a meal costing not less than twenty-five cents. Such licensee shall not sell liquor to any resident of the city or town in which his hotel is situated, neither shall he maintain or keep a bar-room or bar at which liquor is sold."

On a *viva voce* vote the amendment offered by Mr. Remich of Littleton was adopted.

The question being upon the adoption of the amendment offered by Mr. Batchelder of Keene, as amended by the amendment of Mr. Remich of Littleton, on a *viva voce* vote the amendment was adopted.

Mr. Batchelder of Keene offered the following amendment:

Amend section 7 of the bill in the seventh line by striking out the words "one thousand" and inserting instead thereof the words "twelve hundred," so that the sixth and seventh lines shall read:

"Second class.—In cities having a population of forty thousand or over, twelve hundred dollars."

On a *viva voce* vote the amendment was adopted.

Mr. Batchelder of Keene offered the following amendment:

Amend section 31 of the bill by striking out lines 34, 35, 36, 37, 38, and 39 of said section, and inserting instead thereof the following: "regular biennial election in 1904, or at a special election held in lieu thereof, and every fourth year thereafter, the question aforesaid shall be submitted to the legal voters in all cities in the state, and to the legal voters in all towns in the state at the regular March election held in 1906, and every fourth year thereafter, upon the written petition of one tenth of the legal voters of such cities or towns, in accordance with the check-list last used in such cities or towns. If a," so that said section shall read:

SECT. 31. From and after the first day of May, 1903, it shall be lawful to engage in the traffic in liquor under the terms of this act in all cities in the state, and in all such towns as shall have accepted by a majority vote of its legal voters the provisions of this act as herein provided. The board of selectmen in towns may, and upon a written petition of one tenth of the legal voters, according to the check-list last used in such town, shall, within thirty days from the passage of this act, cause a special election to be held, at which the sense of the voters shall be taken by secret ballot upon the following question : " Shall licenses for the sale of liquor be granted in this town under the provisions of 'An act to regulate the traffic in intoxicating liquor,' passed at the January session of the general court, 1903?" If a majority of the qualified voters present and voting at said election shall vote in the affirmative on said question, the town clerk shall immediately certify that fact to the state board of license commissioners, who shall forthwith issue licenses under the provisions of this act to be exercised in such town. Any town not having had a special election as hereinbefore provided may vote on said question at its regular March election held in 1904, or at a special election warned to be held within thirty days of said 1904 election. In case a majority of the qualified voters present and voting at said special or said March election, or special instead thereof, shall vote in the negative on said question the town clerk shall immediately certify that fact to the state board of license commissioners, and in such town the provisions of chapter 112, Public Statutes, and all amendments thereto, shall remain in full force and effect, except that the state board of license commissioners may issue licenses of the first, fifth, and sixth classes in their discretion, to be exercised in such town under the provisions of this act. And at the regular biennial election in 1904, or at a special election held in lieu thereof, and every fourth year thereafter, the question aforesaid shall be submitted to the legal voters in all cities in the state, and to the legal voters in all towns in the state at the regular March election held in 1906, and every fourth year thereafter, upon the written petition of one tenth of the legal voters of such cities or towns, in accordance with the check-list last used in such cities or towns. If a majority of the qualified voters present and voting as aforesaid shall vote in the negative upon said question, the city or town clerk shall immediately certify that fact to the state board of license commissioners, and in such city or town the provisions of chapter 112, Public Statutes, and all amendments thereto, shall then be in full force and effect, except that the state board of license commissioners may issue licenses of the first, fifth, and sixth classes, in their discretion, to be exercised in such city or town, under the provisions of this act.

The question being upon the adoption of the amendment, Mr. Remich of Littleton offered the following amendment to the amendment offered by Mr. Batchelder:

Amend section 31 by striking out all of said section as amended by the amendment offered by Mr. Batchelder and inserting in place thereof the following:

SECT. 31. From and after the first day of May, 1903, it shall be lawful to engage in the traffic in liquor, under the terms of this act, in all cities and towns in the state as shall have accepted by a majority vote of its legal voters present and voting the provisions of this act as herein provided. The officers of every city or town whose duty it is to call a special meeting of the legal voters of their respective cities or towns shall call a meeting, according to the statutes made and provided, on the second Tuesday of May next, at which special meeting and at each biennial election thereafter in November in the towns and in the cities at the biennial election in 1906 and every fourth year thereafter the sense of the voters shall be taken by secret ballot upon the following questions: " Shall licenses for the sale of liquor be granted in this city or town under the provisions of 'An act to regulate the traffic in intoxicating liquor,' passed at the January session of the general court, 1903?" If a majority of the qualified voters in any city or town present and voting at said town or city election, shall vote in the affirmative on said question, the clerk of the city or town shall immediately certify that fact to the state board of license commissioners, who shall forthwith issue licenses under the provisions of this act to be exercised in such city or town. In case a majority of the qualified

voters of a city or town present and voting at such election
shall vote in the negative on said question the clerk of the
city or town shall immediately certify that fact to the state
board of license commissioners and in such city or town the
provisions of chapter 112, Public Statutes, and all amendments thereto, shall remain in full force and effect.   Except
that the state board of license commissioners may issue licenses of the first, fifth, and sixth classes in their discretion to be
exercised in such city or town under the provisions of this
act.

The question being upon the adoption of the amendment to
the amendment,

(Discussion ensued.)

Mr. Barrett of Dover moved the previous question.
The question being,
Shall the main question be now put?

(Discussion ensued.)

Mr. Barrett of Dover withdrew his motion.

(Discussion ensued).

Mr. Ahern of Concord moved the previous question.
The question being,
Shall the main question be now put?

(Discussion ensued.)

Mr. Remich of Littleton moved that the motion of Mr.
Ahern be laid upon the table.
Mr. Ahern withdrew his motion.
Discussion was resumed upon the question of the adoption
of the amendment offered by Mr. Remich of Littleton to the
amendment offered by Mr. Batchelder of Keene.
Mr. Ahern of Concord moved the previous question.
The question being,
Shall the main question be now put?

(Discussion ensued.)

On a *viva voce* vote the motion did not prevail.

The question being upon the adoption of the amendment offered by Mr. Remich of Littleton to the amendment offered by Mr. Batchelder of Keene,

(Discussion ensued.)

On a *viva voce* vote the amendment offered by Mr. Remich of Littleton was adopted.

The question being upon the adoption of the amendment offered by Mr. Batchelder of Keene, as amended by the amendment offered by Mr. Remich of Littleton, on a *viva voce* vote the amendment was adopted.

Mr. Jones of Franklin offered the following amendment:

Amend by striking out all after the enacting clause and inserting in place thereof the following:

SECTION 1. No person shall sell, or expose or keep for sale, any intoxicating liquors except as authorized by chapter 112 of the Public Statutes or by the provisions of this act; but nothing herein contained shall apply to sales made by a person under a provision of law requiring him to sell personal property, or to the sale of cider or native wines by the makers thereof, not to be drunk on the premises; and any beverage containing more than three per cent. of alcohol by volume at sixty degrees Fahrenheit, as well as distilled spirits, shall be deemed to be intoxicating liquors within the meaning of this chapter.

SECT. 2. The proprietors of *bona fide* drug stores may sell pure liquor of any kind for medicinal, mechanical or chemical purposes, upon the prescription of a registered physician in towns or cities adopting the provisions of this act, and shall not be subject to the second clause of section eight.

SECT. 3. A *bona fide* drug store shall include only such stores as shall be legitimately and actually engaged in the sale of a full line of drugs, medicines, and chemicals of good quality, properly equipped to fill physicians' prescriptions under the direction of a reputable registered pharmacist, and which shall not sell liquor to be drunk on the premises. A *bona fide* hotel, under this act shall include only such hotels as provide lodging and meals for the public, and contain at least ten furnished bedrooms; a *bona fide* summer hotel shall include only such hotels as provide lodging and meals for the public, contain at least twenty furnished bedrooms, and are open for guests in the warm season only.

SECT. 4. In any city or town which votes to authorize the granting of licenses for the sale of intoxicating liquors, as hereinafter provided, licenses of the first four classes mentioned in section nine, and in any city or town licenses of the fifth class mentioned in said section, may be granted annually by the mayor and aldermen of cities, or the selectmen of towns, to persons applying therefor. Every license shall be signed by the mayor or the chairman of the selectmen, and by the clerk of the city or town by which it is issued, and shall be recorded in the office of such clerk, who shall be paid by the licensee one dollar for recording the same. It shall name the person licensed, shall set forth the nature of the license, and the building in which the business is to be carried on, and shall continue in force one year, unless sooner forfeited or rendered void. The clerk of each city or town shall annually in November make a return to the secretary of state showing the number of licenses of each class, the amount received for the same by classes, and the number revoked, if any.

SECT. 5. Notice of all applications for licenses shall be published in the following manner, at the expense of the applicant, to be paid in advance, namely: in cities and towns at least once by the mayor and aldermen or the selectmen respectively, in such newspapers printed therein as they may designate, or if no such newspaper is printed therein, then by posting such notice in some conspicuous place on the premises described in the application for the license, and in two or more places where public notices are usually posted in the neighborhood. Such notice shall set forth the name of the applicant in full, the class of the license applied for, and a particular description of the premises on which the license is to be exercised, designating the building or part of the building to be used, and, if practicable, the street and number, and shall be published or posted at least ten days before the licensing board acts thereon.

SECT. 6. No license to sell intoxicating liquor to be drunk on the premises shall be granted for any building within two

32

hundred feet of a church or public school by the nearest traveled way. If, before the expiration of the ten days following the publication or posting of the notice as required by the preceeding section, the owner of any real estate adjoining the premises described in an application for license to be exercised to sell liquors to be drunk on the premises, notifies the licensing board in writing that he objects to the granting of the license, no license to sell intoxicating liquor to be drunk on said premises shall be granted ; this section shall not apply to *bona fide* hotels and drug stores as defined in this act.

SECT. 7. The mayor and aldermen or the selectmen may at any time refuse to issue a license to a person whom they deem unfit to receive the same.

SECT. 8. Each license shall be expressed to be subject to the following conditions:

First. That the provisions in regard to the nature of the license and the building in which the business may be carried on under it shall be strictly adhered to.

Second. That no sale of intoxicating liquor shall be made between the hours of eleven at night and six in the morning, nor during the Lord's day, nor on any legal holiday, election day or town meeting day, nor any other day when the mayor or selectmen shall so order, except that, if the licensee is an innholder he may supply such liquor to guests who have resorted to his house for food or lodging.

Third. That no liquor except such as is of good standard quality and free from adulteration shall be kept or sold on the premises described in the license.

Fourth. That no sale or delivery of liquor shall be made on the premises described in the license to a person known to be a drunkard, to an intoxicated person, or to a person who is known to have been intoxicated within the six months next preceding, or to a minor for his own use or the use of any other person.

Fifth. That there shall be no disorder, indecency, prostitution, lewdness, or illegal gaming, on the premises described in the license, or on any premises connected therewith by an interior communication. Each license shall be subject to the further condition, that no intoxicating liquors except those the sale of which is allowed by the license shall be kept on the premises described in the license.

Sixth. That the license, or a copy thereof, certified by the clerk of the city or town by which it was issued shall be displayed on the premises in a conspicuous position where it can easily be read.

Seventh. It shall further be expressed in such license that it shall be subject to forfeiture, as herein provided, for breach of any of its conditions, and that in case the licensee is convicted in a court of competent jurisdiction of having violated any of such conditions, his license shall thereupon become void.

SECT. 9.   Licenses shall be of the following classes :

First Class.   To sell liquors of any kind to be drunk on the premises.

Second Class.   To sell malt liquors, cider, and light wines, containing not more than fifteen per cent. of alcohol, to be drunk on the premises.

Third Class.   To sell liquors of any kind at retail not to be drunk on the premises.

Fourth Class.   To sell liquors of any kind at wholesale not to be drunk on the premises.

Fifth Class.   Licenses to proprietors of *bona fide* drug stores to sell liquors of any kind for medicinal, mechanical, or chemical purposes on prescription only.

Licenses for the sale of liquor to be drunk on the premises shall also permit the retail sale of liquor not to be drunk on the premises.

SECT. 10.   The fees for licenses shall be as follows : For a license of the first or fourth class not less than two hundred, nor more than twelve hundred dollars.   For a license of the second or third class not less than two hundred, nor more than five hundred dollars.   For a license of the fifth class, twenty-five dollars.

SECT. 11.   The proprietor or manager of any *bona fide* summer hotel as defined in this act may receive a license of the first class to sell liquor to actual guests only, and the fee for such summer hotel may be placed at such sum, not less than one hundred dollars and not more than twelve hundred dollars, as the board of mayor and aldermen or the selectmen may fix; if such hotel be not located in an organized town or city, the county commissioners shall have the same powers and duties with reference to such hotel and license therefor as the selectmen of towns.

SECT. 12. The board granting a license to sell liquor to be drunk on the premises may require the licensee to close permanently all entrances to the licensed premises other than those from the public street or streets upon which such premises are situated, and may so specify in the license, and in such case the construction or opening of any such entrance shall of itself make the license void. The board shall require such licensee to remove any screen, blind, shutter, curtain, partition, or painted, ground or stained glass window, or any other obstruction, which may interfere with a view of the interior of the licensed premises. No such licensee shall place or maintain, or permit to be placed or maintained, upon any premises used by him for the sale of intoxicating liquor under the provisions of his license, any screen, blind, shutter, curtain, partition, or painted, ground or stained glass window, or any other obstruction, which may interfere with a view of the interior of the licensed premises. No such licensee shall place or maintain, or permit to be placed or maintained upon any premises used by him for the sale of intoxicating liquor under the provisions of his license, any screen, blind, shutter, curtain, partition, or painted, ground, or stained glass window, or any other obstruction, nor shall expose in any window upon said premises, any bottle, cask, or other vessel containing or purporting to contain intoxicating liquor in such a way as to interfere with a view of the business conducted upon the premises. This section is not to apply to licenses of the third or fourth class, or to *bona fide* drug stores or hotels, as defined in this act.

SECT. 13. No license shall be issued until the license fee has been paid to the treasurer of the city or town by which it is to be issued, nor until he has received a satisfactory bond payable to him as such treasurer, in the sum of one thousand dollars, signed by the licensee and by a surety company licensed to do business in this state who shall be jointly and severally liable, and conditioned for the payment of all costs, damage, and fines incurred by violations of the provisions of this chapter. Separate suits may be brought on such bond by any persons at their own expense. Such bond, after approval, shall be filed in the office of the city or town clerk, and a certified copy thereof shall be admissible in evidence, and shall have the same force and effect as the original bond would have if offered in evidence. The secretary of state shall, with the advice of the attorney-general, from time to time, prepare blank license certificates, applications for licenses, and bonds to accompany the same, in conformity with the provisions of this act as now existing and as hereafter amended, and shall furnish said blank certificates, applications, and bonds at cost to the clerks of such towns and cities as shall adopt this act. Said blanks shall be furnished to applicants for licenses by town and city clerks free of charge, and shall be used for all certificates, applications, and bonds required under this act.

SECT. 14. The treasurer of a city or town shall pay to the treasurer of the county one fourth of all moneys received by him for licenses within one month after he receives the same.

SECT. 15. The mayor and aldermen of a city, the selectmen of a town, or any police officer or constable specially authorized by either of them, may at any time enter upon the premises of any person licensed under this chapter, to ascertain the manner in which such person conducts his business, and to preserve order, and such police officer or constable may at any time take samples for analysis from any liquors kept on such premises, and the vessel or vessels containing such samples shall be sealed on the premises by the seal of the vendor, and shall remain so sealed until presented to the assayer for analysis. The city or town shall pay for the samples so taken, if such liquors are found to be of good quality and free from adulteration.

SECT. 16. The mayor and aldermen of the city or the selectmen of the town by which a license has been issued, after notice to the licensee and reasonable opportunity for him to be heard by them, or by a committee of their number, may declare his license forfeited upon proof satisfactory to them that he has violated, or permitted to be violated, any condition thereof. The pendency of proceedings before a court of justice shall not suspend or interfere with the power herein given to decree a forfeiture. If the license is declared to have been forfeited, the licensee shall be disqualified to receive a license for five years after the expiration of the term of the license so forfeited, and if the licensee is the owner of said premises, no license shall be issued to be exercised on the premises described in such forfeited license for the residue of the term thereof. The mayor and aldermen of a city, or the selectmen of a town, may at any time revoke the license of any drug store which in their opinion is not *bona fide* under the terms of this act.

SECT. 17. When a person holding a license for the sale of intoxicating liquors is convicted of the violation of any law relating to the business he is licensed to pursue, the court in which or the magistrate before whom such conviction is had, shall send to the board issuing the license a certificate under seal, showing the time and place of such conviction.

SECT. 18. Whoever, by himself, or his agent or servant, sells or gives intoxicating liquor to a minor, or allows a minor to loiter upon the premises where such sales are made, shall forfeit one hundred dollars for each offence, to be recovered by the parent or guardian of such minor in an action of tort.

SECT. 19. The giving away of intoxicating liquors, or any shifts or device to evade the provisions of this act, shall be deemed an unlawful selling within the provisions of this act. The words " giving away " where they occur in this act shall not apply to the giving away of intoxicating liquors by a person in his private dwelling, unless such private dwelling is a place of public resort.

SECT. 20. In any town or city that votes to grant licenses as provided by this act, no agent shall be appointed as provided by section six, chapter one hundred and twelve of Public Statutes.

SECT. 21. Whoever violates any provisions of his license, or being neither an agent of a city or town for the purpose of selling spirit as authorized by chapter 112 of the Public Statutes, nor licensed to sell intoxicating liquors under the provisions of this act, shall sell or keep for sale any intoxicating liquor in any quantity, shall be fined fifty dollars for the first offense, and for any subsequent offense he shall be fined one hundred dollars, and be imprisoned ninety days.

SECT. 22. Chapter 112 of the Public Statutes and amendments thereto except so far as expressly repealed, or in conflict with this act, or modified by this act, shall be and remain in full force and effect.

SECT. 23. The governor, with the advice and consent of the council, shall annually appoint and commission a competent person as an inspector and assayer of liquors. Such person before receiving his commission shall file with the state treasurer a bond to the state in the penal sum of two thousand dollars, with two or more sureties to be approved by the governor and council, for the faithful performance of his duties. He shall receive an annual salary of five hundred dollars, payable quarterly, and shall inspect and analyze all liquors sent to him by the mayor and aldermen of cities and the selectmen of towns, and shall return to such mayor and aldermen and such selectmen, as soon as may be, a written statement signed by him, of the results of such inspection and analysis. Such statement shall be presumptive evidence of the composition and quality of the liquor to which it relates.

SECT. 24. The selectmen of the several towns and places are directed to insert in their warrants calling town meetings for the annual election in March, 1904, and every fourth annual election thereafter, an article which shall require the sense of the qualified voters to be taken on the following question: "Shall licenses be granted for the sale of intoxicating liquors in this city (town)?" A special election shall be warned in all cities not voting on the second Tuesday of March each year for a vote upon said question on the second Tuesday of March in the year 1904, and every fourth year thereafter, the vote in answer to said question shall be "yes" or "no" by separate ballot, and in taking said vote the check-list shall be used. One special town meeting, or meeting of a city by wards, may be called in any town or city to vote upon the adoption of this act before March, 1904, upon written petition of twenty qualified voters addressed to the selectmen of towns and the mayor and aldermen of cities; but thereafter no vote upon this question shall be taken except as provided above, unless twenty-five per cent. of the legal voters shall so request in writing. The ward clerks of each city shall, within seven days of any such election, make, return to the city clerk of the number of votes cast in favor of and against the adoption of this act; and this act shall be in force, at the expiration of said seven days, in such towns and cities as vote for its adoption.

SECT. 25. This act shall take effect upon its passage.

The question being upon the adoption of the amendment, Mr. Ahern of Concord moved that the House take a recess until 7.30 o'clock. On a *viva voce* vote the motion did not prevail.

The question being upon the adoption of the amendment offered by Mr. Jones of Franklin,

(Discussion ensued.)

On a *viva voce* vote the amendment was not adopted. Mr. Jones of Franklin called for a yea and nay vote.

(Discussion ensued.)

Mr. Ahern of Concord moved that the motion and call for a yea and nay vote be laid upon the table. On a *viva voce* vote the motion prevailed.

On motion of Mr. Kohler of Manchester, at 5.45 the House adjourned.

AFTERNOON.

The House was called to order in afternoon session immediately upon adjournment of the morning session.

LEAVES OF ABSENCE.

Mr. Mitchell of Lancaster was granted leave of absence for the balance of the week on account of sickness in his family and the death of a relative.

Mr. Haines of Newmarket was granted an indefinite leave of absence on account of illness.

Mr. Badger of Newington was granted leave of absence on account of sickness.

On motion of Mr. Nason of Dover, the House took a recess at 6 o'clock until 7.30.

(After recess.)

THIRD READING.

An act authorizing the Concord & Montreal Railroad, lessor, to vote on all stock owned by it in other corporations.

Read a third time and passed and sent to the Senate for concurrence.

UNFINISHED BUSINESS.

Mr. Ahern of Concord called for the unfinished business, it being the following entitled bill, "An act to regulate the traffic in intoxicating liquor," and the pending roll call on the adoption of the amendment offered by Mr. Jones of Franklin.

(Discussion ensued.)

The roll was then called with the following result:

YEAS, 36.

BELKNAP COUNTY. Fecteau, Quimby of Meredith, Sanborn of Sanbornton, Mason of Tilton.

MERRIMACK COUNTY. Graves, Beck, Langmaid, Phillips, Morin of Franklin, Jones of Franklin, Sanborn of Northfield, Walker of Pittsfield, Ela, Burbank, Mason of Wilmot.

HILLSBOROUGH COUNTY. Craine, Ware of Hancock, Sasseville, Lynch, Kane, Newman, Goodwin, Duncklee, Spalding, Moran of Nashua, Desmarais, Dionne, Chase of Weare.

CHESHIRE COUNTY. Amidon, Ramsay, Kellom.

SULLIVAN COUNTY. Lufkin.

GRAFTON COUNTY. Russell of Rumney, Bowen.

COÖS COUNTY. Hutchins of Berlin, O'Connor.

NAYS, 265.

ROCKINGHAM COUNTY. Sawyer of Atkinson, Preston of Auburn, Fellows, Morse of Chester, Darbe, Hardy, Shute, Scammon, Severance, Brown of Fremont, Duntley, Emerson of Hampstead, Brown of Hampton Falls, Quimby of

Kingston, Chase of Newfields, George, Blaisdell, Foye, Nelson, Yeaton, Adams of Portsmouth, Abbott of Salem, Gordon, Young, Dow of Seabrook, Chase of Stratham.

STRAFFORD COUNTY. Howe of Barrington, Mathes, Ramsdell, Libby of Dover, Jewell, Nason, Whittemore, Bunce, Smith of Dover, Barrett, Wesley, Langley, York, Tuttle, Davis of Lee, Felker, Place, McCrillis, Crocker, Warren, Small, Harrity, Etter, Wentworth, Boutin, Andrews, Caverly.

BELKNAP COUNTY. Smith of Center Harbor, Potter, Davis of Laconia, Hull, Prescott, Chase of Laconia, Edwards, Morrill of New Hampton, Rogers.

CARROLL COUNTY. Littlefield, Stevens, Weeks, Fifield, Dow of Conway, Burnell, Philbrick of Effingham, Greene, French, Hoyt of Sandwich, Pollard, Edgerly of Tuftonborough, Blake of Wakefield, Beacham.

MERRIMACK COUNTY. Harris of Boscawen, Morse of Bradford, Durgin, Symonds, Cate, Kennedy, Willis, Matson, Hill, A. W., of Concord, Roby, Woodman, Kimball of Concord, Emerson of Concord, Davis of Concord, Critchett, Mathews of Concord, Hill, E. J., of Concord, Ahern, Donagan, Bunten of Dunbarton, Davis of Franklin, Preston of Henniker, Worthley, Fisk, Tallant, Aldrich, Foss, Pillsbury.

HILLSBOROUGH COUNTY. Farley of Amherst, Barr of Bedford, Gould of Bennington, Shattuck, Pattee, Eaton, Putnam, Whitaker, Ward, Connell, Holt, Cavanaugh, Nyberg, Abbott of Manchester, Chase of Manchester, Donahue, Bartlett of Manchester, Taggart, Sheehan, Bunton, A. S., of Manchester, Farrell, Johnson, Straw of Manchester, McDonald of Manchester, Wright, Barr of Manchester, Dubuc, Carpenter, Morgan, Darrah, Stewart of Manchester, Tonery, Ryan, Trinity, Whalen, Riordan, Sullivan of Manchester, Shaughnessey, Marshall, Couch, Bunton, A. B., of Manchester, Armstrong, Tinkham, Graf, Quimby of Manchester, Dinsmore, Dozois, Gunderman, Janelle, Kohler, Filion, Lemay, Emerson of Manchester, Simpson, Hodgman, Sawyer of Milford, Needham, Kendall, Tuck, Lewis, Lampron, Buckley of Nashua, Ingham, Bussell, Shea, Morse of Nashua, Shenton, Hills of Nashua, Earley, McLane, Jones of New Ipswich, Peabody, Smith of Peterborough, Fitzgerald, Bragdon, Sheldon.

CHESHIRE COUNTY. Ware of Alstead, Gowing, Bemis, Fuller, Holland, Cutler, Maloney, Jones of Keene, Fay, Fitch, Batchelder, Whitney, Goodnow, Moors, Scott, Merrill, Lane of Swanzey, Hall, Dickinson.

SULLIVAN COUNTY. Clark, Hamlin of Charlestown, Chandler, Long, Huntley, Churchill, Walker of Grantham, Aiken, Matthews of Newport, Richards, Philbrick of Springfield, Russell of Sunapee, Ball.

GRAFTON COUNTY. Morrill of Ashland, Davenport, Pierce of Bethlehem, Little of Campton, Gates, Dorothy, Glover, Kimball of Grafton, Pinneo, Howe of Hanover, Whitcher, Carr, Pike of Haverhill, Evans, Goold of Lebanon, Pike of Lebanon, Crossman, Stanley, Remich, Mitchell of Littleton, Blake of Littleton, Converse, Celley, Gould of Plymouth, Ferrin, Houston, Goodrich, Bell.

COÖS COUNTY. Caird, Stewart of Berlin, Smyth, Goss, Vaillancourt, Kent of Berlin, Notterstead, Gallagher, Gathercole, Hicks, Martin, Jordan, Hamlin of Dummer, Bragg, Buckley of Lancaster, Ellis, Trafton, McDonald of Northumberland, Piper, Smith of Pittsburg, Wilson, Harriman, Lennon, Darling, Babcock.

Messrs. Cochran of Windham and Crowell of Londonderry, Center of Litchfield and Swain of South Hampton, and Britton of Wolfeborough and Drake of Freedom, were paired, and the amendment was not adopted.

Mr. Pike of Haverhill offered the following amendment:

Amend the bill by inserting the following new section:

" Every application for license of any class permitted in no-license cities or towns shall be advertised not less than thirty days before such license shall be issued. Such advertisement to be inserted during three successive weeks in some newspaper published in the city or town in which such license is intended to be exercised, and if there is no paper published in such city or town, then the application shall be inserted in the paper having the largest circulation in said town. Such notice shall give the name of applicant, the class of license applied for, and the building or location in which the business is to be carried on, and a similar notice shall be conspicuously posted in two or more public places in said town or city. If any written protest is made, signed by twenty citizens of said city or town, the commissioners shall give a public hearing thereon, and in such case no license shall be issued except by the unanimous action of the full board of license commissioners. In case such license is granted the board shall give the reasons therefor in writing delivered to the party whose name heads the protest."

The question being upon the adoption of the amendment,

(Discussion ensued.)

Mr. Buckley of Lancaster moved the previous question.

The question being,

Shall the main question be now put?

On a *viva voce* vote the previous question was ordered.

The question being upon the adoption of the amendment offered by Mr. Pike of Haverhill, on a *viva voce* vote the amendment was not adopted. Mr. Remich of Littleton called for a yea and nay vote.

(Discussion ensued.)

Mr. Remich withdrew his call for a yea and nay vote.

Mr. Remich of Littleton offered the following amendment:

Amend clause 9 of section 8 by striking out in said clause after the word "bond," in line 40, the following words: "in the sum of double the amount of the license fee paid by him, satisfactory to said board," and inserting in place thereof the words, "of some reliable indemnity company authorized to do business in New Hampshire, in the sum of two thousand dollars."

The question being upon the adoption of the amendment,

(Discussion ensued.)

On a *viva voce* vote the amendment was not adopted.

Mr. Sheehan of Manchester offered the following amendment:

Amend section 8 of said bill by striking out all of subdivision 7 of said section and inserting in place thereof the following: "7. No corporation or association hereafter organized under chapter 147, Public Statutes, and the acts amendatory thereof, shall receive a license unless the same shall be equipped to furnish food and lodging to its members."

The question being upon the adoption of the amendment,

(Discussion ensued.)

On a *viva voce* vote the amendment was adopted.

Mr. Remich of Littleton offered the following amendment:

Amend clause 3 of section 8 by inserting after the words "New Hampshire," in line 8, the following words: "and of the town or city within which he desires to carry on the liquor business."

The question being upon the adoption of the amendment,

(Discussion ensued.)

On a *viva voce* vote the amendment was adopted.

Mr. Remich of Littleton offered the following amendment:

Amend the bill by adding the following section:

"The state board of license commissioners shall require the clerk of the board to furnish at the end of each month to the clerk of each city or town in which licenses are granted a complete and accurate list of the names of all persons to whom licenses have been granted in such city or town during the month, with street and number or location designated in the license; and such lists shall be open to public inspection in the office of the clerk of the city or town."

The question being upon the adoption of the amendment,

(Discussion ensued.)

On a *viva voce* vote the amendment was adopted.

Mr. Remich of Littleton offered the following amendment:

Amend the bill by adding the following section:

"Any druggist holding a license under the provisions of this act, who shall sell any spirituous or intoxicating liquors, in any quantity, to be drunk upon the premises, or who shall permit any spirituous or intoxicating liquors to be drunk upon the premises, unless in case of accident or sickness requiring the immediate administration of a stimulant, shall forfeit his license and shall pay a fine of not less than $200."

The question being upon the adoption of the amendment,

(Discussion ensued.)

Mr. Remich of Littleton withdrew his amendment.

Mr. Remich of Littleton offered the following amendment:

Amend the bill by inserting the following section:

" The treasurer of the board of license commissioners shall annually in the month of July pay to the state treasurer $50,000 to be used by the governor and council to establish, furnish, equip, and maintain a hospital and industrial home for the care, treatment, and reformation of inebriates, dipsomaniacs, and persons who have acquired the morphine, chloral, or cocaine habit, and shall each year thereafter pay the state treasurer such sum as in the opinion of the governor and council may be necessary to maintain said hospital and industrial home, and any balance remaining in their hands shall be disposed of as may be provided in this act."

The question being upon the adoption of the amendment,

(Discussion ensued.)

Mr. Crossman of Lisbon moved the previous question.

The question being,

Shall the main question be now put?

On a *viva voce* vote the previous question was ordered. The question being upon the adoption of the amendment offered by Mr. Remich of Littleton, on a *viva voce* vote the amendment was not adopted.

Mr. Remich of Littleton offered the following amendment:

Amend the bill by inserting the following section:

" The treasurer of the state board of license commissioners, after paying the entire cost of maintaining the office of said board, including all salaries and expenses attaching to the performance of their duties, and after paying all special appropriations required by this act, shall on or before the first day of November of each year pay to the state treasurer any balance remaining in his hand, said balance to be divided by the state treasurer among the towns and cities of the state, as the literary fund is now divided, to be kept and expended by the selectmen of towns and the city council of cities in establishing and maintaining substitutes for the saloon, and for no other purpose whatsoever."

The question being upon the adoption of the amendment,

(Discussion ensued.)

Mr. Small of Rochester moved the previous question.

The question being,

Shall the main question be now put?

On a *viva voce* vote the previous question was ordered.

The question being upon the adoption of the amendment offered by Mr. Remich of Littleton, on a *viva voce* vote the amendment was not adopted.

The bill was then ordered to a third reading. On motion of Mr. Barrett of Dover, the rules were suspended and the bill read a third time by its title.

The question being,

Shall the bill pass?

On a *viva voce* vote the bill passed. Mr. Remich of Littleton demanded a yea and nay vote. The roll was called with the following result:

YEAS, 218.

ROCKINGHAM COUNTY. Preston of Auburn, Fellows, Hardy, Shute, Nowell, Scammon, Brown of Fremont, Duntley, Emerson of Hampstead, Quimby of Kingston, Pridham, Chase of Newfields, George, Payne, Blaisdell, Foye, Nelson, Yeaton, Cogan, Adams of Portsmouth, Newton, Couhig, Brown of Rye, Gordon, Young.

STRAFFORD COUNTY. Mathes, Ramsdell, Libby of Dover, Jewell, Nason, Whittemore, Bunce, Smith of Dover, Barrett, Hayes, Wesley, Langley, York, Tuttle, Felker, Place, McCrillis, Crocker, Warren, Small, Harrity, Etter, Andrews, Caverly.

BELKNAP COUNTY. Hoitt of Barnstead, Clough, Fecteau, Edwards.

CARROLL COUNTY. Littlefield, Stevens, Dow of Conway, Greene, French, Beacham.

MERRIMACK COUNTY. Harris of Boscawen, Morse of Bradford, Beck, Durgin, Symonds, Cate, Kennedy, Willis, Matson, Hill, A. W., of Concord, Roby, Woodman, Kimball of Concord, Emerson of Concord, Davis of Concord, Critchett, Mathews of Concord, Hill, E. J., of Concord, Ahern, Donagan, Bunten of Dunbarton, Jones of Franklin, Davis of Franklin, Preston of Henniker, Worthley, Walker of Pittsfield, Pillsbury.

HILLSBOROUGH COUNTY. Barr of Bedford, Gould of Bennington, Shattuck, Craine, Pattee, Eaton, Putnam, Brown of Greenville, Ware of Hancock, Connell, Cavanaugh, Nyberg, Abbott of Manchester, Chase of Manchester, Donahue, Bartlett of Manchester, Taggart, Sheehan, Bunton, A. S., of Manchester, Farrell, Johnson, Straw of Manchester, McDonald of Manchester, Wright, Barr of Manchester, Dubuc, Carpenter, Morgan, Darrah, Stewart of Manchester, Tonery, Ryan, Trinity, Whalen, Riordan, Sullivan of Manchester, Shaughnessey, Marshall, Couch, Bunton, A. B., of Manchester, Armstrong, Tinkham, Graf, Quimby of Manchester, Scannell, Dinsmore, Dozois, Gunderman, Janelle, Kohler, Filion, Lemay, Lynch, Kane, Newman, Emerson of Manchester, Simpson, Hodgman, Tuck, Lewis, Lampron, Buckley of Nashua, Ingham, Bussell, Shea, Morse of Nashua, Shenton, Hills of Nashua, Earley, Desmarais, Dionne, McLane, Peabody, Sheldon.

CHESHIRE COUNTY. Ware of Alstead, Bemis, Fuller, Holland, Maloney, Jones of Keene, Batchelder, Donovan, Merrill, Sherman of Walpole, Dickinson.

SULLIVAN COUNTY. Hamlin of Charlestown, Chandler, Long, Huntley, Churchill, Walker of Grantham, Aiken, Matthews of Newport, Richards.

GRAFTON COUNTY. Morrill of Ashland, Davenport, Kimball of Grafton, Howe of Hanover, Whitcher, Carr, Pike of Haverhill, Barnard, Goold of Lebanon, Pike of Lebanon, Mitchell of Littleton, Gould of Plymouth, Ferrin, Russell of Rumney, Houston, Goodrich, Bell.

COÖS COUNTY. Caird, Stewart of Berlin, Smyth, Goss, Vaillancourt, Kent of Berlin, Notterstead, Gallagher, Gathercole, Hicks, Martin, Jordan, Bragg, Buckley of Lancaster, Ellis, Trafton, McDonald of Northumberland, Piper, Wilson, Lennon, Darling.

NAYS, 84.

ROCKINGHAM COUNTY. Morse of Chester, Darbe, Severance, Brown of Hampton Falls, Gerrish, Sleeper, Abbott of Salem, Dow of Seabrook, Chase of Stratham.

STRAFFORD COUNTY. Howe of Barrington, Davis of Lee, Wentworth.

BELKNAP COUNTY. Smith of Centre Harbor, Potter, Quimby of Meredith, Morrill of New Hampton, Sanborn of Sanbornton.

CARROLL COUNTY. Weeks, Fifield, Burnell, Philbrick of Effingham, Hoyt of Sandwich, Pollard, Edgerly of Tuftonborough.

MERRIMACK COUNTY. White of Bow, Langmaid, Phillips, Morin of Franklin, Fisk, Messer, Sanborn of Northfield, Aldrich, Ela, Burbank, Mason.

HILLSBOROUGH COUNTY. Whitaker, Ward, Sasseville, Goodwin, Sawyer of Milford, Robinson, Needham, Kendall, Duncklee, Jones of New Ipswich, Bragdon.

CHESHIRE COUNTY. Gowing, Tenney, Cutler, Pierce of Jaffrey, Fay, Fitch, Whitney, Goodnow, Moors, Fox, Scott, Amidon, Lane of Swanzey, Hall, Kellom.

SULLIVAN COUNTY. Clark, Lufkin, Philbrick of Springfield, Russell of Sunapee.

GRAFTON COUNTY. McMurphey, Pierce of Bethlehem, Little of Campton, Dorothy, Glover, Pinneo, Crossman, Stanley, Remich, Blake of Littleton, Converse, Frazer, Celley, Bowen.

COÖS COUNTY. Hamlin of Dummer, Smith of Pittsburg, O'Connor, Harriman, Babcock.

Messrs. Cochran of Windham and Crowell of Londonderry, Center of Litchfield and Swain of South Hampton, and Britton of Wolfeborough and Drake of Freedom, were paired, and the bill passed and was sent to the Senate for concurrence.

On motion of Mr. Remich of Littleton, at 12.30 the House adjourned.

FRIDAY, MARCH 20, 1903.

The House met at 11 o'clock.

Prayer was offered by the chaplain.

33

Mr. Converse of Lyme, for the Committee on Engrossed Bills, reported that they had examined and found correctly engrossed the following entitled bills and joint resolution :

Joint resolution in favor of Horace S. Cummings.

An act enabling the city of Concord to appropriate money for observing Memorial Day.

An act in amendment of Public Statutes, chapter 81, section 2, relating to telegraph, telephone, and electric light companies.

The report was accepted.

Mr. Ingham of Nashua, for the Committee on Incorporations, to whom was referred An act to incorporate The New Hampshire Beneficiary Union, having considered the same, report the same with the following resolution :

Resolved, That the bill ought to pass.

The report was accepted and the bill laid upon the table to be printed.

Mr. McDonald of Northumberland, for the Committee on Appropriations, to whom was referred Joint resolution to appropriate the sum of three hundred dollars for the purpose of turning Silver stream into Success pond in the township of Success and to screen the outlet of said pond, having considered the same, report the same with the following resolution :

Resolved, That the joint resolution ought to pass.

The report was accepted and the joint resolution ordered to a third reading. On motion of Mr. Notterstead of Berlin, the rules were suspended and the joint resolution read a third time and passed and sent to the Senate for concurrence.

Mr. Wright of Manchester, for the Committee on Appropriations, to whom was referred Joint resolution in favor of John M. Stanyan for soldier's pay and bounty, having considered the same, report the same with the following resolution :

Resolved, That the joint resolution ought to pass.

The report was accepted and the joint resolution ordered to a third reading. On motion of Mr. Sawyer of Milford, the rules were suspended and the joint resolution read a third time and passed and sent to the Senate for concurrence.

Mr. Tallant of Pembroke, for the Special Committee on Apportionment, to whom was referred An act to establish a new apportionment for the assessment of public taxes, having considered the same, report the same with the following resolution:

Resolved, That the bill ought to pass.

The report was accepted. On motion of Mr. French of Moultonborough, the bill and report were laid upon the table.

Mr. Ingham of Nashua, for the Committee on Incorporations, to whom was referred An act to incorporate the Connecticut River Power Company of New Hampshire, having considered the same, report the same in a new draft with the following resolution:

Resolved, That the bill in new draft ought to pass.

The report was accepted. On motion of Mr. Buckley of Lancaster, the rules were suspended and the bill in new draft read a first time by its title. The bill was then ordered to a second reading. On motion of the same gentleman, the rules were suspended and the bill read a second time by its title. The bill was then laid upon the table to be printed. On motion of the same gentleman the rules were further suspended and the printing of the bill dispensed with. The bill was then ordered to a third reading. On motion of the same gentleman the rules were further suspended and the bill read a third time and passed and sent to the Senate for concurrence.

Mr. Huntley of Claremont, for the Committee on Appropriations, to whom was referred An act in amendment of chapter 134 of the Public Statutes, relating to the practice of dentistry, having considered the same, report the same with the following resolution:

Resolved, That it is inexpedient to legislate.

Mr. Davenport of Bath, for the Committee on Appropriations, to whom was referred Joint resolution appropriating one thousand dollars ($1,000) for a monument to be erected at Hackensack, N. J., in memory of Gen. Enoch Poor, having considered the same, report the same with the following resolution:

Resolved, That it is inexpedient to legislate.

Mr. Ahern of Concord, for the Committee on Appropriations, to whom was referred An act in amendment of "An act to provide for the survey, location, and construction of the Jefferson Notch road in Jefferson, Low and Burbank's Grant, Crawford's Purchase, and Bean's Purchase, approved March 22, 1901," having considered the same, report the same with the following resolution :

Resolved, That it is inexpedient to legislate, the subject matter having been covered by a bill introduced by the committee.

Mr. French of Moultonborough, for the Committee on Railroads, to whom was referred An act in amendment of chapter 89, Session Laws of 1897, relating to passenger, freight, and railroad police, having considered the same, report the same with the following resolution :

Resolved, That it is inexpedient to legislate.

Mr. Foye of Portsmouth, for the Committee on Roads, Bridges, and Canals, to whom was referred Joint resolution in favor of the Durham Point road in the town of Durham in this state, having considered the same, report the same with the following resolution :

Resolved, That it is inexpedient to legislate.

Mr. Ahern of Concord, for the Committee on Appropriations, to whom was referred An act to aid in the reconstruction of the Magalloway road in Errol, on a practicable route, having considered the same, report the same with the following resolution :

Resolved, That it is inexpedient to legislate as the subject matter has been covered by a bill introduced by the committee.

Mr. Ahern of Concord, for the Committee on Appropriations, to whom was referred Joint resolution relating to a state highway between Massachusetts state line and Fort Point in New Castle, N. H., having considered the same, report the same with the following resolution :

Resolved, That it is inexpedient to legislate as the subject matter has been covered by a bill introduced by the committee.

Mr. Ahern of Concord, for the Committee on Appropriations, to whom was referred An act providing for the construction of certain sections of roads and the completion of a line of public highways already inaugurated by the state in the north regions of the White Mountains, having considered the same, report the same with the following resolution:

Resolved, That it is inexpedient to legislate, the subject matter having been covered by a bill reported by the committee.

Mr. French of Moultonborough, for the Committee on Railroads, to whom was referred An act to amend and extend the charter of the Manchester and Haverhill Street Railway, having considered the same, report the same with the following resolution:

Resolved, That it is inexpedient to legislate.

Mr. French of Moultonborough, for the Committee on Railroads, to whom was referred An act in regard to the rates of fare to be charged by street railway companies, etc., having considered the same, report the same with the following resolution:

Resolved, That it is inexpedient to legislate.

Mr. Ahern of Concord, for the Committee on Appropriations, to whom was referred Joint resolution in aid of changing and repairing the Dixville Notch road in Dixville, having considered the same, report the same with the following resolution:

Resolved, That it is inexpedient to legislate, the subject matter having been covered in a new bill introduced by the committee.

Mr. French of Moultonborough, for the Committee on Railroads, to whom was referred An act to incorporate the Dover & Durham Street Railway Company, having considered the same, report the same with the following resolution:

Resolved, That it is inexpedient to legislate.

Mr. Foye of Portsmouth, for the Committee on Roads, Bridges, and Canals, to whom was referred Joint resolution in favor of the Pawtuckaway Mountain road in the town of Deerfield, having considered the same, report the same with the following resolution:

Resolved, That it is inexpedient to legislate.

Mr. Foye of Portsmouth, for the Committee on Roads, Bridges, and Canals, to whom was referred Joint resolution to appropriate four hundred dollars to repair road leading from Forest Glade cemetery to Diamond Corner in city of Somersworth, having considered the same, report the same with the following resolution:

Resolved, That it is inexpedient to legislate.

Mr. Foye of Portsmouth, for the Committee on Roads, Bridges, and Canals, to whom was referred Joint resolution in aid of the highways of the town of Lee, having considered the same, report the same with the following resolution:

Resolved, That it is inexpedient to legislate.

Mr. French of Moultonborough, for the Committee on Railroads, to whom was referred An act to amend the charter of the Concord, Dover & Rochester Street Railway, having considered the same, report the same with the following resolution:

Resolved, That it is inexpedient to legislate, a substitute having been agreed upon by the parties in interest.

Mr. Foye of Portsmouth, for the Committee on Roads, Bridges, and Canals, to whom was referred Joint resolution in aid of the highways of the town of Madbury, having considered the same, report the same with the following resolution:

Resolved, That it is inexpedient to legislate.

Mr. Foye of Portsmouth, for the Committee on Roads, Bridges, and Canals, to whom was referred Joint resolution in favor of the main highway between Center Ossipee village and Effingham Falls, having considered the same, report the same with the following resolution:

Resolved, That it is inexpedient to legislate.

Mr. Foye of Portsmouth, for the Committee on Roads, Bridges, and Canals, to whom was referred Joint resolution for the appropriation of $200 for the repairing of the Pond road, so called, in the town of Clarksville, having considered the same, report the same with the following resolution:

Resolved, That it is inexpedient to legislate.

Mr. Foye of Portsmouth, for the Committee on Roads, Bridges, and Canals, to whom was referred Joint resolution in favor of mountain road in the town of Orange, having considered the same, report the same with the following resolution:

Resolved, That it is inexpedient to legislate.

Mr. Foye of Portsmouth, for the Committee on Roads, Bridges, and Canals, to whom was referred Joint resolution providing for repairs upon the Crotchet Mountain road, so called, in the town of Francestown, having considered the same, report the same with the following resolution :

Resolved, That it is inexpedient to legislate.

Mr. Foye of Portsmouth, for the Committee on Roads, Bridges, and Canals, to whom was referred Joint resolution in favor of highways and bridges in the town of Barrington, having considered the same, report the same with the following resolution :

Resolved, That it is inexpedient to legislate.

Mr. Foye of Portsmouth, for the Committee on Roads, Bridges, and Canals, to whom was referred Joint resolution in favor of the road leading from Patch's Corner to the Amherst line in the town of Hollis, having considered the same, report the same with the following resolution :

Resolved, That it is inexpedient to legislate.

Mr. Foye of Portsmouth, for the Committee on Roads, Bridges, and Canals, to whom was referred Joint resolution for the appropriation of two hundred dollars for the repairing of the highway running around Newfound lake in Hebron, having considered the same, report the same with the following resolution :

Resolved, That it is inexpedient to legislate.

Mr. Foye of Portsmouth, for the Committee on Roads, Bridges, and Canals, to whom was referred Joint resolution in favor of the main road in the town of Gilsum, having considered the same, report the same with the following resolution :

Resolved, That it is inexpedient to legislate.

Mr. Foye of Portsmouth, for the Committee on Roads, Bridges, and Canals, to whom was referred Joint resolution in favor of the Nelson road, so called, in the towns of Hancock, Harrisville, and Nelson, having considered the same, report the same with the following resolution :

Resolved, That it is inexpedient to legislate.

Mr. Foye of Portsmouth, for the Committee on Roads, Bridges, and Canals, to whom was referred Joint resolution for the appropriation of $500 for the repairing of the highways and bridges in the town of Stark, having considered the same, report the same with the following resolution :

Resolved, That it is inexpedient to legislate.

Mr. Foye of Portsmouth, for the Committee on Roads, Bridges, and Canals, to whom was referred Joint resolution to aid in repairing the highway around Granite lake, so called, lying in the towns of Nelson and Stoddard, having considered the same, report the same with the following resolution :

Resolved, That it is inexpedient to legislate.

Mr. Foye of Portsmouth, for the Committee on Roads, Bridges, and Canals, to whom was referred Joint resolution for the repair of the stage road in Hampstead, having considered the same, report the same with the following resolution :

Resolved, That it is inexpedient to legislate.

Mr. Foye of Portsmouth, for the Committee on Roads, Bridges, and Canals, to whom was referred Joint resolution to appropriate a sum of money to repair the River road near North Rochester, having considered the same, report the same with the following resolution :

Resolved, That it is inexpedient to legislate.

Mr. Foye of Portsmouth, for the Committee on Roads, Bridges, and Canals, to whom was referred Joint resolution in favor of highways in the town of Salem, having considered the same, report the same with the following resolution :

Resolved, That it is inexpedient to legislate.

Mr. Foye of Portsmouth, for the Committee on Roads, Bridges, and Canals, to whom was referred Joint resolution to appropriate a sum not exceeding five hundred dollars to be expended on Blue Job Mountain road in Strafford, having considered the same, report the same with the following resolution :

Resolved, That it is inexpedient to. legislate.

Mr. Foye of Portsmouth, for the Committee on Roads, Bridges, and Canals, to whom was referred Joint resolution in favor of Sand road in the town of Wentworth, having considered the same, report the same with the following resolution :

Resolved, That it is inexpedient to legislate.

Mr. Foye of Portsmouth, for the Committee on Roads, Bridges, and Canals, to whom was referred Joint resolution for aid in keeping in repair the road in Sharon from the brick schoolhouse to the Peterborough line on the McCoy road, having considered the same, report the same with the following resolution :

Resolved, That it is inexpedient to legislate.

Mr. Foye of Portsmouth, for the Committee on Roads, Bridges, and Canals, to whom was referred Joint resolution for an appropriation for repair of highway in Plaistow, N. H., leading from Atkinson Depot to the Haverhill line, having considered the same, report the same with the following resolution :

Resolved, That it is inexpedient to legislate.

The reports were severally accepted and the resolutions reported by the committees adopted.

Mr. Foye of Portsmouth, for the Committee on Appropriations, to whom was referred An act providing for a state system of highway construction and improvement and for the appointment of highway engineers, having considered the same, report the same with the following resolution :

Resolved, That the bill ought to pass.

Mr. Quimby of Meredith, for the Committee on Appropriations, to whom was referred An act in relation to the salary of the judge of probate for the county of Grafton, having considered the same, report the same with the following resolution :

Resolved, That the bill ought to pass.

Mr. Quimby of Meredith, for the Committee on Appropriations, to whom was referred An act to amend sections 14 and 15, chapter 286 of the Public Statutes, relating to the salaries of the judge and register of probate for Belknap county, having considered the same report the same with the following resolution :

Resolved, That the bill ought to pass.

Mr. Pike of Haverhill, for the Committee on Appropriations, to whom was referred An act relating to the salary of the judge of probate of the county of Sullivan, having considered the same, report the same with the following resolution :

Resolved, That the bill ought to pass.

The reports were severally accepted and the bills ordered to a third reading.

Mr. Woodman of Concord, for the Committee on Judiciary, to whom was referred An act in relation to the settlement of paupers, having considered the same, report the same in a new draft with the following resolution :

Resolved, That the bill in new draft ought to pass.

The report was accepted and the bill in new draft read a first time and ordered to a second reading. On motion of Mr. Ahern of Concord the rules were suspended and the bill read a second time by its title. The bill was then laid upon the table to be printed.

Mr. French of Moultonborough, for the Committee on Railroads, reported the following entitled bill, " An act to incorporate the Dunbarton and Goffstown Street Railway Company," with the resolution that the bill ought to pass.

The report was accepted. On motion of Mr. French of Moultonborough, the rules were suspended and the bill read a first time by its title. The bill was then ordered to a second reading. On motion of the same gentleman, the rules were further suspended and the bill read a second time by its title. The bill was then laid upon the table to be printed. On motion of the same gentleman, the rules were suspended and the printing of the bill dispensed with. The bill was then ordered to a third reading. On motion of the same gentleman, the rules were further suspended and the bill read a third time by its title and passed and sent to the Senate for concurrence.

Mr. French of Moultonborough, for the Committee on Railroads, reported the following entitled bill, " An act to incorporate the Concord, Dover & Rochester Street Railway," with the resolution that the bill ought to pass.

The report was accepted. On motion of Mr. French of Moultonborough, the rules were suspended and the bill read a first time by its title. The bill was then ordered to a second reading. On motion of the same gentleman, the rules were suspended and the bill read a second time by its title. The bill was then laid upon the table to be printed. On motion of the same gentleman, the rules were suspended and the printing of the bill dispensed with. The bill was then ordered to a third reading. On motion of the same gentleman, the rules were further suspended and the bill read a third time by its title and passed and sent to the Senate for concurrence.

Mr. French of Moultonborough, for the Committee on Railroads, reported the following entitled bill, "An act to incorporate the Manchester & Haverhill Street Railway Company," with the resolution that the bill ought to pass.

The report was accepted. On motion of Mr. French of Moultonborough, the rules were suspended and the bill read a first time by its title. The bill was then ordered to a second reading. On motion of the same gentleman, the rules were suspended and the bill read a second time by its title. The bill was then laid upon the table to be printed. On motion of the same gentleman, the rules were further suspended and the printing of the bill dispensed with. The bill was then ordered to a third reading. On motion of the same gentleman, the rules were further suspended and the bill read a third time by its title and passed and sent to the Senate for concurrence.

Mr. Woodman of Concord, for the Committee on Judiciary, reported the following entitled bill, "An act in amendment of the charter of the Exeter Gas, Electric Light and Power Company," with the resolution that the bill ought to pass.

The report was accepted and the bill read a first time and ordered to a second reading. On motion of Mr. Small of Rochester, the rules were suspended and the bill read a second time by its title. The bill was then laid upon the table to be printed. On motion of the same gentleman, the rules were suspended and the printing of the bill dispensed with. The bill was then ordered to a third reading. On motion of the same gentleman, the rules were further suspended and the bill read a third time by its title and passed and sent to the Senate for concurrence.

Mr. Tallant of Pembroke, for the Committee on Revision of Statutes, reported the following entitled bill, "An act in amendment of section 7 of chapter 59 of the Public Statutes, and section 13 of chapter 60 of the Public Statutes, relating to the assessment and collection of taxes," with the resolution that the bill ought to pass.

The report was accepted. On motion of Mr. Ahern of Concord, the rules were suspended and the bill read a first time by its title. The bill was then ordered to a second reading. On motion of the same gentleman, the rules were further suspended and the bill read a second time by its title. The bill was then laid upon the table to be printed.

Mr. Gowing of Dublin, for the Committee on Revision of Statutes. reported the following entitled bill, "An act in amendment of section 7, chapter 63 of the Laws of 1897, entitled 'An act to regulate the licensing and registration of physicians and surgeons,'" with the resolution that the bill ought to pass.

The report was accepted and the bill read a first time and ordered to a second reading. On motion of Mr. French of Moultonborough, the rules were suspended and the bill read a second time by its title. The bill was then laid upon the table to be printed. On motion of Mr. Smith of Peterborough, the rules were suspended and the printing of the bill dispensed with. The bill was then ordered to a third reading. On motion of Mr. Howe of Hanover, the rules were suspended and the bill read a third time by its title and passed and sent to the Senate for concurrence.

Mr. French of Moultonborough, for the Committee on Railroads, to whom was referred An act to incorporate the Mt. Belknap Railroad, having considered the same, report the same in a new draft with the following resolution:

Resolved, That the bill in the new draft ought to pass.

The report was accepted. On motion of Mr. French of Moultonborough the rules were suspended and the bill read a first time by its title. The bill was then ordered to a second reading. On motion of the same gentleman, the rules were suspended and the bill read a second time by its title. The bill was then laid upon the table to be printed. On motion of the same gentleman, the rules were suspended and the printing of the bill dispensed with. The bill was then ordered to a third reading. On motion of the same gentleman, the rules were suspended and the bill read a third time by its title and passed. On motion of the same gentleman, the title was amended by striking out the word "Railroad" and inserting in place thereof the words, "Electric Railway Company," so that the title as amended should read, "An act to incorporate the Mount Belknap Electric Railway Company." The bill was then sent to the Senate for concurrence.

Mr. French of Moultonborough, for the Committee on Railroads, to whom was referred An act to incorporate the Manchester, Candia & Deerfield Street Railway Company, having considered the same, report the same in a new draft with the following resolution:

Resolved, That the bill in new draft ought to pass.

The report was accepted. On motion of Mr. French of Moultonborough, the rules were suspended and the bill in new draft read a first time by its title. The bill was then ordered to a second reading. On motion of the same gentleman, the rules were suspended and the bill read a second time by its title. The bill was then laid upon the table to be printed. On motion of the same gentleman, the rules were suspended and the printing of the bill dispensed with. The bill was then ordered to a third reading. On motion of the same gentleman, the rules were further suspended and the bill read a third time by its title and passed. On motion of the same gentleman, the title was amended by striking out the word "Manchester," so that the title as amended should read, "An act to incorporate the Candia & Deerfield Street Railway Company." The bill was then sent to the Senate for concurrence.

Mr. Davenport of Bath, for the Committee on Appropriations, to whom was referred Joint resolution to provide for the treatment of indigent consumptives, having considered the same, report the same with the following resolution:

Resolved, That the joint resolution ought to pass.

The report was accepted and the joint resolution ordered to a third reading.

On motion of Mr. Bell of Woodstock, the rules were suspended and the joint resolution read a third time.

The question being,

Shall the joint resolution pass?

(Discussion ensued.)

Mr. Fontaine of Allenstown moved that the joint resolution be laid upon the table.

On a *viva voce* vote the motion did not prevail.

The question being,

Shall the joint resolution pass?

On a *viva voce* vote the joint resolution passed and was sent to the Senate for concurrence.

Mr. Small of Rochester, for the Committee on Judiciary, to whom was referred An act relating to the time required for filing notice of intention of marriage and the consent of parents to the marriage of minors, having considered the same, report the same with an amendment, and the resolution that the bill as amended ought to pass:

Amend section 1 by inserting after the word " shall " in the second line of said section the words, " in case either of the parties is a non-resident of this state," and by striking out all after the word " sections " in the fourth line, so that said section as amended shall read:

SECTION 1. The notice of intention of marriage required by sections 5 and 6 of chapter 174 of the Public Statutes shall, in case either of the parties is a non-resident of this state, be filed five days before the clerk shall issue a certificate setting forth the facts as required by said sections.

The report was accepted, the amendment adopted, and the bill laid upon the table to be printed.

MESSAGE FROM THE SENATE.

A message from the Honorable Senate, by its clerk, announced that the Senate concurs with the House of Representatives in the passage of the following entitled bills:

An act annexing certain islands in Lake Winnipesaukee to the town of Tuftonborough.

An act to amend section 1 of chapter 46, Session Laws of 1895, relating to annual enumeration of school children.

An act to incorporate the History Commission of Concord.

An act in amendment of "An act to incorporate the Society of Social Friends," approved June 29, 1826, "An act to incorporate the United Fraternity," approved July 6, 1827, and "An act to incorporate the Philotechnic Society of the Chandler Scientific Department of Dartmouth College," approved July 13, 1854, and to authorize the calling of meetings of said corporations respectively.

An act to change the name of the Manchester Heating and Lighting Company of Manchester, N. H.

The message also announced that the Senate concurs with the House of Representatives in the passage of the following bills and joint resolutions with amendments, in the passage of which amendments it asks the concurrence of the House of Representatives:

An act in amendment of chapter 107 of the Session Laws of 1901, relating to the inspection of milk.

Amend section 1 of said bill by striking out all after the word " follows," in the second line of said section, and insert instead thereof the following: " By adding at the end of said section the words, ' provided, however, that any person selling only the product of his own cows shall be exempt from paying any fee for such license,' so that said section as amended shall read : "

SECTION 1.   That section 4 of chapter 107 of the Laws of 1901 be amended as follows: By adding at the end of said section the words, " provided, however, that any person selling only the product of his own cows shall be exempt from paying any fee for such license," so that said section as amended shall read :

" SECT. 4.   Whoever goes about in carriages or makes a business of selling milk, skim-milk or cream, in any such city or town, or offering for sale, or having in his possession with intent to sell, milk, skim-milk or cream, unless a license has first been obtained as provided in the preceding sections, shall be fined not more than ten dollars for the first offense ; and for any subsequent offense he shall be fined fifty dollars, or be imprisoned not more than sixty days, or both ; provided, however, that any person selling only the product of his own cows shall be exempt from paying any fee for such license."

Further amend said bill by adding the following section :

SECT. 2.   All acts and parts of acts inconsistent with this act are hereby repealed, and this act shall take effect upon its passage.

On motion of Mr. Woodman of Concord, the amendments were concurred in.

An act to amend chapter 243 of the Laws of 1901, creating the Grafton Improvement, Manufacturing and Power Company.

Amend section 5 by inserting after the word " river " and before the word " in " in the last line of said section the words, " in as free and convenient a manner as is afforded by the river."

On motion of Mr. Remich of Littleton, the amendment was concurred in.

Joint resolution providing for the repairs and construction of certain state highways, certain highways in unincorporated places, and certain roads in places where such roads cannot be maintained by any local municipality.

Amend by adding at the end thereof the following :

"That the sum of one hundred dollars ($100) be appropriated for repairing the Crotchet Mountain road, so called, in the town of Francestown, one half to be expended in 1903,. and one half in 1904."

On motion of Mr. Remich of Littleton, the amendment was concurred in.

SECOND READINGS.

An act in amendment of section 23 of chapter 79 of the Laws of 1901, in relation to fines.

An act to revive the charter of the Colebrook Water Company, approved February 23, 1897.

Severally read a second time and laid upon the table to be printed.

BILLS FORWARDED.

An act in amendment of section 56, chapter 79 of the Laws of 1901, relating to fish and game.

An act relating to the protection and preservation of ornamental and shade trees in the highways.

Severally taken from the table and ordered to a third reading.

On motion of Mr. Woodman of Concord,—

Resolved, That the Committee on Judiciary be directed to make examination as to what changes in the law are made necessary or expedient by the recent adoption of amendments to the constitution and to report by bill or otherwise.

Mr. Ahern of Concord moved that the House reconsider the vote whereby the report of the Committee on Appropriations, that it is inexpedient to legislate upon the following entitled bill, " An act in amendment of chapter 134 of the Public Statutes, relating to the practice of dentistry," was adopted. On a *viva voce* vote the motion prevailed and the vote was reconsidered. The question being upon the adoption of the resolution reported by the committee, on motion of Mr. Ahern of Concord, the bill was recommitted to the Committee on Appropriations.

On motion of Mr. Smith of Peterborough, the following entitled bill, " An act in amendment of section 1, chapter 31 of the Laws of 1897, entitled ' An act in amendment of section 6 of chapter 83 of the Public Statutes, in relation to the settlement of paupers,' " was taken from the table.

The question being,

Shall the bill be read a third time?

On a *viva voce* vote the bill was ordered to a third reading.

On motion of Mr. Ahern of Concord, the following entitled bill, " An act to amend chapter 96 of the Session Laws of 1901, relating to high schools," was taken from the table. The second reading being in order, on motion of Mr. Ahern of Concord, the bill was read a second time by its title. The bill was then laid upon the table to be printed.

On motion of Mr. Smith of Peterborough, the following entitled bill, " An act in amendment of section 1, chapter 83 of the Public Statutes, entitled ' Settlement of paupers,' " was taken from the table.

The question being,

Shall the bill be read a third time?

On a *viva voce* vote the bill was ordered to a third reading.

On motion of Mr. Remich of Littleton, the following joint resolution, " Joint resolution for an appropriation for the ben-

34

efit of the New Hampshire College of Agriculture and the Mechanic Arts," was taken from the table.

The question being,

Shall the joint resolution be read a third time?

On a *viva voce* vote the joint resolution was ordered to a third reading.

On motion of Mr. Bragg of Errol, at 12.32 the House adjourned.

AFTERNOON.

The House met at 3 o'clock.

THIRD READINGS.

An act in relation to the salary of the judge of probate for the county of Grafton.

An act to amend section 14 and section 15, chapter 286 of the Public Statutes, relating to the salaries of the judge and register of probate for Belknap county.

An act relating to the salary of the judge of probate of the county of Sullivan.

An act relating to the protection and preservation of ornamental and shade trees in the highways.

An act in amendment of section 1, chapter 31 of the Laws of 1897, entitled " An act in amendment of section 6 of chapter 83 of the Public Statutes, in relation to the settlement of paupers."

An act in amendment of section 1, chapter 83 of the Public Statutes, entitled " Settlement of paupers."

Severally read a third time and passed and sent to the Senate for concurrence.

An act in amendment of section 56, chapter 79 of the Laws of 1901, relating to fish and game.

Read a third time and passed and sent to the secretary of state to be engrossed.

Joint resolution for an appropriation for the benefit of the New Hampshire College of Agriculture and the Mechanic Arts.

Read a third time.

The question being,

Shall the joint resolution pass?

On motion of Mr. Taggart of Manchester, the joint resolution was laid upon the table and made the special order for Tuesday, March 24, at 3 o'clock.

An act providing for a state system of highway construction and improvement and for the appointment of highway engineers.

The third reading being in order, on motion of Mr. French of Moultonborough, the rules were suspended and the bill read a third time by its title.

The question being,

Shall the bill pass?

On motion of Mr. Filion of Manchester, the bill was laid upon the table.

Mr. Donahue of Manchester moved that the House reconsider the vote whereby the report of the Committee on Appropriations that it is inexpedient to legislate upon the following joint resolution, "Joint resolution appropriating one thousand dollars for a monument to be erected at Hackensack, N. J., in memory of General Enoch Poor," was adopted. On a *viva voce* vote the motion prevailed and the vote was reconsidered. The question being upon the adoption of the resolution reported by the committee, on motion of Mr. Donahue of Manchester, the joint resolution was recommitted to the Committee on Appropriations.

MESSAGE FROM THE SENATE.

A message from the Honorable Senate, by its clerk, announced that the Senate has passed bills with the following titles, in the passage of which it asks the concurrence of the House of Representatives:

An act to incorporate the Evangelical Congregational Church of Plaistow and the North Parish of Haverhill.

An act for the relief of the town of New Castle.

Severally read a first and second time and referred to the Committee on Judiciary.

An act in amendment of section 2 of chapter 32 of the Laws of 1895, entitled "An act in relation to printing the reports of certain state officers."

An act in amendment of section 2 of chapter 5 of the Public Statutes, relating to the publication and distribution of statutes, journals, and reports.

Severally read a first and second time and referred to the Committee on Revision of Statutes.

On motion of Mr. Filion of Manchester,—

Resolved, That when the House adjourns this afternoon it be to meet Monday evening at 8 o'clock.

On motion of Mr. Filion of Manchester, at 3.25 the House adjourned.

MONDAY, MARCH 23, 1903.

The House met at 8 o'clock in the evening, according to adjournment.

On motion of Mr. Converse of Lyme, at 8.01 the House adjourned.

TUESDAY, MARCH 24, 1903.

The House met at 11 o'clock.

Prayer was offered by the chaplain.

COMMITTEE REPORTS.

Mr. Cavanaugh of Manchester, for the Committee on Judiciary, to whom was referred An act to exempt certain property of the Manchester Young Men's Christian Association from taxation, having considered the same, report the same with the following resolution :

Resolved, That the bill ought to pass.

The report was accepted and the bill laid upon the table to be printed. On motion of Mr. Chase of Manchester, the rules were suspended and the printing of the bill dispensed with. The bill was then ordered to a third reading. On motion of the same gentleman, the rules were suspended and the bill read a third time and passed and sent to the secretary of state to be engrossed.

Mr. Cavanaugh of Manchester, for the Committee on Judiciary, to whom was referred An act authorizing the city of Nashua to exempt the Highland Spring Sanatorium Company from taxation, having considered the same, report the same with the following resolution :

Resolved, That the bill ought to pass.

The report was accepted and the bill laid upon the table to be printed.

Mr. Batchelder of Keene, for the Committee on Judiciary, to whom was referred An act to create and establish an inspector of factories, having considered the same, report the same with the following resolution :

Resolved, That it is inexpedient to legislate.

The report was accepted. The question being upon the adoption of the resolution reported by the committee, on motion of Mr. Lynch of Manchester, the bill and report were laid upon the table.

Mr. Roby of Concord, for a majority of the special committee consisting of the delegation from the city of Concord, to whom was referred An act to extend the Union school district to include the city of Concord, having considered the same, report the same in a new draft with the following resolution :

Resolved, That the bill in new draft ought to pass.

Mr. Durgin of Concord, for a minority of the special committee consisting of the delegation from the city of Concord, to whom was referred An act to extend the Union school district to include the city of Concord, having considered the same, submit the following report :

We, the undersigned, object to the passage of this bill, inasmuch as it does not provide that the same shall be in force when accepted by vote of the several districts interested, and because the provision of the Public Statutes of the state, governing the union of school districts, is sufficient to effect such union when desired by the said district.

We, therefore, would report the following resolution :

Resolved, That it is inexpedient.

> Eddie C. Durgin,
> Joseph E. Symonds,
> Albert P. Davis,
> Ross W. Cate.

The report of the majority of the commitee was accepted and the bill in its new draft read a first time and ordered to a second reading. On motion of Mr. Ahern of Concord, the rules were suspended and the bill read a second time by its title. The bill was then laid upon the table to be printed. On motion of Mr. Ahern of Concord, the rules were suspended and the printing of the bill dispensed with. Mr. Cate of Concord offered the following amendment:

Amend said bill by striking out all of section 6 and insert in place thereof the following: " SECT. 6. This act shall take effect and be in force only when accepted by a majority vote of those present and voting of each of said districts at any legal meeting of the same called for that purpose."

The question being upon the adoption of the amendment,

(Discussion ensued.)

Mr. Ahern of Concord called for a yea and nay vote, and the call pending, moved that the amendment and call be laid upon the table. On a *viva voce* vote the motion prevailed and the amendment and call for a yea and nay vote were laid upon the table.

Mr. Fifield of Conway, for a majority of the Committee on Education, to whom was referred An act requiring state certification of teachers of public schools, having considered the same, report the same with the following resolution:

Resolved, That it is inexpedient to legislate.

Mr. Badger of Newington, for a minority of the Committee on Education, to whom was referred An act requiring state certification of teachers of public schools, having considered the same, report the same in a new draft with the following resolution:

Resolved, That the bill in new draft ought to pass.

Mr. Jones of New Ipswich moved that the report of the minority of the committee be substituted for that of the majority. The question being upon the adoption of the motion,

(Discussion ensued.)

On motion of Mr. Taggart of Manchester, the bill and reports were laid upon the table.

Mr. Cavanaugh of Manchester, for the special committee consisting of the delegation from the city of Manchester, to whom was referred An act enabling the city of Manchester to build and operate an electric lighting plant for the purpose of lighting its streets and public buildings, having considered the same, report the same in a new draft with the following resolution :

Resolved, That the bill in new draft ought to pass.

The report was accepted and the bill in new draft read a first time and ordered to a second reading. On motion of Mr. Filion of Manchester, the rules were suspended and the bill read a second time by its title. The bill was then laid upon the table to be printed. On motion of the same gentleman, the rules were suspended and the printing of the bill dispensed with. The bill was then ordered to a third reading. On motion of the same gentleman, the rules were further suspended and the bill read a third time by its title and passed and sent to the Senate for concurrence.

Mr. Cavanaugh of Manchester, for the Committee on Judiciary, reported the following entitled bill, " An act to amend chapter 40, Laws of 1893, relating to inspectors of buildings," with the resolution that the bill ought to pass.

The report was accepted and the bill read a first time and ordered to a second reading. On motion of Mr. Batchelder of Keene, the rules were suspended and the bill read a second time by its title. The bill was then laid upon the table to be printed. On motion of the same gentleman, the rules were further suspended and the printing of the bill dispensed with. The bill was then ordered to a third reading. On motion of the same gentleman, the rules were suspended and the bill read a third time by its title and passed and sent to the Senate for concurrence.

Mr. Fifield of Conway, for the Committee on Education, reported the following entitled bill, " An act to sever certain residences from the school district of the town of Wilmot and to annex the same to the school district of the town of New London," with the resolution that the bill ought to pass.

The report was accepted and the bill read a first time and ordered to a second reading. On motion of Mr. Fox of

Marlow, the rules were suspended and the bill read a second time by its title. The bill was then laid upon the table to be printed. On motion of the same gentleman, the rules were suspended and the printing of the bill dispensed with. The bill was then ordered to a third reading. On motion of the same gentleman, the rules were further suspended and the bill read a third time by its title and passed and sent to the Senate for concurrence.

BILLS FORWARDED.

An act to revive the charter of the Colebrook Water Company, approved February 23, 1897.

Taken from the table and ordered to a third reading. On motion of Mr. Lennon of Stratford, the rules were suspended and the bill read a third time and passed and sent to the Senate for concurrence.

An act relating to the time required for filing notice of intention of marriage and the consent of parents to the marriage of minors.

Taken from the table and ordered to a third reading. On motion of Mr. Small of Rochester, the rules were suspended and the bill read a third time by its title and passed. On motion of Mr. Small of Rochester, the title was amended by striking out the words, " and the consent of parents to the marriage of minors." The bill was then sent to the Senate for concurrence in the amendments.

An act to abolish capital punishment.

An act to amend chapters 2 and 112 of the Public Statutes, and to provide for the better enforcement of the liquor laws.

An act to enlarge the powers of towns and cities.

An act in amendment of section 7 of chapter 59 of the Public Statutes, and section 13 of chapter 60 of the Public Statutes, relating to the assessment and collection of taxes.

An act in amendment of section 23 of chapter 79 of the Laws of 1901, in relation to fines.

An act to incorporate the New Hampshire Beneficiary Union.

An act to amend chapter 96 of the Session Laws of 1901, relating to high schools.

An act in relation to the settlement of paupers.

An act to establish water-works in the town of Greenville.

Severally taken from the table and ordered to a third reading.

On motion of Mr. Bussell of Nashua, the order whereby the following entitled bill, "An act authorizing the city of Nashua to exempt the Highland Spring Sanatorium Company from taxation," was laid upon the table to be printed, was rescinded. The bill was then ordered to a third reading. On motion of the same gentleman, the rules were suspended and the bill read a third time by its title and passed and sent to the Senate for concurrence.

On motion of Mr. Whitcher of Haverhill, the following entitled bill, "An act to provide for the representation of the state of New Hampshire and the exhibition of its products and attractions at the Louisiana Purchase Exposition at St. Louis in 1904," was taken from the table. On motion of the same gentleman, the rules were suspended and the bill placed back upon its second reading and recommitted to the Committee on Appropriations.

On motion of Mr. Barr of Manchester, the following entitled bill, "An act to provide suitable armory quarters for the National Guard at Manchester," was taken from the table.

The question being,

Shall the bill pass?

(Discussion ensued.)

On motion of Mr. Barrett of Dover, the bill was laid upon the table and made the special order for Wednesday, March 25, at 11 o'clock.

MESSAGE FROM THE SENATE.

A message from the Honorable Senate, by its clerk, announced that the Senate concurs with the House of Representatives in the passage of the following bill, with amendment, in the passage of which amendment it asks the concurrence of the House of Representatives:

An act to provide, in common with the state of Vermont, for the acquisition, building, and maintenance of free bridges across the Connecticut river.

Amend by inserting after the word " devolve " in section 7, line 6, the word " equally."

On motion of Mr. Small of Rochester, the amendment was concurred in. The bill was then sent to the secretary of state to be engrossed.

The message further announced that the Senate concurs with the House of Representatives in the passage of the following entitled bills and joint resolutions :

An act to incorporate the History Commission of Concord.

An act in amendment of section 59, chapter 79 of the Session Laws of 1901, relating to the taking of black bass.

An act in amendment of sections 7 to 10, chapter 27, Laws of 1895, relating to street railways.

An act in amendment of section 13, chapter 27 of the Pamphlet Laws of 1895, relating to street railways.

An act in amendment of section 17 of chapter 285 of the Public Statutes, relating to the state prison.

An act to amend the charter of the Bennington Water-Works Company.

An act to incorporate the New Ipswich, Greenville & Wilton Electric Railway Company.

An act to incorporate the Chester, Fremont & Brentwood Street Railway Company.

An act to incorporate the Meredith & Ossipee Railroad Company.

An act to incorporate the Warren Water and Light Company.

An act to incorporate the Sons of Veterans' Memorial Hall Association.

An act in amendment of section 13, chapter 59, Laws of 1895, relating to the bond of the adjutant-general.

An act fixing office hours in state offices.

An act to incorporate the Epping, Brentwood & Kingston Street Railway.

An act to incorporate the Derry & Salem Street Railway Company.

An act to authorize the Dover & Eliot Street Railway Company to transfer their properties and franchises to the Berwick, Eliot & York Street Railway.

An act relating to the salary of the judge of probate for the county of Carroll.

An act to incorporate the Swift River Railroad Company.

An act to incorporate the Prudential Fire Insurance Company.

An act to incorporate the Uncanoonuc Incline Railway and Development Company.

An act annexing certain islands in Lake Winnipesaukee to the town of Tuftonborough.

An act to incorporate the Maynesboro Fire Insurance Company.

An act to incorporate the Bellman Club of Manchester, N. H.

An act to amend section 1 of chapter 46, Session Laws of 1895, relating to annual enumeration of school children.

An act to incorporate the Dover Loan and Trust Company.

An act to incorporate the Milton Mills & Union Electric Railway Company.

An act to require non-residents to secure a license before hunting deer within the state of New Hampshire, and providing penalties for violation of its provisions.

Joint resolution in favor of William J. Patch.

Joint resolution in favor of Green's basin in Lake Winnipesaukee.

Joint resolution in favor of the widow of Benjamin F. March of Mason.

Joint resolution in favor of the New Hampshire School for Feeble-Minded Children.

Joint resolution appropriating nine thousand dollars for additions and repairs to the Industrial School.

Joint resolution in favor of Horace S. Cummings.

Joint resolution in favor of placing and maintaining buoys and lights in Lake Winnipesaukee and adjacent waters.

SPECIAL ORDER.

(Mr. Small of Rochester in the chair.)

Mr. Fay of Keene called for the special order, it being the following entitled bill, "An act in amendment of section 19, chapter 57 of the Public Statutes, relating to the annual invoice of polls and taxable property."

The question being upon the motion of Mr. Fay of Keene, that the report of the minority of the committee be substituted for that of the majority,

(Discussion ensued.)

At 12.50, on motion of Mr. Fay of Keene, the House took a recess until 2.45 o'clock.

(After recess.)

(The Speaker in the chair.)

Discussion was resumed upon the motion of Mr. Fay of Keene, that the report of the minority of the committee be substituted for that of the majority of the committee.

Mr. Whitcher of Haverhill moved the previous question.

The question being,

Shall the main question be now put?

On a *viva voce* vote the previous question was ordered. The question being upon the adoption of the motion of Mr. Fay of Keene, that the report of the minority of the committee be substituted for that of the majority, on a *viva voce* vote the motion prevailed.

Mr. Hamlin of Charlestown demanded a yea and nay vote.

(Discussion ensued.)

Mr. Hamlin of Charlestown withdrew his call for a yea and nay vote but demanded a division. A division being had, the vote was declared to be manifestly in the affirmative and the report of the minority of the committee was substituted for that of the majority. The bill in new draft reported by the minority of the committee was then read a first time and ordered to a second reading.

On motion of Mr. Filion of Manchester, the following entitled bill, "An act providing for a state system of highway construction and improvement and for the appointment of highway engineers," was taken from the table.

The question being,

Shall the bill pass?

On a *viva voce* vote the bill passed and was sent to the Senate for concurrence.

On motion of Mr. French of Moultonborough, the following entitled bill, "An act to establish a new apportionment for the assessment of public taxes," was taken from the table.

The question being,

Shall the bill be read a third time?

On a *viva voce* vote the bill was ordered to a third reading.

On motion of Mr. Morgan of Manchester, the following entitled bill, "An act in amendment of section 20 of chapter 27 of the Public Statutes, entitled ' County commissioners,' " was taken from the table. The question being upon the adoption of the motion of Mr. Scammon of Exeter, that the bill be indefinitely postponed, Mr. Scammon withdrew his motion. The question being upon the adoption of the motion of Mr. Morgan of Manchester, that the rules be suspended and the printing of the bill dispensed with, Mr. Morgan withdrew his motion. Mr. Morgan of Manchester offered the following amendments:

Amend section 1 of said bill, as amended, by striking out in the fourth line thereof the words " four dollars a day " and inserting in place thereof the words " twelve hundred dollars per year payable in equal quarterly instalments."

Further amend said section 1 by striking out in the 9th line thereof the words " four dollars a day " and inserting in place thereof the words " twelve hundred dollars a year payable in equal quarterly instalments," so that said section 1 as amended shall read as follows:

Section 1. Section 20 of chapter 27 of the Public Statutes, is hereby amended by inserting after the words " three dollars a day " in the fourth line of said section the words " except in the county of Hillsborough where each commissioner shall be paid twelve hundred dollars per year payable in equal quarterly instalments," so that said section as amended shall read as follows: " Sect. 20. Each county commissioner shall be paid by the county treasurer for his services, when employed in business of the county and in inspecting the taxable property of towns, as provided in the preceding section, three dollars a day, except in the county of Hillsborough where each commissioner shall be paid twelve hundred dollars per year payable in equal quarterly instalments, and a reasonable sum for all necessary expenses, upon order of the supreme court, his accounts having been first audited by the court."

Add after section 1 a new section which shall be numbered "two," and which shall read as follows:

SECT. 2. All acts and parts of acts inconsistent with this act are hereby repealed and this act shall take effect April 1st, 1903.

The question being upon the adoption of the amendments,

(Discussion ensued.)

Mr. Chase of Manchester moved the previous question.

The question being,

Shall the main question be now put?

On a *viva voce* vote the previous question was ordered. The question being upon the adoption of the amendment offered by Mr. Morgan of Manchester, on a *viva voce* vote the amendment was adopted. The bill was then ordered to a third reading.

In accordance with the resolution adopted at the morning session, Friday, March 13, Mr. Libby of Gorham called for the special report of the Committee on Appropriations in regard to the appropriations already made and pending at the present session. The report was submitted as follows:

Bills that have been referred to the appropriation committee to date, extraordinary expenses amount to		$835,002.29
Bills reported as ought to pass,	$566,000.29	
Bills cut down from amount asked for,	13,550.00	
Bills reported inexpedient,	176,000.00	
Bills in hands of committee,	79,452.00	
		$835,002.29

The report was accepted.

Mr. Howe of Barrington asked unanimous consent to move a reconsideration of the vote whereby the report of the Committee on Appropriations that it is inexpedient to legislate upon the following joint resolution, " Joint resolution in favor of highways and bridges in town of Barrington," was adopted. Objection was made and unanimous consent was therefore refused.

On motion of Mr. Whittemore of Dover, at 4.55 the House adjourned.

AFTERNOON.

The House was called to order in afternoon session immediately upon adjournment of the morning session.

LEAVE OF ABSENCE.

Mr. Crossman of Lisbon was granted leave of absence for the balance of the week on account of the serious illness of his associate in practice.

THIRD READINGS.

An act to establish a new apportionment for the assessment of public taxes.

The third reading being in order, Mr. Ahern of Concord moved that the rules be suspended and the bill read a third time by its title. The question being upon the adoption of the motion,

(Discussion ensued.)

On a *viva voce* vote the motion prevailed and the bill was read a third time by its title and passed and sent to the Senate for concurrence.

An act to abolish capital punishment.

Read a third time.

The question being,

Shall the bill pass?

On a *viva voce* vote the bill was refused a passage. Mr. Ahern of Concord called for a division, and the call pending, moved that the bill and call for a division be laid upon the table and made the special order for Wednesday, March 25, at 3 o'clock. On a *viva voce* vote the motion prevailed and the bill and call for division were laid upon the table and made the special order for Wednesday, March 25, at 3 o'clock.

An act to establish water-works in the town of Greenville.

The third reading being in order, on motion of Mr. Brown

of Greenville, the rules were suspended and the bill read a
third time by its title. The bill was then passed and sent to
the Senate for concurrence.

An act to amend chapter 96 of the Session Laws of 1901,
relating to high schools.

The third reading having begun, on motion of Mr. Nason
of Dover, the further reading was dispensed with. The bill
was then passed and sent to the Senate for concurrence.

An act in relation to the settlement of paupers.

An act to enlarge the powers of towns and cities.

An act in amendment of section 7 of chapter 59 of the Public
Statutes, and section 13 of chapter 60 of the Public Statutes,
relating to the assessment and collection of taxes.

An act in amendment of section 23 of chapter 78 of the
Laws of 1901, in relation to fines.

An act to incorporate the New Hampshire Beneficiary Union.

An act in amendment of section 20 of chapter 27 of the
Public Statutes, entitled " County commissioners."

Severally read a third time and passed and sent to the Senate
for concurrence.

An act to amend chapters 2 and 112 of the Public Statutes,
and to provide for the better enforcement of the liquor laws.

The third reading being in order, on motion of Mr. Remich
of Littleton, the rules were suspended and the bill read a third
time by its title. The bill was then passed and sent to the
Senate for concurrence.

SPECIAL ORDER.

Mr. Nason of Dover called for the special order, it being
the following joint resolution, " Joint resolution for an appropriation for the benefit of the New Hampshire College of
Agriculture and the Mechanic Arts."

The question being,

Shall the joint resolution pass?

On a *viva voce* vote the joint resolution passed and was
sent to the Senate for concurrence.

On motion of Mr. Hoyt of Sandwich the following entitled
bill, "An act for the better preservation of highways and accommodating public travel," was taken from the table. On

motion of the same gentleman the rules were suspended and the bill put back upon its second reading.

Mr. Hoyt of Sandwich offered the following amendment:

Amend section 4 by adding after the word "those," as found in line 8, the words "shrubs marked or reserved by order of the tree warden growing."

The question being upon the adoption of the amendment,

(Discussion ensued.)

On a *viva voce* vote the amendment was adopted.   The bill was then ordered to a third reading.

On motion of Mr. Howe of Hanover the following entitled bill, "An act to amend chapter 60, section 3 of the Statute Laws of 1891, relating to dog licenses," was taken from the table.

The question being upon the adoption of the amendment offered by Mr. Howe of Hanover,

(Discussion ensued.)

On a *viva voce* vote the amendment was not adopted.   The bill was then ordered to a third reading.

On motion of Mr. Pattee of Goffstown, the rules were suspended and the bill read a third time by its title and passed and sent to the Senate for concurrence.

On motion of Mr. Tallant of Pembroke, at 5.40 the House adjourned.

WEDNESDAY, March 25, 1903.

The House met at 11 o'clock.

Prayer was offered by the chaplain.

COMMITTEE REPORTS.

Mr. Willis of Concord, for the Committee on Engrossed Bills, reported that they had examined, and found correctly engrossed, the following entitled bills and joint resolutions:

An act in amendment of section 17 of chapter 285 of the Public Statutes, relating to the state prison.

35

An act in amendment of section 13, chapter 27 of the Pamphlet Laws of 1895, relating to street railways.

An act to incorporate the Warren Water and Light Company.

An act to incorporate the Epping, Brentwood & Kingston Street Railway Company.

An act to incorporate the Derry & Salem Street Railway Company.

An act to incorporate the Milton Mills & Union Electric Railway Company.

An act to amend chapter 243 of the Laws of 1901, creating the Grafton Improvement, Manufacturing and Power Company.

An act annexing certain islands in Lake Winnipesaukee to the town of Tuftonborough.

An act relating to the salary of the judge of probate of the county of Carroll.

Joint resolution in favor of Green's basin in Lake Winnipesaukee.

Joint resolution in favor of the widow of Benjamin F. March of Mason.

Joint resolution in favor of the New Hampshire School for Feeble-Minded Children.

An act to incorporate the Dover Loan and Trust Company.

An act to incorporate the Meredith & Ossipee Valley Railroad Company.

An act to exempt certain property of the Manchester Young Men's Christian Association from taxation.

An act to incorporate the New Ipswich, Greenville & Wilton Electric Railway Company.

An act to incorporate the Uncanoonuc Incline Railway and Development Company.

An act to incorporate the Swift River Railroad Company.

An act to incorporate the Bellman Club of Manchester, N. H.

An act in amendment of section 13, chapter 59, Laws of 1895, relating to the bond of the adjutant-general.

Joint resolution appropriating nine thousand dollars for additions and repairs to the industrial school.

An act in amendment of sections 7 and 10, chapter 27, Laws of 1895, relating to street railways.

Joint resolution providing for the repairs and construction of certain state highways, certain highways in unincorporated places, and certain roads in places where such roads cannot be maintained by any local municipality.

An act in amendment of "An act to incorporate the Society of Social Friends," approved June 29, 1826, "An act to incorporate the United Fraternity," approved July 6, 1827, and "An act to incorporate the Philotechnic Society of the Chandler Scientific Department of Dartmouth College," approved July 13, 1854, and to authorize the calling of meetings of said corporations respectively.

An act fixing office hours in state offices.

An act to incorporate the Chester, Fremont & Brentwood Street Railway Company.

An act to require non-residents to secure a license before hunting deer within the state of New Hampshire, and providing penalties for violation of its provisions.

An act to amend section 1 of chapter 46, Session Laws of 1895, relating to annual enumeration of school children.

An act in amendment of section 59, chapter 79 of the Session Laws of 1901, relating to the taking of black bass.

An act in amendment of section 56, chapter 79 of the Laws of 1901, relating to fish and game.

An act to incorporate the History Commission of Concord.

Joint resolution in favor of William J. Patch.

An act to incorporate the Prudential Fire Insurance Company.

An act to change the name of the Manchester Heating and Lighting Company of Manchester, N. H.

An act to incorporate the Sons of Veterans' Memorial Hall Association.

Joint resolution in favor of placing and maintaining buoys and lights in Lake Winnipesaukee and adjacent waters.

An act to incorporate the Maynesboro Fire Insurance Company.

An act to amend the charter of the Bennington Water-Works Company.

An act in amendment of chapter 107 of the Session Laws of 1901, relating to the inspection of milk.

An act to authorize the Dover & Eliot Street Railway, and the Eliot Bridge Company, to transfer their properties and franchises to the Berwick, Eliot & York Street Railway.

The report was accepted.

Mr. Tripp of Epsom, for the Committee on Labor, to whom was referred An act requiring the use of the label of the International Typographical Union upon all printed matter of the state, having considered the same, report the same with the following resolution :

Resolved, That it is inexpedient to legislate.

Mr. Roby of Concord, for the Committee on Fisheries and Game, to whom was referred An act in amendment of section 52 of chapter 79 of Laws of 1901, having considered the same, report the same with the following resolution :

Resolved, That it is inexpedient to legislate.

Mr. Roby of Concord, for the Committee on Fisheries and Game, to whom was referred An act in amendment of Laws of 1901, chapter 79, sections 16 and 57, being "An act entitled ' An act to revise the fish and game laws of the state,' " having considered the same, report the same with the following resolution :

Resolved, That it is inexpedient to legislate.

Mr. Roby of Concord, for the Committee on Fisheries and Game, to whom was referred An act relating to taking of shiners or red fins from waters of the state for bait, having considered the same, report the same with the following resolution :

Resolved, That it is inexpedient to legislate.

Mr. Roby of Concord, for the Committee on Fisheries and Game, to whom was referred An act in amendment of chapter 79, Laws of 1901, relating to the fish and game laws of the state, having considered the same, report the same with the following resolution :

Resolved, That it is inexpedient to legislate.

Mr. Bell of Woodstock, for the Committee on Public Health, to whom was referred An act to amend section 3 of chapter 110 of the Public Statutes, relating to pestilential diseases, having considered the same, report the same with the following resolution :

Resolved, That it is inexpedient to legislate, the subject matter being covered by another bill reported by the committee.

Mr. Woodman of Concord, for the Committee on Judiciary, to whom was referred An act to provide for and regulate the inspection and care of steam boilers and all steam generating apparatus, and thereby prevent the loss of life and property, having considered the same, report the same with the following resolution :

Resolved, That it is inexpedient to legislate.

Mr. Woodman of Concord, for the Committee on Judiciary, to whom was referred Joint resolution to provide for the sale of the securities in the state treasury known as the Benjamin Thompson securities, having considered the same, report the same with the following resolution :

Resolved, That it is inexpedient to legislate.

Mr. Batchelder of Keene, for the Committee on Judiciary, to whom was referred An act in amendment of the charter of the Contoocook River Navigation and Improvement Company, having considered the same, report the same with the following resolution

Resolved, That it is inexpedient to legislate.

Mr. Woodman of Concord, for the Committee on Liquor Laws, to whom was referred An act to regulate the traffic in spirituous liquors, having considered the same, report the same with the following resolution :

Resolved, That it is inexpedient to legislate, the subject matter having been included in a bill reported by the committee.

Mr. Woodman of Concord, for the Committee on Liquor Laws, to whom was referred An act in amendment of chapter 112 of the Public Statutes, establishing local option in the sale of intoxicating liquors, having considered the same, report the same with the following resolution :

Resolved, That it is inexpedient to legislate, the subject matter having been included in a bill reported by the committee.

Mr. Woodman of Concord, for the Committee on Liquor Laws, to whom was referred An act to regulate the traffic in intoxicating liquors, having considered the same, report the same with the following resolution :

Resolved, That it is inexpedient to legislate, the subject matter having been included in a bill reported by the committee.

Mr. Woodman of Concord, for the Committee on Liquor Laws, to whom was referred An act to amend the prohibitory law by permitting local option, having considered the same, report the same with the following resolution :

Resolved, That it is inexpedient to legislate, the subject matter having been included in a bill reported by the committee.

Mr. Woodman of Concord, for the Committee on Liquor Laws, to whom was referred An act to prohibit the manufacture of malt and spirituous liquor, having considered the same, report the same with the following resolution :

Resolved, That it is inexpedient to legislate, the subject matter having been included in a bill reported by the committee.

Mr. Woodman of Concord, for the Committee on Liquor Laws, to whom was referred An act in amendment of sections 15 and 23 of chapter 112 of the Public Statutes, relating to the enforcement of the provisions of said chapter, having considered the same, report the same with the following resolution :

Resolved, That it is inexpedient to legislate, the subject matter having been included in a bill reported by the committee.

Mr. Ahern of Concord, for the Committee on Appropriations, to whom was referred Joint resolution in favor of an appropriation for the repair of the Mayhew turnpike and Point road, so called, in the town of Bridgewater, having considered the same, report the same with the following resolution :

Resolved, That it is inexpedient to legislate, the subject matter having been considered in a bill reported by the committee.

Mr. Donahue of Manchester, for the Committee on Insurance, to whom was referred An act for the better regulation of the business of fire insurance and to increase the public revenue, having considered the same, report the same with the following resolution :

Resolved, That it is inexpedient to legislate.

The reports were severally accepted and the resolutions reported by the committee adopted.

Mr. Woodman of Concord, for the Committee on Judiciary,

to whom was referred An act in relation to licensing dogs kept for breeding purposes, having considered the same, report the same with the following resolution :

Resolved, That the bill ought to pass.

Mr. Lintott of Nashua, for the Committee on State House and State House Yard, to whom was referred An act in amendment of section 3 of chapter 7 of the Public Statutes, relating to the state house and yard, having considered the same, report the same with the following resolution :

Resolved, That the bill ought to pass.

Mr. Gowing of Dublin, for the Committee on Revision of Statutes, to whom was referred An act in amendment of section 2 of chapter 32 of the Laws of 1895, entitled "An act in relation to printing the reports of certain state officers," having considered the same, report the same with the following resolution :

Resolved, That the bill ought to pass.

The reports were severally accepted and the bills laid upon the table to be printed.

Mr. Roby of Concord, for the Committee on Military Affairs, to whom was referred An act allowing compensation to majors of battalions in the National Guard in certain cases, having considered the same, report the same with the following resolution :

Resolved, That the bill ought to pass.

The report was accepted and the bill laid upon the table to be printed and then referred to the Committee on Appropriations.

Mr. Quimby of Meredith, for the Committee on Appropriations, to whom was referred Joint resolution appropriating money to be expended for the preservation of the muster rolls, having considered the same, report the same with the following resolution :

Resolved, That the joint resolution ought to pass.

Mr. Quimby of Meredith, for the Committee on Appropriations, to whom was referred An act in relation to the administration of the state prison and to provide for necessary improvements and repairs, having considered the same, report the same with the following resolution :

Resolved, That the bill ought to pass.

The reports were severally accepted and the joint resolution and bill ordered to a third reading.

Mr. Dow of Conway, for the Committee on Appropriations, to whom was referred An act in amendment of chapter 134 of the Public Statutes, relating to the practice of dentistry, having considered the same, report the same with the following amendment and with the resolution that the bill as amended ought to pass : Strike out the figure " 10 " in the fourth line and insert therein the figure "5," so it shall read : " The members of the board shall be paid the expenses necessarily incurred, and $5 a day each for time actually spent in the discharge of their duties."

The report was accepted, the amendment adopted, and the bill ordered to a third reading.

Mr. Woodman of Concord, for the Committee on Judiciary, to whom was referred An act to regulate the speed and operation of automobiles and motor vehicles on highways, having considered the same, report the same in a new draft with the following resolution :

Resolved, That the bill in new draft ought to pass.

Mr. Cavanaugh of Manchester, for the Committee on Judiciary, to whom was referred An act in amendment of, and in addition to, section 3, chapter 105 of the Laws of 1901, in relation to political caucuses and conventions, having considered the same, report the same in a new draft with the following resolution :

Resolved, That the bill in new draft ought to pass.

The reports were severally accepted and the bills in their new drafts read a first time and ordered to a second reading.

Mr. Converse of Lyme, for the Committee on Agriculture, to whom was referred An act to amend section 1 of chapter 33 of the Laws of 1893, relating to the diseases of domestic animals, having considered the same, report the same with the following amendment and with the resolution that the bill as amended ought to pass :

Amend section 1 by inserting after the word "state" as found in the third line the words " and inserting the words three fourths." Also amend section 1 by adding after the word " state " as found in the sixth line the words " three fourths."

The report was accepted, the amendments adopted, and the bill laid upon the table to be printed.

Mr. Farrell of Manchester, for the Committee on Incorporations, to whom was referred An act to amend chapter 184 of the Laws of 1897, entitled "An act to incorporate the Dalton Power Company, as amended by section 1, chapter 221 of the Laws of 1899," having considered the same, report the same with the following amendment and with the following resolution :

Resolved, That the bill as amended ought to pass.

Amend the bill by inserting after the enacting clause a new section as follows and renumbering the other sections by advancing each section one number :

SECTION 1.   Amend section 2, chapter 184 of the Laws of 1897, by adding at the end of said section the words "and said corporation may take, hold, and dispose of stocks and bonds of other corporations," so that said section, as amended, shall read as follows :

SECT. 2.   That said company is hereby authorized to acquire by lease or purchase the property, rights, franchises, privileges, and immunities of any electric company now or hereafter existing in any town or city in said counties of Grafton or Coös, in the state of New Hampshire, or said county of Caledonia and county of Essex, state of Vermont, upon such terms or conditions as may be mutually agreed upon ; and upon such lease or purchase and a transfer and conveyance of the same to the Dalton Power Company, it shall succeed to and enjoy all the rights, privileges, and immunities now enjoyed and belonging to any electric light company, and said corporation may take, hold, and dispose of stocks and bonds of other corporations.

The report was accepted, the amendment adopted, and the bill laid upon the table to be printed.   On motion of Mr. Buckley of Lancaster, the rules were suspended and the printing of the bill dispensed with.   The bill was then ordered to a third reading.   On motion of the same gentleman, the rules were further suspended and the bill read a third time by its title and passed and sent to the Senate for concurrence.

Mr. Roby of Concord, for the Committee on Fisheries and Game, to whom was referred An act in amendment of section 14, chapter 79, Session Laws of 1901, relating to the powers of the fish and game commissioners, having considered the same, report the same with the following resolution ·

Resolved, That the bill ought to pass.

The report was accepted and the bill laid upon the table to be printed. On motion of Mr. Goold of Lebanon, the rules were suspended and the printing of the bill dispensed with. The bill was then ordered to a third reading. On motion of the same gentleman, the rules were further suspended and the bill read a third time and passed and sent to the secretary of state to be engrossed.

Mr. Gowing of Dublin, for the Committee on Revision of Statutes, to whom was referred An act in amendment of section 2 of chapter 5 of the Public Statutes, relating to the publication and distribution of statutes, journals, and reports, having considered the same, report the same with the following resolution :

Resolved, That the bill ought to pass.

The report was accepted and the bill laid upon the table to be printed. On motion of Mr. Smith of Peterborough, the rules were suspended and the printing of the bill dispensed with. The bill was then ordered to a third reading. On motion of the same gentleman, the rules were further suspended and the bill read a third time by its title and passed and sent to the secretary of state to be engrossed.

Mr. Tripp of Epsom, for the Committee on Labor, to whom was referred An act in amendment of section 14, chapter 180, Public Statutes, regulating the hours of labor for women and minors in manufacturing or mechanical establishments, having considered the same, report the same with the following resolution :

Resolved, That it is inexpedient to legislate.

The report was accepted. The question being upon the adoption of the resolution reported by the committee, on motion of Mr. Small of Rochester, the bill and report were laid upon the table and made the special order for Thursday, March 26, at 11 o'clock.

Mr. Foye of Portsmouth, for the Committee on Appropriations, to whom was referred Joint resolution appropriating money for the support of the New Hampshire School for Feeble-Minded Children, necessary school buildings, and to provide a suitable water supply, having considered the same, report the same in a new draft with amended enacting clause, and with the resolution that the joint resolution in the new draft with amended enacting clause ought to pass.

The report was accepted and the joint resolution in its new draft read a first time and ordered to a second reading. On motion of Mr. Remich of Littleton, the rules were suspended and the joint resolution read a second time. The joint resolution was then laid upon the table to be printed.

Mr. Hamlin of Charlestown, for the Committee on Claims, reported the following joint resolution, "Joint resolution in favor of the widow of John W. Jewett of Claremont," with the resolution that the joint resolution ought to pass.

The report was accepted and the joint resolution read a first time and ordered to a second reading. On motion of Mr. Ahern of Concord, the rules were suspended and the joint resolution read a second time. The joint resolution was then laid upon the table to be printed. On motion of the same gentleman, the rules were suspended and the printing of the joint resolution dispensed with. The joint resolution was then referred to the Committee on Appropriations. On motion of the same gentleman, the rules were suspended and the reference to the committee dispensed with. The joint resolution was then ordered to a third reading. On motion of the same gentleman, the rules were further suspended and the joint resolution read a third time and passed and sent to the Senate for concurrence.

Mr. Farrell of Manchester, for the Committee on Incorporations, reported the following entitled bill, "An act in amendment of chapter 208 of the Session Laws of 1899, entitled 'An act to incorporate the Walpole Electric Light and Power Company,' and of an act amending said act passed at the present session," with the resolution that the bill ought to pass.

The report was accepted and the bill read a first time and ordered to a second reading. Mr. Batchelder of Keene moved that the rules be suspended and the bill read a second time by its title. The question being upon the adoption of the motion,

(Discussion ensued.)

Mr. Batchelder withdrew his motion and the bill was ordered to a second reading.

Mr. Whittemore of Dover, for the Committee on Judiciary, to whom was referred An act to exempt certain property of the Keene Young Men's Christian Association from taxation, having considered the same, report the same in a new draft with amended title and with the following resolution :

Resolved, That the bill in new draft with amended title ought to pass.

The report was accepted and the bill in new draft and with amended title read a first time and ordered to a second reading. On motion of Mr. Whitney of Keene, the rules were suspended and the bill read a second time by its title. The bill was then laid upon the table to be printed. On motion of the same gentleman, the rules were suspended and the printing of the bill dispensed with. The bill was then ordered to a third reading. On motion of the same gentleman, the rules were further suspended and the bill read a third time by its title and passed and sent to the Senate for concurrence.

Mr. Dow of Conway, for the Committee on Appropriations, to whom was referred Joint resolution appropriating one thousand dollars for a monument to be erected at Hackensack, N. J., in memory of Gen. Enoch Poor, having considered the same, report the same with the following amendment and with the following resolution :

Resolved, That the joint resolution as amended ought to pass.

Strike out the figures " 1000 " in first line, and the words " one thousand " in fifth line, and insert instead the words " five hundred."

The report was accepted, the amendment adopted, and the joint resolution ordered to a third reading. On motion of Mr. Whitcher of Haverhill, the rules were suspended and the joint resolution read a third time. The question being,

Shall the joint resolution pass?

On motion of Mr. Whitcher of Haverhill, the rules were

suspended and the joint resolution placed back upon its second reading for purposes of amendment. Mr. Whitcher of Haverhill offered the following amendment:

Amend the joint resolution by striking out in the seventh line the word " like " and by inserting after the word " sum " in the same line the words " of one thousand dollars," and by striking out in the fifteenth line the word " like." On a *viva voce* vote the amendment was adopted. On motion of the same gentleman, the enacting clause was amended by striking out " $1000 " and inserting in place thereof " $500." The joint resolution was then ordered to a third reading. Mr. Whitcher of Haverhill moved that the rules be suspended and the joint resolution read a third time. The question being upon the adoption of the motion,

(Discussion ensued.)

Mr. Whitcher withdrew his motion and the joint resolution was ordered to a third reading.

Mr. Donahue of Manchester, for the Committee on Insurance, reported the following entitled bill, " An act in amendment of section 2 of chapter 64 of the Laws of 1899, relating to the firemen's relief fund," with the resolution that the bill ought to pass.

The report was accepted and the bill read a first time and ordered to a second reading. On motion of Mr. Donahue of Manchester, the rules were suspended and the bill read a second time by its title. The bill was then laid upon the table to be printed. On motion of the same gentleman, the rules were suspended and the printing of the bill dispensed with. The bill was then referred to the Committee on Appropriations.

Mr. Roby of Concord, for the Committee on Military Affairs, reported the following entitled bill, " An act amending sections 37, 38, and 40 of chapter 59 of the Session Laws of 1895, as amended by chapter 25 of the Laws of 1901," with the resolution that the bill ought to pass.

The report was accepted. On motion of Mr. Roby of Concord, the rules were suspended and the bill read a first time by its title. The bill was then ordered to a second reading. On motion of the same gentleman, the rules were suspended and

the bill read a second time by its title.   The bill was then laid
upon the table to be printed.

Mr. Whitcher of Haverhill, for the Committee on Judiciary,
reported the following entitled bill, " An act relating to the
publication of the Session Laws," with the resolution that the
bill ought to pass.

The report was accepted and the bill read a first time and
ordered to a second reading.   On motion of Mr. Whitcher of
Haverhill, the rules were suspended and the bill read a second
time by its title.   The bill was then laid upon the table to be
printed.

Mr. Taggart of Manchester, for the Committee on Elections,
reported the following entitled bill, " An act to legalize a vote
taken at the annual town meeting in Boscawen on the second
Tuesday of March, A. D. 1903," with the resolution that the
bill ought to pass.

The report was accepted and the bill read a first time and
ordered to a second reading.   On motion of Mr. Harris of
Boscawen, the rules were suspended and the bill read a second time by its title.   The bill was then laid upon the table
to be printed.   On motion of the same gentleman, the rules
were suspended and the printing of the bill dispensed with.
The bill was then ordered to a third reading.   On motion of
the same gentleman, the rules were suspended and the bill
read a third time by its title and passed and sent to the Senate
for concurrence.

Mr. Dow of Conway, for the Committee on Appropriations,
in accordance with the resolution adopted by the House, submitted the following report of the amount of new appropriations for the ensuing two years:

Bills for new appropriations for next two years
amount to $905,632.29

Amount cut down in committee	$51,050.00
Reported inexpedient . .	219,000.00
Approved by committee . .	635,582.29

$905,632.29

The report was accepted.

SECOND READING.

An act in amendment of section 19, chapter 57 of the Public

Statutes, relating to the annual invoice of polls and taxable property.

Read a second time and laid upon the table to be printed.

On motion of Mr. Fay of Keene, the rules were suspended and the bill read a third time by its title and passed. On motion of the same gentleman, the title was amended by striking out all the words after " An act " and inserting the following: " in amendment of section 4 of chapter 113 of the Laws of 1895, relating to the taxation of bank shares and deposits." The bill was then sent to the Senate for concurrence.

MESSAGE FROM THE SENATE.

A message from the Honorable Senate, by its clerk, announced that the Senate concurs with the House of Representatives in the passage of the following bill, with amendment, in the passage of which amendment it asks the concurrence of the House of Representatives:

An act in amendment of section 79 of chapter 79 of the Laws of 1901, in regard to lobster traps.

Amend section 1 of the bill by striking out in lines 26, 27, 28, and 29 of said section the words " but no indictment shall be maintained unless the name of the owner of the trap or traps shall be carved, painted, or printed in legible letters not less than three fourths of an inch in length on all the buoys connected with such traps."

On motion of Mr. Goold of Lebanon, the amendment was concurred in.

The message also announced that the Senate refuses to concur with the House of Representatives in the passage of the following entitled bills sent up from the House of Representatives:

An act to amend the charter of the New England and Louisiana Land Company.

An act in amendment of so much of chapter 264 of the Laws of the State of New Hampshire, passed at the January session, 1893, as relates to the establishing of a board of street and park commissioners for the city of Manchester.

An act in amendment of chapter 91, section 8, Laws of

1897, relating to the duties of the State Board of Charities and Correction.

An act to amend section 2, chapter 179 of the Public Statutes, relating to the appointment of guardians of insane persons.

The message also announced that the Senate concurs with the House of Representatives in its amendments to the following entitled bill:

An act relating to the time required for filing notice of intention of marriage.

The message also announced that the Senate concurs with the House of Representatives in the passage of the following entitled bills:

An act to amend section 52 of chapter 79 of the Laws of 1901, entitled "An act to revise the fish and game laws of the state."

An act to legalize and confirm the warrant for, and the votes and proceedings at, the annual election and meeting in ward three in the city of Berlin, held the 10th day of March, 1903.

The message also announced that the Senate concurs with the House of Representatives in the passage of the following entitled bill in Senate new draft, in the passage of which new draft it asks the concurrence of the House of Representatives:

An act to amend section 16 of chapter 79 of the Session Laws of 1901, relating to the taking of deer.

Read a first and second time and referred to the Committee on Fisheries and Game.

The message further announced that the Senate has passed a bill with the following title, in the passage of which it asks the concurrence of the House of Representatives:

An act in amendment of an act entitled "An act for the enlargement and extension of water-works of the city of Portsmouth," approved March 10th, 1899.

The first reading having begun, on motion of Mr. Ahern of Concord, the rules were suspended and the bill read a first time by its title. The bill was then read a second time and referred to the Committee on Judiciary.

On motion of Mr. Couhig of Portsmouth, the reference was rescinded and the bill referred to a special committee consisting of the delegation from the city of Portsmouth.

Mr. Small of Rochester offered the following resolution :

Resolved, By the House of Representatives of the State of New Hampshire that application is hereby made to the Congress under the provision of Article Five of the constitution of the United States for the calling of a convention to propose an amendment to the constitution of the United States, making United States Senators elective in the several states by direct vote of the people ; and *Resolved* further, that the clerk of the House is hereby directed to transmit copies of this application to the House of Representatives of the Congress, and copies to the members of the said House of Representatives from this state, also, to transmit copies hereof to the presiding officers of each of the legislatures now in session in the several states, requesting their coöperation.

The question being upon the adoption of the resolution,

(Discussion ensued.)

On motion of Mr. Goss of Berlin, the resolution was laid upon the table.

On motion of Mr. Ahern of Concord, at 12.45 the House took a recess until 2.45 o'clock.

(After Recess.)

On motion of Mr. Donahue of Manchester, the following entitled bill, "An act to confirm, revive, and continue the charter of the Manchester City Fire Insurance Company," was taken from the table. The question being upon the adoption of the resolution reported by the committee, that it is inexpedient to legislate,

(Discussion ensued.)

On a *viva voce* vote the resolution was adopted.

SPECIAL ORDER.

Mr. Roby of Concord called for the special order, it being the following entitled bill, "An act to amend sections 4 and 5

36

of chapter 65 of the Public Statutes, relating to the taxation of savings banks."

The third reading being in order, the bill was read a third time and passed and sent to the Senate for concurrence.

SPECIAL ORDER.

Mr. Barr of Manchester called for the special order, it being the following entitled bill, "An act to provide suitable armory quarters for the National Guard at Manchester."

The question being,

Shall the bill pass?

On a *viva voce* vote the bill passed.

Mr. Barrett of Dover called for a yea and nay vote.

(Discussion ensued.)

Mr. Ahern of Concord moved the previous question.

The question being,

Shall the main question be now put?

On a *viva voce* vote the previous question was ordered.

The question being,

Shall the bill pass?

And Mr. Barrett of Dover having called for a yea and nay vote, Mr. Barrett withdrew his call and on a *viva voce* vote the bill passed and was sent to the Senate for concurrence.

Mr. Roby of Concord moved that the vote whereby the House passed the following entitled bill, "An act to amend sections 4 and 5 of chapter 65 of the Public Statutes, relating to the taxation of savings banks," be rescinded. The question being upon the adoption of the motion, on a *viva voce* vote the motion did not prevail.

Mr. Whitcher of Haverhill called for a division. A division being had, the vote was declared to be manifestly in the affirmative, and the vote was reconsidered.

The question being,

Shall the bill pass?

On motion of Mr. Whitcher of Haverhill, the bill was laid upon the table.

MESSAGE FROM THE SENATE.

A message from the Honorable Senate, by its clerk, announced that the Senate has refused to give a second reading to the following entitled bill sent up from the House of Representatives :

An act in relation to the settlement of paupers.

The message also announced that the Senate has indefinitely postponed a bill with the following title sent up from the House of Representatives :

An act to amend chapter 60, section 3 of the Statute Laws of 1891, relating to dog licenses.

The message also announced that the Senate refuses to concur with the House of Representatives in the passage of the following entitled bill sent up from the House of Representatives :

An act to define the duties of the state treasurer with reference to public funds.

The message also announced that the Senate concurs with the House of Representatives in the passage of the following entitled bills sent up from the House of Representatives :

An act to establish a new apportionment for the assessment of public taxes.

An act in relation to the salary of the judge of probate for the county of Grafton.

An act in amendment of section 1, chapter 67, Laws of 1899, relating to expenses of judges of the supreme court.

An act relating to the salary of the judge of probate of the county of Sullivan.

An act to amend section 14 and section 15, chapter 286 of the Public Statutes, relating to the salaries of the judge and register of probate for Belknap county.

The message also announced that the Senate concurs with the House of Representatives in the passage of the following bills with amendments, in the passage of which amendments it asks the concurrence of the House of Representatives :

An act to authorize the town of Gilmanton to exempt certain property from taxation. Amend by adding after the word " from " in line 2, section 1 of the bill, the word " local."

On motion of Mr. Severance of Exeter, the amendment was concurred in and the bill sent to the secretary of state to be engrossed.

An act in amendment of the charter of the city of Manchester, establishing a board of assessors in place of the assessors provided under the chapter and laws of the state. Amend the title of the bill by striking out the word " chapter " and substituting in place thereof the word "charter."

On motion of Mr. Taggart of Manchester, the amendment was concurred in and the bill sent to the secretary of state to be engrossed.

The message further announced that the Senate has passed a bill with the following title, in the passage of which it asks the concurrence of the House of Representatives:

An act to incorporate the First Congregational church of Wolfeborough, New Hampshire.

Read a first and second time and referred to the Committee on Judiciary. Mr. Beacham of Wolfeborough moved that the rules be suspended and the reference to committee dispensed with.

The question being upon the adoption of the motion,

(Discussion ensued.)

Mr. Beacham withdrew his motion and the bill was referred to the Committee on Judiciary.

On motion of Mr. Nelson of Portsmouth, at 4.41 the House adjourned.

AFTERNOON.

The House was called to order in afternoon session immediately upon adjournment of the morning session.

LEAVE OF ABSENCE.

Mr. Murnane of Somersworth was granted leave of absence on account of illness.

THIRD READINGS.

Joint resolution appropriating five hundred dollars for a monument to be erected at Hackensack, New Jersey, in memory of General Enoch Poor.

Joint resolution appropriating money to be expended for the preservation of the muster rolls.

An act in amendment of chapter 134 of the Public Statutes, relating to the practice of dentistry.

An act in relation to the administration of the state prison and to provide for necessary improvements and repairs.

An act for the better preservation of highways and accommodating public travel.

Severally read a third time and passed and sent to the Senate for concurrence.

SPECIAL ORDER.

Mr. Ahern of Concord called for the special order, it being the following entitled bill, "An act to abolish capital punishment." On motion of the same gentleman the bill and his pending call for a division were laid upon the table and made the special order for Thursday, March 26, at 11 o'clock.

On motion of Mr. Pinneo of Hanover, at 4.53 the House adjourned.

THURSDAY, MARCH 26, 1903.

The House met at 11 o'clock.

Prayer was offered by the chaplain.

MESSAGE FROM THE SENATE.

A message from the Honorable Senate, by its clerk, announced that the Senate refuses a second reading to the following entitled bill sent up from the House of Representatives:

An act for the better preservation of highways and accommodating public travel.

The message also announced that the Senate concurs with the House of Representatives in the passage of the following entitled bills and joint resolution:

Joint resolution in favor of the widow of John W. Jewett of Claremont.

An act to sever certain residences from the school district of the town of Wilmot and to annex the same to the school district of the town of New London.

An act to incorporate the Connecticut River Power Company of New Hampshire.

An act relating to the setting off by the legislature of territory of one town or city on to that of another town or city.

The message further announced that the Senate concurs with the House of Representatives in the passage of the following bill, with amendments, in the passage of which amendments it asks the concurrence of the House of Representatives :

An act to regulate the traffic in intoxicating liquors.

Amend section 1 by inserting the word " firms " after the word " include " in the third line of said section.

Amend section 5 by inserting the words "commissioner or" after the word "any" in the eighth line of said section.

Amend section 6, fifth class, by inserting after the word "only" in the third line of said fifth class the words "and for dealers in hardware, paints and decorating materials to sell alcohol for mechanical and chemical uses only."

Also amend section 6, seventh class, by striking out the period after the figure 8, and insert in place thereof a comma, and add the words "in the discretion of the Board of License Commissioners."

Further amend section 6, eighth class, by striking out the word "and" after the word "distillers" in the first line of said class, and insert in place thereof a comma ; also amend said eighth class by inserting after the word "brewer" in said line the words " and bottlers."

Further amend said section 6 by adding at the end of said section the words "all licenses granted prior to May 1st, 1904, shall expire on that date, all licenses after May 1st, 1904, shall expire May 1st of the following year, and all licensees shall pay for the time from date of issue to the first day of the May following."

Further amend section 7, third class, by striking out the word "twenty" in the third line of said third class, and insert in place thereof the word "eighteen."

Further amend said third class by striking out the word "twenty" in the fifth line of said third class, and insert in place thereof the word "eighteen."

Further amend section 7, fourth class, by striking out the word "twenty" in the third line of said fourth class, and insert in place thereof the word "eighteen."

Further amend section 7, fourth class, by striking out the word "twenty" in the fifth line, and insert in place thereof the word "eighteen."

Amend section 8, subdivision 3, by inserting after the word "city" in the second line in said subdivision the words "or the adjoining town or city."

Further amend section 8, subdivision 7, by striking out after the word "thereof" in the second line of said subdivision the words "shall receive a license."

Further amend section 8, subdivision 9, by inserting after the word "him" in the tenth line of said subdivision the words "provided, however, that no bond shall be accepted for a less amount than five hundred dollars."

Amend section 9 by inserting after the word "on" in the seventh line the words "or in any location where the traffic shall be deemed by said board of license commissioners detrimental to the public welfare."

Amend section 10 by inserting after the word "duties" in the fourteenth line of said section the words "also the sum of one thousand dollars, or as much thereof as may be needed to pay the necessary expenses of the state laboratory of hygiene incurred under the provisions of this act, and all expenditures shall be audited by the governor and council."

Amend section 13 by striking out after the word "die" in the second line of said section the words "or cease to traffic in liquor during the term for which said license was issued, such person, or his duly authorized attorney, or his representative," and insert in place of the words so stricken out the words "his heirs, executors or administrators."

Amend section 15 by striking out after the word "minor" in the third line of said section the words "unless accompanied by his parent or guardian."

Amend section 21 by inserting after the word "any" in the first line the word "commissioner"; also amend said section by inserting the word "selectman" after the word "agent" in the first line.

Amend section 24 by inserting after the word " the " and before the word " special " in the third line the words " commissioners and."

Amend section 31 by striking out in the first line of said section the words " first day " and inserting in place thereof the words " third Tuesday."

On motion of Mr. Batchelder of Keene, the above amendments were collectively concurred in.

Amend section 7, first class, by striking out all after the word " lodging " in said first class.

Mr. Batchelder of Keene moved that the House concur in the above amendment. The question being upon the adoption of the motion,

(Discussion ensued.)

Mr. Darrah of Manchester moved the previous question.
The question being,
Shall the main question be now put?

(Discussion ensued.)

Mr. Darrah withdrew his motion.
Discussion was resumed upon the motion offered by Mr. Batchelder of Keene.

At 12.40, Mr. Hodgman of Merrimack moved that the House take a recess until 2 o'clock. The question being upon the adoption of the motion,

(Discussion ensued.)

Mr. Hodgman withdrew his motion. The question being upon the adoption of the motion of Mr. Batchelder of Keene,

(Discussion ensued.)

Mr. Ahern of Concord moved the previous question.
The question being,
Shall the main question be now put?

On a *viva voce* vote the previous question was ordered. The question being upon the adoption of the motion of Mr. Batchelder, Mr. Remich of Littleton called for a yea and nay vote. The roll was called with the following result:

Yeas, 137.

Rockingham County. Hardy, Foye, Nelson, Cogan, Adams of Portsmouth, Newton, Couhig, Young, Blaisdell.

Strafford County. Mathes, Libby of Dover, Jewell, Nason, Whittemore, Bunce, Smith of Dover, Barrett, Hayes, Wesley, Tuttle, Place, Warren, Small, Wallace, Boutin, Andrews, Caverly.

Belknap County. Clough, Fecteau, Prescott, Chase of Laconia, Edwards, Kimball of Laconia, Rogers.

Carroll County. Stevens, Dow of Conway, Drake, Trickey, Greene, French.

Merrimack County. Harris of Boscawen, Morse of Bradford, Symonds, Cate, Kennedy, Willis, Matson, Hill, A. W., of Concord, Roby, Woodman, Kimball of Concord, Emerson of Concord, Davis of Concord, Critchett, Mathews of Concord, Hill, E. J., of Concord, Ahern, Donagan, Worthley, Hutchins of Pittsfield, Walker of Pittsfield.

Hillsborough County. Woodbury, Barr of Bedford, Craine, Putnam, Cavanaugh, Abbott of Manchester, Donahue, Bartlett of Manchester, Sheehan, Bunton, A. S., of Manchester, Johnson, Wright, Barr of Manchester, Dubuc, Carpenter, Morgan, Darrah, Stewart of Manchester, Tonery, Ryan, Trinity, Whalen, Riordan, Sullivan of Manchester, Bunton, A. B., of Manchester, Scannell, Dinsmore, Dozois, Filion, Lynch, Kane, Emerson of Manchester, Lund, Lampron, Buckley of Nashua, Ingham, Bussell, Collins, Dionne, Sheldon.

Cheshire County. Ware of Alstead, Harris of Chesterfield, Fuller, Holland, Jones of Keene, Batchelder, Donovan, Boyden, Sherman of Walpole.

Sullivan County. Long, Churchill.

Grafton County. Morrill of Ashland, Whitcher, Evans, Goold of Lebanon, Pike of Lebanon, Comings, King, Ferrin, Russell of Rumney, Bell.

Coös County. Caird, Smyth, Goss, Vaillancourt, Kent of Berlin, Notterstead, Gallagher, Martin, Bragg, Libby of Gorham, Buckley of Lancaster, Ellis, Trafton, McDonald of Northumberland, Darling.

NAYS, 202.

ROCKINGHAM COUNTY. Sawyer of Atkinson, Fellows, Hubbard, Morse of Chester, Darbe, White of Deerfield, Shute, Edgerly of Epping, Nowell, Scammon, Severance, Smith of Exeter, Brown of Fremont, Emerson of Hampstead, Lane of Hampton, Brown of Hampton Falls, Quimby of Kingston, Crowell, Pridham, George, Warner, Bickford, Gerrish, Sleeper, Payne, Yeaton, Corson, Brown of Rye, Dow of Seabrook, Swain, Chase of Stratham.

STRAFFORD COUNTY. Howe of Barrington, Ramsdell, Langley, York. Davis of Lee, Felker, McCrillis, Crocker, Harrity, Etter, Wentworth.

BELKNAP COUNTY. Pinkham, Hoitt of Barnstead, Sargent, Smith of Center Harbor, Potter, Davis of Laconia, Hull, Quimby of Meredith, Morrill of New Hampton, Sanborn of Sanbornton, Mason of Tilton.

CARROLL COUNTY. Littlefield, Weeks, Fifield, Burnell, Philbrick of Effingham, Hoyt of Sandwich, Pollard, Edgerly of Tuftonborough, Blake of Wakefield, Britton.

MERRIMACK COUNTY. Graves, White of Bow, Beck, Langmaid, Durgin, Shepard, Litchfield, Bunten of Dunbarton, Tripp, Phillips, Morin of Franklin, Jones of Franklin, Adams of Franklin, Davis of Franklin, Twombly, Fisk, Messer, Sanborn of Northfield, Tallant, Aldrich, Foss, Little of Salisbury, Ela, Burbank, Mason of Wilmot.

HILLSBOROUGH COUNTY. Farley of Amherst, Gould of Bennington, Tobie, Pattee, Eaton, Ware of Hancock, Ward, Farley of Hollis, Connell, Center, Holt, Nyberg, Chase of Manchester, Shaughnessey, Sasseville, Marshall, Morse of Manchester, Couch, Tinkham, Quimby of Manchester, Janelle, Kohler, Newman, Simpson, Goodwin, Hodgman, Sawyer of Milford, Robinson, Needham, Kendall, Tuck, Duncklee, Lewis, Spalding, Hills of Nashua, McLane, Jones of New Ipswich, Peabody, Miller, Smith of Peterborough, Fitzgerald, Bragdon, Chase of Weare.

CHESHIRE COUNTY. Gowing, Tenney, Bemis, Cutler, Pierce of Jaffrey, Maloney, Fay, Fitch, Whitney, Goodnow, Moors, Fox, Scott, Amidon, Fletcher, Merrill, Lane of Swanzey, Ramsay, Hall, Kellom.

SULLIVAN COUNTY. Clark, Hamlin of Charlestown, Chandler, Huntley, Walker of Grantham, Lufkin, Aiken, Matthews of Newport, True, Philbrick of Springfield, Russell of Sunapee, Ball.

GRAFTON COUNTY. McMurphey, Davenport, Pierce of Bethlehem, Calley, Little of Campton, Gates, Dorothy, Foster, Glover, Kimball of Grafton, Pinneo, Howe of Hanover, Carr, Pike of Haverhill, Barnard, Stanley, Remich, Mitchell of Littleton, Blake of Littleton, Converse, Frazer, Chase of Orford, Celley, Gould of Plymouth, Houston, Bowen.

COÖS COUNTY. Hutchins of Berlin, Gathercole, Hicks, Jordan, Tillotson, Hamlin of Dummer, Piper, Smith of Pittsburg, Wilson, O'Connor, Harriman, Babcock, Lennon, and the House refused to concur in the amendment sent down by the Honorable Senate.

Mr. Ahern of Concord moved that a committee of conference be requested on the part of the Senate. The question being upon the adoption of the motion,

(Discussion ensued.)

On motion of Mr. Remich of Littleton, the motion of Mr. Ahern was laid upon the table. Upon motion of the same gentleman, at 1.04 the House took a recess until 2.45 o'clock.

(After Recess.)

The further consideration of the amendments sent down from the Honorable Senate was resumed.

Amend section 16, subdivision second, by striking out the word " ten " in the second line of said subdivision, and inserting in place thereof the word " eleven."

The question being,

Shall the House concur in the amendment?

Mr. Ahern of Concord moved that the House non-concur. On a *viva voce* vote the motion prevailed and the House refused to concur in the amendment.

Further amend section 31 by striking out the word " and " in the next to the last line of said section, and inserting after the word " 6th " and before the word " classes " in said line the words " and 8th."

The question being,

Shall the House concur in the amendment?

Mr. Ahern of Concord moved that the House non-concur. On a *viva voce* vote the motion prevailed and the House refused to concur in the amendment.

On motion of Mr. Whitcher of Haverhill, the motion of Mr. Ahern of Concord, that a committee of conference on the part of the Senate be requested, was taken from the table. The question being upon the adoption of the motion of Mr. Ahern,

(Discussion ensued.)

On *viva voce* vote the motion prevailed. The Speaker appointed as members of such committee on the part of the House, Messrs. Batchelder of Keene, Phillips of Franklin, and Small of Rochester.

Mr. Whitcher of Haverhill offered the following resolution :

Resolved, That when the House adjourns this afternoon it be to meet at 10 o'clock to-morrow morning, and when it adjourns to-morrow it be to meet at 8 o'clock Monday evening.

The question being upon the adoption of the resolution,

(Discussion ensued.)

On a *viva voce* vote the resolution was adopted.

Mr. Whitcher of Haverhill offered the following resolution :

WHEREAS, it appears that all necessary legislative work may easily be accomplished by Friday, the 3d day of April, therefore, be it

Resolved, By the House of Representatives, the Senate concurring, that the present session of the legislature be brought to a final adjournment on Friday, the 3d day of April, at 12 o'clock noon ; and be it further

Resolved, That all reports, bills, and joint resolutions at that time pending in either branch of the legislature be indefinitely postponed.

The question being upon the adoption of the resolution, on a *viva voce* vote the resolution was adopted.

COMMITTEE REPORTS.

Mr. Converse of Lyme, for the Committee on Engrossed

Bills, reported that they had examined and found correctly engrossed the following entitled bills:

An act to amend section 52 of chapter 79 of the Laws of 1901, entitled "An act to revise the fish and game laws of the state."

An act to legalize and confirm the warrant for, and the votes and proceedings at, the annual election and meeting in ward three of the city of Berlin, held the tenth day of March, 1903.

An act relating to the time required for filing notice of intention of marriage.

An act to provide, in common with the state of Vermont, for the acquisition, building, and maintenance of free bridges across the Connecticut river.

The report was accepted.

Mr. Collins of Nashua, for the Committee on Appropriations, to whom was referred An act to provide for the representation of the state of New Hampshire and the exhibition of its products and attractions at the Louisiana Purchase Exposition at St. Louis in 1904, having considered the same, report the same with the following amendment and with the following resolution:

Resolved, That the bill, as amended, ought to pass.

Amend the bill by striking out the words "forty-five" in the second line of section 8 and insert in place thereof the words "thirty-five."

Further amend the bill by striking out all of section 9 and by making section 10 read section 9.

The report was accepted. The question being upon the adoption of the amendments, on a *viva voce* vote the amendments were not adopted.

(Discussion ensued.)

On a *viva voce* vote the amendments were adopted. Mr. Barrett of Dover offered the following amendment:

Amend by striking out in the second line of section 8 the words "thirty-five," and inserting in place thereof the word "ten."

The question being upon the adoption of the amendment,

(Discussion ensued.)

On a *viva voce* vote the amendment was not adopted.

Mr. Barrett of Dover called for a division.

(Discussion ensued.)

Mr. Barrett of Dover moved the previous question.

The question being,

Shall the main question be now put?

On a *viva voce* vote the previous question was ordered. The question being upon the adoption of the amendment offered by Mr. Barrett of Dover, Mr. Barrett called for a yea and nay vote. The roll was called with the following result:

YEAS, 22.

ROCKINGHAM COUNTY. Severance, Brown of Hampton Falls, Quimby of Kingston, George, Bickford, Swain.

STRAFFORD COUNTY. Barrett.

BELKNAP COUNTY. Morrill of New Hampton, Sanborn of Sanbornton.

CARROLL COUNTY. Littlefield.

MERRIMACK COUNTY. Messer, Hutchins of Pittsfield.

HILLSBOROUGH COUNTY. Goodwin, Bussell, McLane.

CHESHIRE COUNTY. Harris of Chesterfield.

GRAFTON COUNTY. Glover, Pinneo.

COÖS COUNTY. Gathercole, Piper, Wilson, O'Connor, Lennon.

NAYS, 264.

ROCKINGHAM COUNTY. Sawyer of Atkinson, Preston of Auburn, White of Deerfield, Hardy, Shute, Scammon, Smith of Exeter, Brown of Fremont, Lane of Hampton, Pridham, Warner, Gerrish, Payne, Blaisdell, Foye, Nelson, Newton, Young.

STRAFFORD COUNTY. Howe of Barrington, Mathes, Libby of Dover, Whittemore, Smith of Dover, Wesley, Davis of Lee, McCrillis, Crocker, Warren, Harrity, Boutin, Andrews, Caverly.

BELKNAP COUNTY. Pinkham, Hoitt of Barnstead, Smith of Center Harbor, Potter, Davis of Laconia, Hull, Prescott, Chase of Laconia, Kimball of Laconia, Quimby of Meredith, Rogers, Mason of Tilton.

CARROLL COUNTY.   Stevens, Weeks, Fifield, Dow of
Conway, Burnell, Philbrick of Effingham, Drake, Trickey,
Greene, French, Abbott of Ossipee, Hoyt of Sandwich, Pol-
lard, Blake of Wakefield, Beacham.

. MERRIMACK COUNTY.   Fontaine, Harris of Boscawen,
White of Bow, Morse of Bradford, Beck, Langmaid, Durgin,
Symonds, Cate, Shepard, Kennedy, Willis, Hill, A. W., of
Concord, Roby, Woodman, Kimball of Concord, Emerson
of Concord, Davis of Concord, Critchett, Mathews of Con-
cord, Hill, E. J., of Concord, Ahern, Donagan, Bunten of
Dunbarton, Tripp, Morin of Franklin, Davis of Franklin,
Twombly, Worthley, Sanborn of Northfield, Tallant, Aldrich,
Foss, Walker of Pittsfield, Little of Salisbury, Ela, Burbank,
Mason of Wilmot.

HILLSBOROUGH COUNTY.   Farley of Amherst, Goold of
Bennington, Shattuck, Craine, Tobie, Pattee, Eaton, Putnam,
Brown of Greenville, Ware of Hancock, Ward, Farley of
Hollis, Connell, Center, Holt, Cavanaugh, Nyberg, Abbott of
Manchester, Chase of Manchester, Donahue, Bartlett of Man-
chester, Sheehan, Bunton, A. S., of Manchester, Johnson,
Straw of Manchester, Wright, Barr of Manchester, Carpenter,
Morgan, Stewart of Manchester, Tonery, Ryan, Trinity,
Whalen, Riordan, Sullivan of Manchester, Shaughnessey,
Sasseville, Marshall, Morse of Manchester, Couch, Bunton,
A. B., of Manchester, Armstrong, Tinkham, Graf, Quimby
of Manchester, Scannell, Dinsmore. Dozois, Janelle, Kohler,
Filion, Lynch, Kane, Newman, Simpson, Hodgman, Sawyer
of Milford, Robinson, Needham, Kendall, Lund, Tuck,
Duncklee, Lampron, Buckley of Nashua, Ingham, Spalding,
Lintott, Morse of Nashua. Shenton, Collins, Hills of Nashua,
Moran of Nashua. Dionne, Jones of New Ipswich, Peabody,
Miller, Smith of Peterborough, Fitzgerald, Bragdon, Sheldon.

CHESHIRE COUNTY.   Ware of Alstead, Tenney, Fuller,
Holland, Cutler, Pierce of Jaffrey, Jones of Keene, Whitney,
Donovan, Moors, Fox, Scott, Amidon, Fletcher, Merrill,
Lane of Swanzey, Boyden, Ramsay, Sherman of Walpole,
Hall, Kellom.

SULLIVAN COUNTY.   Clark, Hamlin of Charlestown, Sherman of Claremont, Chandler, Long, Churchill, Walker of

Grantham, Matthews of Newport, True, Philbrick of Springfield, Russell of Sunapee, Ball.

GRAFTON COUNTY. McMurphey, Morrill of Ashland, Pierce of Bethlehem, Calley, Little of Campton, Gates, Dorothy, Foster, Kimball of Grafton, Howe of Hanover, Whitcher, Carr, Pike of Haverhill, Barnard, Evans, Goold of Lebanon, Pike of Lebanon, Comings, Stanley, Remich, Mitchell of Littleton, Blake of Littleton, Converse, King, Chase of Orford, Gould of Plymouth, Ferrin, Russell of Rumney, Houston, Bell.

COÖS COUNTY. Caird, Stewart of Berlin, Smyth, Goss, Vaillancourt, Kent of Berlin, Gallagher, Hicks, Martin, Jordan, Tillotson, Hamlin of Dummer, Bragg, Libby of Gorham, Buckley of Lancaster, Ellis, Trafton, McDonald of Northumberland, Smith of Pittsburg, Harriman, Darling, Babcock, and the amendment was not adopted.

The bill was then ordered to a third reading.

Mr. Ahern of Concord moved that the rules be suspended and the bill read a third time by its title. The question being upon the adoption of the motion,

(Discussion ensued.)

Mr. Barrett of Dover called for a yea and nay vote, and the roll was called with the following result:

YEAS, 229.

ROCKINGHAM COUNTY. Sawyer of Atkinson, Preston of Auburn, Morse of Chester, Darbe, White of Deerfield, Hardy, Shute, Scammon, Emerson of Hampstead, Lane of Hampton, Pridham, Warner, Gerrish, Blaisdell, Foye, Yeaton, Newton, Young, Swain, Chase of Stratham.

STRAFFORD COUNTY. Howe of Barrington, Mathes, Libby of Dover, Smith of Dover, Wesley, McCrillis, Warren, Small, Harrity, Boutin, Andrews, Caverly.

BELKNAP COUNTY. Pinkham, Hoitt of Barnstead, Smith of Center Harbor, Potter, Davis of Laconia, Hull, Chase of Laconia, Edwards, Kimball of Laconia, Morrill of New Hampton, Rogers, Mason of Tilton.

CARROLL COUNTY. Littlefield, Fifield, Dow of Conway,

Drake, Trickey, Greene, French, Hoyt of Sandwich, Pollard, Blake of Wakefield, Beacham.

MERRIMACK COUNTY.   Fontaine, Harris of Boscawen, Beck, Durgin, Symonds, Cate, Kennedy, Willis, Hill, A. W., of Concord, Roby, Woodman, Kimball of Concord, Davis of Concord, Critchett, Mathews of Concord, Hill, E. J., of Concord, Ahern, Donagan, Bunten of Dunbarton, Phillips, Morin of Franklin, Davis of Franklin, Twombly, Messer, Aldrich, Foss, Walker of Pittsfield, Little of Salisbury, Burbank, Mason of Wilmot.

HILLSBOROUGH COUNTY.   Farley of Amherst, Gould of Bennington, Shattuck, Craine, Tobie, Pattee, Putnam, Brown of Greenville, Ware of Hancock, Ward, Farley of Hollis, Center, Holt, Cavanaugh, Nyberg, Abbott of Manchester, Chase of Manchester, Donahue, Bartlett of Manchester, Sheehan, Bunton, A. S., of Manchester, Johnson, Straw of Manchester, Wright, Barr of Manchester, Carpenter, Morgan, Ryan, Trinity, Whalen, Riordan, Sullivan of Manchester, Shaughnessey, Sasseville, Marshall, Morse of Manchester, Couch, Bunton, A. B., of Manchester, Armstrong, Tinkham, Graf, Quimby of Manchester, Scannell, Dinsmore, Dozois, Janelle, Kohler, Filion, Lynch, Kane, Newman, Simpson, Hodgman, Sawyer of Milford, Robinson, Needham, Kendall, Lund, Tuck, Duncklee, Buckley of Nashua, Ingham, Bussell, Spalding, Lintott, Shenton, Hills of Nashua, Dionne, Jones of New Ipswich, Miller, Smith of Peterborough, Fitzgerald, Bragdon, Sheldon.

CHESHIRE COUNTY.   Ware of Alstead, Gowing, Tenney, Holland, Cutler, Pierce of Jaffrey, Jones of Keene, Whitney, Donovan, Moors, Fox, Scott, Fletcher, Merrill, Lane of Swanzey, Ramsay, Sherman of Walpole, Hall.

SULLIVAN COUNTY.   Clark, Hamlin of Charlestown, Long, Churchill, Matthews of Newport, True, Philbrick of Springfield, Russell of Sunapee.

GRAFTON COUNTY.   McMurphey, Morrill of Ashland, Pierce of Bethlehem, Calley, Little of Campton, Dorothy, Kimball of Grafton, Whitcher, Carr, Pike of Haverhill, Barnard, Evans, Goold of Lebanon, Pike of Lebanon, Comings, Stanley, Remich, Mitchell of Littleton, Converse, Chase of

37

Orford, Gould of Plymouth, Ferrin, Russell of Rumney, Houston, Bell.

Coös County. Caird, Stewart of Berlin, Smyth, Goss, Vaillancourt, Kent of Berlin, Gallagher, Martin, Jordan, Tillotson, Hamlin of Dummer, Bragg, Libby of Gorham, Buckley of Lancaster, Ellis, Trafton, McDonald of Northumberland, Smith of Pittsburg, Darling, Babcock.

Nays, 26.

Rockingham County. George, Bickford, Nelson.

Strafford County. Barrett.

Belknap County. Fecteau, Quimby of Meredith, Sanborn of Sanbornton.

Carroll County. Burnell, Abbott of Ossipee.

Merrimack County. White of Bow, Shepard, Sanborn of Northfield, Hutchins of Pittsfield.

Hillsborough County. Goodwin.

Cheshire County. Amidon, Kellom.

Sullivan County. Walker of Grantham.

Grafton County. Glover, Blake of Littleton, King.

Coös County. Gathercole, Hicks, Piper, Wilson, O'Connor, Harriman,

and the motion prevailed, the rules were suspended, and the bill read a third time by its title. The bill was then passed and sent to the Senate for concurrence.

MESSAGE FROM THE SENATE.

A message from the Honorable Senate, by its clerk, announced that the Senate has granted the request of the House of Representatives for a committee of conference in relation to the Senate amendments to House bill No. 473, entitled "An act to regulate the traffic in intoxicating liquor," and the President has appointed as members of such committee on the part of the Senate, Senators Bickford, Hoyt of District No. 21, and Page.

COMMITTEE REPORTS.

Mr. Roby of Concord, for the Committee on Fisheries and Game, to whom was referred An act to amend section 16 of chapter 79 of the Session Laws of 1901, relating to the taking of deer, having considered the same, report the same with the following resolution :

Resolved, That the bill ought to pass.

The report was accepted and the bill laid upon the table to be printed.

Mr. McDonald of Northumberland, for the Committee on Appropriations, to whom was referred Joint resolution providing for the erection of an elevator or elevators in the state house for the use of members of the Senate, House of Representatives, state officers, employees, and the public, having considered the same, report the same with amended enacting clause and with the following resolution :

Resolved, That the joint resolution with amended enacting clause ought to pass. Amend the enacting clause by striking out all the words after " Joint resolution," and inserting in place thereof the following : " relating to repairs upon the state house."

The report was accepted, the amendments adopted, and the joint resolution ordered to a third reading.

Mr. Wright of Manchester, for the Committee on Appropriations, to whom was referred An act in amendment of chapter 64, Laws of 1899, relating to firemen's relief fund, having considered the same, report the same with the following resolution :

Resolved, That the bill ought to pass.

Mr. Dow of Conway, for the Committee on Appropriations, to whom was referred An act to provide for a revision of the general and public laws, having considered the same, report the same with the following resolution :

Resolved, That the bill ought to pass.

The reports were severally accepted and the bills ordered to a third reading.

Mr. Hoyt of Sandwich, for the Committee on Agriculture, to whom was referred An act in amendment of chapter 33, Laws of 1893, entitled "An act to regulate the compensation for cattle killed by order of the cattle commissioners," having considered the same, report the same with the following resolution :

Resolved, That it is inexpedient to legislate, as the subject matter sought has been incorporated in a bill favorably reported.

Mr. French of Moultonborough, for the Committee on Railroads, to whom was referred An act authorizing the Portsmouth, Kittery & York Street Railway to keep and maintain a ferry on Piscataqua river, and for other purposes, having considered the same, report the same with the following resolution:

Resolved, That it is inexpedient to legislate.

Mr. French of Moultonborough, for the Committee on Railroads, to whom was referred An act to incorporate the Ashland, Sandwich & Wolfeborough Railway Company, having considered the same, report the same with the following resolution:

Resolved, That it is inexpedient to legislate.

Mr. French of Moultonborough, for the Committee on Railroads, to whom was referred An act to amend the charter of the Ashland & Asquam Electric Railway Company, having considered the same, report the same with the following resolution:

Resolved, That it is inexpedient to legislate.

Mr. Bunton, A. S., of Manchester, for the Committee on Banks, to whom was referred An act to incorporate the Keene Trust Company, having considered the same, report the same with the following resolution:

Resolved, That it is inexpedient to legislate.

The reports were severally accepted and the resolutions reported by the committees adopted.

Mr. Newton of Portsmouth, for the special committee consisting of the delegation from the city of Portsmouth, to whom was referred An act in amendment of an act, entitled "An act for the enlargement and extension of water-works of the city of Portsmouth," approved March 10, 1899, having considered the same, report the same with the following resolution:

Resolved, That the bill ought to pass.

The report was accepted. On motion of Mr. Yeaton of Portsmouth, the bill was recommitted to a special committee consisting of the delegation from the city of Portsmouth.

Mr. Bunton, A. S., of Manchester, for the Committee on Banks, reported the following entitled bill, "An act providing for the taxation of building and loan associations," with the resolution that the bill ought to pass.

The report was accepted and the bill read a first time.

The question being,

Shall the bill be read a second time?

Mr. Whittemore of Dover moved that the bill be laid upon the table. On a *viva voce* vote the motion did not prevail.

(Discussion ensued.)

Mr. Barrett of Dover moved that the bill be indefinitely postponed and upon this question called for a division.

(Discussion ensued.)

Mr. Barrett moved that the bill, his motion, and the call for a division be laid upon the table. On a *viva voce* vote the motion prevailed and the bill, the motion to indefinitely postpone, and the call for a division by Mr. Barrett were laid upon the table.

Mr. Buckley of Lancaster, for the Committee on Judiciary, reported the following entitled bill, "An act to exempt from local taxation the hotel property that may be erected in the village of North Stratford in the town of Stratford," with the resolution that the bill ought to pass.

The report was accepted. The first reading being in order, on motion of Mr. Lennon of Stratford, the rules were suspended and the bill read a first time by its title. The bill was then ordered to a second reading. On motion of the same gentleman, the rules were suspended and the bill read a second time by its title. The bill was then laid upon the table to be printed. On motion of the same gentleman, the rules were suspended and the printing of the bill dispensed with. The bill was then ordered to a third reading. On motion of the same gentleman, the rules were further suspended and the bill read a third time by its title and passed and sent to the Senate for concurrence.

Mr. Felker of Madbury, for the Committee on Agriculture, reported the following joint resolution, " Joint resolution in favor of the owners of farm animals slaughtered by the gov-

ernment to prevent the spread of the foot and mouth disease,"
with the resolution that the joint resolution ought to pass.

The report was accepted and the joint resolution read a first
time and ordered to a second reading. On motion of Mr.
Converse of Lyme, the rules were suspended and the joint resolution read a second time. The joint resolution was then laid
upon the table to be printed and then referred to the Committee on Appropriations. On motion of Mr. Converse of Lyme,
the rules were suspended and the printing of the joint resolution dispensed with. The joint resolution was then referred
to the Committee on Appropriations.

Mr. Woodman of Concord, for the Committee on Judiciary,
reported the following entitled bill, "An act in addition to and
in amendment to section 10 of chapter 198 of the Public Statutes, relating to trustees of estates," with the resolution that
the bill ought to pass.

The report was accepted and the bill read a first time and
ordered to a second reading.

Mr. Whitcher of Haverhill, for the Committee on Judiciary,
reported the following entitled bill, "An act in amendment of
sections 3, 4, 5, and 6 of chapter 220 of the Public Statutes,
relating to attachment of real estate," with the resolution that
the bill ought to pass.

The report was accepted and the bill read a first time and
ordered to a second reading. On motion of Mr. Whitcher of
Haverhill, the rules were suspended and the bill read a second
time by its title. The bill was then laid upon the table to be
printed.

Mr. French of Moultonborough, for the Committee on Railroads, reported the following entitled bill, "An act to incorporate the Sandwich Electric Railway Company," with the
resolution that the bill ought to pass.

The report was accepted. The first reading being in order,
on motion of Mr. French of Moultonborough, the rules were
suspended and the bill read a first time by its title. The bill
was then ordered to a second reading. On motion of the same
gentleman, the rules were suspended and the bill read a second
time by its title. The bill was then laid upon the table to be
printed. On motion of the same gentleman, the rules were

suspended and the printing of the bill dispensed with. The bill was then ordered to a third reading. On motion of the same gentleman, the rules were further suspended and the bill read a third time by its title and passed and sent to the Senate for concurrence.

Mr. French of Moultonborough, for the Committee on Railroads, reported the following entitled bill, "An act to revive, amend, and extend the charter of the Alton & Gilmanton Electric Railway Company," with the resolution that the bill ought to pass.

The report was accepted. The first reading being in order, on motion of Mr. French of Moultonborough, the rules were suspended and the bill read a first time by its title. The bill was then ordered to a second reading. On motion of the same gentleman, the rules were suspended and the bill read a second time by its title. The bill was then laid upon the table to be printed. On motion of the same gentleman, the rules were suspended and the printing of the bill dispensed with. The bill was then ordered to a third reading. On motion of the same gentleman, the rules were further suspended and the bill read a third time by its title and passed and sent to the Senate for concurrence.

Mr. French of Moultonborough, for the Committee on Railroads, reported the following entitled bill, "An act to revive, amend, and extend the charter of the Gilmanton & Barnstead Electric Railway Company," with the resolution that the bill ought to pass.

The report was accepted. The first reading being in order, on motion of Mr. French of Moultonborough, the rules were suspended and the bill read a first time by its title. The bill was then ordered to a second reading. On motion of the same gentleman, the rules were suspended and the bill read a second time by its title. The bill was then laid upon the table to be printed. On motion of the same gentleman, the rules were suspended and the printing of the bill dispensed with. The bill was then ordered to a third reading. On motion of the same gentleman, the rules were further suspended and the bill read a third time by its title and passed and sent to the Senate for concurrence.

Messrs. French of Moultonborough, Crossman of Lisbon, Dorothy of Enfield, Kimball of Laconia, Long of Claremont, Hall of Westmoreland, Morgan of Manchester, Ahern of Concord, Bussell of Nashua, Jewell of Dover, and Martin of Colebrook, for a majority of the Committee on Railroads, to whom was referred An act to incorporate the Winnipiseogee Valley Street Railway, having considered the same, report the same with the following resolution:

Resolved, That it is inexpedient to legislate.

Mr. Harris of Boscawen, for a minority of the Committee on Railroads, to whom was referred An act to incorporate the Winnipiseogee Valley Street Railway, having considered the same, report the same with the following amendment and with the resolution that the bill as amended ought to pass.

Amend the bill by adding a new section as follows:

SECT. 14.   This act shall be void and inoperative as to all parts of said railway not constructed and ready for operation within two years from its passage.

Mr. Harris of Boscawen moved that the bill and reports be laid upon the table and made the special order for Tuesday, March 31, at 11 o'clock.

The question being upon the adoption of the motion, Mr. French of Moultonborough offered the following amendment:

Amend by making the hour 3 o'clock instead of 11 o'clock.

The question being upon the adoption of the amendment offered by Mr. French, on a *viva voce* vote the amendment was not adopted.

(Discussion ensued.)

On a *viva voce* vote the amendment was adopted and the bill and reports were laid upon the table and made the special order for Tuesday, March 31, at 3 o'clock.

The Committee on Conference upon the non-concurrence of the House of Representatives in the passage of the amendments of the Senate to the following entitled House bill, "An act to regulate the traffic in intoxicating liquor," reported the same with a recommendation that the Senate recede from its position as to the following amendments:

Amend section 7, first class, by striking out all after the word "lodging" in said first class.

Amend section 16, subdivision second, by striking out the word "ten" in the second line of said subdivision, and insert in the place thereof the word "eleven."

Amend section 31 by striking out the word "and" in the next to the last line of said section, and inserting after the word "sixth" and before the word "classes" in said line, the words "and eighth."

The committee further recommended that the following amendments be adopted :

Amend section 7, first class, by striking out the following words : "If the guest resorts to a house for food only, then he must partake of and pay for a meal costing not less than twenty-five cents."

Amend section 16, subdivision second, by adding at the end of said subdivision the words "unless the town or board of mayor and aldermen of the city where such licensee carries on business shall extend the hours not later than 11 o'clock at night, which said town or board of mayor and aldermen is hereby authorized to do."

> JOHN C. BICKFORD,
> ARTHUR E. HOYT,
> CALVIN PAGE,
> *Senate Conferees.*
>
> FREDERIC E. SMALL,
> LEWIS W. PHILLIPS,
> *House Conferees.*

The report was accepted and on a *viva voce* vote the amendments recommended by the committee were adopted. The bill was then sent to the secretary of state to be engrossed.

SECOND READINGS.

An act in amendment of chapter 208 of the Session Laws of 1899, entitled "An act to incorporate the Walpole Electric Light and Power Company," and of an act amending said act passed at the present session.

The second reading being in order, on motion of Mr. Whitcher of Haverhill, the rules were suspended and the bill read a second time by its title. The bill was then laid upon the table to be printed. On motion of the same gentleman, the rules were suspended and the printing of the bill dispensed with. The bill was then ordered to a third reading. On motion of the same gentleman, the rules were suspended and the bill read a third time by its title and passed and sent to the Senate for concurrence.

An act in amendment of, and in addition to, section 3, chapter 105 of the Laws of 1901, in relation to political caucuses and conventions.

Read a second time and laid upon the table to be printed. On motion of Mr. Whittemore of Dover, the rules were suspended and the printing of the bill dispensed with. The bill was then ordered to a third reading. On motion of the same gentleman, the rules were further suspended and the bill read a third time by its title and passed and sent to the Senate for concurrence.

An act to regulate the speed and operation of automobiles and motor vehicles on highways.

The second reading being in order, on motion of Mr. Ahern of Concord, the rules were suspended and the bill read a second time by its title. The bill was then laid upon the table to be printed.

SPECIAL ORDER.

Mr. Lynch of Manchester called for the special order, it being the following entitled bill, "An act in amendment of section 14, chapter 180, Public Statutes, regulating the hours of labor for women and minors in manufacturing or mechanical establishments."

The question being upon the adoption of the resolution reported by the committee that it is inexpedient to legislate,

(Discussion ensued.)

On motion of Mr. Libby of Gorham, the bill and report were laid upon the table and made the special order for Tuesday, March 31, at 11 o'clock.

At 5.55, on motion of Mr. Ahern of Concord, the House adjourned.

AFTERNOON.

The House was called to order in afternoon session immediately upon adjournment of the morning session.

LEAVE OF ABSENCE.

Mr. Demers of Somersworth was granted leave of absence on account of important business.

THIRD READINGS.

An act in amendment of chapter 64, Laws of 1899, relating to firemen's relief fund.

An act to provide for a revision of the general and public laws.

Joint resolution relating to repairs upon the state house.

Severally read a third time and passed and sent to the Senate for concurrence.

SPECIAL ORDER.

Mr. Scammon of Exeter called for the special order, it being the following entitled bill, "An act to abolish capital punishment."

The question being,

Shall the bill pass?

And upon this question Mr. Ahern of Concord having called for a division, on motion of Mr. Scammon of Exeter, the bill was laid upon the table and made the special order for Tuesday, March 31, at 11 o'clock.

On motion of Mr. Long of Claremont, at 6 o'clock the House adjourned.

FRIDAY, MARCH 27, 1903.

The House met at 10 o'clock, according to adjournment.

LEAVE OF ABSENCE.

Mr. Swain of South Hampton was granted leave of absence for Tuesday, March 30, on account of pressing business.

COMMITTEE REPORTS.

Mr. Willis of Concord, for the Committee on Engrossed Bills, reported that they had examined and found correctly engrossed the following entitled bill:

An act to regulate the traffic in intoxicating liquor.

The report was accepted.

SECOND READING.

An act in addition to and in amendment to section 10 of chapter 198 of the Public Statutes, relating to trustees of estates.

Read a second time and laid upon the table to be printed.

BILLS, ETC., FORWARDED.

An act to amend section 1 of chapter 33 of the Laws of 1893, relating to the diseases of domestic animals.

Taken from the table and referred to the Committee on Appropriations.

An act in amendment of section 3 of chapter 7 of the Public Statutes, relating to the state house and yard.

An act in amendment of section 2 of chapter 32 of the Laws of 1895, entitled "An act in relation to printing the reports of certain state officers."

Joint resolution appropriating money for the support of the New Hampshire School for Feeble-Minded Children, necessary school buildings, and to provide water.

An act relating to the publication of the Session Laws.

An act in relation to licensing dogs kept for breeding purposes.

Severally taken from the table and ordered to a third reading.

An act amending sections 37, 38, and 40 of chapter 59 of the Session Laws of 1895, as amended by chapter 25 of the Laws of 1901.

Taken from the table and ordered to a third reading. On motion of Mr. Roby of Concord, the rules were suspended and the bill read a third time by its title and passed. On motion of Mr. Ahern of Concord, the title was amended by adding after the figures " 1901," the words " in relation to the militia." The bill was then sent to the Senate for concurrence.

On motion of Mr. Buckley of Lancaster,—

Resolved, That the clerk of the House be authorized and instructed to have printed 10,000 copies of House bill No. 473, entitled "An act to regulate the traffic in intoxicating liquor," as finally passed, and to distribute five copies to each member of the House and of the Honorable Senate, and that the secretary of state be instructed to distribute the remainder forthwith to the several clerks of the towns and cities of the state *pro rata* according to population.

On motion of Mr. Marshall of Manchester, at 10.13 the House adjourned.

MONDAY, MARCH 30, 1903.

The House met at 8 o'clock in the evening, according to adjournment.

LEAVES OF ABSENCE.

Mr. Churchill of Cornish was granted leave of absence for the balance of the session on account of urgent business.

Mr. Willis of Concord was granted leave of absence for the balance of the session on account of urgent business.

Messrs. Whitaker and Ward of Hillsborough were granted leave of absence for Tuesday, March 31, for the purpose of attending a funeral.

MESSAGE FROM THE SENATE.

A message from the Honorable Senate, by its clerk, announced that the Senate concurs with the House of Representatives in the passage of the following entitled bills and joint resolutions :

An act in amendment of the charter of the Exeter Gas, Electric Light and Power Company.

An act to amend chapter 60, section 3 of the Statute Laws of 1891, relating to dog licenses.

An act authorizing the city of Nashua to exempt the Highland Spring Sanatorium Company from taxation.

An act authorizing the Concord & Montreal Railroad, lessor, to vote on all stock owned by it in other corporations.

An act to incorporate the Dunbarton & Goffstown Street Railway Company.

An act in amendment of section 22, chapter 27, Laws of 1895, entitled "An act in relation to the incorporation, organization, and regulation of street railway companies, and authorizing the use of electricity as motive power by existing steam railroads."

Joint resolution for an appropriation for the benefit of the New Hampshire College of Agriculture and the Mechanic Arts.

An act to incorporate the Kearsarge Mountain Electric Railway Company.

An act to incorporate the Mt. Belknap Electric Railway Company.

An act to incorporate the Candia & Deerfield Street Railway Company.

An act to incorporate the Manchester & Haverhill Street Railway Company.

An act to incorporate the Concord, Dover & Rochester Street Railway.

The message further announced that the Senate refuses to concur with the House of Representatives in the passage of the following joint resolution :

Joint resolution to encourage the breeding and exhibition of thoroughbred farm animals.

The message also announced that the Senate has passed bills with the following titles, in the passage of which it asks the concurrence of the House of Representatives :

An act to establish the office of medical referee and amending chapter 262 of the Public Statutes, relating to coroners' inquests.

An act in relation to the powers and duties of police commissioners of the city of Manchester.

Severally read a first and second time and referred to the Committee on Judiciary.

The message also announced that the Senate concurs with the House of Representatives in the passage of the following bill, with amendment, in the passage of which amendment it asks the concurrence of the House of Representatives:

An act to legalize a vote taken at the annual town meeting in Boscawen on the second Tuesday of March, A. D. 1903.

Amend by inserting after the word " taken" in the first line, the following: " at the annual town meeting in Boscawen on the second Tuesday of March, 1903."

On motion of Mr. Whitcher of Haverhill, the amendment was concurred in.

The message further announced that the Senate concurs with the House of Representatives in the passage of the following concurrent resolution, with amendment, in the passage of which amendment it asks the concurrence of the House of Representatives:

WHEREAS, it appears that all necessary legislative work may easily be accomplished for Friday, the 3d day of April; therefore, be it

Resolved, by the House of Representatives, the Senate concurring, that the present session of the legislature be brought to a final adjournment on Friday, the 3d day of April, at 12 o'clock noon, and be it further

Resolved, That all reports, bills, and joint resolutions at that time pending in either branch of the legislature be indefinitely postponed.

Amend the foregoing resolution by changing the date of adjournment from Friday, the 3d day of April, to Thursday, the 2d day of April.

Mr. Whitcher of Haverhill moved that the House concur in the amendment sent down by the Senate. The question being upon the adoption of the motion,

(Discussion ensued.)

On motion of Mr. Remich of Littleton, the amendment was laid upon the table and made the special order for Tuesday, March 31, at 11.30 o'clock.

On motion of Mr. Hill of Concord, the following entitled bill, " An act providing for the taxation of building and loan associations," was taken from the table and made the special order for Tuesday, March 31, at 11.35 o'clock.

Mr. Ahern of Concord moved that the following entitled bill, " An act to extend the Union school district to include the city of Concord," be taken from the table and made the special order for Tuesday, March 31, at 12 o'clock. The question being upon the adoption of the motion,

(Discussion ensued.)

Mr. Durgin of Concord called for a division. Mr. Ahern withdrew his motion.

On motion of Mr. French of Moultonborough, the following entitled bill, " An act relating to negotiable instruments, being an act to establish a law uniform with the laws of other states on that subject," was taken from the table and made the special order for Tuesday, March 31, at 12 o'clock.

On motion of Mr. Remich of Littleton, the following entitled bill, " An act requiring state certification of teachers of public schools," was taken from the table and made the special order for Tuesday, March 31, at 12.30 o'clock.

On motion of Mr. Durgin of Concord, at 8.17 the House adjourned.

TUESDAY, MARCH 31, 1903.

The House met at 11 o'clock.

Prayer was offered by the chaplain.

LEAVE OF ABSENCE.

Mr. King of Orange was granted leave of absence on account of the death of his father.

MESSAGE FROM THE SENATE.

A message from the Honorable Senate, by its clerk, announced that the Senate concurs with the House of Representatives in the passage of the following entitled bills and joint resolutions:

An act in amendment of section 1, chapter 31 of the Laws of 1897, entitled "An act in amendment of section 6 of chapter 83 of the Public Statutes, in relation to the settlement of paupers."

An act to exempt certain property of the Keene Young Men's Christian Association from taxation.

An act to provide suitable armory quarters for the National Guard at Manchester.

An act to incorporate the Caledonia Power Company.

An act to incorporate the Peabody River Improvement Company.

An act in relation to the administration of the state prison and to provide for necessary improvements and repairs.

An act providing for a state system of highway construction and improvement and for the appointment of highway engineers.

An act to revive the charter of the Colebrook Water Company, approved February 23, 1897.

Joint resolution in favor of John M. Stanyan for soldier's pay and bounty.

COMMITTEE REPORTS.

Mr. Willis of Concord, for the Committee on Engrossed Bills, reported that they had examined and found correctly engrossed the following entitled bills and joint resolutions:

Joint resolution in favor of the widow of John W. Jewett of Claremont.

Joint resolution for an appropriation for the benefit of the New Hampshire College of Agriculture and the Mechanic Arts.

An act authorizing the Concord & Montreal Railroad, lessor, to vote on all stock owned by it in other corporations.

An act to incorporate the Manchester & Haverhill Street Railway Company.

An act authorizing the city of Nashua to exempt the Highland Spring Sanatorium Company from taxation.

An act relating to the setting off by the legislature of territory of one town or city on to that of another town or city.

38

An act to sever certain residences from the school district of the town of Wilmot and to annex the same to the school district of the town of New London.

An act in amendment of section 1, chapter 31 of the Laws of 1897, entitled "An act in amendment of section 6 of chapter 83 of the Public Statutes, in relation to the settlement of paupers."

An act to incorporate the Caledonia Power Company.

Joint resolution in favor of John M. Stanyan for soldier's pay and bounty.

An act in relation to the administration of the state prison and to provide for necessary improvements and repairs.

An act to incorporate the Concord, Dover & Rochester Street Railway.

An act in amendment of the charter of the city of Manchester, establishing a board of assessors in place of the assessors provided under the charter and laws of the state.

An act to revive the charter of the Colebrook Water Company, approved February 23, 1897.

An act to provide suitable armory quarters for the National Guard at Manchester.

An act in amendment of the charter of the Exeter Gas, Electric Light and Power Company.

An act to exempt certain property of the Keene Young Men's Christian Association from taxation.

An act in amendment of section 22, chapter 27, Laws of 1895, entitled "An act in relation to the incorporation, organization, and regulation of street railway companies, and authorizing the use of electricity as motive power by existing steam railroads."

An act to incorporate the Mt. Belknap Electric Railway Company.

An act to incorporate the Kearsarge Mountain Electric Railway Company.

An act to incorporate the Peabody River Improvement Company.

An act providing for a state system of highway construction and improvement, and for the appointment of highway engineers.

An act to incorporate the Connecticut River Power Company of New Hampshire.

An act to incorporate the Dunbarton & Goffstown Street Railway Company.

The report was accepted.

Mr. Mitchell of Littleton, for the Committee on Judiciary, reported the following entitled bill, " An act in relation to the Lisbon village district," with the resolution that the bill ought to pass.

The report was accepted and the bill read a first time and ordered to a second reading. On motion of Mr. Ahern of Concord, the rules were suspended and the bill read a second time by its title. The bill was then laid upon the table to be printed. On motion of the same gentleman, the rules were suspended and the printing of the bill dispensed with. The bill was then ordered to a third reading. On motion of the same gentleman, the rules were further suspended and the bill read a third time by its title and passed and sent to the Senate for concurrence.

BILLS FORWARDED.

An act to amend section 16 of chapter 79 of the Session Laws of 1901, relating to the taking of deer.

An act in amendment of sections 3, 4, 5, and 6 of chapter 220 of the Public Statutes, relating to attachment of real estate.

An act in addition to and in amendment to section 10 of •chapter 198 of the Public Statutes, relating to trustees of estates.

Severally taken from the table and ordered to a third reading.

An act to regulate the speed and operation of automobiles and motor vehicles on highways.

Taken from the table.

Mr. Remich of Littleton offered the following amendment:

Amend section 1 by striking out the word " ten " in the sixth line of said section and by inserting in place thereof the word " six."

On a *viva voce* vote the amendment was adopted.

Mr. Howe of Hanover offered the following amendment:

Amend section 3 by striking out the word " ten " in the

twelfth line of said section and by inserting in place thereof the word " six."

On a *viva voce* vote the amendment was adopted. The bill was then ordered to a third reading.

Mr. Small of Rochester called for the special order, it being the following entitled bill, " An act in amendment of section 14, chapter 180, Public Statutes, regulating the hours of labor for women and minors in manufacturing or mechanical establishments."

The question being upon the adoption of the resolution reported by the Committee on Labor that it is inexpedient to legislate,

(Discussion ensued.)

Mr. Kohler of Manchester moved the previous question.
The question being,
Shall the main question be now put?
Mr. Sullivan of Manchester called for a yea and nay vote.

(Discussion ensued.)

Mr. Sullivan withdrew his call for a yea and nay vote and called for a division.

(Discussion ensued.)

Mr. Libby of Gorham moved that the report of the committee be laid upon the table.

(Discussion ensued.)

Mr. Libby withdrew his motion.
The question being,
Shall the main question be now put? and Mr. Sullivan of Manchester having called for a division and the counting having proceeded, the vote was declared to be manifestly in the affirmative, and the previous question was ordered.

The question being upon the resolution reported by the committee, Mr. Sullivan of Manchester called for a division. The counting having proceeded, the vote was declared to be manifestly in the negative, and the resolution reported by the committee was not adopted.   The bill was then ordered to a third reading.   On motion of Mr. Lynch of Manchester, the rules were suspended and the bill read a third time by its title.   The bill was then passed and sent to the Senate for concurrence.

SPECIAL ORDER.

Mr. Ahern of Concord called for the special order, it being the following entitled bill, " An act to abolish capital punishment."

The question being,

Shall the bill pass?

On motion of Mr. Scammon of Exeter, the rules were suspended and the bill placed back upon its second reading.

Mr. Bell of Woodstock offered the following amendment:

Amend the bill by striking out all of section 1 after the word "follows" in the eleventh line and inserting in place thereof the following:

SECT. 5. The punishment of murder in the first degree shall be death or imprisonment for life as the jury may determine; and the punishment of murder in the second degree shall be imprisonment for life or for such term as the court having cognizance of the offense may order. If the jury shall find the respondent guilty of murder in the first degree the punishment shall be life imprisonment unless the jury shall add to their verdict the words *with capital punishment.*

On a *viva voce* vote the amendment was adopted.   The bill was then ordered to a third reading.   On motion of Mr. Ahern of Concord, the rules were suspended and the bill read a third time by its title and passed.   On motion of Mr. Buckley of Lancaster, the title was amended by striking out all the words after the word " act," and inserting in place thereof the following, " to regulate the penalty for murder," so that the title shall read as follows: " An act to regulate the penalty for murder."   The bill was then sent to the Senate for concurrence.

On motion of Mr. Ahern of Concord, at 12.30 the House took a recess until 2.30 o'clock.

(After recess.)

Message from the Governor.

To the Speaker of the House of Representatives :

I return to the House of Representatives, in which it originated, House bill No. 298, entitled "An act to provide in common with the state of Vermont for the acquisition, building,
and maintenance of free bridges across the Connecticut river,"
without my signature.

My reasons for the disapproval of this act are :

The bill is very loosely drawn. Its limitations are very
few and by no means definite. But apparently it provides
for the appointment of a civil engineer having a practical
knowledge of bridge work who, in connection with a commission authorized by the state of Vermont, shall proceed after
certain investigations to purchase and free all existing toll
bridges over the Connecticut river between New Hampshire
and Vermont, to construct new free bridges at such points or
places as may seem to them best to promote the public welfare, and to reimburse such towns as have already expended
any money in the freeing of bridges, upon condition that the
state of Vermont shall assume half the expense incurred, and
appropriates $20,000 annually for this purpose until the work
is completed.

The boundary line between New Hampshire and Vermont
is at high water mark on the Vermont side of the Connecticut.
The bridges across the river are therefore all in New Hampshire except perhaps the western abutments. I see no good
reason why we should ask Vermont to assume any part of the
expense of the highways in New Hampshire, or why she
should consent to any such proposition.

The logical result of the passage of this bill would be an
agreement between the representatives of the two states that
in justice we should pay three-fourths or seven-eighths of the
cost of the acquirement of the toll bridges, the construction of
such new ones as in the opinion of the commissioners and engineer may be desirable, and the reimbursement of the towns
that have already freed the bridges in their territory, and having started with this scheme, the probabilities are that we
should feel in duty bound to accept what was recommended

by our engineer.   It comes therefore to this, that the bill authorizes the freeing of all toll bridges over the Connecticut in
New Hampshire, the construction of all needed new ones and
the reimbursement of all towns for all they have expended upon such bridges at the expense of our state treasury.   The
cost cannot be computed.   There is absolutely no limit in the
bill as to the time during which we shall pay $20,000 annual-
ly, and that, when once begun, the project will not call for
several times that sum each year, we have no guarantee.
From the best information I can obtain I judge that at least a
quarter of a million dollars will be required to carry this plan
to completion.

I see no more reason why the state of New Hampshire
should purchase, construct, or maintain bridges across the
Connecticut river than across the Merrimack, the Contoocook,
the Androscoggin, the Cocheco or the Saco, and the passage
of this act, it appears to me, would be unjust discrimination
against the taxpayers of every section of the state, except the
tier of towns along the Connecticut which are generally as
well able to support their own highways as any and which, so
far as I am informed, do not ask for state aid of this kind.

I think we should avoid as far as is practicable the adoption
of projects which will entail upon those who come after us,
for an indefinite period, financial burdens that they may not
be able to bear without great sacrifices.   We have now in
the treasury a large sum received from the United States
government which will be dissipated this year.   The next
legislature will not have it to draw upon and if we are prudent we shall consider this fact and restrain ourselves from
contracting unnecessary obligations which they will have to
discharge.   If this be so, the appropriation of $20,000 an-
nually, practically a perpetuity, for such an object cannot be
defended.

According to the terms of the act, the work contemplated is
not to be proceeded with unless the legislature of Vermont
shall assume half the expense before the first of January, 1905.
At that time another New Hampshire legislature will have
been elected and be ready to assemble, and I think we may
wisely leave to our immediate successors the question whether

the condition of our treasury and the public need warrants the outlay proposed, ascertaining meanwhile, if that is desirable, whether Vermont will join us and if so upon what terms, which can easily be done without giving to an engineer such vast, unlimited, and perpetual powers as this bill proposes.

N. J. BACHELDER,

Governor.

The question being,

Shall the bill pass notwithstanding the objections of His Excellency the Governor?

(Discussion ensued.)

Mr. Britton of Wolfeborough moved the previous question.

The question being,

Shall the main question be now put?

On a *viva voce* vote the previous question was ordered.

The question being,

Shall the bill pass notwithstanding the objections of His Excellency the Governor?

In accordance with the requirement of the constitution, the roll was called with the following result:

YEAS, 162.

ROCKINGHAM COUNTY.   Smith of Exeter, Pridham, Bickford, Foye, Nelson.

STRAFFORD COUNTY.   Libby of Dover, Jewell, Nason, Bunce, Smith of Dover, Felker, Warren, Small, Wentworth, Caverly.

BELKNAP COUNTY.   Pinkham, Smith of Center Harbor, Potter, Davis of Laconia, Prescott, Chase of Laconia, Edwards, Kimball of Laconia.

CARROLL COUNTY.   Stevens, Fifield, Burnell, Drake, Trickey, French, Britton.

MERRIMACK COUNTY.   Graves, Durgin, Kennedy, Roby, Woodman, Emerson of Concord, Davis of Concord, Critchett, Mathews of Concord, Hill, E. J., of Concord, Ahern, Bunten of Dunbarton, Morin of Franklin, Jones of Franklin, Davis of Franklin, Preston of Henniker, Twombly,

Worthley, Messer, Sanborn of Northfield, Hutchins of Pittsfield, Walker of Pittsfield, Little of Salisbury.

HILLSBOROUGH COUNTY. Craine, Pattee, Brown of Greenville, Farley of Hollis, Center, Cavanaugh, Nyberg, Abbott of Manchester, Bartlett of Manchester, Taggart, Sheehan, Bunton, A. S., of Manchester, Carpenter, Morgan, Tonery, Riordan, Marshall, Couch, Bunton, A. B., of Manchester, Tinkham, Quimby of Manchester, Gunderman, Janelle, Lynch, Kane, Newman, Emerson of Manchester, Tuck, Lewis, Lampron, Buckley of Nashua, Bussell, Spalding, Lintott, Morse of Nashua, Shenton, Sullivan of Nashua, Jones of New Ipswich, Peabody, Chase of Weare.

CHESHIRE COUNTY. Ware of Alstead, Tenney, Holland, Cutler, Jones of Keene, Moors, Fox, Scott, Fletcher, Hall, Kellom, Dickinson.

SULLIVAN COUNTY. Clark, Hamlin of Charlestown, Chandler, Long, Lufkin, Aiken, Matthews of Newport, True.

GRAFTON COUNTY. McMurphey, Morrill of Ashland, Davenport, Pierce of Bethlehem, Calley, Little of Campton, Dorothy, Foster, Glover, Kimball of Grafton, Pinneo, Howe of Hanover, Whitcher, Carr, Pike of Haverhill, Barnard, Evans, Goold of Lebanon, Pike of Lebanon, Comings, Remich, Blake of Littleton, Converse, Chase of Orford, Gould of Plymouth, Ferrin, Russell of Rumney, Goodrich, Bell.

COÖS COUNTY. Caird, Smyth, Goss, Kent of Berlin, Gallagher, Gathercole, Hicks, Martin, Bragg, Plaisted, Buckley of Lancaster, Ellis, McDonald of Northumberland, Piper, Smith of Pittsburg, Wilson, O'Connor, Harriman, Lennon, Darling.

NAYS, 80.

ROCKINGHAM COUNTY. Fellows, Morse of Chester, Hardy, Nowell, Scammon, Severance, Brown of Fremont, Duntley, Emerson of Hampstead, Lane of Hampton, Badger, Warner, Gerrish, Brown of Rye.

STRAFFORD COUNTY. Mathes, Whittemore, Barrett, Hayes, Davis of Lee.

BELKNAP COUNTY. Hoitt of Barnstead, Hull, Fecteau, Quimby of Meredith, Sanborn of Sanbornton, Rogers, Mason of Tilton.

CARROLL COUNTY. Littlefield, Dow of Conway, Philbrick of Effingham, Greene, Hoyt of Sandwich, Blake of Wakefield.

MERRIMACK COUNTY. Harris of Boscawen, White of Bow, Beck, Langmaid, Symonds, Cate, Shepard, Kimball of Còncord, Donagan, Tripp, Sanborn of Loudon, Tallant.

HILLSBOROUGH COUNTY. Farley of Amherst, Gould of Bennington, Tobie, Eaton, Putnam, Ware of Hancock, Connell, Chase of Manchester, Donahue, Farrell, Johnson, Straw of Manchester, Wright, Dubuc, Darrah, Shaughnessey, Morse of Manchester, Armstrong, Scannell, Filion, Simpson, Hodgman, Ingham, Miller, Smith of Peterborough, Fitzgerald.

CHESHIRE COUNTY. Gowing, Bemis, Pierce of Jaffrey, Amidon, Lane of Swanzey, Boyden.

GRAFTON COUNTY. Mitchell of Littleton, Bowen.

Coös COUNTY. Hutchins of Berlin, Libby of Gorham,

and the bill passed notwithstanding the objections of His Excellency the Governor. The bill was then sent to the Senate for concurrence.

MESSAGE FROM THE SENATE.

A message from the Honorable Senate, by its clerk, announced that the Senate concurs with the House of Representatives in the passage of the following entitled bill and joint resolutions:

An act to establish water-works in the town of Greenville.

Joint resolution appropriating five hundred dollars ($500) for a monument to be erected at Hackensack, New Jersey, in memory of Gen. Enoch Poor.

Joint resolution appropriating money to be expended for the preservation of the muster rolls.

The message also announced that the Senate has refused a third reading to the following joint resolution, sent up from the House of Representatives:

Joint resolution to appropriate the sum of three hundred

dollars for the purpose of turning Silver stream into Success pond in the township of Success and to screen the outlet to said pond.

The message further announced that the Senate has passed the following joint resolution, in the passage of which it asks the concurrence of the House of Representatives:

Joint resolution appropriating money for screening the outlet of Sunapee lake, so called.

Read a first and second time and referred to the Committee on Fisheries and Game. On motion of Mr. Goold of Lebanon, the reference was rescinded and the joint resolution referred to the Committee on Appropriations.

The message likewise announced that the Senate concurs with the House of Representatives in the passage of the following joint resolution, with amendments, in the passage of which amendments it asks the concurrence of the House of Representatives:

Joint resolution in favor of Ella F. Densmore of Charlestown, Mary F. Lombard of Acworth, Frank G. Smith of Waltham, Mass., Eugene P. Smith of Newport, N. H., and George E. Shattuck of Hinsdale, N. H.

Amend by striking out all after the word "only," in the 15th line, and all of the 16th line.

Further amend by striking out all after the word "kin," in the 19th line, and insert instead thereof the following: "in the following shares: To George E. Shattuck of Hinsdale, the sum of eleven hundred dollars ($1,100); to Ella F. Densmore of Charlestown, four hundred forty dollars and fifty-two cents ($440.52); to Mary F. Lombard of Acworth, four hundred forty dollars and fifty-two cents ($440.52); to Frank G. Smith of Waltham, Massachusetts, four hundred forty dollars and fifty-two cents ($440.52); and to Eugene P. Smith of Newport, four hundred forty dollars fifty-four cents ($440.54).

On motion of Mr. Nason of Dover, the amendment was concurred in.

The message further announced that the Senate concurs with the House of Representatives in the passage of the following bill, with amendment, in the passage of which amendment it asks the concurrence of the House of Representatives:

An act to amend section 14 and section 15, chapter 286 of the Public Statutes, relating to the salaries of the judge and register of probate for Belknap county.

Amend section 2 by inserting after the word " six," in the fifth line of said section, the word " hundred."

On motion of Mr. Ahern of Concord, the amendment was concurred in.

SPECIAL ORDER.

Mr. Whitcher of Haverhill called for the special order, it being the consideration of the following concurrent resolutions with Senate amendment

WHEREAS, It appears that all necessary legislative work may easily be accomplished by Friday, the 3d day of April; therefore, be it

Resolved, By the House of Representatives, the Senate concurring, that the present session of the legislature be brought to a final adjournment on Friday, the 3d day of April, at 12 o'clock noon; and be it further

Resolved, That all reports, bills, and joint resolutions at that time pending in either branch of the legislature be indefinitely postponed.

Amend the foregoing resolution by changing the date of adjournment from Friday, the 3d day of April, to Thursday, the 2d day of April.

On motion of Mr. Severance of Exeter, the House concurred in the concurrent resolution as amended by the Senate.

SPECIAL ORDER.

Mr. Ahern of Concord called for the special order, it being the following entitled bill, "An act providing for the taxation of building and loan associations."

The question being upon the motion of Mr. Barrett of Dover, that the bill be indefinitely postponed and upon this question Mr. Barrett having called for a division,

(Discussion ensued.)

Mr. Barrett withdrew his motion and his call for a division. The bill was then ordered to a second reading. On motion of Mr. Ahern of Concord, the rules were suspended and the bill read a second time by its title. The bill was then laid upon the table to be printed. On motion of the same gentleman, the rules were suspended and the printing of the bill dispensed with. The bill was then ordered to a third reading. On motion of the same gentleman, the rules were further suspended and the bill read a third time by its title and passed and sent to the Senate for concurrence.

SPECIAL ORDER.

Mr. Sheehan of Manchester called for the special order, it being the following entitled bill, "An act relating to negotiable instruments, being an act to establish a law uniform with the laws of other states on that subject."

The question being upon the adoption of the resolution of the committee that it is inexpedient to legislate, upon a *viva voce* vote the resolution was adopted.

SPECIAL ORDER.

Mr. Sheehan of Manchester called for the special order, it being the following entitled bill, "An act requiring state certification of teachers of public schools."

The question being upon the motion of Mr. Jones of New Ipswich, that the report of the minority of the committee be substituted for that of the majority of the committee, Mr. Sheehan of Manchester moved that the bill be indefinitely postponed. The question being upon the adoption of the motion of Mr. Sheehan,

(Discussion ensued.)

Mr. Harris of Boscawen moved the previous question.
The question being,
Shall the main question be now put ?
Mr. Pattee of Goffstown called for a yea and nay vote.

(Discussion ensued.)

Mr. Pattee withdrew his call for a yea and nay vote and called for a division. A division being had, 55 gentlemen voted in the affirmative and 62 gentlemen voted in the negative and no quorum voting, at 5.20 the House was declared adjourned.

AFTERNOON.

The House was called to order in afternoon session immediately upon adjournment of the morning session.

LEAVES OF ABSENCE.

Mr. Cutler of Jaffrey was granted leave of absence for Wednesday, April 1, for the purpose of attending a funeral.

Mr. Morrill of New Hampton was granted leave of absence for to-day and to-morrow for the purpose of attending a funeral.

THIRD READING.

An act in addition to and in amendment to section 10 of chapter 198 of the Public Statutes, relating to trustees of estates.

Read a third time and passed and sent to the Senate for concurrence.

On motion of Mr. French of Moultonborough, at 5.30 the House adjourned.

WEDNESDAY, April 1, 1903.

The House met at 11 o'clock.

Prayer was offered by the chaplain.

MESSAGE FROM THE SENATE.

A message from the Honorable Senate, by its clerk, announced that the Senate concurs with the House of Representatives in the passage of the following entitled bills:

An act to amend chapter 96 of the Session Laws of 1901, relating to high schools.

An act to amend chapter 184 of the Laws of 1897, entitled " An act to incorporate the Dalton Power Company," as amended by section 1, chapter 221 of the Laws of 1899.

An act in amendment of chapter 98 of the Laws of 1901, relating to the duties of tree wardens.

An act to incorporate the Sandwich Electric Railway Company.

An act to revive, amend, and extend the charter of the Alton & Gilmanton Electric Railway Company.

An act to revive, amend, and extend the charter of the Gilmanton & Barnstead Electric Railway Company.

The message also announced that the Senate refuses to concur with the House of Representatives in the passage of the following entitled bills:

An act to enlarge the powers of towns and cities.

An act to provide for the holding of library institutes.

An act to incorporate the Portsmouth & New Castle Street Railway Company.

The message also announced that the Senate concurs with the House of Representatives in the passage of the following bill, with amendment, in the passage of which amendment it asks the concurrence of the House of Representatives:

An act to encourage the planting and perpetuation of forests.

Amend by striking out section 3 and inserting in place thereof the following:

SECT. 3. In order to facilitate the planting of trees as hereinbefore provided, the forestry commission is hereby authorized and directed to contract, without expense to the state, upon terms to be approved by the governor and council, with reputable nurserymen to provide, at a price to be determined upon, seeds and seedlings of timber or forest trees, to landowners for planting within this state in accordance with the terms of section 1 of this act.

On motion of Mr. Hoyt of Sandwich, the amendment was concurred in.

The message also announced that the Senate has passed a bill with the following title, in the passage of which it asks the concurrence of the House of Representatives:

An act relating to the use of trade marks and names.

Read a first and second time. On motion of Mr. Ahern of Concord, the rules were suspended and the reference to committee dispensed with. The bill was then laid upon the table to be printed. On motion of the same gentleman, the rules were suspended and the printing of the bill dispensed with.

The bill was then ordered to a third reading. Mr. Ahern of Concord moved that the rules be suspended and the bill read a third time by its title. The question being upon the adoption of the motion,

(Discussion ensued.)

Mr. Ahern of Concord moved the previous question.

The question being,

Shall the main question be now put?

On a *viva voce* vote the previous question was ordered. The question being upon the adoption of the motion of Mr. Ahern, Mr. Hoyt of Sandwich called for a division. A division being had, 141 gentlemen voted in the affirmative and 58 gentlemen voted in the negative, and the motion prevailed. The bill was then read a third time by its title and passed and sent to the secretary of state to be engrossed.

The message further announced that the Senate concurs with the House of Representatives in the passage of the following bill, with amendments, in the passage of which amendments it asks the concurrence of the House of Representatives :

An act amending sections 37, 38, and 40 of chapter 59 of the Session Laws of 1895, as amended by chapter 25 of the Laws of 1901, in relation to the militia.

Amend by striking out section 2 and inserting in the place thereof the following :

SECT. 2. That section 98 of chapter 95 of the Laws of 1895, as amended by chapter 25 of the Laws of 1901, be amended by striking out the words " two dollars " after the words " band musicians " in the sixteenth line and inserting in the place thereof the words " three dollars."

Further amend by adding the following section :

SECT. 3. All acts or parts of acts inconsistent with this act are hereby repealed, and this act shall take effect upon its passage.

On motion of Mr. Severance of Exeter, the amendments were concurred in.

COMMITTEE REPORTS.

Mr. Hamlin of Charlestown, for the Committee on Claims, reported the following joint resolution :

" Joint resolution in favor of Albert T. Severance and others," with the resolution that the joint resolution ought to pass.

The report was accepted. The first reading having begun, on motion of Mr. Ahern of Concord, the further reading of the joint resolution was dispensed with. The joint resolution was then ordered to a second reading. On motion of Mr. Ahern of Concord, the rules were suspended and the second reading of the joint resolution made in order at the present time. The second reading having begun, on motion of Mr. Ahern of Concord, the further reading was dispensed with. The joint resolution was then laid upon the table to be printed, and then referred to the Committee on Appropriations. On motion of Mr. Ahern of Concord, the rules were suspended and the printing of the bill and the reference to committee dispensed with. The joint resolution was then ordered to a third reading. On motion of Mr. Ahern of Concord, the rules were suspended and the third reading of the joint resolution made in order at the present time. The third reading having begun, on motion of Mr. Ahern of Concord, the further reading was dispensed with. The joint resolution was then passed and sent to the Senate for concurrence.

Mr. Scammon of Exeter, for the Committee on Judiciary, reported the following entitled bill, "An act to legalize and confirm the school board's warrant and the votes and proceedings thereunder at the annual school district meeting in the town of Newfields, held in said town on the fourteenth day of March, 1903," with the resolution that the bill ought to pass.

The report was accepted and the bill read a first time and ordered to a second reading. On motion of Mr. Scammon of Exeter, the rules were suspended and the bill read a second time by its title. The bill was then laid upon the table to be printed. On motion of the same gentleman, the rules were suspended and the printing of the bill dispensed with. The bill was then ordered to a third reading. On motion of the same gentleman, the rules were further suspended and the bill read a third time by its title. The bill was then passed and sent to the Senate for concurrence.

Mr. Scammon of Exeter, for the Committee on Judiciary,

39

reported the following entitled bill, "An act for the relief of the town of New Castle," with the resolution that the bill ought to pass.

The report was accepted and the bill read a first time and ordered to a second reading. On motion of Mr. Scammon of Exeter, the rules were suspended and the bill read a second time by its title. The bill was then laid upon the table to be printed. On motion of the same gentleman, the rules were suspended and the printing of the bill dispensed with. The bill was then ordered to a third reading. On motion of the same gentleman, the rules were further suspended and the bill read a third time by its title. The bill was then passed and sent to the Senate for concurrence.

Mr. Woodman of Concord, for the Committee on Liquor Laws, reported the following entitled bill, " An act relating to the printing of ballots provided for in an act entitled 'An act to regulate the traffic in intoxicating liquor,' approved March 27, 1903," with the resolution that the bill ought to pass.

The report was accepted and the bill read a first time and ordered to a second reading. On motion of Mr. Woodman of Concord, the rules were suspended and the bill read a second time by its title. The bill was then laid upon the table to be printed. On motion of the same gentleman, the rules were suspended and the printing of the bill dispensed with. The bill was then ordered to a third reading. On motion of the same gentleman, the rules were further suspended and the bill read a third time by its title. The bill was then passed and sent to the Senate for concurrence.

Mr. Woodman of Concord, for the Committee on Liquor Laws, reported the following entitled bill, "An act authorizing the license commissioners to license *bona fide* hotels in unorganized towns and places to sell intoxicating liquors," with the resolution that the bill ought to pass.

The report was accepted and the bill read a first time and ordered to a second reading. On motion of Mr. Ahern of Concord, the rules were suspended and the bill read a second time by its title. The bill was then laid upon the table to be printed. On motion of the same gentleman, the rules were suspended and the printing of the bill dispensed with. The bill was then ordered to a third reading. On motion of the same gentleman, the rules were further suspended and the bill read a third time by its title. The bill was then passed and sent to the Senate for concurrence.

Mr. French of Moultonborough, for the Committee on Railroads, reported the following entitled bill, "An act to renew 'An act to incorporate the Glen Junction Transfer Company,' passed January session, 1897, and to amend the same," with the resolution that the bill ought to pass.

The report was accepted and the bill read a first time and ordered to a second reading. On motion of Mr. French of Moultonborough, the rules were suspended and the bill read a second time by its title. The bill was then laid upon the table to be printed. On motion of the same gentleman, the rules were suspended and the printing of the bill dispensed with. On motion of the same gentleman, the rules were further suspended and the bill read a third time by its title. The bill was then passed and sent to the Senate for concurrence.

Mr. Donagan of Concord, for the Committee on Claims, reported the following joint resolution, " Joint resolution in favor of John K. Law and others," with the resolution that the joint resolution ought to pass.

The report was accepted. The first reading of the joint resolution having begun, on motion of Mr. French of Moultonborough, the rules were suspended and the further reading of the joint resolution dispensed with. The joint resolution was then ordered to a second reading. On motion of the same gentleman, the rules were suspended and the second reading of the joint resolution made in order at the present time. The second reading having begun, on motion of the same gentleman, the rules were suspended and the further reading of the joint resolution dispensed with. The joint resolution was then laid upon the table to be printed and then referred to the Committee on Appropriations. On motion of Mr. French of Moultonborough, the rules were suspended and the printing of the joint resolution and its reference to committee dispensed with. The joint resolution was then ordered to a third reading. On motion of the same gentleman, the rules were sus pended and the third reading of the joint resolution made in order at the present time. The third reading having begun, on motion of the same gentleman, the further reading was dispensed with. The joint resolution was then passed and sent to the Senate for concurrence.

Mr. Dow of Conway, for the Committee on Appropriations, to whom was referred Joint resolution appropriating money for screening the outlet of Sunapee lake, so called, having considered the same, report the same with the following resolution :

Resolved, That the joint resolution ought to pass.

The report was accepted and the joint resolution ordered to a third reading.

Mr. Hall of Westmoreland, for the Committee on Railroads, to whom was referred An act to incorporate the North Hampton Street Railway Company, having considered the same, report the same with the following resolution :

Resolved, That it is inexpedient to legislate.

The report was accepted and the resolution adopted.

Mr. Woodman of Concord, for the Committee on Judiciary, reported the following entitled bill, "An act in amendment of section 4 and repealing section 5 of chapter 225 of the Public Statutes, relating to the taking of depositions," with the resolution that the bill ought to pass.

The report was accepted and the bill read a first time and ordered to a second reading, but as the hour fixed by the joint rules when all bills must have been transmitted to the Senate had passed, the bill was indefinitely postponed.

Mr. Andrews of Somersworth, for the Committee on Education, reported the following entitled bill, "An act to equalize school privileges in the town of Bath," with the resolution that the bill ought to pass.

The report was accepted and the bill read a first time and ordered to a second reading. On motion of Mr. Andrews of Somersworth, the rules were suspended and the bill read a second time by its title. The bill was then laid upon the table to be printed. On motion of the same gentleman, the rules were suspended and the printing of the bill dispensed with. The bill was then ordered to a third reading. On motion of the same gentleman, the rules were further suspended and the bill read a third time by its title. The bill was then passed, but as the hour fixed by the joint rules when all bills must have been transmitted to the Senate had passed, the President of the Senate refused to receive the message.

Mr. Woodman of Concord, for the Committee on Judiciary, reported the following entitled bill, "An act severing the homesteads of David A. Welch and others from the town district of the city of Concord and annexing the same to the Union school district of said city of Concord," with the resolution that the bill ought to pass.

The report was accepted and the bill read a first time and ordered to a second reading. On motion of Mr. Woodman of Concord, the rules were suspended and the bill read a second time by its title. The bill was then laid upon the table to be printed. On motion of the same gentleman, the rules were suspended and the printing of the bill dispensed with. The bill was then ordered to a third reading. On motion of the same gentleman, the rules were suspended and the bill read a third time by its title. The bill was then passed, but as the hour fixed by the joint rules when all bills must have been transmitted to the Senate had passed, the President of the Senate refused to receive the message.

Mr. Bunton, A. S., of Manchester, for the Committee on Banks, to whom was referred An act amending the charter of the Portsmouth Savings Bank, having considered the same, report the same with the following resolution :

Resolved, That the bill ought to pass.

The report was accepted and the bill laid upon the table to be printed. Mr. Ahern of Concord moved that the rules be suspended and the printing of the bill dispensed with. The question being upon the adoption of the motion,

(Discussion ensued.)

Mr. Ahern withdrew his motion and the bill was laid upon the table to be printed.

Mr. Converse of Lyme, for the Committee on Engrossed Bills, reported that they had examined, and found correctly engrossed, the following entitled bills

An act to incorporate the Candia & Deerfield Street Railway Company.

An act to amend chapter 60, section 3 of the Statute Laws of 1891, relating to dog licenses.

An act to legalize a vote taken at the annual town meeting in Boscawen, on the second Tuesday of March, 1903.

An act in amendment of chapter 208 of the Session Laws of 1899, entitled "An act to incorporate the Walpole Electric Light and Power Company," and of an act amending said act passed at the present session.

The report was accepted.

MESSAGE FROM THE SENATE.

A message from the Honorable Senate, by its clerk, announced that the Senate concurs with the House of Representatives in the passage of the following joint resolution:

Joint resolution in favor of John K. Law and others.

The message also announced that the Senate concurs with the House of Representatives in the passage of the following bill, with amendment, in the passage of which amendment it asks the concurrence of the House of Representatives:

An act to define the duties of the state treasurer with reference to public funds.

Amend by adding at the end of section 1 the following: "excepting the interest upon such funds as are paid to the treasurer for distribution to the towns and cities of the state, and the interest shall be distributed to such towns and cities proportionately in the same manner as said funds are distributed."

On motion of Mr. Scammon of Exeter, the amendment was concurred in.

The message also announced that the Senate concurs with the House of Representatives in the passage of the following bill, with amendment, in the passage of which amendment it asks the concurrence of the House of Representatives:

An act to exempt from local taxation the hotel property that may be erected in the village of North Stratford in the town of Stratford.

Amend by adding to the end of section 1 the following

words: "provided that the town shall so vote at any legal meeting of the voters thereof," so that said section shall read as follows:

SECTION 1.   That the hotel property erected in the village of North Stratford in the town of Stratford during the year 1903, be and the same is hereby exempt from local taxation for the term of ten years, providing the town shall so vote at any legal meeting of the voters thereof.

On motion of Mr. Lennon of Stratford, the amendment was concurred in.

The message also announced that the Senate concurs with the House of Representatives in the passage of the following bill, with amendment, in the passage of which amendment it asks the concurrence of the House of Representatives:

An act to regulate the penalty for murder.

Amend section 1 by striking out the first eleven lines of said section and inserting in place thereof the following:

SECTION 1.   That section 5 of chapter 278 of the Public Statutes, as amended by section 1, chapter 24, Laws of 1899, is hereby repealed and the following is substituted in place thereof:

Amend the title to the bill by striking out its present title and substituting in place thereof the following:

An act in amendment of section 5, chapter 278 of the Public Statutes, as amended by section 1, chapter 24, Laws of 1899, relating to homicide and offenses against the person.

On motion of Mr. Buckley of Lancaster, the amendment was concurred in.

COMMITTEE REPORTS.

Mr. Newton of Portsmouth, for a majority of the special committee consisting of the delegation from the city of Portsmouth, to whom was referred An act in amendment of an act entitled "An act for the enlargement and extension of the water-works of the city of Portsmouth," approved March 10, 1899, having considered the same, report the same with the following resolution:

Resolved, That the bill ought to pass.

Mr. Foye of Portsmouth, for a minority of the special committee consisting of the Portsmouth delegation, to whom was referred An act in amendment of an act entitled "An act for the enlargement and extension of water-works of the city of Portsmouth," approved March 10, 1899, having considered the same, report the same with the following resolution :

Resolved, That it is inexpedient to legislate.

The reports were accepted. Mr. Ahern of Concord moved that the report of the minority of the committee be substituted for that of the majority. The question being upon the adoption of the motion,

(Discussion ensued.)

On a *viva voce* vote the motion prevailed and the report of the minority of the committee was substituted for that of the majority. The question being upon the adoption of the resolution of the committee that it is inexpedient to legislate, on a *viva voce* vote the resolution was adopted.

Mr. Cavanaugh of Manchester, for the Committee on Judiciary, to whom was referred An act in relation to the powers and duties of police commissioners of the city of Manchester, having considered the same, report the same with the following resolution :

Resolved, That the bill ought to pass.

The report was accepted and the bill laid upon the table to be printed. On motion of Mr. Sheehan of Manchester, the rules were suspended and the printing of the bill dispensed with. The bill was then ordered to a third reading. Mr. Sheehan of Manchester moved that the rules be suspended and the bill read a third time by its title. The question being upon the adoption of the motion,

(Discussion ensued.)

On a *viva voce* vote the motion prevailed. Mr. Ingham of Nashua called for a division. A division being had, 129 gentlemen voted in the affirmative and 63 gentlemen voted in the negative, and less than a quorum having voted, at 12.10 the House was declared adjourned.

AFTERNOON.

The House met at 3 o'clock.

THIRD READINGS.

Joint resolution appropriating money for screening the outlet of Sunapee lake, so called.

An act to amend section 16 of chapter 79 of the Session Laws of 1901, relating to the taking of deer.

An act in amendment of section 3 of chapter 7 of the Public Statutes, relating to the state house and yard.

An act in amendment of section 2 of chapter 32 of the Laws of 1895, entitled "An act in relation to printing the reports of certain state officers."

Severally read a third time and passed and sent to the secretary of state to be engrossed.

Joint resolution appropriating money for the support of the New Hampshire School for Feeble-Minded Children, necessary school buildings, and to provide water.

Read a third time and passed, but as the hour fixed by the joint rules when all bills and joint resolutions must have been transmitted to the Senate had passed, the President of the Senate refused to receive the message.

On motion of Mr. Ahern of Concord,—

Resolved, That the clerk be instructed to make up the payroll of the House, and submit the same to the state treasurer, and the treasurer be authorized to pay the members the sums therein specified, beginning at 12.30 o'clock in the afternoon, April 2.

Mr. Remich of Littleton offered the following resolution:

Resolved, By the House of Representatives, the Senate concurring, that the State Board of Equalization be and hereby is instructed to investigate and report to the next session of the general court, by bill or otherwise, ways and means for carrying into effect the recently adopted amendment to the constitution providing for the taxation of inheritances and franchises.

The question being upon the adoption of the resolution,

(Discussion ensued.)

On motion of Mr. Ahern of Concord, the resolution was laid upon the table.

MESSAGE FROM THE SENATE.

A message from the Honorable Senate, by its clerk, announced that the Senate refuses to concur with the House of Representatives in the passage of the following entitled bills and joint resolutions:

An act relating to the protection and preservation of ornamental and shade trees in the highways.

The message further announced that the Senate concurs with the House of Representatives in the passage of the following entitled bills:

An act in relation to the Lisbon village district.

An act in amendment of section 7 of chapter 59 of the Public Statutes, and section 13 of chapter 60 of the Public Statutes, relating to the assessment and collection of taxes.

An act to legalize and confirm the school board's warrant and the votes and proceedings thereunder at the annual school meeting in the town of Newfields, held in said town on the fourteenth day of March, 1903.

An act for the relief of the town of New Castle.

An act in amendment of section 1, chapter 83 of the Public Statutes, entitled " Settlement of paupers."

An act in amendment of chapter 134 of the Public Statutes, relating to the practice of dentistry.

An act in amendment of section 7, chapter 63 of the Laws of 1897, entitled " An act to regulate the licensing and registration of physicians and surgeons."

An act in amendment of chapter 64, Laws of 1899, relating to firemen's relief fund.

UNFINISHED BUSINESS.

Mr. Sheehan of Manchester called for the unfinished business, it being the consideration of the following entitled bill, " An act in relation to the powers and duties of police commissioners of the city of Manchester."

The question being upon the adoption of the motion of Mr. Sheehan of Manchester, that the rules be suspended and the printing of the bill dispensed with, and upon this question Mr. Ingham of Nashua, having called for a division, Mr. Ingham withdrew his call. The question being upon the adoption of the motion of Mr. Sheehan, Mr. French of Moultonborough called for a division.

(Discussion ensued.)

A division being had, 159 gentlemen voted in the affirmative and 26 gentlemen voted in the negative, and less than a quorum having voted, at 3.40 the House was declared adjourned.

THURSDAY, April 2, 1903.

The House met at 11 o'clock.

Prayer was offered by the chaplain.

MESSAGE FROM THE SENATE.

A message from the Honorable Senate, by its clerk, announced that the Senate concurs with the House of Representatives in the passage of the following entitled bills and joint resolutions:

Joint resolution to provide for the treatment of indigent consumptives.

An act in amendment of section 20 of chapter 27 of the Public statutes, entitled " County commissioners."

An act in amendment of chapter 262 of the Public Statutes, relating to coroners and coroners' inquests.

An act in addition to and in amendment of section 10 of chapter 198 of the Public Statutes, relating to trustees of estates.

An act authorizing the license commissioners to license *bona fide* hotels in unorganized towns and places to sell intoxicating liquors.

An act relating to printing of ballots provided for in an act entitled " An act to regulate the traffic in intoxicating liquor," approved March 27, 1903.

An act to renew " An act to incorporate the Glen Junction Transfer Company," passed January session, 1897, and to amend the same.

The message also announced that the Senate refuses to concur with the House of Representatives in the passage of the following entitled bills:

An act in amendment of chapter 7S of the Laws of 1897, relating to biennial elections.

An act in amendment of, and in addition to, section 3, chapter 105 of the Laws of 1901, in relation to political caucuses and conventions.

An act in amendment of section 14, chapter 180, Public Statutes, regulating the hours of labor for women and minors in manufacturing or mechanical establishments.

An act to provide for the representation of the state of New Hampshire and the exhibition of its products and attractions at the Louisiana Purchase Exposition at St. Louis in 1904.

An act to repeal chapter 112 of the Public Statutes, relating to the sale of spirituous or intoxicating liquor and all amendments thereof and thereto.

The message also announced that the Senate concurs with the House of Representatives in the passage of the following bill, with amendment, in the passage of which amendment it asks the concurrence of the House of Representatives:

An act to amend chapter 40, Laws of 1893, relating to inspection of buildings.

Amend section 2 by striking out all after the word " inspector," in the fourteenth line of said section, and insert instead thereof the following : " so far as the same relates to the building rules of such city or town, or the safety of such building after erected for the purpose for which it is designed. If any such inspector shall refuse to approve of any plan submitted to him as aforesaid, any person aggrieved thereby may appeal from the decision of such inspector to the superior court for the county in which such city or town is situated, either in term time or vacation, and said court shall make such orders thereby as justice may require."

On motion of Mr. Donahue of Manchester the amendment was concurred in.

The message also announced that the Senate concurs with the House of Representatives in the passage of the following bill, with amendment, in the passage of which amendment it asks the concurrence of the House of Representatives:

An act to amend chapters 2 and 112 of the Public Statutes, and to provide for the better enforcement of the liquor laws.

Amend by striking out sections 9 and 10 of said act.

Renumber the succeeding sections.

Further amend by striking out section 16 of said bill and inserting instead thereof the following :

" Nothing in this act shall be construed to in any way conflict with, limit, or restrain any part or parts of an act passed at the January session, 1903, entitled ' An act to regulate the traffic in intoxicating liquor,' and this act shall be in force after the third Tuesday of May, 1903."

On motion of Mr. Whittemore of Dover, the amendment was concurred in.

The message also announced that the Senate concurs with the House of Representatives in the passage of the following joint resolution, with amendment, in the passage of which amendment it asks the concurrence of the House of Representatives :

Joint resolution in favor of Albert T. Severance and others.

Amend by adding after the word " house " in the twelfth line of said joint resolution the following :

" That the sum of fourteen thousand dollars be and hereby is appropriated for each of the years 1903 and 1904 for maintenance and to provide water ; that four thousand five hundred dollars be appropriated for equipment, laundry, painting buildings and general repairs ; and that the sum of ten thousand dollars be appropriated for a school building, the same to include two school-rooms, sewing room, manual training room, and a hall to be used for religious and other purposes for the New Hampshire School for Feeble-Minded Children.

" That Warren F. Langley be allowed and paid the sum of one hundred dollars in full payment of salary for attendance as member of the House of Representatives from the opening of the session until February 18, 1903."

On motion of Mr. Scammon of Exeter, the amendment was concurred in.

The message further announced that the Senate has passed the following joint resolution, in the passage of which it asks the concurrence of the House of Representatives :

Joint resolution in favor of the owners of farm animals killed by order of the U. S. department of agriculture to stamp out the foot and mouth disease.

Read a first time and ordered to a second reading. On motion of Mr. Remich of Littleton, the rules were suspended and the joint resolution read a second time. The joint resolution was then laid upon the table to be printed and referred to the committee on appropriations. On motion of Mr. Remich of Littleton, the rules were suspended and the printing of the joint resolution and its reference to committee dispensed with. The joint resolution was then ordered to a third reading. On motion of the same gentleman, the rules were further suspended and the joint resolution read a third time and passed and sent to the secretary of state to be engrossed.

COMMITTEE REPORTS.

Mr. Cavanaugh of Manchester, for the Committee on Judiciary, to whom was referred "An act in amendment of section 1, chapter 185, Laws of 1901, entitled "An act authorizing the Hillsborough county convention to raise money for the building and repairing of court houses," having considered the same, report the same with the following resolution:

Resolved, That the bill ought to pass.

The report was accepted and the bill laid upon the table to be printed. On motion of Mr. Smith of Peterborough, the rules were suspended and the printing of the bill dispensed with. The bill was then ordered to a third reading. On motion of the same gentleman, the rules were further suspended and the bill read a third time and passed and sent to the secretary of state to be engrossed.

Mr. Woodman of Concord, for the Committee on Judiciary, to whom was referred An act establishing the office of medical referee and amending chapter 262 of the Public Statutes, relating to coroners' inquests, having considered the same, report the same with the following resolution:

Resolved, That the bill ought to pass.

The report was accepted and the bill laid upon the table to be printed. On motion of Mr. Ahern of Concord, the rules were suspended and the printing of the bill dispensed with.

The bill was then ordered to a third reading. On motion of the same gentleman, the rules were further suspended and the bill read a third time by its title and passed and sent to the secretary of state to be engrossed.

Mr. Converse of Lyme, for the Committee on Engrossed Bills, reported that they had examined and found correctly engrossed the following entitled bills and joint resolutions:

An act in addition to and in amendment to section 10 of chapter 198 of the Public Statutes, relating to trustees of estates.

An act providing for the taxation of building and loan associations.

An act in amendment of chapter 262 of the Public Statutes, relating to coroners and coroners' inquests.

An act in amendment of section 20 of chapter 27 of the Public Statutes, entitled "County commissioners."

Joint resolution to provide for the treatment of indigent consumptives.

An act relating to the printing of ballots provided for in an act entitled "An act to regulate the traffic in intoxicating liquor," approved March 27, 1903.

An act to renew " An act to incorporate the Glen Junction Transfer Company," passed January session 1897, and to amend the same.

An act authorizing the license commissioners to license *bona fide* hotels in unorganized towns and places to sell intoxicating liquors.

An act to establish water-works in the town of Greenville.

Joint resolution appropriating five hundred dollars for a monument to be erected at Hackensack, New Jersey, in memory of Gen. Enoch Poor.

Joint resolution in favor of Ella F. Densmore of Charlestown, Mary F. Lombard of Acworth, Frank G. Smith of Waltham, Massachusetts, Eugene P. Smith of Newport, and George E. Shattuck of Hinsdale.

Joint resolution appropriating money to be expended for the preservation of the muster rolls.

An act to amend section 14 and section 15, chapter 286 of the Public Statutes, relating to the salaries of the judge and register of probate for Belknap county.

Joint resolution in favor of John K. Law and others.

An act in amendment of chapter 64, Laws of 1899, relating to firemen's relief fund.

An act to legalize and confirm the school board's warrant for, and the votes and proceedings thereunder at, the annual school district meeting in the town of Newfields, held in said town on the fourteenth day of March, 1903.

An act for the relief of the town of New Castle.

An act to revive, amend, and extend the charter of the Alton & Gilmanton Electric Railway Company.

An act to revive, amend, and extend the charter of the Gilmanton & Barnstead Electric Railway Company.

An act to amend chapter 96 of the Session Laws of 1901, relating to high schools.

An act in amendment of chapter 98 of the Laws of 1901, relating to the duties of tree wardens.

An act to amend chapter 184 of the Laws of 1897, entitled "An act to incorporate the Dalton Power Company," as amended by section 1, chapter 221 of the Laws of 1899.

An act amending sections 37, 38, and 40 of chapter 59 of the Session Laws of 1895, as amended by chapter 25 of the Laws of 1901, in relation to the militia.

An act in amendment of section 2 of chapter 32 of the Laws of 1895, entitled "An act in relation to printing the reports of certain state officers."

An act in amendment of section 3 of chapter 7 of the Public Statutes, relating to the state house and yard.

An act in amendment of chapter 134 of the Public Statutes, relating to the practice of dentistry.

An act in amendment of section 5, chapter 278 of the Public Statutes, as amended by section 1, chapter 24, Laws of 1899, relating to homicide and offenses against the person.

An act to exempt from local taxation the hotel property that may be erected in the village of North Stratford in the town of Stratford.

An act to define the duties of the state treasurer with reference to public funds.

An act in amendment of section 1 of chapter 83 of the Public Statutes, entitled " Settlement of paupers."

An act in amendment of section 7 of chapter 59 of the Public Statutes, and section 13 of chapter 60 of the Public Statutes, relating to the assessment and collection of taxes.

An act in amendment of section 7, chapter 63 of the Laws of 1897, entitled "An act to regulate the licensing and registration of physicians and surgeons."

An act to amend section 16 of chapter 79 of the Session Laws of 1901, relating to the taking of deer.

An act to incorporate the Sandwich Electric Railway Company.

An act to encourage the planting and perpetuation of forests.

An act relating to the use of trade marks and names.

An act in relation to the Lisbon village district.

Joint resolution appropriating money for screening the outlet of Sunapee lake, so called.

The report was accepted.

UNFINISHED BUSINESS.

Mr. Sheehan of Manchester called for the unfinished business, it being the consideration of the following entitled bill, "An act in relation to the powers and duties of police commissioners of the city of Manchester."

The question being upon the adoption of the motion of Mr. Sheehan of Manchester, that the rules be suspended and the printing of the bill dispensed with, and Mr. French of Moultonborough having called for a division, Mr. French withdrew his call. On a *viva voce* vote the motion prevailed. The bill was then ordered to a third reading. On motion of Mr. Sheehan of Manchester, the rules were further suspended and the bill read a third time by its title and passed and sent to the secretary of state to be engrossed.

Mr. Small of Rochester moved that the following resolution be taken from the table:

Resolved, By the Senate of the state of New Hampshire that application is hereby made to the congress under the provision of article five of the constitution of the United States for the calling of a convention to propose an amendment to the constitution of the United States making United States

40

senators elective in the several states by direct vote of the people ; and resolved further that the clerk of the Senate is hereby directed to transmit copies of this application to the Senate of the United States and copies to the members of the said Senate from this state, also to transmit copies hereof to the presiding officers of each of the legislatures now in session in the several states, requesting their coöperation.

The question being upon the adoption of the motion, on a *viva voce* vote the motion did not prevail.

(Mr. Nason of Dover in the chair.)

Mr. Small of Rochester offered the following resolution :

Resolved, That the thanks of this House are due and are hereby unanimously extended to the Speaker, Hon. Harry M. Cheney, for the exceedingly able manner in which he has performed all the duties of his office, for his uniform courtesy to all members, and for his eminent fairness and impartiality.

The resolution was unanimously adopted by a rising vote.

On motion of Mr. French of Moultonborough, the House took a recess of thirty minutes.

(After recess.)

(The Speaker in the chair.)

On motion of Mr. Small of Rochester,—

Resolved, By the House of Representatives, the Senate concurring, that a committee, consisting of one from each county, be appointed by the House, with such as the Senate may join, to wait upon His Excellency the Governor, and inform him that the legislature has completed the business of the session and is ready to receive any communication he may be pleased to make.

The Speaker appointed as members of such committee the following gentlemen : Messrs. Small of Rochester, White of Deerfield, Hoitt of Barnstead, Dow of Conway, Emerson of Concord, Jones of New Ipswich, Dickinson of Winchester, Matthews of Newport, Morrill of Ashland, and Hicks of Colebrook.

Mr. Whitcher of Haverhill offered the following resolution :

Resolved, That the thanks of this House be extended to the gentlemen of the press for the fairness, diligence, courtesy, and accuracy with which the proceedings of this House have been reported.

The resolution was unanimously adopted by a rising vote.

MESSAGE FROM THE SENATE.

A message from the Honorable Senate, by its clerk, announced that the Senate refuses to concur with the House of Representatives in the passage of the following entitled bills:

An act to provide for a revision of the general and public laws.

An act in amendment of section 19, chapter 57 of the Public Statutes, relating to the annual invoice of polls and taxable property.

An act to incorporate the New Hampshire Beneficiary Union.

An act enabling the city of Manchester to build and operate an electric lighting plant for the purpose of lighting the streets and public buildings.

The message also announced that the Senate concurs with the House of Representatives in the passage of the following entitled bill and joint resolution:

Joint resolution relating to repairs upon the state house.

An act providing for the appointment of guardians for minors in certain cases.

The message also announced that by the concurrent resolution previously adopted by the Senate and House of Representatives,—that all reports, bills, and joint resolutions pending in either branch of the legislature on Thursday, the 2d day of April, at 12 o'clock, noon, be indefinitely postponed, the following entitled bill sent up from the House of Representatives was indefinitely postponed:

An act in amendment of section 23 of chapter 79 of the Laws of 1901, in relation to fines.

The message further announced that the Senate concurs with the House of Representatives in the adoption of the following concurrent resolution:

Resolved, by the House of Representatives, the Senate con

curring, that a committee, consisting of one from each county, be appointed by the House, with such as the Senate may join, to wait upon His Excellency the Governor, and inform him that the legislature has completed the business of the session and is ready to receive any communication he may be pleased to make.

The President had appointed as members of such committee, on the part of the Senate, Senators Page, Tilton, and Marvin.

On motion of Mr. Jones of New Ipswich,—

Resolved, That the thanks and appreciation of this House are merited by its officers and employees for the faithfulness, promptness, and efficiency with which they have discharged their duties.

COMMITTEE REPORT.

By unanimous consent, the rules were suspended and the following report of the Committee on Engrossed Bills received:

Mr. Converse of Lyme, for the Committee on Engrossed Bills, reported that they had examined and found correctly engrossed the following entitled bills and joint resolutions:

An act in amendment of section 1, chapter 185, Laws of 1901, entitled "An act authorizing the Hillsborough county convention to raise money for the building and repairing of court houses."

An act establishing the office of medical referee and amending chapter 262 of the Public Statutes, relating to coroners' inquests.

An act in amendment of section 1 of chapter 67 of the Laws of 1899, relating to expenses of judges of the supreme court.

An act in amendment of section 14, chapter 79, Session Laws of 1901, relating to the powers of the fish and game commissioners.

An act to authorize the town of Gilmanton to exempt certain property from taxation.

An act in relation to the salary of the judge of probate for the county of Grafton.

An act relating to the salary of the judge of probate of the county of Sullivan.

An act in amendment of section 2 of chapter 5 of the Public Statutes, relating to the publication and distribution of statutes, journals, and reports.

An act in amendment of section 79 of chapter 79 of the Laws of 1901, in regard to lobster traps.

An act to establish a new apportionment for the assessment of public taxes.

Joint resolution in favor of Albert T. Severance and others.

An act to amend chapter 40, Laws of 1893, relating to inspectors of buildings.

An act to amend chapters 2 and 112 of the Public Statutes, and to provide for the better enforcement of the liquor laws.

Joint resolution in favor of the owners of farm animals killed by order of the U. S. department of agriculture to stamp out the foot and mouth disease.

An act in relation to the powers and duties of police commissioners of the city of Manchester.

Joint resolution relating to repairs upon the state house.

An act providing for the appointment of guardians for minors in certain cases.

The report was accepted.

By the concurrent resolution previously adopted by the Senate and House of Representatives that all reports, bills, and joint resolutions pending in either branch of the legislature on Thursday, the 2d day of April, at 12 o'clock, noon, be indefinitely postponed, the following entitled bills and joint resolutions were indefinitely postponed :

HOUSE BILLS.

An act to regulate the speed and operation of automobiles and motor vehicles on highways.

An act to regulate the speed and operation of automobiles and motor vehicles on streets and highways.

An act protecting sportsmen during deer season.

An act to close Crescent lake, formerly known as Cold pond, in the towns of Unity and Acworth, to ice fishing.

An act to regulate the speed and operation of automobiles nd motor vehicles on highways.

An act to regulate the speed and operation of automobiles and motor vehicles on highways.

An act to prevent fishing through the ice and transporting the same out of the state by non-residents.

An act in relation to licensing dogs kept for breeding purposes.

An act to amend chapter 149 of the Public Statutes, by repealing sections 5 and 7 and enacting substitutes in place thereof.

An act regulating the charges for passenger service on railways in this state and to provide for the sale of mileage books.

An act to incorporate the Winnipiseogee Valley Street Railway.

An act to regulate the speed and operation of automobiles and motor vehicles on the public highways.

An act allowing compensation to majors of battalions in the National Guard in certain cases.

An act for the protection of employees.

An act regulating fares on electric roads.

An act to incorporate the Nashua, Manchester & Concord Railway Company.

An act to prohibit the pollution of the waters of Blood brook, so called, in the towns of Lebanon and Plainfield.

An act in amendment of chapter 121, Laws of 1901, relating to the protection of public rights in New Hampshire.

An act requiring goods made in whole or in part by convict labor to be so stamped.

An act in relation to mileage books.

An act to prevent discrimination in rates by express companies.

An act relating to the use of bait or scent for the purpose of trapping foxes.

An act in relation to the trapping of fur bearing animals.

An act to prohibit fishing through the ice in Crystal lake in the town of Gilmanton.

An act to regulate telephone and telegraph companies.

An act to prohibit the further employment of convict labor of certain kinds at the state industrial school.

An act relating to the salary of the solicitor for the county of Merrimack.

An act to prevent trespassing on railroad tracks.

An act severing the homestead of David A. Welch from the town district system of the city of Concord and annexing the same to the Union school district of said Concord.

An act in amendment of section 21 of chapter 180 of the Public Statutes.

An act extending the liability of railroads for injuries to employees.

An act to protect the lives of freight brakemen, being an amendment of chapter 39, section 1 of the statutes of 1893.

An act to save counties the expense of jury trials in certain cases.

An act prohibiting the manufacture and sale of cigarettes.

An act to extend and regulate the liability of employers to make compensation for personal injuries suffered by employees.

An act relating to foreign corporations doing business in this state.

An act requiring state certification of teachers of public schools.

An act for the regulation of bakeshops and candy factories and to improve their sanitary condition.

An act to amend the charter of the city of Portsmouth in relation to street commissioner.

An act in amendment of the charter of the city of Laconia.

An act amending the charter of the Portsmouth Savings Bank.

An act relating to telephone, telegraph, and electric light companies.

An act authorizing the Claremont Railway and Lighting Company to construct and maintain, as a part of its system, an electric railway and lights in the town of Cornish, and an electric railway in the town of Newport and the acquirement by contract of the property and franchises of the Newport Electric Light Company.

An act to provide for the better equipment of cars for the transportation of lumber and wood.

An act to amend chapter 63 of the Laws of 1897, restricting the so-called " counter prescribing " by druggists or registered pharmacists of drugs and medicines not under the prescription of a regularly qualified physician.

An act to establish a state aid road fund to be subject to the disposal of the Governor and Council, to aid such towns and places as are unable to keep the roads and bridges in these towns or places in suitable repair.

An act amending section 14 and section 20 of chapter 180 of the Public Statutes, relating to the hours of labor.

An act to establish an electric lighting, heating, and power plant in the city of Somersworth.

An act to facilitate the settlement of the estates of deceased persons.

An act in amendment of the charter of Pembroke Academy, increasing the number of trustees.

An act to create and establish an inspector of factories.

An act to prevent the pollution of the Piscataqua river and its tributaries.

An act to amend section 1 of chapter 33 of the Laws of 1893, relating to the diseases of domestic animals.

An act for the permanent improvement of the highways of the state.

An act in amendment of section 13, chapter 41 of the Public Statutes, relating to liens.

An act to prohibit the use of arsenic in embalming human bodies.

An act to extend the Union school district to include the city of Concord.

An act relating to the administration of the state library.

An act to amend sections 4 and 5 of chapter 65 of the Public Statutes, relating to the taxation of savings banks.

An act relating to the publication of the Session Laws.

An act in amendment of sections 3, 4, 5, and 6 of chapter 220 of the Public Statutes, relating to attachment of real estate.

HOUSE JOINT RESOLUTIONS.

Joint resolution relating to the completion of the topographical survey.

Joint resolution for the erection of a statue to President Franklin Pierce.

Joint resolution for an appropriation to complete the screen at the outlet of Lake Winnipesaukee in the city of Laconia.

Joint resolution relating to screening the outlets of Ashuelot and Millen lakes in the town of Washington.

Joint resolution in favor of James J. Parks.

Joint resolution in relation to the New Hampshire reports.

Joint resolution in favor of screening the outlet of Nubanuset lake in the towns of Hancock and Nelson.

Joint resolution in favor of the owners of the animals slaughtered by the government to prevent the spread of the foot and mouth disease.

SENATE BILLS.

An act to provide for the co-operation of the state with towns and cities in the construction and repairs of highways and for the establishment of the office of state highway engineer.

An act to incorporate the First Congregational church of Wolfeborough, New Hampshire.

An act in amendment of section 4 of chapter 37 of the Session Laws of 1895, entitled "An act providing for the appointment of bail commissioners for cities and towns."

An act in amendment of section 29, chapter 266 of the Public Statutes, relating to trespasses and malicious injuries.

An act to incorporate the Nutfield Loan and Trust company.

An act in amendment of sections 6 and 7 of chapter 270 of the Public Statutes, relating to lotteries, gambling, and wagers.

An act in amendment of sections 1, 2, and 5 of chapter 105 of the Session Laws of 1901, approved March 22, 1901, and as amended at the session of 1903.

An act for the relief of the town of New Castle.

An act to incorporate the Evangelical Congregational church of Plaistow, N. H., and the North Parish of Haverhill, Mass.

SENATE JOINT RESOLUTIONS.

Joint resolution authorizing the trustees of the New Hampshire College of Agriculture and the Mechanic Arts to permit certain real estate in Durham to be used as the site of a public library.

Joint resolution in favor of Arthur E. Clarke.

Mr. Small of Rochester, for the joint committee appointed to wait upon His Excellency the Governor, and inform him that the legislature had completed its duties, reported that they had attended to their duty, and that the Governor informed them that he had a communication to lay before the House. The report was accepted, and immediately His Excellency Nahum J. Bachelder, Governor, appeared before the House of Representatives, and delivered the following message :

CONCORD, April 2, 1903.

To the Honorable Senate and House of Representatives :

I have signed or returned to the body in which they originated, all the bills and joint resolutions submitted for my approval.

Having been informed by a joint committee of the Senate and House of Representatives that you have completed the business of the session and are ready to adjourn, I do, by the authority vested in the executive, hereby adjourn the legislature to the last Wednesday of December, in the year of our Lord one thousand nine hundred and four.

NAHUM J. BACHELDER,
Governor.

Thereupon the Speaker declared the House adjourned to the last Wednesday of December, 1904.

JAMES M. COOPER,
Clerk.

A true copy.   Attest :

JAMES M. COOPER,
Clerk.

APPENDIX.

MILEAGE ROLL.

ROCKINGHAM COUNTY.

Atkinson	George A. Sawyer	148
Auburn	Albert E. Preston	56
Brentwood	D. Frank Fellows	92
Candia	Edward E. Hubbard	60
Chester	Augustus P. Morse	78
Danville	Mahlon B. Darbe	150
Deerfield	Woodbury R. White	68
Derry	John P. Hardy	64
"	Greenleaf K. Bartlett	60
"	Albert E. Shute	60
Epping	Joseph A. Edgerly	90
Exeter	Edward E. Nowell	110
"	John Scammon	110
"	Albert T. Severance	110
"	Leonard F. Smith	110
Fremont	Andrew J. Brown	123
Greenland	Lorenzo D. Duntley	110
Hampstead	William A. Emerson	150
Hampton	William E. Lane	150
Hampton Falls	James H. Brown	150
Kingston	George F. Quimby	136
Londonderry	William H. Crowell	52
Newcastle	James W. Pridham	130
Newfields	George L. Chase	100
Newington	Daniel W. Badger	138
Newmarket	Harry W. Haines	102
"	John E. Kent	106
Newton	Ezra N. George	136
North Hampton	John W. Warner	144

Northwood .... James A. Bickford.......... 56
Nottingham .... Edward F. Gerrish.......... 100
Plaistow .... John W. Sleeper............ 138
Portsmouth—
   Ward 1 .... Henry P. Payne............ 132
      " .... Eben H. Blaisdell.......... 132
   Ward 2 .... Morris C. Foye............. 132
      " .... Howard O. Nelson.......... 132
      " .... Harry B. Yeaton........... 128
   Ward 3 .... William Cogan.............. 132
      " .... Albert H. Adams............ 130
   Ward 4 .... Sherman T. Newton........ 132
   Ward 5 .... Jeremiah J. Couhig......... 132
Raymond .... Plummer B. Corson.......... 78
Rye .... George H. Brown........... 132
Salem .... Daniel A. Abbott........... 82
    " .... Howard L. Gordon.......... 75
Sandown .... Charles H. Young.......... 84
Seabrook .... George C. Dow............. 153
South Hampton ...... Frank B. Swain............. 124
Stratham .... Emmons B. Chase.......... 108
Windham .... John E. Cochran........... 70

STRAFFORD COUNTY.

Barrington .... Frank L. Howe............. 130
Dover—
   Ward 1 .... George Fred Mathes........ 122
      " .... Alvah T. Ramsdell......... 122
   Ward 2 .... Frank M. Libby............ 124
      " .... John W. Jewell............ 122
      " .... William F. Nason........... 122
   Ward 3 .... Arthur G. Whittemore....... 122
      " .... Charles C. Bunce.......... 122
   Ward 4 .... Edward D. Smith........... 130
      " .... George D. Barrett.......... 122
      " .... Frank L. Hayes............ 128
   Ward 5 .... John H. Wesley............ 126
Durham .... Charles S. Langley.......... 125

Farmington .... Charles F. York............. 160
    " .... John Tuttle................ 160
Lee .... Ben F. Davis.............. 100
Madbury .... Martin V. B. Felker........ 135
Middleton .... William B. Place............ 180
Milton .... John E. Townsend.......... 170
New Durham .... George H. Jones............ 174
Rochester—
    Ward 1 .... Joel W. McCrillis.......... 152
    Ward 2 .... Fred W. Crocker........... 146
    Ward 3 .... Joseph Warren............ 150
    Ward 4 .... Frederick E. Small......... 146
    " .... Simeon Bergeron........... 150
    Ward 5 .... Horace L. Worcester....... 144
    Ward 6 .... Albert Wallace............ 140
Rollinsford .... Michael B. Harrity......... 140
Somersworth—
    Ward 1 .... Burton Etter............... 150
    Ward 2 .... Fred Wentworth........... 150
    Ward 3 .... Pierre P. Demers.......... 150
    Ward 4 .... Denis J. Murnane.......... 150
    " .... Napoleon Boutin........... 150
    Ward 5 .... Elisha C. Andrews......... 150
Strafford .... Victor L. Caverly........... 160

BELKNAP COUNTY.

Alton .... Charles L. Pinkham........ 100
Barnstead .... Thomas L. Hoitt........... 56
Belmont .... John M. Sargent........... 54
Center Harbor .... Edgar W. Smith............ 86
Gilford .... Fred J. Potter............ 65
Gilmanton .... Elbridge G. Clough........ 112
Laconia—
    Ward 1 .... Albert H. Davis............ 58
    " .... George E. Hull............ 58
    Ward 2 .... Cleophas L. Fecteau........ 56
    " .... Wilber L. Prescott......... 56
    Ward 3 .... Harry S. Chase............ 56

Ward 4 .... Frank A. Edwards........... 58
    "   .... Charles L. Kimball.......... 58
Meredith .... Edward Quimby............ 76
New Hampton .... Frank P. Morrill............ 75
Sanbornton .... Otis S. Sanborn.............. 50
Tilton .... George B. Rogers............ 38
    "   .... Frank L. Mason............. 44

CARROLL COUNTY.

Albany .... Horatio Littlefield........... 290
Bartlett .... Edgar A. Stevens............ 330
Chatham .... Dana A. Weeks............. 362
Conway .... Holmes B. Fifield........... 294
    "   .... Hiram H. Dow............. 308
    "   .... Walter R. Burnell.......... 332
Effingham .... Seth J. Philbrick............ 250
Freedom .... Orrin E. Drake............. 268
Jackson .... George P. Trickey........... 332
Madison .... Roscoe G. Greene........... 270
Moultonborough ...... James E. French........... 100
Ossipee .... Almon F. Abbott............ 238
Sandwich .... Charles B. Hoyt............ 110
Tamworth .... Albert S. Pollard............ 332
Tuftonborough .... John A. Edgerly........... 236
Wakefield .... Simon Blake................ 180
Wolfeborough .... John H. Beacham.......... 236
    "   .... William J. Britton.......... 236

MERRIMACK COUNTY.

Allenstown .... Henri T. Fontaine.......... 14
Andover .... Wilton P. Graves............ 68
Boscawen .... Almon G. Harris............ 14
Bow .... David W. White............. 8
Bradford .... Harlan P. Morse............. 60
Canterbury .... John A. Beck.............. 30
Chichester .... Charles A. Langmaid......... 8

Concord—

Ward 1	....	Eddie Durgin..............	15
"	....	Joseph E. Symonds.........	14
Ward 2	....	Ross W. Cate..............	30
Ward 3	....	Joseph E. Shepard...........	6
Ward 4	....	Eben M. Willis.............	2
"	....	Samuel J. Matson...........	2
"	....	James K. Kennedy.........	2
Ward 5	....	Almon W. Hill.............	2
"	....	Harley B. Roby.............	2
Ward 6	....	Frederic T. Woodman.......	2
"	....	Howard A. Kimball.........	2
"	....	William E. Emerson........	2
Ward 7	....	Albert P. Davis............	4
"	....	William W. Critchett........	4
"	....	Horace O. Mathews.........	2
Ward 8	....	Edson J. Hill..............	2
Ward 9	....	William J. Ahern...........	2
"	....	James J. Donagan...........	2
Danbury	....	Roy Litchfield.............	82
Dunbarton	....	John Bunten..............	76
Epsom	....	Walter H. Tripp...........	28

Franklin—

Ward 1	....	Lewis W. Phillips..........	38
Ward 2	....	Hector Morin..............	40
"	....	Seth W. Jones.............	40
Ward 3	....	Charles W. Adams...........	38
"	....	Curtis A. Davis.............	38
Henniker	....	Arthur G. Preston...........	42
Hill	....	George W. Twombly.........	50
Hooksett	....	Spurzhie E. Worthley........	21
Hopkinton	....	Daniel F. Fisk..............	24
Loudon	....	John B. Sanborn............	58
New London	....	Edwin F. Messer............	80
Northfield	....	Oscar P. Sanborn...........	40
Pembroke	....	John G. Tallant............	18
"	....	Levi L. Aldrich.............	16
"	....	Warren D. Foss..............	16

Pittsfield .... Frank D. Hutchins.......... 58
" .... John A. Walker, Jr.......... 56
Salisbury .... Thomas R. Little............ 36
Sutton .... Herbert L. Pillsbury......... 72
Warner .... Mason T. Ela.............. 40
Webster .... Irvin A. Burbank.......... 32
Wilmot .... Henry K. Mason............ 70

HILLSBOROUGH COUNTY.

Amherst .... George E. Farley............ 92
Antrim .... John N. P. Woodbury....... 70
Bedford .... Ira Barr.................. 46
Bennington .... Frank B. Gould............ 72
Brookline .... Linville M. Shattuck......... 142
Deering .... James S. Craine............ 80
Francestown .... Daniel B. Tobie............. 134
Goffstown .... George Pattee.............. 56
" .... George L. Eaton............ 50
Greenfield .... George H. Putnam.......... 126
Greenville .... Robert Brown, Jr............ 162
Hancock .... Clarence H. Ware............ 88
Hillsborough .... Henry P. Whittaker......... 56
" .... Walter J. A. Ward.......... 56
Hollis .... Elbridge J. Farley.......... 84
Hudson .... Philip J. Connell........... 76
Litchfield .... Isaac N. Center............. 64
Lyndeborough .... Andy Holt................. 116
Manchester—
Ward 1 .... John B. Cavanaugh.......... 40
" .... Olof P. Nyberg............. 40
" .... Joseph W. Abbott........... 42
Ward 2 .... Robert R. Chase............ 40
" .... Kirk C. Bartlett............ 42
.... John J. Donahue............ 40
.... James G. Taggart........... 40
" .... John A. Sheehan........... 36
Ward 3 .... Arthur S. Bunton........... 36
" .... Victor C. Johnson.......... 40

Ward 3	....	Amos G. Straw..............	40
"	....	Frank E. Farrell............	40
..	....	Joseph W. McDonald........	40
"	....	Walter H. Wright...........	40
Ward 4	....	Albert T. Barr..............	40
"	....	Amede Dubuc..............	40
..	....	Orrin D. Carpenter..........	36
	....	William H. Morgan..........	36
	....	Fred C. Darrah.............	40
"	....	Patrick J. Stewart.........	40
Ward 5	....	James F. Tonery............	40
"	....	John J. Ryan..............	40
..	....	Michael J. Trinity..........	40
..	....	Martin J. Whalen...........	40
	....	George P. Riordan..........	40
	....	Martin E. Sullivan...........	40
	....	John J. Shaughnessey.......	40
"	....	Nicholas Sasseville...........	40
Ward 6	....	Horace Marshall............	40
"	....	Almus W. Morse.............	40
..	....	Samuel Couch..............	40
"	....	Andrew B. Bunton..........	44
Ward 7	....	Hanson R. Armstrong........	40
Ward 8	....	Edward L. Tinkham.........	38
"	....	Gottlieb Graf..............	40
..	....	George Ed. Quimby..........	40
	....	Dennis F. Scannell..........	40
"	....	Arthur W. Dinsmore........	40
Ward 9	....	Louis A. Dozois.............	40
"	....	Peter Gunderman...........	40
..	....	Omer Janelle..............	40
	....	Thomas F. Kohler..........	40
..	....	August Filion..............	40
	....	Henry I. Lemay.............	40
"	....	Hugh F. Lynch.............	40
Ward 10	....	John A. Kane..............	40
"	....	Frank P. Newman..........	42
..	....	Frank A. Emerson..........	42

Ward 10 .... William E. Simpson......... 40
Mason .... Benjamin F. March.......... 158
Merrimack .... James C. F. Hodgman....... 56
Milford .... Frederick W. Sawyer......... 96
" .... William N. Robinson......... 96
" .... George H. Needham......... 96
Mont Vernon .... William H. Kendall......... 76
Nashua—
Ward 1 .... Fred C. Lund.............. 70
" .... Andrew J. Tuck............ 73
Ward 2 .... Eugene W. Duncklee........ 75
" .... Frank T. Lewis............. 75
Ward 3 .... John P. Lampron........... 75
" .... Michael H. Buckley......... 72
" .... Thomas E. Ingham.......... 75
Ward 4 .... Charles S. Bussell.......... 74
Ward 5 .... Timothy P. Shea............ 75
Ward 6 .... Charles M. Spalding........ 72
Ward 7 .... Herbert C. Lintott......... 72
" .... Charles M. Morse 75
" .... Enoch Shenton............. 70
Ward 8 .... Charles S. Collins.......... 75
" .... George P. Hills............. 74
" .... John T. Sullivan............ 74
Ward 9 .... John M. Earley............. 72
" .... James H. Moran............ 72
.... Joseph A. Desmarais......... 72
" .... Fereol Dionne............. 74
New Boston .... James N. McLane.......... 68
New Ipswich .... Frederic W. Jones.......... 161
Pelham .... William H. Peabody......... 94
Peterborough .... Arthur H. Miller........... 96
" .... Ezra M. Smith............. 90
Sharon .... John F. Fitzgerald.......... 164
Temple .... DeWitt C. Bragdon.......... 120
Weare .... Horace O. Chase............ 86
Wilton .... Samuel J. Sheldon.......... 108

CHESHIRE COUNTY.

SULLIVAN COUNTY.

Claremont	Hiram G. Sherman	110
"	John W. Jewett	110
"	Ira F. Chandler	110
	Charles H. Long	110
"	Frank P. Huntley	110
Cornish	Winston Churchill	136
Grantham	Harry G. Walker	114
Langdon	Charles M. Lufkin	162
Newport	Frederick W. Aiken	88
"	Charles H. Matthews	88
"	William F. Richards	84
Plainfield	Frank W. True	144
Springfield	Edwin F. Philbrick	112
Sunapee	Charles L. Russell	92
Unity	French J. Straw	134
Washington	Sumner N. Ball	80

GRAFTON COUNTY.

Alexandria	Alvertes N. McMurphey	72
Ashland	John H. Morrill	90
Bath	George E. Davenport	206
Bethlehem	John Pierce, Jr.	254
Bristol	David M. Calley	68
Campton	Jason C. Little	117
Canaan	Horatio B. Gates	112
Enfield	Walter S. Dorothy	120
"	Edwin F. Foster	120
Franconia	Ivory H. Glover	244
Grafton	George B. Kimball	96
Hanover	Albert Pinneo	160
"	Hamilton T. Howe	154
Haverhill	William F. Whitcher	188
"	Daniel E. Carr	178
"	Edwin Bertram Pike	164
Hebron	George B. Barnard	116
Holderness	John H. Evans, Jr.	106
Lebanon	Harry M. Cheney	130
"	John Goold	140

OFFICERS.

INDEX

TO THE

SENATE JOURNAL.

ERRATA.

PAGE 106. Insert at bottom of page the following, "An act relating to domestic insurance companies."

" 141. Line 28, for " Whitefield " read " Nutfield."

" 162. Insert at top of page the following, "An act to change the name of the Gorham Five Cent Savings Bank."

" 168. Line 10, for " 427 " read " 42."

" 188. After line 25 insert the following, " The House of Representatives has passed the following entitled bills and joint resolutions, in the passage of which it asks the concurrence of the Honorable Senate."

" 195. Insert after the 12th line the following, "An act to incorporate the Chester, Fremont & Brentwood Street Railway Company."

INDEX

TO THE

SENATE JOURNAL.

———

INDEX

TO THE

HOUSE JOURNAL.

ERRATA.

Insert at top of page 17:

The ballots were so cast and John K. Law was declared duly elected sergeant-at-arms, and Warren W. Lovejoy, Horatio W. Longa, Martin L. Piper, and John Young were duly elected doorkeepers for the ensuing two years.

John K. Law, Warren W. Lovejoy, Horatio W. Longa, Martin L. Piper, and John Young appeared and were duly qualified by taking the oath of their respective offices.

INDEX

TO THE

HOUSE JOURNAL.

45